OXFORD STUDIES IN ANCIENT CULTURE
AND REPRESENTATION

General Editors
Kathleen M. Coleman   R. R. R. Smith   Oliver Taplin
Peter Thonemann   Tim Whitmarsh

OXFORD STUDIES IN ANCIENT CULTURE
AND REPRESENTATION

Oxford Studies in Ancient Culture and Representation publishes significant interdisciplinary research into the visual, social, political, and religious cultures of the ancient Mediterranean world. The series includes work that combines different kinds of representations that are usually treated separately. The over-arching programme is to integrate images, monuments, texts, performances, and rituals with the places, participants, and broader historical environment that gave them meaning.

Fashioning the Future in Roman Greece

Memory, Monuments, Texts

ESTELLE STRAZDINS

Great Clarendon Street, Oxford, OX2 6DP,
United Kingdom

Oxford University Press is a department of the University of Oxford.
It furthers the University's objective of excellence in research, scholarship,
and education by publishing worldwide. Oxford is a registered trade mark of
Oxford University Press in the UK and in certain other countries

© Estelle Strazdins 2023

The moral rights of the author have been asserted

First Edition published in 2023

Impression: 1

All rights reserved. No part of this publication may be reproduced, stored in
a retrieval system, or transmitted, in any form or by any means, without the
prior permission in writing of Oxford University Press, or as expressly permitted
by law, by licence or under terms agreed with the appropriate reprographics
rights organization. Enquiries concerning reproduction outside the scope of the
above should be sent to the Rights Department, Oxford University Press, at the
address above

You must not circulate this work in any other form
and you must impose this same condition on any acquirer

Published in the United States of America by Oxford University Press
198 Madison Avenue, New York, NY 10016, United States of America

British Library Cataloguing in Publication Data
Data available

Library of Congress Control Number: 2022943691

ISBN 978–0–19–286610–3

DOI: 10.1093/oso/9780192866103.001.0001

Printed and bound in the UK by
TJ Books Limited

Links to third party websites are provided by Oxford in good faith and
for information only. Oxford disclaims any responsibility for the materials
contained in any third party website referenced in this work.

ACKNOWLEDGEMENTS

This book is well travelled. Its roots lie in my DPhil thesis, completed in late 2012 at the University of Oxford. In 2014, I spent over a year travelling and researching in Greece and Turkey in order to deepen my familiarity with the material culture of imperial Greece. Drawing heavily on that research and working in Melbourne, Athens, Oxford, Singapore, and Durham, North Carolina, I devoted 2016 and 2017 to producing the manuscript that forms the immediate basis of this book. The process of revising the manuscript for publication took place in Athens in April and May of 2018, in Cambridge in April and May 2019, and in Brisbane in July to September 2020. Along the way, I have accumulated debts of gratitude to many wonderful people and organizations, whom I am thrilled to have the opportunity to thank here.

Above all, I am grateful to Tim Whitmarsh, who is an inexhaustible treasury of knowledge, advice, encouragement, and patience, all of which are distributed with good humour and kindness, despite his aversion to my use of 'likely' as an adverb; to Ewen Bowie, whose counsel, kindness, constructive criticism, and dinner parties are beyond compare; to Jaś Elsner and Jason König, whose insightful critique of my thesis in their roles as its examiners greatly improved this finished product and who have continued to guide and support me; to Cathy Morgan, who has never ceased to encourage, assist, and endorse me; to Janet Downie for all the mentoring, probing questions, and friendship; and to Nikos Gkiokas for initiating me into the mysteries of material culture at sites throughout Greece and Turkey and for countless other things. I also greatly appreciate the patience, suggestions, guidance, and advice of PAC and PCC—the two Pauls (Cartledge and Christesen)—and of the editors of this series, especially Bert Smith. Thank you, too, to the anonymous press reviewers whose perceptive comments and suggestions sharpened the book, and to Jamie Mortimer, Charlotte Loveridge, and her team at Oxford University Press for fielding my many questions so helpfully.

The Clarendon Fund enabled me to attend the University of Oxford, and the Australian Archaeological Institute at Athens (AAIA), having elected me their Fellow for the academic years 2009–10 and 2017–18, gave me the opportunity to spend almost two years in that wonderful city. Balliol College assisted with a grant from their Financial Hardship Fund in 2012. Thank you too to the Rae and Edith Bennett Travelling Fund and Jessie Webb Scholarship, both administered by the University of Melbourne, which brought me to the UK and Greece, respectively, in the first place. Research in Greece and Turkey in 2014–15 was funded by the Alexander S. Onassis Public Benefit Foundation, the Australian Endeavour

Awards, and the Ίδρυμα Κρατικών Υποτροφιών. I am also grateful to the A. G. Leventis Foundation for funding my position in the Faculty of Classics, University of Cambridge, 2018–20.

The ideas in this book have been shaped for the better by the insights and/or assistance of Lucia Athanassaki; Emily Baragwanath; Caitie Barrett; Alastair Blanshard; Amelia Brown; Nick Brown; George Bruseker; Kostas Buraselis; Annelies Cazmeier; Sophy Downes; Kendra Eshleman; Annabel Florence; Emily Greenwood; Will Guast; Tom Harrison; Patrick Hogan; Dawn Hollis; Liz Irwin; Adrian Kelly; Adam Kemezis; Anna Kouremenos; Shushma Malik; Linni Mazurek; Janette McWilliam; Kit Morrell; Peter Murray; S. Douglas Olson; Ayşe Ozil; Katerina Panagopoulou; Chris Pelling; Andrej Petrovic; Jessica Piccinini; Robert Pitt ('Herodes Attikos—serial killer or just very unlucky?'); Dylan Rogers; Brent Shaw; Tim Shea; Matthew Skuse; Michael Squire; Lis Thomas; Jennifer Tobin; Yiannis Tzifopoulos; Carrie Vout; Greg Woolf; Sonya Wurster; and Alexei Zadorojnyi. I am grateful to you all. I am particularly thankful to the postdoctoral Classics community at Cambridge for the many inspiring conversations and moral support, especially Anna Lefteratou, Claire Jackson, Dan Jolowicz, Livvy Elder, Tom Nelson, Emma Greensmith, and Lea Niccolai. An extra shout-out goes to Manuela Dal Borgo and Tommaso Mari for R0.3 camaraderie and counselling.

Special thanks for the mentorship of Lisa Featherstone and Alastair Blanshard, who have helped me navigate the labyrinth of my early career position at the University of Queensland (UQ), the support of my colleagues in the discipline of Classics and Ancient History at UQ, and to my MPhil student, Jessica Zelli, whose inquisitiveness and enthusiasm for the culture of the Roman east is infectious. I have received invaluable assistance from the Athens staff of the AAIA, especially Stavros Paspalas, Lita Tzortzopoulou-Gregory, Anthoulla Vassiliades, Loula Strolonga, and Myrto Komninou, and from the staff of the British School at Athens (BSA), especially Penny Wilson, Sandra Pepelasis, Tania Gerousi, Amalia Kakissis, Chryssanthi Papadopoulou, Philippa Currie, Vicki Tzavara, Jean-Sébastien Gros, and Bouboulina. Many thanks to Katerina Ierodiakonou, who kindly gave me access to a much needed volume from the Michael Frede collection; Corpus Christi College, Oxford, and its Centre for the Study of Greek and Roman Antiquity; Balliol College and the Faculty of Classics at the University of Oxford; the Faculty of Classics at the University of Cambridge, especially Robin Osborne, Nigel Thompson, Rebecca Flemming, and the C Caucus; Myrto Hatzimichali and Homerton College, Cambridge; the Department of Art, Art History, and Visual Studies, Sheila Dillon, and the Classics Faculty of Duke University, especially Jill Wuenschel, Tolly Boatwright, and William Johnson; the School of Classics at the University of St Andrews; Rhiannon Evans, Chris Mackie, and the Research Centre for Greek Studies at La Trobe University; Hyun Jin Kim,

K. O. Chong Gossard, Andrew Turner, Louise Hitchcock, and the School of Historical and Philosophical Studies at the University of Melbourne; Gülgün Girdivan, Lut Vandeput, and the British Institute at Ankara; Dylan Rogers, Pantelis Paschos, Jenifer Neils, Pandora, and the American School of Classical Studies at Athens. Special thanks to Tyla Cascaes and Carlos Robinson for assistance in preparing the final manuscript, and the HPI School Research Fund at UQ, along with Dolly MacKinnon and Megan Cassidy-Welch, that made their help possible. I am also grateful to the students on the BSA undergraduate course 2014–18, who tolerated countless stories about Herodes Attikos.

For help with images, thanks above all to Stavros Paspalas, Tania Gerousi, and Bert Smith; thanks also to George Spyropoulos, who kindly provided me with images of unpublished artefacts from Loukou, John McK. Camp II, David W. Packard, and the Packard Humanities Institute, and to Erin McGowan for the map of Marathon. Gratitude too to the Greek Olympic Committee (*Ελληνική Ολυμπιακή Επιτροπή*) for permission to photograph the Panathenaic Stadium and its surrounds, and to Ferit Baz, Renate Bol, Sylvie Dumont, Hans R. Goette, Christopher Jones, Diana Kleiner, Charalampos Kritzas, Daria Lanzuolo, Tim Mitford, Anna Moles, David Pettegrew, Joe Rife, Guy Sanders, Søren Lund Sørensen, and David Stronach. Permissions to reproduce the images found in this book were largely funded by grants from the Jowett Copyright Trust, administered by Balliol College, Oxford, the Faculty of Classics, Cambridge, and the School of Literature, Languages, and Linguistics at the Australian National University.

Immense gratitude to the following people who saved me financially, housed, and/or fed me at crucial periods during the write-up: Nikos Gkiokas, Christel Strazdins, Abby Robinson, Lis Thomas and Peter Murray, Mark, Katrina, Freya, and Bruno Strazdins, Sonya Wurster and Paul Daniels, Erin McGowan and Bill Zahariadis, George Bruseker, Alex Cameron, Hannah Gwyther, Anna Moles, Annie Hooton, Sophy Downes, Seth Jaffe, Denitsa Nenova and Hüseyin Çınar Öztürk, Lucia Athanassaki, Liz Irwin, Chryssanthi Papadopoulou, Amalia Kakissis, Anthoulla Vassiliades, Calie, Jorrit, Ido, and Ella Kelder, Dave and Heather Sharman, Nikoleta Charana, Margarita Nazou, Cecilia Gasposchkin, Michalis Iliakis, and Simon Young.

Last but in no way least, heartfelt gratitude to my family and friends, especially Nikos, Mutti and Monty, Mark, Trin, Freya, Bruno, and Ziggy, without whose support nothing that I have achieved would have been possible. Gratitude also to Aivars, whose curiosity about antiquity was happily hereditary.

CONTENTS

List of Figures	xi
Abbreviations	xxi
A Note on Names	xxiii
1. The Future and the 'Second Sophistic'	1

PART I. GLORIOUS PAST, TENSE PRESENT, PENDING FUTURE

2. Back to the Future	29
2.1 Postclassicism, the Canon, and the Future	30
2.1.1 Temporality, Sublimity, and Canonicity in *On the Sublime*	30
2.1.2 Temporality, Beauty, and Culture in Dio Chrysostom's *Oration* 21	37
2.1.3 Competitive and Passive Imitation in Theory and Practice	40
2.2 Remaking Space, Time, and Memory in Arrian's *Periplous*	48
2.3 Novelty and the Problem of Audience with Philostratos and Lucian	59
2.4 Creating Original Artistic Space in Aelius Aristeides' *Sacred Tales*	67
2.5 Conclusion	75
3. Monuments and Rhetorical Materiality	77
3.1 Material Memories	79
3.2 Textual Curation of Artefactual Memory	105
3.3 Rhetorical Materiality	115
3.4 Conclusion	119

PART II. TEXTUAL MONUMENTS AND MONUMENTAL TEXTS

4. The Epitaphic Habit	123
4.1 Speech, Text, Monument	124
4.2 Authority and Dominion: Boundaries and Limina	136
4.2.1 Revising Alexander's Altars in Philostratos' *In Honour of Apollonios of Tyana*	138
4.2.2 Transposing the Pillars of Herakles in Lucian's *True Stories*	142
4.2.3 Reshaping Spatial Memory with Herodes' Herms	147
4.3 Arrian, Alexander, and the Textual Appropriation of Memory	159
4.3.1 The Tomb of Achilles	161
4.3.2 The Tomb of Kyros	166

X CONTENTS

4.4 Herodes Attikos and the Physical Appropriation of Memory	174
4.5 Conclusion	192
5. Commemoration Embodied	**194**
5.1 Statue Honours and Their Limitations	194
5.2 Amplification: Statue Programmes on Monuments	207
5.3 Imaginary Spaces of Honour	217
5.4 Replication	221
5.5 Animation and Writing	237
5.6 Conclusion	243

PART III. CONTROLLING THE FUTURE?

6. The King of Athens	**247**
6.1 The Isthmus of Corinth: Hero, King, Tyrant, God?	251
6.2 Sophistic Tyranny, Imperial Democracy	256
6.3 The King of Words	265
6.4 Roman Philosopher, Greek Tyrant	267
6.5 Herodes and Theseus	277
6.6 Conclusion	302
7. The Politics of Posterity	**305**
Bibliography	309
General Index	347
Index Locorum	360

LIST OF FIGURES

1.1 Andronikos of Kyrrhos' 'Tower of the Winds', Roman Agora, Athens. The rights to the illustrated monument belong to the Hellenic Ministry of Culture and Sports; the monument lies within the responsibility of the Ephorate of Antiquities of the city of Athens, Hellenic Ministry of Culture and Sports/Organization of Cultural Resources Development. Image: D-DAI-ATH-2013/79, Kienast.   15

1.2 Philopappos monument, Mouseion hill, Athens. The rights to the illustrated monument belong to the Hellenic Ministry of Culture and Sports; the monument lies within the responsibility of the Ephorate of Antiquities of the city of Athens, Hellenic Ministry of Culture and Sports/Organization of Cultural Resources Development. Image: Kleiner 1983, pl. IV (DFK 74.20.24).   20

1.3 Detail of the seated Philopappos in Greek himation, central panel, upper register, Philopappos monument. Image: Stuart and Revett 1762–1830, vol. 3, ch. 5, pl. 11.   21

1.4 Detail of Philopappos during his Roman consular procession, central panel, lower register, Philopappos monument. Image: Stuart and Revett 1762–1830, vol. 3, ch. 5, pl. 8.   22

2.1 Base of a statue of Demosthenes dedicated by Marcus Antonius Polemon of Laodikeia in the Asklepieion at Pergamon (Inv. 1932, 6; Habicht 1969, 75–6, no. 33). Image: Author.   45

2.2 Probable statue base from Athens with an inscription honouring Lucius Flavius Arrianos as consular and philosopher. Epigraphic Museum, Athens (*EM* 2868 + 3025 + 3118 + 2990 + 3036; *SEG* 30.159). The image and the rights to the illustrated monument belong to the Hellenic Ministry of Culture and Sports; the monument lies within the responsibility of the Epigraphic Museum, Hellenic Ministry of Culture and Sports/ Organization of Cultural Resources Development.   49

2.3 Double portrait herm of Xenophon and Isokrates or Arrian (?) from Athens. National Archaeological Museum, Athens (Glypta 538). The image and the rights to the illustrated monument belong to the Hellenic Ministry of Culture and Sports; the monument lies within the responsibility of the National Archaeological Museum, Hellenic Ministry of Culture and Sports/ Organization of Cultural Resources Development. Photographer: E. A. Galanopoulos.   52

2.4 Statue base or building masonry bearing parts of a Hadrianic inscription. Now built into the Chrysokephalos Church (Fatih Camii) in Trabzon, Turkey, as a door lintel (Mitford 1974, 160–3, pl. V.2). Image: Tim Mitford.   54

xii LIST OF FIGURES

2.5 Altar dedicated by Aelius Aristeides to Asklepios, most probably from the Asklepieion on Lesbos. Mytilene Museum, Lesbos (Inv. 2253; Charitonidis 1968, 27–8, no. 33, plate 11δ). The image and the rights to the illustrated monument belong to the Hellenic Ministry of Culture and Sports; the monument lies within the responsibility of the Archaeological Museum of Mytilene, Hellenic Ministry of Culture and Sports/Organization of Cultural Resources Development. 74

3.1 Marble portrait bust of Herodes Attikos, found with one of Polydeukion (see Figure 5.17) in Kephisia. National Archaeological Museum, Athens (NM 4810). The image and the rights to the illustrated monument belong to the Hellenic Ministry of Culture and Sports, within the responsibility of the National Archaeological Museum, Hellenic Ministry of Culture and Sports/Organization of Cultural Resources Development. Photographer: E. A. Galanopoulos. 82

3.2 Marble portrait statue of Demosthenes. Ny Carlsberg Glyptothek, Copenhagen (Inv. 2782). Image: Ny Carlsberg Glyptothek, Copenhagen. 83

3.3 Marble portrait statue of Aischines (partially restored) from Herculaneum. National Archaeological Museum, Naples (Inv. 6018). Image: Neg. D-DAI-ROM-31.751. 84

3.4 Marble portrait of Lysias mounted on a modern herm that bears the inscription 'Lysias'. Stanza dei Filosofi, Capitoline Museum, Rome (Inv. no. 601; Mus. no. 73). Image: R. Sansaini, Neg. D-DAI-ROM-54.969; © Roma, Sovrintendenza Capitolina ai Beni Culturali. 85

3.5 Marble portrait bust of Herodes Attikos from Brexiza, Attica. The Louvre (Inv. NIII 2536; Ma 1164). Image: Photo © Musée du Louvre, Dist. RMN-Grand Palais/Thierry Ollivier. 87

3.6 Marble portrait bust of Marcus Aurelius from Brexiza, Attica. The Louvre (Inv. NIII 2535; Ma 1161). Image: Photo © RMN-Grand Palais (Musée du Louvre)/Hervé Lewandowski. 87

3.7 Marble portrait bust of Lucius Verus from Brexiza, Attica. The Ashmolean Museum, Oxford (AN1947.277). Image: © Ashmolean Museum, University of Oxford. 88

3.8 Restored elevation of Herodes' Gate of Eternal Concord, Oinoe, Attica. Image: Mallwitz 1964, taf. 3. 90

3.9 Keystone from the Gate of Eternal Concord, from Oinoe, Attica, with statues of Regilla (L) and Herodes (R). Archaeological Museum of Marathon (Inv. Λ159, Inv. Λ158). The rights to the illustrated monument belong to the Hellenic Ministry of Culture and Sports; the monument lies within the responsibility of the Ephorate of Antiquities of East Attica, Hellenic Ministry of Culture and Sports/Organization of Cultural Resources Development. Image: Author. 91

3.10 Map of Marathon showing Brexiza and the *Mantra tis Grias* or 'Regilla's space'. Image: Erin McGowan; World Hillshade—Sources: Esri, Airbus DS, USGS, NGA, NASA, CGIAR, N Robinson, NCEAS, NLS, OS, NMA, Geodatastyrelsen, Rijkswaterstaat, GSA, Geoland, FEMA, Intermap and the GIS user community. 91

LIST OF FIGURES xiii

3.11 Keystone from the Gate of Eternal Concord, Oinoe, Attica, bearing an inscription relating to Regilla's 'space'. Archaeological Museum of Marathon (*IG* II^2 5189a). The rights to the illustrated monument belong to the Hellenic Ministry of Culture and Sports; the monument lies within the responsibility of the Ephorate of Antiquities of East Attica, Hellenic Ministry of Culture and Sports/Organization of Cultural Resources Development. Image: Courtesy of Hans R. Goette. 92

3.12 Keystone from the Gate of Eternal Concord, Oinoe, Attica, bearing an inscription relating to Herodes' 'space'. Archaeological Museum of Marathon (*IG* II^2 5189). The rights to the illustrated monument belong to the Hellenic Ministry of Culture and Sports; the monument lies within the responsibility of the Ephorate of Antiquities of East Attica, Hellenic Ministry of Culture and Sports/Organization of Cultural Resources Development. Image: D-DAI-ATH-Attika-479, Gösta Hellner. 93

3.13 Arch of Hadrian, Athens. The image and the rights to the illustrated monument belong to the Hellenic Ministry of Culture and Sports; the monument lies within the responsibility of the Ephorate of Antiquities of the city of Athens, Hellenic Ministry of Culture and Sports/Organization of Cultural Resources Development. Photographer: E. Bardani. 94

3.14 Secondary inscription lamenting the death of Regilla on the right pilaster of the Arch of Eternal Concord, from Oinoe, Attica (*SEG* 23.121; Geagan 1964). Archaeological Museum of Marathon. The rights to the illustrated monument belong to the Hellenic Ministry of Culture and Sports; the monument lies within the responsibility of the Ephorate of Antiquities of East Attica, Hellenic Ministry of Culture and Sports/Organization of Cultural Resources Development. Image: Courtesy of Hans R. Goette. 96

3.15 Reconstructed façade of the Library of Kelsos, Ephesos. Image: H. Sichtermann, Neg. D-DAI-ROM-82.1937. 102

3.16 Inscribed limestone sarcophagus of Dionysios of Miletos (T. Claudius Flavianus Dionysios), located opposite the Library of Kelsos in central Ephesos. Image: ÖAW/ÖAI—Archive. 103

3.17 Drawing of Dionysios of Miletos' sarcophagus showing the funerary inscription (*I.Ephesos* 2.426). Image: ÖAW/ÖAI—Archive. 104

4.1 Herm of an unidentified individual with curse inscription below the *membrum*. Epigraphic Museum, Athens (EM 10565; *IG* II^2 13201). The rights to the illustrated monument belong to the Hellenic Ministry of Culture and Sports; the monument lies within the responsibility of the Epigraphic Museum, Hellenic Ministry of Culture and Sports/ Organization of Cultural Resources Development. Photographer: Author. 148

4.2 Curse-inscribed herm of Achilles. Epigraphic Museum, Athens (EM 12466; *IG* II^2 13195). The image and the rights to the illustrated monument belong to the Hellenic Ministry of Culture and Sports; the monument lies within the responsibility of the Epigraphic Museum, Hellenic Ministry of Culture and Sports/Organization of Cultural Resources Development. 149

xiv LIST OF FIGURES

4.3 Two fragments of a curse-inscribed heroic relief from Kephisia (*IG* II^2 13191/3). Archaeological Collection of Kephisia. The rights to the illustrated monument belong to the Hellenic Ministry of Culture and Sports; the monument lies within the responsibility of the Ephorate of Antiquities of East Attica, Hellenic Ministry of Culture and Sports/ Organization of Cultural Resources Development. Image: D-DAI-ATH-Attika 408, W. Wrede. 150

4.4 Curse-inscribed herm (unidentified) or *stēlē* from Oinoe. Epigraphic Museum, Athens (EM 12467; *IG* II^2 13202). The image and the rights to the illustrated monument belong to the Hellenic Ministry of Culture and Sports; the monument lies within the responsibility of the Epigraphic Museum, Hellenic Ministry of Culture and Sports/Organization of Cultural Resources Development. 150

4.5 Curse-inscribed altar dedicated to Regilla, 'the light of the house'. Epigraphic Museum, Athens (EM 10317; *IG* II^2 13200). The image and the rights to the illustrated monument belong to the Hellenic Ministry of Culture and Sports; the monument lies within the responsibility of the Epigraphic Museum, Hellenic Ministry of Culture and Sports/ Organization of Cultural Resources Development. 151

4.6 Portrait head of Herodes' foster-son Memnon from Herodes' Villa at Loukou-Eva Kynouria. Antikensammlung, Staatliche Museen zu Berlin (Inv. Sk 1503). Image: Antikensammlung, Staatliche Museen zu Berlin, Preussischer Kulturbesitz. 152

4.7 Curse-inscribed herm of Polydeukion. Ashmolean Museum, Oxford (AN. Michaelis.177; *IG* II^2 13194). Image: © Ashmolean Museum, University of Oxford. 154

4.8 Curse-inscribed herm of Polydeukion. Epigraphic Museum, Athens (EM 13177; *IG* II^2 3970 + 13190). The rights to the illustrated monument belong to the Hellenic Ministry of Culture and Sports; the monument lies within the responsibility of the Epigraphic Museum, Hellenic Ministry of Culture and Sports/Organization of Cultural Resources Development. Photographer: Author. 157

4.9 Inscribed marble portrait herm of Herodes Attikos. Museum of Ancient Corinth (S1219; *Corinth* 8.1, no. 85). The rights to the illustrated monument belong to the Hellenic Ministry of Culture and Sports; the monument lies within the responsibility of the Ephorate of Antiquities of Corinthia, Hellenic Ministry of Culture and Sports/Organization of Cultural Resources Development. Image: bw_2002_017_07, Johnson 1931, 89, fig. 169, courtesy of the American School of Classical Studies at Athens, Corinth Excavations. 159

4.10 Tomb of Kyros from the north-west, Pasargadae. Image: Stronach 1978, pl. 24. 171

4.11 Ground plan of Herodes Attikos' Villa at Loukou-Eva Kynouria. Image: Courtesy of Giorgios Spyropoulos. 176

LIST OF FIGURES   XV

4.12 *Stêlê* inscribed with an epigram and list of the fallen of the Erechtheis tribe in the Battle of Marathon from the Villa of Herodes Attikos at Loukou-Eva Kynouria. Archaeological Museum of Astros (Inv. 535; Steinhauer 2004–2009). The rights to the illustrated monument belong to the Hellenic Ministry of Culture and Sports; the monument lies within the responsibility of the Ephorate of Antiquities of Arkadia, Hellenic Ministry of Culture and Sports/Organization of Cultural Resources Development. Image: Courtesy of Giorgios Spyropoulos.   178

4.13 Fragment of an inscribed casualty list from the Villa of Herodes Attikos at Loukou-Eva Kynouria. Archaeological Museum of Astros (Inv. 586). The rights to the illustrated monument belong to the Hellenic Ministry of Culture and Sports; the monument lies within the responsibility of the Ephorate of Antiquities of Arkadia, Hellenic Ministry of Culture and Sports/Organization of Cultural Resources Development. Image: Author, Courtesy of Giorgios Spyropoulos.   179

4.14 Fragment of an inscribed casualty list from the Villa of Herodes Attikos at Loukou-Eva Kynouria. Archaeological Museum of Astros (Inv. 587). The rights to the illustrated monument belong to the Hellenic Ministry of Culture and Sports; the monument lies within the responsibility of the Ephorate of Antiquities of Arkadia, Hellenic Ministry of Culture and Sports/Organization of Cultural Resources Development. Image: Author, Courtesy of Giorgios Spyropoulos.   179

4.15 One half of a pair of inscriptions found at Petri, near Nemea, that names Herodes Attikos (*SEG* 41.273). Archaeological Museum of Nemea. The rights to the illustrated monument belong to the Hellenic Ministry of Culture and Sports; the monument lies within the responsibility of the Ephorate of Antiquities of Corinthia, Hellenic Ministry of Culture and Sports/Organization of Cultural Resources Development. Image: Courtesy of Charalampos Kritzas.   183

4.16 Marble portrait bust of a priest, possibly a member of the Vedii Antonini family from Ephesos, found at the Villa of Herodes Attikos at Loukou-Eva Kynouria. Archaeological Museum of Astros. The rights to the illustrated monument belong to the Hellenic Ministry of Culture and Sports; the monument lies within the responsibility of the Ephorate of Antiquities of Arkadia, Hellenic Ministry of Culture and Sports/ Organization of Cultural Resources Development. Image: Courtesy of Giorgios Spyropoulos.   186

4.17 Marble portrait of a priest and member of the Vedii Antonini family from Ephesos. Izmir Archaeological Museum (Inv. 570). Image: ÖAW/ÖAI (A-W-OAI-DIA-128369).   186

4.18 Marble portrait of a priest and member of the Vedii Antonini family, from Ephesos. Izmir Archaeological Museum (Inv. 648). Image: ÖAW/ÖAI (A-W-OAI-DIA-128384).   187

xvi LIST OF FIGURES

4.19 Marble portrait of a priest with crown and member of the Vedii Antonini family. Louvre (MND 1012). Image: © Musée du Louvre, Dist. RMN-Grand Palais/Philippe Fuzeau. — 187

4.20 Marble portrait bust of Hadrian found at the Villa of Herodes Attikos at Loukou-Eva Kynouria. Archaeological Museum of Astros. The rights to the illustrated monument belong to the Hellenic Ministry of Culture and Sports; the monument lies within the responsibility of the Ephorate of Antiquities of Arkadia, Hellenic Ministry of Culture and Sports/Organization of Cultural Resources Development. Image: Courtesy of Giorgios Spyropoulos. — 189

5.1 Inscribed statue base of Arrian from Hierapolis (Komana, Kappadokia). Now built into a modern bridge in Şar, Adana province, Turkey (*SEG* 58.1665). Image: Ferit Baz. — 198

5.2 Marble portrait bust of a 'philosopher' or 'rhetor' from the Olympieion, Athens. National Archaeological Museum, Athens (NM 427). The image and the rights to the illustrated monument belong to the Hellenic Ministry of Culture and Sports; the monument lies within the responsibility of the National Archaeological Museum, Hellenic Ministry of Culture and Sports/Organization of Cultural Resources Development. Photographer: E. A. Galanopoulos. — 202

5.3 Marble statue of a seated philosopher from Rome. Vatican Museum Library (MV/P050). Image: © Governatorato SCV-Direzione dei Musei, all rights reserved. — 203

5.4 Remains of a Nymphaion dedicated to Zeus by Regilla at the site of Ancient Olympia. The rights to the illustrated monument belong to the Hellenic Ministry of Culture and Sports; the monument lies within the responsibility of the Ephorate of Antiquities of Elis, Hellenic Ministry of Culture and Sports/Organization of Cultural Resources Development. Image: D-DAI-ATH-1979/471, Gösta Hellner. — 208

5.5 Reconstruction of the Nymphaion at Olympia by Renate Bol. Image: Bol 1984, pl. 5. — 208

5.6 Reconstruction of the statue programme of the Nymphaion at Olympia, upper level. Image: Bol 1984, fig. 29. — 209

5.7 Reconstruction of the statue programme of the Nymphaion at Olympia, lower level. Image: Bol 1984, fig. 30. — 209

5.8 Marble statue of a bull with an inscription identifying Regilla as the dedicator on its flank, from the Nymphaion at Olympia. Archaeological Museum of Olympia (Inv. 373; *I.Olympia* no. 610). The rights to the illustrated monument belong to the Hellenic Ministry of Culture and Sports; the monument lies within the responsibility of the Ephorate of Antiquities of Elis, Hellenic Ministry of Culture and Sports/Organization of Cultural Resources Development. Image: D-DAI-ATH-1979/467, Gösta Hellner. — 210

5.9 Marble cuirass statue of the emperor Hadrian, from the Nymphaion at Olympia. Archaeological Museum of Olympia (Inv. VI, 1712; Mus. no. Λ 148). The rights to the illustrated monument belong to the Hellenic Ministry of Culture and Sports; the monument lies within the responsibility of the Ephorate of Antiquities of Elis, Hellenic Ministry of Culture and Sports/Organization of Cultural Resources Development. Image: D-DAI-ATH-1979/376, Gösta Hellner. 212

5.10 Marble cuirass statue of an emperor, probably Marcus Aurelius, from the Nymphaion at Olympia. Archaeological Museum of Olympia (Inv. II, 524; Mus. no. Λ 150). The rights to the illustrated monument belong to the Hellenic Ministry of Culture and Sports; the monument lies within the responsibility of the Ephorate of Antiquities of Elis, Hellenic Ministry of Culture and Sports/Organization of Cultural Resources Development. Image: D-DAI-ATH-1979/372, Gösta Hellner. 213

5.11 Marble cuirass statue of an emperor, probably Marcus Aurelius from the monopteros, from the Nymphaion at Olympia. Archaeological Museum of Olympia (Inv. V, 1423; Mus no. Λ 149). The rights to the illustrated monument belong to the Hellenic Ministry of Culture and Sports; the monument lies within the responsibility of the Ephorate of Antiquities of Elis, Hellenic Ministry of Culture and Sports/Organization of Cultural Resources Development. Image: D-DAI-ATH-1979/367, Gösta Hellner. 214

5.12 Marble statue of a male in a toga, from the Nymphaion at Olympia. Archaeological Museum of Olympia (Inv. II, 526; Mus no. Λ 153). The rights to the illustrated monument belong to the Hellenic Ministry of Culture and Sports; the monument lies within the responsibility of the Ephorate of Antiquities of Elis, Hellenic Ministry of Culture and Sports/Organization of Cultural Resources Development. Image: D-DAI-ATH-1979/384, Gösta Hellner. 215

5.13 Marble statue of a male in himation, from the Nymphaion at Olympia. Archaeological Museum of Olympia (Inv. II, 524, S 34, S37; Mus no. Λ 152). The rights to the illustrated monument belong to the Hellenic Ministry of Culture and Sports, within the responsibility of the Ephorate of Antiquities of Elis, Hellenic Ministry of Culture and Sports/Organization of Cultural Resources Development. Image: D-DAI-ATH-1979/444, Gösta Hellner. 216

5.14 Marble portrait bust of Antinoos. National Archaeological Museum, Athens (NM 417). The rights to the illustrated monument belong to the Hellenic Ministry of Culture and Sports; the monument lies within the responsibility of the National Archaeological Museum, Hellenic Ministry of Culture and Sports/Organization of Cultural Resources Development. Photographer: Author. 222

5.15 Marble Egyptianizing portrait statue of Antinoos (possibly as Osiris), from Hadrian's villa at Tivoli. Vatican, Museo Gregoriano Egizio (Inv. 22795 IFC; Mus. no. 99). Image: © Governatorato SCV-Direzione dei Musei, all rights reserved. 222

xviii LIST OF FIGURES

5.16 Marble portrait statue of Antinoos from Delphi. Archaeological Museum of Delphi (Inv. 1718). The rights to the illustrated monument belong to the Hellenic Ministry of Culture and Sports; the monument lies within the responsibility of the Ephorate of Antiquities of Phokia, Hellenic Ministry of Culture and Sports/Organization of Cultural Resources Development. Image: EFA/Ph. Collet. 223

5.17 Marble portrait bust of Polydeukion, found in Kephisia with one of Herodes (see Figure 3.1). National Archaeological Museum, Athens (NM 4811). The image and the rights to the illustrated monument belong to the Hellenic Ministry of Culture and Sports; the monument lies within the responsibility of the National Archaeological Museum, Hellenic Ministry of Culture and Sports/Organization of Cultural Resources Development. Image: Photographer: E. A. Galanopoulos. 224

5.18 The 'Antinoos of Olympia'. Archaeological Museum of Olympia (Mus no. Λ 204, 208). The rights to the illustrated monument belong to the Hellenic Ministry of Culture and Sports; the monument lies within the responsibility of the Ephorate of Antiquities of Elis, Hellenic Ministry of Culture and Sports/Organization of Cultural Resources Development. Image: D-DAI-ATH-Olympia-1440, Hermann Wagner. 224

5.19 Male 'Egyptianizing' statue from the Canopus shrine at Brexiza, near Marathon, possibly Antinoos or Polydeukion. National Archaeological Museum, Athens (Aeg. 1). The rights to the illustrated monument belong to the Hellenic Ministry of Culture and Sports; the monument lies within the responsibility of the National Archaeological Museum, Hellenic Ministry of Culture and Sports/Organization of Cultural Resources Development. Photographer: Anna Moles. 225

5.20 Heroic relief from Herodes Attikos' estate at Loukou-Eva Kynouria, possibly Polydeukion or Achilles. National Archaeological Museum, Athens (NM 1450). The rights to the illustrated monument belong to the Hellenic Ministry of Culture and Sports; the monument lies within the responsibility of the National Archaeological Museum, Hellenic Ministry of Culture and Sports/Organization of Cultural Resources Development. Image: D-DAI-ATH-1972/441, Gösta Hellner. 227

5.21 Heroic relief of Polydeukion found at the Sanctuary of Artemis at Brauron. Archaeological Museum of Brauron (Inv. 1181). The rights of the illustrated monument belong to the Hellenic Ministry of Culture and Sports; the monument lies within the responsibility of the Ephorate of East Attica, Hellenic Ministry of Culture and Sports/Organization of Cultural Resources Development. Photographer: Author. 227

5.22 Mid-second-century, marble portrait statue of a Roman youth from Italy, once assigned as an 'export' type of Polydeukion, now unidentified. Said to have been found at Hadrian's villa at Tivoli. Nelson-Atkins Museum of Art, Kansas City, Missouri. Purchase: William Rockhill Nelson Trust, 34–91/1. Image: Nelson-Atkins Museum of Art. 229

LIST OF FIGURES xix

5.23 Schematic portrait herm of Polydeukion from a fourth-century Roman villa at Welschbillig, Germany. Rheinisches Landesmuseum, Trier (Inv. 18876). Image: RD.1966.98, © GDKE/Rheinisches Landesmuseum Trier. Photographer: H. Thörnig.   230

5.24 Statue base of Polydeukion dedicated by the Delphians to the 'hero of Herodes', found reused in the Roman agora. Archaeological site of Delphi, Roman agora (Inv. 3251; *FD* III.3.1, no. 74). The rights to the illustrated monument belong to the Hellenic Ministry of Culture and Sports; the monument lies within the responsibility of Ephorate of Antiquities of Phokia, Hellenic Ministry of Culture and Sports/ Organization of Cultural Resources Development. Image: EFA/J.-Y. Empereur.   232

5.25 The triconch forecourt of the Peirene Fountain, Ancient Corinth. The rights to the illustrated monument belong to the Hellenic Ministry of Culture and Sports; the monument lies within the responsibility of the Ephorate of Antiquities of Corinthia, Hellenic Ministry of Culture and Sports/ Organization of Cultural Resources Development, and American School of Classical Studies at Athens, Corinth Excavations. Photographer: Author.   234

5.26 Marble statue base of Regilla from the Peirene Fountain, Ancient Corinth. Archaeological Museum of Corinth (Inv. 62; *Corinth* 8.1, no. 86). The rights to the illustrated monument belong to the Hellenic Ministry of Culture and Sports; the monument lies within the responsibility of the Ephorate of Antiquities of Corinthia, Hellenic Ministry of Culture and Sports/Organization of Cultural Resources Development, and American School of Classical Studies at Athens, Corinth Excavations. Photographer: Author.   234

5.27 Left side of the statue base of Regilla from the Peirene Fountain (upside down). Archaeological Museum of Corinth (Inv. 62). The rights to the illustrated monument belong to the Hellenic Ministry of Culture and Sports; the monument lies within the responsibility of the Ephorate of Antiquities of Corinthia, Hellenic Ministry of Culture and Sports/ Organization of Cultural Resources Development, and American School of Classical Studies at Athens, Corinth Excavations. Photographer: Author.   235

6.1 Relief of Herakles or Nero as Herakles carved into the wall of an ancient canal trench of the Corinth Canal, Isthmia. The rights to the illustrated monument belong to the Hellenic Ministry of Culture and Sports; the monument lies within the responsibility of the Ephorate of Antiquities of Corinthia, Hellenic Ministry of Culture and Sports/Organization of Cultural Resources Development. Image: David Pettegrew.   255

6.2 Inscribed letter from Marcus Aurelius to the Athenians regarding Herodes Attikos and the social advancement of freedmen. Epigraphic Museum, Athens (EM 13366; *SEG* 29.127). The image and the rights to the illustrated monument belong to the Hellenic Ministry of Culture and Sports; the monument lies within the responsibility of the Epigraphic Museum, Hellenic Ministry of Culture and Sports/Organization of Cultural Resources Development.   258

XX LIST OF FIGURES

6.3 Odeion of Herodes Attikos and Regilla, Athenian Akropolis. The rights to the illustrated monument belong to the Hellenic Ministry of Culture and Sports; the monument lies within the responsibility of the Ephorate of Antiquities of the city of Athens, Hellenic Ministry of Culture and Sports/Organization of Cultural Resources Development. Photographer: Author. 273

6.4 Marble inscribed *stélé* from the village of Bey, near Marathon. Archaeological Museum of Marathon (Inv. 22; *IG* II^2 3606). The image and the rights to the illustrated monument belong to the Hellenic Ministry of Culture and Sports; the monument lies within the responsibility of the Ephorate of East Attica, Hellenic Ministry of Culture and Sports/Organization of Cultural Resources Development. 278

6.5 The Panathenaic Stadium, Athens. The rights to the illustrated Monument belong to the Hellenic Ministry of Culture and Sports; the monument lies within the responsibility of the Ephorate of Antiquities of the city of Athens, Hellenic Ministry of Culture and Sports/Organization of Cultural Resources Development and *Ελληνική Ολυμπιακή Επιτροπή* (Greek Olympic Committee). Photographer: Author. 283

6.6 Statue base of Polydeukion dedicated by Herodes Attikos at the Sanctuary of Nemesis at Rhamnous. Archaeological site of Rhamnous (Λ505; *SEG* 49.209). The rights to the illustrated monument belong to the Hellenic Ministry of Culture and Sports; the monument lies within the responsibility of the Ephorate of Antiquities of East Attica, Hellenic Ministry of Culture and Sports/Organization of Cultural Resources Development. Photographer: Author. 287

6.7 Front panel of the Leda Sarcophagus found in Kephisia. The rights to the illustrated monument belong to the Hellenic Ministry of Culture and Sports; the monument lies within the responsibility of the Ephorate of Antiquities of East Attica, Hellenic Ministry of Culture and Sports/ Organization of Cultural Resources Development. Image: Courtesy of Hans R. Goette. 288

6.8 Ground plan of the Panathenaic Stadium and surrounds. Image: Travlos 1971, pl. 630. 290

6.9 Sarcophagus with associated altar above the eastern side of the Panathenaic Stadium, Athens. The rights to the illustrated monument belong to the Hellenic Ministry of Culture and Sports; the monument lies within the responsibility of the Ephorate of Antiquities of the city of Athens, Hellenic Ministry of Culture and Sports/Organization of Cultural Resources Development and *Ελληνική Ολυμπιακή Επιτροπή* (Greek Olympic Committee). Photographer: Author. 291

6.10 Altar dedicated to 'the hero of Marathon' (*IG* II^2 6791). Panathenaic Stadium, Athens. The rights to the illustrated monument belong to the Hellenic Ministry of Culture and Sports; the monument lies within the responsibility of the Ephorate of Antiquities of the city of Athens, Hellenic Ministry of Culture and Sports/Organization of Cultural Resources Development and *Ελληνική Ολυμπιακή Επιτροπή* (Greek Olympic Committee). Photographer: Author. 292

ABBREVIATIONS

Abbreviations follow those in the *Oxford Classical Dictionary* (third edition), with the following additions:

MODERN WORKS:

BNJ	Worthington, I. ed. *Brill's New Jacoby* (online). Leiden and Boston.
Corinth 8.1	Meritt, B. D. ed. 1931. *Corinth: Results of Excavations Conducted by the American School of Classical Studies at Athens* VIII.1: *Greek Inscriptions 1896–1927.* Cambridge, MA.
Corinth 8.3	Kent, J. H. ed. 1966. *Corinth: Results of Excavations Conducted by the American School of Classical Studies at Athens VIII.3: The Inscriptions 1926–1950.* Princeton, NJ.
FD III	Daux, G. and A. Salać eds. 1932. *Fouilles de Delphes, III. Épigraphie. Fasc. 3: Inscriptions depuis le trésor des Athéniens jusqu'aux bases de Gélon*, Vol. 1. Paris.
IG II^2	Kirchner, J. ed. 1913–1940. *Inscriptiones Atticae Euclidis anno posteriores.* 4 vols. Berlin.
IG XII, 5	Hiller von Gaertringen, F. F. ed. 1903–1909. *Inscriptiones Cycladum.* 2 vols. Berlin. I: *Inscriptiones Cycladum praeter Tenum* (1903); II: *Inscriptiones Teni insulae* (1909).
I.Ephesos 2	Börker, C. and R. Merkelbach with help from H. Engelmann and D. Knibbe eds. 1979. *Die Inschriften von Ephesos*, Part II: Nr. 100–599 (Repertorium). Bonn.
I.Ephesos 3	Engelmann, H., D. Knibbe, and R. Merkelbach eds. 1980. *Die Inschriften von Ephesos*, Part III: Nr. 600–1000 (Repertorium). Bonn.
I.Olympia	Dittenberger, W. and K. Purgold eds. 1896. *Die Inschriften von Olympia.* Berlin.
I.Smyrna	Petzl, G. ed. 1982–1990. *Die Inschriften von Smyrna. 2 vols.* Bonn.

ANCIENT WORKS:

HL	Aelius Aristeides, *Sacred Tales*
VH	Lucian, *True Stories*
Romance/Rom.	*The Alexander Romance*

A NOTE ON NAMES

I have used Greek spellings for Greek names, except in cases where the name is so familiar in its Anglicized/Latinized form (e.g. Achilles, Lucian, Thucydides, Dio Chrysostom, Strabo) as to be jarring for the reader in a Greek form.

ONE

The Future and the 'Second Sophistic'

The future has an ancient heart.

–Carlo Levi, *Il futuro ha un cuore antico.*[1]

In AD 131, Arrian of Nikomedeia, a member of the Greek elite of western Asia Minor and a Roman citizen, makes a decision to remodel an existing monument to the emperor Hadrian at Trapezous on the Black Sea, whilst carrying out an inspection tour of the region.[2] 'This spot is just made for an eternal memorial' (τὸ […] χωρίον ἐπιτηδειότατον εἰς μνήμην αἰώνιον, *Peripl.* 1.4), he writes to Hadrian in justification for the initiative. In Arrian's mind, Trapezous is perfect for a physical memorial because it is here that the famous Xenophon and the retreating 'Ten Thousand' first came to the safety of the Greek-held Black Sea coast, an exploit immortalized in Xenophon's fourth-century BC *Anabasis.* Arrian's physical memorial will thus 'piggy-back' on the reputation of Xenophon and his text, and the cultural and historical significance of place. Moreover, by undertaking the renovations, textualizing his intentions, and revising Xenophon's literary portrait of Trapezous, Arrian writes himself into this famous spot and its layers of history, shaping them to serve his own commemorative purposes. He reconfigures time, space, and artefact to create memory anew.[3] In doing so, however, he also demonstrates the fragility and mutability of fame, even when it is attached to landscape or artefacts.

Arrian's sentiment here encapsulates what this book is about: the imperial Greek obsession with personal commemoration by means of the pervasive, conscious creation of textual and material culture that positions itself within tradition but is crafted to speak to the future. In exploring how and why elite Roman-era Greeks were compelled to fashion a place in future consciousness via these two deeply connected commemorative strategies—the literary and the material—I argue that imperial Greek temporality was far more complex than scholarship has previously allowed. Indeed, the cultural output of elite Greeks during the Roman empire was shaped by a perspective trained not only on the distant past

[1] Translation of the main title of Levi 1961.
[2] Arrian was governor of Kappadokia at this time; he may also have been descended from Italian settlers in Nikomedeia, adding further complexity to his cultural identity.
[3] This process in this text is explored in detail in Section 2.2.

Fashioning the Future in Roman Greece: Memory, Monuments, Texts. Estelle Strazdins, Oxford University Press.
© Estelle Strazdins 2023. DOI: 10.1093/oso/9780192866103.003.0001

2 FASHIONING THE FUTURE IN ROMAN GREECE

but also simultaneously on the future. This made them particularly alive to both the possibility of creating and the apparent impossibility of controlling 'immortal fame'. This book draws out the tensions, anxieties, and opportunities that attend the construction of fame and the contemplation of posterity against the background of the so-called 'Second Sophistic', and it examines the consequences of this embroilment with futurity on our understanding of the cultural and political concerns of elite imperial Greek society.

This is not the usual approach to the 'Second Sophistic'. This phrase makes its first appearance in Flavius Philostratos' third-century AD collection of anecdotal biographies, the *Lives of the Sophists*. There he uses it to describe a type of oratorical performance that he casts as central to contemporary elite Greek culture. In modern scholarship, however, it has taken on a life of its own.[4] It regularly designates the period of the first three centuries AD in the Greek-speaking eastern empire and elite Greek culture in its relationship to Roman power at that time. I will be using it specifically to signify classicizing patterns of literary and monumental self-representation by elite Roman citizens of Greek origin during this period with a particular focus on the second century AD. Importantly, the temporal displacement inherent in the term gels with the time-bending and (virtual) time-travelling activities of the individuals who appear in these pages, and my focus adheres to the spirit and complexity of Philostratos' overall construction.

Philostratos attaches the phrase not to a specific period but to a distinct theatrical type of *epideixis*, in which the rhetor delivers his speech in the guise of a historical or occasionally mythological figure.[5] He juxtaposes this 'later sophistic ($\mu\epsilon\tau$' $\dot{\epsilon}\kappa\epsilon\dot{\iota}\nu\eta\nu$)', which he specifies 'must not be called "new" ($o\dot{\nu}\chi\dot{\iota}$ $\nu\dot{\epsilon}\alpha\nu$), for it is old ($\dot{\alpha}\rho\chi\alpha\dot{\iota}\alpha$ $\gamma\dot{\alpha}\rho$), but rather "second" ($\delta\epsilon\nu\tau\dot{\epsilon}\rho\alpha\nu$ $\delta\dot{\epsilon}$ $\mu\hat{\alpha}\lambda\lambda\rho\nu$)' to an 'ancient sophistic' ($\dot{\alpha}\rho\chi\alpha\dot{\iota}\alpha$ $\sigma\sigma\phi\iota\sigma\tau\iota\kappa\dot{\eta}$) that explored more philosophical themes (*VS* 1.0.481).[6] These speeches were mostly improvised, with the audience proposing the theme to the performing rhetor.[7] Philostratos traces the roots of his topic to the fourth-century BC Athenian orator Aischines (*VS* 1.0.481): he grounds it in classical Athens, just as the men he describes choose classical themes for their speeches, pepper them

---

[4] Philostratos was writing in the late 230s or early 240s. On Philostratos and his corpus, see (with bibliography) Bowie 2009, 19–32; Elsner 2009, 3–18. On the various usages of the 'Second Sophistic' in scholarship, see Whitmarsh 2005, 3–22; Miles 2018, 12–15.

[5] See Whitmarsh 2005, 4–22. For concise and clear discussion of the branches of Greek rhetoric and epideictic in particular, see Webb 2006, 27–46; 2009, 15–20, 26; Pernot 2015. For the extent of sophistic performance culture, see Whitmarsh 2005, 23–40.

[6] For Philostratos' $\tau\dot{\alpha}\varsigma$ $\dot{\epsilon}\varsigma$ $\ddot{o}\nu\rho\mu\alpha$ $\dot{\nu}\pi\sigma\theta\dot{\epsilon}\sigma\epsilon\iota\varsigma$ meaning 'performances *in persona*', see Whitmarsh 2001, 42. *Contra* Wright (1968, 7) for 'definite and special themes'. All translations are my own unless otherwise indicated. This translation follows Wright 1968 with significant alterations.

[7] Whitmarsh 2005, 66, with bibliography; also, Kennedy 1974, 17–22; Russell 1983, 106–28; Swain 1996, 92–6.

with classical quotations, and for the most part employ the archaizing Attic dialect.[8] These characteristics, moreover, spill over into other literary genres.

As a result, the past that fascinated Roman-era Greeks has traditionally been conceived of as limiting and dwarfing their cultural output, so that, for a long time, scholars regularly dismissed imperial Greek literature as derivative and mimetic of the classical canon.[9] That view was reinforced by a long-established tendency to see the culture of archaic and classical Greece as both purer and simply better than that of the imperial period, and by the privileging of originality stemming from romanticism.[10] This scholarly aversion was thus deeply linked to negative modern aesthetic judgements of the Second Sophistic.[11] Aesthetic appraisal, however, is largely determined by social and cultural context, so that a piece of art can be appreciated to vastly different degrees at different times and in different places.[12] Moreover, a thing of extraordinary and enduring beauty comes to be labelled as such only once enough individuals respond to it with positive emotions over large spans of time.[13] This should be a very personal and individual reaction that is repeated on a vast temporal and quantitative scale, but in reality personal response to art is always shaped by the authority of tradition and the dictates of fashion. This is particularly relevant to modern scholarship and what it deems worthy of study.[14]

More recent, theoretically informed scholarship has avoided aesthetic estimation of elite imperial Greek culture in an effort to create distance between modern pluralist attitudes and older canonizing approaches that are now rightly judged elitist, anachronistic, and conservative.[15] Thus only in the last century and particularly the past fifty years or so with the theoretical turn in classics have imperial Greek texts been seen as worthy of exploration. Even so, they have primarily been approached as material for probing social, cultural, political, and historical questions rather than aesthetic ones. Indeed, the texts have proved so good to think with that, if one traces the relevant scholarship, we gain a snapshot of contemporary cultural and intellectual history as much as an insight into the past.[16] One therefore wonders if the history of Second Sophistic scholarship might have been

---

[8] See Swain 1996, 17–64; Whitmarsh 2005, 4–8, 41–56, both with extensive bibliography.

[9] See, e.g., Bompaire 1958.

[10] On the preference for the 'purity' of early Greece, see Whitmarsh 2013a, 1–7, especially 2.

[11] The most extreme expression of this distaste is to be found in van Groningen 1965, 41–56.

[12] Cf. Nelson and Olin 2003, 7.   [13] See Hall 2017.

[14] Cf. Nelson and Olin 2003, 2: 'a monument is what art history chooses to celebrate and proclaim a monument'. Also see Dickenson's (2017, 3–31) discussion of a scholarly assumption that increased monumentality in public space in the Roman period is indicative of social, political, and cultural decline.

[15] For the issue of scholarship and aesthetic worth, see Hall 2017. On the application of 'aesthetics' to the ancient world, see Destrée and Murray 2015, 1–12. On the formation of new theoretically founded canons, see Gorak 1991, 221–60.

[16] Whitmarsh 2005, 10. See 6–10 for a survey of that cultural history.

different, given the modern world's preoccupation with originality, had Philostratos not redefined it from 'new' to 'second'.

The resistance to assigning aesthetic value to Roman-period Greek texts and to granting them a status equivalent to classical literature can be seen most clearly in scholarly dissatisfaction with the defining genre of Philostratos' Second Sophistic: *epideixis*. The surviving speeches have regularly been judged as poor art: '[a]s speakers, most sophists left nothing but a few quotes in Philostratos' *Lives* that do not make us regret the loss of the rest of their production. The texts that have reached us complete and in their original form do not inspire much enthusiasm either'.[17] An enormous part of this negative appraisal must derive from the incongruity of a performative genre like oratory being preserved as silent and immobile text, when in practice it 'would have been dynamized by clothing, props, gesture, intonation, vocal texture, complemented by the surroundings, and framed by an ongoing dialogue with the audience'.[18]

The discrepancy between modern experience of the written word and ancient performed speech has led Martin Korenjak to intimate that Roman-period Greeks engaged in sophistic activities had no interest in posterity and were focused solely on the rise and further rise of their present star.[19] If we are to believe Philostratos' depiction of sophistic culture, contemporary fame did depend largely on one's epideictic ability and the one-off, improvised, oral nature of this genre posed an obstacle to the persistence of fame beyond the performative moment. I will call this the 'sophistic dilemma'.[20] For fame to accrue, one's performance must be remembered and replayed either through the recollections passed on by the initial audience or through the dissemination and consumption of a textual record.[21] Although incongruous with the genre of improvised *epideixis* and thus treated ambivalently in many imperial Greek texts,[22] the monumentalizing capacity of text was embraced as one way of extending fame. Consequently, many literary works produced at this time are cast as though they are 'recordings' of a previous epideictic moment, even if that performance never occurred in reality.[23]

Korenjak's position thus overlooks the fact that authors commit to 'conversing with posterity' the moment they consign their speeches and works of other genres to writing.[24] At the same time, it applies a modern aesthetic assessment to ancient

---

[17] Korenjak 2012, 253.　　[18] Whitmarsh 2005, 24; cf. Webb 2006, 32–4.

[19] Korenjak 2012, 254–6.　　[20] See Strazdins 2008.

[21] Thomas (2003, 162–88) describes the tension between *epideixis* and written publication in classical times.

[22] As well as the spectre of *epideixis* and artistic achievement, this ambivalence is based to some extent on responding to Plato's *Phaidros* and its attitude to rhetoric and writing. See Trapp 1990, 141–73.

[23] Examples include the speeches of Dio Chrysostom, Lucian, and Aelius Aristeides, Apuleius' *Florida* and *Apologia*.

[24] The phrase 'conversing with posterity' forms part of the title of Korenjak's chapter.

material and fails to grasp imperial Greek sensitivity to the performativity and materiality of writing. James Porter, for one, has convincingly argued that, in the minds of ancient Greeks, written texts were understood to retain an aspect of their author's voice and were thus considered to be a kind of auditory recording or 'voiceprint'.[25] When one read a text, Porter suggests, one heard its composer's voice and to possess the text was in some sense to experience the performance.[26] Access to this experience, however, depended on reading the text in the right kind of way. That method may have been at the fingertips of imperial Greeks, since it was part and parcel of their cultural comprehension of textuality, but it tends to elude the modern critic, who can approximate but not reconstruct sensory authenticity. Angelos Chaniotis has made much the same point with respect to the performativity of inscriptions, a topic explored in chapter 4, and our tendency to access the ancient world only in a visual capacity.[27] Thus reading in the modern world is not a sound basis on which to judge the quality of ancient performative texts and our cultural preconceptions of what constitutes great literature interfere with our ability to interpret it.

Philostratos' specificity about the oratorical nature of the Second Sophistic (*VS* 1.0.481) is disingenuous, however, since the contents of the *Lives of the Sophists* do not sit entirely comfortably with his definition. His sophists are *pepaideumenoi*, who vie for recognition in the public domain, and are characterized first and foremost as teachers and performers of rhetoric.[28] They are, however, also more than this. Philostratos' sophists represent their native or adopted cities on imperial embassies, take on priesthoods and administrative positions in their local government, perform liturgies, and make liberal benefactions to those cities with which they are associated.[29] They are competitive and status driven, often bi- or even tri-cultural, and their success is regularly measured in political influence, a following of students, and rivalry with other sophists.[30] Moreover, despite Philostratos' broad temporal scope, the vast majority of his examples do come from the first three centuries AD and he passes over the intervening period from Aischines by mentioning three orators whom he brings up only to reject as unworthy of comment (*VS* 1.18.510–11).

---

[25] Porter 2006, 314. See also the rich, extended discussion of Shane Butler (2015, esp. 11–58) on texts as recordings of voice.

[26] For an excellent analysis of aesthetic materiality and the differences between ancient Greeks and ourselves, see Porter 2010. On the animation of written text and its (in)abilities to capture speech, see especially 308–64.

[27] Chaniotis 2012, 303.

[28] On *paideia*, see the discussion of Whitmarsh 1998 and 2001, 90–132, with bibliography.

[29] See Bowersock 1969. Cf. the qualifications of Bowie 1982. See also Schmitz 1997.

[30] The prime example from *VS* is Polemon and Favorinus (1.8.490–1, 1.25.536, 1.25.541). See Gleason 1995, xxvii–xxviii, 27–8, 46–8. Again, on the social and political status of sophists, see Bowersock 1969.

An appreciation of this broader Philostratean context has led to more recent, more generous appraisals of imperial Greek literature. According to these, the repetition, citation, and reinvention of the classical past becomes a politically motivated creative exercise in shaping and promoting elite Greekness in the face of the Roman present.[31] This position has been particularly influenced by post-colonialism. Ewen Bowie and Simon Swain have both made this argument, although Swain rightly stresses that imperial Greek writers regularly and expediently identify politically, if not culturally, with Rome.[32] Glen Bowersock explicitly rejects the idea of cultural 'renaissance' as a response to Roman rule and focuses primarily on the role Philostratos' sophists play in imperial more so than cultural politics: on their negotiation of and interaction with Roman power in the present.[33] More recently, Maud Gleason, Thomas Schmitz, Tim Whitmarsh, and Joy Connolly have explored the strongly performative and competitive context of elite Greek culture during the empire as well as the ability of sophists to play with their self-identity, so that their posturing as 'Roman', 'Greek', 'Syrian', 'Athenian' is fluid and strategic.[34] Kendra Eshleman has added an extra layer by detailing comparatively the social dimensions of sophistic and early Christian identities.[35] Despite their differences, all these scholars rightly perceive artfulness and complexity in the texts and see the participants in the Second Sophistic as being primarily concerned with their own time, rather than the past, and with cultural and social aspects of personal identity. This book builds on these studies by arguing that we can gain a more robust appreciation of these issues by also examining elite Greeks' concern for their place in posterity, and that this concern directly impacts our understanding of their political as much as their cultural present.

Tony Spawforth, developing Andrew Wallace-Hadrill's 'cardiac' model of Roman acculturation, has flipped the agency in the relationship between Greek culture and Roman power by arguing that the classicizing tendency in the eastern provincial elite was elicited and promoted by a centralized programme from the

---

[31] Schmitz 1997 and Whitmarsh 2001 are particularly strong on this aspect. See also Porter 2005, 42–3; Webb 2006, 36–7; Whitmarsh 2013b, 57–78. For examples of newer scholarship which approach the Second Sophistic broadly, see Webb 2006; Kemezis 2011; 2014; Eshleman 2012; König 2014; Johnson and Richter 2017.

[32] See Bowie 1974, 166–209; Swain 1996. Note that this is a refocusing of an older view that was trained on nationalism rather than culture that stems from Rohde 1960 [1914]. On Rohde's Second Sophistic, see Whitmarsh 2011, 210–24.

[33] See Bowersock 1969.

[34] See especially Gleason 1995; Schmitz 1997; Connolly 2001, 75–96; Whitmarsh 2001 and 2005. On the issue of identity, see also Perkins 2009; Eshleman 2012, 1–20.

[35] Eshleman 2012.

Augustan period onwards.[36] This policy encouraged a return to Greek *polis* values and identities as a way of dispersing and neutralizing potential Greek political resistance to Roman rule. If Roman-era Greeks were focused on the differences between themselves and their neighbours, it was unlikely they would consider a unified opposition to Rome. Greek fascination with the past thus becomes a form of Roman control. A crucial by-product of this profitable argument is the identification of a genuine Roman concern over the potential for Greek elites to disrupt imperial harmony. This concern opens the door to understanding the messages of imperial Greek cultural expression as doing real political and not just cultural work, especially if we allow its exponents a stake in the future. I will argue this position throughout what follows.

With increasing scholarly esteem for the Greek literature of the empire came a more concentrated application of literary theory, one consequence of which was to question the historicity of Philostratos' 'cultural movement'. Adam Kemezis, for instance, presents Philostratos' project as a cultural history which possesses its own geography and narrative that would not have been immediately recognizable to his peers, and which traces the progression of the Second Sophistic from the exiled Aischines in Ionia, back to Athens, then onwards to Rome.[37] The question then arises, what was Philostratos trying to achieve with his catalogue of sophists? I explore this question against the background of Roman Greece, elite Greek political ambitions, and Roman imperial power in chapter 6.

Addressing the same concern for the *Lives of the Sophists*' historicity, Whitmarsh has persuasively argued that the diversity of imperial Greek literature and the multiple visions of imperial society from different cultural, social, and political perspectives it contains have been subsumed and thus underexplored by a scholarly tendency to accept Philostratos' depiction of the period as authoritative.[38] From Whitmarsh's point of view, we should be examining postclassicism rather than the Second Sophistic, a term that would embrace the Hellenistic period as well. What is particularly promising about this approach is that it conceives of Hellenistic and imperial Greek literature as a new phase in a cultural continuum from classical times. It casts its exponents as building (something new) on existing foundations rather than as deteriorating into decadent ruin. Another consequence

---

[36] Spawforth 2012. Wallace-Hadrill 2008, 361: 'it makes no sense to speak of "hellenisation" and "romanisation" as if they were separate phenomena [...]. Think of Rome as a great heart, at the centre of the arterial system of its empire. In the diastolic phase, the heart draws blood from the entire system of its empire, literally sucking blood, drawing to itself all the wealth, the goods, the ideas, crafts and technology of the Mediterranean. In the systolic phase, it pumps blood back out again, transformed by oxygenation into "Roman" blood'.

[37] Kemezis 2011, 3–22. Cf. Whitmarsh 2015, 49. See also Schmitz 2009; Eshleman 2012, 1–20, 125–48.

[38] Whitmarsh 2013a, 3–5; see also Brunt 1994.

has been a shift away from using imperial Greek literature largely as a means of accessing cultural history to a focus on the literature itself.[39] This is the culmination of its rehabilitation to something worth studying in its own right as a form of art. Such a position opens the door to analysing imperial Greek literature seriously as aspirational of canonicity and to assessing the impact of this on our understanding of the canon, imperial Greek culture, and the dynamics of interaction between elite Greeks and Rome.

Given the generous reapplication of the 'Second Sophistic' label and newer scholarship's identification of imperial Greek literature as everything from self-reflexive, playful, creative, multifarious, to forming an aesthetic of postclassicism, and even as a different (i.e. earlier) variety of postmodernism, it is surprising that there have not been more attempts to trace the same processes in material culture as well.[40] This is not to suggest that imperial Greek material culture is poorly studied; there are many fine scholarly works that are both stimulating and useful.[41] Scholarship on creative emulation, eclecticism, and contextual meaning with respect to Roman ideal sculpture, for example, parallels work done on imperial Greek texts.[42] Nevertheless and idiosyncratically, imperial Greek artefacts and architecture tend to fall under the rubric 'Roman', whereas the literature is designated 'Greek', terms that imply cultural affiliation as well as simply language. So the impetus to study both media on the same terms involves a crossing of traditional, if anachronistic and fairly arbitrary, disciplinary lines.

Interdisciplinarity is certainly increasing, led in particular by some of Jaś Elsner's work on Pausanias, Alexia Petsalis-Diomidis' account of Aelius Aristeides and the healing cult of Asklepios at Pergamon, and Zahra Newby's account of Greek athletics in the Roman world.[43] Nonetheless, when imperial Greek monuments and artefacts are considered alongside text, the juxtaposition and mutual rhetoric is rarely a focus of discussion. Verity Platt, for example, combines text and artefact in a brilliant exploration of the ancient experience of divine epiphany, but her attention is (understandably) trained on that phenomenon rather than the intermediality of imperial Greek culture.[44] Laura Nasrallah's study of early Christian texts within the spatial context of the Roman empire goes some way to exploring

---

[39] Recent examples include Kim 2010; Downie 2013; ní Mheallaigh 2014; LaValle Norman 2019; Greensmith 2020; Jolowicz 2021; Leon 2021.

[40] ní Mheallaigh 2014 casts Lucian's works and by extension Second Sophistic literature as postclassical and (anachronistically) to an extent postmodern. Cf. Nasrallah 2010, 29.

[41] See, e.g., Smith 1998, 56–93; Galli 2002; Puech 2002; Perry 2001; 2005; Gleason 2010, 125–62; Nasrallah 2010; Mazurek 2018.

[42] An accessible example is Perry 2005. See also Ma 2006 on connoisseurship in viewing.

[43] Newby 2005; Elsner 2007d, 29–48; 2007e, 49–66; Petsalis-Diomidis 2010. Many contributions to Alcock, Cherry, and Elsner 2001 can be counted here too.

[44] Platt 2011.

this phenomenon in the second century.[45] Michael Squire, exceptionally, takes intermediality as his central topic, building on earlier examinations of the Greek literary practice of *ekphrasis* to place text and art on equal footing and to explore their interpenetration.[46] These topics, the intermediality of imperial Greek culture and *ekphrasis*, are important elements of chapter 3 below. Squire's approach opens new ways of exploring culture that are particularly relevant to imperial Greece, since euergetism and literary composition were both pursuits of the Greek elite and it is possible to study the same individual through both media. One wonders, then, do the same concerns, positionings, engagements with contemporary and past culture identified in Second Sophistic literature also shape material art? This is one puzzle probed throughout the present work, especially in chapters 3 through 5.

My approach is interdisciplinary rather than intermedial. In what follows there is a stronger emphasis on the texts of the Second Sophistic, but it is heavily supplemented and enriched by analysis of material culture, especially inscribed material culture within the commemorative land- and cityscapes of Roman Greece. Intermediality remains an important concept for thinking about imperial Greek culture, however, because the texts and monuments themselves regularly demonstrate engagement with the well-developed Greek discourse of competition between text and artefact. Imperial Greek literature is saturated with monuments and commemorative spaces, and imperial Greek monuments discourse with the architectural matrices of Roman imperial cityscapes, Greek architectural and artistic traditions, and the spaces of Greek history and literature. Physical monuments thus cannot be analysed adequately without considering the historical and literary record in addition to architectural influences, and textual monuments require engagement with their spatial, cultural, and historical contexts alongside their literary function. One aim of this book is to demonstrate the importance of these dual streams of culture—the literary and the material—to any explication of imperial Greece.

Recent explorations of cultural memory in the Roman empire, moreover, have emphasized the role of landscape and architecture in preserving and shaping commemoration as well as the important functions such 'memoryscapes' can perform in the production of literary and material art.[47] In the eastern Roman

---

[45] Nasrallah 2010.

[46] Squire 2009. Newby 2005 is also relevant here. On the concept of intermediality in this sense, see Wagner 1996, 15–18; Squire 2009, 297–9. Note that sections of Thomas (2007, 207–35) apply this approach, which he labels 'experiencing architecture'. On the western empire, see, e.g., Elsner and Meyer 2014.

[47] This initiative has been led by Karl Galinsky's *Memoria Romana* project. See Galinsky 2015, 1–22, as well as the eclectic essays in that volume and Galinsky 2014 and 2016. See also the earlier collection of Cordovana and Galli 2007.

empire, the Greek past was ever present in physical land- and cityscapes. The quality of that past depended on a nexus of factors, such as the 'plurality of peoples [...] their ethnicities, languages, histories, and religions' that created their memories and invested place with meaning.[48] This notion of cultural memory as a constellation of elements helps to explain its constant evolution as new versions of established tales were told or the past came to mean something different to the present.[49] Its inherent mutability, moreover, means memory is often specific to place, so that intensely local memories can exist and signify something to small communities at the same time as those communities share in larger recollections with broader horizons.[50] Given that imperial Greek *pepaideumenoi* are regularly involved in the production of material culture, might they not then take cultural memory, especially that which is attached to place and objects, and embed themselves within it in ways that dialogue with, reinterpret, and redirect existing meaning, much as they do with the literary-historical memory in their texts?[51] In the present work, I will extend the study of the reapplication and manipulation of cultural memory to consider how it is used to converse with the future in both literature and material culture.

In addition to paying insufficient attention to the interpenetration of imperial Greek monuments and literature, recent scholarship has failed to produce a sophisticated conception of temporality to match its subtle approaches to culture, identity, and power.[52] This book explores this added dimension. The link between the present and the past is everywhere in modern scholarship, largely due to the impossibility, given the history of Second Sophistic studies and the 'classicizing' nature of the literature itself, to extract it from its Roman context. The relationship of Greek culture to Roman power still rightly penetrates almost all investigations.[53]

There is, however, no consideration of the Second Sophistic's engagement with the future, even though one result of the collision between Greek culture and Rome is an unmistakeable awareness of large spans of time. Despite the interests of modern scholarship, this awareness is not unidirectional, but rather counterbalanced by an equal and opposite preoccupation with the future. Restricting

---

[48] Galinsky 2015, 1. See also Thomas 2007, 165–78.

[49] Halbwachs 1980, 69; Galinsky 2015, 2. See Erll 2010, 1–9, on the development of the concept of 'cultural memory' in scholarship, and Erll 2011, 13–37, on the field of memory studies.

[50] See Galinsky 2015, 2–3. Also Van Dyke 2008, 278; Alcock 2015, 24.

[51] This follows Pierre Nora's concept of *lieux de mémoire*. See Nora 1996, xv. See Thomas 2007, 165, for Greeks creating cultural narratives around material objects. On the concept of 'collective memory', see Halbwachs 1992; Assman 1995, 125–33; Erll 2011, 13–37.

[52] See Lianeri 2016 for recent attempts to consider the relationship of Greek and Latin historiography to the future.

[53] See Whitmarsh 2001, vii, on the ubiquity of the spectre of Roman power in imperial Greek literature.

temporal investigation thus limits our capacity to appreciate the full range of aspirations and meanings embedded in imperial Greek cultural output. It is striking that the relationship of authors, especially poets, to eternity is a common theme in Greek literary studies from Homer to the Hellenistic epigrammatists, as well as for Latin literature, but no similar work has been done on the Second Sophistic.[54] The vicissitudes of posthumous reception should not restrict scholarly probing. Imperial Greek authors were not cognizant of what form their reputation might take two thousand years down the track, but this does not mean that they were uninterested in shaping it. As Whitmarsh notes, when they wrote, 'the future was entirely up for grabs'.[55]

A different account of temporality, therefore, allows us to ask new questions. For example, since Philostratos' sophists lived and breathed the Greek 'canon', how cognizant were they of their own relationship to it and the (im?)possibility of one day being part of it? Does allowing imperial Greeks a stake in the future change our understanding of their social, cultural, or political present? Just what were the commemorative aspirations of authors/monumentalizers, and where did they think their artworks belonged in relation to cultural monuments of the past? For whom were they writing/building—past, present, or future? This book aims to show that it is all three at once and that a full appreciation of imperial Greek culture in the context of its present cannot be achieved without exploring its relationship to the future. Indeed, throughout what follows, I argue imperial Greek fascination with the past is founded in concerns about the future. The constant interaction with and imitation of past greats allow the writers of the Second Sophistic to revive them.[56] The desire to do so has several pay-offs for the promotion of one's own place in literary history that will form the subject of chapter 2 and provide background to the rest of the book.

First, engagement with the past privileges and enlivens a concept of Greekness that is independent of the empire. It thus situates imperial Greek literature within an established tradition, so that its innovations, breakings away, and reimaginings can be recognized and processed by those versed in Greek culture. To this end, a shared rhetoric of social and cultural homogeneity infuses contemporary perceptions of the future.[57] Greeks and Romans did not possess a sense of technological progress leading to qualitative social transformation and, at least rhetorically, constructing a future culturally identical to the present ensured a suitably qualified audience to receive one's cultural interventions. Exactly what might constitute the

---

[54] See Kerkhecker 1999, 11–16, for a succinct summary of Greek poets and their relationship to eternity from Homer to Hellenistic times with relevant bibliography.

[55] Whitmarsh 2013a, 6.   [56] See Webb 2006, 32–7, especially 35.

[57] E.g. Hor. *Carm.* 3.30.1–9, where poetic 'eternity' is measured by the continuation of a Roman religious rite.

future is nevertheless rarely articulated in Greek and Roman texts. In fact, Brent Shaw has now decisively demonstrated that in economic and practical terms the Romans did not possess a notion of the future equivalent to our own—'time that is densely populated with things that are planned, known and solidly pictured'—as evinced by a failure either to organize for it in concrete ways or to borrow against its projected capital.[58] Although this holds true more broadly for politics and society, amongst elite imperial Greeks, the notion of their own, if isolated and to a large degree abstract, futurity was buttressed by the concept of monumental permanence and the canon of great literature. It is in fact elite authors to whom Shaw permits the anomalous capacity to imagine a notional future.[59] For elite imperial Greeks, however, this future remains largely conceptual beyond its embeddedness in often concrete and commemorative space, and its tethering to cultural history that frequently interweaves with a denser historical consciousness.

Imperial Greek engagement with monumentality is one way in which futurity and historical consciousness are manifested and is intimately connected to the notion of the Greek literary canon. Indeed, an argument can be made that Philostratos' canonization of the 'Second Sophistic' in his *Lives of the Sophists* is a rearguard action to preserve pagan Hellenic culture in the face of a changing, increasingly Roman and Christian, world rather than an accurate representation of imperial culture (see further chapter 6). Contextualizing one's own cultural output in the company of the works of the past and projecting the reception of both into future time is a way of rhetorically insuring one's continuing relevance.[60] As Michael Cole has detailed, culture 'creates an (artificial) continuity between past and future'.[61] Authors and monumentalizers of this period, I argue, make the past work for their own commemoration.

The second pay-off is that reviving the past assigns meaning and priority to specific Greek texts that create a language of cultural influence and power for the initiated. Third, it conflates the present and the past in order to imbue one's own works with pedigree at the same time as creating a level playing field, so that the works of past greats can be contested. Accepting that imperial Greeks were writing and building with their future as much as the past or present in mind is to grant them canonical potential: to take their cultural output seriously as art and to admit to the power of tradition and culture to define (aesthetic) value. It is not my intention to make aesthetic judgements of the worth of imperial Greek literature or monuments. Rather, I wish to underline the fact that Roman-period Greek

---

[58] Shaw 2019; quotation from p. 6.

[59] Shaw 2019, 22 (Pliny and Tacitus). See also the discussion of Tamiolaki 2016 on Lucian, and LaValle Norman 2019 on Methodius.

[60] Cole (1993; 2016) posits that people create a conception of the future in the present based on past experience, which is then materially enforced.

[61] Cole 1993, 251.

authors and monumentalizers were deeply concerned with their works' reception and to make the case that such concerns merit careful study.

Canonicity is thus central to elite imperial Greek temporality, partly because notions of what it meant to be part of the canon extended beyond literary prominence. This is revealed in the signs of elite status propagated and therefore valued by contemporary Greeks. Not only is placement within a library or acknowledgement by one's peers through quotation, emulation, or rivalry desirable, but statue honours, civic benefactions, and embeddedness in a pepaideutic genealogy of pre-eminent teachers and students are also crucial. Indeed, all these latter aspects operate on both a political and cultural plain to promote the canonical aspirant in broader historical consciousness.

The tradition of Greek literature was, therefore, an important spur in imperial Greek efforts at self-commemoration, but the Roman present also played a significant energizing role. Karl Galinsky has recently wondered whether the imperial Greek obsession with the past could 'not have taken place anyway without being a response to Roman domination?'[62] Greek literature was from its beginnings classicizing to a greater or lesser extent and that would no doubt have persisted into later periods had Greece remained politically 'free'. The nature and practice of imperial Greek classicism, however, which this book explores and re-evaluates, was largely dependent on the advent of the Roman present. On a basic historical level, the economic boost from Roman investment in Greek cities, combined with the cessation of internecine warfare, allowed Greek culture to flourish. Moreover, as Spawforth has demonstrated, the impetus for provincial elites to display the right kind of Hellenism largely came from Rome.[63] The connectivity of empire and the benefits of Roman citizenship aided the scale of Greek cultural expression too, as well as enhancing an already well-developed awareness of the mutability of fortune.[64] The role played by the synergy of the Greek past and Roman present in the shaping of imperial Greek artistic aspirations is thus a major theme explored in the present work.

How, then, does this Greek cultural contest between past, present, and future fit into the broader context of the empire? And what role does material culture perform? Far from culturally resisting the Roman empire, as Roman citizens who were often active in the Roman political and administrative machine, elite imperial Greeks found themselves with access to vast resources of wealth and privilege. This is another factor which differentiates this period, its literature and monuments, from earlier eras. Peter Brown has called it the 'age of ambition'. The demonstration of *philotimia*, as expressed by civic benefactions or service, patronage, and sophistic virtuosity, amongst the provincial elite was regularly rewarded

---

[62] Galinsky 2015, 6.   [63] Spawforth 2012.   [64] See, for example, Hdt. 1.5.4.

with citizenship, administrative office, and consequently the means for upward mobility through the Roman system.[65] This phenomenon is evinced by a dramatic increase in the number of provincial members of the Roman Senate over the first few centuries AD.[66] More and more elite Greeks found themselves with meaningful status and the ability to influence both local and wider concerns within the empire.

Moreover, the ability to construct monumental memorials and to mark the civic landscape with benefactions became a genuine option to a broader range of individuals. This in turn gave more provincial elites access to the traditional honour system of Greek *poleis*, which had intensified and flourished during the Hellenistic period and which centred on the public granting of a statue to be placed prominently in public space.[67] Nevertheless, despite this continuing avenue to public honour, Greek *pepaideumenoi* no longer felt the need to wait for the *dêmos* or monarchs to grant them honours but instead constructed their own monuments of their own accord.[68] Occasional examples of a wealthy *pepaideumenos* from the Hellenistic period raising a monument with the ultimate intention of self-commemoration do exist. Andronikos of Kyrrhos, for instance, built a late second to early first century BC horologion in the vicinity of the Roman Agora at Athens, referred to now as the 'Tower of the Winds' (Figure 1.1).[69] The same man constructed a sundial at the sanctuary of Poseidon on Tenos with an inscription honouring himself as an astronomer and 'second Aratos' (δεύτερον| [Ἄρα]τον, *IG* XII, 5 891, ll.1–2).[70] Such cases are rare, but stand as precedents to the intensification and amplification discernible in imperial Greek activities. In the classical past, a man's fame, come by through artistic or cultural prowess, could by accident create a memorial to him, such as Pindar's house in Thebes that was protected by Alexander the Great during his sacking of the city out of respect for the poet's works.[71] In the imperial period, in contrast, an ever increasing number of Greek elites, sometimes backed or even coerced by Roman authority, at other times driven by their own volition or (in the case of essential civic structures) through *force majeure*, had the option to create their own physical memorial and integrate it into the civic or sacred landscape of any given *polis*.[72]

---

[65] Brown 1978, 27–53; Whitmarsh 2005, 12.

[66] Hopkins 1974, esp. 116. On specifically Greek senators, see Halfmann 1979; Syme 1988, 1–20. See also Whitmarsh 2005, 12; Thomas 2007, 6–7; Dickenson 2017, 333–9. For a concise (social, cultural, political) overview of Greek elites in the empire, see Rizakis 2007.

[67] On the Greek tradition of honorific statues, see especially Ma 2013 and Stoop 2017.

[68] See Thomas 2007, 6, on public benefaction as a means of advancing personal power and status.

[69] On this monument, see von Freeden 1983; Kienast 2014; Webb 2017.

[70] Although the beginning of Aratos' name is restored, he is mentioned again in the inscription as being a model for Andronikos.

[71] Arr. *An.* 1.9.10; Plut. *Alex.* 11.12; Dio Chrys. *Or.* 2.33; Plin. *HN* 7.109. Cf. Thomas 2007, 179.

[72] See Mitchell 1987; Thomas 2007, 5–13. Zuiderhoek 2009 gives a detailed account of the profile of elite benefaction in Asia Minor.

FIGURE 1.1 The astronomer Andronikos of Kyrrhos' 'Tower of the Winds' in the Roman Agora, Athens. This monument is a rare extant example of Hellenistic euergetism by a Greek *pepaideumenos* that was specifically commemorative.

Civic infrastructure could be imperially funded, civically funded, privately funded, or some combination thereof, a spectrum that allowed a lot of room for the wealthy elite Greek to make his/her beneficent monumental mark.[73] Yet this capacity to enhance one's prospects of establishing a lasting reputation had the potential to be less well received in the present. The power of elite Greeks in their respective *poleis* could cause friction between themselves, their *dêmos*, and other members of the local elite. Arjan Zuiderhoek, however, has argued convincingly that the intensity of public giving in this period was propelled by a need to mitigate the very tension caused by the growing social divide between the small number of extremely wealthy citizens and the many poor, and to combat the

---

[73] See Mitchell 1987; Zuiderhoek 2009; 2013, 173–92. See Smith 1998, 70–7, for Philopappos' monument, the Library of Kelsos, and the Nymphaion of Herodes Attikos. See Burrell 2009 for monuments in Ephesos. See Alcock 2002, 51–75, for the Athenian agora.

increasing political oligarchization at the local level. He explains that 'the central paradox of ancient munificence [was that] a phenomenon which ostensibly seems to alleviate existing social inequalities by redistributing a (tiny) portion of elite wealth in fact served to perpetuate the same inequalities by means of a naturalisation of elite dominance'.[74] If the *dêmos* were receiving the kind of gifts they needed and expected, the system worked; if, however, the *dêmos* were unhappy with the type or extent of benefaction, conflict arose.[75] This precarious balance between self-promotion and civic acceptance is a focus of chapter 6 in the context of the divide between elite self-presentation and the judgement of posterity.

Roman wealth and status are what enable the massive scale of provincial building activities in the imperial period, but what drives it is autopsy of the remains of monuments from the Greek past, the pre-existing Greek habit of elite euergetism, the imperial practice of embedding ideology into civic centres through monumentalizing benefactions, and the very presence of the many public and collective spaces in cityscapes that could be exploited for personal promotion.[76] The word monument/monumental derives from the Latin *monumentum*, which implies commemoration and covers anything that brings someone or something to mind, whether text, architecture, inscription, sculpture, or coin.[77] Architecturally, this quality can be applied by design in the initial intention of a building's construction or it can adhere to a structure over time due to the associations a population makes between the building and the past.[78] Greek has σῆμα/σημεῖον ('sign') and μνῆμα/μνημεῖον ('memorial'). The first implies a fixed, conspicuous construction, differentiated from its surroundings and society; the second an object within a community that connects it to the past.[79] Both were regularly used of tombs, the former especially of the tombs of

---

[74] Zuiderhoek 2009, 116. See also Lendon 1997, 89.

[75] Zuiderhoek 2009, 66–77, 138–9. See also Lendon 1997, 1–106, especially 84–9.

[76] Thomas 2007, 6, 11; Zuiderhoek 2009, 93. Thomas (2007, 170) establishes the change in public space from classical to Hellenistic times. On changes from Hellenistic to Roman times, see Dickenson 2017. See also Dickenson and van Nijf 2013, xi–xxi, and the papers in that volume on public space, especially Zuiderhoek 2013, 173–8. On euergetism and the relationship of imperial Greek benefactors to the imperial administration, see Mitchell 1987; Boatwright 2000; Zuiderhoek 2009. See also Lendon 1997, 84–9; Alcock 2002, 36–98. On the origins and early development of Greek euergetism, see Gygax 2016. Kousser 2015 identifies the mutual influence of Greek and Roman commemorative strategies on each other's monuments.

[77] See Meadows and Williams 2001, esp. 42–6, on the range of meanings associated with *monumentum* in Latin and especially its association with the goddess Moneta and republican coinage. The Greek equivalent is μνημοσύνη.

[78] Thomas 2007, 2–3; see 1–6 on monumentality in general. This dual route to monumentality was detailed first by Alois Riegl in 1903 with respect to the drafting of a law defining how to select buildings in European cities to preserve as monuments. It is most accessible and translated into English by Forster and Ghirardo as Riegl 1982, 21–51. See also Nelson and Olin 2003, 1–2.

[79] Thomas 2007, 166. *LSJ* s.v. σῆμα 3, σημεῖον 1.1, 1.5; μνῆμα, μνημεῖον.

heroes in Homer. Throughout this book, I argue that imperial Greeks' awareness of the potential for material culture and physical landscape to become monumental underscores their own material efforts and infuses their literary endeavours as well. In both cases, they expect their works to mean something to the future, even if that future is imperfectly envisaged. Nevertheless, the chance involved in a physical structure or commemorative landscape maintaining a sense of monumentality over time concurrently haunts the cultural output of the Second Sophistic and infects it with a chronic sense of pathos: how to control future reception from the present? This issue is explored especially in chapters 4 through 6.

Importantly, imperial Greeks inherited the Roman conception of the connection between temporality and the meaning of buildings. As Edmund Thomas has detailed, for imperial Romans in particular buildings loomed large in their constructions of time, with the hours in the day regularly defined by the position of the sun with respect to specific constructions or their shadows, and later by public sundials.[80] For the most part Romans also conceived of time linearly and teleologically, with the future lying ahead and the past behind.[81] Monumental buildings stood as physical evidence of the Roman past and new constructions aimed at a similar presence in the future. Thus the connection between what has been achieved and what will be accomplished was real and continuous in this material sense.

Greek conceptions of time followed similar spatial lines except in the realm of prophecy and dreams, where they were reversed: the future lay at one's back because it was unknown and, hence, could not be seen, whereas the past stretched out in front, open to scrutiny.[82] Time was anchored, moreover, to significant events (e.g. the Persian Wars), so that classical Greeks were inclined to focus on foundations and origins of architecture rather than its potential to speak to the future.[83] Innovations in temporal measurement, such as the Seleukid Era, which established linear, progressive, and accumulative conceptualization of time were postclassical developments and provided the building blocks for but not the achievement of complex futurity.[84]

This is not to say that the Greeks did not possess a concept of commemorative monumentalization: already Homer's epics are full of grave markers (σήματα) and

---

[80] Thomas 2007, 169.

[81] On Roman conceptions of time, see Bettini 1991, 113–93.

[82] See Thomas 2007, 170, with Bettini 1991, 152, 157. Note, however, that Bettini identifies the same inverse relationship in Latin when the reference is to 'knowing' the future, but that this was inherited from Greece (151–7).

[83] On Greek and Roman ideas of relative time, see Feeney 2007, 7–42. On Greeks as most interested in architectural foundations, see Thomas 2007, 170.

[84] On Seleukid time and the postclassical nature of linear and progressive temporal conceptions, see Kosmin 2018; on such ideas as insufficient to produce a complex future, see Shaw 2019.

burial mounds (τύμβοι) left by the past.[85] These 'signs' of dead heroes, however, are significant in the poems precisely because of their ultimate impermanence—their tendency to come to ruination or to lose their identification.[86] Thus from their foundation, these Homeric tombs are symbolic of an inevitable and eternal loss of κλέος ('fame') that epic song can forestall, at least temporarily.[87] This double-edged vision of fame and the signs of fame—that construction leads necessarily to destruction—remains central to Greek cultural output in Roman times. Indeed, one of the most persistent anxieties attached to imperial Greek commemoration is the discomforting sense that the more one strives for remembrance, the more certain oblivion becomes.

A number of factors enhanced the traditional focus of imperial Greeks on foundations with the added dimension of future projection. These included their familiarity with large-scale public construction and multitemporal land- and cityscapes, the awareness of architecture's commemorative, communicative, and ideological possibilities, the latter of which Rome was particularly accomplished at harnessing, as well as the ability to fund or at least contribute to its realization. Thus the appreciation of reputation's ability to persist over vast expanses of time that accompanied the rich Greek literary tradition also infused imperial Greek relationships with material culture. Art and architecture too could be loaded with cultural meaning and conceived as possessing the potential to speak to the future.[88] The changing attitude can be detected in the second-century travel writer Pausanias' frustrated observation that:

The Greeks are terribly prone to be more wonderstruck (ἐν θαύματι τίθεσθαι) by foreign sights than those at home; for whereas distinguished men have committed to writing the pyramids in Egypt most precisely, the Treasury of Minyas and the Walls of Tiryns they have not led into memory at all (οὐδὲ ἐπὶ βραχὺ ἤγαγον μνήμης), though they are no less a wonder (οὐδὲν ὄντα ἐλάττονος θαύματος). (9.36.5)

Pausanias' project is at least in part to rectify this oversight and record the wonders of Greece for posterity: to convert its monuments and sites of cultural memory into encompassing, interpretative text and, in the process, establish his vision of Greece's physicality as authoritative.

The incorporation of any artefact into literature is never neutral, and the manipulation of and anxiety over meaning as applied to a textualized monument is central to this book. In fact, there are very few passages that I discuss that do not

---

[85] Purves 2010 examines the interrelatedness of space and time in archaic and classical Greek literature.

[86] Garcia Jr 2013, chapter 4.   [87] See Kurke 2013, 55–72, for this notion in Pindar.

[88] Thomas 2007, 170–8. See Thomas 2007, 167, on the different attitudes to Mycenaean ruins of Thucydides and Pausanias: the former was 'sceptical about the historical significance of buildings', whereas the latter saw ruins as signs of ancient greatness. Cf. Thuc. 1.10.2 on power and architecture with respect to Athens and Sparta. See also Nelson and Olin 2003, 6–7.

include either a monument proper or, at least, a metaphoric implication of one. This textual materiality, the extent of which I will consider in detail in chapter 3, is a feature of imperial Greek literature that builds on the concerns over future memory already present in the Homeric poems as well as the intense materiality of Hellenistic texts.[89] It also reflects in literature individual experiences of the saturated monumental cityscapes of the Greek-speaking east, Rome herself, and the numinosity of culturally significant landscapes.

A well-known material example that brings together all these factors—text, monument, memory-rich location, careful curatorship of personal identity aimed at posterity, as well as tension over its control—is the funerary monument of Gaius Julius Antiochos Epiphanes Philopappos. This memorial was erected on the Mouseion hill in Athens during the years AD 114–16 (Figure 1.2). The grandson of the last king of Kommagene, who retained that honorary title,[90] Philopappos was a Roman citizen and consul, who settled in Athens where he became Archon.[91] As R. R. R. Smith has shown, the monument is drenched in imagery that stresses both the Greek and Roman aspects of his character, especially in his dual representations in, respectively, Greek traditional costume and seated pose (Figure 1.3), and Roman consular dress during the procession to mark his inauguration (Figure 1.4). His Greek persona is flanked by statues of his togaed grandfather (representing both royal ancestry and Roman citizenship) and the Makedonian, Seleukos I, from whom the Kommagenian royal family claimed descent.[92] This tri-cultural visuality is matched by bilingual inscriptions that situate him in Athens, the Greek and the Roman worlds respectively.[93]

The monument's prominent position on the Mouseion hill associates him with cultural production, both in its popular connection with the Muses and long-established affinity with Mousaios.[94] It thus taps into that aspect of Greek

[89] On commemorative architecture in the *Iliad* as temporary and tied to the conflict between orality and textuality, see Garcia Jr 2013, especially chapter 4, and Ford 1992, 131–46. For a summary of Greek ideas on poetic immortality, see Kerkhecker 1999, 11–16. Porter 2010, 453–523, examines the materiality of Hellenistic epigram.

[90] See Mason 1974, 120–1, for official and literary use of $\beta\alpha\sigma\iota\lambda\epsilon\acute{\upsilon}\varsigma$; at this time, it was generally reserved for the emperor. See also Section 6.2 and Strazdins 2019.

[91] On Philopappos and his monument see Kleiner 1983; Thompson 1987, 14; Smith 1998, 70–3.

[92] Smith 1998, 71–3. See also Miles 2000, 29–36.

[93] His Greek representation is given a Greek label with the usual Athenian naming conventions: 'Philopappos, son of Epiphanes, of the deme of Besa'. Two inscriptions, one in Latin (left pilaster) and one in Greek (right pilaster) signal his most important titles in the Roman and Greek worlds respectively: 'Gaius Iulius Antiochus Philopappus, son of Gaius, of the Fabian tribe, consul, and Arval brother, admitted to the praetorian rank by the emperor Caesar Nerva Trajan Optimus Augustus Germanicus Dacicus' and 'King Antiochos Philopappos, son of King Epiphanes, son of Antiochos'. Smith 1998, 71–3. See Kleiner 1983, 14–15, for the inscriptions. The Greek inscription on the right pilaster is now lost, but was recorded by Kyriakos of Ancona in the fifteenth century (see Kleiner 1983, 23–7).

[94] See Kleiner 1983, 12, on Mousaios and the Muses.

20 FASHIONING THE FUTURE IN ROMAN GREECE

FIGURE I.2 The remains of the façade of Philopappos' funerary monument (AD 114–16), Mouseion hill, Athens. The monument is sited to be visible from the Akropolis and the Areopagos.

society which was most valued in Roman times. Significantly, the tomb stands within the city walls, a privilege extended to very few and most often to great benefactors.[95] This, combined with the title of βασιλεύς in the right pilaster

[95] See Arafat 1996, 192–3.

FIGURE 1.3 Detail of the seated Philopappos in Greek himation with bare chest. Drawing by Nicholas Revett.

FIGURE 1.4 Detail of the lower central panel of the façade of the Philopappos monument, showing Philopappos during his Roman consular procession. Drawing by Nicholas Revett.

inscription and architectural references to the triumphal arch of Titus in Rome,[96] places the monument in collusion as well as competition with imperial structures. This practice finds its height in Athens with the works of Herodes Attikos a generation later. Yet the dependency on Trajan in Philopappos' Roman titles defuses this effect and reveals the limits of a Roman citizen's power.[97]

Philopappos' monument demonstrates the preoccupation of the age with creating a lasting image that has currency in both the 'classical' Greek world and contemporary Roman empire. The use of Trajan's titles and depiction of eminent ancestors is much the same process as Arrian's evocation of Hadrian and Xenophon at the beginning of his *Periplous* (see above). Moreover, identities which might seem to be at odds—the anachronistic Greek, Kommagenian, and Makedonian, alongside the ectopic Roman—are here placed contiguously to build an

---

[96] See Thompson 1987, 14; Miles 2000, 33–5. Thompson also compares the tomb to *scaenae frons* architecture.
[97] Miles 2000, 33–5.

illustrious whole and, importantly, placed in a position that is itself laden with cultural significance. Using the past, Philopappos' monument fuses his Greek and Roman credentials into a multifaceted funerary identity that will be the face he presents to posterity. Nevertheless, despite this careful structuring of a complex commemorative identity, later in the same century, Pausanias describes it as follows:

The Mouseion is a small hill, opposite the Akropolis, inside the ancient ring-wall, where they say Mousaios used to sing and died and was buried; later a memorial ($\mu\nu\hat{\eta}\mu\alpha$) was erected there for a Syrian ($\grave{\alpha}\nu\delta\rho\grave{\iota}$ [...] $\Sigma\acute{\upsilon}\rho\omega$). (1.25.8)

Pausanias, too, structures his description according to both the past and the present, but his interest is in the hill rather than the monument or the detailed nature of the man it represents. Pausanias' reduction of Philopappos from an individual with impeccable aristocratic Greek and Roman credentials—from Archon, King, and Consul—to an anonymous Syrian reveals an aspect of personal commemoration that greatly concerned men such as Philopappos, Arrian, and Pausanias, and to which I will return time and again: once one has distributed cultural output, either literary or material, into the public eye, one can no longer shape its reception.[98]

A lack of control over posterity haunts elite Greek *pepaideumenoi*: they can fashion themselves in whatever way they please, but how to preserve that image for the future? Thus elite Roman-era Greeks embody a paradox. Their membership of an old, rich culture drives them to forge their own lasting presence in cultural memory, but the temporal and cultural perspective afforded by the Roman empire alerts them to the improbability of this task. It enhances their awareness of the fickleness of fame and the mutability of fortune, especially for the deceased who can no longer actively construct reputation. As a result, monumental constructions of personal identity, in the same way as textualized monuments, are always points of conflict over the power to assign meaning.[99] This book explores how imperial Greeks attempt to overcome this commemorative problem by using intertextual and intermedial strategies to reassert control over their relationship with posterity.

The evidence on which I draw comes from the first three centuries AD, with the majority deriving from the second century. There are two main reasons for this focus. First, this is the period in which Philostratos' 'Second Sophistic' is concentrated, and the fame associated with the cultural, political, and social activities described by Philostratos permeates beyond the boundaries of his text. Further,

---

[98] See Miles 2000, 34–6, for problems of representation relating to this monument.

[99] On the role of discourse in defining monuments for specific audiences and purposes, see Elsner 1994b. See further Sections 3.1 and 3.2.

most of the authors whom I discuss were active during the second century AD, making it the hub of literary testimony. Second, the available evidence reveals that the practice of elite euergetism in the Greek-speaking east was most prevalent during this period: '[t]he boom in elite public giving visible in the cities of the Roman Empire from the later first century AD onwards was unprecedented. When it was over, in the early third century, it was never repeated on the same scale'.[100] Furthermore, there was a clear peak in civic benefaction in the mid-second century with a corresponding rise and fall in the first and third centuries respectively.[101] Associated with elite euergetism was a concomitant civic honouring of the euergetist that usually entailed an honorific or building inscription and often a statue.[102] Given the interdisciplinary character of my exploration of commemoration, this epoch forms the natural limit of my inquiry. Additionally, the wealth of material available makes the prospect of going beyond the third century or introducing Christian evidence a step too far if sufficient attention is to be paid to it. These extra dimensions, however, certainly provide clear and exciting avenues for future comparative investigation.[103]

Another reason for focusing on the second century is Herodes Attikos (*c.* AD 101–*c.*177), who is the central hero of Philostratos' *Lives of the Sophists*, the text that defines the Second Sophistic, and the most accomplished rhetor of his day. Herodes' family came from the deme of Marathon, but had also held Roman citizenship for four generations.[104] He was fabulously wealthy and regularly used that wealth to grant benefactions in the form of public buildings to important Greek cities and sanctuaries, like Athens, Corinth, Olympia, and Delphi.[105] He also built magnificently on private land, so that he has left a substantial material footprint behind. Herodes is thus a central focus of this book because he is the quintessential example of a cultured provincial Greek elite and can be studied in detail from both a literary and material perspective. Herodes is joined in these pages by other Philostratean sophists, such as Dio Chrysostom, Favorinus, Aelius Aristeides, and Polemon, and several who failed to make his catalogue, like Arrian, Lucian, Pausanias, and even the North African, Latin-speaker Apuleius. They are a diverse group from a range of eastern provinces. What unites them is their first- to second-century date, their presence in both material and literary evidence, and/or

---

[100] Zuiderhoek 2009, 1. See also Thomas 2007, 7–8.   [101] Zuiderhoek 2009, 18–21.

[102] See Zuiderhoek 2009, 122–40, on public honorific language, expectations, and implications. See also Reitz 2012, 317–21, on building inscriptions as influencing how architecture is viewed and appreciated.

[103] See, for example, the recent brilliant exploration of the 'aesthetics of hope' in Methodius' *Symposium* by LaValle Norman 2019, and Nasrallah's 2010 examination of Christian apologist responses to the built environments of the Roman empire.

[104] Herodes' great-grandfather, Tiberius Claudius Herodes, gained citizenship under Nero; see Ameling 1983a, 13; Tobin 1997, 14.

[105] On Herodes and sanctuaries, see Strazdins 2022a.

their powerful engagement with material artefacts and their own futurity in their writings.

During the above discussion, I have indicated which chapters of the book align with the issues at hand. Here I will present a brief overview of the shape of the book as a whole. Chapter 2 examines imperial Greek conceptions of temporality and the problem of being postclassical for authors who aspire to canonicity. I analyse several strategies used by a number of authors to carve out their own creative space. The chapter demonstrates that imperial Greek temporality was far more complex than merely an obsession with 'classicism', as well as how important its full exploration is to appreciate properly the dynamics of contemporary elite Greek culture. Chapter 3 traces the same concern for the future and use of similar strategies in the monuments of imperial Greece. In doing so, it draws out the political implications of this concern for futurity. It also establishes the intensive interweaving of text and artefact in imperial Greek culture, and examines some reasons for this density. The chapter reveals how highly tuned elite Greeks were to the inherent meanings of monuments, as well as their desire to control those meanings and some of the mechanisms they use to do so. Chapter 4 compares how inscriptions are deployed in literature to Herodes Attikos' use of them on his private estates. In particular, the chapter analyses how inscriptions are used to discourse on authority, dominion, and power, to overwrite existing spatial and historical meaning, and to stake claims for individual immortality. An important outcome of this analysis is the identification of a tendency to contextualize an inscription as epitaphic when reframing it as commemorative no matter what its ostensible purpose. This tendency emerges in part from imperial Greek awareness of the vulnerability of posthumous fame. Chapter 5 argues that elite imperial Greeks find honorific statues unsuitable as a commemorative object and examines the strategies and mechanisms they employ, both literary and material, to overcome this commemorative problem. Chapter 6 switches focus to the reception of Herodes Attikos, and how his carefully shaped monumental image was reimagined by Philostratos. In particular, I demonstrate how Philostratos uses the example of Herodes and the rhetorical roles of tyrant, king, hero, and philosopher to discourse on the relationship between provincial elites, their fellow citizens, Greek culture, and imperial power. Chapter 7 concludes the book and draws out the broader implications of the preceding discussions.

This book, then, takes a remedial look at the commemorative efforts of elite imperial Greeks by exploring the intersection of euergetism and Philostratos' 'Second Sophistic'. More importantly, it considers an alternative explanation for the imperial Greek obsession with the 'classical' past: that as well as asserting cultural relevance in the Roman world, imperial Greeks require the context of the past to shape their own cultural output as worthy of future canonicity. Imperial Greeks believe they, just like their classical predecessors, are producing great works of art that could mean something to the future. Consequently, a full appreciation of their works and contemporary cultural history requires that they are examined with this in mind. Indeed, one crucial historical question raised by this investigation is: if we grant imperial Greeks a stake in the future, how does that affect our comprehension of their Roman present? At its heart, this book is an exploration of two very human and universal motivations: how to be remembered and how to be remembered in the way one desires. The strategies, 'successes', and 'failures' here defined are testimony to the power these impulses wield over any individual cognizant of his/her own mortality, and the affinities and discontinuities we all share with others distant in time and space.

PART I

Glorious Past, Tense Present, Pending Future

The future is not knowable in the telling, only in the remembering.

– Michael Cole, 'Remembering the Future'[1]

[1] Cole 1993, 263.

TWO

Back to the Future

You cannot back into the future.

— Frank Herbert, *Dune*.[2]

Part I of this book constructs a literary and material backdrop against which the subsequent chapters will unfold. This chapter focuses on how imperial Greek authors mediate the spectre of the classical canon at the moment they come to write. How to make space for one's own contribution amidst such celebrated fare? The great authors of the classical Greek past do not exhibit the same sense of spectral pressure. A feature of their works is an assumption that they are composing for hypothetical future as well as present audiences. 'A possession for all time' (κτῆμα […] ἐς αἰεί, Thuc. 1.22.4) is necessarily crafted as canonical from its inception.[3] Imperial Greek authors also compose with the future very much in mind but this aspect of their writing is often overshadowed by their especially complex relationship to the past: it is something to revere, to engage, to contest, and most importantly, as this chapter argues, something from which to depart. The past, moreover, offers the promise of future fame through the example of the continuing eminence of a Plato, Thucydides, or Sophokles. Aspirational imperial Greek authors thus cannot ignore the past but must rather develop strategies for successfully 'backing into the future'.

In order to establish how ambitious Greek authors in the empire negotiate the problem of being postclassical, I begin by outlining ideas of what constitutes 'classic' and 'canonical' literature, and how one might go about rivalling it. I do so by drawing on ancient and modern literary criticism. *On the Sublime* and Dio Chrysostom's *Oration* 21 form a particular focus in the context of imperial Greek oratory. The chapter will then dissect two common strategies employed by imperial Greek authors, namely competitive imitation and the use of novelty/ originality, to determine how they construct literary temporality and how this impacts on their sociocultural reality. The authors examined—Arrian, Longinos, Philostratos, Lucian, and Aelius Aristeides—cover a range of genres, including

[2] Herbert 1965, 388.

[3] Cf. Hdt. 1.1.0. On Thucydides and writing for the future, see Greenwood 2006, 1–18. See Lucian's *How to Write History* 5, on the care required in historical writing to live up to Thucydides' ideal. See now Leon (2021) for this futuring as a feature of imperial Greek historiography.

Fashioning the Future in Roman Greece: Memory, Monuments, Texts. Estelle Strazdins, Oxford University Press.
© Estelle Strazdins 2023. DOI: 10.1093/oso/9780192866103.003.0002

oratory, geographical writing, and biography, in order to demonstrate how pervasively concerns about the future permeate contemporary literature. Themes that are particularly important for this chapter are the relationship between the orator/author and his audience, the performative and agonistic context that underlies much Greek literature of the period, and the tension between text and speech. I argue that imperial Greek authors use the context of the past to negotiate their own potential canonicity in a hypothetical future. The pendant chapter of this first part of the book will explore the interpenetration of text and monuments in imperial Greek culture and how the material world reflects the same complex commemorative preoccupations of its textual counterpart.

2.1 POSTCLASSICISM, THE CANON, AND THE FUTURE

My initial focus here will be on the framework of literary temporality and sublimity constructed by the rhetorical treatise *On the Sublime* and its implications for postclassical canonicity. This picture will then be refined by Dio Chrysostom's analysis of temporal and cultural issues surrounding contemporary artistic production in his *Oration* 21. Finally, *On the Sublime*'s formulation of how to maximize the canonical potential of literary imitation will be examined alongside literary and material responses to imitation of the classical past. My discussion of these two texts lays the groundwork for understanding the strategies exploited by imperial Greek authors to address posterity that form the focus of subsequent sections.

2.1.1 Temporality, Sublimity, and Canonicity in On the Sublime

On the Sublime is a work of Greek literary criticism composed in a Roman context and attributed in the manuscript tradition to one 'Longinos'. The author has sometimes been identified with the grammarian Cassius Longinos, active in the third century AD, but the treatise is now assumed to date from the first century of the same era.[4] For the sake of convenience, I will refer to the author as Longinos rather than Pseudo-Longinos or 'Longinos'. This treatise is generically anomalous, although a precursor, possibly also called *On the Sublime* and written by Caecilius of Kaleakte in the first century BC, is known only via Longinos' text.[5] In criticism of *On the Sublime*, it has long been argued that Longinos' subject is

---

[4] Heath 1999, 43–74. For the first-century date and attribution, see Russell 1964, xxii–xxx. See also Grube 1965, 340–2; Whitmarsh 2001, 57. Boyd 1957 suggests the author is a Dionysios Longinos of the first century, but see the refutation of Russell 1964, xxvi. Porter (2001, 76–7; cf. 2016, 1–5) observes that Longinos is never as specific in his treatise as those trying to date him want him to be.

[5] Caecilius also wrote a treatise called *On the Style of the Ten Orators*, which solidified that canon.

'great writing' not simply writing in the grand style, as τὸ ὕψος ('the sublime') might imply.[6] Thus sublimity in this conception is a quality of writing that cannot be reduced to stylistics. James Porter, however, has rightly asserted that this is an assumption that removes the text from its larger tradition and would like to conceive of Longinos as differentiating instead an art of the sublime.[7] These two positions need not be mutually exclusive, since, despite the text's clear engagement with the notion of a sublime style, within this work, there is also a consciousness of shared greatness amongst canonical texts, so that writing sublimely becomes a strategy to achieve canonicity. One of the primary aims of *On the Sublime*, therefore, is to advocate for and advise on ways of attaining literary eminence.

One well-known passage (14.1–3) dispenses specific guidance on how to approach literary production in a postclassical world. In doing so, it demonstrates a number of principles essential to understanding the constraints imperial Greek authors responded to in their literary self-positioning. In this section, I will take a closer look at these issues, drawing on modern theory as an aid in parsing this postclassical framework. In the passage, Longinos promotes three modes of literary production in a hierarchy of increasing sublimity. The first and least desirable is 'emulation' (ζῆλος):[8] 'How might Homer have said this same thing, how would Plato or Demosthenes or, in history, Thucydides have made it sublime (ὕψωσαν)?' (14.1).[9] This is precisely the act performed by Philostratos' sophists when they take to the stage and request a theme from the past to be proposed by their audience. Longinos' focus on ζῆλος rather than μίμησις, however, promotes the imitation of canonical authors' outlook and process rather than regurgitation of their works or style. The second mode subjugates ζῆλος to competition, as one's literary achievements are rather to be judged by past greats: 'How would Homer or Demosthenes, had either been present, have listened (ἤκουσεν) to this passage of mine? How would that passage have affected them?' (14.2). This is a directive to conceive of one's work as worthy of canonicity from a contemporary perspective. The final mode overthrows the authority of the canon by adopting a temporal outlook that privileges future reception over the present and removes the judgement of the quality of one's work from known parameters: 'If I write this, how would all eternity receive it (ὁ μετ᾽ ἐμὲ πᾶς ἀκούσειεν αἰών)?' (14.3).[10]

Futuring reception in this manner neatly breaks down the boundaries of the canon, rendering it anachronistic in its present form. This does not make the

---

[6] As pointed out by Grube 1957, 355–60. Cf. Grube 1965, 342.

[7] Porter 2016, 7–17.

[8] See Russell 1964, 113, on the conflation of ζῆλος and μίμησις in Longinos. Cf. Whitmarsh 2001, 58.

[9] All translations of *On the Sublime* are based on Russell in Russell and Winterbottom 1989 with frequent alterations.

[10] Cf. Russell 1981, 79.

existing canon obsolete—to completely oust it would enforce a cultural break and create an entirely new tradition lacking the requisite cultural impact.[11] The pre-existence of classic literature, therefore, is a prerequisite to the production of new classic texts. To become great in one's own right within an existing tradition, moreover, one must respond to the influence of a great forerunner,[12] and precisely how one responds becomes a measure of one's own potential canonicity.

Like much postclassical art, imperial Greek literature is hyperaware of its position in history, but it is under-acknowledged in scholarship that this awareness is multidirectional. As demonstrated by Longinos' text, not only are imperial Greek authors immersed in the classical canon, but they are also cognizant that the rich literary past signals the possibility of their own famous future. This 'consciousness of history', to use T. S. Eliot's terms, involves an intentional balance between tradition and originality that injects imperial Greek literature with its plurality, richness, and responsiveness to social and cultural realities.[13]

In attempting to address posterity, plurality is particularly important because it allows the text to adapt over time so that it can be accommodated by new and successive audiences. Frank Kermode, who critiqued, extended, and revised Eliot's ideas on what constitutes 'classic' literature, argues persuasively that the ability of a text to provide a plurality of interpretations—to fail 'to give a definitive account of itself'—is indicative of the modern classic.[14] This precept is equally applicable to all postclassical art. Equivocation, openness, plurality are natural creative responses to composing vis-à-vis an established canon, but in order for them to be effective they also require a competent audience, who can appreciate and assimilate their cultural nuances. In this there is an element of chance; it is not uncommon for works to fall into obsolescence for long periods only to be revived by sudden interest at a much later date.[15] To paraphrase Kermode, through 'acts of historical understanding' an audience can change an old piece of art and release its power to please.[16] What this 'historical understanding' involves in practice is the audience creating its own moveable perception of history that avoids conceiving of 'now' as the most advanced and worthy of epochs.[17] Equally, in the context of imperial Greek literature, it can rescale the pre-eminence of 'then' (i.e. classical Greek literature). Thus a moveable temporal perspective of both author and

[11] See Eliot 1945, 24–5, on the need for continuity between past and future in order to produce great literature.

[12] See Bloom 1973, 3–18; 1994, 8. Cf. Eliot 1932a, 15; 1945, 19; Kermode 2004a, 33–4.

[13] Cf. Eliot 1945, 14–19, who believes postclassical literary creativeness requires rather an *unconscious* balance between tradition and innovation.

[14] Kermode 1975, 114.   [15] See Kermode 1975, 43–4; 2004a, 33–6.

[16] Kermode 2004a, 36; cf. Kermode 1975, 75.

[17] What Eliot (1932c, 74–5) calls the '*over-estimation of the importance of our own time*'; the emphasis is his. See also Kermode 2004a, 43.

audience can transform a literary canon into something malleable and open; it allows for the imagination of many potential canons and, most importantly, it makes entering any one of these hypothetical canons a genuine possibility. Playing with temporal perspective makes competition with canonical texts viable.

Despite its title, *On the Sublime* struggles to provide a clear indication of precisely what it means by sublimity.[18] For example, in the following passage, Longinos points to the impossibility of being able to accurately quantify or qualify sublimity, but that the quality is necessary for enduring fame:[19]

Sublimity (τὰ ὕψη) is a kind of eminence (ἀκρότης) and excellence (ἐξοχή) of discourse. It is the source of the distinction of the very greatest (οἱ μέγιστοι) poets and prose writers and the means by which they have invested (περιέβαλον) their own glory (ταῖς ἑαυτῶν […] εὐκλείαις) with eternal life (τὸν αἰῶνα). For the extraordinary (τὰ ὑπερφυᾶ) induces ecstasy (ἔκστασιν) rather than persuasion (πειθώ) in hearers (τοὺς ἀκροωμένους); and the wondrous (τὸ θαυμάσιον) combined with bewilderment (ἐκπλήξει) always proves superior to the persuasive (πιθανοῦ) and charming (χάριν). This is because persuasion on the whole is something we can control, whereas amazement and wonder exert irresistible power and force (δυναστείαν καὶ βίαν ἄμαχον) and get the better of every hearer.   (*Subl.* 1.3–4)

Longinos here stresses the importance of the relationship between author and audience, and the qualities that allow the audience to be overcome by the text are 'bewilderment'/ 'amazement' (ἔκπληξις) and 'wonder' (θαυμάσιον). This idea surfaces also in modern theory, where canonical texts are held to exhibit strangeness/novelty combined with beauty,[20] or 'have to administer shock; […] leap out of their context, disrupt it, and cause a kind of delight mingled with dismay'.[21] The indeterminacy of these requirements—both ancient and modern—is striking and indicates the eternal subjectivity of aesthetic judgement and its dependency on taste, fashion, and convention.[22] Indeed, the subjectivity applied to literary aesthetic is why canonical texts require a competent reader, one who can assimilate the text or be assimilated by it.[23] By using the term 'ecstasy' (ἔκστασις) above, Longinos likens the experience of great literature to divine possession and points once more to the need for an audience capable of displacement: of the ability to stand outside itself, its own time and expectations.

---

[18] On Longinos and his conception of 'the sublime', see Porter 2016, xvii–xx, 1–36. On just how hydra-headed the concept is, see Stephen Halliwell's review of Porter 2016 in *BMCR* 2016.09.25.

[19] See Segal 1959 for the importance of eternity to Longinos in *On the Sublime*. See also Innes 1995a, 120–1; Porter 2001, 79.

[20] Eliot 1945, 14; Bloom 1994, 3. Cf. Feeney 1995, 310: 'great works can or even must break the bounds of interpretive possibility, redefining the critical practice needed to read them, addressing an audience which is not (yet) there'.

[21] Kermode 2004a, 50. Cf. Kermode 2004b, 19, 22–3. See also Porter 2012, 50.

[22] See further Classen 1995, 515–16, 518–19, on the role of fashion in aesthetic appreciation.

[23] See Kermode 1975, 43–4, 118, on audience assimilation; cf. Bloom 1994, 3.

Philostratos' *Lives of the Sophists* catalogues men bound by the literary conventions of their day to imitate the past in order to achieve contemporary fame in the practice of *epideixis*. More often than not, their audiences come to have expectations fulfilled not confounded,[24] so the production of novelty is always fraught and the balance between accruing contemporary and aiming at future fame is a regular point of tension in Second Sophistic texts.[25] In this context, one risk associated with novelty is that its effect might only work once, and thus the wrong kind of novelty may impede in addressing posterity. According to Longinos, something affective only during momentary performance can never be truly great;[26] rather the way to achieve a lasting literary presence is to affect one's target audience repeatedly, irresistibly, and diversely:

When a man of sense and literary experience (ἐμπείρου λόγων) hears (ἀκουόμενον) something many times over, and it fails to dispose his mind to greatness (μεγαλοφροσύνην τὴν ψυχὴν) or to leave him with more to reflect upon than was contained in the mere words, but comes instead to seem valueless on repeated inspection, this is not true sublimity (οὐκ ἂν ἔτ' ἀληθὲς ὕψος εἴη); it endures only for the moment of hearing (μέχρι μόνης τῆς ἀκοῆς σωζόμενον). Real sublimity contains much food for reflection, is difficult or rather impossible to resist, and the memory of it is strong and ineffaceable (ἰσχυρὰ δὲ ἡ μνήμη καὶ δυσεξάλειπτος). (*Subl.* 7.3)

This is an example of Longinos attempting to explain what the sublime is and how to recognize it. In doing so, he also strives to shape how literature is both produced and received by constructing his text as a handbook and himself as the supreme arbiter of literary quality. He thus casts his text as indispensable to both a contemporary and future learned audience and its indeterminacy becomes a strategy to encourage repeated contemplation. Longinos here highlights the educational qualities of his text to embed it in elite imperial Greek cultural praxis.[27]

The passage also stresses the expertise of the auditor, and a knowledgeable audience is regularly cast as both an enabling and limiting factor in the production of imperial Greek literature. In terms of *epideixis*, shared immersion in *paideia* ensures that each time a sophist performs, an agonistic intellectual relationship exists between audience and orator: the audience is challenged to 'get' the obscure in-jokes and references; the sophist is required to continually entertain and engage.[28] Importantly, the audience is as central as the speaker in creating the

---

[24] On the relationship between audience and oratorical performer in this period, see Korenjak 2000.

[25] On this issue, see further below under Section 2.3 and Strazdins 2008. On the Greeks' relationship with novelty in general, see D'Angour 2011.

[26] See Greenwood 2006, 10, for Thucydides on the same topic.

[27] See Classen 1995, 522, on the connections of rhetoric and criticism with elite education in Greek culture. Cf. Clark 1951, 13, with special reference to imitation.

[28] On the relationship between audience and sophist, see Korenjak 2000; Webb 2006. See also Lauwers 2012 on read knowledge and performed knowledge in a sophistic context.

fictive world of declamation, since it plays the role of the civic body to whom the speech is addressed and, consequently, its members are transported to the speech's temporal and spatial setting along with the orator.[29] This same agonistic context, although less immediate, exists in written compositions as well, in the tension between innovation and tradition that is habitual in imperial Greek texts.

A work cannot be great in a vacuum but needs the right medium in which to resonate, or, in the case of the above passage, on which to imprint itself: the final clause describes the sublime work as a mental vestige, as though it were an inscription carved into the minds of the audience. This materiality of memory and commemoration is a central theme in imperial Greek culture and one that will recur throughout what follows. At the same time, Longinos reveals that audiences are primed with a preconception of what a great work should contain and how it should affect their minds.[30] Moreover, he offers yet another means of transportation, this time by removing the passivity of the auditor and uniting author and audience into the role of composer, as 'we come to believe we have created what we have only heard' ($\dot{\omega}_S$ $\alpha\dot{\upsilon}\tau\dot{\eta}$ $\gamma\epsilon\nu\nu\dot{\eta}\sigma\alpha\sigma\alpha$ $\ddot{o}\pi\epsilon\rho$ $\ddot{\eta}\kappa o\upsilon\sigma\epsilon\nu$, 7.2). The right relationship between author and audience can thus recreate a pre-existing work in the moment of hearing/reading.

The focus on the learned audience and their expectations implies that the author of *On the Sublime* leaves no room for the novel work that cannot be assimilated by its audience. No allowance is conceded to the piece that jars, shocks, or mystifies, since the introduction of material that is contrary to what an audience has been primed to accept would risk rejection. Although Longinos damns novelty and sees it as a fad (5.1), his choice of sublime fragments for discussion tends to be of those that do jar, shock, or mystify.[31] Notably, in their shockingness they can become instant classics. So, for example, he recalls a moment in Demosthenes' *On the Crown* (18.208), in which the orator dismisses blame from the Athenians after the battle of Chaironeia by swearing by the *Marathonomachoi*. In this moment, according to Longinos, Demosthenes:

deifies his audience's ancestors [...] He inspires the judges with the temper of those who risked their lives. He transforms his demonstration into an extraordinary piece of sublimity and passion ($\mu\epsilon\theta\epsilon\sigma\tau\alpha\kappa\dot{\omega}_S$ $\epsilon\dot{\iota}_S$ $\dot{\upsilon}\pi\epsilon\rho\beta\dot{\alpha}\lambda\lambda o\nu$ $\ddot{\upsilon}\psi o_S$ $\kappa\alpha\dot{\iota}$ $\pi\dot{\alpha}\theta o_S$), and into the convincingness of this unusual ($\xi\dot{\epsilon}\nu\omega\nu$) and supernatural ($\dot{\upsilon}\pi\epsilon\rho\phi\upsilon\dot{\omega}\nu$) oath.   (*Subl.* 16.2)

Despite Longinos offering the example of this one sentence that both affects Demosthenes' immediate audience and transforms his speech into an instant

---

[29] Webb 2006, 33.

[30] This notion ties into Eliot's ideas on tradition. See Eliot 1932a; 1932b.

[31] See Porter 2001, 83. Cf. Hertz 1983; Guerlac 1985. On the necessity of a shocking novelty in great works, see Kermode 2004a, 49.

36 FASHIONING THE FUTURE IN ROMAN GREECE

classic, revealing such a dual effect was possible in Demosthenes' day and should be so still, the vast majority of his examples derive from authors who were active in the fourth century BC or earlier. It is their unusual, powerful, or amazing way of expressing themselves, moreover, which has made them candidates for Longinos' treatise. Thus this contradiction within Longinos illustrates the risk that an author who aspires to a place in posterity must take—the possibility of contemporary failure in the moment they shock, jar, or mystify. No contemporary authors manage to achieve, in Longinos' opinion, the striking brilliance which Demosthenes demonstrates. Nevertheless, in this circumstance, the discrepancy between what is possible and what is demonstrable emphasizes the temporal gap between Demosthenes' text and Longinos' criticism—Demosthenes becomes an instant classic only from the distance of several centuries.

Returning to the passage that began this section (14.1–3), in which Longinos urges ambitious authors to aim their works at the future, the generative imagery of the final lines becomes significant in the context of Demosthenes' speech as an instant-yet-belated classic:

It would be even more stimulating to add, 'If I write this, how would all eternity receive it?' But if a man shrinks at the very thought of saying anything that is going to outlast his own life and time, then must all the conceptions (τὰ συλλαμβανόμενα) of that man's mind be like some half-formed (ἀτελῆ), blind embryo (τυφλὰ ὥσπερ ἀμβλοῦσθαι), all too abortive for the life of posthumous fame (τὸν τῆς ὑστεροφημίας ὅλως μὴ τελεσφορούμενα χρόνον).

(*Subl.* 14.3)

An author's ideas are here compared by Longinos to a foetus, an analogy which designates one's writings as akin to one's children.[32] Offspring play an important role in any individual's posthumous commemoration, in that they extend one's own life by their internal memories and by acting as walking memories through sharing physical resemblance. In using this metaphor, *On the Sublime* invests literary works with the essence of their author and their circulation in society ensures a form of continued physical existence. The use of the verb ἀκούειν in particular highlights that an author's writings possess an independent life: both the great canonical writers of the past and the hypothetical future readers are conceived of as 'hearing' the work, as though it has a voice of its own. Although this is the usual way Greek prose denotes reading, it is based on the habitual practice of reading aloud that renders texts 'deposits of voice'.[33] Consequently, for the author of *On the Sublime*, if one's writings are not designed to speak to future audiences, they remain forever 'malformed' (ἀτελής; cf. τυφλός, 'blind') and

---

[32] On the imagery of procreation here see Walsh 1988, 266, and Whitmarsh 2001, 59 n. 76.

[33] 'Deposits of voice': Porter 2006, 314–23. On ἀκούειν meaning 'to read', see Schenkeveld 1992.

can only 'miscarry' (ἀμβλόομαι; μὴ τελεσφορούμενος).[34] Significantly, this imagery recalls Longinos' requirements for sublimity: novelty coupled to wondrous beauty. Novelty alone is insufficient and may in fact produce monstrosity.[35] Yet the moveable temporal perspective advocated by Longinos allows reception to evolve: a onetime monster might become a latter-day god.

2.1.2 *Temporality, Beauty, and Culture in Dio Chrysostom's* Oration *21*

In his twenty-first oration, Dio Chrysostom (*c.* AD 40/50–*c.*110/120) addresses some of these same issues, but in a far more pessimistic way. This first-century dialogue, contemporary with Longinos' treatise, is about 'beauty' (τὸ κάλλος), specifically male beauty, with the relationship between (the Greek) past and (the Roman) present a secondary focus. Both these themes are foregrounded in the opening:

> How sublime (ὑψηλός) the youth is and handsome; and, further, his form (τὸ εἶδος) is ancient (ἀρχαῖον), such as I have not seen in modern images (τῶν νῦν), but only in those very old ones (τῶν πάνυ παλαιῶν) dedicated at Olympia. The later images (ὕστερον εἰκόνες) are always revealed as increasingly inferior (χείρους) and ignoble (ἀγεννεστέρων), partly on account of their creators, but mostly because their subjects are like the images. (21.1)

Here the failure of contemporary art is identified as the fault of both the deficient skills of the artists and the inferiority of their subject matter. Decline in beauty, moreover, is connected to two issues: a decline in character and manliness, as demonstrated by reference to the paradigm of athlete statues at Olympia; and artifice, as shown by the subsequent discussion of the effeminization of beautiful youths of the present day. In this context, the eunuch, whose primary use is as an object of 'depraved lust' (ὕβρις), becomes the ideal of masculine beauty (21.2). This practice finds its despicable exemplum in the emperor Nero's lust for a young man, whom he castrates, names after his second wife, Sabina, and has live as a woman (21.6–8; cf. Suet. *Ner.* 6.28).

The emphasis on uncontrived, classic, 'manly' beauty as specifically Greek in the dialogue is indicated in three ways: first, in the accusation that, unlike Greeks, Persians most admire feminine beauty (21.3–6); next, the allusion to Greece's loss of freedom to Rome ('for the race of lions is now extinct [in Europe], though formerly they were to be found in Makedonia', 21.1); and, finally, the discussion that concludes the dialogue on differences in beauty according to ethnicity, in which Dio stresses that the statue is 'perfectly Greek' (Ἑλληνικὸν ἄκρως, 21.15).

---

[34] Cf. Segal 1959, 124: 'what is sublime, in short, is eternal, and what aims at eternity becomes sublime'. This reflects Eliot (1945, 24–5) on the classic.

[35] For novelty potentially creating monstrosity, see Lucian, *Prometheus in Words* 3. Cf. *Zeuxis* (Section 2.3).

38 FASHIONING THE FUTURE IN ROMAN GREECE

This distillation of Greek beauty is then applied to literary art when Dio is challenged by his interlocutor on his tendency to find reasons to disparage his fellow men. He defends himself as follows:

Perhaps you look down on me and believe that I am babbling because I am not talking about Kyros and Alkibiades, as the smart men (οἱ σοφοί) do, still even now (ἔτι καὶ νῦν), but about Nero and such other radical (νεωτέρων) and inglorious (ἀδόξων) subjects that I call to mind. The reason for this is that I do not much like the tragic poets nor try to emulate (ζηλοῦν) them; for I know that it is a disgrace to name people of the present day (τοὺς νῦν ὄντας) in a tragedy, but rather some ancient matter (ἀρχαίου τινὸς [...] πράγματος) is necessary and one not very credible. Yet men of former times (ἔμπροσθεν) were not ashamed to name contemporaries (τοὺς τότε ὄντας) whether in speaking (λέγοντες) or in writing (γράφοντες); but those of the present day strive to name the ancients in all cases.

(21.11)

Like Longinos, Dio here points to the control audiences possess over artistic production and reception. The audience of the present day wants only to hear about the classical past, an impulse not restricted merely to those genres whose conventions demand ancient/mythic subjects, such as tragedy, but to all speaking and writing.[36] This makes contemporary material appear defective, when really it is the audience's blindness to the present and focus on the past that creates the illusion that modern topics amount to poor quality.

At the same time, Dio implies that writing about the distant past is artistically inauthentic. He elaborates this notion through the example of devious booksellers who doctor freshly composed works so as to appear old: 'knowing that ancient (ἀρχαῖα) books are in demand [...] they bury the worst examples of our day (τὰ φαυλότατα τῶν νῦν) in grain so that they take on the same colour (τό γε χρῶμα ὅμοια) as the old ones and, having destroyed them anyway (προσδιαφθείροντες), they sell them as old' (21.12).

This metaphor forces the reader to reassess the notion presented at the beginning of the dialogue that present-day statues are inferior because they reflect inferior subjects, since in this case a poorly composed work disguised as an ancient text immediately finds an appreciative audience. The example of Nero's eunuch, moreover, who was dressed up as a woman and was readily accepted as a woman by the court while it was profitable to do so, shows that the consumers of rapidly aged books are complicit in the trick. The social cachet attached to consuming ancient literature makes the selling of artificially aged books a performance enabled by an audience that literally buys into it. The dialogue's opening lines are thus revealed as an ironic portrayal of a prevailing and unfounded assessment

---

[36] See Classen 1995, 518–19, on Graeco-Roman authors' awareness of conventions, rules, and genre traditions.

of contemporary Greek art that fails to conform to the demands of a backwards-looking audience. The theme of artistic decline was also current in Latin literature, as exemplified by Tacitus' *Dialogus*. Dio's construction of Greek art in these terms can thus be understood as pushing back in particular against Roman conceptions of the contemporary state of Greek literature as well as the degenerative rhetoric of the influence of Greek culture on Rome more broadly (e.g. Juv. *Sat.* 3; Cic. *ad Quint.* 1.1).

Additionally, the 'ancient colour' ($\chi\rho\hat{\omega}\mu\alpha$ $\check{o}\mu\omega\iota\alpha$ [...] $\tau\hat{o}\hat{\iota}\varsigma$ $\pi\alpha\lambda\alpha\hat{\iota}o\varsigma$) the books acquire from the grain infers a change in perception of their rhetorical 'style' (commonly expressed by $\chi\rho\hat{\omega}\mu\alpha$). This seepage of superficial quality into the content of the books mimics the moveable perspective advocated by Longinos, so that an audience removed temporally from a text, even if this displacement is only an illusion, approaches that text with fresh and accommodating eyes. Though an indictment of contemporary literary criticism, the success of the artificially aged books holds out a promise of positive future reception for contemporary authors. This must be the thrust behind the accusation that ageing the books in grain 'destroys them' ($\pi\rho\sigma\sigma\delta\iota\alpha\phi\theta\epsilon\acute{\iota}\rho\sigma\nu\tau\epsilon\varsigma$), since by gifting them the veneer of antiquity one forestalls them meeting a (potentially) more appreciative posterity in their own right.

Dio's sublime and beautiful youth is thus in part symbolic of Greek culture, which has been deformed from its classical perfection by the inferior artistry of imitation, the influence of foreign power, and most damningly by the demands of a superficial audience. For this reason, Dio laments that, should a true beauty actually appear, he will 'pass unnoticed' ($\pi\lambda\epsilon\acute{\iota}\sigma\tau\sigma\upsilon\varsigma$ $\lambda\alpha\nu\theta\acute{\alpha}\nu\epsilon\iota$) or 'be misused' ($\mu\epsilon\theta$' $\ddot{\upsilon}\beta\rho\epsilon\omega\varsigma$; $\pi\rho\grave{o}\varsigma$ $o\dot{\upsilon}\delta\grave{\epsilon}\nu$ $\dot{\alpha}\gamma\alpha\theta\acute{o}\nu$, 21.2). In Dio's estimation, therefore, contemporary audiences have lost the ability to judge artistic quality and a modern classic will not receive the 'acclaim' ($\check{\epsilon}\pi\alpha\iota\nu\sigma\varsigma$) it deserves, so that it will 'quickly vanish from public consciousness' ($\tau\alpha\chi\grave{\upsilon}$ $\lambda\acute{\eta}\gamma\epsilon\iota\nu$ $\kappa\alpha\grave{\iota}$ $\dot{\alpha}\phi\alpha\nu\acute{\iota}\zeta\epsilon\sigma\theta\alpha\iota$, 21.2). We are reminded that none of Longinos' sublime examples come from his contemporaries. The unrecognized beauty is clearly not a classic beauty (i.e. not a replication of classical models), but rather a modern sublime creation that its audience cannot accommodate. More than this, it is also a specifically 'Greek' creation. Dio's insistence on this point indicates his confidence in both the continuity and vibrancy of a progressive Greek culture, the failure of which results from the incompetence and misplaced priorities of its Roman(-period) audience.

Dio's use of $\sigma\sigma\phi\sigma\acute{\iota}$ ('the wise') as arbiters of artistic quality recalls Longinos' talk of the need for vast literary experience in a worthy critic, as well as his text's attempts to teach an audience how both to produce and to receive literary art.[37] In

---

[37] See Classen 1995, 522, for this notion applied to rhetorical treatises and literary criticism in general.

Dio's presentation, however, these wise men uphold the status quo, so that their judgements bow to the coercive power tradition possesses over the identification and codification of great works of art.[38] This makes them less 'wise' than 'savvy' as to broader contemporary audience appeal. In addition, Dio's story of the artificially aged books must also be a veiled swipe at the profession of sophistry which prided itself on imitating the past in speech and personal image and which, despite his own sophistic activities, Dio was prone to denigrate.[39]

Oration 21 thus spotlights the temporal and cultural complexities of contemporary artistic production, as well as critiques what modern scholarship perceives as the political dimension of imperial Greek literature: its promotion of the Greek cultural past as a form of resistance to the political reality of the Roman empire. This speech aims instead to expose the limitations that a fascination with the past places on artistic sublimity and equates classical imitation with sociocultural as well as political acceptance. Both Longinos and Dio, therefore, intimate that lasting fame and the continuity of Greek cultural excellence requires a disengagement from the present through the courage to invest in the future.

A by-product of Dio's argument, however, is the exposure of slavish artistic imitation as an efficient pathway to contemporary fame and fortune. An easy method of cultivating authority, this kind of imitation nevertheless limits the reach of fame, since it facilitates the potential for the secondary author to be subsumed by his forerunner and to plagiarize rather than (re)create. How then to strike a balance between present and future artistic impact? The next section considers this issue in relation to literary imitation.

2.1.3 Competitive and Passive Imitation in Theory and Practice

Ancient literary criticism more broadly delineates variations on imitation involving differing levels of authorial individuality. The first-century BC rhetorician Dionysios of Halikarnassos, for instance, describes two kinds: one which is natural that comes 'through intensive instruction' (ἐκ πολλῆς κατηχήσεως) and 'familiarity' (συντροφίας), and one which is artificial that is achieved 'by following the rules of the craft' (ἐκ τῶν τῆς τέχνης παραγγελμάτων, *On Dinarchos* 7). Dionysios notes that these types of imitation apply to both literature and art, and can envision no scenario in which imitation enables modern orators to reproduce the quality of canonical figures (8). Nevertheless, he does promote

---

[38] On the issue of aesthetic appeal in art and classical criticism, see Hall 2017.

[39] For a discussion of Dio's relationship to both philosophy and sophistry, see Whitmarsh 2001, 192–4 and 2005, 17–19. Cf. Moles 1978. On Dio's relationship to the 'Second Sophistic', see Jackson 2017.

imitation via the natural method of many models rather than a single author.[40] Longinos also differentiates between varieties of imitation, but rather than 'natural' and 'artificial', he distinguishes between passive 'possession' and active 'contestation', the adoption of which depends on the skills and ambition of the imitating author:[41]

Many are possessed by a spirit not their own (ἀλλοτρίῳ θεοφοροῦνται πνεύματι). It is like what we are told of the Pythia at Delphi: she is in contact with the tripod near the cleft in the ground which, so they say, exhales divine vapour, and she is thereupon made pregnant (ἐγκύμονα) by the supernatural power and forthwith prophesies as one inspired (χρησμῳδεῖν κατ᾽ ἐπίπνοιαν). Similarly, the genius of the ancients (τῆς τῶν ἀρχαίων μεγα-λοφυΐας) acts as a kind of oracular cavern and effluences flow from it into the minds (ψυχάς) of their emulators (ζηλούντων) [...]. In all this process there is no plagiarism (κλοπή). It resembles rather the impression (ἀποτύπωσις) of good character (καλῶν ἠθῶν) in statues (πλασμάτων) and works of art (δημιουργημάτων). Plato could not have put such a brilliant finish on his philosophical doctrines or so often risen to poetic subjects and language, if he had not tried and tried wholeheartedly to compete for first place (πρωτείων) against Homer, as a young competitor (ἀνταγωνιστὴς νέος) against an established marvel (ἤδη τεθαυμασμένον). Equally very eager for rivalry (φιλονικότερον) and as if crossing spears (διαδορατιζόμενος), not unprofitably (ἀνωφελῶς), but to become the best (διηριστεύετο).

(*Subl.* 13.2–4)

The idea of μίμησις as possession is a metaphor usually applied to the inspiration a poet in particular, but later also a writer of prose, receives from the muses or other divine figure. It is used alternatively to represent inspiration from an earlier author as through links on a chain only when the ultimate source remains divine.[42] Longinos here adopts the Hellenistic innovation of stipulating the canonical author as the source and thus bundles the essence of a writer into his words, just as the essence of the god is contained in the Pythia's prophecies. In this case, the ancient author speaks through the medium of the modern author with the implied result that the latter loses his own identity.

This possessive version of μίμησις is particularly common in reference to Homer, and becomes a topos in later Greek prose from the Hellenistic period onwards and, through it, into Latin.[43] Famous examples include Ennius' dream of Homer, in which he is informed by the bard himself, through metempsychosis and an intermediary peacock, that he is in fact the reincarnation of the father of

---

[40] See Perry 2002, 158–63, for a discussion of the promotion of eclectic imitation in Greek and Latin rhetorical theory; and Too 1998, 210–12, for a comparison of Dionysios and Longinos on the notion of imitation.

[41] See Whitmarsh 2001, 62–4, for a discussion of Longinos' views on the application of τέχνη to natural talent.

[42] See Russell 1964, 114–15, with Plato, *Ion* 533c–e.   [43] See Brink 1972.

Greek epic.[44] A similar claim is made about Stesichoros being Homer reincarnate in an epigram of one of the Antipaters.[45] The imagery of the Homeric spring is also common in Hellenistic writing, as is the idea of Homer as a fountain from which later authors drink.[46] Although Longinos stresses that channelling Homer does not equate to plagiarism, his comparison of the inspired work to a statue—a lifeless counterfeit—invests it with an immediate derivative inferiority. Moreover, it attributes stagnancy to the later author's work, in that statues are rooted to a particular spot and do not have the freedom to travel and announce themselves far and wide as words do. Here, the long-dead Homer shapes the art of his successor, so that the modern author produces a monument to Homer rather than himself. Such derivative reapplication of another's memorial in the production of literary art is mocked in Lucian's *Charon or the Inspectors*, in which the ferryman relates how Homer became seasick as he conveyed him across the Styx and vomited up his verses, which Charon then salvaged and stored so that he could later bring them out to recite (7).[47] Homer here creates material versions of his poetry which Charon then treats as monumental commemorative artefacts and repurposes to demonstrate his own erudition.

James Porter characterizes this imitative channelling as both the aim and result of the backward-looking imperial Greek perspective: 'utterly possessed by the classical past, in the end one simply *is* classical'.[48] This classicism, however, is a sleight of hand, in that such transformative and transportive imitation aims at inserting the postclassical author firmly into the company of the canon by bringing the past into the present, but the result is instead the impression of being stuck in the past. Passive imitation thus loses the contest for future reputation before it even begins.

Longinos, however, provides an alternative mode of imitation by comparing the immovable, second-rate Homeric reproduction to Plato, who is presented as dynamically battling with the spectre of Homer instead, metaphorically 'crossing spears' ($\delta\iota\alpha\delta\text{o}\rho\alpha\tau\iota\zeta\acute{o}\mu\epsilon\nu\text{o}\varsigma$) with him as befits a contest between Homeric heroes for immortal fame.[49] Moreover, although Plato too drinks from the Homeric spring, he actively diverts and directs the flow (*Subl.* 13.3).[50] What is at stake in active competition is the possibility of displacing Homer's absolute primacy, assuming a

---

[44] See Aicher 1989 for this dream as a technique used by Ennius to legitimize his artistic choices and ease his audience into his innovative style. See also Brink 1972, 556–60.

[45] See Brink 1972, 557–60.

[46] See Brink 1972, 553. See Guerlac 1985, 288 for Longinos borrowing Plato's own metaphor of bodily irrigation to describe his imitation of Homer. Cf. Russell 1964, 116.

[47] This image draws on a repulsive painting by Galaton (described in Ael. *VH* 13.22), in which Homer is represented as vomiting his poetry that is then drunk by other later poets. See Kim 2010, 16.

[48] See Porter 2006, 347. The emphasis is Porter's.

[49] See Segal 1987 for the idea of the writer as hero in Longinos. Cf. Innes 1995b, 323–33; Porter 2001, 66; Whitmarsh 2001, 60–1.

[50] See Innes 2002, 267–9, on Longinos' view of Plato as the model for attaining sublimity through imitation. Cf. Russell 1981, 78.

share of his fame, and asserting one's own literary supremacy; the risk is failure and relegation as another Homeric imitator. Thus for Longinos real canonical success can come only through a risky decision to meet the past great head-on and proclaim one's own authority: to become monumental (i.e. 'an established marvel', ἤδη τεθαυμασμένος, 13.4) in one's own right, one must compete (i.e. become a 'rival', ἀνταγωνιστής, 13.4).[51] Passive possession, in contrast, is cast as a process of feminization, as exemplified by the imagery of the Pythia impregnated by the god's presence.[52] Thus in Longinos' view passive imitation cannot lead to canonicity since it threatens both to destroy an individual's identity and, in the process, to unman him.

The battle of Homer and Plato collapses time to bring the two great authors together. Several scholars have noted the spatial and temporal dislocation associated with this move and interpreted it to different ends,[53] primarily as either reflective of the treatise's own aspirations to eternity or as indicative of the limitations of being postclassical.[54] Porter, who adopts the latter position, argues that Longinos' classicism ties him to a derivative postclassical age, since his examples reaffirm the primacy of the canon. As he sees it, the treatise aims to teach its audience how to identify, reproduce, and respond to the sublime, how to bring the past into the present and how to project that past into the future.[55] What Porter misses is that, instead of projecting the past into the future, Longinos advocates rather for the competition between the past and the present to be futured. In this way, he urges contemporary authors to recapture the perspective of past writers and, instead of reproducing their works, reproduce their approach to literary production. While acknowledging the primacy of literary forbears at the time of composition, this method does not set that primacy in stone. It is thus an approach in which anything is possible since it subjugates the judgement of the past and the present to that of the future. Plato battles Homer and succeeds in slotting himself into the canon but, from an imperial Greek standpoint, Plato himself is a treasured cultural relic, as venerable to the modern writer as Homer. Thus only through commitment both to competing with rather than simply reproducing the past and to a moveable temporal perspective can an imperial Greek writer ever reach canonical heights.

---

[51] Segal (1959, 124–6) interprets Longinos as saying that μίμησις is the key to sublimity and a way of approaching the past greatness of ancient writers and achieving greatness oneself. This model does not take into consideration the need for competition and the levelling capacity of a futuring of perspective.

[52] Walsh 1988, 266–8. See also Whitmarsh 2001, 59, on the implicit power relationship in this reproductive metaphor. Cf. ní Mheallaigh 2014, 13–15.

[53] On the creation of this spatial and temporal dislocation, see especially Too 1998, 196–202.

[54] On the former, see Segal 1959; on the latter, see especially Whitmarsh 2001, 66–71, who notes the importance of freedom for Longinos in enabling the production of great art. Hertz 1983 and Guerlac 1985 also note that *On the Sublime* causes forms of dislocation and displacement, either with respect to speaker/writer and the auditor/reader, or the rhetorician and the fragments he quotes.

[55] Porter 2001, 77–85.

Longinos' unease over the potential loss of identity associated with passive imitation, with becoming the 'new' so-and-so, can also be traced in the figure of Herodes Attikos in Philostratos' *Lives of the Sophists*. Herodes (*c.* AD 101–*c.*177) is Philostratos' central hero and greatest example of the sophistic art; how Philostratos crafts him, therefore, is indicative of the third-century author's own attitudes to imperial Greek literary culture.[56] In the text, Herodes is twice hailed by his contemporaries as being equal to a past great and on both occasions he distances himself from the compliment or, at least, recasts it with his own spin. In the first instance, in discussing Herodes' style, Philostratos says that he was inseparable from Kritias and that all Greece hailed him as one of the ten, referring to the canon of ten Attic orators (*VS* 2.1.564).[57] Herodes deflects the compliment by saying that he is, at least, better than Andokides. In this way, Herodes asserts his own critical judgement of the canon and slots himself into it by displacing one of its established members. Importantly, although his oratory approximates that of Kritias, it is via his own oratorical identity that he affirms himself as canonical. In the second case, Philostratos describes how, at the Olympic games, all Greece cried out to Herodes (βοησάσης ἐπ' αὐτῷ τῆς Ἑλλάδος), 'you are like Demosthenes!' (1.25.539), and again he brushed it off by saying he would rather be like Polemon. He was referring to Marcus Antonius Polemon (*c.* AD 90–*c.*144) of Laodikeia, who was most active in Smyrna and is Philostratos' secondary focus in the *Lives*, in that he is presented by him as the greatest sophist in the generation before Herodes.[58]

Material evidence reveals that there might be more to this anecdote than simply its placement within the chapter that deals with the life of Polemon. A white marble statue base found in the Asklepieion at Pergamon near the Roman bath, in front of the north portico and opposite the theatre, bears the following inscription (Figure 2.1):[59]

Δημοσθένην
Δημοσθένους
  Παιανιέα
  Πολέμων
κατὰ ὄναρ

Demosthenes
son of Demosthenes
of the deme of Paiania
Polemon [erected a statue of him]
according to a dream.

---

[56] On Herodes' career, see Graindor 1930; Ameling 1983a; Tobin 1997, 13–67; Galli 2002.
[57] See Schmitz 1997, 226–7, on this episode.
[58] On Polemon, his life, writings, and career, see Gleason 1995, 21–81; Reader 1996, 7–46.
[59] Inv. no. 1932, 6. See Habicht 1969, 75–6, no. 33, plate 11; Puech 2002, 399–401, no. 210.

FIGURE 2.1 Base of a statue of Demosthenes dedicated by Marcus Antonius Polemon of Laodikeia in the Asklepieion at Pergamon (Inv. 1932, 6; Habicht 1969, 75–6, no. 33). He refers to himself only as 'Polemon', but Demosthenes is identified by his name, his patronymic, and his deme. Height: 1.04 m; Width: 0.41 m; Depth: 0.41 m.

Polemon here uses the literary trope of an inspirational dream, which by this time was a commonplace, to legitimize this self-aggrandizing monument representing the greatest of Attic orators.[60] The arrangement of the inscription with two lines

---

[60] See Brink 1972, 560–5, on the inspirational dream as a literary trope from the Hellenistic period onwards. Gleason (1995, 25) argues the monument must stem from Polemon seeing Demosthenes in a

beginning with *Δ* parelleled by two beginning with *Π* creates a chiasmus between Demosthenes and Polemon, equating them and thus visually indicating that the monument honours both men. Moreover, the wording of the inscription constructs an unexpected hierarchy of fame. Polemon refers to himself by a single name only, in keeping with the practice on his Smyrnaean coinage.[61] This, in contrast to other epigraphic references to him that include the gentilician and occasionally praenomen, intimates he is confident that his fame is so vast that anyone who reads the inscription will be aware of exactly who Polemon is.[62] Demosthenes, on the other hand, requires his patronymic and deme affiliation for secure identification.[63] The naming choices also locate Demosthenes in a specifically Athenian context while gifting Polemon a more universal bearing. The selection of single-name self-representation by Polemon also neatly masks his Roman citizenship, hence highlighting that the field of honour for both men is Greek *paideia*. That Polemon's oratorical brilliance was to some extent dependent on his famed predecessor would have been advertised by the statue, whether marble or bronze, placed upon the base in its original use. This Demosthenic visual dominance undermines the claim of Polemon's single name, an effect absent from the inscription if considered in isolation. Thus, even in this material context, $\mu\iota\mu\eta\sigma\iota\varsigma$ threatens to overwhelm a celebrated rhetor's reputation. That the inscription is attached to a statue within an important sanctuary at Pergamon shows that Polemon nevertheless expects his fame to last in a broad imperial and Hellenic context as long as the inscription, and that the god Asklepios, whose method of communication with mortals is via dreams, sanctions the monument's honorific messages.

Herodes' response to being compared to Demosthenes in Philostratos' *Lives* should thus be interpreted in the context of Polemon's association with that orator, which may well have extended to the epithet 'new Demosthenes'.[64] In such a circumstance, Herodes' stated desire to be considered instead the equal of Polemon provides a strategy to counter concerns over the potential loss of identity that emulation threatens. Herodes' comment contrives to bring two modern orators into the foreground and neatly pushes the anachronistic Demosthenes off stage. He signals his wish to strive with a contemporary and makes the case for his peer, Polemon, to be considered greater (or at least more relevant)

---

dream; Petsalis-Diomidis (2010, 267–8), however, more convincingly proposes that the dream should rather have featured Asklepios. These options need not be mutually exclusive, but it is more probable that Polemon simply uses the dream trope as a pretext for creating the monument.

[61] See Klose 1987, 44.C.19–36, 45.B.13–21, 46.1–2, 4–17, 19–42; Amandry and Burnett, with Mairat 2015, nos. 3.172, 3.174–83.

[62] See Puech 2002, 396–406, nos. 209–11.   [63] See Puech 2002, 400.

[64] See Philostr. *VS* 1.25.542–3, for Polemon's channelling and imitation of Demosthenes.

than the canonical Demosthenes, who is traditionally judged the greatest orator of all.[65]

In Longinos, although μίμησις is the means by which to engage with past greats, it can lead only to personal oblivion if the aspiring author fails to consider the audiences of the future over those of the past or present (14.3). This sentiment underlies the thrust of the final section of *On the Sublime*, in which not only is the Greek response to loss of political freedom alluded to and critiqued (as maintained by Whitmarsh and, to a lesser extent, Porter and Segal)[66] but also contemporary writers' slavish imitation of past greats. For Longinos, as for Dio, it is the backwards-looking perspective of the Greeks which causes them to fail in the literary field. Just as 'a slave could never be an orator' (δοῦλον δὲ μηδένα γίνεσθαι ῥήτορα, 44.4), so 'greatness of mind (τὰ ψυχικὰ μεγέθη) wanes, fades, and becomes dreary when men spend their admiration on their mortal parts (τὰ θνητά) and neglect to grow (αὔξειν) the immortal (τἀθάνατα)' (44.8). Longinos is here referring overtly to physical and material desires but, given the focus on eternity throughout the treatise (1.3, 4.7, 9.3, 14.3, 36.2, 44.1, 44.9), he can equally be critiquing a preoccupation with both the present and the past that neglects the potential of 'future fame' (ὑστεροφημία, 44.8). This despite both Longinos' treatise and Dio's *Oration* 21 warning against the contemporary failure predicated by practising the exhortation to address eternity.

Imitation that looks to the future can, therefore, only be agonistic. It must emulate in order to subsume literary authority at the same time as striving to supersede.[67] Emulation can be as explicit as claiming to be the 'new' so-and-so (e.g. the new Homer, the new Demosthenes, or the new Xenophon),[68] or manipulating an earlier author's identity in some other subtler manner. Importantly, assuming the identity of another is also to seize his fame. While this process can be a positive, symbiotic relationship that promotes a renewal or revival of the past and its great authors, imitation that is overtly competitive involves instead a rewriting of the past, an act which displaces the great forerunner and attempts to make him obsolete. The agonistic quality of this form of imitation regularly crystallizes as a desire to create a context in which to be understood and from which to depart: I am a bit like so-and-so; if you keep him in mind, you'll see how

---

[65] See Rutherford 1992, 156–7; in particular, Hermogenes' presentation of Demosthenes as superior to all others. Also: Innes 1995a, 115; 2002, 276–81; Puech 2002, 399–400; Petsalis-Diomidis 2010, 269.

[66] Segal 1959; Porter 2001, 77–85; Whitmarsh 2001, 66–71.

[67] Bloom (1973, 3–18; 1994, 8) argues for the need for an 'oedipal' psychological tension between forerunner and aspirant.

[68] See Schmitz 1997, 46–7 esp. n. 25, for references to this phenomenon, including Nikanor as the 'New Homer and the New Themistokles', Arrian as the 'New Xenophon', Herakleitos of Rhodes as 'the Homer of medical literature'.

48 FASHIONING THE FUTURE IN ROMAN GREECE

I'm different (i.e. better?).[69] I turn now to an example of competitive imitation in action by examining the relationship established between Xenophontic space and the contemporary Roman landscape encountered by Arrian of Nikomedeia at Trapezous as presented in his *Circumnavigation of the Black Sea* (*Periplous.*).

2.2 REMAKING SPACE, TIME, AND MEMORY IN ARRIAN'S *PERIPLOUS*

Arrian of Nikomedeia (*c.* AD 86–*c.*160) is practised at fictionalizing himself and his social roles within his literary efforts. For this reason, his mastery of the complexities of the relationship between imitation of past literary greats and assertion of his own authorial voice is impressive. Arrian's protean literary self-fashioning is enhanced by the range of his personal accomplishments and his ability to straddle numerous, potentially dissonant sociocultural identities: a wealthy Bithynian and Roman senator, who was fluent in Greek and Latin, a philosopher, military commander, Roman provincial governor, historian, friend to the emperor, writer; he was *entre plusieurs mondes*, to paraphrase Pierre Vidal-Naquet.[70] Importantly, this versatile self-image is reflected in other presentations of the man, both literary and material, indicating the success of his self-fashioning. In the later second-century, for instance, Lucian calls him 'a man among the first Romans and devoted throughout his life to [Greek] culture ($\pi\alpha\iota\delta\epsilon\acute{\iota}\alpha$)' (*Alex.* 2). Honorific inscriptions relating to Arrian also focus on a dual Roman/Greek, statesman/thinker identification. An inscription on a statue base in Athens, for instance, reads (Figure 2.2):[71]

Λ · $\Phi\lambda$ · $\mathring{A}\rho\rho\iota\alpha\nu\grave{o}[\nu]$
$\mathring{v}\pi\alpha\tau\iota\kappa\grave{o}\nu\ \varphi\iota\lambda\acute{o}[\sigma o]$
$\qquad\varphi o[\nu]$

L(ucius) Fl(avius) Arrian
consular and philoso-
       pher.

---

[69] Schmitz (1999, 78) argues that, in *epideixis*, the identity of the speaker was entirely subsumed by the character he was playing. The counterargument that slavish *mimēsis* was not the goal is more convincing; see Webb 2006, 27–46; Guast 2016.

[70] Vidal-Naquet 1984, 309–94. For biographical information, see Halfmann 1979, 146–7; Stadter 1980, 1–18; Syme 1982; Bosworth 1988, 16–25; 1993, 226–32; Fein 1994, 174–80; Madsen 2009, 68–70; Carlsen 2014, 210–13. On Arrian's bi-cultural nature, see Swain 1996, 242–8; Madsen 2006, 70–1; 2009, 119–26.

[71] See Peppas-Delmouzou 1970, 377–80; Oliver 1970a, 338. See also Bowersock 1967, 279–80; Stadter 1980, 14; Oliver 1982, 122–9; Liddle 2003, 14.

FIGURE 2.2 Inscription honouring Lucius Flavius Arrianos as consul and philosopher from Athens, probably a statue base, Epigraphic Museum (*EM* 2868 + 3025 + 3118 + 2990 + 3036; *SEG* 30.159). Preserved height: 0.51 m; Width: 0.51 m; Depth: 0.20 m.

Indeed, the majority of surviving inscriptions identify Arrian as a [Greek] philosopher and either [Roman] consular or governor of Kappadokia.[72] The example above is particularly noteworthy in how the Greek text conforms to Roman inscriptional conventions: it translates typical Latin abbreviations, defines them with Latin interpuncts, and inserts spaces between words to aid visual comprehension in the usual practice of Latin epigraphy. Visually, then, the text presents a thorough blending of Greek and Roman traditions befitting Arrian's own self-presentation.[73]

[72] See *Corinth* 8.3, 56; Bowersock 1967. There is also the biography of Cassius Dio, entitled Ἀρριανὸς ὁ φιλόσοφος: see Wirth 1963, 221–3; Stadter 1967, 155–61. Note that a metrical inscription dedicated by a Proconsul Arrian has also been discovered in Cordoba, Baetica, Spain. See Bosworth 1976 with bibliography. Beltrán Fortes (1992, 171–96), however, dates the altar based on stylistic comparison with other Baetican altars to the early third century; thus, he argues, the inscription either transcribes an earlier inscription of Arrian's or it was composed by a different man.

[73] On cultural blending in imperial period inscriptions, see Graham 2013 and further Section 4.1.

It has long been acknowledged that the most common role Arrian plays is that of Xenophon.[74] In *On Hunting*, for instance, he claims that his pursuits since youth have been those of Xenophon (1.4) and he gives orders as Xenophon in his *Battle Order against the Alani*. Yet Arrian's repertoire includes a *Tactical Handbook* describing an idealized reconstruction of the Hellenistic Macedonian army followed by a description of the Roman cavalry's ceremonial manoeuvres.[75] Thus he also embraces the role of Alexander, whose campaigns he describes in the *Anabasis*, while advertising his own strategic skills. Moreover, he is keenly attuned to generic conventions, imitating Herodotean Ionic Greek, for example, in his presentation of Nearchos' voyage in the *Indika*. This exemplary role-playing is emblematic of imperial Greek authors, such as Lucian. Unlike Lucian, however, Arrian does not divulge his literary twists with a dramatic stage wink; rather, he expects exceptional erudition from his readers and for them to work to decipher the layers in his art.[76] Most importantly, Arrian also maintains a separate identity that competes with his model as much as it honours him, as Longinos represents Plato doing with Homer.

Arrian's *Periplous* (*c.* AD 131) brilliantly illustrates the literary strategy of competitive imitation and brings to bear all his sociocultural and political complexity on its construction of spatial commemoration. Ostensibly, it describes the coast of the Black Sea as part of an inspection tour conducted during Hadrian's reign and is framed by a letter addressed to that emperor. Arrian also mentions a letter in Latin (6.2, 10.1), which must be the official report appended to the literary letter in Greek. At the same time, it interweaves earlier literary constructions of the landscape and history of this storied region, in particular Xenophon's, to create a new authoritative vision of the Black Sea and its surrounds.

It begins:

We came to Trapezous, a Greek city (πόλιν Ἑλληνίδα), as that Xenophon (ὁ Ξενοφῶν ἐκεῖνος) says, founded on the sea (θαλάττῃ), a colony of the Sinopeans (Σινωπέων ἄποικον); and gladly we looked down (κατείδομεν) on the Euxine Sea (τὴν μὲν θάλατταν τὴν τοῦ Εὐξείνου) from the same spot (ὅθενπερ) as Xenophon and you (σύ).[77]   (*Peripl.* 1.1)

The addressee, cast in the familiar 'you' (singular) of a friend, is the emperor Hadrian, and ὁ Ξενοφῶν ἐκεῖνος is the classical author. This sentence conflates

---

[74] On Arrian and Xenophon, see Stadter 1967, and, more fully, Stadter 1980; Bosworth 1993, 272–5; Bowie 2016, 409–14. On the name Xenophon, see Stadter 1980, especially 2–3. Rood 2011 discusses Arrian's allusions to Xenophon throughout the *Periplous*.

[75] On these two texts, see Bosworth 1993, 253–72; Devine 1993, 312–37; DeVoto 1993.

[76] Rood 2011 shows this extremely well by reference to Arrian's engagement with Xenophon and Herodotos in the *Periplous*. I am grateful for discussion of this section and my ideas about this text with Jaś Elsner and Tim Rood in early 2009 as part of an internal Oxford examination. Other than Rood on this text, see Bosworth 1993, 242–53; Silberman 1993, 276–311, and 1995, vii–xlv; Zadorojnyi 2018; and Braund 1994, 178–204, for the *Periplous* in the context of the region.

[77] The text used here is that in Liddle 2003.

centuries by drawing the three men together and situates them in a single very specific place at the limits of the Roman empire. Space and time are here made to serve Arrian's literary design. By mentioning 'that Xenophon', Arrian invests the spot on which he stands with a history that was celebrated in Xenophon's *Anabasis of Kyros*.[78] The phrase ὡς λέγει ὁ Ξενοφῶν ἐκεῖνος draws the reader's attention to the relevant passage, where the verbal echoes between Arrian's and Xenophon's accounts of their mutual arrivals are close: 'they came to the sea (θάλατταν) at Trapezous, a Greek city (πόλιν Ἑλληνίδα) founded on the Euxine Sea (τῷ Εὐξείνῳ Πόντῳ), a colony of the Sinopeans (Σινωπέων ἀποικίαν)' (Xen. *An.* 4.8.22). Arrian presents his arrival as almost a replay of Xenophon's and, in doing so, places himself as the inheritor of the classical author's voice. Nevertheless, there are significant differences between the two passages, which are surprising and pointed, given that ὡς λέγει ὁ Ξενοφῶν suggests a direct quotation. Arrian thus demonstrates the repetition and variation that has so concerned modern scholarship of the Second Sophistic, but his purpose here is primarily to tip his readers off to his conception of Trapezous as Xenophontic space and his requirement for them to know the relevant passages of the *Anabasis* in order to understand his own literary process fully.

Contiguously, Arrian acknowledges his complex relationship with the classical author that has been thoroughly discussed in modern scholarship.[79] Arrian regularly refers to himself as Xenophon and carefully distinguishes the other earlier Xenophon with labels such as ἐκεῖνος (*Peripl.* 1.1, 2.3; *On Hunting* 16.7, 21.2, 25.4) or ὁ πρεσβύτερος (*Peripl.* 12.5, 25.1), although on occasion he omits the qualifier altogether (e.g. *Peripl.* 13.6), a strategy designed to create ambiguity and a sense of instability about Arrian's personal identification:[80] is it distinction, descent, or assimilation? In favour of the last, James Oliver has suggested that a double herm in the National Archaeology Museum at Athens, one portrait of which is securely identified as Xenophon,[81] also bears the likeness of Arrian (*Glypta* 538; Figure 2.3).[82] There is no hard evidence for this classification but it is a compelling suggestion that merges the two authors physically to

---

[78] Cf. Liddle 2003, 91; Rood 2011, 139–41.

[79] See Stadter (1967; 1980, 2) for the suggestion that Arrian's full name was Lucius Flavius Arrianos Xenophon. It is as likely to be an honorary title (Ameling 1984). The *Battle Order against the Alani*, in which Arrian issues orders as 'Xenophon' (10, 22) and seems to draw on a speech by Kyros in Xenophon's *Education of Kyros* (5.3.34–45), as well as employing anachronistic Hellenistic military terms used by the Alexander historians (Stadter 1980, 48; Bosworth 1993, 265–7), lends weight to the suggestion that identification with Xenophon is primarily a literary move.

[80] Note that Xenophon talks about himself in the third person and uses his own name 250 times in the *Anabasis*.

[81] Minakaran-Hiesgen 1970, 112–57, especially figs 4, 10, 13, 26.

[82] Oliver 1972, 327–8. See also Bosworth 1993, 275; Petsalis-Diomidis 2010, 103–6, fig. 24. See Helbig 1886, 71–8, especially 72, 77–8; Benndorf 1899, 250–4, especially 254, fig. 138; Richter 1959, 168.2, figs 967–70.

52 FASHIONING THE FUTURE IN ROMAN GREECE

FIGURE 2.3 Double portrait herm of Xenophon and Isokrates or Arrian (?). National Archaeological Museum, Athens (Glypta 538). Height: 0.32 m. Top: Lateral view. Bottom: (L) Xenophon; (R) Isokrates or Arrian (?).

match Arrian's own textual fusion and the *Periplous'* engagement with Xenophontic space.[83]

Arrian's literary and personal identification with Xenophon has regularly been assessed as emulation, but there is also a strong element of competition.[84] The coupling of ἐκεῖνος with Xenophon's name, for instance, is loaded. The word is the distal pronoun and contains a spatial element: it denotes someone who is literally or metaphorically distant in time or space. Yet it can also stand alone in the singular to denote someone who is so famous that their name need not be mentioned.[85] In this context, Arrian turns the tables on Xenophon, in that his coupling of the word to Xenophon's name as an adjective, instead of letting either stand alone, highlights that there is another Xenophon from whom the classical author needs to be differentiated. The reader is meant to know that this unnamed Xenophon is Arrian himself. Here ἐκεῖνος assigns the classical Xenophon to the derivative role and suggests that Arrian is the first person to spring to mind when the appellation 'Xenophon' is used. This is taking Polemon's single name in contrast to the more elaborate identification of Demosthenes on the Pergamon statue base one step further.

Arrian's near quotation of the *Anabasis*, therefore, is better interpreted as a rewriting: a competitive act that produces a different (arguably better?) version. In addition, ἐκεῖνος serves to highlight Xenophon's absence and antiquity; he is distant in both time and space from this moment shared between Arrian and Hadrian within the letter, and Arrian and Hadrian's statue in Trapezous. He stands in the background of an intimate moment between the emperor and his provincial governor, acting as the glue that binds the two via their shared knowledge of his writings and, equally, to that place.

The most striking difference between Xenophon's and Arrian's mutual descriptions of their arrivals at Trapezous is the repeated use of θάλαττα by Arrian instead of Xenophon's θάλαττα followed by πόντος. The repetition points to the earlier passage of Xenophon's *Anabasis*, in which the Greeks first catch sight of the Black Sea and the famous cry of θάλαττα θάλαττα is raised (4.7.24). Although, as argued by Tim Rood, the fame of this shout is a phenomenon predominantly of the last two hundred years,[86] Arrian has gathered himself, Hadrian, and Xenophon virtually in Trapezous through his reworked replaying of Xenophon's own arrival, which consciously renders the disparities (θάλαττα/πόντος) in stark relief. The allusion depends on Hadrian's knowledge of Xenophon's text rather than Arrian's appeal to the fame of the phrase. It is a game of erudition and obscurity, as is common amongst literary elites in Arrian's age.

---

[83] Cf. Petsalis-Diomidis 2010, 103, on the herm.

[84] Cf. Bosworth 1993, 275; Stadter 1980, 50–9, on the *Cyn.*; Rood 2011.

[85] The word is used in the singular in speeches in the first four books of the *Odyssey* to refer almost exclusively to the absent Odysseus, often without any other signifier of the referent's identity.

[86] Rood 2004, 11–13.

This allusion is strengthened by Arrian's claim to have looked down on the Euxine Sea from the same place as Xenophon, since it was that first sight of the sea on Mt Theches that brought the cry from the Ten Thousand and in Xenophon's account of arriving at Trapezous there is no mention of gazing at the sea. It is therefore improbable that Arrian's reference to standing in the same spot as Xenophon is meant literally. He stresses the location of Hadrian's statue as Trapezous and mentions the neighbouring temple of Hermes (*Peripl.* 2), neither of which is perched on a remote mountaintop.[87] In addition, a large marble block bearing remnants of an inscription dedicated to Hadrian that may well stem from Arrian's memorial forms part of the Chrysokephalos Church (Fatih or Ortahisar Camii) in modern Trabzon (Figure 2.4). Its size (2.53 × 0.60 × 0.46 m) dictates that it would not have been sourced from a distant site.[88]

FIGURE 2.4 Statue base or building masonry bearing parts of a Hadrianic inscription that probably came from the monument renovated by Arrian at Trapezous. The inscription has been almost entirely over-written by an Arabic one; its remnants are traced in chalk on the lower border. Now built into the Chrysokephalos Church in Trabzon as a door lintel (Mitford 1974, 160–3, pl. V.2). Preserved length: 2.53 m; Height: 0.60 m; Depth: 0.46 m.

---

[87] On this, see also Rood 2004, 145–7. On a possible site for the cairn, see Mitford 2000; 2018a, 349, 373–6, pl. 43.

[88] Mitford 1974, 160–3, pl. V.2; 2018a, 392–3; 2018b, 542–3, no. 84; Liddle 2003, 92–3; Silberman 1995, 23 n. 4. Only four words of the inscription remain, running along the bottom border of this lintel block: Ἁδριανῷ Σεβαστῷ δημαρχικῆς ἐξουσίας ('to Hadrian Augustus of/from tribunician power').

The allusion to the sight of the sea on Mt Theches is, however, intentional. Arrian here collapses distance, as he has already collapsed time, in order to invest the place he has chosen for Hadrian's statue and altars with greater history. He recasts the backdrop of Xenophon's famous scene to suit his own commemorative purpose and, essentially, repackages Xenophon's work into a neater, tighter unit which combines two significant passages, integrating them as it virtually disintegrates the distance between Mt Theches and Trapezous. In doing so, he stakes a claim for that piece of the literary canon by both assimilating the Xenophon passages and competitively displacing them.[89] He makes Xenophon write for Hadrian and himself at the same time as he removes Xenophon's absolute authority over the continuing significance (i.e. the future history) of the *polis*-colony.[90]

The third participant in this virtual gathering is the emperor Hadrian or, more precisely, his statue, which Arrian tells us points out to the sea (1.3). Hadrian did make an inspection tour of the Kappadokian frontier in AD 123/4 or 129, and the statue was probably commissioned to commemorate that visit.[91] Nevertheless, in its current form, it is a poor memorial, since, according to Arrian, it does not resemble the emperor in any way ($\tau\dot{\eta}\nu$ $\delta\dot{\epsilon}$ $\dot{\epsilon}\rho\gamma\alpha\sigma\dot{\iota}\alpha\nu$ $o\ddot{v}\tau\epsilon$ $\ddot{o}\mu o\iota\dot{o}s$ $\sigma o\iota$). Due to the mimetic qualities of statues and the belief that they replace the person they represent, the poor state of Hadrian's image casts doubts on his prior physical presence. The 'you' ($\sigma\dot{v}$; 1.1), with whom Arrian and Xenophon gaze at the sea, therefore, could well be the statue itself rather than the emperor at an earlier time. Arrian's request that Hadrian send a statue carved in his true likeness from Rome (1.4) is thus a way of ensuring that the emperor really will stand in this historic place for all time to come. He stresses his intimacy with Hadrian but, more than this, he sets himself up as the arbiter of Hadrian's form and the public representation of that form.[92]

The fringe-like quality Arrian invests in the place he has chosen for Hadrian's statue and associated altars is significant. They will mark the limit of the empire where it meets the sea and the statue is posed to point out to the sea and the region beyond absolute Roman control. This arrangement aligns with Alexander's practices of monumentalizing the reach of his conquests, such as the twelve altars he ordered constructed on the Hyphasis in India, just before his army began the long trek back to Babylon (*An.* 5.29.1: $\mu\nu\eta\mu\epsilon\hat{\iota}\alpha$ $\tau\hat{\omega}\nu$ $\alpha\dot{v}\tau o\hat{v}$ $\pi\acute{o}\nu\omega\nu$; cf. Philostr. *VA* 2.43), or the altars at Sestos and Abydos he established to commemorate his crossing of a similar watery boundary in the Hellespont (*An.* 1.11.6–7).[93] Since Arrian's

---

[89] Rood (2011, 142–3) makes a similar argument.

[90] A number of scholars have noted Arrian's evocation of Xenophon in the landscape; see Braund 1994, 29–30, 180–1; Silberman 1993, 305; Petsalis-Diomidis 2010, 103; Rood 2011, 145. Crucially, they miss his efforts to assert the primacy of his own influence in the landscape.

[91] Liddle 2003, 92.   [92] Cf. Zadorojnyi 2013, 373.

[93] For the pose of the statue as signifying power and domination, see Brilliant 1963, 130; Calandra 1996, 136; Rood 2011, 142–3.

56 FASHIONING THE FUTURE IN ROMAN GREECE

Anabasis may have been composed before the *Periplous* and given the clear allusions to Xenophon's *Anabasis* in the *Periplous* (1.1, 2.3, 11.1, 12.5, 13.6, 14.4, 16.3, 25.1), it is possible to see the shade of Alexander also lurking in the background of this opening scene.[94] This allusion is strengthened by other famous ghosts. Arrian addresses Hadrian at the beginning of the letter with name and select titles, including the elements Τραϊανός and Σεβαστός. Alexander was an important model for Trajan and his military activity (e.g. Cass. Dio 68.29.1, 68.39.1), and Hadrian acquired his predecessor's name on becoming emperor to represent his late adoption and help legitimate the succession. The pointing adlocutio pose, moreover, is associated with Roman generalship and imperium, and the title Augustus conjures the *princeps* who also admired Alexander and used him as a model.

If a remembrance of Alexander is intended, Arrian's efforts to reshape the statue can be interpreted in two ways: first, as a promise to Hadrian to celebrate him in literature as he already has or intends to the Makedonian king (i.e. to give an account of the emperor that is worthy and which represents him accurately to posterity); second, as a promise to improve on Xenophon's *Anabasis* with his own version. Arrian's marking of the landscape here continues a programme of shaping Hadrian's image at the same time as asserting his role as an extension of Hadrian's imperial power. Therefore it may well presage a more extensive literary effort.[95] Arrian certainly makes a number of other physical interventions in the landscape on Hadrian's behalf. He raised a Latin inscription in his name at Sebastopolis-Dioskourias (modern Sukhumi), the eastern limit of the Roman empire,[96] and in a different Sebastopolis (modern Sulusaray) in Kappadokia he erected a *stêlê*

---

[94] The dating of Arrian's works is notoriously difficult. The *Periplous* can be dated to AD 131/2, but the sequence and date of the major historical works—the *Anabasis* and *Indika*, the *Parthika*, the *Events after Alexander*, and the *Bithyniaka*—remain unclear. Stadter (1980, 179–85) examines the evidence and the opposing views of Bosworth, who dates the *Anabasis* early (Bosworth 1980, 4–7, 8–11), and Wirth 1963, who dates it later. Carlsen (2014, 211–13) also favours a later date, but Bowie (2016, 412–14) convincingly argues for the *Anabasis* being Arrian's first historical work, probably falling after the *Discourses*. In Strazdins (2022b) I argue that there is an allusive intertextual connection via μνήμη and τὸ χωρίον between the second preface of Arrian's *Anabasis* and this first chapter of the *Periplous*, for which the best explanation is that the *Anabasis* refers back to the *Periplous*, but that Arrian already had Alexander in mind as the subject of a projected *Anabasis* when he wrote the *Periplous*. Note that Leon (2021, 115–21) argues for a date in the 120s.

[95] On Arrian wielding imperial power, see Petsalis-Diomidis 2010, 101; Zadorojnyi 2013, 373. See also Mitford 1974, 161–3, for Trabzon's strategic importance during the early second century.

[96] Had[rianus...] | per Fl. A[rrianum] | leg[(atum) Augusti pr(o) pr(aetore) Cappadociae]. See *L'Année Epigraphique* 1905, 44, no. 175; Stadter 1980, 11; Silberman 1995, vii–x; Petsalis-Diomidis 2010, 101; Mitford 2018b, 550, no. 99. Braund (1994, 194–5, pl. 13) questions the restoration of Arrian's name and supplies a photograph of the now lost fragment. He notes also that Arrian mentions no building on his behalf at Sebastopolis. For bibliography, see Braund 1994, 195 n. 87. For the original publication and reconstruction, see Rostovtzeff 1909, 1–22.

in Greek, celebrating Hadrian's adoption of Lucius Ceionius Commodus in AD 137.[97]

Arrian's monumental renovation at Trapezous, moreover, extends from the statue to the accompanying altars and applies metaphorically to the literary history of Trapezous and both the *Anabasis* of Xenophon and that of Arrian. These altars are equally inadequate because the stone is 'rough' ($\tau\rho\alpha\chi\acute{e}os$) and 'the inscription carved unclearly' ($\tau\grave{\alpha}\ \gamma\rho\acute{\alpha}\mu\mu\alpha\tau\alpha\ [...]\ o\mathring{v}\kappa\ e\mathring{v}\delta\eta\lambda\alpha\ \kappa\epsilon\chi\acute{\alpha}\rho\alpha\kappa\tau\alpha\iota$; 1.2). The poor artwork of Hadrian's statue, combined with the 'inaccurately carved' ($\mathring{\eta}\mu\alpha\rho\tau\eta\mu\acute{e}\nu\omega s$ $\gamma\acute{e}\gamma\rho\alpha\pi\tau\alpha\iota$) Greek inscription written 'by barbarians' ($\mathring{v}\pi\grave{o}\ \beta\alpha\rho\beta\acute{\alpha}\rho\omega\nu$; 1.2), belies the Greekness with which Arrian and Xenophon invest Trapezous ($\pi\acute{o}\lambda\iota\nu$ $\mathring{E}\lambda\lambda\eta\nu\acute{\iota}\delta\alpha$; *Peripl.* 1.1; Xen. *An.* 4.8.22).[98] This works both to stress the frontier character that Arrian is trying to apply to Trapezous and to enhance Arrian's authority over Hadrian's public image. Additionally, the $\pi\acute{o}\lambda\iota s\ \mathring{E}\lambda\lambda\eta\nu\acute{\iota}s$ is finally Hellenized by Arrian, who marks it with both Greek and imperial Roman artefacts: the reworked inscription and altars, and a true likeness of the emperor Hadrian.

Arrian's description of the 'rough stone' ($\lambda\acute{\iota}\theta os\ \tau\rho\alpha\chi\acute{v}s$; *Peripl.* 1.2) combined with the ambiguous spatial and temporal context also conjures the 'stones' ($\lambda\acute{\iota}\theta o\iota$; Xen. *An.* 4.7.25) which the Ten Thousand piled up to make a cairn as a commemoration of the sight of the sea on Mt Theches. Arrian vows to replace the inferior altars with clearly inscribed marble ($\beta\omega\mu o\grave{v}s\ \lambda\acute{\iota}\theta ov\ \lambda\epsilon v\kappa o\mathring{v}\ [...]\ \mathring{e}\gamma\chi\alpha\rho\acute{\alpha}\xi\alpha\iota$ $e\mathring{v}\sigma\acute{\eta}\mu o\iota s\ \tauo\hat{\iota}s\ \gamma\rho\acute{\alpha}\mu\mu\alpha\sigma\iota\nu$, *Peripl.* 1.2) and, in doing so, enhances his claim to control the historical memory of Trapezous.[99] Not only has he rewritten Xenophon, he will also bring the mountain to the sea, reconstruct his memorial, and direct it to another purpose.

The dilapidated state of the current statue and altars, and Arrian's initiatives to replace them with better, newer, more accurate, and more monumental structures are a commentary on the superiority of Arrian's literary authority in comparison to Xenophon's. Arrian's *Anabasis* is, after all, a monument to Alexander and his conquest of the east rather than the tale of a retreat from the east by the remnants of a mercenary Greek army. Additionally, Arrian's activities at Trapezous act to commemorate the power and reach of a Roman emperor, for whom he serves as a general and an administrator, whereas Xenophon and the Ten Thousand's memorialize their partially successful escape from an ill-fated foreign expedition. This contrast is significant in the context of Trajan's Parthian campaign

---

[97] See Mitford 1991, 194–6, no. 8, taf. IX.

[98] On the cultural complexities of Arrian's *Periplous*, see Madsen and Rees 2014, 1–8. On the altars, inscription, and statue, see the rich discussions of Rood 2011, 148–9, and Zadorojnyi 2018.

[99] Zadorojnyi (2018, 58–60) correctly stresses that both $e\mathring{v}\delta\eta\lambda os$ and $e\mathring{v}\sigma\eta\mu os$ refer to the legibility of the inscription.

(AD 115–17), which although unsuccessful still left the province of Kappadokia, over which Arrian was legate, firmly under Roman control, and looks forward to Arrian's own successful repulsion of the Alani (AD 135).

Thus Arrian reuses historical memory and the fame of Xenophon to commemorate both himself and Hadrian.[100] The statue and altars that will stand in Trapezous mark the place where the famous Xenophon stood in classical times, where the contemporary emperor may have once stood, and where Arrian has come to raise a μνήμην αἰώνιον ('everlasting memorial', *Peripl.* 1.4) to that emperor. For all the reasons that Arrian has alluded to in this opening passage, it is a place ἐπιτηδειότατον ('absolutely made for', 1.4) the memorial he proposes. He invests that 'spot' (χωρίον, 1.4) with a complex temporality that connects it back to the classical past, the recent past, the present, and that shapes its meaning for the future, a meaning that has been created intertextually by Arrian himself. This is combined with a complex textuality: a monument within a literary, allusive casting of an official report within a personal letter to the emperor.

Additionally, Arrian's description of the statue—'for it/he points out to the sea' (ἀποδείκνυσι γὰρ τὴν θάλατταν, 1.3)—the posture and the use of θάλαττα again, almost have the effect of animating it and supplying it with a voice to cry out the word.[101] This illusion is enhanced by the statue's bearing being the only aspect of the memorial Arrian finds acceptable. It is as though the image, in all its inadequacy, has been compelled by its surrounds to assume the pose of its own volition. So, although Arrian is the only person truly present, his text endows the site of Hadrian's statue with the power to collapse centuries and kilometres so that both Hadrian and Xenophon are brought to stand beside him and to relive a moment, which only Xenophon ever truly experienced, and to preserve that moment for the future. Moreover, by textualizing it, he makes the moment and the site of the statue moveable, spatially and temporally. In this way, Arrian becomes the guardian, publisher, and arbiter of the fame of Hadrian in particular, but also that of Xenophon, as it relates to this particular place: he builds a μνήμην αἰώνιον and then textualizes it to secure it for the future and a wider audience.[102]

Arrian's text is itself liminal, in that it marks a boundary between how Trapezous has previously been conceived in the historical memory and how Arrian proposes it should be conceived in the future. Hadrian's statue, placed by a temple of Hermes, himself the guardian of boundaries, forms the fulcrum. In this respect, if the identification is correct, the Athenian double herm (Figure 2.3) is an apt

---

[100] Compare Porter (2001, 75–6) on Pausanias' appeals to historical meaning.

[101] Rood (2004, 154) disagrees, noting that neither Arrian nor Hadrian is actually recorded as crying out the word. In Rood 2011, 142–3, however, he revises his position and implies this phrase is behind Arrian's description, that he is interested in the spot as visited by Xenophon, and that Hadrian's statue points to Xenophon's sea.

[102] Cf. Rood 2011, 147 and 149. See also Zadorojnyi 2018.

representation of Arrian's literary programme: Janus-like, Xenophon looks back to the historical memory and represents that memory, and Arrian looks forward with a reinterpretation and reapplication of that memory. Moreover, Arrian is in no way passive in this passage: his renovation of Hadrian's memorial does not let the emperor steal the limelight. He inserts himself into the scene actively, and both Hadrian and Xenophon depend on him for the commemoration which they receive. It is Arrian who creates an official and a literary record of the moment, who marks and alters the landscape of Trapezous, and who constructs his own literary supremacy.

Arrian reuses historical and cultural memory to create a new authoritative vision of Trapezous. He exploits and manipulates Xenophon's famous account. He controls and shapes the memorial to Hadrian. All these acts reveal him to be savvy as to the vicissitudes of one's future fame, artistic reception, and the capacity of material culture, especially textualized material culture, to communicate commemorative messages. The positioning of this one complex paragraph laden with meaning at the very beginning of his work only enhances this impression. On the basis of its geographical position, literary tradition, and genre conventions, Trapezous seems an otherwise odd place to commence a *Periplous*, which one would expect to begin from the Bosporos.[103] Moreover, it demonstrates the kind of μίμησις of which Longinos approves: a competitive embracing, which creates a context for one's own efforts, and concurrent displacement of the ancient illustrious model.

Finally, Arrian is also highly conscious in this work of the power of posterity to manipulate one's reputation as he describes the fluctuating historical fortunes of the locales he visits.[104] This historical consciousness is regularly manifested in imperial Greek literature as a deep ambivalence over one's individual prospects of successful and lasting commemoration, and it will be a theme to which I continually return. In the following sections, I will move away from the idea of imitation and look more closely at the unease that attends another strategy for escaping the shadow of the classical past: the injection of novelty/originality into speech and text.

2.3 NOVELTY AND THE PROBLEM OF AUDIENCE WITH PHILOSTRATOS AND LUCIAN

Longinos theorizes and Arrian demonstrates that imitation that looks to the future can only be agonistic, and Longinos and Dio Chrysostom propose that

---

[103] See Silberman 1993, 286–90; Liddle 2003, 22–32; Rood 2011, 139–42, on the features of the *Periplous* as a genre.

[104] Rood 2011, 147–60.

investing in the future necessitates mortgaging reception in the present. The focus of this section will be on the tensions that form in imperial Greek epideictic culture around this latter situation, especially in relation to the production and reception of novelty. In what follows, I explore authorial strategies for negotiating novelty and tradition, oral performance and literary composition, present acclaim and future fame at the interface of author and audience. My main focus will be on Philostratos' portrait of Philagros but Lucian and Longinos will provide context for the discussion.

Newness is denoted by two words in Ancient Greek—νέος, καινός—and their compounds. Although both can have the idea of either 'newness in time' or 'newness in kind', in the imperial period, the former is more regularly applied to time and the latter to type.[105] It is the idea of newness in kind that interests me here. For καινός the cognate noun is καινότης and it usually entails a level of strangeness, which can be either positive or negative.[106]

In sophistic culture, the inherent eccentricity and ambivalence of καινότης are the qualities that can make or break a speech due to the competitive performance environment. Not only does a rhetor contend with his peers, who regularly form part of his audience, but also with the crowd more broadly, who must be transported to the speech-world, entertained, moved, and challenged in a satisfying manner.[107] Hyper-critical, intellectual spectators in sophistic centres like Athens are but one extreme and acclaim can be based on entirely different criteria. In his 'Life of Favorinus', for example, Philostratos explains that this eunuch-sophist enchanted audiences at Rome, who were unable to understand Greek, simply by his tone of voice, facial expressions, rhythms, and his habit (which Philostratos himself finds distasteful) of singing an epilogue to his speeches (*VS* 1.8.491–2). Philostratos also records the emperor Trajan telling Dio Chrysostom: 'I don't understand what you're saying but I love you as I love myself' (*VS* 1.7.488). Moreover, Aelius Aristeides describes his own moments of oratorical brilliance as being akin to a torrent of words that his admirers could barely follow (*Oration* 52.22 = *HL* 4.22).[108] So the expertise of one's public matters in shaping response and, although sophists can entertain diverse crowds, the intertextual, erudite quality of imperial Greek literature anticipates an audience of peers.

Pushing the envelope of novelty too far, therefore, risks performative disaster, the destruction of contemporary reputation, and concurrent undermining of social status. Indeed, the quest for novelty (καινόσπουδον), Longinos tells us, is

---

[105] D'Angour 2011, 19, 66–79. Cf. Tilg 2010, 172–3, on the usage of καινός.

[106] D'Angour 2011, 29, 79–84 (for καινός associated with metal working and craft), 90.

[107] On the relationship between audience and sophist, see Korenjak 2000; Whitmarsh 2005, 23–40; Webb 2006. On the performativity of sophistic culture more generally, see Schmitz 1999 and 2017; Connolly 2001. On the spaces of performance, see Thomas 2017.

[108] On this comment by Aristeides, see Downie 2013, 124.

double-edged and a cause of both success and failure (*Subl.* 5.1). Conforming to performative norms, however, limits a rhetor's ability to address audiences of the future, who will consume the performance via the incongruous medium of writing.[109] My discussion of sophistic negotiation of audience, novelty, and fame begins with Philostratos' account of the second-century Philagros of Kilikia.

In Philostratos' *Lives of the Sophists*, the Kilikian Philagros makes a disastrous visit to Athens. His failures in the city are regularly interpreted as due to his inability to successfully negotiate Athenian sophistic identity politics.[110] This is undoubtedly one layer of Philostratos' anecdote, but just as important to Philagros' experiences in Athens is his characterization as a non-conformist on an artistic level. Initially, he fails to impress his Athenian audience through attempting to produce a new kind of speech:

As I have heard from those older than myself ($\tau\hat{\omega}\nu\ \pi\rho\epsilon\sigma\beta\upsilon\tau\acute{\epsilon}\rho\omega\nu$), his introductory speech gave offence, because they thought it had a novel-sounding flow ($\nu\epsilon\alpha\rho\omega\eta\chi\acute{\eta}s$) and was disconnected in its ideas ($\delta\iota\epsilon\sigma\pi\alpha\sigma\mu\acute{\epsilon}\nu\eta\ \tau\grave{\alpha}s\ \acute{\epsilon}\nu\nu o\acute{\iota}\alpha s$); they even thought it was puerile ($\mu\epsilon\iota\rho\alpha\kappa\iota\acute{\omega}\delta\eta s$). For into his encomium ($\acute{\epsilon}\gamma\kappa\omega\mu\acute{\iota}o\iota s$) of the Athenians, he inserted a lament ($\theta\rho\hat{\eta}\nu o s$) for his wife who had died in Ionia.[111]   (*VS* 2.8.579)

This passage juxtaposes the experimental oratorical artist with the authority of the learned, sophistic(ated) Athenian audience. Philostratos defers specifically to the adjudication of 'those older' than himself ($o\acute{\iota}\ \pi\rho\epsilon\sigma\beta\acute{\upsilon}\tau\epsilon\rho o\iota$), ostensibly designating those who were present at the Kilikian's oration. There is nevertheless an implied sense of wisdom and command that is strengthened by $o\acute{\iota}\ \pi\rho\epsilon\sigma\beta\acute{\upsilon}\tau\epsilon\rho o\iota$ being key sources exploited by Philostratos in the compilation of his *Lives*. These $\pi\rho\epsilon\sigma\beta\acute{\upsilon}\tau\epsilon\rho o\iota$, a group who ideologically correspond to Dio Chrysostom's $\sigma o\phi o\acute{\iota}$, expressly object to the novelty of Philagros' sound and arrangement of ideas. So the strangeness of novel expression is here critiqued by the authority of tradition. Moreover, Philagros is accused of sounding 'youthful' ($\mu\epsilon\iota\rho\alpha\kappa\iota\acute{\omega}\delta\eta s$), an uncomplimentary characteristic of style that is particularly damning when juxtaposed to $o\acute{\iota}\ \pi\rho\epsilon\sigma\beta\acute{\upsilon}\tau\epsilon\rho o\iota$. Most interestingly, Philagros is condemned for replacing praise of the Athenians (a topic which surely focused on the achievements of the past, as for example did the *Panathenaic Oration* of Aelius Aristeides) with a personal, modern, and foreign concern. This infringes on the sophistic fiction in which the speaker transports the audience into another reality. Longinos too criticizes such off-topic interruption to an oration, comparing it to indulging in 'drunken'

---

[109] See Korenjak 2012 for the suggestion that imperial Greek sophists were uninterested in posterity because the dictates of *epideixis* meant their compositions were designed for success in the moment of performance rather than as written literature.

[110] See, e.g., Bowersock 1969, 92–3; Papalas 1979; Anderson 1993, 36–7, 85; Whitmarsh 2005, 33–4; Kemezis 2011, 3–4, 11–12; Eshleman 2012, 7–10.

[111] See Wright 1968, 208 for $\delta\iota\epsilon\sigma\pi\alpha\sigma\mu\acute{\epsilon}\nu\eta$ instead of $\acute{\epsilon}\sigma\pi\alpha\sigma\mu\acute{\epsilon}\nu\eta$.

(ὥσπερ ἐκ μέθης), 'pedantic' (σχολικά), 'personal emotions' (πάθη [...] ἴδια ἑαυτῶν), which the audience cannot share, so that the orator 'makes an exhibition of himself' (ἀσχημονοῦσιν) (*Subl.* 3.5). The focal shift from topic to speaker breaks the sophistic spell.

On the Sublime also damns puerility (τὸ μειρακιῶδες), calling it the opposite of greatness and explaining that it emerges through attempts at originality:[112]

What do I mean by 'puerility'? A pedantic (σχολαστικὴ) thought, so over-worked (περιεργασίας) that it ends in frigidity (ψυχρότητα). Writers slip into it through aiming at originality/strangeness (περιττοῦ), artifice (πεποιημένου), and above all charm (ἡδέος), and then coming to grief on the rocks of tawdriness (ῥωπικὸν) and affectation (κακόζηλον).
(3.4)

As Longinos describes it, puerility stems from trying too hard: from attempting to produce a work that is cleverer and more innovative than the ability of the author allows. This accusation of literary failure, however, may not be the last word. We have also seen that the ability of the audience to accommodate change is a key factor in the production of sublimity and that literature that later becomes classic can be received as unusual or difficult in its moment of production.

Philagros' innovation here is unexpected to the point that it cannot be assimilated by his present audience since it disrupts the necessary suspension of disbelief; he therefore becomes an object of derision. The attempt to inject his discourse with individual details, however, is an effort to imbue it with personality, a trait which might differentiate his work from that of his peers and which promotes Philagros' authorship rather than his model or subject matter. The audience in Athens, the centre of the sophistic world, however, wants its expectations fulfilled. While Philostratos' account does emphasize the politics of sophistic performance and how breaking with tradition is dangerous for contemporary reputation, at the same time, it subtly mocks the Athenian crowd's inflexible traditionalist response. On a separate occasion, in the life of Philiskos of Thessaly, for example, Philostratos singles out 'innovative sound' (καινοπρεπὴς ἦχος, *VS* 2.30.623) as a positive attribute.[113]

Philostratos' Philagros, however, is a radical who is consumed by his own orations becoming literature. This tendency can already be identified in the personalization of his encomia of Athens, but is also at the heart of the well-known incident in which, having been challenged by Herodes' students in Athens both on his identity and his use of language, he declares that an 'outlandish word' (ἔκφυλον ῥῆμα), implying non-classical and non-canonical, comes from the 'classic'

---

[112] See Russell 1964, 73, for sublimity as the mean between turgidity (τὸ οἰδοῦν) and puerility. Cf. Arist. *Eth. Nic.* 1125a 17–34.
[113] See Whitmarsh 2005, 55, on Philiskos.

($\dot{\epsilon}\lambda\lambda\acute{o}\gamma\iota\mu os$) work of Philagros (*VS* 2.8.578–9).[114] This assertion turns the derision of Herodes' students on its head by claiming canonical status based on an idiosyncratic set of criteria. That Philagros is operating outside of known parameters is highlighted by Herodes' admonition to him when he writes to demand an apology: 'it seems to me that you are not performing your proem well ($o\dot{v}$ $\kappa\alpha\lambda\hat{\omega}s$ $\pi\rho o o\iota\mu\iota\acute{\alpha}\zeta\epsilon\sigma\theta\alpha\iota$)' (*VS* 2.8.579). Herodes' critique here is thus based on Philagros' failure to adapt his performance appropriately to his present audience and to prime them for its quirks.

Lucian of Samosata (born *c.* AD 120) provides a point of comparison to Philagros' disregard for his contemporary reception. Known for his satirical oratory, Lucian also displays an uneasy relationship with novelty but directly flags the issue to shape audience response. It is well known that a number of Lucian's works focus on minimizing what he considers incorrect audience reactions.[115] This is especially true of the introductory speeches—the oratorical form Herodes accused Philagros of getting wrong. His *Zeuxis*, for example, uses *ekphrasis* to educate his admirers on how to look beyond novelty to *technê*.[116] The speech opens with a lament that novelty ($\kappa\alpha\iota\nu\acute{o}s$, $\kappa\alpha\iota\nu\acute{o}\tau\eta s$) and strangeness ($\xi\epsilon\nu\acute{\iota}\zeta\omega\nu$) are the only things considered of value in his works, while their technical skill, intellect, and beauty are ignored (*Zeuxis* 2).[117] Lucian then compares his predicament to that of two others: the painter Zeuxis (fifth to fourth century BC), whose work fascinated its audience primarily on account of its curious subject matter rather than his excellent technique (3–7); and Antiochos I *Sôtêr* (*c.*324–261 BC), who won a battle by spooking the opposing cavalry with the sight and sound of his exotic elephants (8–11).[118] In both cases, the audience fails to see the truth behind these spectacles. Antiochos' achievement smacks of cheap trickery that is effective only for its inherent novelty, but Zeuxis blames his audience for failing to see the true mastery behind his innovations. Both Antiochos' and Zeuxis' audiences, therefore, respond positively but incorrectly.

As Lucian describes it, the novelty in Zeuxis' painting centres on its depiction of a family of centaurs, creatures well known for their volatility and wildness. The painting's focus is on the mother suckling her children (4). Like Arrian's reconfiguration of Xenophontic space in the *Periplous*, Lucian's *ekphrasis* of the classical painter's depiction of domestic centaurs emulates the image in words while laying

---

[114] On this, see Whitmarsh 2005, 33–4.

[115] See, for example, Nesselrath 1990, 129–32; Romm 1990, 86–7; Branham 1985; ní Mheallaigh 2014, 1–38.

[116] See Branham 1985, 238–9.

[117] Cf. *Prometheus in Words* 3, in which Lucian stresses he would destroy a piece that exhibited only novelty and lacked beauty.

[118] Nesselrath (1990), 129–32, sees the two stories as illustrating the possible reactions (rejection or acceptance) Lucian might have to someone who praises $\kappa\alpha\iota\nu\acute{o}\tau\eta s$ in his work.

claim to its form, interpretation, and subsequent fame. He describes the painting twice, first recounting its composition in all its novelty. The second description changes its reception, so that rather than the surprising aspects drawing attention, Zeuxis' skill and techniques are detailed as each element is recast in Lucian's terms. That Lucian calls his assessment of the painting's technical skill 'amateur' ($ἰδιώτης$, 5) is a dig at the superficiality of his own audience: though they be ignorant of the subtleties of his technique, they should still be able to sense its greatness.[119] His treatment of Zeuxis' painting is thus a challenge to spectators and readers to receive his own work adequately. That the classical Zeuxis had to wait for the Roman-period Lucian's scrutiny for worthy appreciation, moreover, intimates that any failure by Lucian's contemporary spectators to admire his art might well be rectified by audiences of the future.

The brand of innovation that Lucian exploits in his oeuvre functions by playing with expectations. It seems to have developed from the epideictic orator's need to entertain and to differentiate himself from other such performers.[120] It is, more-over, a technique that bleeds from epideictic into other contemporary forms.[121] Novelty in this sense is less about originality and more about surprise—about repurposing and recombining tradition in a startling way.[122] Importantly, Lucian's signposting and its contextualization within tradition allows his audience to accommodate and thus appreciate it, assuring his contemporary fame. Unlike Philagros' genre-breaking departures, therefore, his work is aimed very much at the present.[123] The contemporary focus explains Lucian's tendency to anticipate and try to defuse criticism of his innovations.[124]

[119] Romm (1990, 86–7), in contrast, suggests that Lucian's description reveals that he too is overwhelmed by its novelty and is uninterested in its skill. But, although Lucian spends his time describing the painting's aesthetic qualities, he stresses Zeuxis' extraordinary skill as the most important element (*Zeuxis* 5).

[120] On Lucian's self-construction and *epideixis*, see Romm 1990; Branham 1985; Saïd 1993; Dubel 1994; Dobrov 2002; Goldhill 2002, 60–107; Humble and Sidwell 2006.

[121] One example is the novel, on which see Tilg 2010. On the connection between the novel and *epideixis*, see Whitmarsh 2005, 86–8. Bowie (2008, 17–38) gives an introduction to the novel that situates it in its literary context. A huge and expanding body of recent scholarship (particularly over the past thirty years) exists on the ancient novel. See Whitmarsh 2008 and Cueva and Byrne 2014 for an indication of the range of scholarly concerns.

[122] See the extended discussion of the range of Lucian's novelty in ní Mheallaigh 2014, 1–38. E.g. he imagines unseen places (e.g. the moon in *True Stories*); he combines disparate genres (e.g. comic dialogue in *Twice Accused*; see Branham 1989, 11–63, on Lucian and Old Comedy).

[123] For example, Polemon's surviving *controversiae* on who died more gloriously at the battle of Marathon, Kallimachos, or Kynegeiros, also exhibit this brand of novelty. Kynegeiros' father, for instance, claims his son was 'the first human to engage in a naval battle on land' ($πρῶτος ἀνθρώπων ἐναυμάχησεν ἐκ γῆς$, *Kynegeiros* 8).

[124] See also *You're a Prometheus in Words* and *Dionysos* 5, with Branham 1985.

Many of Lucian's works are thus concerned with the correct balance between canonical imitation, novelty, and audience reception in the quest for lasting fame, and he provides a number of different perspectives. The ekphrastic lesson in the *Zeuxis*, for instance, not only highlights how novelty can overshadow skill but also the dangers of imitating the canon too closely. The painting Lucian describes is in fact a copy of Zeuxis' lost original by an anonymous artist. Here, 'slavish imitation' of the classic artist (ἀντίγραφος [...] ἀκριβεῖ τῇ στάθμῃ μετενηνεγμένη, *Zeuxis* 3) results in complete loss of identity for the copyist.[125] His *True Stories* (2.5–29) makes a similar point through the narrator's visit to the Isle of the Blessed, populated solely by canonical authors and characters: it is impossible to be original and canonical at the same time, and one cannot successfully reinvent characters or plots central to canonical texts because their existing representation is too monumental. Although Lucian here trumps Longinos' instruction to imagine the past greats as one's audience and instead gains direct access to them, their fixed, frozen-in-time state means he can gain no greater insight into their experience than what he has already gleaned from reading about them.[126] Any who do try to change their fates and add to or alter their stories fail.[127] At the opposite extreme, in his *Death of Peregrinus*, Lucian details what happens when novelty-seeking goes too far. The eponymous phony philosopher's constant re-invention of himself in more and more extreme ways in order to maintain the attention of the crowd ultimately ends in his self-immolation at Olympia. Here, the desperate pursuit of novelty results in a ludicrous death rather than apotheosis and artistic immortality.[128]

Lucian's depiction of individuals trapped by their own stories on the Isle of the Blessed is indicative of the constraints of contemporary literary production, especially epideictic oratory, and again resembles an apology for Lucian's own conformity.[129] Moreover, his narrator's subsequent departure from the Isle to continue his own story intimates that true artistic originality lies in abandoning canonical models for the unknown.[130] Lucian's negotiation of and attempts to

---

[125] On the issue of the painting being a copy, see Perry 2005, 91–4; Anguissola 2014, 119.

[126] See Kim 2010, 157–8, for other examples of accessing the past, including direct contact with those living as the ancients did, dream interactions, and encounters with ghosts. Cf. Swain 1996, 79–87. See Kim 2010, 161, on the characters' fixed state.

[127] Kim 2010, 168–73.

[128] On this text as Lucian's self-condemnation for his own novelty-seeking ways, see the excellent discussion of Fields 2013. See also König 2005a.

[129] Cf. ní Mheallaigh 2014, 248, on contemporary literary conformity; see 246–50 on how competition, performance, and literary-cultural posterity are manifested in this text; see 206–60, for an exploration of the *True Stories* against the mimetic culture of imperial Greek literature.

[130] Attempts to break free of Homer regularly still depend on his text. Examples include Philostratos' *Heroikos*, which uses the autopsy of Protesilaos as a greater authority (see Kim 2010, 175–215; Aitken and

control audience expectations and responses to novelty are social as much as artistic strategies because the orator's status depends on his public reception.

The experiences of Philagros in Herodes' Athens, the centre of the sophistic world, again highlight the dangers to social status in deviating from the accepted epideictic script. The Kilikian breaks the rules of sophistic performance once more in a subsequent display by reperforming an already published, much celebrated speech instead of improvising.[131] Philagros' epideictic misstep here is regularly assessed as a failed attempt to hoodwink his audience and falsely inflate his reputation for epideictic oratory, a judgement encouraged by his speech being hijacked and ridiculed by Herodes' pupils.[132] Philostratos' designation of Philagros as 'brilliant' (λαμπρός, *VS* 2.8.578) and his attainment of the Chair of Rhetoric in Rome (*VS* 2.8.580), however, point to an alternate interpretation. Philagros' repetition is a deliberately transgressive and innovative act that is intended both to invest his own work with greater literary clout and to promote written composition over spoken improvisation. By reproducing a previously successful performance, he aims to cement his name to that particular work and to give its fame increased longevity: he treats his earlier epideictic speech as literature. In this scenario, Philagros is doing precisely what Herodes accused him of: he is directing his speech beyond his present audience to a hypothetical future. Writing, in this case, allows old and new material to be distinguished, the showcasing of individuality, and the capacity to claim credit for brilliant composition.[133] In this particular sophistic context controlled by Herodes Attikos, even though the scrutiny offered by the written text works against Philagros, his outrage at being mocked for reusing his own art (*VS* 2.8.579) reveals his preparedness to attach greater permanency to it at the risk of his present reputation.

In this episode, Philostratos' sympathies ostensibly lie with Herodes and his students, and he is critical of Philagros' epideictic *faux pas* but, at the same time, the act of writing the sophists and their lives essentially creates the canon of the Second Sophistic and, in the sense of commitment to the written word and using it to invest one's novel ideas with authority, Philostratos' practice approaches that of Philagros more so than that of Herodes.[134] I will return to Philostratos' presentation of Philagros' difficult relationship with Athens in chapter 6.[135] For now, his apparently misplaced innovation demonstrates once more how

---

Maclean 2001; 2005), and 'pseudo-documentary fiction', which depends on the discovery in a material context (e.g. a tomb) of an autobiographical text that describes the author's experiences during the Trojan War. On the latter, see Hansen 2003 and ní Mheallaigh 2008.

[131] On this episode, see Eshleman 2012, 7–10; Kemezis 2011, 3–4 and 11; Papalas 1979.

[132] See, e.g., Kemezis 2011, 11: 'inferior talent'; cf. 12.

[133] Cf. D'Angour 2011, 167, on music and poetry.

[134] On Philostratos writing the canon of the Second Sophistic, see Eshleman 2008, 396; 2012, 125–7.

[135] See Section 6.3.

important audience reception is to creating a positive impression and reputation, as well as his voluntary investment in the potential for present and future audiences to respond quite differently. I turn now to another of Philostratos' sophists who solves the problem of audience reception in a unique way by creating an alternative textual reality controlled by the author in which anything is possible and immortal fame is ineffaceable.

2.4 CREATING ORIGINAL ARTISTIC SPACE IN AELIUS ARISTEIDES' *SACRED TALES*

Aelius Aristeides (AD 117–after 181) was from Hadrianotherae in Mysia, but spent much of his active career in Smyrna. As a sophist, he faced a unique problem brought on by a sudden and debilitating illness—the inability to declaim epideictically. As he tells it, the sickness that began as his greatest setback ended as a personal and professional triumph. He constructs this image textually via a number of strategies centred on the manipulation of space, time, audience, and commemorative artefacts. After completing his rhetorical training in Smyrna under Alexander of Kotiaion and Polemon, and Athens under Herodes Attikos, Aristeides began a promising sophistic career.[136] He set off for Rome with the intention of advancing it further at the centre of empire; along the way, however, a cold developed into the great illness that would plague his body, but shape his art.[137] His *Sacred Tales* (*Hieroi Logoi*, *HL*),[138] an unusual collection of five complete autobiographical discourses and one fragment, commemorate his physical, spiritual, and oratorical journey over the next twenty-six years guided by the healing-god Asklepios.[139]

For Aristeides, the advent of his sickness marked the end of his sophistic career (*HL* 4.14), the natural path to sociocultural success, contemporary fame, and a relationship with posterity. During a two-year stay at the Asklepieion in Pergamon, however, Asklepios both personally oversaw his recovery from illness and directed his re-engagement with *epideixis*. Aristeides refers to this as his ἡ ἐν Περγάμῳ καθέδρα (*HL* 2.70; 3.44), meaning 'period of inactivity in Pergamon',

---

[136] Behr 1968, 10–22.   [137] Behr 1968, 23–5.

[138] Note that I will refer to *HL* 1–5, but that these correspond to *Orations* 47–52, so that *HL* 1 = *Oration* 47, *HL* 2 = *Oration* 48, and so on. Translations follow Behr 1981 with some amendments.

[139] Behr 1968, 23: note that the years 155–165 are absent from the text. On Aristeides' entwining of physical and rhetorical healing, see Baumgart 1874, 95–120. See also Downie 2013, who places Aristeides' devotion to rhetoric at the centre of the *HL* and traces how his religious investment in Asklepios and his experience of his own body aid his rhetorical triumph. Petsalis-Diomidis 2010 focuses on religion and Aristeides' relationship with Asklepios. Pernot (2002, 369–83) constructs the 'triangle aristidien' (371), constituting medicine, religion, and rhetoric. On Aristeides' relationship to pain, see King 2017, 129–56.

68 FASHIONING THE FUTURE IN ROMAN GREECE

but he is probably also alluding to the sought-after Chairs of Rhetoric (known as *Καθέδραι*) in Athens and Rome. The reference is on the one hand ironic, since these chairs were beyond Aristeides' reach at the time, and on the other an assertion that his residency in Pergamon rivals them in importance. His time at the Asklepieion is not inactive, after all, but is presented as a period of 'physical training' (*ἄσκησις*, *HL* 4.18) which both cures his illness and recreates him as a pre-eminent fluent orator.[140]

As with all cures related to Asklepios cult, Aristeides receives his instructions via dreams, a process bestowing legitimacy on his claims: that the god sometimes dispenses medical and at others or even concurrently rhetorical advice via dreams is a process that fits comfortably within contemporary social and religious comprehension.[141] Thus Aristeides creates a divine context for his unusual literary activities.[142] It is also integral to Aristeides' construction of an original voice. Janet Downie argues compellingly that, rather than manifesting as a vehicle of rhetorical perfection, Aristeides' authorial voice must naturally exceed conventional rhetorical bounds because it comes from the god. His form is experimental, bewildering, disjointed, because his voice too is unprecedented.[143] His eventual physical recovery, moreover, only adds further veracity to his assertions of divine favour and revelation. Evidence for backlash against these claims do exist (e.g. *Or.* 28 is an apology for boasting that Athena co-authored a hymn with him), but in the *Sacred Tales* he can silence such criticisms by omitting them.[144]

Asklepios prescribes oratory and, indeed, exemplary, competitive, and improvised oratory as the cure for Aristeides' illness. To become well again, he must take his rightful place in contemporary sophistic culture, so his professional success is tied directly to his physical recovery. Asklepios creates the oratorical framework for Aristeides' works, assuring him:

'Your speeches are to be outstanding like those of Sokrates, Demosthenes, and Thucydides'. And one of the distinguished personages, who came before me, was pointed out (*τῶν ὑπὲρ ἡμᾶς τοῖς χρόνοις ἐνδόξων ἐδείχθη τις*), in order that I would be especially moved to speak. And the god commanded me to go to the Temple Stoa, which is at the Theatre, and to offer to him the very first fruits (*τό γε σφόδρα πρῶτον ἀπάρξασθαι*) of these improvised (*αὐτοσχεδίων*) competitive (*ἀγωνιστικῶν*) orations. (*HL* 4.15)

---

[140] On Aristeides' treatments as oratorical training, see Downie 2013, 116–17. On agonistic physical performance and the imagery of initiation in contemporary oratory, see Korenjak 2000, 195–9, 214–9.

[141] Cf. Petsalis-Diomidis 2010, 133.

[142] On Aristeides' shaping of 'divine time' through the structure of his text, see Tagliabue 2016.

[143] Downie 2013, 128. Cf. Pearcy 1988, 379. See also Korenjak 2005; Petsalis-Diomidis 2010, 129, 132.

[144] See the discussion of Downie 2013, 141–2, on *Oration* 28.

Aristeides is to be understood, then, in relation to these famous individuals, rather than to any of his contemporaries, and as their equals.[145] He thus conforms to the imperial Greek tendency to contextualize one's own innovation by reference to canonical authors and, like Lucian in the *True Stories*, he converses directly with past greats, including Plato (4.57), Lysias (4.59), and Sophokles (4.60). His greatest contemporaries, meanwhile, trip and sprawl silently nearby in the street (σοφιστὴς τῶν ἐφ' ἡμῶν καὶ μάλα τῶν ἐπιφανῶν [...] ἀνατραπεὶς ἔκειτο, 4.61). Also like Lucian's Isle of the Blessed, Aristeides' dreamscape is simultaneously atemporal (in that the past and present exist all at once) and eternal. The 'distinguished personage' described above is a classical model, who 'was displayed' (ἐδείχθη) for Aristeides as though he were an artefact or memorial. The presentation of this figure by the god Asklepios suggests that immortality through exceptional oratorical performance is possible and that Aristeides can be monumentalized alongside him. That this particular past great remains anonymous is Aristeides' way of asserting his supremacy. Moreover, the verb ἀπάρχεσθαι ('to offer first fruits') signals the religious, sacrificial character of Aristeides' activity, as well as the bountiful harvest implied to follow.[146]

How, then, does this divinely ordained, therapeutic *epideixis* work out for the ailing sophist? After going to the Temple of Hygeia, Aristeides meets his friend Sedatius and tells him of the god's directive to orate, despite his inability to breathe (*HL* 4.17). It is a feature of Aristeides' illness that his ailments are of a kind that physically precludes him from orating—intestinal difficulties, breathing problems, catarrhs, throat swellings, spasms.[147] Charles Behr has even suggested that the physical complaints were a product of stage fright, so that it is Aristeides' mind rather than his body that fails him.[148] It is an attractive solution, given that successful oratorical performance is the key to his cure, but is also indicative of a scholarly desire to psychologize and diagnose Aristeides according to modern social and cultural norms.[149] In the *Sacred Tales*, however, it is specifically his body that is unfit, so much so that he tells Sedatius he will simply go through the motions of speaking in the hope of satisfying the god by striking a pose and saying a few words. His friend, however, protests that the cure is less about words and

---

[145] Cf. *HL* 4.62: 'When I was giving a rhetorical display in my dream and was winning much approval, and someone in my audience said in praise, "Just as so-and-so" (ὡς ὁ δεῖνα), whom he admired (ἐθαύμαζε) most of the ancients, I dreamed that my teacher, who was present, grew restless and said, "Will you not also add such-and-such?" (οὐ προσθήσεις τὸν καὶ τόν). And he intended to mention others in turn, since no one man should be compared to me'.

[146] Petsalis-Diomidis 2010, 142–3.

[147] See Pearcy 1988, 386, for Aristeides' laryngeal symptoms and their interference in his literary activities.

[148] Behr 1968, 45 n. 17.

[149] On scholarly psychologizing, see Petsalis-Diomidis 2010, 122–5; Downie 2013, 22–8.

more about the exertion of oratory, since he knows of another who overcame disease by sweating it out while speaking (thus rebalancing his Hippocratic humours),[150] and he offers himself as an audience (*HL* 4.17). As Aristeides describes it, however, the cure lies less in physiology and more in performative embodiment.

The theme proposed is, 'while Alexander is in India, Demosthenes advises it is time to act':

I immediately accepted the portent (φήμην) of Demosthenes speaking again (αὖθις λέγοντα) and of the subject, which was about rule/supremacy (ἡγεμονίας). And pausing a little, I contended (ἠγωνιζόμην), and my new strength was such as is of the god's devising, and the year seemed not to have been passed in silence (σιωπῆς), but in training (ἀσκήσεως). This was the beginning (ἀρχὴ) of the practice (μελέτης) of oratory (λόγων) for us (ἡμῖν), and so we returned to it (ἐπανήλθομεν). (*HL* 4.18–19)

As demonstrated by Downie, Aristeides' god-directed bathing, vomiting, and fasting are the 'training' (ἄσκησις) that allows him to return to improvised *epideixis*. His body is shaped by his suffering in order to become an adequate vehicle for his voice, and the god inspires his words. This strikes chords that once more resonate socially and culturally—the competitive physicality of athletics and the inspiration of mystery initiation[151]—as he essentially unites Longinos' modes of passive and active μίμησις. The shift from 'I' to 'we' indicates how integral his partnership with Asklepios is. Moreover, the 'portent' of Demosthenes 'speaking again' implies Aristeides' assumption of his mantle; Aristeides rather than Polemon is the 'new Demosthenes' here. Thus it is especially fitting that this first oratorical triumph on the topic of 'supremacy' is made in the region of the theatre at the Pergamene Asklepieion, where it is probable his audience would extend beyond Sedatius to nearby votive and honorific statues, including Polemon's own dedication of Demosthenes.[152] The topic excites Aristeides because it offers the opportunity to surpass his model as highlighted by his animated self performing before the immobile and silent image of the classical orator.

The combination of a healed body and the god's rhetorical teachings leads to a kind of oratorical *aristeia*, in which Aristeides' ability to control his 'breath' (πνεῦμα) also reveals his embodiment of the 'divine presence' (πνεῦμα):

It was my experience that when I received my problems and stood ready for the contest (ἀγῶνα), I was at a loss and scarcely recovered from my failure of breath (ἐπιλείποντος τοῦ

---

[150] See Downie 2013, 124.

[151] Downie 2013, 116–17. On these aspects of contemporary oratory, see Korenjak 2000, 195–9, 214–9. On performative excess and personal theatre, see Connolly 2001.

[152] See Petsalis-Diomidis 2010, 267–9, on the viewing culture of the Asklepieion and the presence of classical Greek figures.

πνεύματος); but as I proceeded in the introduction, I was able to manage and regulate my breath more easily; and as my speech went on, I was filled with strength (δυνάμεως) and lightness (κουφότητος) and strung my words together (συνείρειν) so well that the audience scarcely followed them. And in my opinion, the spectacle (τὸ θέαμα) was greater than what was heard (τὸ ἀκρόαμα). (*HL* 4.22)

Through speaking, Aristeides himself becomes a 'wonder' or 'spectacle' (θέαμα). The mental image created by Aristeides of his words flowing together approximates the visualization of written text in the Greek world, with its absence of word-division and punctuation. That the spectacle is more for the eyes than ears can therefore be read to imply his voice becomes instant text (i.e. his speech is a process of 'writing aloud'),[153] and given his surrounds, the θέαμα can be interpreted here as a monumentalized image (i.e. a statue) of Aristeides declaiming with accompanying inscription. His textually monumentalized body thus approximates both an honorific statue and a votive offering to Asklepios to match the votive artefact of the *Sacred Tales* itself.[154]

Elsewhere, Aristeides again makes his body and its care an object of wonder. In particular, in book two, he takes a series of performative baths dictated by the god (*HL* 2.21; 2.51–5; 2.74–8; 2.82). Most of these occur in extreme conditions and are designed to cast Aristeides as heroic, but many also occur before audiences who respond to his efforts with enthusiastic applause.[155] In the final bath of book two, for instance, after being sent by Asklepios to Ephesos to speak, Aristeides explicitly connects his bathing exploits to his oratory:

[Asklepios] ordered a cold bath and I bathed in the gymnasium at Koressos. The spectators (οἱ ὁρῶντες) wondered (ἐθαύμαζον) no less at the bath than at my words. But the god was the cause of both. (*HL* 2.82)

Consequently, audience is vitally important to Aristeides' literary design. He constantly supplies internal dream and external waking audiences for both his medical and his oratorical performances. Everything he does must be witnessed, and the *Sacred Tales* gives the impression of a life lived in perpetual performance. Indeed, when he almost died in a plague at Smyrna, he dreams the process of death as that of an actor at the end of a play about to remove his buskins (*HL* 2.40). Equally, the promise of his relationship with posterity is something he witnesses as a spectator himself and then records. He dreams he sees Egyptian school children, for example, performing one of his hymns (*HL* 3.4); he is told by

---

[153] On texts as 'written aloud', see Porter 2010, 351–3, with Barthes 1975, 66–7. Also see Porter's discussion of the process of composition in creating (verbal) monuments (500–3).

[154] On the *Sacred Tales* as a votive offering, see Downie 2013, 155–81. Cf. Pearcy 1988, 377–8; Petsalis-Diomidis 2006; 2010, 133, 139–40 with *HL* 5.36.

[155] On Aristeides' baths in book two, see Downie 2008; 2013, 87–126.

72 FASHIONING THE FUTURE IN ROMAN GREECE

a dream philosopher that he has surpassed Demosthenes in 'reputation' (ἀξίωμα, *HL* 4.19).

Ewen Bowie, however, has pointed out that we have very little evidence for the reality of Aristeides' resurgence on the imperial sophistic stage, as presented by the redemptive healing narrative of the *Sacred Tales*. Moreover, he correctly interprets Aristeides' frequent dreams of imperial favour as indicative of anxiety over the absence of a close relationship with emperors, such as his teacher Alexander of Kotiaion possessed, and a concern that this ultimately demonstrates a lack of success in comparison to other rhetorical performers.[156] This assessment is backed up by Philostratos' disparaging assessment of Aristeides' extempore oratory in his *Lives of the Sophists* (*VS* 2.9.582–3, 585). Aristeides' thoughtful and deliberate process—'I am not a vomiter (ἐμούντων) but a perfectionist (ἀκριβούντων)' (*VS* 2.9.583)—is entirely incompatible with Philostratos' presentation of improvised *epideixis* as the pinnacle of cultural expression.[157]

Concerning Aristeides' relationship to posterity, however, this apparent failing is intriguing primarily for how it affects our understanding of his attempts to address it. The medium of his conversation with future audiences is the written text, and through the text he supplies himself with countless audiences, he performs countless successful improvised speeches, communes with past literary greats, is honoured by emperors, and speaks with the gods. This codification of success in the book removes his achievements from the immediate present and opens them to the future. The god's agency and Aristeides' failure to perceive Asklepios and, hence, his own trajectory completely is communicated by the sudden shifts in space and time, the porous borders between the waking and dream world, and Aristeides' inability to adequately and vividly describe the latter precisely.[158] Thus, even though he worries that his periods of withdrawal from society and his unconventional career may have handicapped his success,[159] he places his faith in the belief that his communion with the god, so similar to Athena's promotion and care for the Homeric Achilles or Odysseus, will ensure his literary posterity (*HL* 5.56).

As well as using his text to provide his own marvelling spectators, Aristeides exploits its ability to create commemorative space via its conjuring of an eternal divine dream world in which honorific monuments take form. As a thank offering for acclaim he received from a series of improvised choral performances, for instance, Aristeides decides to dedicate a tripod and composes an elegiac couplet

---

[156] Bowie 2012, 229–36. [157] See Korenjak 2012.

[158] See Whitmarsh 2004, 444–5; Petsalis-Diomidis 2006, 196–203. Cf. Petsalis-Diomidis 2010, 109, 130; Platt 2011, 288.

[159] On Aristeides' efforts to evade public service and cast this evasion as due to his devotion to oratory, see Downie 2013, 155–81.

honouring the god to inscribe upon it. The god intervenes in a dream, however, and changes the couplet to be about Aristeides rather than himself: 'Aristeides, not invisible (οὐκ ἀφανὴς) to the Greeks, dedicated this, | The glorious charioteer of everlasting words (μύθων ἀενάων κύδιμος ἡνίοχος)' (*HL* 4.45). Aristeides here becomes the audience for his own divine honouring. Through its invocation of the tradition of epinician odes, the inscription not only alludes to sophistry's adoption of athletic exertion as a metaphor for its own trials, but also places Aristeides both in the company of and in competition with the likes of Pindar and Bakkhylides. The sophist's supremacy is indicated by his ability to be both 'charioteer' and (self-)commemorative singer. Moreover, his fame and his vocation are god-sanctioned:

it seemed in every way to be fitting to keep on with oratory, as our name (ὄνομα ἡμῶν) would live even among future men (τοῖς ὕστερον ἀνθρώποις), since the god happened to have called our speeches 'everlasting' (ἀενάους). (*HL* 4.47)

It is consequential that the god identifies Aristeides in the inscription by a single name and that Aristeides refers to his oratory as a joint effort ('we', 'our') once more. This both highlights their intimacy and replicates Aristeides' own process in the material world, where like Polemon he felt comfortable that his single personal name would be recognizable and sufficient for his identification for an extended period to come.[160] This is demonstrated by an altar dedicated to Asklepios in Mytilene (Figure 2.5):[161]

[Ἀ]ριστεί-
δης Ἀσκλη-
πιῷ Σωτῆρι
  εὐχήν

Aristeides [offers]
to Asklepios
the Saviour
a prayer/vow.

Since this dedication is an altar, it most likely comes from the sacred precinct of the island's Asklepieion. The single name and the way it and the prayer embrace 'to Asklepios the Saviour' on the stone highlight the intimacy between Aristeides and Asklepios. The altar stands as an eternal representation of a transitory sacrifice

---

[160] Puech 2002, 140; Downie 2013, 11. For other epigraphic instances of Aristeides using only a single name (all on altars dedicated to gods), see Jones 1978, 231–4; Puech 2002, 138–9 nos. 40–2; Tanriver 2013, 42–6. For Aristeides and inscriptions in general, see Petsalis-Diomidis 2010, 117–20.

[161] Museum of Mytilene, inv. no. 1078. Charitonidis 1968, 27–8, no. 33, plate 11δ; Robert 1980, 7–8; Puech 2002, 139–40, no. 43.

FIGURE 2.5 Inscribed altar dedicated by Aelius Aristeides to Asklepios on the island of Lesbos, most probably in the Asklepieion, Archaeological Museum of Mytilene (Inv. 2253; Charitonidis 1968, 27–8, no. 33, plate 11δ). He refers to himself only as 'Aristeides' and Asklepios as the 'saviour'. Height: 0.33 m; Width: 0.19 m; Depth: 0.17 m.

confirming the reciprocity between god and man, the vow made or the prayer offered. Its simplicity in comparison to the elegiac dedication of the dream tripod emphasizes the greater freedom literary text has over inscribed text to shape self-presentation. Importantly, Aristeides' focus on his closeness to Asklepios in his writings is the primary reason for the dedicator of the altar being identified with him. Thus his literary self-presentation has here bled into the material world as a social strategy and then defined scholarly interpretations of the dyad Aristeides-Asklepios.

The porous borders that the *Sacred Tales* creates between divine dream world and mortal reality render Aristeides' textual commemorative strategies rhetorically ineffaceable, whether or not anyone reads his *Sacred Tales* or the dedicatory inscriptions on his temple offerings in waking reality. The text itself, moreover, becomes a new space for original artistic expression that bypasses contemporary audiences and their control over social and cultural prestige. Like Philagros, Aristeides aims the spotlight at himself but within the safety of his own textual universe in which positive audience response and his own canonicity are predetermined. The text and its story of success clearly function as a votive offering to

Asklepios.[162] More than this, however, Aristeides makes himself and his suffering body the subject of the discourses, so that the text turns his very existence into a votive artefact that is also a commemorative object/wonder ($\theta \acute{\epsilon} \alpha \mu \alpha$).[163] This is achieved primarily via the often self-supplied audience to witness and marvel at his every action and achievement (both real and imaginary).

Thus the *Sacred Tales* makes an active intervention in the sophistic culture of the Roman east by shaping an original performative persona—the sickly orating $\theta \epsilon \hat{\iota} o s \ \dot{\alpha} v \acute{\eta} \rho$ ('holy man')[164]—based on religious devotion, divine favour, and its miraculous epiphany in both Aristeides' physical recovery and his oratorical brilliance. That this persona operates both within and without sociocultural norms, in that it capitalizes on religious and athletic paradigms at the same time as embracing restricted engagement in the social obligations of elite provincial society, creates new artistic space that has the potential to speak to the present but, through its commemorative focus, is designed primarily to address posterity. It also makes a strong case for the commemorative importance of writing. In particular, it highlights the text's ability to use the context of the past to reshape present realities for the consumption of posterity via an image carefully curated to be worthy of the canon.

2.5 CONCLUSION

Imperial Greek authors are fascinated by the classical past, but this fascination should not be mistaken for fixation. Instead, the greatness of the literary past signals the possibility of an even greater future and inspires a number of artistic and social strategies aimed at positioning oneself within a hypothetical future canon. Whether it be the adoption of a moveable temporal perspective to create a level playing field; competitive imitation to simultaneously piggyback on and leapfrog over a famous forerunner; or novelty and investment in writing to differentiate oneself from past greats and present aspirants, the construction of creative space which abuts or builds on top of the canon of great literature remains central. Celebrated classical paradigms are thus regularly used as both a context and a springboard for one's own innovations and commemorative posturing. Imperial Greek fascination with the past in this conception is less about political escapism than aspirations for future cultural eminence.

[162] See Downie 2013, 155–81. See also Pearcy 1988, 377–8; Petsalis-Diomidis 2006; 2010, 133, 139–40 with *HL* 5.36.

[163] See Petsalis-Diomidis 2010, 111, for Aristides' body as a landscape of pilgrimage. Cf. Platt 2011, 263–4.

[164] See Fields 2008, 163–6; Petsalis-Diomidis 2010, 135–40; Downie 2013, 31. Note that Empedokles (*c.*492–*c.*432 BC) might have been a classical model for Aristeides.

These techniques that try to negotiate the divide between contemporary acclaim and the praises of posterity reveal that imperial Greek temporality was far more complex than simply an adherence to 'classicism', as well as how important its full exploration is to gain a complete appreciation of the dynamics of elite imperial Greek culture. Via their dual fixation on the poles of past and future, these authors transform literature into a sociocultural forum for self-aggrandizement that serves to advertise their own conceptions of their place in the Roman empire. How they offset the context of the classical canon with contemporary sociocultural reality signals the type of temporal scale they hope to inhabit: one in which Rome is diminished against the Greek cultural continuum or one in which Rome features as an important element in one's identity. The literary moves considered here are also largely applicable to the physical monuments left by Greeks during the same period and it is to physical monuments and literary materiality that I now turn.

THREE

Monuments and Rhetorical Materiality

> It is the stones (λίθοι) that reveal the dignity ($\sigma\epsilon\mu\nu$ό$\tau\eta\tau\alpha$) and greatness (μέ$\gamma\epsilon\theta$ος) of Hellas.
>
> – Dio Chrysostom, *Orations* 31.159.
>
> You've got to put your name on stuff or no one remembers you.
>
> – Donald J. Trump.[1]

This chapter builds on the previous one by spotlighting material culture and its presence in literature more intensely. The well-known competitive and performative nature of imperial Greek society is directed not just at its own time but, as shown by chapter 2, also at audiences and rivals of the future. Contemporary cultural production is thus as much about ensuring the persistence of a prominent public identity beyond one's own lifetime as about the initial creation and promotion of that identity in the present. This preoccupation can be traced in both material culture and literature, but how it is manifested is influenced by two factors: the layered, multi-temporal physicality of monumental cityscapes and memorial landscapes in the Roman empire; and the dense materiality of contemporary rhetorical culture. This chapter establishes and explores these two aspects of imperial Greek culture and its interweaving of text and artefact. It does so by analysing several examples of multivalent monuments, examining the use of text to shape and control monumental meaning, and demonstrating how these two streams of culture are fundamental to the Greek paideutic system. I argue that imperial Greeks use both the monumental and the literary to signal their innovations and relevance while creating and exploiting a powerful cultural framework in which to embed them.

Greek monuments and texts of this era are regularly intermedial, in that they draw consciously on long and rich interweaving discourses of both text and image. This characteristic of imperial Greek aesthetics has been analysed by Michael Squire in relation to the concept of 'iconotexts'.[2] Peter Wagner provides a

---

[1] Quoted in E. Johnson and D. Lippman, 'Trump's "Truly Bizarre" Visit to Mt. Vernon', *POLITICO* 10/04/2019 (https://www.politico.com/story/2019/04/10/donald-trump-mount-vernon-george-washington-1264073).

[2] Squire 2009, 300.

Fashioning the Future in Roman Greece: Memory, Monuments, Texts. Estelle Strazdins, Oxford University Press.
© Estelle Strazdins 2023. DOI: 10.1093/oso/9780192866103.003.0003

definition of 'iconotexts', describing them as both works of art which reveal 'interpenetration of words and images in a concrete sense' and those 'in which one medium is only implied'.[3] Squire uses this concept profitably to examine the mutual, often insinuated, interaction between text and image in the Roman imperial period and how shared literary and visual resources shape aesthetic conception and reception.[4] This characterisation of intermedial texts and objects as mutually interpenetrative is particularly useful when interpreting imperial Greek cultural output. Not only are the texts saturated with commemorative artefacts and landscapes, but physical monuments draw on myth, history, literary tradition and those same memory-laden landscapes to construct a rich culturally significant context. The long Greek literary habit of comparing text to monument and designating text as monumental, a topic examined in chapter 4, also encourages this interweaving of media and aesthetic traditions. My analysis here is interdisciplinary rather than intermedial, but the texts and artefacts themselves regularly demonstrate this latter quality and recognizing it can aid in drawing out implied meanings. My examples, moreover, are taken both from the physical remains of Roman-era Greek monuments in Attica and at Ephesos, and from the rich textual tradition of imperial Greece.

This chapter provides an overview of how these factors impact imperial Greek commemorative aspiration and process, and sets up the contiguous exploration of literary and material expression as the best means of elucidating it. As such, as well as demonstrating the usefulness of this interdisciplinary methodological approach, it also lays groundwork for Part II of the book, which concentrates specifically on the literary and physical deployment of inscribed individual monuments, namely tombs and honorific statues, as vehicles for the construction of personal commemoration and the mediation of its attendant concerns.

Initially, the chapter will focus on monuments and how their physical and metaphoric contextualization reconfigures and redeploys the past to make provocative commemorative claims. The section will concentrate on Herodes Attikos, but the discussion will be supplemented by the Library of Kelsos and the tomb of Dionysios of Miletos in Ephesos in order to show that Herodes' approach to monumentalization is not isolated. The second section explores the impact of contemporary monumental building on imperial Greek commemorative thinking and how text is regularly used to shape and control monumental messages. A particular focus here is texts involving travel and the explication of physical land- and cityscapes, such as Arrian's *Periplous* and Pausanias' *Description of Greece*. The final section explores the material aspects of contemporary rhetorical training and culture by reference to Lucian's *On the Hall* to demonstrate how embedded the interweaving of text and artefact is in imperial Greek aesthetic thought.

---

[3] Wagner 1996, 16; see 15–17 for fuller discussion.   [4] See Squire 2009, 300–428.

3.1 MATERIAL MEMORIES

This section examines a variety of imperial Greek material culture that can be considered intermedial in its interaction with the literary and historical record to create material memories. In doing so, it will demonstrate that the same concerns with acknowledging the classical tradition while reformulating commemorative meaning that was traced in the literature of the Second Sophistic in the previous chapter can be identified in the art and architecture of imperial Greece as well. Initially, I will examine the portrait type of Herodes Attikos to show how he contextualizes it within Hellenic tradition and deploys it to shape his image for posterity in provocative ways that resonate both culturally and politically. The section will then move to analyse a commemorative arch on Herodes' Marathonian estate that layers meaning by engaging with Greek and Roman visual and literary traditions, and with the commemorative landscapes that surround it. I will then briefly show how two funerary monuments from Ephesos—the Library of Kelsos and the burial of Dionysios of Miletos—plug into the same cultural and political currents. Although these monuments might seem disparate, they all engage with visual and verbal traditions to address posterity in idiosyncratic ways. The range of media—portrait bust, arch, library-heroon, and sarcophagus—demonstrates how pervasive this practice was in the Roman east, and the deep concern imperial Greeks had with shaping their commemorative identities authoritatively in stone.

Roman art, an umbrella beneath which imperial Greek art has by default sheltered, was long approached in modern scholarship from a similar perspective to imperial Greek literature. This is best seen with Roman statuary, particularly Roman ideal sculpture, which was regularly cast as an exercise in imitating the classical Greek achievement. Indeed, artistic value for modern scholars lay in rediscovering the form of the Greek original assumed to lie behind the Roman copy. More recent investigation, in contrast, has focused on assigning Roman sculpture a value that lies in original expression as well as eclectic reconfiguration and reapplication of Greek, but also Egyptian, Italian, or other local/indigenous models.[5] This approach homes in on the function of art in social space and the desires of the patron who commissioned it.[6] Physical context is thus all important and the element that completes a sculpture's, painting's, or even building's identity.[7] Imperial Greeks were highly tuned to the significance of context and

---

[5] For how to approach Roman copies, see Vermeule 1977, 1–19; Perry 2002; 2005, 1–17; Gazda 2002, 1–15; Stewart 2003, 231–6; Hallett 2005; Wyler 2006; Varner 2006; Small 2008; Anguissola 2014; Di Napoli 2016. On the eclecticism and syncretism of Roman art, and what may be considered 'classical' see Elsner 2006; cf. Thomas 2007, 6–11, on architecture.

[6] Stewart 2003, 234–6; Hallett 2005, 433–5; Perry 2005, 50–77; Mazurek 2018.

[7] See Perry 2005, 56.

their material endeavours regularly draw on commemorative spaces and landscapes.

The common rhetorical education of elites and their shared repository of visual knowledge, a topic discussed in the section on 'Rhetorical Materiality', played a crucial role in this sensitivity to spatial meaning. This common education has been pinpointed as also underlying the Roman-period desire for statuary that drew on Greek models. Workshops were responding to demand prompted by literary anecdotes or *ekphraseis* of Greek art, and φαντασία ('inner visualisation') played an important role in representing gods and heroes in an affective way.[8] Both imperial Greek literature and material art, then, draw on classical *exempla* to create their own innovative expressions that, because of these *exempla*, are easily assimilated within their cultural context.[9] This aspect of contemporary aesthetics is another indication of its intermediality, and a strong motivating factor in the need to consider both text and artefact in order to understand most clearly the commemorative aspirations of the imperial Greek elite.

Few *pepaideumenoi* who have left a literary trace have also bequeathed monumentalizing architecture; indeed, Herodes Attikos and, to a far lesser extent and in another's name, Arrian are the clearest examples. This is largely due to the rich inscriptional and literary record surrounding Herodes, especially in Attica, so that his contributions have been easy to identify in the archaeological record. When it comes to other sophists, we have the odd confirmed burial, such as the grave of Dionysios of Miletos in Ephesos or T. Flavius Damianos outside Ephesos on the road to Magnesia.[10] By comparison to other contemporary material remains, these monuments tell us that these individuals adhere comfortably to the broad range of funerary customs of the day. Damianos' tomb, moreover, shows every indication of demonstrating the same kind of dynastic concerns identified in a number of Herodes' monuments discussed in the chapters which follow.[11] By far the most prevalent evidential medium is that of statue dedications on extant marble bases. Once again, however, the only secure identification of an actual portrait pertains to Herodes Attikos, and it is with this image that I begin my discussion. Tentative portrait identifications of other imperial Greek authors will be analysed in chapter 5.[12]

---

[8] Stewart 2003, 235; see Perry 2005, 150–71, on Philostratos' third-century *In Honour of Apollonios of Tyana*, in which the eponymous sage explains that viewers of an image created by an artist through φαντασία must employ the same process and use their own mental image in order to evaluate the artist's work accurately (*VA* 2.22.5).

[9] The messages of Roman art are not fixed or uniform, as argued by Hölscher 2004, but must be interpreted via local and individual contextualization. See Elsner 2006, 274–5; Squire 2009, 86–7.

[10] Rife 2009, 114–19; Quatember and Scheilbelreiter-Gail 2017.

[11] See Quatember and Scheilbelreiter-Gail 2017.   [12] See Section 5.1.

Despite the paucity of (confidently assigned) representations of other imperial Greek sophists and authors, there are ten extant versions of Herodes' single portrait type, as well as several headless statues.[13] This makes Herodes the most represented male figure outside the imperial family except for his foster-son Polydeukion, who features in chapters 4 to 6 below.[14] Figure 3.1 (cf. Figure 3.5) shows a bust of Herodes' portrait type now on display in the National Archaeological Museum, Athens.[15] It was discovered, along with one of Polydeukion (see Figure 5.17) and a black marble arm assumed to belong to a statue of his Ethiopian foster-son Memnon (see Figure 4.6), during construction work in 1961 on a private house in the Athenian suburb of Kephisia and has thus been associated with his villa there. Most of Herodes' portraits have been found in areas where he had private holdings, so he probably set them up himself rather than their being a reflection of a communal or individual honouring of the man.[16] Other examples come from sanctuaries or locations of importance to Herodes, including the sanctuary of Nemesis at Rhamnous, the Egyptianizing complex at Brexiza (part of his Marathon estate),[17] and close by the tomb of the Athenians at Marathon.[18] Like the bust from Kephisia, these other portraits have regularly been discovered with those of individuals with whom Herodes wanted to demonstrate intimacy. At the Marathon *soros*, his bust was found with one of Faustina the Younger, at Brexiza with his imperial pupils Marcus Aurelius and Lucius Verus, and the same two companions were found with him again at Rhamnous. Thus these examples must also have been raised on Herodes' directive to show his closeness to the imperial family.

That Herodes has a portrait type which is codified and copied is in itself significant. It testifies to his desire to shape his image for both his contemporaries and posterity in a consistent and recognizable way. Additionally, the luxury of a

---

[13] See Goette 2019, 226; Smith 1998, 78–9; Tobin 1997, 71–6; Fittschen 2021, no. 22, 42–6, taf. 20–3. The portraits have been studied by Richter 1965c, 286, figs 2043–44, 2047–49; Datsoulis-Stavridis 1978; Bol 1998; Goette 2019; Fittschen 2021, no. 22. See also, Walker 1989 on a pentelic head of Herodes from Winchester City Museum (now in the British Museum), whose provenance appears to be Alexandria. Goette (2019, 228) plausibly suggests Alexandria Troas instead. Note that Voutiras 2008 argues that a portrait head in the Royal Ontario Museum of Toronto is a second portrait type of Herodes Attikos. There is certainly a resemblance between this portrait and Herodes', but also enough difference to suggest that the Toronto head was riffing on Herodes' portrait (or vice versa) in a similar way to second-century portraits of youths drawing on the image of Antinoos (see Section 5.4).

[14] Smith 1998, 78.

[15] Inv. no. 4810. See Vanderpool 1961, 299–300, pl. 97.1; Richter 1965c, 286, fig. 2047; Datsoulis-Stavridis 1978, 214–18, figs 1–4; Datsoulis-Stavridis 1985, 50–1, pl. 50–3; Romiopoulou 1997, no. 92; Kaltsas 2002, 346, fig. 734.

[16] Tobin 1997, 75.   [17] Papaioannou 2018, 340–1, 343–5.

[18] Note, however, the portrait from Winchester (Walker 1989). If this portrait did come from Alexandria and not Alexandria Troas, as posited by Goette (2019, 228), either Herodes had an estate there, which would fit his efforts to mark important cultural landscapes, or the portrait had been brought there through the antiquities' trade.

FIGURE 3.1 Marble portrait bust of Herodes Attikos found in Kephisia with one of Polydeukion (see Fig. 4.17). National Archaeological Museum, Athens (NM 4810). Height: 0.64 m.

specific, repeated portrait suggests power, wealth, influence, and fame. It is the kind of recognition great classical cultural figures and Roman emperors receive, the latter of whom use their official portraiture to spread a homogenous presence throughout the empire. Multiple representations of wealthy benefactors in specific civic centres had a similar effect in microcosm.[19] Herodes' example, however,

---

[19] See, e.g., Dillon's 1996 discussion of Vedius Antonius in Ephesos, and Quatember and Scheilbelreiter-Gail 2017 on the extensive material evidence for this family in Ephesos. Also now see Kalinowski 2021.

reveals that the efforts of such individuals need not be restricted to a single city, but rather their presence could mark shrines, sanctuaries, civic centres, and private lands across the empire as well.[20] Evidence for statues of Philostratos' most prominent sophist exists in Athens and Eleusis, in the regions around Marathon, on his private estates at Kephisia and in the Peloponnese, in Corinth, Olympia, Delphi, and at Ephesos.[21] His material presence extends much farther, even to Rome, but here I am concerned specifically with his portrait.

As demonstrated by R. R. R. Smith, Herodes' image draws on features associated with the posthumous bronze statue of Demosthenes by Polyeuktos (*c.* 280 BC) from the Athenian agora that survives in various Roman-era marble copies (Figure 3.2). It exhibits a similarly modest, downturned posture of the head and

FIGURE 3.2 Marble portrait statue of Demosthenes; copy of the bronze statue by Polyeuktos in the Athenian Agora. Found in Campania and acquired in 1929 by the Ny Carlsberg Glyptotek, Copenhagen (Inv. 2782). Height without plinth: 1.92 m.

[20] Cf. Quatember and Scheilbelreiter-Gail 2017, 229, on the Vedii Antonini in Rome, Tralleis, and Sardis. See Strazdins 2022a on Herodes in the province of Achaia.
[21] See Tobin 1997, 71–4, 295–331; Bol 1998, 118–26.

FIGURE 3.3 Marble portrait statue of Aischines (partially restored), found at Herculaneum. National Museum, Naples (Inv. 6018). Height: 2.10 m.

serious, thoughtful furrowing of the brow.[22] His short, unstyled hair recalls Demosthenes as well, but also Aischines (Figure 3.3),[23] and the full beard and overhanging, thick moustache channel Lysias (Figure 3.4) and Aischines again.[24] His portrait thus draws on the material representations of these classical period orators. His eyes are deep set and heavy lidded; he wears a himation (with tunic) wrapped closely around him and bunched at the left shoulder in a modest, constraining manner. The lack of styling of the hair in comparison to contemporary imperial portraits which show heavy use of the drill is particularly striking. All this contributes, as Smith argues, less to a paradigmatic image of a Greek intellectual (although it certainly riffs on this imagery as well) and rather more to a classical *polis* orator-politician—a leader of the *dêmos*.[25] As such, despite having numerous other modes to choose from—benefactor, consul, teacher—he

---

[22] Smith 1998, 78. For Demosthenes' portrait, see Richter 1965b, 215–23, figs 1397–510; Ma 2006, 326–9.
[23] Richter 1965b, 212–15, figs 1369–90; Smith 1998, 78–9.
[24] For Lysias, see Richter 1965b 207–8, figs 1340–5; Smith 1998, 78–9.
[25] Smith 1998, 79.

FIGURE 3.4 Marble portrait head of Lysias, mounted on a modern herm that bears the inscription 'Lysias'. Stanza dei Filosofi, Capitoline Museum (Inv. no. 601; Mus. no. 73), Rome. Height of head: 0.29 m.

constructs a self-representation that is Hellenic, local, and traditional and, by drawing on famous models, familiar and thus intelligible in an expected way.[26]

Portraits of prominent men from the Greek east in fact show a large variety of combinations of Hellenic and Roman, intellectual and political characteristics.[27] They regularly 'cite' aspects of famous portraits of classical orators or statesmen, Hellenistic philosophers, or Roman emperors:[28] an image like Herodes', therefore, is a product of connoisseurship that speaks to connoisseurs.[29] When a Greek *pepaideumenos* viewed it, he would simultaneously see Herodes, Demosthenes, Aischines, Lysias, philosopher, orator, politician, and would make a judgement about the character that Herodes was trying to project based on his own learned opinion, experience of classical art, and knowledge of Greek literature and history.[30] Portraits like Herodes' collapse time and space for their audience in

---

[26] Cf. Ma 2006, 332. See also Smith 1998, 79: this was an unusual choice that became popular in the second century.
[27] Smith 1998, 79–84; Borg 2004.
[28] On the notion of citation/quotation in statuary, see Varner 2006.
[29] On connoisseurship in the viewing of Greek art, see Ma 2006.
[30] See the discussion of Ma 2006, esp. 329, for ways of viewing copies of earlier honorific statues, which must be a similar process to viewing an image that is influenced by earlier honorific statues.

a similar way to texts like Arrian's *Periplous*. Like Aristeides conversing with the greats in his dreams, moreover, Herodes channels them through his image. His ability to choose this form of representation was made more acceptable by the change in the imperial portraiture of the Antonines from the time of Hadrian onwards.[31] Prior to Hadrian's adoption of a glamorous, bearded and styled metropolitan portrait,[32] very few bearded portraits were produced in the eastern empire. This circumstance must reflect the continuing influence of Alexander's beardless image and the eastern elites' political conformity in following Roman imperial styles that drew on the Makedonian's representation, as well as the deeply conservative and conventional nature of honorific statues.

As noted above, the display of Herodes' portraits tended to be contextualized in commemorative space and with other portraits of prominent individuals. On two occasions at Rhamnous and Brexiza, his portrait (Figure 3.5) was combined with those of the glamorous, cosmopolitan, Roman emperors Marcus Aurelius (Figure 3.6) and Lucius Verus (Figure 3.7).[33] How might this triad have been received? Would Herodes' portrait have taken on a more intellectual cast as his role of imperial tutor was highlighted? Given that the emperors appear cuirassed as a sign of their imperium, one intended message of the group is certainly a play on the trope of the Greek philosopher who speaks truth to power, usually in the form of a foreign king. In its public setting, this would suggest to the average viewer that Herodes is a mediator and representative of imperial power in Attica, but also in the role of tutor or philosophical adviser that he has the potential to direct and shape the application of that power as well. In an Athenian context, the paradigm in this case is Solon and Herodotos' story of his encounter with Kroisos, the king of Lydia (1.29–33). One might also think of Sokrates, however, or even Aristotle.[34] Herodes' arrangement of these busts thus draws on a line of distinguished Athenian

---

[31] See Smith 1998, 91; Borg 2004.   [32] See Borg 2004 on the glamorous metropolitan style.

[33] Note that the triads from Brexiza and Rhamnous are copies, but those from Rhamnous are extremely fragmentary. See Petrakos 1999a, 291–3 with figs 204 and 205. Mazurek (2018, 620–1) connects a Polydeukion bust from Brexiza with the Brexiza triad, making it a quartet. Evidence for a Polydeukion bust at Rhamnous does not exist. Herodes' father, however, had raised a statue of Hadrian and one of Antinoos previously. See Petrakos 1999b, 126, no. 158; Karanastasi 2019.

[34] See Galli 2002, 165. He argues that the slight left twist to Herodes' portrait head (i.e. as one faces it— Herodes actually turns to his right) is an allusion to expressions of the Type B portrait of Sokrates. See Richter 1965a, s.v. Sokrates Type B, figs 503, 513, 524–6, 560–2, 563a, 569. He asserts the existence of this allusion based on the reported discovery of a bust of Sokrates along with those of Marcus, Lucius, and Herodes at Brexiza. This is what Dodwell (1819, 161) reports as described in Fauvel's notebooks according to a certain L. Dubois, but Petrakos (1995, 68–9, 114–18), using Fauvel's notebooks, does not mention the Sokrates bust, and Tobin (1997, 253) is adamant that it was found elsewhere in Marathon, although she does not say where. The Sokrates bust was already lost in 1934 (Neugebauer 1934, 95). The discovery of Sokrates with this group would enhance my argument, but the evidence for it is too sketchy to be reliable. On Sokrates' portraits, see Lapatin 2006. Note that Galli also stresses that Herodes' portrait strongly shapes him as a teacher.

FIGURE 3.5 Marble portrait bust of Herodes Attikos found at the Sanctuary of the Egyptian Gods at Brexiza, now in the Louvre (Inv. NIII 2536; Ma 1164). A fragmentary bust of Herodes from Rhamnous closely follows the same type. Height: 0.62 m.

FIGURE 3.6 Marble portrait bust of Marcus Aurelius, found at the Sanctuary of the Egyptian Gods at Brexiza, now in the Louvre (Inv. NIII 2535; Ma 1161). A fragmentary bust from Rhamnous follows this type closely. Height: 0.62 m.

FIGURE 3.7 Marble portrait bust of Lucius Verus, found at the Sanctuary of the Egyptian Gods at Brexiza, now in the Ashmolean Museum (AN1947.277). A fragmentary bust from Rhamnous follows this type closely. Height including base: 0.85 m.

wise men and advisers as well as the literary traditions associated with them. He expects his audience to then apply these models to his own aspirations and the present political reality. This reveals that the casting of his image is as much a political as cultural choice.

The setting of the triad in the Sanctuary of Rhamnousian Nemesis, however, undermines this picture of imperial co-operation. By this time, the goddess was inseparable from the Battle of Marathon, so that a mistaken tradition existed that the sanctuary was founded to honour the goddess for her role in the victory.[35] Pausanias, for example, tells us that the cult statue of Nemesis at Rhamnous was carved from Parian marble brought by the Persians to Greece in preparation for a victory monument, but that Nemesis fell on them at the Battle of Marathon for their *hubris* (Paus. 1.33.2–3). The cult statue thus replaced the Persians' aborted victory monument and served as both sacred object and monument to the Athenian victory.

Herodes' portrait, then, must have created tension and discomfort for any viewer able to detect the politician-orators it cites and their legacy in connection

---

[35] Pottery and votives indicate worship of the goddess at the site dates to at least the early sixth century BC (Petrakos 1999a, 190–7).

to Athenian freedom: Demosthenes' ultimate failure to inspire a successful resistance to Philip II of Makedon; Aischines' apparent betrayal and capitulation to the foreign power.[36] Where would Herodes be deemed to fall on such a scale in this setting that was so closely associated with resistance to foreign invaders?[37] The military dress of the emperors only heightens the discord, especially if the viewer were privy to knowledge of Herodes' trial before Marcus for tyranny over the Athenians in AD 174.[38] The images of the emperors and the historical and cultural memory attached to the sanctuary of Nemesis are here made to serve Herodes' equivocal self-fashioning: his portrait becomes the fulcrum of interpretation, depending on how the viewer prioritizes its models and the traditions associated with its setting. Importantly, Herodes expects the viewer not only to be able to read the influences behind his own representation, but also to know the legends and literary associations of Nemesis and Rhamnous. At Brexiza, so close to the *soros* itself, the messages would be similar if slightly less immediate. Herodes' choice of where to display and how to contextualize his commemorative portrait in this case raises questions about his relationship to both Athens and Rome, and, as we will see in chapters 5 and, more fully, 6, this issue is pivotal to his commemorative efforts and reception. The discordance of his image in the empire indicates that contemporary society is unlikely to be his primary target audience.

Herodes' commemorative consciousness was highly developed and his attempts to embed himself into the landscape of the empire remain impressive. Importantly, these efforts gravitated to places that were meaningful to Greek culture and history, including Athens (the cultural capital), Corinth (the provincial capital), Isthmia, Delphi, Olympia (all panhellenic sanctuaries), Thermopylai (the site of Spartan and Thespian heroics), and Alexandria Troas (a city closely associated with the site of Troy).[39] His large-scale building in public space was complemented by extensive smaller-scale, experimental creations on his private lands. Unlike his portrait, his architectural efforts tend to blend Greek and Roman aspects in the manner typical of the period, but his deployment and contextualization of material culture are idiosyncratic and draw on literary and historical traditions.

---

[36] On how someone might view the allusion to the portrait of Demosthenes, see Ma 2006, 326–9.

[37] Although the sanctuary had been rededicated to Augustus' wife, Livia, in AD 45/6, the Greek sources continue to refer only to Nemesis (see Petrakos 1999a, 288–91; 1999b, 123–4, no. 156). Herodes' conformity to this custom (see *SEG* 49.209, Section 6.5) is particularly striking given his role as priest of the imperial cult in Athens, and his father's earlier dedication of a statue of Hadrian and one of Antinoos at Rhamnous (see Petrakos 1999b, 126, no. 158; Karanastasi 2019). On these issues and Herodes' triad of busts, see further Strazdins 2022a and In press. On the rededication to Livia in the context of Claudius' early reign and imperial cult, see Stafford 2013.

[38] This incident is discussed in detail in Sections 6.2 and 6.4.

[39] If the British Museum portrait head did indeed come from Alexandria—the burial place of Alexander the Great—it conforms to the same pattern.

One such example is the commemorative arch raised on his Marathonian estate (Figures 3.8 and 3.9). This unusual construction uses an established form to create a novel personal statement of individual and familial identity, as Maud Gleason perceptively argues in her examination of biculturality in Herodes' commemorations for his Roman patrician wife Regilla.[40] The arch stood at an artificial boundary, serving as the gateway into an enclosure encircled by substantial stone walls with a circumference of 3,300m that occupied the pass leading from the Avlona valley to Oinoe and further on to Marathon (Figure 3.10).[41] What the enclosure contained is impossible to ascertain from the current state of the remains, but remnants of hypocaust tiles point to a villa.[42] This arch drew on the Roman practice of building commemorative and triumphal arches; in particular,

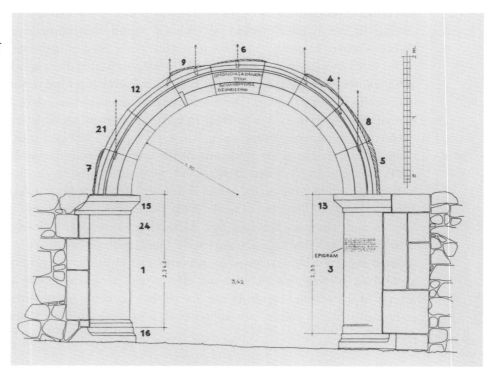

FIGURE 3.8 Elevation plan of Herodes' Gate of Eternal Concord.

[40] Gleason 2010, 135–42. See also Geagan 1964; Mallwitz 1964; Ameling 1983b, 117–20; Tobin 1997, 242–9; Galli 2002, 134–8.

[41] McCredie 1966, 35–7; Vanderpool 1970, 43. See also Galli 2002, 134–8, 178–203; Papaioannou 2018, 340–3.

[42] See Vanderpool 1970, 44; Tobin 1997, 242–9. McCredie (1966, 36–7) notes that despite the wall being impressive in dimensions, its purpose would not have been military due to its erratic line and lack of strategic positioning. Petrakos (2002, 89) suggests the original family villa.

MONUMENTS AND RHETORICAL MATERIALITY 91

FIGURE 3.9 Keystone from the Gate of Eternal Concord with life-size statues of Regilla (L) and Herodes (R) as they are currently displayed in the Archaeological Museum of Marathon (Inv. Λ159; Inv. Λ158). The inscription on the keystone facing into the room relates to Regilla's 'space'.

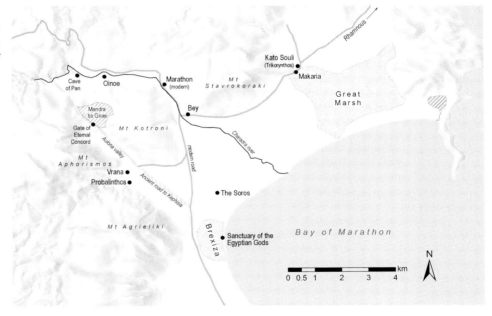

FIGURE 3.10 Map of Marathon showing Brexiza and the *Mandra tis Grias*.

the paired inscriptions on the keystones on either side of the arch connected it to Hadrian's arch in Athens and detailed the nature of the delineation it straddled. On the external face, an inscription announced (*IG* II² 5189a; Figure 3.11):

FIGURE 3.11
Keystone showing the inscription relating to Regilla's 'space', Archaeological Museum of Marathon (*IG* II² 5189a).

ὁμονοίας ἀθανάτου
   πύλη
Ῥηγίλλης ὁ χῶρος
εἰς ὃν εἰσέρχει

Eternal Concord's
   Gate;
Regilla's is the space
which you are entering.

On the internal face, it reads (*IG* II² 5189; Figure 3.12):

ὁμονοίας ἀθανάτου
   πύλη
Ἡρώδου ὁ χῶρος
εἰς [ὃν εἰσέ]ρχε[ι]

Eternal Concord's
   Gate;
Herodes' is the space
which you are entering.

On the honorific arch raised to Hadrian in Athens (*c.* AD 131/2; Figure 3.13) that separated the classical city centre from the region of the Olympieion and the Ilisos

FIGURE 3.12 Keystone showing the inscription relating to Herodes' 'space', before it was moved to the Archaeological Museum of Marathon. The inscription is now very faint and barely legible (*IG* II² 5189).

river, the respective inscriptions are: 'This is the Athens of Theseus, the former city' (αἵδ' εἴσ' Ἀθῆναι Θησέως ἡ πρὶν πόλις) and 'This is the city of Hadrian and not the city of Theseus' (αἵδ' εἴσ' Ἀδριανοῦ καὶ οὐχὶ Θησέως πόλις). The mention of Theseus is designed to recall the pillar supposedly raised by that hero at the Isthmus of Corinth that bore mirrored inscriptions dividing the Peloponnese from Ionia.[43] Gleason equivocates on whether Herodes is imitating Hadrian imitating Theseus or trying to bypass the Hadrianic middleman, seeing this distinction as dependant on which of Herodes' cultural leanings we assume he was trying to stress.[44] Placed in the context of his other monuments, however, discussed in detail in the chapters to follow, Herodes' arch is clearly referencing (and competing with) both rulers. It is doing so, moreover, via both the literary and architectural record.[45] Despite this, Herodes' arch marks a very different, far more personal division than those of either Hadrian or Theseus.

---

[43] Herodes' arch inscription: *SEG* 23.131. Hadrian's arch inscription: *IG* II² 5185. Theseus' pillar: Strabo 3.5.5; 9.1.6–7; Plut. *Thes.* 25.4. See Tobin 1997, 243–4; Gleason 2010, 135–8, on the intertextual nature of the inscriptions. See also Ameling 1983b, 118–20 nos 97 and 98.

[44] Gleason 2010, 136–7.

[45] Note also that two arches that copy the architectural form of Hadrian's arch were set up in Eleusis in honour of Demeter and Kore, and Antoninus Pius. So, the arch form in Attica was strongly associated with the emperors.

FIGURE 3.13 Arch of Hadrian, *c.* AD 131/2, Athens. Built to honour the emperor on his visit to Athens when he oversaw the inauguration of the completed Temple of Olympian Zeus. As with Herodes' arch, there are paired inscriptions, one on either side.

Herodes' arch commemorates his marriage (*c.* AD 141) via the phrase ὁμόνοια ἀθάνατος (literally, 'eternal unanimity/oneness of mind') and for this reason the area designated as Regilla's was probably a wedding present.[46] While Theseus'

---

[46] Tobin 1997, 246; Ameling 1983b, 118–19. Note that Petrakos (2002, 89) suggests the area may have enclosed the original family estate, which Herodes modified and gifted to Regilla. Cf. Papaioannou 2018, 342.

pillar marks a simple territorial division and Hadrian's arch creates a territorial and temporal division between his Roman Athens and Theseus' Greek city,[47] Herodes' arch, in contrast, at the same time as memorializing his marriage, delineates also a separation of territory, gender, social roles (husband/wife), and cultural affiliation (Greek/Roman). The inscription denoting eternal unanimity, however, stresses rather unification over division: the marriage of Herodes and Regilla fuses these discrete elements into a single multifaceted identity.[48] Moreover, the Greek ὁμόνοια ἀθάνατος translates the Latin *concordia aeterna*, which was an imperial slogan used to promote the marriage of Antoninus Pius and Faustina, especially on coins.[49] Thus this arch places Herodes in a succession of heroic and imperial figures as well as in a position of rivalry with them, and it draws on literary and material traditions to do so. Via the intertextual references to Hadrian's arch, moreover, Regilla, whose family traced its line to Aeneas, metonymically assumes the role of Hadrian and Herodes that of Theseus, and the marriage therefore fuses Roman emperor and Athenian king into an eternal union made flesh in this culturally diverse family.

All this becomes more complex when Regilla dies. At some point after this event, Herodes adds another inscription carved in small letters (1.3–1.5 cm high) on the eastern pillar at eye level, so that it must be read up close.[50] The new poetic inscription celebrates Herodes' former happiness and laments his current sorrow (Figure 3.14):[51]

> Ἆ μάκαρ ὅστις ἔδειμε νέην πόλιν, οὔν[ο]μα δ'αὐτὴν
> Ῥηγίλλης καλέων, ζώει ἀγαλλόμενος.
> Ζώω δ'ἀχ[ν]ύμενος τό μοι οἰκία ταῦτα τέτυκται
> νόσφ[ι] φίλης ἀλόχου καὶ δόμος ἡμιτελής.
> ὡς ἄρα τοι θνητοῖσι θεοὶ βιοτὴν κεράσαντ[ες],
> χά[ρ]ματα τ' ἠδ' ἀνίας γείτονας ἀμφὶς ἔχο[υν].

> Ah, blessed is he who has built a new city, calling it
>   by Regilla's name; he lives in exultation.
> But *I* live in grief because this dwelling of mine has been built
>   without my beloved wife, and my home is half complete.
> For the gods, in truth, having blended life for mortals,
>   pour out joys and griefs as neighbours side by side.

---

[47] On the complex phrasing of Hadrian's inscriptions and just what the two cities constitute, see Adams 1989, 10–17.

[48] Gleason (2010, 138), in contrast, sees it as marking 'shifting perspectives on identity and difference'.

[49] Cf. Geagan 1964, 149–56, especially 152 n. 11; Tobin 1997, 243–4; Gleason 2010, 138. See also Ameling 1983b, 118–19, for the encomiastic commonplace of ὁμόνοια.

[50] Geagan 1964; Tobin 1997, 247; Skenteri 2005, 67; Gleason 2010, 140.

[51] *SEG* 23.121. Text from Geagan 1964, 151. See also Ameling 1983b, 117–18, no. 99; Tobin 1997, 247–8; Skenteri 2005, 67–72; Gleason 2010, 140.

FIGURE 3.14 Secondary poetic inscription on the Gate of Eternal Concord commemorating the death of Regilla, Archaeological Museum of Marathon (*SEG* 23.121; Geagan 1964). It is inscribed just below eye level (1.4 m from the base) on the eastern pillar to one's right as one walks through the arch into 'Regilla's space' in small lettering (height: 0.013–0.015 m).

The poem moves from a joyous past to a dismal present to a timeless, philosophical contemplation of the human condition. Although the third-person perspective of the first couplet has generally been interpreted as coming from a passer-by impressed by Regilla's space and the happiness of the harmonious marriage the gate signifies,[52] Gleason has convincingly argued that it, too, is best placed in Herodes' mouth. It thus vividly highlights the gulf between Herodes prior to Regilla's passing and the present Herodes of the poem's second couplet, who mourns his loss with all the immediacy and intimacy of the first person.[53] The poem is full of Homeric allusions and the imagery of building, which have been well discussed by Gleason and Daniel Geagan.[54] One of these comes through the figure of Protesilaos and the words δόμος ἡμιτελής ('house half-complete', *Il.* 2.701), which describe the state of the home the warrior leaves to his grieving wife at the moment of his death. In Herodes' epigram, the gender roles are reversed, so that he fulfils the part of Protesilaos' wife, Laodameia, and the arch now comes to represent the division between life and death, and the ruin of the marriage it formerly upheld.[55]

---

[52] Geagan 1964, 152; Tobin 1997, 248; Galli 2002, 135; Skenteri 2005, 70.

[53] Gleason 2010, 141. Note that Herodes' authorship (or, at least, commissioning) of this poem is confirmed by a corresponding elegiac poem of six verses that describes Herodes' sorrow over the death of a beloved son found built into a tomb in Kephisia (*SEG* 26.290). See Ameling 1983b, 143, no. 140; Tobin 1997, 225–6.

[54] Geagan 1964, 149–56; Gleason 2010, 140–2; also Galli 2002, 134–8.

[55] Cf. Gleason 2010, 142.

Through this inscription, Herodes transforms the commemorative function of the arch from one of celebration to one of mourning and it comes to stand in for a funeral monument to Regilla.[56] The effect on the unaware viewer would be sudden and shocking, especially since the design of the arch and its inscriptions draw the visitor in while initially holding back the news of Regilla's passing. As one approached the enclosure, one would see the arch with the inscription of eternal concord and, nearby, seated statues of Regilla and Herodes in a *naiskos* that were probably added at the same time as the epigram (Figure 3.9).[57] As one walked through the arch, however, the eye would be drawn to the secondary inscription unmasking the fallacy of the arch's joyous first impression. The eye-level positioning and small-scale writing that approximates personal graffiti more so than monumental inscription (Figures 3.8 and 3.14) encourages the viewer to empathize with Herodes emotionally by forcing the viewer to assume the position of the author/inscriber somatically. This too would alter the meaning of the nearby *naiskos* and statues from portraits of a happy couple to participants in a scene typical of classical funerary art.[58] Finally, on the internal face of the gate, one would discover the identity of the bereaved husband, whose seated presence beside his wife in the *naiskos* now signals the living death of his all-encompassing grief. This effect is enhanced by the liminality of the arch form that highlights the transition between life and death, joy and sorrow. In this way, the visual and verbal narrative of the doubly inscribed arch forces the viewer to engage with Herodes' desolation and empathize with the suddenness of its advent, which the statue suggests turned the man himself to stone. In this respect, the secondary funerary inscription and the statues work together to draw on literary and mythological tradition to cast Herodes as a new Laodameia. Separated by death, Herodes creates a simulacrum of his spouse, but ultimately discovers the only way to reunite with her is to join her in death, as symbolized by his own statue.[59] Laodameia becomes a cultural touchstone for Herodes' pain and another means of encouraging empathy in the viewer. Herodes' arch thus engages with the myth of Protesilaos and Laodameia both textually and visually. The monument,

[56] Note that Gleason 2010 considers the epigram to transform the arch into a commemorative structure, but it was of course already commemorative, and the transformation is specifically funerary.

[57] See Mallwitz 1964, 160–2; Tobin 1997, 245–6. Note that the arch is regularly reconstructed with the statues sitting either side of the gate, as in the Marathon museum at Vrana (Figure 3.9), but Mallwitz argues convincingly in favour of a *naiskos* containing the statues off to the side of the gate based on archaeological evidence and the descriptions of early European travellers to Greece, such as Chandler 1776, 166 (chapter 36).

[58] Cf. Galli 2002, 137, on the seated Regilla possibly being intended as a funerary statue.

[59] On the various versions of Laodameia's story, see Bettini 1999, 9–28, especially with nn. 15–18. See further with respect to this arch, Strazdins forthcoming.

moreover, concurrently comments on the impossibility of eternity for mortals and promotes commemoration as a substandard but necessary replacement.

This memorial arch that sits on private land is a strange, novel structure to begin with—as Gleason notes, 'even Roman emperors did not put up honorific arches to themselves'.[60] Its later transformation, however, makes it still more unique. The intertextual, intercultural monument overlays a Thesean, Hadrianic Herodes with a womanly,[61] grieving, exanimate replacement, the latter of whom the viewer is directly enticed to identify with. The monument is thus as much about Herodes' heroic emotional experience as about Regilla's death. The monument demands that its viewers feel like Herodes and redefines the landscape of the estate as one saturated by his grief. If the viewers comply, they acquiesce to Herodes' personal reformulation of not only the immediate vicinity, but also the broader cultural, historic, and political sphere of influence the arch stakes out.

Its private nature enabled Herodes to experiment in such grand imperial terms initially and the stately form encouraged its re-designation as a unique funerary monument that stood within an already powerful memorial landscape spotted by famous tombs. In such a schema, Herodes' dead wife and his own heroic grief become interwoven into a commemorative narrative punctuated by such luminaries as the fallen Athenians and Plataians of Marathon, who, following the directive of the inner keystone's inscription, find themselves interred not in that famous plain but rather in 'Herodes' space' (Ἡρώδου ὁ χῶρος).[62] The extent of this space remains pregnantly undefined beyond being external to that of Regilla. Does it encompass Marathon? Attica? Greece? The οἰκουμένη ('inhabited world')? The inscription surely prompts the viewer to contemplate this issue and come to their own conclusion.

This spatial redefinition and its location on a private estate, albeit one that spread over much of the deme of Marathon, thus makes the question of audience important. Who would have seen the transformed arch? Herodes' family, household, and the extensive workforce required to run and farm the estate?[63] Important visitors with ties to Herodes from across the empire? The local populations of the tetrapolis? Travellers from the sea to Oinoe via the Avlona valley? Travellers to

---

[60] Gleason 2010, 135. See Galli 2002, 134–8, for Herodes as presenting himself as a city founder in the private domain. Galli also compares the arch to the Triopion in Rome, which is associated with Regilla's death too.

[61] See Gleason 2010, 142, for the 'poetic reversal of gender identification'.

[62] Cf. Steinhauer 2009, 278, on the Gate inscription suggesting Herodes owned large portions of Marathon. See Petrakos 2002 (cf. Papaioannou 2018, 340, 342) for an inscription (c. AD 138–43; SEG 53.220) composed by Herodes that claims his estate, which he names 'Attikos' after his father, stretches to east and west of Mt Kotroni, south over the plains of Avlona and vast tracts of Marathon. See also Bowie 2013, 251–3.

[63] For an overview of the commercial and private agricultural activities of Herodes' estate at Marathon, see Papaioannou 2018, 340–5, with bibliography.

or from Kephisia via the ancient road that skirted 'Regilla's space'?[64] All of these are probable targets. One important group, who was known to frequent Herodes' Marathon estate, was the Klepsydrion—the exclusive dining club of Herodes' ten favourite students (*VS* 2.10.585–6), sourced from around the empire and referred to expansively by Alexander the Clay Plato as 'the Greeks' (οἱ Ἕλληνες, *VS* 2.5.571) when he requests their recall to Athens to hear him speak.[65] Herodes here has the opportunity to indoctrinate the next generation of guardians of Hellenic culture with the centrality and primacy of his heroic, Homeric and Thesean identity to the landscape of Marathon, an identity that can couple with Rome without compromising its Hellenic continuity or territorial control.

The funereal metamorphosis of the arch implies, in addition, that Herodes also conceived of it addressing audiences beyond his lifetime. This is particularly suggested by Herodes' name appearing only on the inside face of the keystone—to understand Herodes' identity built into this arch, one could not simply pass by, one had to enter the walled enclosure and engage with it more intimately.[66] Such a reading of the arch requires an especially attentive spectator, but the combination of text and monument works to guide any observer to see the arch through Herodes' eyes. Another major audience, then, would be those who frequented or owned the land in the future and who would have the leisure to explore its semantic range.

At the same time, that the act of adding a small, subsidiary inscription changed the monument's possible interpretation so significantly highlights the dangers of relying on monumental forms to address posterity as well as Herodes' keen grasp of this issue. Note that the epigram's reference to city-founding (ἔδειμε νέην πόλιν) can be read either as an ironic, self-deprecating nod to the impotency of Herodes' arch compared to Hadrian's, or as an example of the implied threat contained in many of Herodes' monuments that engage with Roman emperors (discussed in subsequent chapters). That threat intimates that spatial, cultural, and even historic memory are up for grabs if one looks beyond a present audience, and that the compliance of the Greek elite in Roman rule is crucial but not guaranteed.

The importance of controlling commemorative messages and channelling monumental meanings is demonstrated starkly by the folktale that adhered to Regilla's space in modern times. The area is known as η μάντρα της γριάς ('the old woman's sheepfold') and the legend behind the name is reported by Richard Chandler in his *Travels in Greece* (1776):[67]

---

[64] On the road, see Soteriades 1933, 32. See also Papaioannou 2018, 342, with n. 137.

[65] See also Mazurek 2018, 613–15, who discusses the audience for Herodes' Sanctuary of the Egyptian Gods.

[66] Cf. now Papaioannou 2018, 368 n. 144.

[67] On Chandler's expedition, see Constantine 2011, 188–209.

near the vestiges of a small building, probably a sepulchre, was a headless statue of a woman sedent, lying on the ground. This, my companions informed me, was once endued with life, being an aged lady possessed of a numerous flock, which was folded near that spot. Her riches were great, and her prosperity was uninterrupted. She was elated by her good fortune. The winter was gone by, and even the rude month of March had spared her sheep and goats. She now defied Heaven, as unapprehensive for the future, and as secure from all mishap. But Providence, to correct her impiety and ingratitude, commanded a fierce and penetrating frost to be its avenging minister; and she, her fold, and flocks were hardened into stone.[68]

This traveller's tale reveals what became of Herodes' monumental narrative. Indications of the original story remain: Regilla's wealth and prosperity (perhaps originally gleaned from the 'eternal concord' inscriptions); that the enclosure belonged to a woman; that there was a shocking reversal in her fortune; most importantly, that the spot somehow marks and commemorates this woman's death in stone. What is lost, along with the ability or inclination to read the inscriptions and the fading of collective local memory, are identity and details. Eugene Vanderpool believed the 'old woman's sheepfold (μάντρα)' appellation is in fact ancient (μάνδρα; 'enclosure') and possibly even contemporary with Regilla's life.[69] If this were the case, Herodes' arch would be extremely successful in its secondary phase as effectively a funeral monument. Its association with Herodes, however, who used its renovation to embed his emotions in the landscape and redefine historical and cultural memory, is completely erased. This effect of time is reflected in the different states of preservation of the keystone inscriptions: the face exposed to the elements for so many centuries bore Herodes' name, while that inscribed with 'Regilla' lay protected, so that the former is now barely legible, while the latter remains uneffaced.

Herodes' arch is just one example of the careful crafting of identity in monumental form that draws on a range of visual and literary traditions for the consumption of posterity demonstrated by imperial Greek *pepaideumenoi*. In the process, it also reveals that they were working through the same anxieties over commemoration, identity, and the reconfiguration of the past in material culture as in the literary media examined in chapter 2.[70] The Philopappos monument is another instance and many more exist.[71] Herodes Attikos, for example, also rebuilt the Panathenaic stadium of Lykourgos in Athens,[72] replacing and updating the fourth-century BC classical structure to make it his own at the same time as symbolically overwriting the memory of one of Athens' great orators,

---

[68] Chandler 1776, 166 (chapter 36).   [69] Vanderpool 1970, 45–6.

[70] See Dickenson 2017, 339, on reference to the past in the built environment of imperial-period agoras.

[71] For other examples see Smith 1998, 70–7; Burrell 2009; Gleason 2010.

[72] See Tobin 1997, 165.

benefactors, and statesmen,[73] much as Arrian reshaped the commemorative landscape of Trapezous to sideline Xenophon. As mentioned previously, only a smattering of literary artists were in the same kind of position of wealth and influence as Herodes, so that a few scattered funerary monuments, some inscribed *stêlai*, and inscribed statue bases are the only material traces we possess of them. Nevertheless, they were surrounded by Greek elites of similar resources to Herodes, many of whom associated themselves with *paideia* and Hellenic traditions.[74] Moreover, there is surely substantial evidence now lost to us. Aelius Aristeides, for instance, speaks of his estate (*HL* 4.48) and Philostratos describes the extensive holdings of Damianos of Ephesos (*VS* 2.23.606), who married into the prominent Vedii Antonini family and whose monopteros funeral monument on his villa grounds outside Ephesos has been convincingly interpreted as a dynastic statement.[75] Greek *pepaideumenoi* were therefore well aware of the commemorative possibilities of material culture and its potential to shape a lasting identity.

One noteworthy example of a monument that negotiates commemorative identity in a similar way to Herodes' gate is the library-heroon of Tiberius Julius Kelsos Polemaianos, a member of the elite of Sardis, a benefactor at Ephesos, a Roman military commander, consul (AD 92), and proconsul of Asia (*c.* AD 106). This public building-cum-tomb was raised in central Ephesos during the end of Trajan's and early phases of Hadrian's reign (*c.* AD 112–17; Figure 3.15). R. R. R. Smith, Abigail Graham, Barbara Burrell, and Edmund Thomas have discussed its combination of Greek and Roman elements in detail;[76] I am more interested, however, in its broader commemorative function.

The four female statues on the lower storey of the reconstructed façade represent traditional Greek cultural virtues of Wisdom (σοφία), Excellence (ἀρετή), Knowledge (ἐπιστήμη), and Good Judgement (ἔννοια). Three of the four statues on the second storey (only the bases stand) were most likely of Kelsos in his various personal and career guises: military commander (cuirass statue), Greek civilian/intellectual (himation), Roman citizen (toga).[77] The final statue was of his son, who began the library's construction but died before its completion. This façade thus claims that Kelsos' successful Roman career was underpinned by his Greek *paideia*, a notion of which the library itself is a powerful testament, and by extension that the empire too is founded on Greek culture and men like Kelsos.

---

[73] Welch 1998, 137–8. On the originality of Herodes' public benefactions and their novel combinations of 'Greek' and 'Roman' aspects, see Galli 2002. On Lykourgos and Athens, see Hanink 2014.

[74] See Boatwright 1993; Smith 1998; Kalinowski 2021.

[75] See Quatember and Scheilbelreiter-Gail 2017 on the elaborate funerary monument of this sophist. The Vedii Antonini family bequeathed extensive benefactions to Ephesos. See now Kalinowski 2021.

[76] Smith 1998, 73–5; Thomas 2007, 8–11; 2014, 78–82; Burrell 2009, 78–82; Graham 2013, 398–402.

[77] See the scholarly works listed in the previous footnote. Burrell 2009, 81: the inscription of *ennoia* is of late-antique date and replaces an unknown earlier virtue.

FIGURE 3.15 Reconstructed façade of the Library of Kelsos, Ephesos, c. AD 112–17. The upper register shows only the bases for the statues of Kelsos and his son; the lower register shows replicas of female statues representing Greek virtues.

This message of cultural potency is heightened by its placement in the centre of the provincial capital of proconsular Asia. By combining a dynastic (in the inclusion of both father and son) representation of Greek tradition with Roman power and asserting the primacy of the former, Kelsos' library, like Herodes' image at Rhamnous and Brexiza, insinuates that its Greek context might be more enduring than its Roman present.

Additionally, that the main dedicatory inscription across the façade names Kelsos in the accusative and that the individual statues represent virtues or biographical aspects of the kind one regularly finds inscribed on statue bases gives this library-heroon the veneer of a particularly magnificent honorific statue.[78] Kelsos' identity is

[78] Stewart (2003, 169) suggests the statue analogy in relation to the virtue statues on Kelsos' library, noting they correspond to virtues typically inscribed on bases, but this is also clearly true of the *cursus honorum* statues.

FIGURE 3.16 Inscribed limestone sarcophagus of Dionysios of Miletos (T. Claudius Flavianus Dionysios), Ephesos. The sarcophagus sits in an alcove opposite the Library of Kelsos and to the right of the Gate of Mazaios and Mithridates.

too multifaceted to be expressed by a single statue type, and one statue is not remarkable enough to represent his achievements. His monument thus draws consciously on the visual tradition of the honorific statue, but magnifies it to encompass his family's commemorative ambition. Why this Greek idiom was aggrandized in this manner will be a central issue of my discussion of honorific statues in chapter 5.[79]

Not every Greek cultural figure could monumentalize on the scale of a Kelsos or Herodes. Indeed, economy is one explanation for the prominence of commemorative material culture in their writings. An illustrative example of a remarkably more low-key level of funerary monumentalization but with similar commemorative positioning comes in the tomb of Titus Claudius Flavianus Dionysios (c. AD 140), which stood opposite Kelsos' library-heroon in Ephesos. It consisted of a simply decorated sarcophagus with a Greek inscription (Figures 3.16 and 3.17):[80]

---

[79] Note that, as a library, this monument combines 'visuality, literature and architecture' and provides a physical analogue to the dense commemorative materiality of contemporary literature. See Thomas 2014, 78–81. See also the extended discussion of Porter 2010, 453–535. For the visual rhetoric of the library, both inside ('functional') and out ('hegemonic'), as well as its placement within Ephesos, see Eidson 2013.

[80] Eichler 1969, 136–7; Vetters 1978, 199, fig. 3, pl. 3; *I.Ephesos* 2.426; Puech 2002, 231–2, no. 99.

T. Κλαύδιος
   Φλαουιανὸς
   Διονύσιος
      ῥήτωρ

T(itus) Claudius
   Flavianus
      Dionysios
         Rhetor

As inconspicuous and humble as this may seem, it would have stood out in its simplicity and for the single social role and Greek virtue contained in the epithet of 'rhetor' amidst the other lavish funerary monuments and buildings in this busy sector of Ephesos.[81] Moreover, even though the inscription is only in Greek, in the basic juxtaposition of name and occupation Dionysios signals his possession of both Greek culture and Roman citizenship, and the form of a limestone sarcophagus is a choice more closely associated with Roman than Greek traditions. As well as Kelsos' library, the tomb also lies nearby an audience hall that was used by sophists and philosophers as well as the governor.[82] Dionysios' sarcophagus, therefore, is sited within the same area of Ephesos that he would have haunted as a practising sophist—a fitting resting place reflected in the first epigraph of chapter 4 (Cavafy, *Tomb of the Grammarian Lysias*).[83] The simplicity of his tomb and funerary inscription simultaneously differentiates him from and embeds him within the cosmopolitan cultural heart of Ephesos, thus making his tomb an essential element in a greater commemorative material narrative. It is this aspect on which Philostratos concentrates in his description of Dionysios' passing, which begins by quoting Perikles' funeral oration in Thucydides 2.43.3:

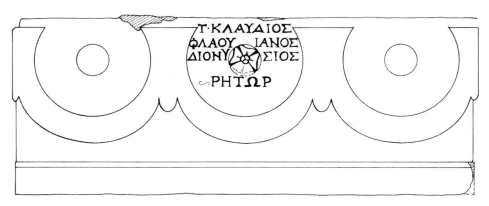

FIGURE 3.17 Drawing of Dionysios of Miletos' sarcophagus with funerary inscription (*I.Ephesos* 2.426).

---

[81] On the precinct as crammed with important tombs, see Rife 2009, 116–18. On the development of its monumental programme over time, see Burrell 2009, and p. 87 on Dionysios' burial in particular.
[82] Engelmann 1993, 105–11; 1995, 86–7; Rife 2009, 116–17.
[83] See chapter 4; cf. Engelmann 1993, 87.

'The entire earth is the grave of famous men' (ἀνδρῶν μὲν οὖν ἐπιφανῶν πᾶσα γῆ τάφος), but the tomb (σῆμα) of Dionysios is in the most famous (ἐπιφανεστάτῃ) city Ephesos, for he was buried in the agora in the most important (κυριώτατον) part of Ephesos, where he passed away (κατεβίω).   (*VS* 1.22.526)

Philostratos' phrasing places Dionysios' death and interment in the very place where he gained his great reputation. He thus gives Dionysios a famous literary context for his simple burial to match his honorific physical interment within the central civic confines of this important cultural and political city of Roman Asia Minor. He also implies that Ephesos' fame is partially dependent on its eternal embrace of Dionysios.

All these monuments draw on visual and verbal traditions to shape their own idiosyncratic commemorative narratives. The range of artefacts discussed and the distant locations of Attica and Ephesos reveal how prevalent these practices and concerns were among Greek *pepaideumenoi*. In particular, the same need to future reputation that was traced in Second Sophistic literature in the previous chapter is also apparent in its material production. This discussion, moreover, has pointed to how aware imperial Greeks were of the ability of stone to shape memory and how attuned they were to the messages of monuments. Philostratos' literary shaping of Dionysios' commemorative intent, for instance, demonstrates the ability of text to repackage and reinterpret material memories. Herodes' layering of meaning via inscriptional and sculptural additions to his Arch of Eternal Concord provides the same insight as well as showing that plastic interventions can affect interpretation as much as verbal ones. The following section dives deeper into imperial Greek engagement with the inherent meanings of monuments and explores the use of text as a means of shaping and controlling those messages for one's own commemorative purposes.

3.2 TEXTUAL CURATION OF ARTEFACTUAL MEMORY

In his *Isthmian Oration* in honour of Poseidon, Aelius Aristeides has the following to say about Corinth:

While travelling about the city, you would find wisdom (σοφὸν) and you would learn (μάθοις) and hear (ἀκούσειας) it from its inanimate objects (ἀψύχων). So numerous are the treasures of images/inscriptions (γραμμάτων) all about it, wherever one might simply glance, throughout the streets themselves and the porticoes. And further the gymnasiums and schools are lessons (μαθήματα) and stories (ἱστορήματα).[84]

(46.28)

---

[84] Translations after Behr 1981.

Here Aristeides endows the physical materiality of Corinth with the ability to communicate its knowledge, memories, and essence to the astute observer.[85] He presents the fabric of the city as a witness to its own existence and as capable of interrogation about its many and varied experiences. The richness of its potential to disseminate knowledge is highlighted by two features: Aristeides' prior identification of the city as a hub of commerce and trade as well as a refuge, so that the whole world floods into the city by land and sea and departs again enriched culturally, spiritually, or fiscally (46.22–7); and his subsequent invocation of its legendary and historic past, so that these stories are intertwined with both the space of the city and artefacts associated with it, such as the *Argo* (46.29). This monumental communicative capacity is extended yet further by the double sense of γράμμα, which is regularly used to mean a letter or writing, but in the plural can signify a picture where the γράμματα are conceived of as the lines delineating the image.[86] This notion extends the concept of text retaining traces of the voice to that of physical artefacts retaining an imprint of the lives lived in and around them.

Aristeides' awareness of stone's ability to preserve and communicate meaning reflects both the richness and continuing presence of past Greek material culture in the empire and imperial Greek inheritance of Roman conceptions of the interweaving of time and buildings.[87] This is exemplified by the commemorative and calculated intent behind much construction in the empire, particularly by emperors themselves or local rich and powerful individuals like Herodes Attikos. During the Antonine period, the empire reached its greatest extent and was held together, as Edmund Thomas has indicated, not only by the extensive official use of Latin and Greek, common law and custom, but also by architectural affinities.[88] Indeed, Roman public buildings were invested with messages of empire, identity, and power, specifically through imperial benefaction or dedication, the presence of official imperial statuary, and the use of Roman imperial architectural styles.[89] Moreover, messages of imperial hierarchy and cultural belonging were also reflected in the inscriptions emblazoned on public buildings.[90] The role of inscriptions in the futuring of imperial Greek culture is a central topic of Part II of the book.

The eclecticism in how this monumental ambition was expressed, however, was partly due to the increasing diversity of citizenship and senatorial membership,

---

[85] See Petsalis-Diomidis 2008, 142, on this passage and the chapter in general for the themes of travel and landscape and how they are intertwined with notions of the body and divinity in Aristeides' works.

[86] See *LSJ* s.v. γράμμα. On the similar polyvalence of γράφειν/γραφή, see Lissarrague 1992; Boeder 1996, 149–65; Squire 2009, 147–8.

[87] See chapter 1.

[88] Thomas 2007, 6. See also Dickenson's account (2017, esp. 202–392) of the increasing monumentalization of agoras in Greece during the Roman period. Cf. Evangelidis 2014.

[89] Thomas 2007, 6.   [90] See Graham 2013 on Ephesos.

which promoted 'dynamic interaction and reciprocal cultural influence' between Rome and her provinces.[91] For the wealthy provincial elite, monumental benefaction was one way to promote one's position both on a local and imperial stage, and to weave regional traditions and connections with broader imperial ideologies.[92] The non-elite, for whom such lavish expression was not possible, nevertheless immersed themselves in the same currents through the decoration and form of their funerary monuments or small contributions to larger building projects, as well as simply experiencing the metamorphosis of public space around them.[93] Moreover, conceptual aggrandizement accompanied technical advances in building materials and techniques, allowing new and more impressive architectural feats. Just as rhetorical expression was focused on performance and appearance, so too architecture became preoccupied by decoration and image.[94] Thus aspirational builders designed their monumental benefactions with the expectation that those who came to use the construction would also view it as art and engage with its decorative programme to interpret communicative intent. All this combined to make monumental buildings loom large in the thoughts and ambitions of imperial subjects. This preoccupation is evinced by the physical engagement with the cityscape and sites of cultural memory exemplified in both the public building of Kelsos and Herodes' private monuments, discussed in the previous section, as well as the contemporaneous materiality of literature.[95]

At the same time, however, Aelius Aristeides' literary perspective suggests that architectural constructions have their own stories to tell that have little to do with individual or imperial ideology and much more to do with their autopsy, with the buildings' involvement in the life of the city and the pervasive but insubstantial residue of those interactions and ordeals: just as text materializes voice and speech, so too monuments materialize memories. This aspect of monumentality is something the financer cannot control and is the kind of meaning that attaches to a building over time, often unexpectedly; it is the sort of monumental memory that

[91] Thomas 2007, 6. See also Dickenson 2017, 333–43. On senatorial diversity, see Hopkins 1974, esp. 116. On specifically Greek senators, see Halfmann 1979; Syme 1988, 1–20; Whitmarsh 2005, 12. For a concise (social, cultural, political) overview of Greek elites in the empire, see Rizakis 2007.

[92] On elite Greek benefaction in this period, see Zuiderhoek 2009. On its origins and development, see Gygax 2016. On combining cultural influences, see Thomas 2007, 6–13. See also Mitchell 1987; Waelkens 1987. See Thomas 2013 for the complex interaction of Greek and Roman elements with the introduction of western architectural forms to the eastern empire. For Athens in particular, see Thompson 1987.

[93] Thomas 2007, 7, 11; Van Dyke 2008, 277–8.

[94] Thomas 2014, 68; Dickenson 2017, 338.

[95] See Thomas 2007, 12, on the mental impact of monuments and Thomas 2014 for the shared conceptual language of rhetoric and architecture in Longinos (*Subl.* 12.3–4). See Nasrallah 2010, 30–50, on monuments acting as a form of address to public and, especially, emperor. See also Benediktson 2000, 6, 90–126, 139–50; Porter 2011.

adheres to ruins.[96] Depth of monumentality and commemoration is what an elite benefactor hopes will fasten onto his/her constructions to increase the longevity of their significance in the communities that matter to him/her. It is the key to enduring commemoration and architectural sublimity.[97] In a place like Corinth, with its powerful Greek heritage, destruction by Mummius, and refoundation as a Roman colony under Julius Caesar, its cityscape and architectural matrix would surely have witnessed fantastic and shocking events: if these walls could speak indeed.

The attempt to access such architectural or artefactual stories is a feature of imperial Greek literature, most obviously of 'travel' narratives, such as Arrian's *Periplous*, Pausanias' *Description of Greece*, Aelius Aristeides' *Sacred Tales*, Lucian's *On the Syrian Goddess*, the novels, or Philostratos' *In Honour of Apollonios of Tyana*, to name but a few. Asking artefacts to divulge their knowledge/ memories is another tactic deployed to connect to and contest the past as well as forge how the present is futured and packaged for posterity. When artefacts speak in these tales, however, their voices are filtered through the authority of individual authors, who shape the stories they might tell in specific and deliberate ways.[98] When Arrian in the role of Roman Governor of Kappadokia describes his arrival at the river Phasis in the *Periplous*, for instance, he notes:

On the left of one entering the Phasis sits the goddess Phasine. Judging by her attributes (τοῦ σχήματος τεκμαιρομένῳ), she is Rhea; for she has a cymbal in her hand and lions beneath her throne, and sits just like the one by Pheidias in the Athenian Metroon. Here too is displayed (δείκνυται) the anchor from the *Argo*. This object, made of iron, does not look old to me (οὐκ ἔδοξέ μοι εἶναι παλαιά) – although it is not the size of modern anchors (τὰς νῦν ἀγκύρας), and the shape has been altered in some way – but appears more recent (νεωτέρα). But also conspicuous (ἐδείκνυτο) are some old fragments (παλαιά θραύσματα) of a stone one, and it is rather these one would guess, which are the remains (τὰ λείψανα) of the anchor of the *Argo*. (Arr. *Peripl.* 9.2)

Here Arrian interprets these sacred and mythic artefacts built into the local landscape of the empire's periphery for Hadrian and a cultured Roman/Greek audience.[99] He translates the local goddess into a consumable and relatable form for someone at the cultural centre of empire, where an originally foreign goddess in Kybele has already been conflated with Rhea. In particular, he chooses to

---

[96] On the concept of architectural monumentality in general, see Choay 2001, 1–17; Thomas 2007, 1–6.

[97] On the notion of architectural sublimity and the interconnectedness of rhetorical and architectural terminology, see Thomas 2014; 2015; cf. Benediktson 2000, 90–120, 127–45; Porter 2010, 490–4, and 2011.

[98] On this idea, see Elsner 1994b. See the similar point made by Squire 2009, 355, in relation to Philostratos the Elder's *Imagines*.

[99] On this passage, see Silberman 1995, 28–9; Petsalis-Diomidis 2010, 102.

compare this statue to one in Athens by a famous classical artist (cf. Paus. 1.3.5), who was believed responsible for the Zeus at Olympia, one of the seven wonders of the ancient world, and both the Athena Promachos and Parthenos of the Athenian Akropolis. He thus indulges Hadrian's affection for Athens and Athenian classical art, and he enriches the Black Sea coast with powerful ectopic and anachronistic cultural touchstones. Moreover, his assimilation of Phasine to Rhea is based on the physical attributes of the statue: the pose, the accoutrements, the form and content. It is an art-historical judgement made on stylistic and formal comparison.

The basis of that comparison is broad, in that it consists of the fact she is seated in the same way as Pheidias' statue, has a cymbal and lions, but it enables anyone who has seen the Athenian version to visualize the Phasian one. Arrian thus employs a shared cultural (i.e. visual and literary) repertoire to create a context for his ekphrastic narrative. Moreover, the lack of detail sits well with a judgement itself based on distant memory.[100] An equivalent attempt to match an exotic goddess with Kybele and through Kybele to Rhea is also made by Lucian in *On the Syrian Goddess* 15, in which he provides proofs for the Syrian goddess' identification with Rhea, again based on iconography and accoutrements.[101] As Jaś Elsner has shown, Lucian highlights the difficulties 'in marrying the visual style of Syrian deities with their representation in Greek nomenclature' and, further, that these difficulties arise in the first place because of ethnic diversity in the Roman east.[102] Thus Lucian's project is fundamentally different from Arrian's, who reveals no friction in his identification of Phasine as Rhea. Where Lucian shows the fracture lines of imperial ethnicities, Arrian presents a homogenous imperial gaze that is enforced from the centre he represents in this text.

The second artefact requires further interpretation: it is claimed as the anchor of the *Argo*, the ship Jason sailed to Kolchis, but it does not look quite right to Arrian. As a discerning viewer, moreover, he can spot the real one, placed conveniently and conspicuously nearby, its antiquity and authenticity evident in its state of stony ruination. Much like Dio Chrysostom's artificially aged books (*Or.* 21.12), the apparently newish iron anchor attempts the impression of antiquity but fails to trick Arrian's learned scrutiny.[103] In making the effort, however, the locals at Phasis demonstrate the preoccupation of the age with connecting their own stories to those of the Greek past: the fabricated iron anchor is analogous to imperial Greek literary fascination with and manipulation of classical Greek writings. Arrian is on hand, however, to show the locals how things

---

[100] On this kind of connoisseurship in Pausanias, see Elsner 2007e, 51–8.
[101] See Lightfoot 2003, 257–63; Elsner 2007e, 61–2. [102] Elsner 2007e, 62.
[103] On this type of learned viewing in relation to Pausanias, see Pretzler 2010.

should really be done in his knowledgeable correction and identification of the neglected stone fragments lying nearby.

Tim Rood has perceptively noted that the verb δείκνυται ('it is pointed out') is used in this first section of the *Periplous* to highlight mythic artefacts or locations in particular and, in this way, these ancient elements are connected verbally to the pose of Hadrian's statue at Trapezous, who points (ἀποδείκνυσι, 1.3) to a sea that is simultaneously Xenophontic, Hadrianic and, as shown in chapter 2, rendered Arrianic.[104] Arrian thus uses historical artefacts and mythic landscapes to make this distant land knowable and to subdue it beneath the intellectual categorization of imperial control,[105] at the same time as capturing his interpretations in an authoritative text. Just as he intends to fix Hadrian's memorial at Trapezous so that it is a fitting commemoration, so he grafts new and appropriate meaning to the Black Sea littoral. He thus curates the signs of the Phasian/Trapezousian past for both present and future readers by allowing the landscape to tell only the story that he prescribes. The same authoritative thinking is revealed in the two inscriptions mentioned in chapter 2 that Arrian erected, respectively, in Sebastopolis-Dioskourias and Kappadokian Sebastopolis, one in Latin and one in Greek, both relating to Hadrian, which physically mark the extent of the Roman empire in terms pertinent to its cultural and political centres.[106] For Arrian, the signs of the Black Sea's past are very much possessions of the present to be manipulated and pieced together into a new commemorative narrative.[107] His textualization of artefacts is thus an attempt to control their innate messages.

Pausanias' *Description of Greece*, probably written between the years AD 165–80, also tells selective, interpretive, and instructive stories of the Greek past in the present (3.11.1) via its artefacts, architecture, rituals, and traditions, to construct a personal vision of a textualized museum of Hellenism.[108] Where once his text was considered useful primarily as a reference work for monuments and religious practice, it is now accepted and analysed as a carefully constructed literary account with topographic, historical, cultural, and religious goals.[109] His literary

---

[104] Rood 2011, 143.   [105] See Braund 1986, 38–9. Cf. Whitmarsh 2012, 467.

[106] See Section 2.2; Mitford 1991, 194–6, no. 8, taf. IX; *L'Année Epigraphique* 1905, 44, no. 175; Stadter 1980, 11; Silberman 1995, vii–x; Petsalis-Diomidis 2010, 101. Rostovtzeff 1909; Braund 1994, 194–5, pl. 13.

[107] On artefacts always being possessions of the present, see Olivier 2011. Cf. Lucas 2005, 32–60.

[108] On Pausanias as a textual museum, see Shaya 2015, 633; on subjectivity and turning 'the gaze' into text, see Elsner 2007b. On Pausanias' origins and the text's date, see Bowie 2001, 21–5, and on Pausanias' careful design, see Hutton 2010.

[109] See the seminal studies of Habicht 1985; Alcock, Cherry, and Elsner 2001; Knoepfler and Piérart 2001; Hutton 2005; Pretzler 2007. See Hutton 2005, 20–9, for scholarly attitudes to Pausanias, and 2017, 359, for the two main perceptions: 'diligent and uninspired antiquarian' vs 'active participant in the self-conscious urbanities of the Second Sophistic'.

interaction with artefacts is more varied than Arrian's but, like Arrian and Aristeides, he also uses objects and landscapes to unlock and shape interpretations of the Greek past.

Pausanias' two primary modes of engagement with Greece's physicality are the sort of art-historical analysis used by Arrian and Lucian, and the use of artefacts and ruins as touchstones for cultural history, especially of religious practice.[110] This latter approach corresponds more closely with Aristeides' casting of the built environment as a container of lessons and stories. Pausanias' Greece is therefore less a physical entity and more a landscape of layered histories, traditions, and rituals. Jaś Elsner has demonstrated, for instance, that his description of the altars at Olympia follows the order and processes of sacrifice rather than any spatial relationship or physical configuration.[111] Similarly, in the Athenian agora, more often than not he mentions a particular piece of art simply to launch into a historical and cultural narrative that is linked to the entity behind the artefact rather than the object itself. This is indeed his main approach when encountering statuary of a secular variety, such as the honorific statues to Philip II, Alexander, and his successors before the Odeion of Agrippa (1.8.6–13.9).[112] Occasionally the statue's material is noted (1.8.2), but the more detailed *ekphraseis* and acknowledgements of famous artists assigned to cult statues (e.g. Argive Hera, 2.17.4) are not replicated.[113] The difference between the way Pausanias treats statues of gods and historical individuals must have to do with the clues that the idiosyncrasies of cult statues give to specific religious practice (e.g. Argive Hera's pomegranate, the significance of which Pausanias declines to discuss out of respect for a religious prohibition). This stands in contrast to the relative uniformity of honorific poses, a commemorative problem I focus on in chapter 5.[114]

As has long been noted, for the most part, Pausanias concentrates on the pre-Roman past.[115] Two important exceptions to this archaizing programme are the emperor Hadrian and Herodes Attikos.[116] The former is regularly praised for his generosity to Athens and Greece, especially with respect to building (e.g. 1.5.5; cf. 8.43.3–6 on Antoninus Pius); the grandest building efforts of the latter are too wondrous for Pausanias to omit (1.19.6: θαῦμα, 'wonder'; 7.20.6: ἀξιολογώτατα,

---

[110] On Pausanias' fusion of an art-historical and religious approach, see Elsner 2007c, 12–19; 2007d. On Pausanias' literary landscape, see Hutton 2005.

[111] Elsner 2007c, 15–16.

[112] See also König 2005b, 158–204, on Pausanias and Olympic victor statues.

[113] Cf. Hutton 2017, 363–4.

[114] On Pausanias' avoidance of breaking religious taboos, see Foccardi 1987.

[115] See Swain 1996, 330–56.

[116] See Thomas 2007, 203, for other exceptions, notably Trajan, Antoninus Pius, and Pythodoros at Epidauros. See also Madsen 2014, 32; Bowie 1996.

'most remarkable'). He thus conceives of them as significant enough to be included among Greece's great monuments from a future perspective: not mentioning them could undermine his literary project in the minds of later readers. Thus here Pausanias demonstrates the movable perspective Longinos advocated but in relation to material culture rather than canonical texts. He acknowledges the agonistic relationship between contemporary benefactions and culturally revered monuments, and the aspirational quality of the former that have been conceived with posterity as much as the past and the present in mind. In doing so, he defers to the judgement of future audiences and, at the same time, reveals that his conception of Greece is in fact multi-temporal rather than simply archaizing.

Pausanias' anchoring of Greece to objects and landscape signals his own vast programme of canonization,[117] in which artists, authors, artefacts, rituals, and history are authenticated and legitimized by their physical traces. This is what Verity Platt describes as the 'numinosity' of Pausanias' Greece.[118] This 'numinosity', however, is often creative, consisting of living rather than absent or ghostly traditions and rituals that are relevant to and suggested by physical space and the material that occupies it, as though the legends and the artefacts grow from the ground itself, entwined, complete, and, importantly, accessible to the observant viewer. Pausanias' trained and perceptive eye transforms them into textual explication. One such example is a statue of Theseus representing one of the Troizen legends that Pausanias mentions on the Akropolis:

The next [story] is that Aegeus placed boots and a sword under a rock as tokens for the child, and then sailed away to Athens; Theseus, when sixteen years old, pushed the rock away and departed, taking what Aegeus had deposited. There is an image ($\epsilon\dot{\iota}\kappa\dot{\omega}\nu$) of this story ($\lambda\acute{o}\gamma o\upsilon$) produced ($\pi\epsilon\pi o\acute{\iota}\eta\tau\alpha\iota$) on the Akropolis, everything in bronze except the rock ($\chi\alpha\lambda\kappa o\hat{\upsilon}$ $\pi\acute{\alpha}\nu\tau\alpha$ $\dot{o}\mu o\acute{\iota}\omega\varsigma$ $\pi\lambda\dot{\eta}\nu$ $\tau\hat{\eta}\varsigma$ $\pi\acute{\epsilon}\tau\rho\alpha\varsigma$). (1.27.8)

Here the limestone of the Akropolis, the sacred heart of Athens, participates in the artistic rendering of this myth about Athens' legendary king that took place in the lands around Argos. The Attic stone that conceals the tokens becomes a metaphor for Theseus' true identity and birthright. Pausanias does not describe the statue here, but the story he tells stands in place of the description and the statue embodies this tale so that the details of the rendering must be supplied by the imaginations of the readers. There are surely many ways to represent this tale in bronze and the only definite detail is the participation of the Akropolis rock.

---

[117] See Porter 2001 on Pausanias' project resembling Longinos' canonizing of great textual moments. Cf. Thomas 2007, 177.

[118] Platt 2011, 218: Pausanias' tales of epiphanic experience 'imbue physical topography with sacred presence'. See also Alcock 1996.

This is a similar ploy to Arrian's relation of the goddess Phasine's statue to Pheidias' Rhea, in that the images already extant in the minds of his audience supply the details of the description and make the story of Theseus into a concrete monument. Pausanias' Greece, therefore, is in fact malleable in the form of its commemorative crystallization and open to the quirks of reader imagination and interpretation. As much as he creates a canon of Greek artefacts and traditions, then, he also opens that canon to the interpretative creativity of future audiences. Pausanias thus demonstrates a very different attitude to material culture than that shown by Arrian or Herodes Attikos, both of whom try to control an artefact's interpretation as much as possible.

Pausanias' Greece is further ambiguated by the gaps in his description. Even though artefact after artefact gives access to, opens an exegesis on, and makes present the past, Pausanias selects only those things he deems 'most worthy of memory' ($\tau \grave{a}$ $\delta \grave{\epsilon}$ $\mu \acute{a} \lambda \iota \sigma \tau a$ $\mathring{a} \xi \iota a$ $\mu \nu \acute{\eta} \mu \eta \varsigma$, 3.11.1) and suppresses the most sacred specifics, cutting short his authoritative insights for the uninitiated, as we saw with the example of Argive Hera's pomegranate.[119] Pausanias' literary construction of the materiality of Greece has, like Aristeides' Corinth, its own cultural, religious, and historical stories to tell, some of which cannot be transcribed in words or intellectualized. His text is thus also a museum that demands interaction with its artefacts rather than merely remote observation; *paideia* alone in this instance is not enough.[120] This applies also to the constructions and objects that he finds unworthy of mention—those things that do make the cut can be appreciated fully only in company with the rejects. Pausanias entices the reader to embody his experience, so that Greece (a Greece that is 'always already' in the past) exists for posterity only in his footsteps and through his eyes, even if those eyes are open to the prospect of the future's power to reconfigure and redefine meaning.

The textual curation of the material past, present, and future by Aristeides, Arrian, and Pausanias highlights imperial Greek awareness that artefacts and monuments require control, lest their commemorative messages be misinterpreted.[121] This control can be about preservation, in that two problems which the incorporation of an inscription or monument into text overcomes are destruction of context, should a physical monument lose its dedicatory inscription or some other mishap befall it, and the danger that one's monument might be

---

[119] See Hutton 2005, 14–16.

[120] Platt 2011, 223, and more generally 215–24; cf. Elsner 1992, especially 22–7; 2001b, 18; Thomas 2007, 177. See also Petsalis-Diomidis 2007 on the intertwining of epiphany, landscape, and travel in Severan literary and material culture.

[121] See, relatedly, Beard 1991, 58, on the power of writing to control experience. Cf. Beard 1998, 81–8, on words and artefacts' mutual abilities to supplement each other.

ignored or appreciated solely for its artistic merit rather than its commemorative purpose. In the first instance, the text creates a stable context for the monument, which then becomes moveable. In the second, a textualized monument immediately enables the targeting of an appropriate and specific audience.

Textualization, however, can also be about redefinition and dominance, about shaping reception via authoritative interpretation. This notion goes back to Sokrates in Plato's *Phaidros* (esp. 275b–276a) and has been elaborated by Charles Martindale with respect to the reception of texts.[122] Martindale argues that textual meaning is generated entirely by readers, so that no matter what strategies an author puts in place his/her intention is lost as soon as the work is disseminated. This is an extreme position that minimizes the effect of culture and history on audience comprehension, two factors which mediate between the producer and receiver. The stories monuments (or texts) from the past tell may indeed be refracted via countless intermediaries (other readers, writers, viewers, builders), thus destabilizing meaning, but they also function within a broad cultural complex of shared knowledge.[123] Meaning is therefore subject to the interpretive and creative gaze of the receiver, but his/her analytical capacities, instilled by the sociocultural milieu, maximize the potential for meaningful exchange. This is what Aelius Aristeides is getting at in his touching description of the story-laden architecture of Corinth: buildings have their tales to tell, but they need to be unlocked by the right kind of viewer. Arrian's and Pausanias' engagement with the landscapes of Roman Greece and Asia Minor provide an interpretative key by which to channel an artefact's communicative power.

To enhance their readers' access to the materiality of their texts, imperial Greek authors, such as Arrian, Pausanias, and Aristeides, rely on shared cultural conceptions. One important element in this is the rhetorical training undergone by the upper levels of Roman and imperial Greek society, which created common reserves of rhetorical *topoi* that could then be exploited in the crafting of speeches and texts. These *topoi* functioned alongside techniques such as *ekphrasis* to enhance reader interpretive capacity but also made material elements such as monuments and commemorative landscapes especially popular elements of contemporary literature. This density of materiality in literature and its effects form the subject of the following section.

---

[122] Martindale 1993, 3–4. See, however, pages 1–10 for a detailed discussion of the nuances of textual agency and reception. See also Martindale 2006; 2013. On Plato's *Phaedros* in this context, see Derrida 1981, esp. 130–54.

[123] Whitmarsh 2006a, 106; Fowler 2000, 201–2; cf. Kahane 2011, 829; Squire 2015. Compare also Elsner's argument that discourse shapes and defines monumental meanings in the guise of history, in Elsner 1994b. See Olivier 2011 for the application of this idea to archaeology and material culture.

3.3 RHETORICAL MATERIALITY

The shared education of the literate elite provided access to common verbal and visual cues that were integral to the art of public speaking and the creation of contemporary literature.[124] Ekphrastic description, a well-known myth or historical episode, or comparison of a novel artefact with a famous touchstone were methods employed to create a desired image in the reader's mind.[125] The rhetorical techniques of ἐναργεία ('vividness') and σαφήνεια ('clarity') were specifically designed to bring a 'subject before the eyes' or turn 'listeners into spectators' by activating visual memories.[126] The prevalence of these techniques and the variety of ekphrastic subject matter—Lucian's *Zeuxis*, for instance, offers an *ekphrasis* of both a painting and a battle—indicate just how intertwined word and image were in Greek rhetorical thought. *Ekphrasis* and cultural or historical touchstones, therefore, worked by accessing an auditor's internal repository of imagination, which in turn derived from their personal experience of materiality in the world.[127] Due to the subjectivity inherent in this strategy, for it to succeed, rhetors would need to be confident that their audience shared a similar mental storehouse of images to their own, so that their words would conjure a relatable 'inner vision' or φαντασία.[128] This, Ruth Webb convincingly argues, was one of the key elements underlying the elite's common rhetorical education, since it guaranteed a basic communal imaginative visual repertoire, and yet another reason for authors and orators of the day to use classical paradigms to create their novel works.[129]

An important aspect to all this is the materiality of memory in Greek and Roman perceptions: mentally stored knowledge was regularly conceived of as existing in material form. From classical times onwards, how memories are created was understood as the imprinting of a mental wax tablet, the differing memory

---

[124] See Webb 2009, 14, and 10–13 for *ekphrasis* and declamation; Elsner 1995, 24–8; 2014, 24–31, especially 27–9; Squire 2009, 142–3.

[125] On *ekphrasis*, see Squire 2009, 139–46. On the variety of ways to understand and approach *ekphrasis*, see the essays in Bartsch and Elsner 2007.

[126] Webb 2009, 8, 38, 105. She does not cite sources for the quotations but later notes equivalent passages from Plutarch on Thucydides (*Artax.* 8.1) and Longinos on Herodotos (*Subl.* 26.2) on p. 20. Cf. Theon, *Progymnasmata* 119, 1.32, and Nikolaos, *Progymnasmata*, p. 70, ll. 5–6. See also Squire 2009, 142–4, Bartsch and Elsner 2007, i, and especially Elsner 1995, 25, who stresses the necessity of clarity (σαφήνεια) and discusses Hermogenes on seeing through hearing. Porter (2010, 356) also highlights the role of the sound attached to the written words to effect ἐναργεία.

[127] See Webb 2009, 10, 38, 107; Squire 2009, 244.

[128] See Squire 2009, 143, with bibliography, and Fowler 1991, 35; Bartsch and Elsner 2007, ii; Webb 2009, 105–30.

[129] Webb 2009, 122. See also Tompkins 1980, 202–6.

capabilities of various individuals described by the depth of imprint and quality of wax.[130] This notion is related to the specifically Stoic conception of φαντασία, whereby an object 'imprinted itself upon and in some sense altered the soul'.[131] The art of memory as described by rhetorical theorists also conceived of memory creation as occurring within an imagined physical space: memories were attached, like furniture or paintings, to the superstructure of the mind, conceptualized as a building with many rooms or something similar, and retrieved by wandering through it.[132] Consequently, memory marks the virtual landscape of the mind, much as monuments and inscriptions mark the civic landscape in reality, and the orator's voice imprints the page with written words. The common training undertaken by rhetors and authors therefore elucidates how the intense materiality of texts and the textuality of art in the imperial period was encouraged by the desire to communicate intended meaning effectively within cultural constraints.

Lucian's *On the Hall* is one example of a text that directly confronts the interrelationship between rhetoric and image and the communicative possibilities of both media. This short introductory speech considers the correct way to respond to visual beauty by evaluating the relative power of verbal and visual material.[133] It provides two points of view via different *personae* on speaking within magnificent surrounds. The key questions are whether words or images are more memorable, and whether they work in partnership or competition, both of which are central concerns of imperial Greek commemorative efforts.

At the beginning, the first speaker claims that a beautiful setting urges one on to speak and, at the same time, improves one's words (13). From this point of view, the two media are partners in creating a better product and the monumental takes an auxiliary position to the verbal. When this persona retires, he is replaced by ἕτερος λόγος ('the other opinion') who asserts that visual objects are more impressive than words. His main point, illustrated by a comparison of Sirens, whose singing merely causes delay, to the Gorgon, whose gaze petrifies for eternity, is that words are fleeting, whereas images remain (19). Nevertheless, that his audience is more enamoured by the hall's artwork than his speech (18) leads him to describe the artworks in some detail, to make what he calls a word-painting

[130] Whitehead 2009, 15–26. Cf. Le Goff 1992, 65; Small 1997; Danziger 2008, 31–4; Webb 2009, 111–12; Butler 2015, 40–2. See also Pl. *Tht.* 191c–e; Arist. *Mem.* 450a 30–2.

[131] Elsner 1995, 26. For a discussion of φαντασία as it relates to the connection and tension between literature and the visual arts, with bibliography, see Benediktson 2000, 162–88.

[132] Whitehead 2009, 27–37. See also Le Goff 1992, 65–8; Bergmann 1994, 225–7; Webb 2009, 110–13. On ancient Greek understanding of memory and how it worked in general, see Yates 1966, 1–49; Danziger 2008, 24–41; *Rhet. Her.* 3.16.28–24.30; Quint., *Inst.* 11.2; Arist. *De an.* 427b 18–20; Cic. *De or.* 2.354–60.

[133] On this speech, see Goldhill 2000; 2001, 160–7; Newby 2002a; 2002b; Thomas 2007, 229–35; Squire 2009, 239–47; Webb 2009, 172–4. On Lucian's introductory speeches in general, see Branham 1985; Nesselrath 1990.

($\dot{\eta}$ $\gamma\rho\alpha\phi\dot{\eta}$ $\tau\hat{\omega}\nu$ $\lambda\acute{o}\gamma\omega\nu$, 21), and so in fact to engage in the practice of the first speaker.[134] Moreover, his descriptions range beyond the images themselves to recontextualize them within broader cultural history (e.g. the painting of Orestes' murder of Aigisthos is connected to Euripides' and Sophokles' plays). The second speaker's oration is therefore a contest between words and the physical image in an attempt to control the innate messages of the latter, which (if left to its own devices) 'subjects the spectator to its power ($\tau\grave{o}\nu$ $\theta\epsilon\alpha\tau\grave{\eta}\nu$ $\dot{\upsilon}\pi\acute{\alpha}\gamma\epsilon\tau\alpha\iota$)' (20).

The first persona's scenario is essentially that of a monument incorporated into text and the second's is more like an inscription applied to a material artefact. In both cases the two media end up working together, but the first foregrounds speech, while the second uses words to frame the physical monument. The authority of the two speakers has been of primary scholarly concern.[135] Both are compelled to describe the hall verbally by their visual experience, which adds weight to the first speaker's position.[136] At the very conclusion to the piece, however, the second speaker requires the audience to close their eyes, thus removing the visual competition for their attention. He demonstrates, therefore, that only in not seeing images, can an audience truly appreciate words (32). This notion underlies the principles of *ekphrasis*: an epideictic *ekphrasis* performed before the object the speaker is trying to conjure in words would risk becoming superfluous.[137] Moreover, any imaginative divergence sparked by the words vis-à-vis the object would open the door to incongruity and cognitive dissonance. Both speakers' authority thus appears shaky under scrutiny because the relationship between word and image is one of shaping context and meaning, of controlling innate messages, and intellectualizing sensory perception.[138] Separately, each medium is subject to the interpretation of the viewer or auditor; together, meaning is channelled and defined at the point of reception to limit interpretative response. The kinds of narratives text can create for artefacts, however, are multiple and varied, thus destabilizing and delegitimizing each individual rendition.

This variance and instability are directly reflected in both the oratorical memory technique of the 'mind palace' and the rhetorical process attached to the viewing of collections of art for the educated elite in imperial times. The former allows for

[134] See Goldhill 2001, 165; Squire 2009, 241–2; cf. Goldhill 2000, 49. See also Lucian's *Alex.* 3 and *Imagines* 3 for the idea of a 'word painting' or 'image in words'.

[135] Newby 2002b, 133; Webb 2009, 173 (ambiguous authority); Goldhill 2001, 163–4 (first speaker authoritative, based on an allusion to Plato's *Republic* and the use of the mendacious Herodotos as a champion of autopsy). See Momigliano 1958 (esp. 8 on Lucian) on Herodotos' reputation in antiquity. Cf. Thomas 2007, 232–3 (second speaker authoritative, based on the self-undermining language of the first speaker).

[136] Squire 2009, 241–2.

[137] See Webb 2009, 172, on the problems of *ekphrasis* applied to a visually available object.

[138] On the second speaker's attempts to intellectualize visual experience, see Newby 2002b, 131–3. Cf. Newby 2002a, 129.

the same subject matter to be organized in diverse ways to create different improvised *epideixeis*, and the latter encourages the viewer to construct different narratives based on how s/he moves about the display and the individual ideas stimulated by that sequence.[139] Lucian's *On the Hall* thus combines a demonstration of epideictic process and skill with the implication that leaving a lasting impression is particularly tough when one attempts to do so via the immaterial and endlessly malleable medium of speech. In this context, its physical images and architecture also stand as metaphorically representative of the materiality of text. The ambivalence directed towards the commemorative capacity of speech contrasts pointedly with the typical posturing of the vast literary tradition by implying that physical structures might just be more lasting than words.[140] This is ἕτερος λόγος' point when he says that the visual image (unsupplemented by words) speaks for itself and brings the viewer under its power. In this conception, reception is controlled by the object rather than its viewer, as implied by Aristeides' description of Corinth and the architectural stories it emits for the perceptive observer.[141] Nevertheless, even though the object has its own stories, it still requires the right kind of audience to unlock them. What one person learns from Corinth's monumental matrix may be very different from another. This potential for multiple readings is what prompts Arrian's and Pausanias' textual curation of material memory.

On the Hall thus casts monuments, artefacts (and even texts themselves) as sites of contention. These media strive to control memory and meaning but, because of their vulnerability to the power of others' words and their dependency on context, that meaning can be manipulated through their inclusion in artfully constructed literary texts or via physical recontextualization. This means that, while a viewer's cultural comprehension can aid the reuse, manipulation, or supplementation of an artefact when appropriating it along with its cultural baggage and incorporating it into a different physical or literary setting, any such recontextualized object becomes subject to the potential for re-interpretation and exploitation by others. The writers and monumentalizers of the Second Sophistic are versed in this complex interplay of intention, authority, and reception that renders any given memorial a site of conflict over identity, power, meaning, and memory.

How both monumental and textual messages might be controlled once they are publicly disseminated is one of the most prevalent anxieties associated with

---

[139] Bergmann 1994, 226; Newby 2002a, 112. For an example of this variance in relation to Lucian's *On the Hall*, compare Newby 2002a, 118–25, and Thomas 2007, 233–4.

[140] See further Section 4.1.

[141] Note also that the first speaker describes the hall as distinctly remembering his words like a quick-learning listener (ὡς ἄν τις εὐμαθὴς ἀκροατὴς διαμνημονεύων τὰ εἰρημένα, *On the Hall* 3).

personal commemoration in the imperial age. The first and to a large extent the second speakers' words in *On the Hall*, for instance, are above all designed to control and redirect the images' visual power, to reduce them to symbols.[142] This process is precisely that undertaken by individuals in both literary and monumental attempts to craft a self-image for posterity through the application of inscriptions to physical monuments, the incorporation of artefacts into artistically composed texts or carefully curated physical contexts, and the transformation of texts into metaphoric monuments, all central topics of Part II of this book. The acknowledgement of an image's or object's own power to disseminate ideas is, nonetheless, a confession that the potential exists for the ultimate failure of all three strategies.

3.4 CONCLUSION

This chapter has examined the prominence of materiality and monumentality in imperial Greek literature and established some reasons for its density, including the saturation of land- and cityscapes with cultural memory and the newer, culturally mixed and often politically charged constructions that began to redefine them; the benefit of shared verbal and visual resources; the focus in rhetorical education on *ekphrasis* and culturally potent *topoi*; and, above all, the desire to shape and control the cultural and political messages attached to monuments and commemorative landscapes. The interpenetration of imperial Greek texts and visual arts highlights that both media exploit the same borrowings of past cultural meanings in combination with more contemporary social and political frameworks to create a context in which one's own novel commemorative efforts are to be interpreted. These two contiguous streams of culture (the textual and the material) combine and diverge continuously in the quest for meaningful contemporary cultural, political, and social posturing, and a presence in future cultural consciousness. That physical creations are clearly designed as memorials elucidates the subtler futuring of the literature.

What the material efforts discussed here show particularly well, however, is the precision and rhetorical nature of individual representation: Herodes' vividly Hellenic portrait with its ambivalent presence in the Roman world; Dionysios' simple yet honorific Roman and Greek burial in a cultural and political centre; Kelsos' magnificent Roman and Greek burial *as* a cultural centre. The care taken in creating monumental meaning suggests that a similar concern over controlling one's memory underpins imperial Greek material as much as literary production.

---

[142] Cf. Newby 2002b, 133. See also, Squire 2009, 240, 242.

This situation is highlighted by Aristeides' acknowledgement that artefacts have an inbuilt ability to communicate, which Arrian, Lucian, and Pausanias demonstrate must be channelled and controlled. Imperial Greek engagement with both media thus reveals self-conscious and self-reflexive experimentation with temporal positioning, individual and collective identity, power, culture, and canonicity. In all cases, context becomes the key to unlocking meaning, and the reconfiguration and reapplication of the past buttress a sense of cultural continuity to create the impression of both grand achievement and a receptive audience capable of accurate (or at least adequate) interpretation whether in the present or the future. Part II of the book, to which I now turn, provides a more in-depth study of the interdependency of text and monument in imperial Greek negotiation of identity, power, culture, the past and the future with a focus on two monumental forms specifically designed to preserve individual memory: tombs and honorific statuary.

PART II

Textual Monuments and Monumental Texts

The Tyrian ship, sacred to Herakles, which he captured in the attack, [Alexander] dedicated to Herakles and inscribed an epigram on it, either of his own composition or someone else's. The epigram is not worthy of remembrance (οὐκ ἄξιον μνήμης); that's why I didn't bother recording it (ἐγὼ αὐτὸ ἀναγράψαι ἀπηξίωσα).

— Arrian, *Anabasis* 2.24.6.

FOUR

The Epitaphic Habit

Nearby, on the right as you enter the library
of Beirut, we buried the learned Lysias
the grammarian. The location is most appropriate.
We placed him near those things of his he may
remember even there – annotations, texts, grammatical analyses,
writings, tomes of ample commentary on Greek idioms.
Thus his tomb will be seen and honoured by us,
each time we make our way towards the books.

> – C. P. Cavafy, *Tomb of the Grammarian Lysias.*[1]

Are we surprised that men die? Monuments gape apart,
death comes even to stones and names.

> – Ausonius, *Epigrams* 37.9–10.[2]

The eastern Roman empire was littered with inscribed monuments and the desire to embed one's presence into the landscape was a powerful driving force behind the building works and benefactions of elite Greeks in the Roman imperial era. This chapter concentrates on imperial Greek fascination with inscriptions and aims to accomplish two things. First, it will explore the ways in which inscribed monuments are integrated into literary texts and how these textualized memorials are used to construct new temporalities and commemorative meanings. Second, it will analyse the commemorative deployment of physical inscriptions that act in similar ways to the literary examples. I argue that imperial Greeks use commemorative landscapes and the monuments embedded within them to create a context for their innovative, future-conscious artistic endeavours, and the temporal and cultural meanings they generate function socially and politically as much as culturally. The commemorative capacity of the artefacts discussed below is emphasized by how they are shaped by text or their physical deployment as epitaphic, whether they be boundary markers, altars, honorific inscriptions, or casualty lists. Tombs and epitaphs are thus a focus of the chapter.

During the imperial period, there was an intensification of intellectual interest in inscriptions from the past which corresponded to a significant increase in new

[1] Translated by Sacheroglou, in Hirst 2007, 61.   [2] Translated by Fowler 2000, 193.

Fashioning the Future in Roman Greece: Memory, Monuments, Texts. Estelle Strazdins, Oxford University Press.
© Estelle Strazdins 2023. DOI: 10.1093/oso/9780192866103.003.0004

inscriptional dedications across the empire in both languages.[3] The κλέος-creating qualities of honorific inscriptions in particular made them an attractive medium to be exploited by imperial Greeks in their efforts to self-commemorate.[4] The proliferation of monumental benefaction in the east and the building predilection of emperors such as Hadrian, moreover, helped thrust the relationship between word and monument to the fore in the minds of individuals trying to future their cultural presence.[5] Writing the already marked landscape into texts is the natural extension of this elite monumentalizing compulsion, and the interaction of textual and material culture is consequently a prevalent theme in contemporary Greek literature. In what follows, I will consider how this relationship plays out in several texts—Philostratos' *Lives of the Sophists* and *In Honour of Apollonios of Tyana*, Aelius Aristeides' *Sacred Tales*, Lucian's *True Stories*, and Arrian's *Anabasis of Alexander*—and what it can tell us about the temporal and cultural positioning of imperial Greek artistic production. I will also examine some examples of real inscriptions and how Herodes Attikos (re)deploys them to a comparable end with posterity in mind. The first section establishes significant influences on elite imperial Greeks in their literary engagement with monuments and the metaphoric application of the monumental to text. The second section explores literary and physical engagement with inscribed monuments that mark boundaries. The third and fourth sections examine literary and physical examples of the appropriation of cultural memory for one's own commemorative purposes.

4.1 SPEECH, TEXT, MONUMENT

This section will survey some of the primary influences that are assumed and manipulated by Greek writers of the imperial period and how their approach fits into the Greek tradition of literary materiality. It will also establish the complexity of experiential factors that feed into imperial Greek engagement with inscribed monuments. Imperial Greek authors arrive at the medium of inscriptions with significant cultural baggage. An inscription is itself monumental, and a long history exists of both partnership and friction between text and physical construction. Each is recognized as a means of memorialization from the very beginnings of Greek literature—Homer's epics marry tomb and song as partners in memory

---

[3] Woolf 1996, 22. See also MacMullen 1982; Meyer 1990; Bodel 2001, 15–25; Graham 2013, 386–8.

[4] See Svenbro 1993, 62, 164, on honorific inscriptions as machines 'designed to produce *kleos*'.

[5] On Hadrian and his civic building in the Greek east, see Boatwright 2000. On Roman monumentality, especially in the Antonine period, see Thomas 2007. On the intricacies of imperial Greek euergetism, see especially Zuiderhoek 2009.

preservation—but the relationship between them is never entirely neutral.[6] Sometimes they compete for commemorative supremacy; at other times, text and monument collude to create either a physical or a textual memorial.

Roman-era Greek writers and monumentalizers draw on the attitudes and practices of the past, but their relationship to any particular influence is never unilateral or set. Their literary works are thus distinguished by artful engagement with the interface between text and monument, and characteristically experiment with and mingle different modes of textuality, as illustrated by the discussion of Arrian's *Periplous* in chapter 2. Moreover, this experimental and plural approach was also expressed in monumental form, so that physical monuments of the period reflect the intricacy and stratification of their textual counterparts.

The interdependency of fame, memory, text, and monument is apparent already in the *Iliad* and *Odyssey*, which act to perpetuate the κλέος ('fame'/ 'glory') of their respective heroes and, concurrently, that of the poet who composed them. Over time they become conceptualized as literary monuments to both hero and author, and as the primary and greatest monuments of their kind against which all others are to be measured.[7] Further, within these poems, commemorative song defines the role of tombs as memorials to the κλέος of their inhabitants.[8] Significantly, the identification of the tomb is purely oral, since Homeric society is largely pre-literate.[9] In a world where inscriptions do not aid memorialization, monuments can be suspect or anonymous, as at *Iliad* 23.326–33. Here Nestor speculates on the significance of a tree stump between two white stones with an area cleared around it. He suggests that it may have been a tomb-marker (σῆμα) of someone long dead (and since forgotten) or, alternatively, a turning post.[10] What is important here is that no one remembers what the marker signifies and no inscription or celebratory song exists as an aid to identification. This is where the efficacy of a monument can fall down: it gains its

---

[6] See Steiner 2001, 252–9, especially 253–5, for tombs in the *Iliad* and *Odyssey*. On 253, she says: '[a]ccounts of the commemoration of the dead in epic song regularly harness the two kinds of memorialization to one another, showing how frequently each depends on the other and builds on its character and claims: no artefact without the speech that disseminates its message, and no verbal renown without some monument to spark it off'. Cf. Day 1989, 27. On commemorative architecture in the *Iliad* as temporary and tied to the conflict between orality and textuality, see Garcia Jr 2013, especially chapter 4, and Ford 1992, 131–46. On the interdependency of monument and text in commemoration, see Stewart 1990, 54. For a succinct account of the development of Greek ideas on poetic immortality, see Kerkhecker 1999, 11–16.

[7] For example, see Moles 1999, 32–41, for Thucydides engaging with Homer's epics and the idea of a textual monument.

[8] See *Od.* 24.80, 4.584; *Il.* 7.87–91 (here the tomb adds to the κλέος of the slayer as well as the slain). See Steiner 2001, 253–4; Porter 2010, 476–9.

[9] See, however, as a possible indication of writing, the well-known example of the σήματα λυγρά ('baneful marks') Bellerophon is given by Proteus to take to the king of Lykia at *Il.* 6.168.

[10] See also Steiner 2001, 253; Porter 2010, 477–8; and Sourvinou-Inwood 1995, 108–39, for a discussion of grave monuments in Homer.

meaning from its context and sometimes the viewer is not capable of interpreting the clues to its signification without verbal or written prompting. The same problem applies to oral or written memorialization: perhaps a song did once exist, which told the story of whoever was interred beneath the stump to which Nestor refers, but it has now faded from memory. Thus both media have their limitations: all things being equal, a monument is long lasting but its context is unstable; a text is better able to explain its own context but is more fragile.

Yet the fragility of text is the very thing that later authors deny as they cast their medium as the victor in the quest for immortalization.[11] The seminal expressions of this sentiment in the two languages are the opening of Pindar's *Pythian* 6 (especially lines 5, 7–14; θησαυρὸς ὕμνων, 'treasury of songs') and Horace's *Odes* 3.30.1–9 (*monumentum aere perennius*, 'monument more enduring than bronze').[12] Both authors stress the inability of time to wear away or obscure their words as it might a physical construction and, in addition, Horace arrogates the fame of his odes to himself. Yet Horace's future gaze extends only so far. He limits his own fame by tying it to Rome, its rituals, and institutions: it exists 'for as long as the priest and the silent virgin climb the Capitol' (*Carm.* 3.30.8–9). To remove his work from this Roman context is similar to removing a monument or statue from its original position: at least some of its intended meaning is lost. Moreover, both authors draw on a hypothetical physical structure in casting their poems as verbal monuments, and in the Horatian passage, the mental monument stands in for Horace himself, acting virtually as his σῆμα ('tomb').[13]

This image of text assuming one's own place in the world is a development of the idea of the grave marker (σῆμα) replacing a dead individual in the community, a notion which existed in Greek thought from archaic times: the grave monument 'became the (metonymically derived) symbol for the deceased's new persona [...] that is, his memory'.[14] Thus the grave monument is the means by which the memory of the dead is kept alive in the minds of others. Sarah Cormack perceptively describes it as a 'mirror' both of its inhabitant's life and of civic architecture. In this conception, the cemetery becomes a city of the dead, and the city proper is intricately connected to its mortuary neighbour by personal bonds between the living and dead, and by how the dead have left their imprint on the physical structure of the city.[15] Indeed, this is one of the central metaphorical functions of

---

[11] On this issue, see Benediktson 2000, 5–6, 12–39.

[12] Woolf (1996, 25 n. 15) notes Horace is adapting Pindar to a Roman context. On Horace's engagement with the collision of text and art, see Benediktson 2000, 127–39. Compare also Isokrates, *Paneg.* 4.186 and *Antid.* 15.7.

[13] On poet's tombs and literary reception, see now Goldschmidt and Graziosi 2018.

[14] See Sourvinou-Inwood 1995, 108–297, quotation from p. 120. Cf. Derderian 2001, 3–4; Porter 2010, 465–6.

[15] See further Cormack 2004, 46–9.

any civic monument bearing an individual's name, no matter what its practical purpose. Herodes' Odeion of Regilla in Athens, for instance, is functionally a hall for public speaking or musical performance, but it was dedicated to stand as a memorial to his dead wife and, by association, to himself and his desire to commemorate her. Importantly, the tomb is also atemporal, in that it marks the cessation of a life but concurrently aims to perpetuate the memory of that life; it thus creates a past and a future for someone with no present.[16]

Although the grave monument renews an individual's memory in the minds of his community, death still robs that individual of speech and it is only through inscription that the dead continue to speak.[17] It is in no small part for this reason that graves are traditionally associated with communication and the development of writing.[18] The vast majority of extant inscribed epigrams are funerary or dedicatory.[19] Both reveal a preoccupation with naming, with leaving the sign of one's identity in a sacred or public place.[20] In archaic grave inscriptions, for instance, it is usual that both the grave monument ($\sigma\hat{\eta}\mu a$) and the deceased are referred to, most often in the formula 'I am the $\sigma\hat{\eta}\mu a$ of X'.[21]

The presence of so many inscriptions in different communal contexts has led to scholarly debate over whether or not inscriptions were read by the public, especially in the scholarship of Hellenistic and archaic epigrams.[22] Despite epigrams themselves consistently speaking directly to an imagined audience, often conceived of as passing by through chance, Peter Bing has argued that very little evidence exists for any public interest in inscriptions and that an audience for this style of poetry appeared only after it developed into a literary genre collected in books during the Hellenistic period.[23] This position overlooks that some impetus for these collections must have existed in the first place. Literary authors, moreover, have good reason to downplay the efficacy of physical monuments: a text's ability to travel both geographically and temporally, to assign and preserve context, and to withstand the elements is the very reason writers employ to claim that their medium is superior in the preservation of fame.

Bing's position is further undermined by the design of inscribed epigrams that aims to attract and aid reading, implying that they must have been regularly

---

[16] Cormack (2004, 47) understands the tomb as eroding time, but it in fact bridges temporal disruption and reconfigures time.

[17] Cf. Sourvinou-Inwood 1995, 142.

[18] See Derderian 2001, 3, on graves and the development of writing.   [19] Bettenworth 2007, 69.

[20] Cormack 2004, 123. Cf. Beard 1991, 46, on votive inscriptions.

[21] Sourvinou-Inwood 1995, 147, 279–80. Cf. Day 1989, 16–17.

[22] On Graeco-Roman literacy more generally, see Harris 1989; Humphrey 1991; Bowman and Woolf 1994; Johnson and Parker 2009; Bagnall 2011.

[23] Bing 2002, 40–2.

read.[24] Inscriptions in the imperial period, in particular, were specifically crafted to enhance visual comprehension, even by the illiterate, through their positioning and other motifs capable of shaping meaning.[25] Such aids to understanding included physical hierarchies of language;[26] the repetitive, conventional, and abbreviated units of Latin inscriptions that came to be adopted in the Greek;[27] the close relation of architectural inscription and statuary (itself formulaic) that aided identification of the individuals involved;[28] the use of interpuncts, indentations, and vine leaves or other elements to highlight sections, break up the text, and create language patterns.

The object on which the text is inscribed, moreover, helps to direct understanding: the form of a tomb and its location in a cemetery announces that writing upon it will be epitaphic; a statue in a public place will bear an honorific statement.[29] High levels of illiteracy would not necessarily impede the size of an inscription's audience either, since if only one person amongst those gathered around a monument were capable of deciphering the words, s/he may well read it to the rest.[30] This is surely pointed to by the metaphor of the stone's voice, present in so many epitaphs, the efficacy of which depends on 'people [...] accustomed in reading stones aloud'.[31]

Even though a monument is aesthetically pleasing, however, and its inscription is set out in a manner that encourages and assists comprehension, it still may not succeed in attracting readers, even should a passer-by show interest in the monument itself. Plutarch's *On Oracles at Delphi* 395a–b gives just such a scenario, which has been taken as evidence of both interest in inscriptions—in that it describes the typical spiel given by Delphi's trained guides that included a description and explanation of many of the inscriptions—and disinterest—in that the learned audience on this particular occasion requests they skip over this material.[32]

---

[24] Day 2010, 31.

[25] Graham 2013, 386–7. Cf. Thomas 2007, 12. On inscriptions as visual media, see Eastmond 2015; Leatherbury 2017; Cooley 2018.

[26] E.g.: was Latin placed above Greek; were the Latin letters larger; which name came first; was one or the other language placed on a protruding architectural member that caught the light throughout the day versus being confined to a shadowy recess; were the letters painted red or appended in bronze?

[27] Graham 2013. See 408–9 on the changes in Greek inscriptions and the impact of Latin formatting. Cf. Woolf (1996, 28), who cites RIP and QED as modern analogues; the latter, however, would be quite challenging for the illiterate and is never inscribed publicly. On the readability of public inscriptions (including for the illiterate), see also Thomas 1992, 65–100; Bodel 2001, 15–3.

[28] Graham 2013, 388, also cites the reinforcement of images on coins.

[29] See Cormack 2004, 143–6, on tombs. Cf. Cooley 2000, 8–9, on a viewer needing to understand a monument's overall purpose in order to understand its inscription visually.

[30] See Day 2010, 17, 23, 26–75, on this practice. Cf. van Nijf 2000, 23; Graham 2013, 386–8.

[31] Chaniotis 2012, 301.

[32] Bing (2002, 61) uses this section as evidence for reader apathy towards inscriptions, whereas Day (2010, 44) uses it to show that, at major religious sites, the explication of inscriptions was important. On this

These same tourists then discuss at some length the colour of the bronze Nauarchs' statues on the Spartan dedication celebrating victory over the Athenians at Aegospotami in 405 BC. Here, an audience of *pepaideumenoi* does pay more attention to the aesthetics of a monument than to its inscriptional accompaniment. This is a choice, however, based on the present topic of conversation within the dialogue and the fact that the learned viewers—completely capable of reading the inscription—already understood the significance of what they were seeing. Instead, it is evidence that a range of possible engagements with epigraphy existed alongside sets of viewers with varying interpretative proficiency, the less competent of whom still had open to them avenues leading to understanding.

Even if no correlation existed between the increase in the number of civic inscriptions produced during the early empire and the number of people actively reading them, there was a clear growth in individual desire to construct a personalized inscribed monument in public space.[33] Imperial Greek literature certainly evinces a fascination with such monuments and the fragility of monumental meaning in the face of authorial literary design allows the creation of new interpretations. These cultural, social, and literary influences attached to inscriptions and monuments pervade the consciousness of imperial Greek authors, who use public engagement with inscriptions to manipulate them for their own purposes. I turn now to two quite different examples of imperial Greek authors engaging with the contemporary epitaphic habit to exploit the tension between text, monument, speech, and meaning with the goal of shaping and controlling individual commemoration.

In his *Lives of the Sophists*, Philostratos relates an anecdote about the death of Polemon (*VS* 1.25.543–4) in which voice and inscription, body and tomb compete. In the story, Polemon is ironically left with a voice but no body, the direct result of which is that the current whereabouts of his tomb are a mystery.[34] Although Philostratos associates Polemon with Smyrna throughout his 'Life', he denies that city his tomb (τάφος), while acknowledging that several burial places there are said to belong to him (*VS* 1.25.543).[35] He then proceeds to list the various false tombs, the majority of which are marked by statues of the man.

---

text as representing Delphi as a site of Greek memory, see Jacquemin 1991. See Witschel 2014, 114–24, on how visitors of varying literacy, social rank, and epigraphic/monumental interest to the forum might interact with inscribed monuments.

[33] See Graham 2013, 387; Zuiderhoek 2009.

[34] On Philostratos' presentation of Polemon in general, see Campanile 1999.

[35] Tombs reputed to belong to great men or gods are a *topos*. The tomb of Ramesses VI and the temple of Amenophis III were both said to be tombs of Memnon; see Gardner 1961, 97. For the tomb of Zeus on Crete, see Cook 1925, 940–3; 1940, 1173. Homer was also said to have a tomb on Ios. In Philostratos' *VA* 8.31.3, Apollonios is denied a known extant tomb.

Finally, Philostratos places the tomb in Laodikeia where Polemon's ancestors were buried, but states that this version is only 'truer' ($\dot{a}\lambda\eta\theta\acute{\epsilon}\sigma\tau\epsilon\rho a$) than the others, not definitive.[36] This uncertainty is odd given the centrality of tombs in the creation of personal commemoration, the contemporary and posthumous fame which Philostratos assigns to Polemon (he is second only to Herodes Attikos in the *VS*), and the expectation that a grave of a prominent individual should be marked by a fitting inscription.

Philostratos' focus on the confusion over Polemon's tomb makes sense in the context of the manner of his burial, in that he was interred while still living and speaking, thus removing the requirement for an inscribed $\sigma\hat{\eta}\mu a$. Polemon suffered severe arthritis and decided to be buried alive to starve to death instead of continuing to suffer (*VS* 1.25.543–4).[37] Philostratos places two statements in the dying man's mouth, supposedly cried out as he was already 'inside the tomb' ($\dot{\epsilon}\nu\ \tau\hat{\omega}\ \sigma\acute{\eta}\mu a\tau\iota$) and it was being sealed, which defy the usual rituals of burial: 'Close it ($\ddot{\epsilon}\pi a\gamma\epsilon$)! Close it ($\ddot{\epsilon}\pi a\gamma\epsilon$)! Never shall the sun see me silent ($\sigma\iota\omega\pi\hat{\omega}\nu\tau a$)', and 'Give me a body and I will declaim ($\delta\acute{o}\tau\epsilon\ \mu o\iota\ \sigma\hat{\omega}\mu a\ \kappa a\grave{\iota}\ \mu\epsilon\lambda\epsilon\tau\acute{\eta}\sigma o\mu a\iota$)!' (*VS* 1.25.544).[38] These statements and, indeed, the live burial subtract the body—the lifeless thing that usually stands in as the $\sigma\hat{\eta}\mu a$ of the man until it is replaced by the grave monument—from the equation. Polemon thus presents himself to the mourners as a disembodied voice. In this respect, it is the tomb itself that speaks with the voice of the (not yet) dead and it is this voice that we hear, rather than those of the living reading the epitaphic inscription. The $\sigma\hat{\eta}\mu a$ cannot perform its metonymic function if its inhabitant still lives. Polemon's two commands are thus at odds, since he wishes to be interred while still speaking, yet requires a body in order to declaim. In effect, he illustrates his liminal position as not fully alive and not quite dead: he can still speak but can no longer use his voice in its usual social function, that of epideictic oratory. Moreover, the detail that all but one false Smyrnaean tomb are marked by a statue of Polemon—another stand-in for the living/dead man—only draws attention to the lack of a body in Laodikeia.[39]

Having the tomb speak is precisely the aim of grave inscriptions, even though their sentiments are eternally repetitive and usually composed post-mortem by the

---

[36] Compare Philostratos' *VA* 8.30–1, in which he lists numerous potential places of death for Apollonios, but knows of no tomb, only a shrine in Tyana. See Elsner 1997.

[37] Campanile (1999, 306) interprets this as self-sacrifice for the ideal of rhetoric.

[38] Rife (2009, 119 n. 65), following Civiletti (2002, 501–2 n. 92), suggests that $\ddot{\epsilon}\pi a\gamma\epsilon$ here means 'Close it!' instead of the usual translation of 'Quickly', from the sense of 'laying on', 'applying' or 'putting' of $\dot{\epsilon}\pi\acute{a}\gamma\omega$. See *LSJ* s.v. $\dot{\epsilon}\pi\acute{a}\gamma\omega$ 7. This is apt, given Polemon was not expecting to die imminently. See Campanile 1999, 306, for the theatricality of this event.

[39] For a discussion of each of Polemon's potential tombs and the function of funerary statues, see Rife 2009, 119–26. Philostratos' phrasing here is particularly interesting, in that he speaks of the body specifically lying under the statue(s) ($\dot{v}\varphi'\ \hat{\omega}\ [\dot{a}\gamma\acute{a}\lambda\mu a\tau\iota]$ and $\dot{v}\pi\grave{o}\ \tau o\hat{\iota}\varsigma\ \chi a\lambda\kappa o\hat{\iota}\varsigma\ \dot{a}\nu\delta\rho\iota\hat{a}\sigma\iota\nu$, *VS* 1.25.543), as though the statue is rooted to the remains of the man.

living.[40] Funerary epigrams are inherently performative, moreover, because they both preserve performed speech in stone and, when read aloud, re-enact that original performance and recall both the individual for whom they speak and the rites of burial.[41] Importantly, the inscribed stone must borrow a living voice to communicate, and its otherwise mute nature mocks its claims to speak for the dead amongst the living.[42] Philostratos' tale of Polemon's live burial pokes fun at the idea of the talking grave and, by extension, the sophistic quest for κλέος ἄφθιτον ('immortal fame'), since graves which permit their inhabitants to continue speaking with their own voice are the stuff of heroic myth.[43]

Elsewhere in the *Lives*, Polemon has been established as a character who sees his profession as the natural inheritor of heroic effort.[44] One anecdote, for example, reveals just how closely Polemon considers the disciplines of epideictic oratory and physical combat to be aligned, as he quips at a gladiator about to do battle and sweating with fear: 'you are in as great an agony as though you were about to declaim' (*VS* 1.25.541).[45] Speaking was an essential quality of the Homeric hero, as exemplified by Odysseus and as explained by Phoenix at *Iliad* 9.438–43; in his downtime from battle, even Achilles entertained himself with songs of 'the great deeds of men' (κλέα ἀνδρῶν, *Il.* 9.189).[46] Nevertheless, a hero's deeds rather than words define him and it is telling that, of the many who tried, only Herakles, whose greatness lay purely in his physical prowess, achieved immortality and then only in some versions of his story.

In this context, the comparison of epideictic speech to heroic exploit belittles the former and undermines sophistic claims to immortality via rhetoric. This is clearly shown by Polemon's living burial parodying the process of apotheosis.[47] It is driven home further by the ultimately anonymous fate of the sophist's tomb and yet another Philostratean anecdote. In the latter, Antoninus Pius rejects a replacement rhetor for the dead Polemon on an embassy, but accepts a speech of his delivered by another, which leads the Smyrnaeans to claim he had come back to

---

[40] See Chaniotis 2012, 300.

[41] See Day 2000, 37–57. Cf. Day 2007, 32, 37. Cf. Chaniotis 2012, 307–9.

[42] Cf. Bing 2002, 48–52; Svenbro 1993, 47. See also Thomas 1992, 61–5, on inscriptions on inanimate objects giving them a voice. See Chaniotis 2012, 300–2, on the epitaph creating the *illusion* of communication between living and dead.

[43] E.g. Achilles' ghost at his tomb in Eur. *Hec.* 109–15, Philostr. *VA* 4.11–16, Ov. *Met.* 13.441–50.

[44] On the sophists as modern Homeric heroes, striving for supremacy in both words and deeds, see Coté 2010, 475–502.

[45] Skopelian is another of Philostratos' sophists with heroic characteristics; see *VS* 1.21.519 (oratory as combat); *VS* 1.21.516 (fantastic birth).

[46] On this, see Coté 2010, paragraphs 34–42.

[47] Campanile (1999, 307) draws a parallel with Christian martyr narrative, but the concept of apotheosis is more immediate within the context of the *VS*.

life (ἀναβεβιωκέναι) to aid them (*VS* 1.25.540).[48] Here, Polemon does declaim with another's body and his words transcend his own passing. In this respect, Philostratos' representation of Polemon has him outdoing Horace since his words do not stand as a memorial to him, but rather he is cast in an almost god-like mould, supplying the members of the Smyrnaean embassy with inspiration as though he were a muse. Philostratos' anecdote achieves a form of apotheosis for Polemon, but it also places him in the role of a past great to be emulated and performed by others, essentially displacing him temporally to be associated with the canonical writers of the classical period. The body he invokes as needing in order to declaim thus turns out to be his corpus of literature.[49] Intriguingly, it is a Roman emperor who puts him in this position by forcing the Smyrnaean delegation to be ventriloquized by Polemon. Antoninus here plays with the cultural capital in which imperial Greeks are so invested for his own entertainment, and his request reduces Polemon to a cultural artefact of sorts, making him more quaint than immortal.

That Polemon's grave later lacks adequate identification, despite his tomb's initial ability to speak with his voice, highlights the plight of speech vis-à-vis text and of a monument without an inscription. Polemon's Philostratean death, moreover, is illustrative of the sophistic dilemma:[50] one's contemporary fame is all about the ability to speak off the cuff, but one's future fame depends on leaving evidence of that speech behind in textual form or in a monumental commemoration of greatness. In seeking to never stop speaking, Polemon thus denies his grave its own future voice in the form of an inscription to speak on his behalf to (and through) future generations. By committing to the spoken word, Polemon fails to leave a lasting mark, underscoring his inability to control his reputation once dead.

The proximity of the phrasing used in describing Polemon's interment (ἐν τῷ σήματι) and his demand for a body (δότε μοι σῶμα) alludes to the Pythagorean and Orphic dictum σῶμα σῆμα, in which the body is considered the tomb of the soul, and invites the reader to make the substitution. If this were to occur, Polemon's command regarding declamation would be: 'Give me a tomb (σῆμα) and I will

---

[48] On this episode, see Rife 2009, 126, who connects it to the earlier scene in which Polemon replaced the aged Skopelian on a similar embassy. Rife notes that Polemon's words (δότε μοι σῶμα καὶ μελετήσομαι) recall Patroklos' to Achilles (δὸς δέ μοι ὤμοιιν τὰ σὰ τεύχεα θωρηχθῆναι|αἴ κ' ἐμὲ σοὶ ἴσκοντες ἀπόσχωνται πολέμοιο|Τρῶες, *Il.* 16.40–2), words Polemon did quote when he took Skopelian's position. Once again, this indicates Polemon's belief in the heroic nature of his profession. Cf. Campanile 1999, 310–11, who notes that Polemon's demand for a body parallels the well-known saying of Archimedes, 'Give me a place to stand and I will move the earth' (δός μοι ποῦ στῶ καὶ κινῶ τὴν γῆν).

[49] Cf. Campanile 1999, 313. Note that she implies the 'body' is Polemon himself, resurrected by Antoninus' will, but I read her discussion to suggest *corpus* of literature.

[50] See Strazdins 2008.

THE EPITAPHIC HABIT 133

declaim!'[51] Not only does this point to Polemon's 'unorthodox role as funeral orator at his own tomb',[52] but also to the intense ambivalence of imperial Greek writers towards the potential of lasting commemoration, which is distant from either Pindar's or Horace's claims to certain literary immortality. If given a tomb, as he has been, Polemon will in fact fall into silence and, at least on the level of possessing a definitive funerary monument, into obscurity. Yet at the same time Philostratos' biography has preserved several tombs for him, and here the text proves more effective than the monument itself.

Nevertheless, in the sophistic world presented by Philostratos, commitment to the written word is never complete, making text of any description, including epigraphy, problematic. The difficulty of self-memorialization for exponents of improvised *epideixis* was a very real problem, and the challenge to make a speech transcend the performative moment was ever present. Philostratos no doubt exaggerates the extent of the tension between the written and spoken word, but the issue does feature in other authors too, as Aelius Aristeides explains in his *Sacred Tales*. In the following dream, Aristeides perceives a treatment he must shortly undergo, which he then explains to two doctors who appear as his internal audience within the vision. While awaiting the right moment to begin the treatment, one doctor requests some entertainment:

'Why then,' said the doctor, 'did you not declaim for us in the meantime?' 'Because, by Zeus,' I said, 'it is more important (σπουδαιότερον) for me to revise some things which I have written (τινα τῶν γεγραμμένων), for I must also converse with men of later times (τοῖς ὕστερον ἀνθρώποις διαλέγεσθαι)'. And at the same time I indicated that I was pressing myself (ἐπειγοίμην), in case something should happen first. And he augured many years for me. And I said, 'I would wish to live many years if I am destined to be engaged in words (εἰ μέλλοιμι ἔσεσθαι πρὸς λόγοις).'[53]   (*HL* 5.52)

Here Aristeides privileges written text over oral declamation, sees his legacy lying in the written word, and admits he is driven by the fear of dying before he can achieve literary immortality. For Aristeides, the conflict between speech and writing that we see in Philostratos' portrait of Polemon does not exist to the same extent, even though he does feel public, social pressure to declaim and even writes a speech in his own defence, *Against Those Who Criticize Him Because He*

---

[51] See Pl. *Cra.* 400b–c, *Grg.* 493a, with Ewegen 2014, 125–44, especially 130. See Rife 2009, 126, on σῶμα σῆμα and Polemon's epigrammatic phrasing. See Cormack 2004, 124–7, on the tomb as an inviolable house of the dead body in Asia Minor. Note also that the play on σῶμα σῆμα, combined with Polemon's various tombs and his regular conflation of rhetorical and martial brilliance, may well be an allusion to Alexander's tomb in Alexandria, known as the '*Sḗma*' or '*Sṓma*' (see further below on the tomb of Achilles).

[52] Rife 2009, 126.

[53] Translations adapted from Behr 1981. Note that *HL* 5.52 = *Oration* 51.52. *HL* 1 = *Oration* 47; *HL* 2 = *Oration* 48; *HL* 3 = *Oration* 49; *HL* 4 = *Oration* 50; *HL* 5 = *Oration* 51; *HL* 6 = *Oration* 52.

134 FASHIONING THE FUTURE IN ROMAN GREECE

Does Not Declaim (*Or.* 33). Rather, he conceives of the two arts working together, with speaking being more immediate and writing taking that immediacy and preserving it for posterity. Writing for Aristeides is thus simply a greater commemorative investment, and it is the idea of self-commemoration through physical monumentalization that instead sits uncomfortably with his outlook. This can be seen particularly in his dreams, in which monuments regularly appear as inappropriate for a man who wields words.

In one such dream Aristeides is first given the honour of being crowned by a 'public gathering' (σύλλογος δημοτελής) before the hearth of Olympian Zeus 'because of his speeches' (λόγων ἕνεκα) and because 'he is invincible in oratory' (ἔστιν ἀήττητος περὶ λόγους, *HL* 4.48). Where this hearth is exactly is difficult to determine due to the disorienting conflation of reality and dream in this section of the text. Just prior to this vision, Aristeides had made a votive offering to Olympian Zeus in the temple of Zeus Asklepios at Pergamon, so this could be the intended setting. The act of crowning, however, invokes Olympia and its games, thus tapping once more into the common metaphor of athletics for the exertions and glory of oratory. The hearth here is called 'also ancestral' (καὶ πατρῴου), which in combination with the public ceremony, as though at an 'assembly' (ἐκκλησία), and the involvement of the 'sacred herald' (κήρυκα ἱερόν) situates the vision simultaneously on Aristeides' estate and at the panhellenic sanctuary via dream superimposition. Aristeides' technique here is comparable to Arrian's efforts of translating Mt Theches to Trapezous in the *Periplous*, but Aristeides' landscapes do not entirely merge into a single concrete space.[54]

Still within the vision, Aristeides then wanders over to the garden of Asklepios in front of his ancestral home and, to the right of the temple, he discovers a common tomb for himself and Alexander the Great. This enormously pleases Aristeides due to its import for his chosen career:

I rejoiced and interpreted that we both had reached the peak (τὸ ἄκρον), he in military and I in oratorical might (ὁ μὲν τῆς ἐν τοῖς ὅπλοις δυνάμεως, ἐγὼ δὲ τῆς ἐπὶ τοῖς λόγοις). And besides, it also occurred to me, that this man was very important in Pella, and that those here would be proud of me. I thought that I heard (ἀκοῦσαι) and saw (ἰδεῖν) such things, and that I spoke to myself (πρὸς ἐμαυτὸν εἰπεῖν) and calculated some of these things by the statue of Zeus, and some in the temple of Asklepios before my house. (*HL* 4.49)

Here, Aristeides' fame and achievement are built into the immortal dreamscape that mirrors and overlays both the landscape of his estate and a public sanctuary central to Greek identity. The familiar markers of the hearth and statue of Zeus, the temple of Asklepios, and Aristeides' house serve to give substance to the dream vision, in which his public honour before the assembly is replicated in

---

[54] See Section 2.2.

his private appropriation of Alexander's body and tomb. Possession of the Makedonian's body is an assertion of inheritance: the space reserved for him to lie eternally beside the greatest of all Greeks and the equal share of tomb assigned to each indicates Aristeides has matched Alexander's achievements. This is an affirmation not only of personal brilliance but also of the genius of Greek cultural production, placing cultural achievement on the level of political and martial supremacy. In light of the Greek east's subservience to Rome, this is a common claim, both sincerely and ironically, in imperial Greek literature. The specific claim to have equalled Alexander's military might with rhetoric is made also by Arrian in his *Anabasis of Alexander* (1.12.5), a text that I will discuss shortly; the desire to achieve this goal may therefore have been a rhetorical commonplace. Aristeides, however, outdoes even Arrian by demonstrating the truth of his claim through the physical evidence of the double tomb.

Like Arrian in the *Periplous* again, Aristeides folds time and space for the purposes of self-promotion to bring the entombed Alexander to his estate/the sanctuary of Zeus at Olympia. Importantly, the double grave is situated between the approving, apparently public, cult statue of Zeus and the private temple of his patron Asklepios. Not only is this association of the greatest of Greeks—Alexander and Aristeides—accepted by the gods, but the 'wondrous scent of incense' (εὐωδίας θαυμαστῆς θυωμάτων, *HL* 4.49) that comes from both Alexander's portion of the tomb and the one awaiting Aristeides hints, by negating any suggestion of corruption, at a god-sanctioned immortality of reputation for both.[55] Moreover, that Aristeides is still alive in the dream world and his half of the grave is empty reflects a kind of living apotheosis that promotes him to outstrip even Alexander's fame.

It is important that Aristeides voices what he sees within the dream ('I seemed [...] to speak to myself', *HL* 4.49) and writes it also on the page. Rehearsing the vision orally itself mirrors the *Sacred Tales*' casting as transcripts of orations.[56] The subsequent narration in writing is a process of solidifying the dream and satisfying Asklepios' votive requirements. Since the dream grave lacks an inscription, Aristeides is able to shape its meaning via this transcription. Given that he fails to occupy the sepulchral space reserved for him, that meaning is clearly that a monumental tomb may be fitting for the deeds of Alexander, but it fails to commemorate properly the words of Aristeides, which keep him alive both in this world and the next.

That Aristeides' greatest successes and the promise of immortal fame occur within his dreams undermines his commemorative vision, since this double grave,

---

[55] See the Iliadic deaths of Sarpedon, Patroklos, and Hektor, and the gods' temporary preservation of their bodies via ambrosia and nektar, both of which emit pleasant scents, with Garcia Jr 2013.

[56] For the *HL* as public performance texts, see Whitmarsh 2004, 441; Petsalis-Diomidis 2010, 124–7.

for example, cannot be visited in reality.[57] Aristeides combats this impression by making others dream of both the treatments for his disease and his oratorical success, so that his dream world becomes a stable realm potentially populated by all sleepers and not just specific to Aristeides himself. Recording his dreams in writing thus enables him to capture his special relationship with the god, its physical effects, promises of eternal glory, and manifestation in his oratorical triumphs witnessed by adoring audiences. So, unlike Polemon, whose performative and declamatory interment symbolizes his lack of a persistent post-mortem literary presence, Aristeides rejects the grave monument for a written legacy.

Neither Polemon's nor Alexander's tombs in the texts considered above had an inscription. This allowed Philostratos and Aristeides to exploit the sophistic tension between text, speech, and monument in order to shape idiosyncratic commemorative messages. Their ability to do so stemmed from their familiarity with the public and sacred inscriptions that surrounded them and their consequent conversance with the physicality and variety of form and substance of the engraved text.[58] This imperial Greek epigraphic awareness leads to experimentation with different modes of textuality in both literature and physical constructions. Real inscriptions were regularly employed for solemn purposes, such as votive dedications, funerary epigrams, or inscribed laws. Their symbolic value, therefore, lends gravitas to virtual inscriptions, whether fictional or genuine.[59] In the section that follows, I will analyse some imperial Greek texts that play off this symbolic value, alongside their epitaphic potential, to deploy textualized inscriptions to enhance commemorative authority. I will also show how some physical inscriptions can utilize the same tradition to reconfigure commemorative landscapes in a very personal way.

4.2 AUTHORITY AND DOMINION: BOUNDARIES AND LIMINA

Inscriptions were regularly employed as boundary markers and therefore assertions of authority and dominion over space. This is true of milestones (*milliaria*) as much as the more definitive boundary stone or *horos*, since milestones included the names of officials and consuls. Claiming space with an inscription could also be far grander. An important imperial example was Augustus' *Res Gestae*, the monumentalized text of which was inscribed on or in the vicinity of temples dedicated

---

[57] See Whitmarsh 2004, 446, on the potential for ironic readings of the text.

[58] On the partnership between object and text in creating meaning, see Beard 1998. See Davies 2005, 284–6, on the materiality of the inscribed surface. See also Zadorojnyi 2013, 366.

[59] Cf. Zadorojnyi 2013, 368.

to the imperial cult in Galatia and, possibly, elsewhere in the eastern empire.[60] Although the text varied slightly in different contexts,[61] these inscriptions were designed as monumental-textual incarnations of Augustus as *princeps*, his legacy, and both his and Rome's relationship to the empire in his own words.[62] Moreover, these inscriptions were self-consciously copies that referenced the original in Rome, the centre of the empire, where the man and his tomb were too.[63] Like a textualized monument, therefore, each copy spread a largely uniform message. As well as publishing the achievements of Augustus in populous centres of the east, the *Res Gestae* inscriptions connected more-distant regions with Rome, and marked the reach of Augustus' (and, by extension, Rome's) power. In chapter 2, we saw a similar process at work in Hadrian's statue and altars that were renovated by Arrian at Trapezous. Moreover, both Hadrian's statue and altars and Augustus' monumental texts tie their accomplishments to Rome and the ideology of empire, and both, given their grounding within the physicality of empire, are tailored equally to contemporary and future audiences.

This practice of physically indicating one's territory and reach is the same process attributed to Alexander the Great in literary sources. He too is represented as marking the landscape he passes through, whether at the extent of his travels with altars and statues, like those by the river Hyphasis, or with altars at points of historical significance, such as either side of the Hellespont to demonstrate his own piety in comparison to Xerxes' hybris.[64] That this tradition existed allowed later authors to add inscriptional elements to Alexander's constructions, thus manipulating the message for their own literary agenda. Moreover, Alexander himself is presented as a monumental interpreter and manipulator, particularly in the *Romance* tradition, and thus acts as an exemplar in this practice for imperial Greek authors.[65] Unlike the overtly imperial ideology present in the monuments of Augustus and Hadrian, the inscriptional efforts attributed to Alexander in literary sources tie his achievements to himself, to the ambitions of the man and his role in creating a new tradition, although his personal commemorative efforts do often convey an imperialistic message. At the same time, Alexander's monuments imprint territory that is often empty and strongly foreign (at least to a

---

[60] See Cooley 2009, 6–18. On the distribution of the *Res Gestae* and the possibility that they may have been instigated internally within Galatia rather than stemming from an imperial programme, see Cooley 2009, 18–22.

[61] Cooley 2009, 19, 22–30.   [62] See Elsner 1996.   [63] Elsner 1996, 38; Cooley 2009, 18.

[64] On the Hyphasis, see Arr. *An.* 5.29.1–2; Diod. 17.95.1–2; Curt. 9.3.19; Plut. *Alex.* 62.7–8; Just. 12.8.16; Strabo 3.5.5. See Bosworth 1995, 356–7, who is convinced of their historicity. On the Hellespont, see *An.* 1.11.6–7; Liotsakis 2019, 175–6; Leon 2021, 58.

[65] See Stoneman 1995; Zadorojnyi 2013, 377–82. For a succinct overview of the development and dating of the *Romance* tradition, see Whitmarsh 2018, 129–33, with bibliography. Leon 2021, 57–60, touches on this by highlighting Alexander's engagement with literary texts.

Greek audience). His lonely memorials at the Hyphasis in particular are designed to set a precedent and are aimed more at eternity than his present sociocultural context.

In addition, Alexander's marking of boundaries or frontiers is symbolically aligned with the mythological heroic traditions of Herakles and Dionysos: Herakles transgressed and defined the boundaries of the known world (e.g. the Pillars of Herakles) in his role as the hero who mediated between the mortal and divine;[66] Dionysos both came from and ventured into the far east, and the myth of his conquest of India appears to have grown out of Alexander's own expedition.[67] Indeed, in Arrian's *Anabasis*, Dionysos and Herakles are both referred to as conquerors of India (4.28.1–5; 5.1.1–2; 6.3.4–5).[68] All these individuals—Alexander, Augustus, Hadrian, Dionysos, Herakles—are united in attempting to employ the power of an inscribed monument to denote dominion and authority over physical, cultural, and/or political space.

In this section, I will analyse examples of inscriptions incorporated into texts as well as physical inscriptions in the landscape which are designed to perform the same functions and which play on the established history, whether real or invented, of these imperial statements of power and ownership to make personal commemorative claims. I begin with an episode in Philostratos' *In Honour of Apollonios of Tyana*, in which Apollonios' engagement with Alexander's altars on the Hyphasis revise their meaning for posterity. I then demonstrate how Lucian plays on the Pillars of Herakles in his *True Stories* to redefine original artistic space. Finally, I show how Herodes Attikos reconfigures commemorative landscapes to enhance his own memory through the use of curse-inscribed herms.

4.2.1 Revising Alexander's Altars in Philostratos' In Honour of Apollonios of Tyana

At the end of book two of the *Apollonios*, the eponymous philosopher and his companion Damis journey into India; when they arrive at the furthest point of Alexander's eastern journey, they happen upon the following:

They came to the Hyphasis. About thirty *stadia* further on they found altars with this inscription: 'To my father Ammon, my brother Herakles, Athena of Forethought, Olympian Zeus, the Kabiri of Samothrace, the Sun of India, and Apollo of Delphi'.

---

[66] Romm 1992, 17–18, 115.

[67] See Whitmarsh 2018, 147. On Alexander, Dionysos, and the east, see Blanshard 2007. See also Stoneman 1995 on the *Alexander Romance*, Dionysos, and Herakles. Strabo (3.5.5) interprets the altars as an emulation of Herakles and Dionysos.

[68] Cf. Plut. *De fort. Rom.* 326b, in which Alexander's desire to go further than Dionysos and Herakles is cited. See also Curt. 8.10.2, 8.11.2, 8.14.11, 9.2.29; Strabo 15.1.6–9.

They say there was also a bronze *stêlê* dedicated there with the engraving, 'Alexander stopped here' (Ἀλέξανδρος ἐνταῦθα ἔστη). We must suppose that the altars were set up by Alexander to honour the limit of his own rule (τὸ τῆς ἑαυτοῦ ἀρχῆς τέρμα τιμῶντος), while it seems to me that the Indians across the Hyphasis dedicated the *stêlê*, presumably in order to highlight that Alexander had advanced no further.[69]   (2.43)

The Hyphasis is traditionally the boundary between the known and the unknown world. Since the travellers arrive at the very spot where Alexander turned back, they are quite literally following in his footsteps.[70] As such, the act of going beyond these altars is loaded. That Apollonios' journey extends further than Alexander's immediately places the sage in competition with the conqueror and it is the wise man who achieves more.[71] The motif of travel is often used to mirror character development in any narrative: Alexander strives to conquer the inhabited world and, in doing so, gain immortality; his journey into India brings him closer to the limits of the earth, but also ironically closer to his death, a notion that is explicitly explained to him by a group of Indian wise men in Arrian's *Anabasis.*[72]

King Alexander, each man is master of just so much of the earth as this on which we stand; and you being a man resembling other men, except that you are full of activity (πολυπράγμων) and presumptuous (ἀτάσθαλος), are roaming over all this earth far from your home, troubled yourself and troubling others (πράγματα ἔχων τε καὶ παρέχων ἄλλοις). But not so long from now (ὀλίγον ὕστερον), having died (ἀποθανὼν), you will govern just so much of the earth as is sufficient to bury your body (ὅσον ἐξαρκεῖ ἐντεθάφθαι τῷ σώματι).[73]

(7.1.6; cf. 7.2.2–4; *Rom.* 3.6)

Once more we see a connection between one's tomb and one's achievements: everything Alexander does in life will ultimately be expressed to posterity only through the form of his grave. In this way, Alexander's absolute mortality is displayed and his attempts to conquer the world come to seem pointless (cf. 7.2.3). In comparison to the Makedonian's quest for glory, Apollonios seeks only wisdom. This wisdom derives from his travels, which allow him both to understand the wonders at the ends of the earth and return to the centre of the

---

[69]   Translations adapted from Jones 2005a.

[70]   See Romm 1992, 116–20, for the immediate change in the narrative of Philostratos once the Hyphasis is crossed to reflect the usual catalogue of wonders present in any description of India.

[71]   See Elsner 1997, 30–1, for the parallelism between Alexander and Apollonios in Philostratos' text. See also Romm 1992, 116–20; Whitmarsh 2012, 464–5. See van Dijk 2009 for parallels between Apollonios and Odysseus.

[72]   On Arrian's foreboding of Alexander's death and critical position towards his excesses, see Bosworth 2007, 447–53. This is also a strong theme of the *Alexander Romance.*

[73]   Note that πολυπράγμων here probably also carries connotations of its secondary meaning of 'inquisitive'.

world to defeat an emperor.[74] This quest to understand the world and probe its limits is partially modelled on the inquisitive and interpretative Alexander of the *Alexander Romance* tradition, whose intellect is regularly applied to inscribed monuments.[75] Knowledge in Philostratos' text, however, gives Apollonios authority and power that is not attached to dominion over a particular place, but which is applicable and available to him anywhere in the empire or beyond. He also contrasts favourably to Plutarch's Alexander, whose philosophic Hellenism is progressively eroded on his journey east.[76] Accordingly, Apollonios' achievement in surpassing Alexander is a triumph for philosophy over military might and statesmanship, and ultimately allows the wise man to transcend death (*VA* 8.30), the very goal Alexander desired but failed to achieve.

In Philostratos' tale, Apollonios' supremacy is confirmed by others' spontaneous expressions of awe or acknowledgement of quasi-divinity, such as the people of Tyana believing him to be the son of Zeus (*VA* 1.6) and all Greece gathering at Olympia to see him after his trial before Domitian, where they can barely keep from doing obeisance to him: 'Greece was not far from being disposed to bow down (προσκυνεῖν) to him; they thought him a holy man (θεῖον ἡγούμενοι ἄνδρα) precisely because he never boasted (κόμπον) about his deeds' (*VA* 8.15).[77] Apollonios' disposition is as different from Alexander's as can be and yet he instinctively receives the signs of adulation that Alexander had to coerce from his followers. He, like Aristeides, becomes an object of wonder for countless audiences.[78]

Moreover, the second inscription, the one attributed to the Indians, serves to put Alexander's achievements into a perspective that exceeds the Hellenocentric conception of the audience whom Philostratos is addressing. The simplicity and directness of the three words—Ἀλέξανδρος ἐνταῦθα ἔστη—stand in contrast to the elaborate labelling of Alexander's dedication, which excludes his own name. The implication is that Alexander did not think he needed to specify his name, given his self-positioning in relation to the gods that he does identify: only one man could fulfil the familial connections he claims on the altar. In comparison, the Indians' plaque does use Alexander's name and neglects to mention his divine associations. The single personal identifier is itself a nod to his vast fame and

---

[74] See Elsner 1997, 24.

[75] On the Alexander of the *Romance* as an interpreter of monuments and explorer, see Stoneman 1995; Zadorojnyi 2013, 377–82. Although later additions, *Rom.* 2.41 (Alexander builds an arch to mark the limit of the world, then immediately goes beyond it) and *Rom.* 2.38 (he attempts to explore the seabed) highlight how these qualities become central to his character.

[76] See Whitmarsh 2002.

[77] See Platt 2011, 293–332, on the viewing of sacred images in the *VA* leading to wisdom. See especially 331, where she lists instances of Apollonios being treated as though he were divine, all of which correspond to characteristics ascribed to Alexander.

[78] Cf. Elsner 1995, 27, on Apollonios as an object of pilgrimage.

achievement, but it also humanizes him by stripping him of self-invested pseudo-divinity. Thus his ultimate failure is highlighted over his successes.

In this respect, the Indian bronze *stêlê* stands as an epitaph to the Makedonian and ἐνταῦθα recalls the common funerary variant ἐνθάδε. It thus portends that Alexander's death stems from this very moment of enforced retreat.[79] Additionally, it manages to do this in the present of Apollonios, since he is the first Greek to see it, so that the prediction occurs simultaneously at Apollonios' advent and in the past at the moment when the bronze *stêlê* was initially set up. This temporal layering is further complicated by Alexander's continuing presence in the landscape via natural features and monuments, such as this *stêlê*, associated with his conquests,[80] so that not only the monuments themselves but also Alexander exist in two temporal frames. Apollonios' crossing of this boundary and leaving it behind, however, forces Alexander indelibly into the past. It is at this moment that both Alexander's and the Indians' inscriptions fail in their purpose. Once the sage passes the Makedonian's altars, they no longer designate the easternmost progress of Greek knowledge and culture. Once he goes beyond the Indian plaque, he defies its warning to those Greeks, written as it is in Greek lettering, who might wish to outdo Alexander, and he breaches both the boundary of the known and unknown, as well as that which had divided western Greek and eastern Indian knowledge.

The dominion and authority claimed by both inscriptions are thus rendered empty rhetoric and Apollonios is promoted in contrast as a superior contemporary paradigm, whose investment in wisdom allows him to navigate India more successfully than Alexander and to prevail against the might of Rome. Philostratos, too, as his biographer and explicator, lays claim to a portion of his fame and achievement. This role of outdoing illustrious models and concurrently showcasing Philostratos' literary triumph is one which Apollonios fulfils throughout Philostratos' text.[81] In this, the text reflects the preoccupations of elite Greek authors, who champion the priority and continuity of Greek culture in the Roman world and is complementary to Aristeides' vision of sharing a common grave with Alexander, which he evades occupying (discussed above).

This is a lot to read into two textualized inscriptions, yet there is a palpable depth of meaning to them despite their brevity, since the significance of a single wise man and his companion going beyond the apogee of Alexander the Great's conquests would readily strike any *pepaideumenos* in the early centuries of the common era, given the weight applied by Greeks and Romans to the Alexander

---

[79] Note that Alexander's death is portended in most historical accounts, but is more closely tied to his return to Babylon (e.g., Plut. *Alex.* 73–7; Arr. *An.* 7.24–8; Justin 12.13.3–10). In the *Romance*, however, his death is regularly pointed to throughout his campaigns and especially in India.
[80] See Elsner 1995, 30 n. 49, for these features.   [81] See Platt 2011, 295.

legend. What is striking in this case is how the process is tied to monumental writing in a historically meaningful spatial context, and how Apollonios' journey uses the paradigm of Alexander's own experiences with ancient monuments in both the historical and *Romance* traditions to surpass him. Philostratos (via Apollonios) thus overwrites Alexander, reconfiguring space, time, and the historical narrative that ties the two phenomena together. More than this, he overwrites an inscribed ὅρος ('boundary marker') in such a way that its commemorative force becomes epitaphic.

4.2.2 Transposing the Pillars of Herakles in Lucian's True Stories

Lucian's *True Stories* again taps into the Alexander tradition of marking space but, in contrast, uses the idea of a boundary marker determining the known world to weigh the dangers and benefits of artistic originality, for which Alexander's seemingly unstoppable march into the unknown is the perfect historical analogue.[82] Two discrete yet allusively connected monuments serve this purpose. The first appears at the text's beginning. After the narrator explains that his narrative is a lie and motivated by a desire to leave something for posterity (1.4), he sails off with his crew from the Pillars of Herakles (1.5: ἀπὸ Ἡρακλείων στηλῶν).[83] These are generally identified with the rocks on either side of the straits of Gibraltar, where they mark the western-most point of the known world in the antique imagination and form the gateway to Ocean.[84] Their precise position and form (rocks, bronze *stélai*), however, is not set, with Strabo detailing their march westwards as the known world expanded (3.5.5).[85] Shortly after crossing this boundary, the narrator's ship is thrown off course by a lengthy storm, reminiscent of that which takes Odysseus and his crew into the unknown (*Od.* 9.67–83).[86] Then, at the first place they visit, they discover the following:

We had advanced from the sea through the woods about three stades, when we saw a *stélê* of wrought bronze, inscribed with Greek letters (Ἑλληνικοῖς γράμμασιν), but faint (ἀμυδροῖς) and worn (ἐκτετριμμένοις), that said: 'To this point came Herakles and Dionysos'. Not far off were two footprints on rock; one very large, the other smaller; it seemed to me the smaller was from Dionysos, the other from Herakles. We did obeisance (προσκυνήσαντες) and went on.   (*VS* 1.7)

---

[82] On the parallels between the *VH* and the Alexander tradition, see Aerts 1994.

[83] On the complexity and playfulness of this preface and how it works against the expectations of historical works, see ní Mheallaigh 2014, 159–60; 2009, 11–13. See McIver 2016 for Lucian's play with Socratic, Homeric, and Odyssean truths in the *True Stories*. See also Romm 1992, 211–14; Whitmarsh 2006a, 114; Kim 2010, 142; von Möllendorf 2014, 529–30.

[84] Romm 1992, 17, 147.

[85] In the *Alexander Romance*, the pillars exist in the east. See Stoneman 1995, 162–3

[86] See McIver 2016, 243, for how Lucian's preface parallels Odysseus' introduction to the tale of his wanderings in *Odyssey* 9; Kim 2010, 142–3.

If the Pillars of Herakles designate the extent of the known mortal world, this bronze pillar and associated footprints mark the limits of mythic travel by the greatest of heroes in Herakles and the 'least' of the twelve Olympians in Dionysos.[87] This *stêlê* thus supersedes the established *stêlai* of Herakles. Ostensibly, it serves the same purpose as the inscriptions set up by Alexander and the Indians in Philostratos' *Apollonios*—it is celebratory, a challenge, and a warning. Like Alexander's altars, the pillar evinces the achievement of Herakles and Dionysos in reaching this point and, at the same time, sets itself up as a deed that is possible to surpass, simply by going that little bit further. In this, it is significant that Lucian places this boundary at the very beginning of his story.[88] It serves to announce just how 'far out' this adventure will be and how little it will resemble any other traveller's tale that has come before, simply because it is situated in a world outside the literary record.[89] Equally, it presents a cautionary marker, since it emphasizes that no mortal has traversed this spot, much as the Indians' plaque warned that no Greek had gone beyond the Hyphasis. In literary terms, it highlights the risks of novelty and blazing a trail into new literary territory.[90] Venturing into unknown lands empty of one's fellow man is a lonely and unpopular enterprise—one's works require an audience after all.

Alexander is alluded to in the travellers' act of *proskynêsis* ('bowing down') and in the narrator's ability to interpret the monument, a quality strongly associated with the Makedonian in the *Romance* tradition.[91] That the inscription is again based on those attributed to Alexander, combined with the imprints of Herakles' and Dionysos' feet—the marking of the land itself with their physical presence—ground the story in reality and give authority to the invented tale through the support of material artefacts, all the while luxuriating in its fictional nature (*VH* 1.4).[92]

---

[87] On this passage and the associations of Dionysos and Herakles, see Georgiadou and Larmour 1998, 70–5.

[88] ní Mheallaigh 2014, 181, makes a similar point, reached independently.

[89] Cf. ní Mheallaigh 2014, 255.

[90] See ní Mheallaigh 2009, 13–20, for this episode as dramatizing the desire to engage in literary *mimêsis* of the classical canon and the dangers to originality and authorial authority in doing so. Cf. her richer discussion in 2014, 208–16.

[91] See Stoneman 1995 on Alexander and monuments in the *Romance*.

[92] Cf. Philostr. *Her.* 13.3, on the footprints left by Protesilaos; and Lucian, *A Teacher of Rhetoric* 9, in which a student on the steep, difficult path to *paideia* is shown by his teacher the faint footprints of Demosthenes and Plato, with ní Mheallaigh 2014, 209. See Taylor 2011, 94–7, on the erotic associations of rock-cut graffitied feet and the heightening of this effect when the footprint is combined with a name in the genitive, as both Herakles and Dionysos are on the pillar. If Lucian is playing on this association, the different sizes of the footprints may jokingly imply a pederastic relationship between Herakles (as the *erastês*) and Dionysos (as the *erômenos*). Cf. Levine 2005, 62–3. Note that Langdon (1985, 268–9) unconvincingly interprets the footprints that Levine and Taylor cite as erotic as simply commemorative (i.e. 'I was here'). See ní Mheallaigh 2014, 159–60, on Lucian's gleeful framing of his true lies.

At the same time, the frame of autopsy serves to mock the extravagant and fanciful claims of genuine historiography and geography.[93]

If following the paradigm of the *Odyssey*, the storm that brings the travellers to this monumental beginning signals the intervention of a hostile god. In the case of the narrator and his companions, however, who go where gods and heroes feared to tread, the agency in this story is very much human. That the lettering on the bronze pillar is faint and worn, moreover, highlights its antiquity as well as stressing that the travellers' advent has made even Dionysos and Herakles' exploratory efforts passé.[94] At some point, only the footprints will be left without the supplementation of the inscription and, much like the tomb/turning post indicated by Nestor in the *Iliad*, no one will remember their significance. Moreover, like the paired inscriptions in the *Apollonios*, there is an epitaphic quality to such boundary markers: to leave one's mark in this way is to become part of the past; the footprints run out and the writing fades. Lucian again uses this metaphor to highlight the risk of new cultural production. Even if one does make a splash in the present, time is fickle and one's ability to withstand the judgement of posterity is ever fragile and uncertain.

This same ambivalence to literary longevity is expressed in another inscribed monument that appears much later in the text:

Λουκιανὸς τάδε πάντα φίλος μακάρεσσι θεοῖσιν
εἶδέ τε καὶ πάλιν ἦλθε φίλην ἐς πατρίδα γαῖαν

Lucian, dear to the blessed gods, saw all these things
and back again he went to his beloved homeland.   (*VH* 2.28)

This epigram is composed by Homer and inscribed by the narrator himself near the harbour of the Isle of the Blessed on a pillar of beryl, the same substance from which the house of the gods is also constructed. This occurs close to the end of the second book after Lucian has spent some time cavorting on the island populated, as Lawrence Kim notes, solely by illustrious figures from the Greek literary canon, either authors or characters.[95] Lucian asks Homer to compose the epigram to commemorate his visit to this canonical realm. He has therefore learnt the importance of physically memorializing achievement from the practice of Dionysos and Herakles at the beginning of book one.

This inscribed *stêlê* recalls the golden pillar of Euhemeros' story of the island of Panchaia, which was engraved with the deeds of Ouranos, Chronos, and Zeus, whom Euhemeros identified as great men of the past rather than immortal gods

---

[93] See Georgiadou and Larmour 1998, 28–40, on the *VH*'s relationship to historiography and storytelling.

[94] Cf. ní Mheallaigh 2014, 255.   [95] Kim 2010, 157–8, 162.

(Diod. 6.1.4–10).[96] If Lucian is alluding to Euhemeros, he is placing himself in a similar position to these men-cum-gods and highlighting that all the characters on the island, mythic and historical, were once simply men like him who were later aggrandized and mythologized. It is the act of writing them that immortalizes them, and Lucian's self-inscription is a bid to receive similar treatment in the eyes of posterity.

The allusion to Euhemeros concurrently highlights, however, the tradition of Homer's untruthfulness in order to taint the sentiments contained in the epigraph. This is a rare instance in the corpus of Lucian in which he inserts his own name into his writings.[97] Simon Goldhill well describes the layered and theatrical self-sabotage: 'Lucian immortalizes his name […] in a third-rate epigram by a fictionalized and untrustworthy poet on a monument in an unseeable afterlife, recorded in a work which boasts of its own falsehood'.[98]

But exactly how does this epigram fail? For one, it creates a poor parody of the *Odyssey*. Homer places 'Lucian' in the initial position of ἄνδρα ('the man'/ Odysseus) and his own and Odysseus' entire tales are blandly captured in two lines.[99] This not only brings Lucian into the island's literary population by extending the control Homer has over the rest of the island to Lucian's own story,[100] but Lucian's act of personally inscribing Homer's dictation stresses that, in this reality, canonicity is possible only through accepting the inescapable influence of the existing canon. This—the fixing of Lucian's literary life in stone—should render the epigram epitaphic, especially given its placement on the Isle of the Blessed and its inscription on a *stêlê* that alludes to other epitaphic inscriptions. Instead, however, Homer's hexameter verses in place of the expected funereal elegiacs reveal it is rather a snatch of heroic epic. While satisfying Lucian's literary mission to hybridize genres, this also highlights Homer's literary limitations, in his inability to compose in anything other than hexameter. The inscribed pillar is, therefore, a proclamation

[96] On Euhemeros and his account, see Ferguson 1975, 102–10; Holzberg 1996, 621–8; Winiarczyk 2002; P. Christesen, 'Euhemeros of Messene' in *BNJ*.

[97] Goldhill 2002, 64–5. It happens four times, twice in the body of a work, twice the salutation of a letter. On four further occasions the name appears in titles or subtitles.

[98] Goldhill 2002, 65. ní Mheallaigh (2009, 22–3) rightly sees this as ironizing the reader's search for the author in the authorial persona of the text. Cf. ní Mheallaigh 2014, 256–8. See 171–81 for an excellent discussion of Lucian's use of his own and others' names.

[99] McIver (2016, 244–5) notes that Lucian's epigram is specifically modelled on *Od.* 1.82–3.

[100] See Kim 2010, 160–2, 168–72, on the characters condemned to live Homer's construction of them for eternity. Odysseus' letter to Kalypso explaining that he made a mistake in not accepting her offer of immortality has been seen by McIver 2016 as rewriting Homer's epic, but as noted by Kim (2010, 170–2), Odysseus can only express his desire to escape Homer's narrative along with Helen and Thersites without being able to realize it. Kim 2010, 172–3: Lucian 'becomes a "character", like the other heroes, of his own (admittedly brief) Homeric narrative'; cf. McIver 2016, 242–3.

of immortality by a poet whose genius is shown up to be as repetitive and formulaic as the literary lives endured by the island's population.

That Lucian can and does leave the island, thus escaping Homer's influence, signals his rejection of the obligation to seek canonicity through eternal engagement with the canon. The *stêlê* thus finds itself advertising the greatest achievement of all—eluding death—to an eternal captive audience, including Alexander himself and numerous literary luminaries. Thus, no matter how great the accomplishments of the island's canonical figures in life, they are confronted on their arrival with an effort that, unlike the *stêlê* of Herakles and Dionysos, cannot be outdone.[101]

In this respect, Lucian's inscription finds another intertextual counterpart in Kritias' description in Plato's dialogue of that name of a pillar made of *oreichalkinos* within the sanctuary of Poseidon on Atlantis that records the god's laws and the archive of the first princes (119c). *Oreichalkinos* was also one of the main building materials for the temple, just as Lucian's pillar is made from the same material as the house of the gods. This combined with the allusion to Euhemeros' pillar places Lucian on the level of the gods and, more specifically, Poseidon. In this context, the agency behind the Odyssean storm that initiated his 'far out' adventure and brought him to Dionysos and Herakles' pillar is revealed as entirely his own, which in escaping the canon's control can create a space of original artistic production capable of enchanting new audiences.[102] Lucian's *stêlê* thus connects to the *stêlê* of Herakles and Dionysos to redefine the spatial dominance of the Pillars of Herakles yet again, thus marking out a new boundary between known and unknown, canonical imitation, and artistic originality.

What should be a triumphant authorial moment in *True Stories* is nevertheless regularly interpreted in light of the mendacity claimed at the beginning of the work. As Karen ní Mheallaigh explains: 'by inscribing his name into the world of *True Stories*, the author himself comes under erasure, for if the reader is to follow the contract of reading faithfully, (s)he must deny Lucian's existence along with that of all other beings and events in the narrative'.[103] The allusion to Kritias'

---

[101] See Mairs 2011 for the competitive and interactive nature of travellers' cumulative graffiti, which is transferable to the rival inscriptions of Lucian, and Dionysos and Herakles. See also Adams 2007, 215.

[102] Georgiadou and Larmour (1998, 213) perceptively connect the harbour placement of the *stêlê* to the Pharos of Alexandria that stars at the conclusion to Lucian's *How to Write History* (61–3), in which the narrator both encourages authors to reach out to posterity via artistic achievement and urges budding historians to embrace the attitude to posterity demonstrated by Sostratos of Knidos, the lighthouse's architect. According to Lucian's text, Sostratos carved an epigram containing his name and achievement into the structure, covered it with gypsum, then engraved the name of the reigning king on top, knowing that eventually the stucco would fall off to reveal his own. Sostratos' creative act was thus designed to address posterity more so than the present in a way that monumentalizes Longinos' movable temporal perspective.

[103] ní Mheallaigh 2014, 176.

Atlantis via the *stêlê* works in much the same way: it highlights the fictionality of Lucian's tale and unmasks the authority invested in it by an imaginary inscribed stone artefact as false. Lucian's literary inscription therefore destabilizes everything one would normally assume to be concrete about a text, authorial identity, and the medium of inscription. This, however, is precisely the point: literary immortality is not possible in a milieu that regurgitates the past, but the consequences of abandoning the context of that past strips potential audiences of their cultural understanding and is a gamble on the receptivity of an unknown future. Once again, we see intense ambivalence attached to the literary project of self-commemoration, which remains impossible to secure, even at the moment a text seems to solidify literary immortality.

4.2.3 Reshaping Spatial Memory with Herodes' Herms

I turn now to an example that exploits the same associations of inscriptions with authority, dominion, spatial definition, and epitaphic commemoration but this time in the material world, in Herodes Attikos' use of portrait herms inscribed with curses to mark sites of emotional importance to him. Apart from one anomalous inscription found in the sanctuary of Nemesis at Rhamnous, all examples of Herodes' curses were established on his private estates. They have thus been found in the regions around Marathon and Kephisia, and at Loukou in the Peloponnese. An example discovered on Euboia suggests the family also had a villa there.[104] Herodes placed the curses on free-standing portrait herms (15) (e.g. Figures 4.1, 4.2), statue bases (5), reliefs (1) (e.g. Figure 4.3), and *stêlai* or altars (4) (e.g. Figures 4.4, 4.5).[105] Here, I am interested specifically in the portrait herms of his three favoured foster-sons (τρόφιμοι): Polydeukes (always referred to epigraphically by the diminutive Polydeukion), Achilles, and Memnon.[106]

The heroic names of these boys and their scant biographic history has been used to place them among the twenty-four children who, Philostratos reports, were introduced into Herodes' household to help his dim-witted son, Attikos Bradua, learn his letters by each being given a name beginning with one letter of the Greek alphabet (*VS* 2.1.558).[107] The reasons for their presence in the household aside, Herodes became extremely attached to them, so that when all three died young, he mourned them excessively and raised curse-inscribed monuments to them.[108]

---

[104] Tobin 1997, 114; see also Graindor 1930, 115.

[105] Tobin 1997, 114. The *stêlai*, as noted by Tobin, may also be herms, but are too fragmentary to assign to this category with any certainty. On the altar of Regilla (*IG* II² 13200, EM 10317), see Ameling 1983b, 160 no. 147; Guarducci 1978, 230–5, who interprets it as a statue base.

[106] Note that curses also occur on objects dedicated to Regilla.   [107] So, Gazda 1980.

[108] See Tobin 1997, 113–43, for the find spots, descriptions, and transcriptions of twenty-five curse inscriptions set up by Herodes. Cf. Ameling 1983b, 23–9, nos 147–70. For further clarification on the

FIGURE 4.1 Herm of an unidentified individual with curse inscription below the *membrum*. Epigraphic Museum, Athens (EM 10565; *IG* II² 13201).

Vibullus Polydeukion, Herodes' favourite, was a Roman citizen of equestrian rank (*IG* II² 3969; see Figure 6.6 for the inscription and Figure 5.17 for his portrait

inscriptions for which Tobin notes no findspot, see Lenormant 1866, 383 no. 191; 385 no. 199; Lolling 1873; Kastorxis 1882; Graindor 1914, 360–62; 1930, 116 n. 4. Some have vague recorded findspots: Rhamnous, Bey, Kephisia.

THE EPITAPHIC HABIT   149

FIGURE 4.2 Curse-inscribed herm of Achilles. Epigraphic Museum, Athens (EM 12466; *IG* II² 13195). Height: 1.5 m; Width: 0.30 m; Depth: 0.24 m.

FIGURE 4.3 Two fragments of a curse-inscribed heroic relief within a *naiskos* (*IG* II² 13191/3). Archaeological Collection of Kephisia. A youth stands on the left holding the reins of a horse, who raises its right foot, on the right. There is a tree behind the horse. The curse is inscribed in three columns: one to the left of the youth, one between the youth and the horse, the last between the legs of the horse.

FIGURE 4.4 Curse-inscribed herm (unidentified) or *stēlē* from Oinoe. Epigraphic Museum, Athens (EM 12467; *IG* II² 13202). Height: 0.80 m; Width: 0.28 m; Depth: 0.24 m.

FIGURE 4.5 Curse-inscribed altar dedicated to Regilla, 'the light of the house', found in the ruins of a temple-like structure that was converted into a church (Agios Ioannis Theologos). Epigraphic Museum, Athens (EM 10317; *IG* II² 13200). Height: 0.58 m; Width: 0.48 m; Depth: 0.85 m.

bust), but nothing is known of the other two, except that Philostratos tells us Memnon was dark-skinned and designates him as Ethiopian in comparison to a dark-skinned Indian in the *Apollonios of Tyana* (*VA* 3.11; Figure 4.6).[109] The use of the label Ethiopian is most probably intended to indicate exoticness more so than accurate geographic or ethnic origin. It is a way of tapping into the literary tradition of Ethiopians living at the ends of the earth and being closer to the gods than other humans. This stresses Herodes' wealth and reach, demonstrating that he is capable of having a young man with such mythic connotations amongst his retinue.[110]

[109] Graindor 1915b was first to suggest that the portrait head in Berlin belonged to Memnon, and that the dark-skinned 'Menon' of Philostr. *VA* 3.11 was one and the same Memnon. See Figures 5.20 and 5.22 for portraits that have been tentatively proposed for Achilles.

[110] See Allen 2017 for Herodes' inclusion of Memnon in his retinue as an attempt to exceed local identities and shape an imperial identity for himself.

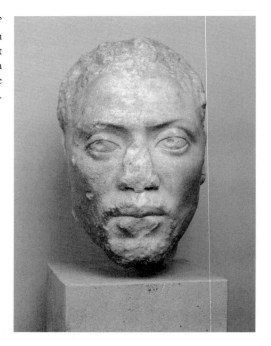

Figure 4.6 Portrait head of Herodes' 'Ethiopian' (Philostr. *VA* 3.11) foster-son Memnon, found at Herodes' Villa at Loukou-Eva Kynouria, probably from a bust or herm. Antikensammlung, Staatliche Museen zu Berlin (Inv. Sk 1503).

As though he were traumatized by his own collecting habit and the cultural vandalism it entailed, on which I will focus in Section 4.4 of this chapter, Herodes' curse inscriptions become more and more explicit about exactly whom they are targeting. An initial dedication is followed by up to three clauses often chiselled in different hands, which points to their inscription occurring at different times. The first clause targets those who will come to own his land in the future, who might wish to move or destroy the monuments and who are threatened with infertile earth, unnavigable seas, and miserable death but who are also promised favours should they take care of the monuments.[111] Another clause, unique to Herodes' curses, follows. It precludes tampering with specific elements: the ἐπιθέματα ('things covering' or 'things on top'), ὑπόστημα ('support' or 'underpinning'), and βάσεις ('bases'). It is unclear to what the first two terms refer. Jennifer Tobin plausibly proposes the head of the statue/herm, a fillet, or a wreath for the ἐπιθέματα and shaft of the herm for the ὑπόστημα.[112] The specificity and singularity of this clause implies Herodes had his own difficulty with vandals. There is little evidence of this on the actual stones, although a herm of Achilles (*IG* II² 3977) that is otherwise without a curse shows a seventeen-line erasure and a heroic relief from Kephisia (Figure 4.3) reveals signs of deliberate damage. Finally,

---

[111] See Tobin 1997, 115, for the text. This is the curse inscription in its most complete form. Cf. *IG* II² 13188; *IG* II² 13192.

[112] Tobin 1997, 116.

a third clause is added, which curses anyone who even influences another to move or destroy the monuments: 'whoever commands ($\pi\rho o\sigma\tau\acute{a}\xi\epsilon\iota\epsilon\nu$) another or governs the intentions ($\gamma\nu\acute{\omega}\mu\eta\varsigma\ \breve{a}\rho\xi\epsilon\iota\epsilon\nu$) or colludes with the intentions ($\gamma\nu\acute{\omega}\mu\eta\ \sigma\upsilon\mu\beta\acute{a}\lambda o\iota\tau o$) [of another] concerning displacing ($\kappa\epsilon\iota\nu\eta\theta\hat{\eta}\nu a\iota$) or demolishing ($\sigma\upsilon\nu\chi\upsilon\theta\hat{\eta}\nu a\iota$) any of these [is cursed]'. Tobin is right to caution against using the presence or lack thereof of specific clauses as indicative of a set chronology, but there is clearly a development in Herodes' cursing practice.[113] This evolution indicates that Herodes was becoming more and more obsessed with safe-guarding the memory of his dead loved ones.

Importantly, the curses are specifically directed at a future audience—those who will come to own his land (e.g. *IG* II² 13195, ll. 1, 3: $\~{o}\sigma\tau\iota\varsigma\ \epsilon\~{\iota}\ \acute{o}\ \breve{\epsilon}\chi\omega\nu\ [\ldots]\ \tau\grave{o}\nu\ \chi\hat{\omega}\rho o\nu$). His cursing practice and growing paranoia should therefore be interpreted as an implicit acknowledgement of the inevitable impermanence of one's commemorative efforts rather than simply a fear of contemporary vandals. It also binds the monuments to the land itself, an effect that is enhanced by the form of the monument. Herms are an especially Attic medium and are regularly used to denote boundaries.[114] Through their connection with the god Hermes, moreover, they were associated with learning and protection (the very benefits Herodes offered his foster-sons). They were also connected to the passage to the underworld, through Hermes Psychopompos, and were regularly used as grave markers and as localized shrines.[115]

The curses intensified these funerary associations, since they were commonplace on tombs in Asia Minor, although Herodes' use of them is almost unique on the Greek mainland.[116] The correlation indicates that he considered these media to be performing the same commemorative function as tombs and he wanted to attach a similar sanctity to his monuments. The notion of the herm as a localized shrine and the effect of the curses binding the memorials to a specific place was exploited by Herodes in the heading or dedicatory inscriptions that identified the individual represented in the portrait and embedded some aspect of their relationship to Herodes in the surrounding landscape.

One such example, dedicated to Polydeukion, comes from Herodes' estate in Kephisia and is now in the Ashmolean Museum in Oxford (Figure 4.7; *IG* II² 13194, ll. 1–4):[117]

---

[113] Tobin 1997, 145–7. Her caution comes in response to Ameling 1983b, 23–5, who uses the form of the curses to create a relative chronology of death for Regilla and the foster-sons.

[114] Tobin (1997, 154–7) succinctly lays out the Attic associations of herms.

[115] Wrede 1986, 42–4; see 55–8 on classical-period herms receiving offerings as localized shrines.

[116] See Tobin 1997, 148–9; Cormack 2004, 146. On funerary curse inscriptions more generally, see Lattimore 1942, 106–25; Robert 1978; Strubbe 1991; Cormack 2004 123–46. Strubbe 1997 catalogues known funerary curse inscriptions.

[117] See Tobin 1997, 121–3. Ameling 1983b, 163 no. 158. On Polydeukion's herms and their association with baths, see Galli 2002, 166–8.

FIGURE 4.7 Curse-inscribed herm of Polydeukion found in a church at Kephisia. Ashmolean Museum, Oxford (AN.Michaelis.177; *IG* II² 13194). Height: 1.43 m; Width: 0.28 m; Depth: 0.23 m.

ἥρως Πολυδευκίων
ταῖσδέ ποτ' ἐν τριό-
δοις σὺν σοὶ ἐπε-
στρεφόμην

Hero Polydeukion,
once, at these cross-
roads with you I used
to wander about.

The heading assigns Polydeukion the status of hero,[118] thus providing an example of a herm as a localized shrine, and embeds Herodes' experiential memories, feelings of loss, and Polydeukion's presence in the region it marks. Another from Varnava near Marathon, this time dedicated to his foster-son Achilles, reads (*IG* II² 3977, ll. 1–12):[119]

Ἡρώδης Ἀχιλλεῖ
ὅς βλέπειν σε ἔχοιμι
καὶ ἐν τούτῳ τῷ
νάπει· αὐτός τε
καὶ εἴ τις γ' ἔτερος,   5
κἀκεῖνοί [γ', ἔ]ση με-
μνημένο[ς τῆ]ς ἡ-
μετέρας φιλίας ὅ-
ση ἡμεῖν ἐγένετο·
ἱερὸν δέ σε Ἑρμοῦ ἐ-   10
φόρου καὶ νομίου
ποιοῦμαι

Herodes to Achilles
So that I may see you
also in this
grove; I myself and
anyone else [who comes here],   5
and to that man at least, you will be
remembered for
our great friendship
that we shared.
Sacred to Hermes,   10
the guardian and shepherd,
I render you.

---

[118] See further Section 5.4.

[119] This herm does not bear a curse, but shows 17 lines of erased text, which was probably a curse clause. See Wilhelm 1933, 168–72; Tobin 1997, 277–8.

156 FASHIONING THE FUTURE IN ROMAN GREECE

This heading ties a specific spot to a broader remembrance of extended emotional experience attached to close friendship and again suggests a continued lingering presence. The notion that people and significant events could live on in specific locales was current. Herodes' younger contemporary Pausanias, for example, tells us that the Marathon plain was haunted by its own heroes: 'at Marathon every night you can hear horses neighing and men fighting' (Paus. 1.32.4).[120] Philostratos, in his *Heroikos*, presents another such spiritual example, in describing the footprints left by the shadowy, reanimated, and immortal Protesilaos, which act as evidence of his reality and the sacredness of the space he occupies for the Phoenician sailor (*Her.* 13.3).[121] The evocation of crossroads in the first herm's inscription heightens the sense of a haunted locale, since crossroads were sacred to both Hekate and Hermes, gods of transition and communication between the worlds of the living and dead.[122] By tapping into these ideas of continued, if ghostly, post-mortem heroic existence and the signs it can leave, Herodes is once more creating a context for the passer-by of how to understand the monument and its function within its surrounds and commemorative tradition.[123] He elevates his personal emotional experiences to a heroic register, even though they are tied to repeated, relatively mundane activities conducted with the boys, such as hunting or eating. For example, a herm from Kato Souli announces (Figure 4.8; *IG* II² 3970; EM 13177):[124]

> Πολυδευ-
> κίωνα, ὃν ἀν-
> θ' υ[ἱ]οῦ ἔστε-
> <ρξ>εν καὶ ἐνθά-
> δε Ἡρώδης <ἀν>-   5
> έθηκεν ὅτι ἐν-
> θάδε καὶ περὶ
> θήραν εἶχον.

> Polydeukion,
> whom, as though he
> were a son,
> Herodes loved. And here
> Herodes set him up   5
> because here also
> they used to hunt.

---

[120] On Marathon as a commemorative landscape, see Galli 2002, 178–9; Jung 2006; 2013, 263–6.

[121] See also Apollonios of Tyana's interview with Achilles at his grave in Philostr. *VA* 4.11–16 with Grossardt 2008.

[122] Johnston 1991.

[123] See Luce 2013 for a discussion of Herodes' herms in the tradition of bucolic poetry.

[124] *SEG* 21.1092; Ameling 1983b, no. 161; Tobin 1997, 130–1.

FIGURE 4.8 Curse-inscribed herm of Polydeukion, Epigraphic Museum, Athens (EM 13177; *IG* II² 3970 + 13190). Height: 1.50 m; Width: 0.28 m; Depth: 0.21 m.

Another herm records, 'here we would eat together and we would all make a libation' ([κ]αὶ ἐνθάδε συνεσιτο[ῦ]- | μεν καὶ συνεπισπένδομεν; Figure 4.1; *IG* II² 13201; EM 10565).[125] The repeated use of ἐνθάδε in these inscribed texts adds to the sepulchral, commemorative character of the herms in its recollection of funerary epigram (ἐνθάδε κεῖται), much like the Indians' plaque noted by Apollonios of Tyana beyond Alexander's altars at the Hyphasis (see Section 4.2.1). The portraits, however, express the eternal potential of reanimation associated with statues and the heading inscriptions provide activities of everyday life carried out again and again, through the use of the imperfect tense and the reactivation provided by every individual reading.[126] Here, it is Herodes himself who attempts to reanimate them by imprinting the dead boys' lives and, indeed, the dead boys alive onto the landscape. This intention is humorously captured by Philostratos' description of Herodes' efforts in raising statues and reliefs to his foster-sons in remote areas that inserts a quality of stop-motion animation into the project: 'so he put up statues

---

[125] Findspot unknown. Ameling 1983b, no. 151; Tobin 1997, 141–2.
[126] On statue animation, see Section 5.5.

(ϵἰκόνας) of them hunting ($\theta\eta\rho\dot\omega\nu\tau\omega\nu$), having hunted ($\tau\epsilon\theta\eta\rho\alpha\kappa\dot\sigma\tau\omega\nu$), and about to hunt ($\theta\eta\rho\alpha\sigma\dot\sigma\nu\tau\omega\nu$)' (*VS* 2.1.558–9).

Philostratos is gently mocking Herodes' excess here, but it highlights his efforts to ritualize his emotional connection to the dead boys, which is also picked up in Lucian's descriptions of Herodes continuing to prepare meals for them (*Demon.* 24, 33).[127] As on the Arch of Eternal Concord,[128] Herodes here aims to redefine space and demands that the viewer of the herms embody his experience, so that his emotions can be transferred to and lived by countless others, a potential enhanced by the everyday, identifiable activities described. The repetition and extent of his erection of the herms—the desperate need to capture many individual memories and have them replay as though on a loop through their inscriptions and images—reveals that Herodes ultimately doubted the capacity of stone to coalesce and convey memories adequately. One monument was never enough because stone is immobile, cold, dead. It also accentuates his need to claim the memory-laden landscapes of Greece as his own (cf. Ἡρώδου ὁ χῶρος; *IG* II² 5189; Figure 3.12) and that his commemoration of his loved ones was primarily about his own experiences and his attempt to establish his centrality to those spaces.

The citizens of Corinth or someone close to Herodes appear to have followed his example shortly after his own death and raised a portrait herm of their own. This memorial of Herodes was found in 1919 near New Corinth and now resides in the museum at Ancient Corinth (Figure 4.9).[129] The inscription reads:

Ἡρώδης
ἐνθάδε
περιεπάτει

'Herodes used to walk here'

The use of ἐνθάδε again points to the grave and, as in the case of the boys, adds to the incongruity of attempting to capture repeated activity, life, and spatial ownership in a stone monument.

The textual and material inscriptions discussed above that are located at boundaries are used by authors, literary characters, and monumentalizers to indicate authority, dominion, power, to overwrite existing spatial and historical meaning, and to stake claims for individual immortality. Despite such grand aims, their epitaphic quality regularly undermines these messages to highlight instead mortality and the fragility of memory. In the case of Philostratos' Apollonios, the superseding of the conqueror Alexander brings the potential longevity of Rome's own dominance into question and underscores the continuing crucial impact of Greek culture and its gatekeepers on the functioning of power. The Pillars of Lucian point the way to enduring vibrancy for Greek culture but emphasize the

---

[127] See further Section 6.4. [128] See Section 3.1.

[129] The head was broken off but fits cleanly onto the body. See *Corinth* 8.1, no. 85; *SEG* 2.52; Philadelpheus 1919, 38–40; 1920, 170–80; Johnson 1931, no. 169; Tobin 1997, 73 no. 1; 297 c.i; Ameling 1983b, no. 194.

FIGURE 4.9 Inscribed marble portrait herm of Herodes Attikos, Archaeological Museum of Corinth (S1219; *Corinth* 8.1, no. 85). Height: 1.84 m; Width: 0.29 m; Depth: 0.255 m.

contiguous risk of literary oblivion, and Herodes' herms overwrite spaces of cultural memory with individual emotion, the impact of which depends on the empathy of the passer-by. The following section takes a closer look at such processes of redefinition in relation to Arrian's Alexander. It moves away from the epitaphic inscriptions analysed above to focus rather on the appropriation for personal commemoration of the cultural and historical memory attached to tombs proper.

4.3 ARRIAN, ALEXANDER, AND THE TEXTUAL APPROPRIATION OF MEMORY

In this section, I consider two tombs in Arrian's *Anabasis of Alexander*: Achilles' in book one and Kyros' in book six. I focus on the way both Arrian and his Alexander appropriate cultural and historical memory in order to embed themselves within established tradition in a way that redefines that tradition for the future, and how funerary monuments function as sites used by both author and protagonist to negotiate mortality, identity, power, and fame.[130]

---

[130] Leon (2021) has recently argued that Arrian is more concerned for a future than present audience, and sees Arrian and similar historians as part of a 'counterculture' in comparison to Philostratos' sophistic

The role of tombs as symbols of status, identity, and propagators of fame, especially in literature, evolves from their function as the σήματα of those interred within them—that is, the representations and replacements of the deceased and the foci of communal memory.[131] Indeed, this metonymic function lies behind the wise Indians' warning to Alexander, quoted above, that in the end he owns only as much of the earth as will hold him, either while living and standing upon it or dead and interred within it (Arr. *An.* 7.1.6). The interchangeability of tomb and body again stems from Pythagorean and Orphic doctrine, in which the 'body' (σῶμα) is the 'tomb' (σῆμα), 'sacred enclosure' (περίβολος), and 'prison' (δεσμωτήριον) of the soul (Pl. *Cra.* 400b–c). The ability of the tomb to replace the body, however, is ultimately impermanent, as the lines from Ausonius at the beginning of this chapter elucidate. Tombs thus give a false impression of eternal commemoration, since, like statues (the focus of chapter 5), they are open to appropriation and reclassification, and like fame, their fate lies in the hands of others.[132] As such, they perfectly illustrate the inescapable truth faced by all those who strive to be remembered: at some point, inevitably, one's memory will fade and, equally horrifying, once dead, one's control over that memory ceases.[133] Arrian's *Anabasis of Alexander* employs the tombs of Achilles and Kyros as loci of contested meaning and memory to explore these themes and to connote cultural and political implications within the contemporary Roman empire.

In the *Anabasis*, Arrian retells Alexander's story in a way that enhances his personal authority over the subject of the greatest of all Greeks. His *Anabasis* is therefore less a history of Alexander's campaigns and more a study of one man's desire—Alexander's, but also Arrian's—to craft an eternal reputation. That desire is set against the backdrop of the reality that one cannot control how one's fame is propagated post-mortem. At the beginning of the *Periplous*, Arrian manipulated and reinterpreted the *Anabasis* of his namesake Xenophon in a way which tried both to emulate and to supersede the classical author, and which claimed control of the memory attached to Trapezous. In the *Anabasis*, he instils into his Alexander a similar awareness of the ability of time and other people to manipulate fame and memory. Arrian's Alexander thus displays a desperate need both to honour the dictates of the past and to propagate and control his own

---

scene. His monograph unfortunately appeared too late to be integrated into this discussion in detail, but our analyses are complementary. I suggest that this 'counterculture' is in fact quite mainstream and applicable to a number of genres.

[131] See Carroll 2011, 65–9.

[132] See Fowler 2000, 193–217, esp. 201–2, on the re-applicability and transience of monuments in Latin literature. Cf. Kahane 2011, 829.

[133] See Martindale 1993, 2–4, for an insightful discussion of Shelley's *Ozymandias* along these lines.

commemoration. Indeed, it is with the literary tradition that he admonishes his reluctant troops at the Hyphasis by using the very Homeric sentiment: 'it is sweet both to live with excellence ($\dot{a}\rho\epsilon\tau\hat{\eta}$) and to die leaving behind immortal fame ($\dot{a}\pi o\theta\nu\acute{\eta}\sigma\kappa\epsilon\iota\nu$ $\kappa\lambda\acute{\epsilon}os$ $\dot{a}\theta\acute{a}\nu\alpha\tau o\nu$ $\dot{\nu}\pi o\lambda\epsilon\iota\pi o\mu\acute{\epsilon}\nu ovs$)' (5.26.4).[134] Arrian's *Anabasis* mediates Alexander's desire for eternal reputation and the improbability of the fulfilment of that desire through the Makedonian's interaction with monuments to ancient or mythic men that are or become corrupted. In doing so, he also constructs and self-consciously frustrates his own project of piggy-backing on the fame of another.

4.3.1 *The Tomb of Achilles*

The *Anabasis*' textual monuments serve as markers of collective memory and media through which both Alexander and Arrian muse on the vicissitudes of future fame. At the grave of Achilles, for instance, Arrian records that Alexander laments his lack of a Homer to herald 'his memory to posterity ($\dot{\epsilon}s$ $\tau\dot{\eta}\nu$ $\ddot{\epsilon}\pi\epsilon\iota\tau\alpha$ $\mu\nu\acute{\eta}\mu\eta\nu$)' (1.12.1).[135] There is a long literary tradition that invests Achilles' tomb at Troy with meaning as well as a history of pilgrimage, beginning with Alexander and including Julius Caesar (Luc. 9.964–99), Hadrian (Philostr. *Her.* 8.1), and Caracalla (Herodian 4.8.1–5; Cass. Dio 78.16.7). It is Alexander's encounter with Troy that informs the visits of later pilgrims.[136] He crowns Achilles' grave (*An.* 1.12.1; cf. Plut. *Alex.* 15.4), bemoans his lack of a Homer (*An.* 1.12.1; cf. Plut. *Alex.* 15.4; Cic. *Arch.* 24; *Rom.* 1.42), and switches some of his armour for some that was previously dedicated in the temple of Athena (*An.* 1.11.7–8).

---

[134] See Bosworth 1980, 203 (on *An.* 5.26.4): in the vulgate, Alexander visited all the tombs of the heroes and gave appropriate offerings (Diod. 17.17.3; Just. 11.5.12). For further acts of Alexander in the *Anabasis* that show his investment in famous mythic and historic traditions, and his own desire to carve himself into the heroic landscape, see: *An.* 1.9.10 (saving Pindar's house); 1.11.5 (sacrifice to Protesilaos); 1.11.7 (Alexander switches his own armour for some in the temple of Athena); 1.12.1–5 (the delayed second preface); 1.16.5 (Alexander visits the wounded and listens to their tales of glory); 2.3.7 (the Gordian knot); 2.5.9 (Alexander claims decent from the Herakleidai); 2.7.8–9 (Alexander recalls Xenophon and his ten thousand); 3.3.1–2 (Alexander must visit the oracle of Ammon to rival Perseus and Herakles); 5.1.5 (Alexander spares Nysa because Dionysos founded it as a monument to his wanderings); 6.9.3 (Alexander carried the shield he took from Troy with him into battle); 6.9.5 (Alexander's desire to perform glorious deeds and have a glorious death); 7.9.6 (Alexander lists his achievements).

[135] This concern of Alexander derives from the vulgate tradition; cf. Plut. *Alex.* 15.4; Cic. *Arch.* 24; *Rom.* 1.42.

[136] Lucan's tale of Caesar's visit to Troy is probably invention; see Rossi 2001, 313. Caesar marks the landscape in a comic, accidental way when he tramples unwittingly over Hektor's grave (Luc. *Civil War* 974–9). Caracalla, however, imitates the actions of Alexander. On pilgrimage to Troy, see Minchin 2012. On Caesar and Troy, see Rossi 2001; Tesoriero 2005. On the presence of Homer's Troy at Ilion and Roman reconfigurations of cultural memory there, see Rose 2015. On Apollonios of Tyana's interview with Achilles at his grave in Philostr. *VA*, see Grossardt 2008. See also Alcock 2005, 159–63.

He alters the landscape in significant ways that portend his future success. The act of crowning is reverential, but when taken in the context of Alexander's habit of building memorials at the extent of his travels, it is also making the claim of having superseded the Homeric hero: Achilles set foot in Asia, but he did not conquer it and even died before the sack of Troy.[137] Moreover, switching the armour (a detail unique to Arrian's account) takes a piece of the Trojan War story and merges it with the story Alexander is about to compose through his campaigns in Asia: he both installs himself in Troy and takes Troy with him, and it is here that Arrian stakes his claim to be Alexander's Homer (1.12.4–5).

As a point of comparison to highlight the poignancy of Arrian's work, in describing the same episode Plutarch follows Alexander's reverential treatment of Achilles' grave with an anecdote about someone asking him if he would not also wish to see the lyre of his namesake, Paris-Alexandros. Alexander rejects the idea, saying he would rather see the lyre of Achilles (*Alex.* 15.4–5). The placement of this episode and the parallel drawn with the Trojan prince is designed to undermine Alexander's Achillean pretensions, as well as draw attention to his precarious identification with Hellenism. Plutarch's complex portrait of Alexander, in whom the philosophic and the irrational, the Greek and the barbarian/oriental contend, stands in stark contrast to Arrian's Alexander, the greatest of Greeks who is obsessed with the construction and preservation of his future reputation.[138] Arrian's version, therefore, would never brook such a subversive tale, not at least at this programmatic moment.[139] Although Plutarch also highlights that one's own reputation and, hence, commemoration cannot be controlled, he does so in a way that mocks Alexander and destabilizes his identity.

In tying both his and Homer's compositions to this famous grave, Arrian stresses the line of inheritance: his history is the heir to the *Iliad* and Alexander is the heir to Achilles.[140] More importantly, Alexander will complete what Homer's Achaians began: the conquest of Asia. The insertion of the Second Preface at this point announces a change of focus and narrative. From this moment on, Arrian's prose Alexander 'epic' truly begins. Its inception at Achilles' tomb invests it too with the quality of a lasting memorial and, consequently, takes up the challenge thrown down by Alexander concerning his future memorialization (1.12.1).[141] Further, the lack of a physical inscription on the grave allows Arrian to bend the tomb's message to his own commemorative ends and use it to

---

[137] Cf. Marincola 1989, 187, on Arrian's Alexander challenging Xenophon's achievement; Whitmarsh 2018, 146–7, on the *Romance*'s Alexander superseding Achilles.

[138] See Whitmarsh 2002 on Plutarch's Alexander.

[139] Cf. Moles 1985, 164, on Arrian's *Anabasis* as prose encomium.   [140] Moles 1985, 163.

[141] See Whitmarsh 2018, 146, for Alexander's concern over his lack of an adequate commemorator stemming from popular narrative tradition.

set both himself and Alexander up as supreme in their respective fields and, importantly, as symbiotic.

As identified by John Moles, Arrian's use of ὁρμάομαι (1.12.4) at this point elucidates the parallel between Alexander setting out into Asia and Arrian embarking on his history.[142] Their two tasks inform and depend upon each other. The word also conjures the idea of epic 'paths of song'.[143] Indeed, by using this particular verb, Arrian gives his history (ξυγγραφή 'narrative'/'inscription' 1.12.4, cf. 1.0.3; συγγράφω 1.0.1, 1.0.2, 1.0.3) a spatial dimension that corresponds to the continent of Asia. Ὁρμάομαι conjures epic and ἡ ξυγγραφή references specifically the opening of Thucydides: 'Thucydides the Athenian wrote down/ inscribed (ξυνέγραψε) the war of the Peloponnesians and the Athenians' (1.1.1).[144] In addition, the phrase parallels Herodotos as well: 'I will advance (προβήσομαι) further into my history' (1.5.3).[145] Thus in this one sentence Arrian alludes to Thucydides and Herodotos, compares his task with that of Homer's through the spatial context of the Second Preface, and by implication places himself in the company of these canonical authors from the perspective of his future readers.

Arrian then goes further and solidifies the idea of Asia as a monumental surface upon which he will inscribe Alexander's story through the use of ἀναγράφω (1.12.5; cf. 1.0.1, 1.0.2, 1.0.3) and the spatiality of τὸ χωρίον (1.12.2; 'the gap'/'empty space', ostensibly left by inadequate documentation of Alexander). While ἀναγράφω can simply signify 'to write down', it has as its primary meaning 'to engrave or inscribe publicly' as one does on a monument.[146] 'Placing' or 'hanging up', as though in dedication, is a common implication of the prefix *ana-* when combined with verbs of positioning, as in ἀνατίθημι ('to dedicate') or ἀνάκειμαι ('to be set up', 'to be dedicated'). Thus this spatial, dedicatory prefix gives the action of writing a similarly sacred and monumental essence. Whereas Achilles' tomb is clearly marked out by tradition at Troy, in Arrian's text Asia becomes a rival memorial to Alexander, inscribed and invested with meaning by the words of Arrian.

In a similar vein, within the Second Preface, there is a play between what is known, what is unknown, and what has been or must be revealed.[147] According to Arrian, Alexander's exploits 'are far less known (πολὺ μεῖον γιγνώσκεται) than the most trivial deeds of old (τὰ φαυλότατα τῶν πάλαι ἔργων)' (1.12.2) and have

---

[142] Moles 1985, 164 n. 9, on the connection of ὁρμάομαι with progression and travel.

[143] See Ford 1992, 42–8, with relevant bibliography. For earliest usage, see Hes. *Op.* 659; *Hom. Hymn to Hermes* 464–5.

[144] See Moles 1985, 164, on the Thucydides reference.

[145] Moles 1985, 164 n. 9. Cf. Hdt 1.1.0 and Arr. *An.* 1.12.4.

[146] See Moles 1985, 166, and 1999 on ἀναγράφω and historical writings as metaphoric inscriptions.

[147] Cf. Moles 1985, 163–5.

'not been worthily revealed' (οὐδὲ ἐξηνέχθη [...] ἐπαξίως, 1.12.2). It is this failure of revelation regarding Alexander that creates the great 'gap' (τὸ χωρίον) in the literary-monumental record. That Alexander's deeds are more obscure than those of Xenophon's Ten Thousand or the achievements of the Sicilian tyrants, as claimed by Arrian (1.12.2), is clearly an exaggeration. Arrian, himself, in the concluding passage of his history states: 'I believe that at that time there was no race of men nor any city nor any individual whom the name of Alexander had not reached' (7.30.2).[148] Alexander's fame is (or at least was) ubiquitous. On the one hand, this failure of revelation is a dig at the inadequate artistry of previous Alexander historians, who pale in comparison to Pindar and Xenophon; on the other, it is creating artistic space for Arrian's own contribution.

There must, therefore, be a different thrust to Arrian's claims that Alexander's deeds 'had not been worthily revealed' (οὐδὲ ἐξηνέχθη [...] ἐπαξίως, 1.12.2). Ἐκφέρω as well as having the sense of 'publishing' is also commonly used of carrying some material object out into the light, especially of bringing corpses out for burial.[149] This implication, combined with the physicality of τὸ χωρίον ('the [empty] space'), the setting of Achilles' tomb, and the established connection between σῆμα and σῶμα, gives Arrian's literary Alexander memorial the specific quality of a grave monument and one which has been obscured from sight prior to Arrian's unveiling.

In his *Events after Alexander*, Arrian relates that Ptolemy eventually takes possession of Alexander's body and inters it in his capital (9.25; cf. Diod. 18.3.5, 18.26–8; Strabo 17.1.8; Paus. 1.7.1; Curt. 10.10.20). The potency of the aura still attached to his tomb, known as the *Sêma* or *Sôma*, in Arrian's day derived from the symbolic value of Alexander's Hellenism and astounding achievements in life. That he had previously been interred elsewhere in Alexandria and before that in Memphis (Paus. 1.6.3, 1.7.1; Curt. 10.10.20; cf. *Rom.* 3.34), as well as the competition amongst the successors to possess the body, frees Arrian to make his own claim for it and to conceive yet another, this time metaphoric tomb, embedded in the landscape of Alexander's greatest successes.[150] The spatial element is created by Arrian through ὁρμάομαι (1.12.4) and τὸ χωρίον (1.12.2)—the gap in the literary record, but also the as-yet-unconquered territory of Asia and the empty papyrus awaiting Arrian's words. He combines this with the concept of a literary monument, which is built through the inscriptional connotations of ἀναγράφω (1.12.5) and ξυγγραφή (1.12.4). These two features of

[148] Moles 1985, 167 n. 39, notes that this picks up Arrian's claim in the second preface that his 'name is not unknown to men' (ὄνομα...οὐδὲ ἄγνωστον ἐς ἀνθρώπους, 1.12.5), thus comparing Arrian to Alexander again.

[149] See *LSJ* s.v. ἐκφέρω, AI.2.

[150] On Alexander's tomb(s), see Chugg 2002; Erskine 2002; Saunders 2006; on the tomb's name as *Sêma* or *Sôma*, see Fraser 1972, vol. 2, 32–3.

Arrian's account lay Asia out, and concurrently shape Arrian's *Anabasis*, as an inscribed funerary monument to Alexander.[151] Arrian thus claims Alexander's commemoration as his own, just as he took Xenophon's literary space in the *Periplous* and raised an 'immortal memorial' ($\mu\nu\dot{\eta}\mu\eta\nu$ $a\dot{\iota}\dot{\omega}\nu\iota\sigma\nu$, 1.4) to Hadrian and himself to both mirror and overshadow that constructed by Xenophon's Ten Thousand. In this respect, Arrian presents himself as the author of Alexander's achievements and fame, rather than merely their scribe. Here it is the historian who creates history out of the past's remains.

Further to this idea, in book four of the *Anabasis*, Arrian reports that Kallisthenes had claimed 'that Alexander and the deeds of Alexander were made clear ($\dot{a}\pi\dot{\epsilon}\varphi a\iota\nu\epsilon$) by him ($\dot{\upsilon}\varphi$' $a\dot{\upsilon}\tau\hat{\omega}$) and by his history ($\tau\hat{\eta}$ $a\dot{\upsilon}\tau\sigma\hat{\upsilon}$ $\xi\upsilon\gamma\gamma\rho a\varphi\hat{\eta}$)' (4.10.1). Kallisthenes here grasps keenly an author's control over how his/her subject is interpreted. Oddly, then, Arrian finds this sentiment distasteful, even though he sees himself as the only writer to illuminate Alexander as he truly deserves and should thus at least empathize with Kallisthenes' aim. Yet Arrian finds the following statement of Kallisthenes equally concerning: 'he did not come to acquire reputation ($\delta\dot{\delta}\xi a\nu$ $\kappa\tau\eta\sigma\dot{\delta}\mu\epsilon\nu\sigma$) from Alexander, but rather to make ($\pi\sigma\iota\dot{\eta}\sigma\omega\nu$) Alexander famous ($\epsilon\dot{\upsilon}\kappa\lambda\dot{\epsilon}\hat{a}$) to men' (4.10.2). The issue is that Kallisthenes fails to understand that the historian and the hero are partners in fame (1.12.5):[152] Alexander achieves *as* Arrian composes. Kallisthenes' statements, in contrast, not only reveal his lack of agency in his composition but also that his task is isolated from Alexander's efforts. Kallisthenes' literary representation of Alexander is thus flawed as indicated by its encomiastic quality completely at odds with his personal and well-known opposition to Alexander's excesses.[153] Through placing himself as the author of Alexander's exploits, Arrian concurrently sidelines the inadequate writings of his rivals.

This funerary monument created by Arrian is, moreover, not Alexander's alone. The *Anabasis*—canonical and famous from its inception—makes Arrian himself worthy of canonicity. As such, he is 'not obscure' ($\sigma\dot{\upsilon}\delta\dot{\epsilon}$ $\ddot{a}\gamma\nu\omega\sigma\tau\sigma\nu$) because Alexander's 'story' ($\sigma\ddot{\iota}\delta\epsilon$ $\sigma\dot{\iota}$ $\lambda\dot{\delta}\gamma\sigma\iota$),[154] which serves to identify and commemorate both the great man and himself (1.12.4–5), replaces his own name on this literary gravestone. The repeated use of $\dot{a}\nu a\gamma\rho\dot{a}\varphi\omega$ ('to write down'/'inscribe') and its presence so close to Arrian's listing of those things which he will not mention about himself (i.e. country, family, offices—all of which are items of the kind one

---

[151] See Strazdins (2022b) for the intertextual nexus of the Second Preface, Arrian's *Periplous*, and Xenophon's *Anabasis* that centres on the shared language of inscription, $\tau\dot{\sigma}$ $\chi\omega\rho\dot{\iota}\sigma\nu$, and the idea of $\dot{a}\nu\dot{a}\beta a\sigma\iota$.

[152] Cf. Bosworth 1988, 33–5; 1995, 75.

[153] See Arr. *An.* 4.10.1–11.9 with Bosworth, 1995, 72–90.

[154] I agree here with Moles 1985, 167, who sees $\sigma\ddot{\iota}\delta\epsilon$ $\sigma\dot{\iota}$ $\lambda\dot{\delta}\gamma\sigma\iota$ as referring to the *Anabasis, contra* Bosworth 1972, 168, who considers the phrase to refer to all Arrian's works.

does inscribe on monuments[155] and especially includes in epitaphs) drives home the sepulchral metaphor.

So Arrian here builds an inscribed grave monument on the literary landscape of Asia that memorializes Alexander and, at the same time, himself better than any physical structure and better than any previous literary attempt. Ptolemy may take possession of Alexander's body, but Arrian takes possession of his fame and inters it within the pages of his *Anabasis*. Arrian thus seals his authority and dominion over Alexander's story and its place in cultural history. Indeed, his literary Alexander memorial marks the apogee of the territory of Alexander histories in much the same way Alexander marked the extent of his travels to signal martial and political supremacy. As with Aelius Aristeides and his common grave with the Makedonian, military might is equated to literary skill (*An.* 1.12.5; cf. *HL* 4.49), the historian becomes a hero, and the book crystallizes into a (funerary) monument. Arrian here uses the epitaphic potential of inscription to claim cultural hegemony.

4.3.2 The Tomb of Kyros

Alexander's encounter with another tomb, that of Kyros the Great, is employed by Arrian to discourse on the mutability of fortune, the limits of empire, and the frailty of posthumous reputation. At the end of book six (6.29.4), Alexander returns to Persia and discovers the ransacking of Kyros' tomb. In this passage, there are three competing claims staked for authority over the tomb: Arrian's, Alexander's, and Kyros'. Although it is described pre-looting, it is never revealed to the reader from Kyros' viewpoint, the one that matters if we wish to decipher any form of intentionality from it, even though all the participants in this passage—Arrian, Alexander, and Kyros—attempt to claim it, even construct it, as their own interpretive space.

Arrian's description of the tomb is an assertion of his authority over the past, and particularly over Alexander's and Kyros' respective memorialization. He shapes his account to underscore the fragility of commemoration and one's inability to control it in the future. In the *Anabasis*, Kyros' tomb begins as a ransacked monument (6.29.4). It is then 'reconstructed' by Arrian through a lengthy description of it in its prior pristine state, the evidence for which is taken from the autopsy of Aristoboulos (6.29.4–6):

The tomb of that famous (ἐκείνου) Kyros was in Pasargadae in the royal park; around it a grove of all sorts of trees had been planted and was irrigated, and deep grass grew in the meadow. The tomb itself in the lower parts was made of stones cut square and was

---

[155] See Moles 1985, 166.

rectangular in form. Above was a roofed stone chamber; it had a door leading into it so narrow that it was only just possible for a single man of low stature to get through with much distress. In the chamber lay a golden sarcophagus ($\pi\acute{v}\epsilon\lambda o s$), in which the body ($\sigma\hat{\omega}\mu a$) of Kyros had been buried. A couch stood by the sarcophagus with feet of wrought gold; a Babylonian tapestry served as a covering and purple cloaks as a carpet. On it there was a Median sleeved garment and other tunics of Babylonian workmanship. Both Median trousers and robes dyed the colour of hyacinths lay there, as Aristoboulos says, some deep purple, some of other shades, with metal collars, Persian swords and golden earrings set with stones; a table stood there also. Between the table and the couch lay the sarcophagus ($\pi\acute{v}\epsilon\lambda o s$) containing the body ($\sigma\hat{\omega}\mu a$) of Kyros.

This description is capped off by recording the inscription, spoken in the voice of Kyros, written on the monument in Persian, but translated into the Greek of Arrian in the text.

The tomb is then 'deconstructed' as Arrian describes its interior again, this time in its looted and vandalized state, which is how it appeared to Alexander when he arrived at the monument:

Alexander [...] found everything else carried out ($\tau\grave{a}$ $\mu\grave{\epsilon}\nu$ $\check{a}\lambda\lambda a$ $\kappa a\tau a\lambda a\mu\beta\acute{a}\nu\epsilon\iota$ $\dot{\epsilon}\kappa\pi\epsilon\phi o\rho\eta\mu\acute{\epsilon}\nu a$) except the sarcophagus and the couch. Even the body of Kyros they had violated ($\kappa a\grave{\iota}$ $\tau\grave{o}$ $\sigma\hat{\omega}\mu a$ [...] $\dot{\epsilon}\lambda\omega\beta\acute{\eta}\sigma a\nu\tau o$), for they had removed the lid of the sarcophagus and had thrown out the corpse ($\tau\grave{o}\nu$ $\nu\epsilon\kappa\rho\grave{o}\nu$ $\dot{\epsilon}\xi\acute{\epsilon}\beta a\lambda o\nu$).   (6.29.9)

Finally, Alexander's orders to Aristoboulos on how to restore the tomb are cited (6.29.10). Strabo also follows the account of Aristoboulos and describes (in less detail) the tomb's surroundings and contents, segueing straight into the description of its destruction, and ending his account with the inscription (Strabo 15.3.7).[156] Quintus Curtius, on the other hand, describes only the looted tomb and the persecution of the satrap Orxines (Curt. 10.1.30–8). Plutarch mentions that the tomb was rifled, identifies the culprit, and records the inscription (*Alex.* 69.1–3).[157] Arrian's is by far the longest account and his arrangement creates the most pathos and irony.

In detailing the tomb first in its pristine state, Arrian stresses his ownership of Alexander's experience, in that he sees the tomb in a state Alexander does not, but desperately wished to. This discrepancy is underscored by the change from past to present tense at the moment Alexander discovers the tomb looted ($\kappa a\tau a\lambda a\mu\beta\acute{a}\nu\epsilon\iota$, 6.29.9): Kyros' memorial, seen with the historian's gaze, had been pristine; now, in Alexander's experience, it is ravaged. Although Alexander tries to put it back together again, he can never equal the perfection of Arrian's pre-looting description.[158]

---

[156] On Strabo's account see Roller 2018, 880.

[157] See Bosworth 1988, 46–55, on Arrian's and Strabo's accounts of the looted tomb.

[158] In the *Romance*, Kyros' tomb is intact, but Alexander does repair other dilapidated tombs and sanctuaries (e.g., Ammon, A1.30; Proteus, A1.32)

The Makedonian's attempt, capped off with his 'royal seal' (τὸ σημεῖον τὸ βασιλικόν; a detail that exists only in Arrian), is merely an approximation, because the looters have also marked the tomb, removing objects and vandalizing parts of its structure.

Arrian, on the other hand, details Kyros' tomb in the order that a visitor would have seen it prior to its ransacking (thus approximating Kyros' intentionality), with one exception: the inscription is held back until just before the interior is redescribed in its devastated state. If a tomb is meant to speak with the voice of the dead, Arrian here silences Kyros for as long as possible. When he does allow him to speak, it is not the Persian of the original, but Arrian's Greek translation. Kyros' native voice is denied him and his message is appropriated and translated into Arrian's work. This is Arrian ensuring the monument is understandable to his Greek audience;[159] nevertheless, Kyros' intent is filtered through Arrian's interpretive account.

Moreover, unlike the other authors who append the inscription to their relation of this episode, he inserts it immediately before he describes the results of the tomb's ransacking. It reads: 'Mortal! I am Kyros son of Kambyses, who founded the Persian empire and who was ruler of Asia. Do not then begrudge me my monument! (Μὴ οὖν φθονήσῃς μοι τοῦ μνήματος)' (6.29.8). Although this is essentially the same inscription recorded by Strabo (15.3.7) and, therefore, must stem from Aristoboulos, Arrian cites it at a point that makes the whole episode's meaning to his version of Alexander's story clear. The irony and pathos are all too apparent as it is immediately followed by a description of the destruction witnessed by Alexander: Kyros' body, strewn in pieces around the tomb, is mocked by his own silent voice that claims a measure of immortality. The scene that meets Alexander's eyes thus makes a travesty of the tomb's role in protecting and replacing the body, which in its broken and discarded state becomes simply a 'corpse' (νεκρός). Kyros' golden sarcophagus, in comparison, stands slightly damaged, but unmoved (6.29.9). Thus the trappings of royal burial survive, but the royal body and identity are dismantled. Arrian's arrangement of the story produces this pathos to emphasize how easily a memorial's meaning can be upended.

Indeed, Alexander's reconstruction of the tomb partially annexes Kyros' memory and his monument for himself. Alexander's 'kingly sign' (τὸ σημεῖον τὸ βασιλικόν) redefines Kyros' tomb (τάφος, 6.29.10), just as Arrian's placement of the inscription makes its message intelligible for his audience in precisely the way he wants it to be. The impotent inscription, which stands as the liminal element between the pristine and the desecrated monument, is an exegesis on the mutability of fortune and the absolute nature of mortality. In Plutarch's version of the same incident, this notion is spelt out:

[159] Compare his assimilation of Phasine to Rhea in *Peripl.* 9.2 (Section 3.2).

Then, having discovered that the tomb (τάφον) of Kyros had been rifled (διορωρυγμένον), he put to death the perpetrator, even though the culprit was a prominent Makedonian from Pella, named Polymachos. Having recognized (ἀναγνούς) the inscription on the tomb, he ordered it to be engraved below in Greek letters (Ἑλληνικοῖς […] γράμμασιν). It ran thus: 'Mortal, whoever you are and from wherever you come, for I know that you will come (ὅτι ἥξεις οἶδα), I am Kyros, the one who won the empire (κτησάμενος τὴν ἀρχήν) for the Persians. Do not, therefore, begrudge (μὴ […] φθονήσῃς) me this little earth which covers my body (τοὐμὸν σῶμα περικαλύπτει)'. These words, then, deeply affected Alexander, who was reminded of the lack of clarity (ἀδηλότητα) in and the capriciousness (μεταβολήν) of life.   (*Alex.* 69.2–3)

Alexander's reaction here to the frailty of life, fortune, and memory recalls Xerxes' tears at Abydos in Herodotos, when he gazed down on his forces in all their strength just prior to their crossing of the Hellespont and was filled simultaneously with joy over his power and sorrow at human life's impermanence (Hdt. 7.45.1–46.2). Plutarch's allusion to Herodotos and the knowledge of Xerxes' subsequent failure at Salamis (8.40–96), where he also gazed down on the theatre of battle, underscores that all great power and ambition is eventually broken. The setting of the ransacked tomb, moreover, emphasizes the futility of Alexander's efforts to control his commemoration and the inevitability of his imminent death.

In Plutarch, it is Alexander who interprets and translates Kyros' inscription, in the process making the foreign words understandable to a Greek audience. Alexei Zadorojnyi perceptively describes this as an ideological and alphabetical colonization,[160] and it aligns Alexander psychologically with Kyros despite their cultural differences. The association and comparison of Alexander and Kyros, based both on their imperialistic bent and their cultural hybridity, was a common theme in imperial Greek texts, where Alexander appears as a natural 'successor'.[161] Indeed, that Alexander takes the side of Kyros over the Makedonian vandal shows that in this instant his identity as famed king and imperialist is being stressed over his cultural origins.[162] The allusion to Herodotos' Xerxes only heightens this effect. Moreover, the inscription itself is prescient: Kyros has been waiting for Alexander in order to teach him this lesson on mortality, memory, and ambition.[163] The inscription thus gains its complete meaning only in the moment Alexander 'recognizes' (ἀναγνούς) it on the looted tomb. That same lesson was lost on the Makedonian vandal and this must form part of Alexander's motivation in translating the Persian: the hope that, if the looter had understood the

---

[160] Zadorojnyi 2013, 382.

[161] See Whitmarsh 2018, 135–6, 148–9, for references and discussion.

[162] Cf. Mossman 2006, 292. See Brosius 2003, 174–5, on Alexander's respect for Kyros.

[163] Cf. Slater 2009, 72, on *Rom.* 2.27; Zadorojnyi 2013, 382. Cf. Herodes' curse inscriptions' use of ὅστις εἶ at Tobin 1997, 115.

inscription, he would have let Kyros' memorial stand. Plutarch's Alexander here adopts the role of monumental interpreter that characterizes his *Romance* alter ego.[164]

Judith Mossman claims that Arrian is, in contrast, uninterested in Alexander's psychological reaction to the destruction of Kyros' tomb apart from noting that he wished to find those responsible.[165] The same lesson is clearly implicit, however, in Arrian's version of this incident: Alexander's distress ($\dot{\epsilon}\lambda\dot{\upsilon}\pi\eta\sigma\epsilon$, 6.29.4) stems from the realization that death comes to all great kings/empires and makes them impotent in the face of posterity. His reaction is accentuated by his own regret ($o\dot{\upsilon}\delta'$ $\dot{\epsilon}\pi\dot{\eta}\nu\epsilon\iota$, 6.30.1) over burning Persepolis down, which Arrian mentions directly after the tomb incident. That Alexander's own corpse was understood to have rested inside a golden coffin in Alexandria, moreover, until Ptolemy X exchanged it for a glass, crystal, or alabaster one (Strabo 17.1.8; Diod. 18.26.3; Curt. 10.10.13), only heightens the pathos of Arrian's description and his assimilation of the Makedonian and Median kings.

Alexander's need to see the tomb directly upon his return to Persia from India foreshadows his own corpse's later history as an Alexandrian tourist attraction for other imperialists, such as Caesar (Luc. 10.14–52), Augustus (Suet. *Aug.* 18; Cass. Dio 51.16.5), Septimius Severus (Cass. Dio 76.13.2), and Caracalla (Cass. Dio 78.7–8, 22–3; Herodian 4.8.9). From Alexander's point of view, then, the tomb must be reconstructed because of Kyros' standing as former ruler of Asia and on account of the trouble he took over his funerary monument. Alexander's own fame depends on that of his predecessors: the more impressive they were, the more remarkable his achievement in surpassing them. Not much prior to the Pasargadae episode, this is stressed in Arrian's text when Alexander's desire to achieve the desert march to Gedrosia is attributed primarily to his need to outdo ($\dot{\epsilon}\rho\iota\nu$ $\dot{\epsilon}\mu\beta\alpha\lambda\epsilon\hat{\iota}\nu$ $\pi\rho\dot{o}s$) Kyros and Semiramis (6.24.2–3). Protecting Kyros' memory is thus a surrogate for Alexander's hopes for the longevity of his own. It is tempting too to see here in Arrian's rivetted attention to Alexander's pain over an emperor and empire brought low an allusion to the cyclical nature of history in the vein of Herodotos (e.g. 1.5.4) and a warning of Rome's own inevitable if still inconceivable failure, as well as the power a historian wields over its representation.

Given the historical fascination with Kyros' inscription, it is intriguing that no trace of it exists on what has been identified as Kyros' tomb at Pasargadae (Figure 4.10) and no obvious place on the architectural members from where it

---

[164] See Stoneman 1995.

[165] Mossman 2006, 291. See also Zadorojnyi 2013, 381: Plutarch alone engages with the psychological impact on Alexander.

FIGURE 4.10 Tomb of Kyros from the north west, showing the surrounding area, Pasargadae.

may have been lost or removed.[166] The only genuine possibility is the door, which is now missing but whose opening is notably diminutive (1.39 × 0.78 m) and not the usual setting for Achaemenian inscriptions. In fact, as David Stronach notes:

it was certainly never a standard Achaemenian practice to place inscriptions on tombs. Of the seven rock-cut tombs of the royal family that are to be found near Persepolis, only that of Darius the Great bears any identification. The remainder are anonymous and so again is the virtually intact, free-standing Gur-I Dukhtar tomb, which appears to have been built in imitation of the tomb of Kyros.[167]

A. B. Bosworth, on the other hand, is certain there was a now lost inscription seen by the Greeks on the tomb.[168] He bases this assumption on the persistent reports in Greek literature and on the fact that the received version of Darius' tomb inscription from Onesikritos, another of Alexander's companion historians, does convey the essence of sections of the physical inscription on the real tomb at Naqsh-i Rustam.[169] Strabo's report (15.3.8) of Onesikritos here, however,

---

[166] For detailed discussion of the tomb, known as the 'Tomb of the Mother of Solomon', and its identification, see Stronach 1978, 24–43. See also Herzfeld 1901; Stronach 1985.
[167] Stronach 1978, 26 (see plate 185a for the Gur-i Dukhtar tomb).
[168] Bosworth 1988, 50 n. 37.
[169] Onesikritos' version of Darius' inscription from Strabo 15.3.8: 'I was a friend to friends; I was the best horseman and archer; as a hunter I was a master; I could do everything'. See Jacoby 1923, 134 F 35; Whitby 2016, 134 F 35. For a discussion and translation of Darius' physical inscription and tomb iconography, see Briant 2002, 211–16. See also Kent 1950, 138.

contains only the gist of a fraction of what was unintelligible language, both in its written cuneiform and spoken version, passed on through Persian intermediaries. Thus Stronach's suggestion that the Makedonians saw inscriptions mentioning Kyros in the palace that were translated for them into Greek and that these inscriptions became associated with the textual rather than physical tomb in the retellings of the campaigns (and then the re-retellings by Roman-era historians) is more compelling as well as a fascinating insight into the textualization of tradition.[170]

Plutarch's, Arrian's, and Strabo's versions of the inscription are close and derive from Aristoboulos.[171] Strabo also cites Onesikritos, however, who records a far simpler epitaph that corresponds in its first clause to a type of Greek funerary epigram that was frequently used from classical into Roman imperial times: $\dot{\epsilon}\nu\theta\acute{a}\delta$' $\dot{\epsilon}\gamma\grave{\omega}$ $\kappa\epsilon\hat{\iota}\mu\alpha\iota$ $K\hat{\nu}\rho\sigma$ $\beta\alpha\sigma\iota\lambda\epsilon\grave{\nu}s$ $\beta\alpha\sigma\iota\lambda\acute{\eta}\omega\nu$ ('here I lie, Kyros King of Kings', 15.3.7).[172] $\ddot{E}\nu\theta\acute{a}\delta\epsilon$ $\kappa\epsilon\hat{\iota}\tau\alpha\iota$ is a common formula, with the stone speaking about the deceased: 'here lies X'. The palace inscriptions associated with Kyros, which were recorded in three languages (Old Persian, Elamite, Babylonian, though never of course Greek) one below the other, are equally simple in their sentiments: 'I am Kyros the King, an Achaemenian' (CMa); 'Kyros the Great King, son of Kambyses the King, an Achaemenian...' (CMb); 'Kyros the Great King, an Achaemenian' (CMc).[173] It is easy to see how these could produce both Onesikritos' epitaph and the more complex one of Aristoboulos if translated into a Greek cultural context in which $\kappa\lambda\acute{\epsilon}os$ $\ddot{a}\phi\theta\iota\tau\sigma\nu$ ('undying fame') was an irresistible concept. The evidence indicates, then, that the tradition of the inscription on Kyros' tomb developed through the Greek literary sources and that the particularly pathetic tenor was invented by Alexander historians. In this case, the entire purpose of the Greek versions of the inscription is to address Alexander's ambitions in the face of mortality, the weight of the past, and the judgement of posterity. This relationship between Alexander and monuments from the past also becomes one of the most persistent themes of the *Romance* tradition, in which the memorials of dead kings or ancient shrines simultaneously spur his divine ambitions and portend his death.[174]

Significantly, Arrian's Alexander fails to fix Kyros' tomb in one important particular: the body cannot be reconstructed; only what is salvageable can be

---

[170] See Stronach 1978, 26.

[171] Strabo records: 'O man, I am Kyros, I acquired for myself the rule ($\tau\grave{\eta}\nu$ $\dot{a}\rho\chi\grave{\eta}\nu...\kappa\tau\eta\sigma\acute{a}\mu\epsilon\nu os$) over the Persians and am King of Asia; do not begrudge me my monument ($\mu\grave{\eta}$ $o\mathring{\nu}\nu$ $\phi\theta\sigma\nu\acute{\eta}\sigma\eta s$ $\mu\sigma\iota$ $\tau\sigma\hat{\nu}$ $\mu\nu\acute{\eta}\mu\alpha\tau os$)' (15.3.7).

[172] Note that Onesikritos reports it was Greek written in Persian letters ($\dot{\epsilon}\pi\acute{\iota}\gamma\rho\alpha\mu\mu\alpha...\ddot{E}\lambda\lambda\eta\nu\iota\kappa\acute{o}\nu$, $\Pi\epsilon\rho\sigma\iota\kappa\sigma\hat{\iota}s$ $\kappa\epsilon\chi\alpha\rho\alpha\gamma\mu\acute{\epsilon}\nu\sigma\nu$ $\gamma\rho\acute{a}\mu\mu\alpha\sigma\iota\nu$, 15.3.7)!

[173] See Kent 1950, 116; Stronach 1978, 26. Herzfeld (1901, 41) argues there was a similarly simple inscription on the tomb. Note that these palace inscriptions probably derive from Darius who sought to associate himself with Kyros' prestige. See Briant 2002, 63.

[174] See, e.g., *Rom.* A1.30, A1.32, A/L1.33–34, A1.42; A/L3.24; L3.28. This aspect is also a feature of oracles he encounters, e.g., L3.5–17. See Stoneman 1995 for the *Romance* Alexander as a solver of riddles and interpreter of monuments.

placed back inside the sarcophagus, a circumstance that once more stresses Alexander's impotence against death and oblivion. In contrast to Plutarch's version, Alexander's lack of control is underscored by his inability to find and punish the culprits (6.29.11). Moreover, he changes the dynamics of the monument by securing the entrance and placing his seal upon it, a detail which is unique to Arrian and again without archaeological trace.[175] This aligns with his act of switching armour at Troy: he embeds a part of himself into Kyros' reconstructed tomb, a monument that fails to preserve memory as it was designed to do, thus asserting both his dominance over Kyros and his new role as protector of his predecessor's fame.[176] The act also points, however, to the future appropriation and manipulation of his own renown by the Diadochoi and countless authors.

In contrast, Arrian's description of the tomb prior to its looting stresses his achievement as a historian: he can cause the vandalism to be non-existent through the power of his narrative. Yet he also demonstrates his authority over the monument's broader representation. He makes Kyros' memory perfect, but perfect according to Arrian, and he records the alternative in describing the vandalism and Alexander's imperfect reconstruction. In this way, Arrian highlights the superiority of his power to shape and preserve Alexander's memory, while at the same time acknowledging that no monument (including a literary one) is incorruptible and no empire (even that of the Romans) is eternal.

Arrian's account of Alexander at Achilles' grave thus promotes his own cultural and artistic expertise within Greek tradition; his retelling of Alexander's visit to Kyros' tomb, in contrast, implicitly attaches a terminus to any iteration of empire and any crafting of individual memory. More than this, however, Arrian's, Philostratos', and Lucian's literary reinterpretations of the trail-blazing progression of Alexander's conquests and his loaded interaction with the monuments of the past reveal just what an exceptional paradigm the conqueror was for imperial Greek commemorative and artistic process. The Makedonian's historical advent and the narrative tradition that adhered to his achievements were so transformative as to provide, via the metaphor of advancement into the unknown, a route to original expression and creative possibility, whether cultural, aesthetic, or even political. At the same time, Alexander's own reconfiguring of spatial meaning, his untimely death and its consequences point to the pitfalls of such revolutionary ambitions. This double-edged commemorative dynamic accounts for the epitaphic quality of the literary monuments within these imperial Greek accounts, as well as physical artefacts such as Herodes' herms. The following section switches focus to material culture again but examines similar acts of cultural and commemorative

---

[175] The only original markings found on the tomb are tool marks and half of a badly damaged, double rosette within a rayed disk on the pediment above the door that Stronach 1971 interprets as a religious symbol, probably indicating belief in Ahuramazda. The upper half is missing with the capstone.

[176] Cf. Curt. 10.1.32: Alexander places a gold crown and his own robe on Kyros' coffin.

4.4 HERODES ATTIKOS AND THE PHYSICAL APPROPRIATION OF MEMORY

Here my attention turns to Herodes Attikos' appropriation of inscriptions from the memorial for the fallen Athenians at the Battle of Marathon in 490 BC in order to enhance his own project of personal commemoration. This physical claiming of an artefact from the past and creating a new personal context for it provides a material analogue to the literary examples discussed in the previous section. It demonstrates that the imperial Greek elite were negotiating the same concerns through literary and material culture. Before addressing this subject, however, I will make a brief detour to examine Hadrian's intervention at Ajax's tomb at Troy, as described in Philostratos' *Heroikos* (8.1), since it provides a neat transition between the activities of Alexander and those of Herodes.

According to Philostratos' Vinedresser, the emperor Hadrian reconstructed the tomb of Ajax after it was destroyed by a high tide. This act resonates with Alexander's repair of Kyros' tomb and creates similar associations. In particular, the emperor's focus is on the body: he kissed the bones, wrapped them, and then restored the tomb.[177] In the text, this intervention is intended to add veracity and authority to the Vinedresser's narrative about the extreme size of heroes' bones. Depending on how the audience reads it, however—how convinced it is by the Vinedresser's tales—it either enhances the glory of Hadrian or mocks his gullibility. The precise literary character aside, much like Alexander's treatment of Achilles and Kyros, Hadrian's actions indicate his reverence for and attempt to assert authority over the figure of Ajax. His actions are consistent, moreover, with the emperor who granted monumental benefactions to the cities of the Greek east, while simultaneously creating his own monumental legacy:[178] restoring a Homeric hero's tomb at the site of Troy embeds the emperor into the history and landscape of a region of major importance for both Greece and Rome.[179] The hero's tomb stands due to the emperor's generosity and his name will be forever associated with this historic landmark. In contrast to Alexander's act of exchanging armour with Achilles, which plundered the relics of Troy to enhance his own reputation, Hadrian's appropriation of cultural memory restores and protects Greek cultural legacy, while promoting its virile, martial, but importantly long-past aspects that are traditionally valued by Rome.

---

[177] Cf. Paus. 1.35.4–5 in which the destruction of the tomb is recorded, but not Hadrian's intervention.
[178] See Boatwright 2000.   [179] On Romans at Troy, see Erskine 2001, 225–53.

The Trojan War was significant in this respect, but some of the most revered events to evince classical Greek virtue for Romans and imperial Greeks alike were the Persian Wars and their famous battles—Marathon in 490 BC, Thermopylai and Salamis in 480, and Plataia in 479.[180] On the one hand, they had been used by Greeks as an exemplum of resistance to foreign powers from the fourth century BC onwards; on the other, Roman emperors turned that disruptive potential into one of unification, equating barbarian threats beyond the empire's borders, especially to the east, with the Persian threat seen off by the 'classical' Greeks. At the same time, Roman propaganda established classical Athenians and Spartans, who formed the primary resistance to Darius and Xerxes, as positive paradigms and role models for Roman-era Greeks, in their maintenance of manly vigour despite being rich in culture (especially in the Athenians' case).[181] This formed part of a larger Roman impetus to keep provincial Greeks focused on their *polis*-based past and ancient territorial rivalries as a means of control.[182] Nevertheless, despite Rome's best efforts, in the culture of the eastern empire, references to the Persian Wars were always loaded with the potential to be interpreted subversively instead of as a dutiful expression of collective imperial belonging. For one thing, it demonstrated what Greeks could do when they banded together.

We have already seen Herodes Attikos exploit this double-edged dynamic in both public and private space in his arrangement of his own bust in the company of Marcus Aurelius and Lucius Verus at Rhamnous and Brexiza, as well as claiming the region of Marathon as his own via the keystone inscription on his Gate of Eternal Concord.[183] In what follows, I will examine how he incorporates it into the decorative programme of his Peloponnesian villa as well via the appropriation of Athenian casualty lists from the Battle of Marathon.

The villa, situated by the Loukou monastery near modern Astros and close to the ancient village of Eua (Paus. 2.38.7) in the region known as Kynouria in antiquity, was mostly constructed by Herodes and his father, Attikos, although it was begun sometime during the Flavian era.[184] The wealth of material, particularly sculptural, combined with elaborate buildings and gardens, as well as numerous water features, invoke parallels with aspects of Hadrian's villa at Tivoli, and suggest that it was designed as much as a museum as a country retreat for Herodes and his family (Figure 4.11).[185]

---

[180] Spawforth 1994. See also Jung 2006, 205–24. On Greek representations of Trojans in literature/art and the Persian Wars, see Erskine 2001, 61–92.

[181] Spawforth 1994, 243–7; see also Proietti 2012, 108–10.

[182] On this topic, see Spawforth 2012.   [183] See Section 3.1.   [184] Spyropoulos 2009, 12–13.

[185] On the design of the villa, see Spyropoulos 2006b; 2009, 11–22. On the emulation of Tivoli, see Tobin 1997, 292; Spyropoulos 2009, 12–19. On museums and collecting in Roman culture, see Rutledge 2012, especially 1–30. The villa plan was published in the Capitoline Museum's *L'età dell'angoscia* exhibition catalogue 2015. On the importance of water to the display, see Rogers 2021.

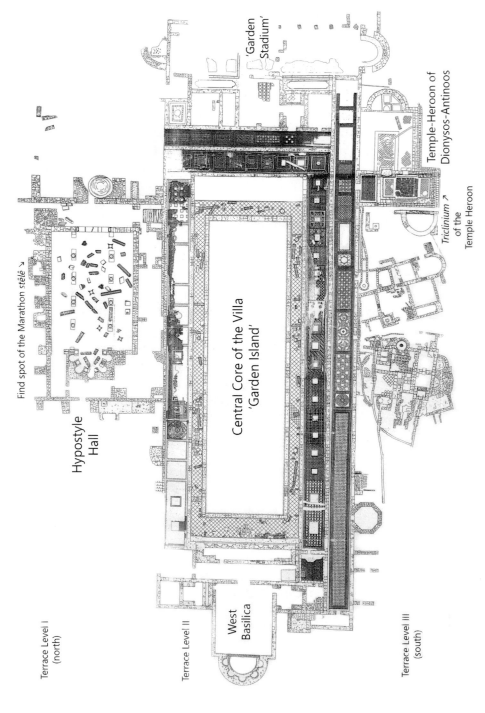

FIGURE 4.11 Ground plan of the central portion of Herodes Attikos' Villa at Loukou-Eva Kynouria.

John Bodel has shown, from the early principate onwards, Roman elites of the Western empire began to embed a commemorative programme into their country houses, often associated with the shrine to the *Lares*.[186] He convincingly argues that the artefacts discovered in these circumstances—honorific statues or inscriptions, along with ancestor portrait busts and funerary masks—suggest that 'a man's country house, and not his tomb, might serve as his most enduring monument'.[187] This notion fits well with the Roman attitude of entangling a man's identity with his property, which regularly saw the obliteration of disgraced citizens' houses. Why this practice centred on rural villas lies in the constraints on public commemorative display that came to bear on Roman citizens once Rome became the emperor's city and public building was mostly undertaken by the imperial family.[188] The less populous and less prestigious nature of provincial centres made self-promoting benefaction less appealing than, as Bodel suggests, targeting a select group of social peers in one's own house.[189] At the same time, the proliferation of public honorific monuments, granted by senate, *boulê*, or *dêmos*, devalued the honour through overcrowding.[190] Herodes certainly did not shy away from provincial benefaction, primarily because it was the provinces that preserved the commemorative landscapes he wanted a slice of: Marathon, Thermopylai, Athens, Olympia, Delphi, Isthmia, Alexandria Troas, Corinth amongst others. Nevertheless, his villa at Loukou displays all the signs of approximating this villa-as-monument habit of the imperial west.

Herodes' villa has yielded heroic mosaics featuring the labours of Herakles and Achilles towering over Penthesileia at the moment of her death; statues of athletic victors, gods and goddesses, an Achilles-Penthesileia complex, Antinoos in the guise of Dionysos or an athlete and in Egyptianizing form; busts of various emperors and members of the imperial family, members of Herodes' family and his beloved foster-sons (τρόφιμοι); many other unidentified male and female portraits; numerous heroic and funerary reliefs; and a set of Asklepios reliefs that may have come from the Asklepieion in Athens.[191]

One intriguing find, excavated in June 2000 from an early Christian kiln,[192] is an inscribed *stêlê* that has since been identified as one of ten commemorative *stêlai*

---

[186] Bodel 1997.

[187] Bodel 1997, 32 (quotation), 26–32 (villa artefacts), 20–6 (tombs on villa lands), honorific display (18–20); villa destruction (7–11).

[188] Bodel 1997, 30. See also Eck 1984, 139–45.

[189] Bodel 1997, 30.   [190] Bodel 1997, 30; cf. Eck 1984, 145.

[191] On the finds, see Spyropoulos 2009, 11–22; cf. Tobin 1997, 333–54. On the sculpture and mosaics, see Spyropoulos 2006a; 2001; Spyropoulos and Spyropoulos 1996. A fascinating feature is the matching of mosaics to statuary, so that the Achilles-Penthesileia complex was placed behind a mosaic depicting the same scene.

[192] Spyropoulos 2009, 23; 2006a, 192; Steinhauer 2009, 122.

FIGURE 4.12 *Stêlê* of the fallen of the Erechtheid tribe in the Battle of Marathon, found at the Villa of Herodes Attikos at Loukou-Eva Kynouria. Archaeological Museum of Astros (Inv. 535; Steinhauer 2004–2009). Height: 0.68 m; Width: 0.558-0.57 m; Depth: 0.265-0.285 m.

(one for each tribe), raised for the Athenian fallen in the Battle of Marathon in 490 BC (Paus. 1.32.3; cf. Thuc. 2.34.5–6, who mentions the tomb).[193] There were at least two such polyandreion monuments for the 192 dead Athenians—one by the *soros* at Marathon and a similar, less-extensive one as part of a general Persian War memorial in Athens at the city cenotaph (δημόσιον σῆμα).[194] This particular *stêlê*, however, if indeed from the early fifth century, most probably comes from the *soros*.

The inscription is headed by the name of the Erechtheis tribe (the first in the sequence), followed by an epigram, and then a list of twenty-two names arranged in a distinctive checkerboard fashion (Figure 4.12).[195] Below this the stone terminates and appears to have been deliberately cut, so the list of names may have been longer.[196] Two other fragments bearing letters arranged in

---

[193] Spyropoulos 2009; Steinhauer 2010. Cf. Steinhauer 2004–2009; 2009, 122.

[194] See Olson 2016, 50–6; Petrovic 2013, 47–53. On rituals associated with and the social, political, and ideological function of the commemoration of Athenian war dead, see Low 2012; cf. Arrington 2015.

[195] The inscription was first published in Steinhauer 2004–2009, 680. Spyropoulos 2009 included photographs, and he presented it at a conference in Kalamata on the importance of the Battle of Marathon to civilization in October 2010. See also https://www.archaiologia.gr/blog/2010/11/30.

[196] A mason's mark is associated with Roman-period reworking of the stone.

THE EPITAPHIC HABIT 179

FIGURE 4.13 Fragment of another *stêlê* found at the site of the Villa of Herodes Attikos at Loukou-Eva Kynouria. Archaeological Museum of Astros (Inv. 586).

FIGURE 4.14 Fragment of another *stêlê* found at the site of the Villa of Herodes Attikos at Loukou-Eva Kynouria. Archaeological Museum of Astros (Inv. 587).

the same checkerboard manner have also been found, one within the villa's Hypostyle Hall, the other built into a path leading from it to the north part of the villa's core (Figures 4.13 and 4.14).[197] The intact *stêlê* also bears markings that show it was joined to something else. Herodes thus probably had more than one and most likely all ten *stêlai* set up inside his villa. The current excavator, Giorgios Spyropoulos, holds that they were originally displayed within the Hypostyle Hall, interpreted as the villa's formal reception room (Figure 4.11).[198]

---

[197] Spyropoulos 2009, 23–4; Ameling 2011, 11, 21.
[198] Spyropoulos 2009, 13, 24. Cf. Papaioannou 2018, 347. The large and heavy *stêlê* (h. 0.68m; w. 0.558–0.57m; d. 0.265–0.285m) is unlikely to have been moved far by the monks of Loukou, although Tobin did note a lime kiln in the vicinity; see Tobin 1997, 335.

The *stêlê*, then, is a survivor from the monument to the fallen *Marathonomachoi*, which once stood at their Marathonian tomb. It caused a stir upon its discovery, largely due to the power that the narrative of the victory of the greatly outnumbered free Athenians and Plataians over the mass of eastern Persian slaves holds over western imaginations. The main scholarly interest in the *stêlê*, therefore, has been squarely on what the epigram says (i.e., how were these heroes remembered at their tomb in words?) and whether it is the genuine article. No one has been particularly interested in what Herodes was doing with it in his private villa approximately 200 km from Marathon beyond seeing it as another example of imperial Greek fascination with the past.

The first line of the epigram is very difficult to read and no definitive transcription has been established;[199] the most reliable version comes from Marco Tentori Montalto, based on autopsy and the production of a squeeze.[200] I reproduce his version of the epigram below with a translation:

Φἐμὶ· καὶ hόσστις ναίει hυφ' Άōς τ' ἔσσχατα γαίἐς,[201]
τōνδ' ἀνδρōν ἀρετὲν πεύσεται, hōς ἔθανον
βαρνάμενοι Μέδοισι καὶ ἐσστεφάνōσαν Άθένας,
παυρότεροι πολλōν δεχσάμενοι πόλεμον

I declare: even whoever dwells beneath Eos at the ends of the earth,
Will learn of the *aretê* (excellence/virtue/valour) of these men, how they died
Fighting the Medes and how they crowned Athens,[202]
Having taken on the war, a few against many.

Due to the autopsy of Pausanias, who reported seeing *stêlai* engraved with the names of the dead for each tribe on the *soros* in his *Description of Greece* (1.32.3), there has been speculation that Herodes' *stêlai* are not original. Arguments for

---

[199] Steinhauer 2004–2009, 690–1 (drawing by Skouloudhi on p. 691); Spyropoulos 2009, 42–5. Spyropoulos' photos show the stone with a clear covering on which recognized letter forms have been marked, thus obscuring the markings on the stone itself. Discussion of the epigram before Tentori Montalto's newest version can be found in: Steinhauer 2004–2009; Steinhauer 2009, 122–3; Spyropoulos 2009; Steinhauer 2010; Ameling 2011; Proietti 2012; 2013; Petrovic 2013; Tentori Montalto 2013; Janko 2014. A brief summary of discussion exists in Pitt 2014–15, 51. See now also Olson 2016; Proietti 2020.

[200] Tentori Montalto 2014. Note that the squeeze is now in the archive of *Inscriptiones Graecae* at the Berlin-Brandenburgische Akademie der Wissenschaften.

[201] The remaining issue is that there are two vertical strokes between *ΦΑΟΣ* and *ΕΣΣΧΑΤΑ*. If the first is not a fault in the stone, and the squeeze in particular appears to show it is a deliberate stroke, Proietti's (2012, 99–101) and Janko's (2014, 12) readings of aspiration, *hΕΣΣΧΑΤΑ*, would be correct, *contra* Tentori Montalto (2014, 35). The translation above reflects this, although confirmation requires direct study of the stone and squeeze. Janko's suggestion of ὑ<πὲρ> φάος for Tentori Montalto's ὑφ' Άως is also possible if improbable.

[202] Or 'because they died fighting the Medes and because they crowned Athens', with causal ὡς after verb of learning, see *LSJ* s.v. VI.I and Petrovic 2013, 60.

and against an early fifth-century date have been made on both epigraphic and stylistic grounds, with consensus falling on authenticity and 480 BC.[203] Andrej Petrovic, however, has suggested a date between 480 and 475 BC, and most likely after the Greek victories at Salamis and Plataia. Using Steinhauer's *editio princeps* that begins with φῆμις ('oracular utterance'), he posited that the epigram responds triumphantly as a form of oracular criticism to the 'medizing' Delphic oracles, which told the Athenians to 'flee to the ends of the earth' (φεῦγ᾿ ἔσχατα γαίης, Hdt. 7.140) rather than defend Attica against Xerxes' invasion in 480–79 BC.[204] His argument still works with the epigram in its present form, if *ΦΕΜΙ* is taken ambiguously to be both the first person singular form of the verb and the vocative of φῆμις, so that the stone can be understood to apostrophize the oracle at the same time as addressing the passer-by. In this case, it celebrates not only the unexpected victory at Marathon, but also that the Athenians defeated the Persians again at the naval Battle of Salamis, after defying the overt meaning of the oracle and, via Themistocles' reinterpretation, abandoning the city. It is probable, then, that the final form of the *stêlê*'s inscription that included both epigram and casualty list was achieved shortly after 479 BC.

Spyropoulos argues convincingly that the memorial was moved from Marathon to Loukou after AD 165, around the time when Herodes lost most of his family.[205] Pausanias' report, then, probably indicates that Herodes snatched the *stêlai* after Pausanias had passed through Marathon, or even that Pausanias tells us about what used to be there rather than what still was. Therefore, although the *stêlai* might be copies or from somewhere other than the tomb of the Athenians at Marathon, the weight of evidence argues against it. More important than its authenticity for my purposes (and I believe Herodes') is that this *stêlê* is intended to commemorate the fame of the glorious Athenian dead, even to the ends of the earth.

---

[203] Authentic based on epigraphy: Keesling 2012; Tentori Montalto 2014, 34–7; cf. Steinhauer 2004–2009, 681–6; 2010. Copy based on stylistics: Proietti 2013, 26–9. She concedes the casualty list and tribal heading may be original, but sees the epigram as a late edition because, in her opinion, it is not very good or fitting, and its appearance on the stone is cramped and off kilter; see Proietti 2013, 28; 2012, 101–3, 105–8. There is logic to the latter position, in that a *stêlê* at the *soros* does not require explanation, but once moved, it needs verbal supplementation to explain its origin. Petrovic 2013, Olson (2016, 47–50), and Ewen Bowie (pers. comm.), however, have presented fifth-century parallels for the epigram, revealing its language is not unusual. Moreover, Proietti's spatial arguments can be upended to ask why such a significant gap would exist between heading and list were the epigram later. Butz 2015, discussing letter forms and arrangement, concludes the stone is either original or an excellent reproduction. Cf. Ameling 2011, 20–3. Note the left-side moulding also indicates a fifth-century date. Proietti 2020 recasts her position of a two-phase inscriptional process to argue the *stêlê* dates from the early 480s and the epigram from the 470s. For examples of archaizing inscriptions that date to the first centuries AD, most of which do not reproduce an older inscription, see Lazzarini 1986, 147–53, figs 1–4.

[204] Petrovic 2013, 58–61. Cf. Proietti 2020.   [205] Spyropoulos 2009, 20.

Spyropoulos bases his argument for the date of the *stêlai*'s transfer on a traceable shift in the design of the villa from a museum-like structure to a focus on honouring the dead. As well as re-siting the Marathon *stêlai*, a number of other innovations were made. The temple of Dionysos-Antinoos was transformed into a Heroon-cenotaph. A series of statues of dancing figures were removed from display and replaced by niches filled with reclining representations of members of Herodes' deceased family and portrait busts.[206] Herodes went on to establish games and feasts for the dead at this location. He set up heroic statues, including an Achilles and Penthesileia group, and a copy of the Pasquino group (seen by Colonel Leake in the 1820s),[207] as well as athletic victors. He also established funerary reliefs, some of which stemmed from other classical period tombs.[208] Finally, he included among this wealth of artefacts representations of his own family, Roman emperors, and heroic reliefs of his foster-sons.

Herodes' act of resituating the Marathon inscriptions provides a specific physical example of self-commemoration through the appropriation of earlier commemorative strategies. The incorporation of the entire honorific memorial to the fallen of Marathon would have enhanced the prestige of the monumental mausoleum he was constructing at Loukou. Moreover, the act required effort and audacity. It reveals a greater concern for his own renown than for the protection of one of classical Athens' most important monuments, and suggests ownership or at least curatorship of the Marathon legend.[209] As mentioned above, the battle became a symbol of Greek identity in the Roman world and of 'the proper role of provincial Greek aristocracy' in Roman eyes.[210] S. Douglas Olson interprets this role as glorifying the city of Athens despite the reality of Roman rule. Herodes' activities in Athens, including elaborate benefaction and displays of rhetorical prowess, fit well into this context, in which he equated himself with the *Marathonomachoi*.[211]

As we have seen, the conflation of martial excellence with literary brilliance is commonplace in imperial Greek literature, especially in relation to Alexander the Great. Infrequent, however, is military might placed side by side with building, since that is the domain of emperors. A third-century inscription from Petri near

---

[206] See Spyropoulos 2006b, 24, for an illustration of these representations.

[207] Leake 1830, 488–9. Given Herodes' familial associations, this group probably represented Ajax carrying Achilles rather than Menelaos carrying Patroklos.

[208] See Spyropoulos 2009, 20; 2006b; Papaioannou 2018, 347–8, on the Heroon, reliefs, feasting.

[209] Ameling (2011, 21) perceptively notes that the sanctity of tombs was not critical to Herodes, who incorporated elements from other fifth-century memorials as well. The possibility that he despoiled the Marathon memorial is something Proietti (2012, 112–13) thinks a step too far even for Herodes. von Moock 1998 explains that the reuse of earlier funerary monuments in Attica is not unusual. His examples, however, tend to be Hadrianic period reuse of Augustan or Julio-Claudian monuments (see nos. 175, 192, 205, 212, 214, 216, 231, 261, 264).

[210] Olson 2016, 63.   [211] See further Section 6.5.

FIGURE 4.15 One half of a pair of third-century inscriptions found at Petri, near Nemea. Archaeological Museum of Nemea. The inscription names Herodes Attikos as a paradigm of building and Hellenic culture. The inscriptions were cut down to be used as building material and incorporated into a Christian tomb (*SEG* 41.273). Height: 0.49 m; Width: 0.71 m; Depth: 0.145 m.

Nemea is pertinent in this context (Figure 4.15).[212] It outlines the descent of a certain Flavianus' family from himself to an Aristomenes, six generations removed, and focuses on Aristomenes' constructions as a sign of the family's worth (τοῦ τάδε ἔργα τέτυκται, l. 7). In it, Flavianus compares himself to Herodes Attikos both in looks and in his and his descendants' capacity as great builders, claiming in Homeric terms, 'Herodes alone of the Achaeans won glory equal to me (μοι ἴσον κλέος), | just as he matches me in the form of his appearance' (ll. 9–10). In Flavianus' vision, Herodes and himself become the best of the Achaeans specifically through their monumentalizing activity. So here an example of warrior glory is equated to commemorative construction that perhaps found its exemplar in Herodes' Marathonian posturing.[213]

As shown in chapter 3 and detailed further in chapter 6, Herodes' ties to Marathon were strong.[214] He came from that deme, owned much of the surrounding land,

---

[212] On this inscription see Kritzas 1992; Jones 2014.

[213] Note that the inscription also draws on Herodes' Homeric self-fashioning, since a statue base dedicated to Regilla from Corinth (*Corinth* 8.3, no. 128; Inv. no. 1658) refers to Herodes as 'the great' (μέγας, l. 3), 'standing out from others' (ἔξοχος ἄλλων, l. 3), reaching the peak 'of every excellence' ([παντ]οίης ἀρετῆς, l. 4), 'much talked about among the Hellenes' (Ἑλλήνων…περίβωτον ἁπάντων, l. 5) and 'a son (of Greece) greater than them all, the flower of Achaia' ([κρέσ]σονα δ' αὖτε π⟨ά⟩ϊν ἄνθος Ἀχαιιάδος, l. 6). See also Schowalter 2014, 166–9.

[214] See Sections 3.1 and 6.5. See also Bowie 2013, 251–3.

traced his line back to Miltiades (*VS* 2.1.546–7), Marathon's victorious general, and named one of his daughters Elpinike after Miltiades' child. Moreover, he set up busts of at least himself, Polydeukion, and Faustina the Younger near the *soros*. He worked his family's connection to the battle into iconographic elements such as those on the so-called 'Leda Sarcophagus' from Kephisia, which was probably made for Elpinike and her husband (Figure 6.7). He frequented and made dedications at the sanctuary of Rhamnousian Nemesis, whose cult was intricately connected with the battle.[215] It begs the question, then, why take the *stêlai* to Loukou and not his villa near Marathon? The Marathonian plain was a powerful landscape of cultural memory that contained numerous antique tombs as well as Herodes' Sanctuary of the Egyptian Gods (itself a nod to Hadrian's villa at Tivoli).[216] Alternatively, why not to his villa at Kephisia, where most of his family actually were buried?

One answer must lie in the character of the Loukou villa's decorative programme. The Marathon *stêlai* were only one of the artefacts on display there. If the kind of gathering involved with museum-like collections asserts that identity is a form of 'wealth (of objects, knowledge, memories, experience)',[217] then the identity that Herodes projects in connection to the artefacts at Loukou is one concerned first and foremost with his and his family's commemoration.[218] By taking the *stêlai*, Herodes displaces and appropriates the significance attached to them and forces them into the role of honouring his personal dead with all the glorious tradition of the *Marathonomachoi*, who were worshipped as heroes in imperial times (Paus. 1.32.3).[219] When considered in the context of the other finds, the *stêlai* of the Marathon fallen serve less as an example to be emulated and more as a guide to how Herodes and his family should be conceptualized. Their meaning is determined by how they are placed within relations of significance—that they were in the formal reception hall, and the amount of space they would have occupied, must matter—and, equally, how a viewer might approach and move about the broader display.[220]

The aesthetic properties of the *stêlê* are important in this respect, because it is not simply an inscription, but rather an artistically inscribed, three-dimensional narrative of glorious death and, as such, very much at home amidst heroic and

---

[215] On the finds associated with Herodes near the *soros*, see Tobin 1997, 275–6; see also the discussion of Perry 2001, especially 482–3 on Herodes' iconographic links to Marathon on the Leda Sarcophagus and 485–9 on the attribution to Elpinike. Cf. Galli 2002, 158–60. On Herodes' connection to Marathon in general, see Galli 2002, 178–9; Proietti 2012, 110–12. For all Herodes' building activities at and around Marathon, see Tobin 1997, 241–83; Papaioannou 2018, 339–45.

[216] On this shrine and Herodes, see Mazurek 2018.   [217] Clifford 1988, 218.

[218] For a concise summary of the display, see Papaioannou 2018, 248–50.

[219] See also *IG* II² 1006, ll. 26–7; Matthaiou 2003, 197–8.

[220] Hooper-Greenhill 2000, 50, on relations of significance; cf. Bergmann 1994, 225–7, on the pluralities of meaning possible within artistic displays, depending on how, and the order in which, one views them. The finds associated directly with the Hypostyle Hall by Spyropoulos (2001, 22) include: a torso of Hermes, bust of a male in a toga, portrait of Dionysos, statue of Athena, portrait bust of Mithras, portrait of Herodes, portrait of Korê, fourth-century BC grave *stêlê*, two more grave *stêlai*, a statue base, several other unidentified or headless busts. For all the finds in the villa, see Spyropoulos 2001, 20–30.

funerary art.[221] Patricia Butz has highlighted that the names almost form a square, suggesting that the break at the bottom of the stone was deliberate to create this effect, and that their *stoichedon*, 'checkerboard' arrangement draws the eye and encourages the perception of multidirectional legibility. This impression invests the inscription with a quasi-magical quality, as though it might contain esoteric knowledge from the Greek past beyond its ostensible commemorative text.[222] The checkerboard arrangement also recalls isodomic ashlar masonry so typical of Athenian and Roman monumental buildings.[223] The *stélê* thus builds the concept of monumental architecture into its self-presentation. Fittingly, it references too the distribution of the Athenian hoplite phalanx that destroyed the Persians.[224]

The visually captivating Marathon *stélê* that draws one in to read its narrative of glorious death, added to the transformation of the temple of Antinoos-Dionysos into a heroon and the introduction of feasts for the dead according to the require-ments of hero-cult, as well as the proliferation of heroic and funerary art,[225] reveal that Herodes was constructing a commemorative monumental anthology of Hel-lenic heroic virtue for the benefit of himself and his predominantly deceased family. This must be why the *stélai* had to come all the way to Loukou instead of to Marathon or Kephisia, because it is at Loukou that Herodes chose to honour his dead and embed them amongst examples of his culture's most honoured dead, such as the deified Antinoos, Achilles, Herakles, and the *Marathonomachoi*. It is an act that transfers the memory-laden Marathonian landscape to Arkadia and makes the past glories of Athens hinge on one man's commemorative obsessions.

One fascinating find evinces that Herodes' memorial outlook extended beyond his own family to include a broader vision of Greek heroic virtue that truly incorporated contemporary elites into heroic tradition. As mentioned, there are numerous unidentified portrait sculptures associated with the villa at Loukou. One of these bears a striking resemblance, down to the distinctive hairknot and associated scheme of six radiating forelocks, to the member of the Vedii Antonini family from Ephesos (Figure 4.16) whose portrait type was identified by Sheila Dillon (Figures 4.17, 4.18, and 4.19).[226]

---

[221] On the importance of the viewing experience of inscriptions, see Beard 1998, 83–8; Cooley 2018.

[222] Butz 2015, 89–96. The arrangement appears on the magical healing *Stélê* of Moschion from Sakha in Lower Egypt, which calls its own arrangement *stoichedon* and states it should be read in multiple directions (89–90). Keesling 2012 argues for *plinthedon* style. See Squire 2009, 137–9, on multi-directional inscrip-tions on *tabulae Iliacae*.

[223] Steinhauer 2004–09; Petrovic 2013, 54.   [224] Steinhauer 2004–09, 683; Butz 2015, 91.

[225] See Spyropoulos 2009, 20.

[226] Dillon 1996, with extensive bibliography. Spyropoulos 2006a, 113–14 no. 9, 117 fig. 23; Spyro-poulos suggests this is a member of the same family, but not the same individual, and has since identified the portrait as T. Flavius Damianos. See also Smith 1998, 81–2. Izmir Inv. no. 648 (Figure 4.18), was identified as T. Flavius Damianos by Keil 1932, col. 31; see also Alzinger 1970, col. 1614; Fittschen 2021, no. 26, 50–4, taf. 28. Dillon 1996, however, argued convincingly for the three previously known portraits of this individual from Ephesus (Figures 4.17–19) as all being of the same man and as representing M. Claudius P. Vedius Antoninus Sabinus or his son M. Claudius P. Vedius Antoninus Phaedrus Sabinianus. Szewczyk

Figure 4.16 Portrait of a priest, probably a member of the Vedii Antonini family from Ephesos, found at the Villa of Herodes Attikos at Loukou-Eva Kynouria. Archaeological Museum of Astros. Height: 0.70 m.

Figure 4.17 Portrait of a member of the Vedii Antonini family without priestly crown, found at Ephesos. Izmir Archaeological Museum (Inv. 570). Height: 0.31 m.

2015 narrows the field to M. Claudius P. Vedius Antoninus Sabinus, but this identification is not definitive; see further Quatember and Scheilbelreiter-Gail 2017, 226–8. The portrait from Loukou most closely matches that of Izmir Archaeological Museum, Inv. no. 570 (Figure 4.17). Spyropoulos published the bust in the Capitoline Museum's *L'età dell'angoscia* exhibition catalogue 2015 and discussed it in presentations at ISAW in New York and at the Scuola Italiana di Atene in 2017.

THE EPITAPHIC HABIT 187

FIGURE 4.18 Portrait of a priest and member of the Vedii Antonini family, found at Ephesos. Izmir Archaeological Museum (Inv. 648). Height: 0.35 m.

FIGURE 4.19 Portrait of a priest and member of the Vedii Antonini family. Louvre (MND 1012). Height: 0.38 m.

The Loukou version is particularly interesting because it resembles most closely the unadorned head of Figure 4.17, but preserves the rolled fillet headdress of the two priestly versions from Ephesos, while lacking the bust crown. It thus strengthens the case for all four portraits representing the same man. The presence of this bust at Loukou opens the possibility that other currently anonymous portraits might belong to other members of the Hellenic elite from the breadth of the eastern empire.[227] Both Herodes and the Vedii Antonini were great benefactors to their respective cities and Herodes would have known the family from his time as Corrector of Asia.[228] He abided some while in Ephesos and was honoured there by at least one statue, set up in the precinct of the Artemision.[229] The Loukou bust is fittingly heroic for Herodes' overall decorative scheme, with bare chest and *himation*, in comparison to the more modestly attired honorific examples from Ephesos that also sport a tunic.

Alongside this broad display of elite Hellenic virtue, Herodes incorporates Roman emperors, and here Antinoos, with his likely connection to imperial cult, also plays a role.[230] The boy from Bithynia, who was deified by Hadrian, takes on a bridging, mediating function between the two cultures, which is expressed beautifully by a cuirass bust of Hadrian sporting a winged Antinoos portrait in place of the Gorgoneion. The Greek beauty, beloved of Hadrian, takes on the Gorgon's apotropaic functions, bestowing the emperor with the power to petrify in battle, and the cuirass, the symbol of his imperium, is empowered by his new Greek god (Figure 4.20).[231] Note that both these portraits were probably arranged with busts of Herodes and his family on an exedra associated with the nymphaion at the west end of the central peristyle.[232]

Like Arrian in the Second Preface of the *Anabasis*, Herodes too creates a cultural lineage and glorious context for his own efforts. Indeed, the resettlement of the Marathon memorial is analogous to an author inserting an inscription into his text and manipulating its meaning for his own literary ends. Unlike Arrian, however, Herodes does so in the framework of both Greek cultural and former political greatness and current Roman power. Arrian may have been between two worlds for Pierre Vidal-Naquet, but at Loukou Herodes demonstrates his immersion in both and that, importantly, is how he shapes his identity

---

[227] Note that some of these portraits are likely later third-century additions, along with Severan-period emperors; see Papaioannou 2018, 350. See Fittschen 2021, no. 25, 48–50, taf. 26, 27, for another example of a portrait from Loukou with copies elsewhere, including from Dion.

[228] On this family see Kalinowski 2021.

[229] *I.Ephesos* 3.640; See also Ameling 1983b, no. 77; Tobin 1997, 330–1.

[230] On Antinoos and the imperial cult, see Vout 2007, 12–13; 113–20.

[231] Spyropoulos 2006a, 106 no.2, 105 fig.16; Spyropoulos in Calandra and Adembri 2014, no. 18. See further Strazdins (In press) on the Gorgon associations, the suggestion the wings invoke Eros, and why Herodes presented Hadrian in this way. The bust will be discussed in Spyropoulos (In press) and has featured in talks he gave at ISAW in New York and McMaster University.

[232] See Spyropoulos 2006a; Rogers 2021, 102–3.

THE EPITAPHIC HABIT 189

FIGURE 4.20 Marble cuirass protome of the Emperor Hadrian with the head of Antinoos in place of the Gorgoneion from Herodes' villa at Loukou-Eva Kynouria. Archaeological Museum of Astros. Height: 0.635 m.

for posterity.[233] The display approaches a new, modern, multicultural, and multi-traditional Pindaric Ode in material form.

The plurality of representation also supports a plurality of interpretation and how one might receive the *stêlê* for the fallen *Marathonomachoi* within this eclectic display is hard to pin down. The glory of those who fought off the Persians sits in tension with the many busts of Roman emperors but, at the same time, the Hellenic elite as mediators and friends of Roman power, and as an authoritative cultural force, create the impression of imperial harmony, as though the emperors are just another link in this glorious chain. Images like the Hadrian-Antinoos bust take this a step further to imply that Rome's power is sustained by Greek underpinning, just like the statues on Kelsos' library façade in Ephesos.[234]

[233] Vidal-Naquet 1984, 309–94.
[234] On the Hadrian bust in this context, see Strazdins (In press).

As evinced by his curse-inscription habit (see Section 4.2.3), Herodes was not immune to the nuances of and problems with his collecting practice, as well as the difficulty of maintaining such a carefully constructed display and its plural messages. The pedantry he displayed in the increasingly specific language of the curses is thus ironic and extraordinary, given his removal of the inscribed casualty *stêlai* from Marathon. In some way, he must have conceived of these artefacts as belonging to him rather than to the *dêmos* of Athens or the deme of Marathon. Nevertheless, both the curse inscriptions and the transposed Marathon memorial indicate the potential to redefine and redirect a monument's commemorative intention, as well as Herodes' need to control how his and his family's virtue is commended to the future.

The display of wealth, including cultural wealth, is a claim to a type of prestige on which political power is based.[235] The question of the villa's audience is therefore important. If considered as a country retreat, the villa was unlikely to receive many visitors beyond family, friends, and the extensive staff necessary to run the estate.[236] Such a secluded context renders the villa a personal project of familial commemoration for Herodes' benefit in life and for his descendants after him. The villa, moreover, was probably passed to the imperial family at some point after Herodes' death, given later decorative adjustments which integrate them into the villa to a greater extent while maintaining Herodes' centrality. The Hypostyle Hall, however, as the primary site of formal reception at the villa, is the most public space on this private estate.[237] Anyone who did come there, whether on official business or as a guest, would have passed through it and seen the Marathon *stêlai*. Maria Papaioannou estimates that the villa's grounds occupy 20,000 m^2 and that it controlled commercial activities further afield such as the production of wine and olive oil, animal husbandry, game hunting, and stone quarrying.[238] It also had easy access to ports in the bays of Astros and Thyreatis. Thus numerous members of the surrounding communities or regular visitors to the region probably met Herodes or his representatives in this hall. Such guests might have included the inhabitants of the large town of Eua or frequenters of the healing sanctuary of Polemokrates (Paus. 2.38.6), as well as merchants and/or consumers of local produce and raw materials, and possibly even local adherents of Antinoos or imperial cult.[239]

Here is another reason why the Marathon *stêlai* had to come to the Peloponnese rather than to Herodes' villas at Marathon or Kephisia. Herodes' 'Hero of Marathon' persona was not popular in Attica,[240] but it might have impressed or at

---

[235] Pearce 1995, 105.   [236] Tobin 1997, 333–4; Butz 2015, 88.

[237] On formal reception basilicas, see Papaioannou 2018, 347.

[238] Papaioannou 2018, 345, 351.

[239] See Papaioannou 2018, 351, on the possible commercial activities of the villa.

[240] See further chapter 6.

least been accepted by the more removed locals around Loukou. It also offered this hyper-Athenian the opportunity to 'troll' the Peloponnesians, whose ancestors famously missed the Battle of Marathon. What is clear is that such elaborate and potentially controversial self-fashioning is best expressed in the private sphere—no cityscape within the Roman empire existed in which Herodes could embed such a personal and provocative identity without experiencing backlash.[241]

The context of the *stêlê*'s display, then, shifts focus from an artefact that marks the birth of the Classical age as we know it to Herodes and his family, who become the stars around which the symbols of Hellenic and Roman imperial culture constellate. There is in this private space a rescaling of past glories and present political realities that shapes Herodes Attikos as the distillation and culmination of Graeco-Roman heroic tradition. The past and present are made to work for his commemoration at the same time as the decorative programme and ritual activity associated with the villa solidify and codify Herodes' renowned, excessive, performative, almost Homeric grief to shape a multifaceted heroic identity.[242] The *epideixis* involved in this mourning gives him the excuse to become more and more elaborate in his monumental building. Here in the villa, his identity draws broadly and aggressively on Greek heroes, including Achilles, Herakles, and especially the *Marathonomachoi*. In this way, Herodes pushes the boundaries between the adoption of a persona from the past and his contemporary persona in how he presents himself to the present and the future. It is very much the same self-conscious play with temporal positioning and the preservation of memory found in the textual works of such authors as Arrian and Lucian, but in the face of inevitable oblivion it emits a far more desperate character. Herodes' commemorative urgency approaches that of Arrian's Alexander rather than that of Lucian or Arrian himself. Towards the end of his life, Herodes became increasingly preoccupied with leaving a lasting mark for posterity through the manipulation of exemplars, both Greek and imperial Roman.

In this context, the Marathon *stêlê*'s authenticity—the element that has so concerned modern scholars—becomes largely irrelevant.[243] If the *stêlê* is a very good copy of a fifth-century BC memorial, it does not lose its commemorative value. There was no stigma attached to the copying of famous Greek sculptures in Roman imperial times. Indeed, copies of originals were highly valued and could be treated as though they were equivalent to the original masterpiece (e.g. Lucian's

---

[241] Again, see chapter 6.

[242] Spyropoulos (2009, 20) sees the mourning as genuine. On Herodes' extravagant mourning, see also Section 6.4; Tobin 1997, 248–9; Gleason 2010, 157–62; and Strazdins (forthcoming).

[243] For a discussion of the dynamics of authenticity and *mimêsis* in imperial Greek literature, see ní Mheallaigh 2014, 232–40. On the topic of authenticity in general, see Higbie 2017.

Lover of Lies 18).[244] Moreover, if the replicated object were well-known enough, it became 'exceptionally effective in broadcasting socially relevant information because of [its] capacity to evoke multiple memories and associated narratives'.[245] In such a scenario, replication was as effective as originality.

The clearest difference in viewer interpretation if the stones were part of the original memorial rather than copies would be a greater emphasis placed on Herodes as the inheritor and arbiter of the glorious tradition of the *Marathonomachoi*. The overall meaning, however, would not change, especially since, in a world before photography or mass media, one would have to see the originals closely and, depending on the precision of replication, even require original and copy side by side to discern any differences between them. This possibility is negated by the distance between Loukou and Marathon.[246] If the *stêlai* were copies, part of their purpose was no doubt precisely to prompt the viewer to consider how the presence of the originals might impact the display. Concern for authenticity in this case, then, is more something in which modern scholars and those with a stake in Greek national identity or notions of 'western civilization' are invested. The Battle of Marathon has a revered place in the history of western culture and identity formation. The discovery of its original memorial is hugely significant in those terms, but, if it is Herodes' use of the stones one is interested in, their originality or replication is inconsequential. Given the context of the villa's artistic programme, it was the idea of the memorial, how it harmonized with the villa's other artefacts, and how Herodes' family fitted within that tradition that truly preoccupied Herodes Attikos.

4.5 CONCLUSION

The reuse of historical, literary, or monumental memory and the claiming of authority over the famous and their memorialization allows imperial Greeks to create a culturally meaningful context for their own commemorative efforts. Such manipulation of the cultural and historical record, however, inadvertently highlights the inability of anyone to control his or her future reputation. This conundrum suffuses imperial Greek literary and material art with a sense of pathos. Though they strive to shape how they will be perceived within cultural history, their efforts are hampered by an awareness of the vulnerability of fame and reputation posthumously, especially when it is attached to a textual or physical artefact. A striking element in engagement with the commemorative capacity of

---

[244] On the culture of Roman-era copying, see Vermeule 1977, 1–19; Gazda 2002, 1–24; Perry 2002; 2005, 1–17; Hallett 2005; Varner 2006; Wyler 2006; Small 2008; Anguissola 2014; Di Napoli 2016.

[245] Anguissola 2014, 120.   [246] See Small 2008, 235, on Roman appreciation of copies.

epigraphy that emphasizes this pathos is that, no matter what an inscription's ostensible purpose, it is regularly reinterpreted or reshaped as epitaphic.

Importantly, inscribed monuments in imperial Greek art are always situated in concrete commemorative landscapes, whether imaginary or real: they are not the abstract memorials of Pindar or Horace. One explanation for this arises in the fact that Pindar and Horace had no realistic hope of attaching their names to a physical monument nor do their works intimate a desire for such commemoration. Whereas Philostratos' many wealthy elite sophists were quite capable of granting or, at least, contributing to significant monumental benefactions to various cities that would carry their name into the future and actively sought to do so. The significant sites of Greek history thus become multitemporal spaces and the monuments within them act as time machines that communicate between the temporal layers and allow the projection of fame into the future as well as acting as portals to the past. In this way, imperial Greek writers and monumentalizers can extract their own cultural efforts and carefully shaped identities from the immediate Roman present and place them rather in a grander cycle of history, where Rome becomes just another empire destined ultimately to subside. Imperial Greeks can thus position themselves as central to the preservation of its power. This multidirectional, temporally expansive perspective rescales Greek and Roman history and shifts focus to a hypothetical future moment, when someone looking back might see imperial Greeks as an equal notch on a long, culturally inclusive timeline or, potentially, as its culmination. Thus imperial Greeks make the past work for themselves and their own commemoration. The evocation of Alexander or the emulation of Homer serves as a starting point for something greater. These are not individuals in whose shadows to cower, but paradigms from which to depart.

FIVE

Commemoration Embodied

The idol in ashes, to be swept away with the trash.
– C. P. Cavafy, *In the Outskirts of Antioch.*[1]

Building on the 'Epitaphic Habit', this chapter takes a closer look at one specific type of inscribed monument: the honorific statue. Statues are examined here separately because of their mimetic qualities and special ability to replace the individual whom they represent, both in a physical sense and as metaphoric representations of some facet of consciousness or identity. Expressly designed as commemorative artefacts, statues should be desirable honours. As this chapter argues, however, imperial Greek texts and aspects of how statues are deployed in reality suggest instead that an honorific statue is insufficient and ultimately unsuitable for personal commemorative ambition. The chapter begins by establishing the place of statue honours in the empire and their perceived commemorative limitations and will then move on to examine several literary and material strategies employed by imperial Greeks that are designed to counter these disadvantages. In particular, I consider how statue programmes on monuments are used to amplify commemorative claims; how texts can create carefully tailored, imaginary, and inviolable spaces of honour; how the replication of private portrait types can extend fame to a broader audience; and how literature can remove the limitations of the honorific statue by animating it and instilling personality. Herodes Attikos will again form the focus of the material discussion, but the texts are drawn from a much broader field, including Favorinus, Apuleius, Aelius Aristeides, Polemon, Philostratos, Arrian, and Dio Chrysostom.

5.1 STATUE HONOURS AND THEIR LIMITATIONS

As a widespread practice, the granting of statue honours emerged in Greek cities at the end-of-the-fifth/beginning-of-the-fourth century BC.[2] Statues were a

---

[1] Translated by Sacheroglou, in Hirst 2007, 61.
[2] Ma 2013, 4; Stoop 2017, 3. See also Keesling 2017, 19–52.

Fashioning the Future in Roman Greece: Memory, Monuments, Texts. Estelle Strazdins, Oxford University Press.
© Estelle Strazdins 2023. DOI: 10.1093/oso/9780192866103.003.0005

prestigious means of celebrating benefactors of the city and served to acknowledge generosity or service. They could be public or private dedications; each became increasingly frequent from the second century BC onwards into the Roman period, and both types influenced and encouraged each other.[3] The individual honoured could be one of the city's own citizens or a foreigner who took a particular interest in a given locale.[4] Indeed, statues were the most common honour given to Roman benefactors in Greece.[5] Usually, an honorific image required ratification by a city's assembly, so that no statue could occupy public space without the approval of the *dêmos*.[6] Honorific statues, therefore, were a long-standing, civic-based, traditional system to signify reciprocity and power relationships between benefactor, city, and dedicator.

This specificity was important for sophists, who journeyed around the empire and formed distinct relationships with discrete *poleis*. The purpose of their images, therefore, differs markedly from statuary of the imperial family, whose repeated, mostly replicated images were a means of extending their presence physically throughout the empire as well as within the minds of their subjects.[7] Honorific statues, in contrast, continually reminded a community of a particular debt owed to the statue's subject and, at the same time, fulfilled that debt. Their message was thus tightly controlled by local civic authorities.[8] Their particularity could limit their commemorative potential as well as any imperial connotations: not only were they restricted to one place, but they tended to be commissioned or granted for a single distinct achievement or event, such as an athletic victory, or a discrete civic service. An honorific statue thus records a single moment in time and represents the tension between a specified and universal identity.

Public, highly frequented spaces—the agora, gymnasium, theatre, or a sanctuary—were the most desirable settings for one's statue, and the more it could present an obstacle to passing crowds, the more likely it was to be noticed and its significance registered.[9] By its fixity, durability, and visibility, a statue maximized its potential to extend one's fame well beyond the present and to a broad cross-section of society. At the same time, the statue gained meaning from

---

[3] See Ma 2006, 325; 2007, 203–4; 2013, 7–11.   [4] Stewart 1979, 115–16; Ma 2013, 4–5.

[5] Højte 2002, 55; Stoop 2017, 3–36.   [6] Stoop 2017, 4.

[7] See Ando 2000, 228–45, especially 232–9. See Elsner 1998, 54, on the ubiquitous nature of imperial images. See also Severian of Gabala, *On the Creation of the World* 5.5; Fronto, *Ep.* 4.12.6.

[8] Martin 1996, 53. Cf. Welsh 1904–05, 35; Smith 1998, 56, 61; Henderson 2002, 155–71, especially 161; Ma 2006, 326, 329; 2007, 213–14; 2013, 45–63; Platt 2007, 250. See Steiner 2001, 265–81, on the negotiation between *dêmos* and honorand with respect to honorific statues and encomia. See Ma 2007, 203–4, on Hellenistic honorifics in particular. Cf. van Nijf 2000 on Termessos.

[9] Stewart 2003, 136–40. See Ma 2013, 67–98, on Hellenistic cities, but his discussion is largely transferable to Roman Greek cities. See Dickenson 2017, 396–401, for agoras remaining vibrant civic centres, frequented not in the capacity of museums, but as a 'multipurpose public space' (400). Cf. Evangelidis 2014; Witschel 2014, 121–2.

those surrounding it, with the whole contextualizing the individual in a distinct, local honorific tradition. This broad communicative potential was nevertheless hampered in the Roman imperial period by the sheer number of statues dedicated: 'statues functioned as major punctuators of urban space and constituted an entire population in themselves, both at Rome and across the empire'.[10] Their abundance did not increase the likelihood of ancient viewers being particularly conscious of them, however, and one's own honour could easily get lost in the crowd.[11] This issue of crowding was intensified by the more desirable places for display attracting the most examples.[12] A related problem that also decreased the impact of individual dedications, was that, over time, the busiest thoroughfares and most frequented communal spaces might change. Indeed, for this reason, the re-siting of a statue could draw attention back to a monument that by its very fixity had fallen out of public consciousness.[13] Nevertheless, such an effect was possible only if the subject's identity and reasons for the initial dedication were preserved.[14]

Statuary has a theoretical advantage over other forms of memorialization, in that its inherent qualities and conventions facilitate recognition of its subject: the conformity of imperial images, accoutrements of cult statues, or recognizable honorific types such as athletes, philosophers, and soldiers, for instance.[15] This very conformity, however, could also blur and obscure accurate identification.[16] In a world before mass media, those who could identify the living model for any given portrait would be limited to those who knew that individual by sight, provided its features genuinely resembled the subject or, at least, that all his or her statues had a uniform likeness.[17] A statue's dedication was thus essential to its honorific function: without an inscription, the image was simply an ornament and, 'without a statue, the inscribed base was merely a civic record'.[18]

The inscription thus helped strengthen the connection between living model and artefact. The dedicator was usually the subject of the inscription and the represented individual the object. The statue itself was rarely mentioned: for

---

[10] Kellum 2015, 424. See also Stewart 2003, 118–56. Note the reservations of Stoop 2017.

[11] Stewart 2003, 118; see also Witschel 2014 on the increase and abundance of writing in imperial cities, on the concentration of monuments at the most frequented spaces in a city, and how these spaces of honour often developed around monuments associated with the imperial family. See especially 114–24 on how visitors of varying literacy, social rank, and epigraphic/monumental interest to the forum might interact with inscribed monuments.

[12] On Hellenistic cities in particular and the spatial relationships of their statues, see Ma 2013, 68–151.

[13] Stewart 2003, 149; Smith 2016, 1.   [14] Cf. Cooley 2000, 8–9.

[15] See Ma 2007, 204; Platt 2007, 259. See Zanker 1995 on the diachronic development of the image of the intellectual. See Witschel 2014, 122–3, on inscriptional uniformity allowing literate (and illiterate) viewers to understand the main message of a monument in a glance.

[16] Ma 2013, 125.   [17] Cf. Platt 2007, 259.

[18] Smith 2016, 3. Cf. Smith 1998, 56, 61; 2007, 84; Ma 2007, 205; Platt 2007, 251.

example, 'the *dêmos* dedicates X'.[19] John Ma well describes how the statue's metonymic function is complicated by the absence of the phrase, 'a statue of', which draws attention to the discreteness of the image and its subject:[20]

the statue, not mentioned but immediately thought of when the text is read, is both absent (in the text) and present (in indisputably physical form, bronze or marble, before the viewer-reader), like the represented person, personally absent yet present through the image.[21]

This slight metonymic ambiguity opens the door for the literary reinterpretation of representational meaning.

Conventions of inscriptional expression meant that the language of honour was comprehensible throughout the empire.[22] Subtle differences did occur between east and west, and even between different cities in the same region; some inscriptions preserve more individuality than others. In general, however, honorific inscriptions were largely generic.[23] Labels such as 'philosopher', 'sophist', 'teacher', 'rhetor' and virtues that drove the award such as $\dot{\alpha}\rho\epsilon\tau\dot{\eta}$ or $\dot{\alpha}\nu\delta\rho\epsilon\dot{\iota}\alpha$ were regularly employed, along with titles associated with imperial administrative, civic, or sacred positions.[24] A statue base from Olympia commemorating Philostratos, for example, marks him as a man of words:[25]

> Ἀγαθῇ Τύχῃ
> Δόγματι τῆς Ὀλυμπι-
> κῆς βουλῆς [*vac.*] Φλ. ℘
> Φιλόστρατον Ἀθη-
> ναῖον, τὸν σοφιστήν
> ἡ λαμπροτάτη πατρίς
> ℘   ℘

> To Good Luck.[26]
> By the decree of the Olympi-
> an *boulê* [*vac.*], Fl(avius) ℘
> Philostratos the Athe-
> nian, the sophist,
> his most radiant fatherland [dedicates (a statue of) him].
> ℘   ℘

[19] See Ma 2007, 205–15; 2013, 15–63, for the grammar of honorific inscriptions and the politics of this grammar.

[20] On the ability of statues to become the individual, particularly the god, whom they depict, see especially Elsner 2007d, 38–48.

[21] Ma 2007, 209. See Ma 2013, 15–43, for a detailed discussion of honorific grammar. Cf. Henderson 2002, 161.

[22] Stewart 2003, 166.   [23] Stewart 2003, 166–9, 28–35; Stoop 2017, 3–7.

[24] See the ample examples in Puech 2002. See also Smith 1998, 63–4.

[25] *I.Olympia*, no. 476; Puech 2002, 377–8, no. 200.

[26] On this common formula, see Thomas 2007, 172.

198 FASHIONING THE FUTURE IN ROMAN GREECE

FIGURE 5.1 Inscribed statue base of Arrian from Hierapolis (Komana, Kappadokia), built into a modern bridge in Şar, Adana province. The block lies on its left side, so that the inscription begins in the bottom left corner of the image (*SEG* 58.1665). Height: 1.075 m; Width: 0.498 m; Depth: 0.516 m.

Whereas one for Arrian from Hierapolis in Kappadokia[27]—the site of a sanctuary of the Syrian goddess Enyo or Ma—that is now built into a modern bridge records his imperial positions rather than his literary talents (Figure 5.1):[28]

Φλ. Ἀρριανὸν 𝒮 πρεσ.
καὶ ἀντιστρ. 𝒮 τοῦ
Σεβαστοῦ τὸν εὐ-
σεβέστατον καὶ δι-
καιότατον ἡγε-   5
μόνα 𝒮 ἡ ἱερὰ σύν-
[ο]δος τοῦ Ἀπόλλω-
νος 𝒮 ἐπιμελείᾳ
Μ. 𝒮 Ἰουνίου 𝒮 Ἀρχί-
ου τοῦ διὰ βίου ἱε-   10
ρέως 𝒮

Fl(avius) Arrian 𝒮 *legatus*
Augusti 𝒮 *pro*
praetore, most pi-

---

[27] Komana (modern Şar in Adana province, Turkey).
[28] Baz 2007, 123–7. On the translation of πρεσβευτὴν καὶ ἀντιστράτηγον τοῦ Σεβαστοῦ see Mason 1974, 78–9, 153. This was the official title given to governors or generals of imperial provinces.

ous and very
fair gov-
ernor, ✒ the sacred assem-   5
bly of Apollo
[dedicates (a statue of) him] ✒ by the undertaking of
M(arcus) ✒ Junius ✒ Archi-
as, for life the   10
priest ✒.

The translations above are awkward, but follow as closely as possible the layout of the inscriptions and demonstrate how conventional honorific dedications were, the way vine leaves or gaps can be used to highlight names and act as punctuation, as well as the recurrence of Roman-style abbreviations in second-century Greek inscriptions.[29] This formulaic language made it difficult to assert the kind of individuality necessary for a far-reaching, meaningful, and lasting reputation, but at the same time, was necessary in order to be understood correctly within local, contemporary social, political, and cultural parameters. Honorific statues thus affirm communal values through their lack of differentiation.[30]

These examples also underscore another consequence of dedicatory formulas: the lack of control the honorand had over the mode of his or her honouring, even though s/he might have been required to fund it.[31] For a public monument, as the two above, it is always a collective civic unit (*boulê*, *polis*, *dêmos*, 'the sacred assembly of Apollo') that dedicates the image, even if the impetus comes from someone else or a particular representative of the larger group (e.g. the Athenians or Marcus Junius Archias).[32] This issue is addressed by Apuleius (*c*. AD 125–after 170) of Madauros in North Africa, an orator, novelist, and philosopher, whose literary output, although in Latin, harmonizes with the kind of works produced by sophists in the Greek east.[33] In his *Florida* 16, he uses language to turn himself into the statue that the Carthaginian senate is granting him to stress how the honour wrests away his autonomy:[34]

Seeing that, in this way, I have set up (*institui*) the whole period of my life (*omne uitae meae tempus*) for you to approve (*probare*), to whom I have fixedly dedicated (*firmiter*

---

[29] On these issues, see Graham 2013.

[30] Ma 2006, 332; Stoop 2017. See Woolf 1996, 29–34, for the use of epigraphy to fix the individual's place in society, history, and the cosmos.

[31] Veyne 1990, 125. See also Steiner 2001, 265–81; Ma 2007, 214; 2013, 45–63.

[32] Ma 2013, 45–63, especially 49–55: the statue is a representation of the 'process of honouring, rather than (or as well as?) a homage to the honorand' (48). See also Stoop 2017, 5.

[33] Although he boasts of his ability in Greek, Apuleius' surviving works are all in Latin. On Apuleius as a Latin sophist, see Harrison 2000, 1–38; 2001, 1–2; Lee 2005, 20–5; Sandy 1997, 92–175.

[34] See Too 1996, 137–41, 145–6.

dedicaui) myself for all time (*in perpetuum*). I will never do anything so large, anything so small, without your knowledge and approval.   (16.3)

Apuleius therefore implies that all his future achievements will be regulated by Carthage through the image and honours they ascribe to him.

The confines of the relationship between man and city as represented by the honorific statue is one element against which imperial Greek authors and monumentalizers push back. How Apuleius retakes control of his reputation will be a subject I return to below. Another literary example, however, comes from Favorinus' (*c.* AD 85–*c.*155) *Corinthian Oration*, addressed to the citizens of Corinth in response to the removal of his statue from the city.[35] Exactly why the statue was removed is unclear, but it was probably the city's response to reports that Favorinus had fallen out of Hadrian's favour.[36] In the speech, Favorinus uses his image's specificity to protect his reputation, stressing that the statue represents his relationship with Corinth alone rather than Favorinus the man in all his facets. He does this by using language which marks it as a citizen who has not received the treatment that he lawfully deserves: 'the Corinthians themselves banished him (ἐκβαλεῖν αὐτὸν), not only without holding any trial, but also without having any charge at all to bring against him' (37.16). At the same time, he creates distance between man and artefact ('the image of my body', τὴν εἰκὼ τοῦ σώματος, 37.8) by highlighting that it depicts his interaction with Corinth only prior to its erection, so that its removal in response to a perceived recent transgression is an error on the city's behalf that violates the honorific transaction (37.31; cf. 37.22).

Favorinus' characterization of his image accentuates one of the fundamental functions of statuary: to replace or assume the position of the individual upon whom the image is modelled.[37] This is particularly seen in the case of gods, whose cult images both embodied the god and made him/her present.[38] Philostratos' *Heroikos* reflects this belief in a story about Hektor's statue at Troy, in which an affront to the statue is dealt with by the apparition of the legendary hero himself (19.1–7). In his dream visions, Aelius Aristeides regularly interacts with the gods in the form of their cult statues (Athena as Pheidias' cult image on the Akropolis, *HL* 2.41–3; Serapis in seated form, *HL* 3.47; Asklepios, *HL* 4.50).[39] Favorinus

---

[35] This text is preserved as Dio Chrysostom's *Or.* 37. On this speech see: Gleason 1995; König 2001; Whitmarsh 2001, 119–21 (all focus on identity); Platt 2007, 262–6 (focus on statue rededication). See Barigazzi 1966, 298–346, for a general discussion of the text.

[36] See Gleason 1995, 5, 146–8; Holford-Strevens 1997, 192–6; Stewart 2003, 287–8. See also Philostr. *VS* 1.8.489–90 for two possible reasons: a charge of adultery with a consular's wife or avoidance of elite civic liturgies.

[37] See Steiner 2001, 3–78, on statues replacing or replicating an individual. See also Bussels 2012, 9–23.

[38] See Spivey 1997, 442–59, 452–3; Elsner 2007c, 11; Platt 2011; Bussels 2012.

[39] See Platt 2011, 261–3. She refers to this as Aristeides' 'agalmatophany' (262). Note that *HL* 2.41–3 = *Oration* 48.41–3; *HL* 3.47 = *Oration* 49.47; *HL* 4.50 = *Oration* 50.50.

also exploits this idea, explaining that his statue was erected as a substitute for him only once the Corinthians failed to convince him to stay in their city in person (37.8).

Despite the meaning attached to an honorific statue by its accompanying inscription, its context remained fragile. As well as the effects of time, the enemy of all commemoration, a statue could be removed, rededicated, inscribed with additional unrelated material, or separated from its original inscription, all circumstances which irrevocably change its intended meaning.[40] A lack of inscription could lead to confusion over who in fact was represented, as in Philostratos' *Heroikos* 19.5, where the identity of a statue of Hektor is doubted. At *Heroikos* 9.6, on the other hand, in which the cult statue of Protesilaos is described as worn and altered by both time and the repeated attentions of worshippers, the value of the statue and its ability to stand in for the hero is implicitly questioned: '[t]ime has worn it away (περιτρίψας δὲ αὐτὸ ὁ χρόνος) and, by Zeus, those who anoint it and seal their vows here have changed its form (ἐξηλλάχασι τοῦ εἴδους). But to me this is nothing; for I spend time with him, and I see him (αὐτὸν βλέπω), and no statue (ἄγαλμα) could be more pleasant than that man (ἐκείνου)' (9.6–7). Here importance is laid on seeing Protesilaos in living, breathing reality—in his true form—rather than the statue, whose altered shape—τὸ εἶδος (literally 'that which is seen')—no longer adequately replaces the reanimated hero. The inaccuracy of the statue's appearance impacts on its ability to perform its designated job (cf. Arr. *Peripl.* 1.3–4 on Hadrian's statue).

Looks, therefore, can be deceiving, a situation that impacts on the interpretation and identification of portraits. Apart from Herodes, none of Philostratos' sophists have been securely recognized in stone. Bases and honorary inscriptions exist in reasonable numbers, but no portraits.[41] This in part reflects that most statue dedications were granted for benefactions rather than 'intellectual' pursuits, so that a sophist was unlikely to receive an honorific portrait without contributing something substantial to the city.[42] Herodes' representations are so plentiful because of his own self-commemorating efforts rather than public civic awards. His portrait, moreover, was securely identified only with the discovery of the Corinthian herm (Figure 4.9), which bore both portrait and inscribed name.[43] It is probable, therefore, that we have more sophistic portraits, but we have no way of firmly identifying them.

---

[40] See Ma 2013, 61–2; Ng 2016.   [41] See Puech 2002 for a catalogue of many of the inscriptions.

[42] Smith 1999, 452.

[43] Johnson 1931, no. 169; Tobin 1997, 73, no. 1, 75. There are fewer honorific dedications for Herodes than one might expect, given his generous benefactions throughout the Greek world. This may be an accident of preservation, may reflect the apparent unpopularity he experienced in Athens (see chapter 6), or may be on account of Herodes' predilection for having his family rather than just himself honoured in public contexts.

FIGURE 5.2 Marble portrait bust of a 'philosopher' or 'rhetor'. National Archaeological Museum, Athens (NM 427). An identification with Polemon has been suggested on the basis of its findspot at the Olympieion and Philostratos' description of his speech at the temple's dedication in AD 131 (*VS* 1.25.533). Height: 0.51 m.

Where an identification has been proposed for other sophists, the argument has been made on grounds of context, epigraphy, and a dose of wishful thinking. Anton Heckler, for instance, has suggested that a bust in the National Museum in Athens (NM 427) represents Polemon of Laodikeia for the tenuous reason that it was discovered at the Olympieion in Athens, and Polemon delivered the oration at its dedication before Hadrian in AD 131 (Figure 5.2).[44] There is no solid indication for accepting this designation. Circumstantial evidence, however, does make it an apt representation of this sophist. The twist of the subject's head and the upwards and leftwards roll of his eyes, for instance, fits well with Philostratos' description of Polemon's speech on the occasion: 'he, as was his habit, having fixed his gaze (στήσας τοὺς ὀφθαλμοὺς) on the thoughts that were already presenting to his mind, flung himself into his speech' (*VS* 1.25.533).[45] The portrait, moreover, is bearded, with a furrowed brow and receding hairline, and of the bare-chested himation type, suggesting broad adherence to philosophical ideals.[46]

---

[44] Hekler 1940, 125, figs 6 and 7 on pp. 122–3. See also von Schefold 1943, 180–1; Richter 1965c, 285, figs 2034–7.
[45] Cf. Zanker 1995, 246.   [46] See Zanker 1995, 226; Smith 1998, 65, on this himation type.

FIGURE 5.3 Marble statue of a seated philosopher with the base inscribed 'Aristides of Smyrna', possibly Aelius Aristeides. From Rome, late second or early third century AD. Vatican Museum, Library (Inv 64440 b). Height: 1.64 m.

More secure, but only marginally, is a seated statue of Aelius Aristeides in the Vatican (Figure 5.3).[47] The inscription on the side of its base—Ἀριστίδης Σμύρνεος—which provides the identification, has been judged modern largely due to the variant rendering of both Aristeides' name (Ἀριστείδης) and the adjective Σμυρναῖος. The statue's authenticity cannot be doubted on such grounds, however, since Claude Brixhe has shown that such alternative phonetic spellings were common in Aristeides' day.[48] Moreover, the variant spelling may well have been introduced when the original supporting plinth, now missing but extant when the statue was acquired by Pope Pius IV (AD 1559–65), was replaced.[49] The statue's identity can be called into question, however, on account of the frequent use of this seated 'Epicurean' type to represent 'intellectual laymen' rather than professional philosophers or orators, and its deployment as symbolic of this quality in private portrait galleries that aimed to show the many strings to an

---

[47] See Richter 1965c, 287, figs 2051, 2053.   [48] Brixhe 1984, 46–62.
[49] Richter 1965c, 287. See also the discussion of Petsalis-Diomidis 2010, 119, who notes that, if the statue is genuine, it must be connected to Aristeides' visit to Rome in c. AD 144 or 155.

individual's bow.[50] The identification is therefore once more circumstantial and the inscription may simply reflect Aristeides' popularity as a master orator in the sixteenth century and have appealed specifically to Pius on account of Aristeides' devotion to his god. An appropriate-looking statue was then inscribed with his name and in this way became a representation of Aristeides. In chapter 2, I discussed a double portrait herm that sports the likenesses of Xenophon and perhaps Arrian (Figure 2.3). Again, it is Arrian's personal assimilation to Xenophon that suggests this attribution and no other evidence. The possible images of Polemon and Arrian in particular demonstrate scholarly desire to attribute a visage fitting to these authors' literary presence and the power their textual representation still wields over our constructions of them.

With portraits from the imperial period, as R. R. R. Smith has warned, it is thus easy to fall into a double-edged biographical fallacy, whereby, when the subject is unknown, the portrait type is assumed to establish the kind of man represented (philosopher, soldier, athlete) or the biography of a known individual determines the interpretation of his or her portrait (e.g. Polemon was a rhetor; therefore he is represented as a rhetor).[51] Philostratos stresses that his subjects were often elegant, luxurious men, but this element is not to the fore in Herodes' representations, our only certain assignation.[52] The tendency to read identity into stock representations is encouraged by the imagery tapping into long-established visual tradition, and the form of citational representation involved was aided by the frequent display of reproduced 'classic' busts and statues in private household galleries.[53] As Herodes Attikos' portrait reveals (see Figures 3.1, 3.5), images could draw on famous, much-copied *exempla* such as Demosthenes (Figure 3.2), Aischines (Figure 3.3), and Lysias (Figure 3.4), but how those allusions might be interpreted depended largely on the display context. Assimilation to classical or Hellenistic intellectual paradigms, such as those of Plato or Epikouros, for instance, are common in the portrait herms of Athenian *kosmêtai* from the gymnasium,[54] but the classical models of Herodes' portrait represent far more than simply knowledge and education when displayed in the company of emperors at Rhamnous.[55]

Throughout the imperial period, however, the imagery associated with *pepaideumenoi* became progressively more diffuse,[56] as popular features developed to match prevailing fashions centred on Rome. The 'philosopher's beard', for example, began as relatively short in assimilation to the emperor Hadrian and

---

[50] Zanker 1995, 230. Cf. the statue programme on the library of Kelsos in Section 3.1.
[51] Smith 1998, 60–1; 1999, 450–1.   [52] See Smith 1998, 78–9, on his portrait.
[53] See Ma 2006.
[54] On the *kosmêtai*, see Graindor 1915a; Zanker 1995, 220–1; Smith 1998, 79–80; Krumaich 2004.
[55] See Section 3.1.   [56] Smith 1999, 450.

became fuller over the course of the second and third centuries.[57] This increasing elaboration, moreover, was made possible by advances in sculptural technology, and it opened 'philosophical' elements to reinterpretation and redeployment as glamorous cosmopolitanism.[58]

The insecurity of statue identification, moreover, was heightened by generic statue types encouraging reuse and rededication. Economic hardship has been floated as an explanation for this phenomenon,[59] but since it also occurred in prosperous cities, there must have been other contributing factors. Julia Shear has convincingly posited an alternative explanation for the rededication of Greek statues as Roman benefactors in the cities of the Roman east. She argues it was a strategy to show the honorand as both a Roman citizen and a member of the city in order to indicate that the city in question had powerful friends on whom it could count.[60] The practice of rededication is condemned, however, by the men whom it might affect, such as Favorinus in the *Corinthian Oration* and Dio Chrysostom in his *Rhodian Oration*.[61] Both authors underscore the incongruity of the representation of one person labelled by the name of another, whose identity is in no way comparable. This is what Favorinus refers to when he speaks of statues having a 'Greek character, but Roman fortune' (*Or.* 37.40). This phrase stresses the cultural divide, but there is also a temporal aspect, given the primacy of the Greek statue. As an example, he cites an image of Alkibiades that was reassigned to the emperor Nero (37.40). The infamy of the individuals concerned adds a sense of the ridiculous: are we to see both Nero and Alkibiades in the statue and, if so, what claim is being made? Has Nero become the 'new Alkibiades', as Polemon was labelled the 'new Demosthenes', or is it merely the beauty of the statue that is being annexed rather than character traits?[62] Favorinus considers the two identifications to exist simultaneously, while Dio, who focuses on more generic examples such as statues of young men rededicated with the names of old men, understands the statue to have become the second individual.[63] In his

---

[57] Zanker 1995, 217–26. See, however, the reservations of Smith (1999, 453; 1998, 59–61), who notes that although the 'period face' certainly existed and was important, it did not dictate portraiture to the degree assumed by Zanker. Cf. Vout 2003 on how Hadrian's beard might be interpreted. Cf. Borg 2004, 157–9.

[58] Borg 2004 on glamorous cosmopolitanism.

[59] See especially Platt 2007, 254–6, and Shear 2007, 223, with accompanying bibliography. Blanck (1969, 99–105) makes the case for economic hardship. See also Kinney 1997, 134–5.

[60] See Shear 2007, 242–6. Her focus is a group of bases from the Athenian Akropolis which bear both the original Greek and a secondary Roman inscription.

[61] See also Cic. *To Atticus* 6.1.26; Plut., *Ant.* 60; Paus. 2.17.3; and Alcock 2002, 60.

[62] On Polemon as a 'new Demosthenes', see Section 2.1.3; Philostr. *VS* 1.25.539; Pergamon Asklepieion inv. no. 1932, 6. See Habicht 1969, 75–6, no. 33, plate 11; Puech 2002, 399–401, no. 210. Cf. Platt 2007, 258, on how/if changing a label alters the image.

[63] Cf. Shear 2007, 224–5. See also Platt 2007, 258–60.

view, rededicating an honorific statue undermines the whole system, since an honour which persists or is destroyed on the whim of a magistrate (31.9) is no honour at all:

> If they will say that it is both necessary and expedient to honour men of a later time also, is it not the very reverse of this to insult (ὑβρίζειν) the men who in the past have received these honours? For what no man of former times would have chosen to accept if he had known that this was going to happen, is it at all reasonable to suppose that any man of the present day is glad to accept when he sees what is being done?[64]   (31.30)

As Dio conceives it, rededication shares much in common with Roman memory sanctions or *damnatio memoriae*.[65] In the empire, memory sanctions took various forms, from the complete obliteration of images, the removal of inscribed names, the partial removal of an image, to the re-sculpting of an image.[66] The process, however, rarely destroyed the public memory of the victim but rather commemorated the disgrace, since the specificity of erasure or modification usually left no doubt as to original identity,[67] and this was often exploited to stress an association or conquest.[68] In the case of less famous individuals in contemporary times, however, rededication may well eradicate commemoration entirely, since their identity was not so welded to the monument in the public imagination.

Elite imperial Greeks attempt to counter these commemorative issues by producing their own material or literary statues and by employing various strategies to control their meaning and reception. Honorific images signify permanence and are thus the antithesis to improvised epideictic oratory. Epideictic texts, which form the basis of discussion below, regularly exploit this polarity in combination with the incongruity of an inanimate monument embodying a living person to negotiate tensions between such concepts as life and death, self-identity and perceived identity, communication and silence, orality and writing, transience and eternity. Moreover, the distinctive 'affective and performative' qualities of a statue lends its textualized version the ability to imbue the text itself with these characteristics, as well as gifting the ephemeral *epideixis* a sense of solidity and permanence.[69] A point of such physicality and focus aids both memorization and oral transmission. A textualized statue also allows authors to break free of commemorative conventions and manipulate the monument for their own purposes. For those with enough means, moreover, honorific statues become insufficient for adequate physical

---

[64] Translation adapted from Cohoon 1940.

[65] On *damnatio memoriae* (modern terminology for a set of ancient practices), see Elsner 2003, 211–19; Stewart 2003, 267–83; Flower 2006, 197–275; Platt 2007, 263–66.

[66] Elsner 2003, 211–19; Platt 2007, 263–5; Harrison 1990; Varner 2004, especially 1–20; 2015.

[67] Elsner 2003, 211–19. See also, Bodel 1997, 7–11, on destroyed Roman aristocratic villas as monuments to disgrace.

[68] Elsner 2003, 214–18; cf. Platt 2007, 264–5.   [69] See Steiner 2001, 252, on textualized statues.

commemoration as well, a situation offset by the commissioning and raising of statues oneself. In what follows, I will examine several strategies for overcoming the perceived limitations of honorific statues in both literature and material culture.

5.2 AMPLIFICATION: STATUE PROGRAMMES ON MONUMENTS

In chapter 3, I argued that the façade of Kelsos' library in Ephesos, with its series of statues depicting aspects of his career and traditional Greek virtues, approximates an aggrandized version of an honorific statue.[70] This form of visual rhetoric via a statue programme is not uncommon on elite monuments in the Roman east. Not only does its amplification of honorific concepts make one's message more striking and imposing, it also largely wrests back control from civic authorities of how one's reputation is shaped. One can thus create more personal public statements, as well as choose the context of their viewing and type of monument on which they appear.

One such example that makes a political, cultural, and personal statement about how to be thought about and remembered is Herodes Attikos' funding of the nymphaion at Olympia, which was dedicated by his wife Regilla. This fountain house was constructed within the Altis by AD 153 and was, along with the Philippeion and the honorific monument of Ptolemy II and Arsinoë II, the only dedication of such scope celebrating mortals within the sacred precinct.[71] Today the fountain house is remembered on site only by two basins: one semi-circular on a tier above a larger rectangular one with the bases of matching circular monopteroi at the extremities (Figure 5.4). Several statues, statue fragments, and bases from the decorative programme, however, also survive and are displayed or stored in the museum.

Following Renate Bol's reconstruction, above the two basins there was an ornate façade with two rows of eleven rectangular niches, one above the other, filled by twenty-four statues (Figure 5.5).[72] The lower row housed images of the imperial family and the upper row statues of Herodes', with a statue of Zeus at the centre of each row. To the left of Zeus on the upper row stood Herodes, his father, his mother, his eldest surviving son Attikos Bradua, and his daughter Athenais sharing a base with her younger brother Regillus; to Zeus' right stood

---

[70] See Section 3.1.

[71] On the date, see Bol 1984, 98–100; Tobin 1997, 321. On other nymphaia constructed in the second century in civic centres in Greece, see Dickenson 2017, 363–70. On Roman-era Greek nymphaia more broadly, see Aristodemou 2018.

[72] Bol 1984 corrects the reconstruction of Adler 1892. See Bol 1984, 1–12, for the excavation and early reconstructions. Tobin (1997, 314–22) presents a summary of the architectural design along with alterations and repairs made after its completion. Also see the discussion of Herodes as benefactor via the nymphaion, in Galli 2002, 222–7.

FIGURE 5.4 Remains of a Nymphaion dedicated to Zeus by Regilla and displaying four generations of the imperial family below four generations of Herodes' family. Site of Ancient Olympia. Bases of the lower register are visible and the base of the western monopteros.

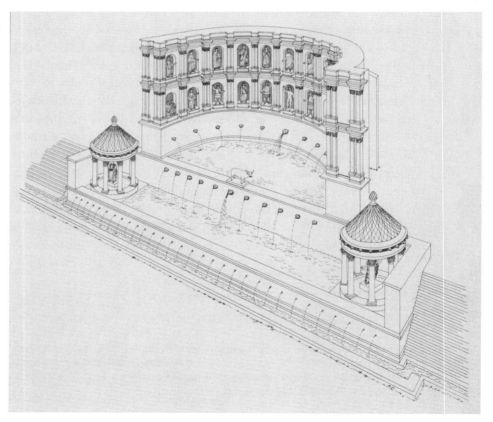

FIGURE 5.5 Reconstruction of the Nymphaion by Renate Bol.

Regilla, her father, mother, grandfather, and her and Herodes' daughter Elpinike (Figure 5.6). On the lower row, to Zeus' left stood Hadrian, his wife Sabina, Marcus Aurelius, Faustina the Younger, and Lucilla; to Zeus' right were Antoninus Pius, his wife Faustina the Elder, Lucius Verus, Domitia Faustina, and two children sharing a base (probably Annia Faustina and T. Aelius Antoninus) (Figure 5.7).[73] The statues of the imperial family are slightly taller than those of Herodes' and have been reconstructed as occupying the lower row for this reason. The monopteroi at either end of the lower basin were most likely built at a date

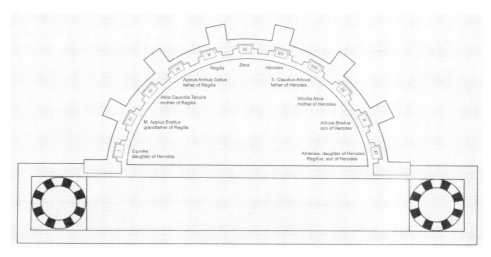

FIGURE 5.6 Reconstruction of the statue programme of the Nymphaion at Olympia, upper level.

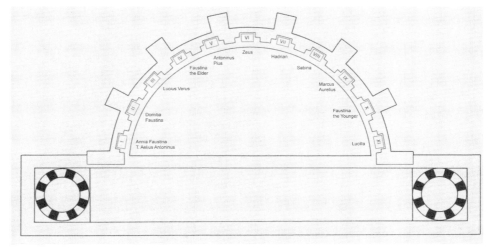

FIGURE 5.7 Reconstruction of the statue programme of the Nymphaion at Olympia, lower level.

[73] See Bol 1984, 50–8, and insert 4.

after the initial construction to replace original fountains with a statue of Marcus Aurelius (in the eastern monopteros) and one of Herodes (in the western).[74] Both Bol and Tobin plausibly suggest that these last two statues were raised around AD 175 after Herodes returned to Greece from his trial for tyranny before Marcus Aurelius in Sirmium, an event discussed in detail in chapter 6.[75]

Four generations of Herodes' family thus stood above the same generational spread of the imperial family. According to the inscriptions on the bases, the statues of Herodes' family were dedicated by the city of Elis and those of the imperial family by Herodes.[76] The nymphaion as a whole, however, was dedicated to Zeus by Regilla, probably when she was priestess of the local cult of Demeter Chamyne.[77] A life-size bull, which according to Bol's reconstruction stood at the division between the upper and lower basins, is inscribed with 'Regilla, Priestess of Demeter, [dedicated] the water and the things around the water to Zeus' (Figure 5.8).[78] Thus the fountain is both a private and a public dedication. The bull no doubt stands as a permanent commemoration of an ephemeral sacrificial

FIGURE 5.8 Marble statue of a bull with inscription identifying Regilla as the dedicator on its flank from the Nymphaion at Olympia. Archaeological Museum of Olympia (Inv. 373; *I.Olympia* no. 610). Height: 1.05 m; Length: 1.60 m.

[74] Tobin 1997, 318–21; cf. Bol 1984, 58–67.
[75] See Section 6.2 and 6.4 below; Tobin 1997, 321.
[76] See Bol 1984, 113–41.
[77] Tobin 1997, 321.
[78] *I.Olympia*, no. 610.

offering and thus demonstrates Herodes and Regilla's piety and immersion in Greek religious traditions, since bulls were the core sacrifice at the Olympic Games. As well as being associated with water and Zeus through, for example, the rape of Europa, the bull is also connected to Athens' legendary king, Theseus, via his efforts to tame and subsequently sacrifice the Marathonian bull (Paus. 1.27.10; Plut. *Thes.* 14.1) and by the myth of the Minotaur. Elsewhere, Herodes makes deliberate monumental choices to align himself with Theseus and to highlight his connection to the deme of Marathon in order to shape himself as the inheritor of the legacy of the Athenian triumph over the Persians and to naturalize his dominance over the city of Athens.[79] The bull on the nymphaion is therefore presumably intended as a nod to Theseus as well.

As Jennifer Tobin has shown, the parallel generations of Herodes' and the imperial families represent continuity and stability, both in imperial rule and in euergetism and patronage of sacred Greek sites and, by extension, Greece more broadly.[80] Herodes' connection to Athens would also make the viewer think of Hadrian's Panhellenion and reinforce the symbolic centrality of Athens to Greece's relationship with Rome.[81] The grouping stresses the friendship shared between Herodes and the emperors and that there is a partnership, or indeed equivalence, between his own and the imperial family. The off-setting of the portrait rows and slight difference in statue size project a more ambiguous message: an implication exists that Herodes' line is a lesser adjunct to the imperial family and yet at the same time a higher power behind or overseeing its actions. A viewer would then be left with the impression that Rome's capacity to rule is created and maintained by the *paideia*-wielding Greek elite.

The emperors and emperors-to-be all wear cuirasses, announcing their imperium, in the sense of their right to rule and its foundation on Roman military might (Figures 5.9, 5.10, 5.11), and Herodes' father Attikos, as well as Regilla's male relatives, are togaed as civilians (Figure 5.12).[82] Herodes and his sons, on the other hand, wear Greek dress (Figure 5.13). Attikos' and Herodes' culturally diverse costumes parallel the iconography on the Philopappos monument (Figures 1.2–1.4), on which the ancestor who secured Roman citizenship was represented in a toga, but Philopappos himself wore the himation to stress his Greekness.[83] This arrangement is equally fitting for Herodes, who can convey

---

[79] See further Section 3.1, Section 4.2.3, and chapter 6 (*passim*).

[80] Tobin 1997, 317. On the interpretation of the monument's sculptural programme, see also Smith 1998, 75–7; Galli 2002, 225.

[81] On the Panhellenion, see Spawforth and Walker 1985; Jones 1996; Spawforth 1999; Riccardi 2007.

[82] For descriptions of the individual statues, see Bol 1984, 151–96. Note that Bol reconstructs one headless togaed statue as Herodes, but Smith (1998, 77) more convincingly assigns it to Herodes' father.

[83] Smith 1998, 77.

FIGURE 5.9 Marble cuirass statue of the emperor Hadrian from the Nymphaion at Olympia. Archaeological Museum of Olympia (Inv. VI, 1712; Mus. no. Λ148). Height with head: 1.85 m.

both affiliations while promoting in Olympia, the sacred heart of Greece, his self-appointed personal role as the great second-century purveyor of Greek culture.[84]

As well as highlighting Herodes' personal Greekness, the monument underscores the depth of his connection to Rome through Regilla's family. She came from a wealthy patrician background that, like Rome's first emperor, counted Aeneas as an ancestor, and her male forbears could boast of numerous consulships.[85] In keeping with other Herodean monuments that present him and Regilla as a unit, the bicultural nobility of the family is a major theme.[86] This, combined with their arrangement above the imperial family and the location of the fountain within the Altis at Olympia, constructs Herodes' family as performing a mediating role between the seat of Roman power and the traditions and people of Greece. This

---

[84] Cf. Galli 2002, 226, and Nasrallah 2010, 35–44, on the rhetorical dimension of the monument.
[85] Tobin 1997, 76.   [86] On this quality see Gleason 2010, 130–5; Smith 1998, 77.

FIGURE 5.10 Marble cuirass statue of an emperor, probably Marcus Aurelius, from the Nymphaion at Olympia. Archaeological Museum of Olympia (Inv. II, 524; Mus. no. Λ150). Height without plinth: 1.76 m.

effect is enhanced by the statues of Herodes' family being dedicated by the Eleians and Herodes himself dedicating the imperial statues, a circumstance which places Herodes in the position of representing the Eleians (and by extension Greece) in interacting with and giving honour to the emperors. Importantly, it is the Eleians who bestow this prestige upon him, delivering the impression that Greece has chosen this role for him rather than him creating it himself.[87] Moreover, the two central statues of Zeus convey divine approval of the arrangement.

The addition of the monopteroi with separate statues of Marcus Aurelius and Herodes after the latter's acquittal at the Sirmium trial for tyranny in AD 174 attempts to restate Herodes' pre-eminence and strives to remove any suggestion that the tight relationship between him and the imperial family has in any way

---

[87] Cf. Ma 2013, 223–5, on the significance of extravagant family dedications at Delphi by Aitolians during the period the sanctuary was under their control, and 226–8 on Olympia.

FIGURE 5.11 Marble cuirass statue of an emperor, probably Marcus Aurelius from the monopteros, from the Nymphaion at Olympia. Archaeological Museum of Olympia (Inv. V, 1423; Mus no. Λ149). Height without plinth: 2.11 m.

faltered.[88] In this case, Herodes wears a toga. The additions also realign the monument to stress Herodes' intimacy (and equality?) with Marcus in particular. Significantly, the representations of the emperors replicate official iconography. The cuirass imagery of Hadrian, for instance, is one of his most common early depictions with twenty complete or fragmentary examples surviving from the eastern empire, Egypt, and North Africa.[89] The monument thus intimates the approval and involvement of official channels and promotes Herodes' role in shaping the imperial image in Greece.

According to Lucian, Herodes' extravagance drew the condemnation of the Cynic philosopher, Peregrinus Proteus. In an inversion of the charges usually brought against Greek cultural artefacts by Romans, he accused Herodes of making the Greeks soft by providing the Altis with such a luxurious Roman-style fountain. In a demonstration of the slippery fickleness that is a focus of

[88] See further Section 6.2. [89] See Gergel 2004.

FIGURE 5.12 Marble statue of a male in toga (Roman civilian) from the Nymphaion at Olympia. Archaeological Museum of Olympia (Inv. II, 526; Mus no. Λ153). Height without plinth: 1.76 m.

Lucian's piece, Peregrinus then revised his position at the next Olympiad to placate the disapproving crowd with an encomium of Herodes' innovation (*Peregr.* 19–20). Lucian's text indicates that many Greeks at the games approved of Herodes' intervention in the sacred landscape, but in the figure of Peregrinus also critiques contemporary striving for fame through novelty.[90] His narrator appears positively aligned with Herodes' religious euergetism but the nymphaion is really a material example of the same phenomenon. Herodes integrates a new, culturally expansive monument, modelled on imperial precursors,[91] into an ancient sacred Hellenic landscape in order to make an immediate political and cultural impact and shape his and his family's image for posterity.

Herodes and Regilla thus use the sacred precinct of the Altis and well-known imperial images to create a carefully curated yet ambivalent identity. Rather than

---

[90] Fields 2013.
[91] For example, Hadrian's nymphaion in the Athenian agora. See Longfellow 2011, 107–62.

FIGURE 5.13 Marble statue of a male in himation (Greek civilian) from the Nymphaion at Olympia. Archaeological Museum of Olympia (Inv. II, 524, S 34, S37; Mus no. Λ152). Height: 1.69 m.

simple alignment with Roman imperial power, Herodes and Regilla assert their control over how that power is experienced by the population, imply it depends on Greek elites, even offer themselves as a potential alternative. They also affirm an unbroken connection with powerful Greek traditions, much like the trio of busts Herodes set up at Rhamnous and Brexiza but on a grander scale.[92] At Olympia, not only is this religious tradition, but also the dynastic imperial tradition of Philip II, Alexander, and the Ptolemaic kings. The nymphaion thus engages with contemporary monumentalizing culture and instils a sense of permanence in its Greek iconography that hints its Roman context may be less enduring. This kind of elaborate material self-fashioning is possible only via such a substantial benefaction,

---

[92] See Section 3.1. In this context, also see Allen 2017 on Herodes' inclusion of Memnon in his retinue as an attempt to shape an imperial identity.

even though the personal touches are created through the thoughtful deployment and combination of individual statues.

The type of iconography and the association of emperors and gods with private citizens are not unique to the nymphaion of Herodes and Regilla, but are reflected in other lavish benefactions across the Greek east, such as Plancia Magna's rebuilding of the main city gate at Perge in AD 121.[93] Nevertheless, the capital needed to fund such a monument in its entirety was available only to a select few. What is conspicuous about Herodes and Regilla's nymphaion is its existence within a Panhellenic sanctuary rather than the confines of a civic centre, a circumstance compatible with Herodes' wider attempts to mark places of cultural and historical importance to Greeks. The monument also highlights that in public, panhellenic space, Herodes' monumentalizing focus is squarely on his family as a whole, so that his commemorative impulse is less personal than dynastic.[94] Herodes and Regilla thus create a narrative of cultural belonging, religious piety, and political power through their deployment of a carefully curated programme of many individual statues, a narrative impossible to express with such nuance through a single honorific dedication.

5.3 IMAGINARY SPACES OF HONOUR

In literature, instead of building a larger monument on which to place a personalized statue programme, a common means of transcending the confines of civic honouring is to create one's own meaningful, if imaginary, context for it. This section will explore this commemorative option in texts of Favorinus, Aristeides, and Polemon, and argues that all three authors use the written word to create sacred spaces of honour in which their images are elevated.

An imaginary context of honour is Favorinus' ultimate solution to Corinth's removal of his statue in the *Corinthian Oration*. Since the physical statue has vanished, Favorinus' speech re-raises and re-dedicates a virtual version of it in the precinct of the goddess, Fame:

> 'Someone, I say ($\varphi\alpha\mu\iota$), will yet remember ($\mu\nu\acute{\alpha}\sigma\varepsilon\sigma\theta\alpha\iota$) me',
> as Sappho very beautifully says, and far more beautifully Hesiod:
> 'But rumour/fame ($\varphi\acute{\eta}\mu\eta$) is never utterly destroyed,
> which many people voice ($\varphi\eta\mu\acute{\iota}\xi\omega\sigma\iota$); she is a goddess'.

[93] For a detailed discussion of Plancia Magna's gate and her euergetism, see Boatwright 1993, 189–207. For other parallels to Herodes' nymphaion, see Bol 1984, 83–95.

[94] Cf. the exedra at Delphi which supported statues of Herodes, Regilla, Elpinike, Regillus, and Athenais, on which see Tobin 1997, 303–5. On Herodes' project in Panhellenic compared to local sanctuaries, see Strazdins 2022a.

I myself will raise you up ($\dot{a}\nu a\sigma\tau\dot{\eta}\sigma\omega$) beside the goddess, from where nothing shall tear you down—not earthquake, not wind, not snow, not rain, not jealousy, not enemy; but even now I perceive you standing there ($\dot{\epsilon}\sigma\tau\eta\kappa\acute{o}\tau a$). Before now forgetfulness ($\lambda\acute{a}\theta a$) has tripped up ($\check{\epsilon}\sigma\phi\eta\lambda\epsilon$) and deceived ($\dot{\epsilon}\psi\epsilon\acute{v}\sigma a\tau o$) others too, but opinion ($\gamma\nu\acute{\omega}\mu\eta$) has done neither to any good man, by which ($\mathring{\eta}$ [$\gamma\nu\acute{\omega}\mu\eta$]) you stand upright for me like a man ($\kappa a\tau$' $\check{a}\nu\delta\rho a$ $\mu o\iota$ $\dot{o}\rho\theta\grave{o}s$ $\check{\epsilon}\sigma\tau\eta\kappa as$). (37.47)

In the Hesiodic context (*Op.* 763–4), $\varphi\acute{\eta}\mu\eta$ means 'rumour', but in Favorinus' oration, alongside the quotation of Sappho, it is better taken as 'fame'. The ambiguity, however, juxtaposes the rumours that led to Favorinus' disgrace with his rehabilitation of his reputation through speech, a situation highlighted by the focus on speaking and memory in the Sapphic and Hesiodic verses. The speech thus creates its own space of honour for the missing statue. Unlike the library of Corinth, before which the physical statue stood, the precinct of Fame extends universally, and the resurrected image becomes a metaphor for the written text of Favorinus' oration. He apostrophizes it as, $\mathring{\omega}$ $\lambda\acute{o}\gamma\omega\nu$ $\dot{\epsilon}\mu\mathring{\omega}\nu$ $\sigma\iota\gamma\eta\lambda\grave{o}\nu$ $\epsilon\check{\iota}\delta\omega\lambda o\nu$ ('o silent image of my words', 37.46), which is precisely what text is: silent until read again. That his imagery of the re-erected statue withstanding potential threats reflects that of Horace's and Pindar's literary monuments,[95] and that he uses Sappho and Hesiod to establish the supremacy of his wider, non-Corinthian reputation casts them as peers and rivals in the quest for literary immortality. What Favorinus manages to do that these other authors do not is turn his literary monument/toppled honorific civic dedication into a sanctified and inviolable votive offering to the goddess Fame. Indeed, earlier in the speech, he suggests that this is how the Corinthians should treat their civic dedications, saying: 'each of these statues which has been erected by your city [...] is instantly invested with the attributes of sanctity ($\tau\grave{a}$ $\tau\mathring{\eta}s$ $\dot{o}\sigma\acute{\iota} as$), and the city should defend it as a votive offering ($\dot{a}\nu a\theta\acute{\eta}\mu a\tau os$)' (37.28).[96]

Aelius Aristeides performs a similar sleight of hand with a portrait statue of his own in the *Sacred Tales*, only he uses the reality-bending frame of a dream to pull it off rather than an abstract holy precinct. Aristeides dreams that he and a certain Zenon are at the temple of Asklepios in his adopted hometown of Smyrna, where he finds a statue of himself in the temple's vestibule:[97]

I examined ($\pi\epsilon\rho\iota\epsilon\sigma\kappa\acute{o}\pi o\upsilon\nu$), as though in this vestibule, a statue of me ($\dot{a}\nu\delta\rho\iota\acute{a}\nu\tau a$ $\dot{\epsilon}\mu a\upsilon\tauο\hat{\upsilon}$). At one time I saw it as if it were of me, and then again it seemed to be a great ($\mu\acute{\epsilon}\gamma as$) and beautiful ($\kappa a\lambda\acute{o}s$) statue of Asklepios. Then I recounted ($\delta\iota\eta\gamma\epsilon\hat{\iota}\sigma\theta a\iota$) to Zenon himself these things which appeared to me in my dream. And the part about the statue seemed to be exceedingly honourable ($\sigma\phi\acute{o}\delta\rho a$ $\check{\epsilon}\nu\tau\iota\mu o\nu$). Again I saw the statue as if it were in the long portico of the gymnasium.[98] (*HL* 1.17)

---

[95] See Section 4.1.   [96] Cf. Dio Chrys. *Or.* 31.89. See also Barigazzi 1966, 332 (on 37.28).

[97] On this episode, see also Platt 2011, 264–5; Downie 2013, 64–6.

[98] Translations adapted from Behr 1981.

The dream frame here allows Aristeides to conflate himself with the god, so that his statue is both mortal and divine.[99] Dreams are the usual mode of the god's communication, a circumstance that makes the conflation more significant: it is the god who shows Aristeides that they are one (cf. *HL* 4.50). The image does not gain meaning, however, until Aristeides relates the experience within the dream to his friend, Zenon. He thus supplies himself with yet another internal audience and makes himself an object of wonder once more.[100] It is in the telling that the honour of the god-man double-vision becomes manifest and, following this verbalization, the statue appears rather in the portico of the gymnasium, a very common location for honorific statues of rhetors and philosophers to be found.[101] In this, the validity of the honorific image is tied to the art of speaking and suggests that only in words can such immortality truly be claimed.

The two surviving *epideixeis* of Marcus Antonius Polemon, in contrast, use speech to turn a pair of corpses that become the focus of a competition over glory into statues. These orations form a pair of *controversiae* on the theme of the valour of Kynegeiros and Kallimachos at the battle of Marathon. According to tradition, the father of the fallen man who had shown the greatest courage was awarded the honour of delivering the funeral oration at Athens. The fathers of Kynegeiros and Kallimachos both lay claim to that right.[102] Legend had it that Kynegeiros died having lost either both hands or, alternatively, just his right hand while either pursuing fleeing Persians or attempting to keep one of their ships on shore. Kallimachos, in contrast, died after receiving many wounds and, in some versions, being pierced by so many arrows and spears that his body was held upright even after he died.[103] In Polemon's speeches, both hands and body are repeatedly made statue-like, and each father claims their lifeless son as a victory monument (τρόπαιον: *Kynegeiros* 10, 39; *Kallimachos* 61).[104] With the focus on the monumental, Kallimachos' father has more to work with and it is he who appears victorious in the end (*Kallimachos* 65). Throughout the speech, he transforms his son into a statue in as many ways as possible, at one point apostrophizing him as:

O revered votive offering (ἀνάθημα) of war! O noble statue (ἄγαλμα) of Ares! O polemarch, terrible likeness (εἴδωλον) of the polemarch god, enclosed all around (περιβεβλημένον) with the missiles of Asia! O only one putting on the equipment of war! O figure (σχῆμα) of

---

[99] Cf. Downie 2013, 65.   [100] Cf. Section 2.4.

[101] See Platt 2011, 265, on this episode revealing the transmission of divine blessing from sacred to paideutic space. On philosophers and orators in bath-gymnasium complexes, see Newby 2005, 235–46.

[102] See Reader 1996, 33–40, for Classical and Hellenistic representations of both men and their deeds at Marathon.

[103] See Reader 1996, 36–9.

[104] References to either son as statue, victory monument, fortification, or tree: *Kynegeiros* 7, 10, 22–3, 30, 33, 39; *Kallimachos* 3, 10, 11, 12, 51, 54, 58, 60, 61.

freedom, O figure (σχῆμα) of Marathon! O [figure] not letting Greece lie down! O [figure] greater than nature! (*Kallimachos* 51–2)[105]

Kallimachos' father addresses his dead son repeatedly as an inanimate object, image, or effigy, which serves to strip away his humanity and vigour layer by layer. Moreover, in the process, he is brought closer to the divine, as though his frozen state rarefies him. The words used to describe Kallimachos are varied and pointed. Firstly, σεμνὸν ἀνάθημα ('sacred offering') is that which is set up or dedicated to a deity, often after victory in war.[106] This is what Favorinus told the Corinthians they should treat their honorific statues as (*Or.* 37.28). Next, he is called Ἄρεως ἄγαλμα ('statue of Ares'). Though often simply a word for statue, ἄγαλμα regularly has the sense of a votive offering as well.[107] This implies that Kallimachos is simultaneously an offering to Ares and a representation of Ares. Finally, he is termed δεινὸν εἴδωλον ('terrible image') of the polemarch god. Polemarch was Kallimachos' magisterial title. It is not used elsewhere of Ares,[108] so the phrase most probably refers to Kallimachos himself as an idol or divine image.

This fleshy statue is surrounded by the weapons of the Persians as though by a wall and, given the religious terminology and semantic relationship between περιβάλλω and περιβόλιον/περίβολος ('the area surrounding a temple'), the implication is that the lifeless Kallimachos stands in a sacred precinct and has become a statue of something divine.[109] Statues of gods were considered in Greek ritual to be the gods themselves in that they housed the gods' divinity.[110] Yet, at the same time, a cult statue was also just an empty shell, as noted by Pythagoras in the form of a rooster in Lucian's *Dream or the Cock* 24, when he says that outwardly cult statues are glorious chryselephantine images with gleaming accoutrements, but inside their hollow spaces are struts, nails, pitch, clay, and even mice and rats (cf. *Iupp. trag.* 8). Kallimachos too has a double nature—divine and dead—since περίβολος was also the term used to describe the enclosure around a tomb.[111] So Kallimachos' mortality coexists with his apparent divinity, and it is at this point that the language of sacred images ceases and the language of enduring freedom begins. This dead/divine doubling of Kallimachos, moreover, highlights the role of the cult statue as the point of contact and communication between human and god. Kallimachos' glory lies in the perception of his corpse as an inhuman, god-like statue within a sacred precinct by the Persians who retreat in the face of this marvel, thus turning the corpse surrounded by weapons on the plain of Marathon into a *tropaion*. This organic *tropaion* then becomes the first monumentalizing commemorative effort of the Persian Wars.

---

[105] For commentary on this passage, see Reader 1996, 362–7. Translations follow Reader 1996 with alterations.

[106] Reader 1996, 363, with bibliography. [107] Reader 1996, 364–5, with bibliography.

[108] Reader 1996, 365. [109] Cf. Reader 1996, 366. [110] Platt 2011, 77–123.

[111] See Cormack 2004, 29–30, on the application of this word to tomb enclosures.

The example of Polemon's Kallimachos is different from those of Favorinus' and Aristeides' statues, in that the transformation is of a corpse rather than an honorific image, but all three use language to create sacred spaces of honour in which their images are elevated. Polemon uses Kallimachos' corpse to reshape the commemorative landscape of Marathon within the textual landscape of his speech. Favorinus and Aristeides use their translated statues to make claims for their oratory or literature, so that the monument becomes symbolic of wider fame that is not anchored to any material artefact. In this way, the new contexts they craft for their monuments ensure rhetorically that any harm that comes to Favorinus' image or any suggestion that Aristeides' statue exists only in his dreams become irrelevant to their enduring reputations. The power of these claims come from the genuine spaces of divinity and honour on which they draw.

5.4 REPLICATION

One aspect of honorific statues that imperial Greeks repeatedly cast as limiting is their specificity to place, event, or moment. A material method to counteract these perceived constraints is replication. This is the means by which emperors spread a uniform and recognizable image of themselves throughout the empire.[112] This imperial practice was adopted by the Greek elite, as we have already seen with Herodes Attikos and the Vedii Antonini,[113] and was one way to shape a desirable image and export it to various target markets. Herodes' project of replication encompassed himself, his family, and his foster-sons. One unusual element of his statue habit was his attempt to emulate Hadrian's creation of the god Antinoos via his heroization of Polydeukion.[114] The success and reach of Antinoos' cult was aided by the adaptability of the Bithynian youth's image (Figures 5.14, 5.15, and 5.16).[115] His worship continued into at least the fourth century AD and images have been uncovered across the empire, as far afield as Britain and Georgia.[116] Drawing on existing classical models and the iconography of gods such as Dionysos, Apollo, Osiris, Hermes, and 'tragic, eroticized heroes such as Ganymede and Narcissus',[117]

---

[112] See Ando 2000, 228–45.   [113] See Sections 3.1 and 4.4.

[114] On Antinoos' deification, see Birley 1997, 247–57; Vout 2007, 12–13; 113–21; Jones 2010, 75–83.

[115] See Vout 2007, 73–85; 100–6, esp. 105; Morewood 2012, 84–5; Moorhead and Stuttard 2012, 132. Christians saw him as a rival to their own universalizing faith; see, e.g., Athanasios, *Apologia contra Arianos* III 5.230. See also Goldhill 2001, 172–3; Galli 2007, 191–4. On issues surrounding reproductions of cult statues and the process of 'iconization', see Gaifman 2006. On Antinoos' image, see Meyer 1991.

[116] Opper 2008, 186; Vout 2007, 13, 62.

[117] Vout 2005, 83. See also Opper 2008, 186; Morewood 2012, 84–5; Moorhead and Stuttard 2012, 132; Vout 2007, 13.

FIGURE 5.14 Marble portrait bust of Antinoos. National Archaeological Museum, Athens (NM 417). Height: 0.67 m.

FIGURE 5.15 Marble Egyptianizing portrait statue of Antinoos (possibly as Osiris) from Hadrian's villa at Tivoli. Vatican, Museo Gregoriano Egizio 99 (Inv. 22795 IFC). Height with plinth: 2.41 m.

COMMEMORATION EMBODIED 223

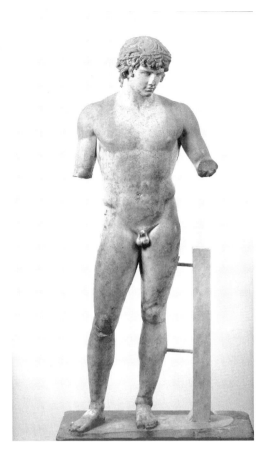

FIGURE 5.16 Marble portrait statue of Antinoos from Delphi. Archaeological Museum of Delphi (Inv. 1718). Height: 1.80 m.

Antinoos' chameleon nature not only made him more accessible to more people but also influenced the types of portraits commissioned by the provincial elite.[118] There was a detectable increase in images depicting young males in the second century AD on the back of the production and propagation of Antinoos' likeness.[119]

One such example is Herodes Attikos' favourite foster-son, Polydeukion, of whom we have more than twenty-five portraits, making him the most represented figure known outside the imperial family.[120] Although Polydeukion (Figure 5.17) appears noticeably younger than Antinoos, his portrait draws on the features of Hadrian's god.[121] The similarities have led to confusion on more than one occasion, such as the Antinoos of Olympia (Figure 5.18) and the male Egyptianizing

---

[118] See Moorhead and Stuttard 2012, 132, on Antinoos as a 'chameleon creation'.
[119] Vout 2005, 91; see also 2006; 2007, 89–96, on identification of Antinoos' image.
[120] Tobin 1997, 101–7; Vout 2005, 91; Jansen 2006 129–207; Fittschen 2021, no. 76, 124–32, taf. 78–81.
[121] See Vout 2007, 85–9, on Polydeukion's play off the figure of Antinoos.

FIGURE 5.17 Marble portrait bust of Polydeukion, found in Kephisia with one of Herodes (see Figure 3.1). National Archaeological Museum, Athens (NM 4811). Height: 0.56 m.

FIGURE 5.18 The 'Antinoos of Olympia'. Archaeological Museum of Olympia (Λ204, Λ208). This marble head was found in the palaestra and initially identified with Polydeukion, but reassigned due to the closeness of its lock scheme to that of Antinoos' statues. Height of head: 0.255 m.

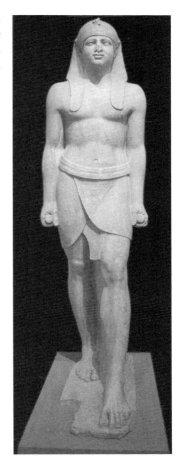

FIGURE 5.19 Male 'Egyptianizing' statue from the Canopus shrine at Brexiza, near Marathon, possibly Antinoos or Polydeukion. National Archaeological Museum, Athens (Aeg. 1).

statues from Herodes' Canopus shrine at Brexiza near Marathon (Figure 5.19).[122] The Olympia Antinoos was initially identified as Polydeukion but has been reassigned based on the similarity between his coiffure and the lock scheme allocated to Antinoos.[123] Although the male Brexiza statues are categorized as Antinoos, the facial features approximate more closely a more mature vision of Polydeukion; the mouth, however, is distorted by the archaic smile and differs markedly from both models.[124] Caroline Vout has perceptively argued that Herodes deliberately creates the ambiguity, both in the visual dialoguing between the Brexiza statues and the portraits of Antinoos and Polydeukion, and by dedicating images of Polydeukion in

[122] On these statues as critique of contemporary Platonic philosophy, see Mazurek 2018.
[123] See Vout 2005, 92; 2007, 87; Weber 1956, 142–8.
[124] See Gazda 1980, 6 n. 34; Tobin 1997, 256–8. See Siskou 2011, 83–8, for the statues as a hybrid Osiris-Polydeukion in imitation of the Tivoli Antinoos statues. Fittschen 2021, no. 76, 130, catalogues the Egyptianizing statues as Polydeukion portraits.

public sanctuaries and setting up portraits of Antinoos in his private villas.[125] These practices invite comparison while also stressing difference. Herodes' statue habit here thus utilizes the same strategy employed by contemporary authors in creating a culturally meaningful context from which to depart with his own innovations. The Olympia Antinoos invites the same viewing methodology with its mouth, eyes, and coiffure that riff on but do not replicate Antinoos' more common representations. A powerful motivation underlying the deliberate ambiguity was for Herodes in turn to be assimilated to Hadrian in the minds of those who viewed Polydeukion's portraits.[126] The benefit of this connection in a Greek context extends to Hadrian's own efforts to encourage a conflation between himself and Zeus, both in his relationship with Antinoos resembling the myth of Zeus and Ganymede, and in his completion and inauguration of the Temple of Olympian Zeus in Athens the year following Antinoos' death.[127]

Herodes' efforts to commemorate Polydeukion, however, go beyond an imprecise assimilation to Antinoos. Herodes heroized Polydeukion in his own right, and he was the only one of the *trophimoi* to receive this honour definitively in Herodes' monumentalizing programme.[128] There is evidence, moreover, of a hero cult at Kephisia. A statue base built into the church of Agios Demetrios near the tombs of Herodes' family is dedicated to the 'hero Polydeukion' and records a list of competitors in games (*IG* II² 3968).[129] These must have been in the boy's honour and indicate, through the assignation of year by agonothetes and archon, that the games were more than a one-off occurrence. An altar whose provenance is unknown, but which probably came from Kephisia, is also dedicated to the 'hero Polydeukion' (*IG* II² 3975) by a certain Asiatikos Lanptreus.[130] A herm of the 'hero Polydeukion', moreover, was set up in Kephisia by a Lucius Octavius Restitutus of Marathon (*IG* II² 3974).[131] Additionally, two heroic reliefs have been found, one from Loukou (Figure 5.20) and one from the sanctuary of Artemis at Brauron (Figure 5.21).[132]

The Brauron relief is particularly striking because the sanctuary was abandoned in Roman times.[133] Jennifer Tobin argues Herodes' dedication was made out of

---

[125] Vout 2005, 92; 2007, 87.   [126] Vout 2005, 92; 2007, 87–8.

[127] See Vout 2007, 13, on Hadrian as Zeus and the Olympieion; also Paus. 1.18.6.

[128] On new 'heroes' in Greek antiquity, including those associated with private honouring, see Jones 2010, 48–65.

[129] Tobin 1997, 229–34; Ameling 1983b, no. 172; Follet 1977; Robert 1979.

[130] Tobin 1997, 234–5; Ameling 1983b, 173, no. 179.

[131] Graindor 1914, 366; Ameling 1983b, 173, no. 178; Tobin 1997, 217–18. For dedications addressing Polydeukion as 'hero' by Herodes or his family, see *IG* II² 3974, II² 3973, II² 4776.

[132] Tobin 1997, 103, 281–2. See also Datsoulis-Stavridis 1977, esp. 143, fig. 21; Daux 1962, 679–81, fig. 21; 1963, 710, fig. 17; Jansen 2006, 160–1; Meyer 1985, 398, no. 14. Note that the relief from Kephisia (Figure 4.3) is too damaged to identify the individual portrayed and the inscription does not record a name.

[133] Tobin 1997, 282; Papadimitriou 1963; Travlos 1988, 55–79.

COMMEMORATION EMBODIED 227

FIGURE 5.20 Heroizing relief from Herodes' estate at Loukou-Eva Kynouria. National Archaeological Museum, Athens (NM 1450). It depicts a youth (Polydeukion? Achilles?) wearing only a cloak and standing in front of a horse in profile. A tree to the youth's right is entwined with a snake and further to his right armour and weapons are piled. A slave holds out a helmet and a funerary amphora stands on a pillar behind the slave. Height: 0.64 m; Width: 1.0 m.

FIGURE 5.21 Heroic relief of Polydeukion from the Sanctuary of Artemis at Brauron. Archaeological Museum of Brauron (Inv. 1181). A youth reclines on a *klinê* and raises a *kantharos* (fragment missing from image) in his right hand. In his left, he holds the reins of a horse, whose head is faintly represented over his left shoulder.

'antiquarian' sentiment or, perhaps, this was one region where Herodes and the *trophimoi* used to hunt (see Philostr. *VS* 2.1.558–9).[134] She is partially correct, in that Herodes would certainly have been attracted to Brauron because of its importance to classical Athenian religion and Artemis' association with rituals of transition for children and youths. Beyond the heroic associations, the feasting of the youth in the relief also taps into Herodes' reanimating impulse discussed in chapter 4 with respect to his herms in its depiction of a necessary daily act.[135] More importantly, however, it is yet another symptom of Herodes' long view, in which the Greek past becomes continuous with the Roman present and an as-yet-malleable future. In this context, for an elite Athenian, the dedication of a heroic relief of a youth prematurely dead amongst the many classical statues of children from the site becomes an unsurprising act. It is of no consequence that no one frequents the sanctuary in the present because the target audience, who is meant to understand Herodes as the inheritor, propagator, and reinterpreter of Athenian ritual tradition, lies in the future. It thus aligns with the imperial quality of his private monumentalization in its attempts to dominate and redefine the spaces and landscapes of Greek memory and religion in Attica and beyond.[136]

There is some doubt as to the identity of the boy in the Loukou relief because he does not fit the usual Polydeukion portrait type, and he has rather been identified as Achilles, of whom we have no secure depiction.[137] Polydeukion was, however, the only one of the three who was definitively heroized and addressed as 'hero' in inscriptions, and he was clearly memorialized to a far greater extent.[138] Hans R. Goette has therefore convincingly argued that the relief depicts Achilles the *trophimos* in the guise of Achilles son of Peleus, who also died young, and does not represent Herodes' Achilles as a hero in his own right.[139] This identification explains also the piled weapons on the right of the relief. The heroic and Homeric names of the *trophimoi* support such casting, and Polydeukion the hero surely appears as (or is at least meant to recall) the Dioskouros Polydeukes in the relief from Brauron as well.[140]

The effectiveness of Herodes' heroizing efforts is difficult to judge: the cult persisted for several years and we have dedications made by those external to

---

[134] Tobin 1997, 282.   [135] See Section 4.2.3.

[136] See further Strazdins 2022a.

[137] For identification as Polydeukion, see Kapetanopoulos 1989; for Achilles, see Karusu 1969, 264; Tobin 1997, 346–7; Goette 2001, 425–6; 2019, 248–50. On this relief in general, see Jansen 2006, 214–19.

[138] See Gazda 1977, 20; 1980, 3–4.   [139] Goette 2001, 426. Jansen (2006, 218) agrees.

[140] Gazda 1980, 4. See also Datsoulis-Stavridis 1977, 132–4, fig. 7, which shows a possible variant of Polydeukion's portrait type in the guise of another unknown hero. The differences in features make it more probable that this image draws on Herodes' iconography of Polydeukion and is a portrait of an unknown individual.

FIGURE 5.22 Portrait of a Roman youth, from Italy, mid-2nd century AD, once assigned as an 'export' type of Polydeukion, now unidentified. Said to have been found at Hadrian's villa at Tivoli. Nelson-Atkins Museum of Art, Kansas City, Missouri. Purchase: William Rockhill Nelson Trust, 34-91/1. Marble, Height: 1.683 m; Width: 0.432 m; Depth: 0.356 m.

Herodes' direct family.[141] Nevertheless, secure evidence for the cult is tied closely to Herodes' holdings in Kephisia, where Polydeukion was buried. Cornelius Vermeule has asserted that it spread around the empire just like Antinoos' based on portraits found at Tivoli and Leptis Magna that he designated as a secondary, 'export' type of Polydeukion, but which have since been assigned to an unknown individual, probably from the imperial family (Figure 5.22).[142] This anonymous portrait, however, does closely resemble the ambiguous Polydeukion-Achilles (?) figure in the Loukou relief, although the statue's jaw is slightly squarer and the fringe more detailed with individuated locks.[143] The affinity nevertheless strengthens the case that the third *trophimos*' visual identification is contained in the relief, given the artistic influence Polydeukion's images appear to have exerted

---

[141] Gazda (1980, 7) notes that the known portraits of Polydeukion differ in quality and workmanship, which would indicate many hands at work in the production of the images, possibly over a significant period. For further discussion of dating, see Lattimore, 1996, 7–9.

[142] Vermeule 1954, 253–5; Gazda 1980, 5–6; Tobin 1997, 106–7, 326; Jansen 2006, 199–201; Fittschen 2021, no. 73, 120–22, taf. 76–7.

[143] Jansen 2006, 208–13, taf. 49, 1 and 2, suggests that a grave *stélē* in the National Archaeological Museum, Athens (NM 3285) belongs to Achilles, but disagrees that the statue from Kansas City (Figure 5.22) could be Achilles because of the differences between the fringes.

FIGURE 5.23 'Schematic' portrait of Polydeukion from a fourth-century Roman villa at Welschbillig, Germany. The identification with Polydeukion is based largely on the lock scheme. Rheinisches Landesmuseum, Trier (Inv. 18876).

on later portraits and the influence Antinoos' representation had on Polydeukion's: the Tivoli and Leptis Magna youth's features should thus be understood as drawing on Herodes' art (or vice versa).

A herm found in a fourth-century Roman villa in Welschbillig, Germany, however, does replicate the main features of Polydeukion's portrait, particularly the lock scheme, if in a more schematic manner without the fine workmanship (Figure 5.23).[144] It was displayed in a gallery of approximately one hundred portrait herms, which formed pillars of a perimeter fence surrounding a shallow pool (*piscina*) and courtyard.[145] This image could be interpreted as evidence for the longevity and extensive geographical influence of Herodes' Polydeukion cult, but in reality the German herm sticks out as a geographic and temporal anomaly. Its display context indicates that it should instead be understood as a product created for aesthetic rather than religious, sentimental, or

---

[144] Wrede 1972, 54–5, 113, no. 80, pls 12.1–2, 14.1–2, 14.4; Gazda 1980, 6–7.
[145] See Wrede 1972, 37, for a reconstruction of the herm gallery and the possible position of the Polydeukion herm.

commemorative reasons.[146] Four more portraits from the National Museum in Athens have been assigned by Alkmini Datsoulis-Stavridis to Polydeukion, even though they diverge from his portrait type.[147] As with the Welschbillig herm, it is as probable that they too are creations inspired by the sombre, contemplative features of Polydeukion's portrait instead of genuine representations of the boy. His signature features were attractive enough to inspire at least four modern copies as well that cannot have been prompted by commemorative impulses.[148]

It is Herodes' aesthetic choices, therefore, that have influenced later artists rather than his efforts to create a hero: these images no doubt owe their similarities to Herodes' Polydeukion portraits through emulation. This makes him a cultural force of significant reach but extracts his and Polydeukion's commemorative identity from the process. The Kephisian games held in Polydeukion's honour were also a private affair, with the competitors coming from Herodes' household and close acquaintances.[149] In comparison to the vast spread of Hadrian's Antinoos cult, then, Herodes' hero Polydeukion pales. Indeed, one last dedication to the 'hero Polydeukion', this time from Delphi, implies a note of scepticism towards the whole project. A reused statue base now in the Roman agora bears the following inscription (Figure 5.24):[150]

Δελφοὶ
Βιβούλλιον
Πολυδευκί-
ωνα σωφρο-
σύνης ἕνε-
κα τὸν Ἡρώ-
δου ἥρωα 𝒮

The Delphians [dedicate a statue of]
Vibullius
Polydeukion
on account of
his moderation,
Herodes'
hero 𝒮

---

[146] Lattimore (1996, 6) notes the villa's owner probably did not know of Polydeukion.

[147] Datsoulis-Stavridis 1977, 130–9, National Archaeological Museum, Athens, nos. 850 (figs 5–6), 2144 (fig. 7), 4913 (fig. 9), 5247 (figs 11–12). Also see Jansen 2006, 180–219, taf. 40–51, for other portraits that draw on Herodes' images.

[148] See Gazda 1980, 2 n. 5 and Gazda 1977, 20–1, for details. Gazda (1980, 7–8) also identifies a possible reflection of Polydeukion in Donatello's bronze statue of David and a youth on Ghiberti's *Gates of Paradise*, both of which support the case for his portrait exerting lasting artistic influence.

[149] Tobin 1997, 230.   [150] *FD* III.3.1, no. 74. Delphi inv. no. 3251.

FIGURE 5.24 Statue base of Polydeukion dedicated by the Delphians to the 'hero of Herodes', found reused in the Roman agora. Archaeological site of Delphi (Inv. 3251; *FD* III.3.1, no. 74). Height: 1.15 m; Width (at the level of the inscription): 0.435 m; Depth: 0.425 m.

'Herodes' hero', the Delphians pointedly call Polydeukion, making the reader wait until the very end of the inscription to find the designation, as though his elevated state were not acknowledged more broadly beyond Herodes' authority of one.[151] The title also puns on Herodes' name and gently mocks Herodes' own posturing as the 'hero of Marathon'.[152]

Although Herodes' cult of Polydeukion was a quite localized parochial affair,[153] Polydeukion's status as hero fits into Greek tradition stretching back to Homeric times in a more comfortable way than Antinoos' deification. The elevation of the latter succeeded due to a number of factors: Hadrian's own efforts in encouraging it; its bypassing the usual senatorial process;[154] the entanglement of the new god with imperial cult; and the Greek elite actively adopting and promoting it, no doubt in the hope of garnering imperial favour.[155] Thus not only was Herodes

---

[151] See Tobin 1997, 305–6, on this dedication. [152] See further Sections 4.4 and 6.5.
[153] Gazda 1980, 5–7.
[154] On the differences between Antinoos' posthumous treatment and the deification of emperors, see Vout 2007, 12–13, 113–21; Jones 2010, 75–83.
[155] Polemon is known to have sponsored the issue of Antinoos coins at Smyrna (see Opper 2008, 186–90) and Herodes had an Antinoos shrine on his estate at Loukou (see Section 4.4). See also Price 1984, 68.

limited in his public commemorative efforts by possessing insufficient authority, but Polydeukion also did not have the mystery or mythic potency of Antinoos—there was no Osirian paradigm on which to build; there was no Zeus and Ganymede. Moreover, in spite of his generous benefactions to Athens and the Greek world, Herodes was considerably less popular than the emperor, especially in Athens.[156] One further aspect that may have doomed Herodes' efforts to local efficacy was that Hadrian was his older contemporary, whose socio-political identity and the institutions in which it functioned still had powerful currency. In contrast, the temporal distance between Philostratos' sophists and their models was vast, a circumstance that allowed them far greater freedom in turning their borrowings and reworkings into new authoritative creations. Nevertheless, Herodes' ambition to commemorate his loved ones on an imperial scale is clear, as is his care to contextualize the process in long-established Greek traditions.

Although Herodes' hero may have failed to make a lasting commemorative impact, an honorific statue base from Corinth reveals that his habit of replicating his family as social and cultural exemplars in stone did. In her comprehensive study of the development and history of Corinth's Peirene fountain, Betsey Robinson notes that a statue of Regilla found in the fountain's triconch court was situated in a 'nostalgic, museum-like arrangement' with other items of cultural significance after the court's remodelling in the later fourth century AD (Figure 5.25).[157] Most probably a 'temporal-hybrid' (i.e., constructed from a mismatched Roman matron's body and late-antique head),[158] the statue stood on a reused base with a secondary inscription that was probably recut for the occasion (*Corinth* 8.1, no. 86; Figures 5.26–7):[159]

[N]εύματι Σισυφίης βουλῆς παρὰ χεύματι πηγῶν
Ρηγίλλαν μ'ἐσορᾶ(ι)ς, εἰκόνα σωφροσύνης
        Ψ   Β

By the command of the Sisyphean *boulê*, beside the stream of the springs,
You see me, Regilla, an image of moderation.
        By decree of the *boulê*.

---

[156] See chapter 6.   [157] Robinson (2011, 252–75) discusses the dating of the court in detail.
[158] Robinson 2011, 282.
[159] That this and another inscription referring to Regilla (*Corinth* 8.3, no. 128, also for her σωφροσύνη) were recut on reused bases was first suggested by Kent (*Corinth* 8.3, 22 n.15). For the findspot and publication of the base, see *Corinth* 8.1, no. 86, where Herodes was identified as the renovator of the triconch court. Robinson (2011, 79–80) traces the history of this proposition from Richardson (1900, 236–7) to *Corinth* 8.3, nos 337, 343, pl. 31, which propose a different donor, but maintain a second-century date. See also Tobin 1997, 298–9. Robinson 2011 notes that the base had been used twice before for bronze statues and that a relief of musical instruments hanging from a cord that would have appeared upside-down on the left face of the base when used for Regilla belongs to one of these earlier configurations (Figure 5.27). Schowalter (2014, 166–83) argues that the inscriptions are original second-century cuttings. If he is correct, their reuse in the fourth century still suggests nostalgia as a motivation.

FIGURE 5.25 The triconch forecourt of the Peirene Fountain, Ancient Corinth, looking towards the fountain's façade and the eastern apse, in front of which the statue base of Regilla was found.

FIGURE 5.26 Marble statue base of Regilla found in front of the middle of the eastern apse of the Peirene Fountain's forecourt, Ancient Corinth, showing the (recut) inscription praising Regilla for her *sôphrosynê*. Archaeological Museum of Corinth (Inv. 62; *Corinth* 8.1, no. 86). Height: 0.35 m; Width: 0.67 m; Depth: 0.67 m.

FIGURE 5.27 Left side of the statue base of Regilla from the Peirene Fountain, Ancient Corinth, showing musical instruments suspended from a rope (upside down), indicating the base was inverted to cut the Regilla inscription. Archaeological Museum of Corinth (Inv. 62). Height: 0.35 m; Width: 0.67 m; Depth: 0.67 m.

A possible motivation for reconstructing Regilla in this way is the quality of *sôphrosynê* ('moderation' or 'self-control') assigned to her, which in late-antique Corinth would have appealed to pagan and Christian viewers alike.[160] Additionally, Regilla's and Herodes' reputations as benefactors would have recalled the great flowering of Greek culture in Roman Achaea in the second century AD. Importantly, this nostalgia coincided with an increased interest in philosophers and rhetoric in the late fourth and early fifth centuries in eastern cities, both as important figures and as defenders of pagan religion and Hellenic culture. These sentiments regularly translated into the portrayal of the famous dead and prominent contemporaries in sculpture.[161] In this scenario, Regilla stands in for her husband and family as a symbol of pagan Hellenic culture in the kind of archaizing display in which Herodes himself indulged.[162] Peirene's forecourt was the perfect spot to tap into this sentiment, given the fountain's history of signifying literary and philosophical inspiration.[163] That another recut and reused base for Regilla in

[160] *Sôphrosynê* was an important Christian virtue. See Schowalter 2014, 181. Stirling 2008, 136–9, describes the religious tension between pagans and Christians in Corinth in the fourth century that created a hostile environment for pagan art, making Regilla's 'moderation' an important element in her rededication. Note also that laws were in place across the empire at the time to repair or recycle elements of irreparable monuments. See Robinson 2011, 274; Alchermes 1994.

[161] Smith 1990, 127–55, 177, on Aphrodisias; Schowalter 2014, 176–8.   [162] See Section 4.4.

[163] On Peirene's association with artistic and philosophical inspiration in late antiquity, see Robinson 2011, 62–3, 274–5.

Corinth also refers to her *sôphrosynê*,[164] as does the Delphic base for Polydeukion above, shows the effectiveness of this inscriptional replication in a changing world. It is the base inscribed with words in Regilla's voice, moreover, which clearly activates the statue in this case, given the portrait belonged to an anonymous late-antique woman. Regilla thus stands at the Peirene fountain in the fourth century because her and Herodes' commemorative programme shaped her in a way that could be accommodated by new and varied audiences and that allowed its effect to be futured.

In the *Corinthian Oration*, Favorinus also champions replication as a means of overcoming the limiting specificity of honorific statues. At the mock trial he instigates for his citizen statue, the image itself speaks in defence of the man.[165] It stresses that Favorinus deserves statues in all cities but that the reasons why specific cities should raise their own bronze Favorinus are idiosyncratic: in Corinth because, like the Roman city itself, he has become Greek (ἀφηλληνίσθη); in Athens because he speaks the Attic dialect (ἀττικίζει τῇ φωνῇ); in Sparta because he loves athletics (φιλογυμναστεῖ); elsewhere, because he is a philosopher (φιλοσοφεῖ); above all, because he attained and dispenses *paideia* (37.25–8).[166] Favorinus here accepts the necessity of a statue's specificity and that real statues do not speak but rather have their stories devised by their dedicators. At the same time, he demonstrates that a single statue cannot encompass an individual. Favorinus' advocation for many statues in many cities, each symbolic of a particular benefaction and civic relationship, is more diversification than direct replication; nevertheless, variation would typically be expressed by the inscription rather than the image, which would conform to honorific norms. That these many statues can be contextualized in a few sentences of oratory, moreover, demonstrates text's greater commemorative efficiency in this instance.

Replication thus allows an individual to spread their personally shaped image beyond a specific locale. As with all commemorative artistic efforts, however, that image is always dependent on audience interpretation. Polydeukion's portrait persists not because Herodes promoted him as heroic but because his visual qualities appealed to either collectors or those commissioning their own images of melancholic youths. Regilla's presence in Corinth endured because the qualities ascribed to her in honorific inscriptions harmonized with both later Christian and pagan values. These instances, along with Favorinus' rhetorical statues, indicate

---

[164] See *Corinth* 8.3, 59–60, no. 128; Schowalter 2014, 166–9.

[165] See Gleason 1995, 13–14; König 2001, 164 and 166, for the ambiguity between man and statue. See also Francis 2003, 581, on Lucian's use of ἀνδριάς in his *Essays in Portraiture*. On the terminology of statues and the difference between ἀνδριάς and ἄγαλμα, see Stewart 2003, 25–8.

[166] On this passage, see Barigazzi 1966, 329–31 (on 37.25–8); Gleason 1995, 16–17; König 2001, 164–7; Whitmarsh 2001, 119–21. All focus on his self-fashioning and his cultural mutability, particularly with respect to Corinth (especially König and Whitmarsh).

once more that individual images stand in individual and specific relation to the community they grace but also that art can transcend its own time and context if it is capable of accommodating new audiences.

5.5 ANIMATION AND WRITING

Aligned with replication in literature is statue animation. This phenomenon allows one's statue to transcend its specificity by freeing it to roam far and wide.[167] Favorinus uses this idea to suggest that his Corinthian statue fled the city rather than that the city deliberately removed it. He counters his own proposition, however, by claiming that no statue has moved of its own accord since the great mythic craftsman Daidalos made images: men are represented on horseback and in motion themselves or even with wings, but 'all maintain their pose ($\kappa\alpha\tau\grave{\alpha}\ \sigma\chi\hat{\eta}\mu\alpha$) and position ($\kappa\alpha\tau\grave{\alpha}\ \chi\acute{\omega}\rho\alpha\nu$)' (*Or.* 37.10). That statues possessed an innate potential to become animate was nevertheless a popular belief, evinced by the chaining of statues to their pedestals, just in case the artwork felt the urge to flee.[168] The animation of statues need not, however, be so dramatic. In Philostratos' *Heroikos*, for example, Hektor's statue at Troy sweats in empathy as athletic games are held in his honour (19.4).[169]

The sweating of statues was a common occurrence that was usually interpreted as an evil omen.[170] In Arrian's *Anabasis*, however, a sweating statue becomes the augur of fame for both Alexander and the author. On Alexander's return to Makedon following the attack on Thebes, Arrian describes an incident in which a statue of Orpheus begins to sweat (*An.* 1.11.2; cf. Plut. *Alex.* 14.8–9).[171] This fantastic event was variously interpreted, but Arrian chooses to mention only one explanation: 'it was clear that makers of epics and choric songs and odes would have much toil ($\pi o\lambda\grave{u}\varsigma\ \pi\acute{o}\nu o\varsigma$) to poetize and sing of Alexander and the deeds of Alexander' (1.11.2). Ironically, despite this prediction, it is the very lack of

---

[167] On the idea of statue animation through time, see Gross 1992. On statue animation in Greek antiquity, see Mayor 2018.

[168] Spivey 1997, 442–3, 446–8 (on Daidalos); cf. Barigazzi 1966, 320–1 (on 37.10); Kassel 1983, 1–12; Freedberg 1989, 33–7; Mossman 1991, 106; Gleason 1995, 13–15; Steiner 2001, 138–44, for numerous examples of moving statues; Stewart 2003, 260–4; Smith 2007, 89–92; Mayor 2018, esp. 45–60, 85–104. See also Plut. *Alex.* 24.4 for the chaining of a statue of Apollo with Merkelbach 1971. See Hom. *Il.* 18.417–18, 375–7, for Hephaistos' moving automata. See also Apollod. *Bibl.* 1.140–2; Ap. Rhod. *Argon.* 4.1639–93; Paus. 8.53.5. For the magical properties attributed to statues, see Faraone 1992 and for the same in Byzantium, see James 1996.

[169] See also Kallistratos' *Descriptiones* for statues possessing life-like characteristics, especially 1.3, 2.3, 3.2, 6.3, 7.3, 9.1, 11.2.

[170] See Bosworth 1980, 97; Poulsen 1945.

[171] See Mossman 1991, 116, for the event in Plutarch.

effective commemoration which Arrian claims a few sentences later compels him to write the *Anabasis* (1.12.2–4). Arrian uses the perspiring Orpheus to highlight the failure of his literary predecessors and sets the scene for his own literary monument and triumph. He drives his point home at the beginning of the Second Preface, stating that 'neither in prose, nor in verse has anyone crafted ($\dot{\epsilon}\pi o\acute{\iota}\eta\sigma\epsilon v$) him, nor indeed is Alexander sung of in lyrics' (1.12.2), the very things the sweating statue was meant to prophesy. So, by interpreting the statue to his own ends and then claiming the prophecy attached to it has yet to be fulfilled, Arrian makes this prodigy as much about himself and his literary ability as he does about Alexander's fame. He thus imbues his composition with divine endorsement.

Favorinus' mention of Daidalos as a statue animator may also allude to Plato's *Meno* 97d (cf. *Euthphr.* 11c–d), in which Sokrates compares the art of sophistry to that of Daidalos' truant images.[172] The metaphor is apt too for both the practice of improvised epideictic oratory and the fame which it can garner. Like Daidalos' statues, each *epideixis* is a fine creation, but it remains only for that performance. The sophist's fame, on the other hand, can be fleeting—existing only for the moment of speaking—or, alternatively, it has the potential to travel. That capacity multiplies should the speech be recorded in writing and thus a Daedalian statue is also a metaphor for text. Favorinus underscores the freedom granted his fame by the circulating text in comparison to the statue through an altered quotation from Homer's *Odyssey*: 'yet Honour, like a dream, takes wing and flies away' (*Or.* 37.9; *Od.* 11.222).[173] Here the original $\psi v\chi\acute{\eta}$ ('ghost' in the Odyssean context, but also 'soul') is replaced by $\tau\iota\mu\acute{\eta}$ ('honour'). The Homeric verse is spoken by Odysseus' mother in the underworld, as she explains that, although he cannot grasp her in his embrace, she is not a 'false image' ($\epsilon\H{\iota}\delta\omega\lambda ov$) but the insubstantial spirit freed by burning the body on the funeral pyre (*Od.* 11.204–22). The 'body' ($\sigma\H{\omega}\mu a$) is thus once more cast as the imprisoner or 'tomb' ($\sigma\H{\eta}\mu a$) of the soul. By extension, the statue becomes the imprisoner of Favorinus' 'honour' ($\tau\iota\mu\acute{\eta}$) which is freed upon its destruction to circulate as text.

In his *Florida* 16, Apuleius, in contrast, characterizes Carthage's control over his honour via its award of a statue as a form of death.[174] Initially, he tells the story of Philemon, a rival of the comic poet Menander, whom he sets up as illustrative of his own predicament.[175] After the performance of his new play was interrupted, Philemon dies in the night and his body is discovered conjoined with the play's text (16.16–17).[176] It is described as though it were a statue, and the

---

[172] Cf. Barigazzi 1966, 321 (on 37.10); Spivey 1997, 446.

[173] On this phrase see Barigazzi 1966, 320 (on 37.9).   [174] See Too 1996.

[175] For the extant fragments of Philemon, see Kassel and Austin 1989, 221–317.

[176] See Lee 2005, 152 (on 16.16–17), on the entanglement of Philemo and the scroll. Cf. Too 1996, 140–1. See Harrison 2000, 117; Hunink 2001, 160; Lee 2005, 147, on other versions of Philemon's death.

commingling of body and text represents the two modes of possible commemoration: monument and written word.[177] This organic image is described as a 'beautiful death' (*formosa mors*), which reworks the Homeric καλὸς θάνατος[178] and opens the possibility of immortality through the glorious deed of writing. Apuleius previously suggested that Philemon was a slave to his audience (16.6–10),[179] rendering his works repetitive and clichéd. Philemon thus achieved contemporary fame, often defeating the now far-more-famous Menander, but his plays do not stand up before the critics of Apuleius' own day (cf. Quintillian 3.7.18; 10.1.72). Hence his statuesque corpse is an apt monument, in that it will not linger.

Apuleius signals his anxiety over relinquishing control over his representation to the Carthaginian senate by likening his living self to an inanimate image or corpse: as soon as he is granted a statue, he loses the ability to speak, the very attribute that garnered fame and honour for him. His first attempt to make a public speech is postponed like Philemon's performance (16.10; 16.19), and then he suffers a wrestling accident (16.20–2), which not only keeps him from the senate, but also takes him from animation to incapacitation:

An acute pain of the intestines began, which eased off just before it finished me off with its virulence, and forced me, like Philemon, to be dead (*letum*) before I had read (*lectum*), to meet my death (*fata*) rather than my deadline (*fanda*), to come to my end (*consummare animam*) rather than the end of my story (*historiam*).[180]   (16.22)

The juxtapositions of *letum/lectum, fata/fanda, animam/historiam* serve to offset death with literary production,[181] and death, here, is aligned with representation in stone or bronze. Apuleius' stupefaction embodies his fears that the statue will fix him in a way that does not adequately represent him (16.32–3). Thus the statue might be a fitting memorial for a single speech, but not a man's whole life.[182] Although a three-dimensional object with texture, volume, colour, it fundamentally struggles to express character and identity in more than one dimension. At the same time, Apuleius indicates that a statue is a fitting monument for the deceased alone, since it represents achieved glories rather than continuing attainments. Apuleius' concern over being typecast is borne out in

---

[177] Lee (2005, 148) sees this as a claim for life equalling literature and that Apuleius offers his literature to Carthage in exchange for a statue. I argue rather that statue and text are opposed.

[178] See Vernant 1991.   [179] Cf. Too 1996, 140.

[180] Translated by Hilton 2001.

[181] *Contra* Lee 2005, 153 (on 16.22): 'These figures […] conceptually intertwine life and literature'. Cf. Connors 1994.

[182] Cf. Ng 2016 on Dio Chrysostom.

the composition of an inscription on a statue base from Madauros, his hometown, which was raised in his honour:[183]

[PH]ILOSOPHO
[PL]ATONICO
[MA]DAVRENSES
CIVES
ORNAMENT[O]
SVO D.D.P.[P.]

To the philosopher
The Platonist
The Madaurensian
Citizens [dedicate]
their own ornament
by Senatorial decree and at public expense.

The inscription characterizes Apuleius in a precise manner—'Platonist', 'philosopher', 'ornament'—that, via *ornamentum*, highlights the honour's inanimate nature: Apuleius embellishes the city through his philosophical activities and their fame in exchange for his immobile, silent image physically adorning its public commemorative space. Apuleius' name is missing from the inscription and one is meant to know, as scholars have assumed, that he is the Platonic philosopher so honoured. Successful sophists would commonly use only a single element of their name without patronymic or other identifying label in inscriptions, as seen with Polemon and Aristeides in chapter 2,[184] but here it is Apuleius' role that defines him for the community. Moreover, his fame, derived from his writings and unattached to the statue, has been used in modern scholarship to ascribe an identity to this anonymous inscription, a role played by the portrait itself in antiquity. This indicates that the philosopher must have been immediately recognizable to most citizens and that the identification of the statue did not depend entirely on the inscription in this case.

In *Florida* 16, Apuleius mentions two statues: one proposed as a private dedication by his friend Aemilianus Strabon and accepted by the senate, and one that he understands the senate will subsequently grant publicly (16.39–44). The present speech is in thanks for the decision to award the private honour, but he proposes to write another piece for its public dedication:

I will also soon compose my thanks in a book (*libro*) written for the dedication of my statue; and I will send that book through all the provinces to represent my praises of your

---

[183] Gsell 1922, 1.2115. See also Tatum 1978, 105–8; Too 1996, 133.
[184] See Sections 2.1.3 and 2.4.

benefaction in every other place throughout the whole world and to continue to do so for all time to come.[185]   (16.47–8)

The composition of the 'book' (*liber*) is a pun on the idea that the written word can make Apuleius free (*liber*) from the constraints of Carthage's representation of him.[186] Like Favorinus' textualized statue, his book will be a moving self-constructed monument that will offset the city's dedication of his image. In this way, he promotes his literature over the statue and makes the monument represent his words rather than his physical self, thus highlighting yet again that a mute memorial cannot serve adequately to reveal the basis and quality of his fame. The book will act as a secondary, detailed, and personalized inscription that explains what the statue means to Apuleius and his art beyond the constraints of civic decrees. Animation, then, allows a statue to move beyond its specific context through time and space and to achieve the same results as the material replication of an image in many different places. The phenomenon, however, can occur only in speech or text and, for this reason, statue animation is regularly used as a metaphor for writing. Additionally, it allows the author to shape and control the statue's honorific message in a way largely impossible with a real statue.

Apuleius' book supplements the civic honour of the statue without rejecting it outright. One of Aelius Aristeides' dreams in the *Sacred Tales*, however, is less accommodating. Instead of turning an animated statue into a travelling book, he makes the case for the superiority of books over statues as memorials. In this vision, while wandering through Athens (*HL* 5.57–67), Aristeides comes across a magnificent temple consecrated to Plato. Some people nearby are discussing the statue of the philosopher inside it as though it were ancient. Aristeides interrupts to correct them, saying: 'it is not possible to say that it is ancient ($\pi\alpha\lambda\alpha\iota\acute{o}\nu$). For the form of the workmanship is shown to be rather recent ($\nu\epsilon\acute{\omega}\tau\epsilon\rho\sigma$), and there was not much regard for Plato in Plato's own lifetime, but […] his reputation grew later ($\mathring{\upsilon}\sigma\tau\epsilon\rho\sigma\nu$ […] $\pi\rho\sigma\mathring{\upsilon}\beta\eta$ $\delta\acute{o}\xi\alpha$)' (*HL* 5.62). Aristeides here demonstrates the same kind of art-historical appraisal we saw in chapter 3 with Pausanias and Arrian.[187] His connoisseur's eye can comprehend and explicate the signs of the statue's production and its relationship to time. When someone suggests there should be more temples of Plato, Aristeides again modifies this view, proposing instead:

'But perhaps it is proper to consecrate temples to the gods, but to honour famous men with the offering of books, since,' I said, 'our most valuable possessions are what we say ($\mathring{\eta}\mu\mathring{\omega}\nu$ $\tau\iota\mu\iota\acute{\omega}\tau\alpha\tau\alpha$ $\mathring{\alpha}$ $\varphi\theta\epsilon\gamma\gamma\acute{o}\mu\epsilon\theta\alpha$). For statues and images are memorials of bodies, but books

---

[185] Note that this reworks Pind. *Nem.* 5.1–6.   [186] Cf. Too 1996, 145–6.
[187] See Section 3.2. Translations after Behr 1981.

of words (τοὺς μὲν ἀνδριάντας καὶ τὰ ἀγάλματα τῶν σωμάτων ὄντα ὑπομνήματα, τὰ δὲ βιβλία τῶν λόγων)'. (*HL* 5.63)

The idea of a temple on the scale of the Parthenon (*HL* 5.61) consecrated to a man of literature seems hubristic, but it plays off the tradition of hero cult and, in Aristeides' dream world, establishes conceptual immortality as the level of recognition great authors should receive.[188] Moreover, Plato's newish statue reflects how true appreciation may come only centuries in the future. This perspective aligns with Dio Chrysostom's concerns about the public's tendency to miss a modern classic (*Or.* 21), Longinos' movable temporal perspective,[189] and the belief that one's devotees have the potential to swell as time passes rather than diminish.

Aristeides' championing of the book as a far more fitting memorial than a statue is a rejection of the established mode of civic honours practised throughout the empire.[190] This is not the kind of acclaim he seeks. He does participate in the traditional civic exchange of benefaction and honour, but even then our evidence can be unusual and decidedly bookish. An inscribed base from Smyrna, for example, honours Publius Aelius Aristeides Theodoros on account of his speeches.[191] Jean Bingen has shown, however, that the dedicators ('the city of the Alexandrians and Hermopolis Magna and the council of the Antinoeis *Neoi Hellenes* and the Hellenes who dwell in the Delta of Egypt and in the Theban Nome') are imaginative constructions by the unknown Smyrnaeans honouring Aristeides as a nod to his nostalgia for his positive experiences in Egypt early in his career. The phraseology draws on Herodotos (2.4), and the monument probably had at least two other invented honorific inscriptions dedicated by Ἰταλοί and Ἑλλάς ('Italians' and 'Greece'), since it appears to be the same bronze statue described by Philostratos (*VS* 2.9.582).[192] This honorific celebration of Aristeides is fitting both to his own tendency to construct imaginative arenas of honour for himself and to imperial Greek literary culture more broadly, with its evocation of the language of civic honours and Herodotos to shape personal idiosyncratic commemoration.

Aristeides, moreover, regularly expresses concern that his absence from public life (*HL* 5.56) gives him poor access to the honorific system. As Janet Downie has compellingly demonstrated, however, the entire narrative of how he gains

---

[188] On temples to Homer in the Hellenistic world, see Brink 1972, 547–67. See also Ael. *VH* 13.22 (Alexandria); Strabo 14.1.37 and Cic. *Arch.* 9 (Smyrna).

[189] See Sections 2.1.1 and 2.1.2.   [190] See also Downie 2013, 181.

[191] *I.Smyrna* 901 (*SEG* 55, 1279). See Robert 1937, 207–22; Bingen 1987; Quet 1992; Puech 2002, no. 44, 140–5. See also Philostr. *VS* 2.9.582; Bowie 2012, 235. See *HL* 4.53 and Petsalis-Diomidis 2010, 118–19, 132–3, for the name 'Theodoros'.

[192] See Bingen 2005, 169–83.

immunity from holding public office is designed to establish and enhance his reputation as an orator: he wants his immunity to be based on his oratorical brilliance and to use the freedom he gains to compose his literary legacy.[193] So, like Apuleius, Aristeides champions the written word as the most appropriate way to memorialize his sophistic career. Within the dream of Plato's temple, he even summons Eudoxos ('he of good repute') as a witness to preserve in writing everything he has seen precisely (ἀκριβείας αὐτὰ αὑτῶι σῶσαι, *HL* 5.66). Aristeides thus stakes his reputation on a personal conviction that his life's works are literature rather than transitory performances and, therefore, the only way they can be preserved for posterity is via writing. It is thus fitting that his words also made him a great euergetist, since, according to Philostratos, his *Monody for Smyrna* convinced Marcus Aurelius to fund the reconstruction of that city after it was devastated by an earthquake (*VS* 2.9.582).

5.6 CONCLUSION

The long tradition of statue honours in Greek cities provided one means of securing a form of permanence in cultural consciousness for prominent citizens and foreign benefactors in the Roman empire. For imperial Greek rhetors, authors, and monumentalizers, however, it was not enough. The varied strategies they employed to try to overcome the perceived limitations of honorific statues were largely aimed at reclaiming control over the shaping of their own representation and reputation—to break free of long-standing commemorative conventions.

Honorific statues may not manage to encapsulate individuality and personality, but statues of individuals could still be manipulated to shape and project a specific ideology. The more one-dimensional they are in this case, the more effective they are at conveying their assigned message. Real statues thus function well as symbols, but poorly as personal monuments. This is one reason for Antinoos' success—his own individuality was subsumed by the gods his images approximated, allowing him to be many things to many people. In his material efforts, Herodes Attikos exploits this characteristic of statues either by combining many such symbols into a complex commemorative narrative on a large monumental benefaction or by using the de-personalized aspect of replication in stone to elevate the deceased: to turn a beloved foster-son into a hero. In both cases, we again see him marking Hellenic sacred or memorial landscapes—Olympia, Brauron, Delphi, Marathon—and his own estates with commemorative identities that compete with or refract imperial messages in contentious ways. This creates an artificial sense of cultural continuity with the classical Greek past and advertises

---

[193] Downie 2013, 157–71, especially 159; see also Petsalis-Diomidis 2010, 144.

Herodes as its inheritor. All this reveals a long view of history that mimics Longinos' movable temporal perspective and that implies Roman power may not ultimately be viewed as its culmination. At the same time, Herodes' efforts promote the importance of provincial Greek elites in enabling, mediating, and shaping Roman governance in the present, so that Roman power is crafted as dependent on Greek *paideia*.

In Second Sophistic literary pursuits, statues are used to construct how the author himself wants to be remembered. The literary statue is thus regularly characterized as the written word that can take a civic-based, single moment in time described by either epideictic speech or honorific statue and make it geographically and temporally movable. As well as giving the author control over his own fame in the present, this strategy signals a desire to speak to the future. Sophistic epideictic oratory was a reasonably late-developing genre that was caught between the dictates of an oral and a literate society.[194] The predominant medium of Greek performance was poetry and oral repetition was always important to its memorialization, even once poetry was recorded in writing.[195] Sophistic *epideixis*, on the other hand, is a performed medium that actively seeks to avoid repetition. The way authors use statues within their texts reveals that they are aware of this dictate but, in recording their speeches and in trying to give their work future currency, are also rejecting it. They express confidence that text can record speech accurately, so that whoever reads it will hear them speak again (Apul. *Flor.* 16.47–8).[196] For these authors, therefore, writing, in contrast to plastic art, captures their speech in all its idiosyncrasy. The textual statue can also be political: Favorinus uses it to push back against Corinth bending to the perceived displeasure of Hadrian, and Apuleius uses it to commend the Carthaginian senate for honouring him, while suggesting their effort is ultimately unsatisfactory. Aristides uses textual monuments to reject the entire system of civic honours, so that his own retirement from public life becomes a sign of his oratorical exceptionalism.

How imperial Greeks take control of individual representation in stone or bronze reveals the extent and potency of their concerns over personal commemoration. It demonstrates their desire to break out of localism, specificity, and typecasting, to address future and geographically far-flung audiences. Their efforts also reveal a tendency to use the idea of an honorific statue to muse on broader political and cultural considerations: to make their statue (whether real or imagined) a player on the stage of empire and history.

---

[194] See the rich discussion of Porter 2010, 312–64. On prose use in Roman Greece, see Whitmarsh 2006b.

[195] See Thomas 1992, 101–27.   [196] On this notion, see Porter 2006, 314–23; Butler 2015.

PART III

Controlling the Future?

Who controls the past controls the future;
who controls the present controls the past.

– George Orwell, *1984.*[1]

[1] Orwell 1949, 204.

SIX

The King of Athens

And thou in this shalt find thy monument,
When tyrants' crests and tombs of brass are spent.

– William Shakespeare, *Sonnets* 107.13–14.

Previously, this book has examined elite imperial Greek strategies for creating a meaningful cultural presence in the future within a postclassical framework and how those strategies resonate culturally, socially, and politically in the Roman empire. This chapter will instead explore the contemporary and near-contemporary reception of Herodes Attikos in the literary record.[2] Throughout the book, I have analysed how Herodes' monuments were consciously and carefully shaped to project a distinct personal and dynastic identity, and how they contribute and respond to the commemorative culture of his day. Despite Herodes' best efforts to control his image, however, other formations of his character and identity have come down to our era through literature. He features in the letters of Marcus Cornelius Fronto, the miscellaneous collection of Aulus Gellius, known as the *Attic Nights*, the topographical narrative of Pausanias' *Description of Greece*, several satires of Lucian, and, most extensively, in the anecdotal 'biographies' of Philostratos' *Lives of the Sophists*.[3] These works enrich, destabilize, and confound Herodes' monumental image. They also often provide context for the material evidence of pushback against Herodes' commemorative impulse, such as his curse inscriptions or the defacement of the 'hero of Marathon' altar.[4] This chapter will examine the most robust literary depiction of Herodes— Philostratos' account—and its collision with both his material footprint and the portrayal of other authors. I argue that Philostratos' portrait draws out the

---

[2] This chapter substantially develops Strazdins 2019, © 2019 by the University of Chicago. All rights reserved.

[3] This chapter will not discuss 'ancient biography' as a genre nor how it differs from 'history'. These are fraught and hotly debated topics, which require more space than is here available. I use the term 'biography' loosely for a work that constructs a narrative of a life based on a series of anecdotes. Key discussions of Greek 'biography' are contained in: Geiger 1985, especially 9–29; 2014; Momigliano 1993; Swain 1997; Hägg and Rousseau 2000; McGing and Mossman 2006, ix–xx; Hägg 2012; de Temmerman 2020.

[4] On the latter, see Section 6.5; on the former, see Section 4.2.3.

Fashioning the Future in Roman Greece: Memory, Monuments, Texts. Estelle Strazdins, Oxford University Press.
© Estelle Strazdins 2023. DOI: 10.1093/oso/9780192866103.003.0006

complexities and discordance in Herodes' character to create a remarkably ambivalent representation of his 'Second Sophistic' and its role in the contemporary Roman empire. At the same time, Philostratos' equivocal fashioning of Herodes demonstrates that the commemorative anxieties identified in previous chapters as characteristic of imperial Greek culture were very real and valid concerns.

Increasing scholarly attention has been paid to Herodes over recent decades, focusing on his cultural identity,[5] the trial for tyranny before Marcus Aurelius in AD 174,[6] his euergetism as imitative of Hadrian and as a mechanism of political influence,[7] and his use of the past to create public memorial identities.[8] Most have approached him from the material record, while largely consulting the third-century *Lives of the Sophists* as a historical source rather than as a work with its own literary and rhetorical agenda.[9] Consequently, there has not been sufficient scrutiny of his image in that text, and too much faith has been placed in the literal reading of the (particularly literary) inscribed word, so that the complexity and contradictions in Herodes' nature are not developed adequately.[10] Moreover, the focus on particular qualities—biculturalism, elite identity, or public benefactions—obscures the bigger, fuller picture of the man and his place in the cultural landscape of Roman Greece as conceived by Philostratos, who himself has largely dominated scholarly conception of imperial Greek culture more broadly.[11]

Such scrutiny of the material record is not surprising: the majority of our evidence for Herodes is monumental, demonstrating his desire to write himself into the landscape as prominently and vastly as possible, and on a grander scale than his sophistic peers.[12] His public benefactions, moreover, were clearly aimed at his contemporaries as well as posterity. That he built so magnificently on private land, however, where his monuments were largely hidden from the public eye, is indicative of a particularly strong ambition to leave a lasting impression for future generations. Herodes' own land was his to shape in any way he chose. Philostratos, moreover, records an exchange between Herodes and the Roman

---

[5] Gleason 2010, especially 156–62; Mazurek 2018.

[6] See Tobin 1997, especially 285–94; Kennell 1997.   [7] Tobin 1997; Galli 2002.

[8] Rife 2008, especially 117–21; cf. Smith 1998; Galli 2002.

[9] See in this respect the otherwise extremely useful Ameling 1983a and 1983b, and the still invaluable Graindor 1930.

[10] On literary inscriptions approximating real inscriptions, but with more existential foci, see Chaniotis 2018. On the difficulties of determining real from virtual inscriptions once they have been incorporated into books, see Bing 1998, 29–38.

[11] See, e.g., on the *VS* and the Second Sophistic: Swain 1991; Brunt 1994; Eshleman 2008; 2012; Schmitz 2009; Kemezis 2011; 2014, 196–228; König 2014.

[12] See Ameling 1983b and Tobin 1997 for catalogues of inscriptions relating to Herodes. See Arafat 1996, 191–2, for the grand scale of Herodes' benefactions and the suggestion they target his contemporaries; cf. Galli 2002.

proconsuls of Achaia, in which Herodes wonders in response to criticism over his private extravagance, 'what difference does it make to you, if I amuse myself with my trifling marbles?' (*VS* 2.1.559). This exchange reveals that the kind of identities and meanings he was shaping did in fact impact public and, more importantly, Roman administrative consciousness.

Herodes certainly wanted his commemorative efforts to last, as indicated by his use of increasingly elaborate curse inscriptions.[13] Nevertheless, this single-minded need to control future reception ironically limits the ability of his works to adapt to new audiences and thus to maintain and assert continuing cultural relevance.[14] The commemorative capacity of Herodes' efforts, therefore, is rather reined in and opened up to subversion. In this chapter, along with Philostratos' portrait, I will concern myself specifically with Herodes' public Athenian benefactions, their semantic function in the literary and physical cityscape, and how his contemporaries and near-contemporaries cast them in their own works. My aim, then, is to reverse the approach of most recent scholarship: I will start with the text and use material culture as one method of elucidating and explicating his literary portrait. Gellius, Fronto, Pausanias, and Lucian appear when they shed light on Philostratos' depiction or Herodes' self-presentation in the material record.

A careful reading of Philostratos, alongside our other sources for Herodes, builds a fascinatingly complex picture of one of the most charismatic and controversial figures of second-century Greece. More than this, it reveals just how influential Philostratos has been in shaping Herodes' memory despite his own best efforts. It provides insight into why Philostratos creates such an intricate and contradictory image of his central character, how his literary construction of Herodes impacts on his own multifaceted identity, the place of elite Greeks in the empire, and the anxiety over personal commemoration that is a feature of the period.

Philostratos' text privileges Athens over any other city in the empire and Herodes Attikos over any other sophist. Athens is the centre of sophistic activity; Herodes is the city's most prominent citizen. Both city and man combine to create and reinforce each other's significance to the extent that the whole sophistic scene seems to be controlled by Herodes and Athens itself becomes his domain.[15] Herodes' 'Life' is placed at the beginning of the larger second book, thus occupying the centre of Philostratos' *Lives*, and is longer than any other *bios*. Only the 'Life of Polemon', Philostratos' secondary focus, comes close to matching it. As Kendra Eshleman has shown, Herodes and Polemon, bound by mutual regard, stand at the centre of a sophistic web, the strands of which are formed by

---

[13] See Section 4.2.3. [14] See Segal 1959, 123–40, and Section 2.1.
[15] Anderson 1986, 83; Civiletti 2002, 30–1; Eshleman 2008, 397–9; 2012, 128–32; Kemezis 2011; 2014, 212; Bowie 2015, 241–2.

teacher-student relationships.[16] Herodes' prominence thus directly reflects Athens' role as the cultural heart of Greece in Philostratos' text. Adam Kemezis has influentially read the *Lives'* as a narrative that explains how this centrality came about after Aischines was exiled from Athens and took the art of epideictic with him.[17] Through Herodes, he argues, the 'Second Sophistic' re-established itself in Athens, following an early flourishing in Asia Minor, and then spread its influence to Rome.[18] This makes it a narrative of a quite narrow cultural conquest that can nevertheless be exploited ideologically. What is interesting, then, is that Philostratos' 'Life of Herodes Attikos' tells a different and more complex tale.

Philostratos is regularly assessed as a eulogist or at least an apologist for the great man.[19] While this assessment is superficially accurate, particularly the perception that Philostratos aims to defend Herodes, a closer look reveals the anecdotal biography to be a complex mix of praise and blame. Herodes appears as a 'larger than life' character, who is ever teetering on the verge of antisocial behaviour at the same time as he dominates sophistic society.[20] Philostratos' criticism can be elucidated by showing how he refracts Herodes through a sophistic lens: just as he defines the Second Sophistic, so he also sketches Herodes by exploiting the types of 'the poor ($\pi\acute{\epsilon}\nu\eta\tau\alpha\varsigma$) and the rich ($\pi\lambda o\upsilon\sigma\acute{\iota}o\upsilon\varsigma$), of heroes ($\mathring{a}\rho\iota\sigma\tau\acute{\epsilon}\alpha\varsigma$) and tyrants ($\tau\upsilon\rho\acute{a}\nu\nu o\upsilon\varsigma$)' (*VS* 1.0.481). More precisely, Philostratos uses the opposing rhetorical concepts of the tyrant and the king, the ambiguous figure of the hero, and the revered figure of the philosopher (who appears as a foil to highlight Herodes' excesses) to meditate on what it means to be an elite Greek in the Roman empire.[21] Herodes is in sharpest relief when he is juxtaposed to Roman emperors and, in this relationship, he comes to resemble Athens' legendary king, Theseus.

One episode within the *Lives of the Sophists* that displays the full spectrum of how Philostratos conceives of Herodes and his ambitions involves the Isthmus of

---

[16] Eshleman 2008, 397; see also 399 and the diagram on 398; Eshleman 2012, 128–32. See also Anderson 1986, 83.

[17] Kemezis 2011; 2014, 212. See also Civiletti 2002, 30–1; Bowie 2015, 241–2.

[18] See Bowie 2004 for variations in the culture of Philostratos' Second Sophistic based on geography, which are far slighter than one would expect.

[19] For example, Tobin 1997, 7: 'Philostratos tries to present the more negative events in Herodes' life [...] in as positive a light as possible [...] he could not completely hide unpleasant facts about Herodes' life. Instead, he tried to defend them or minimize them'. König 2014, 253: 'Herodes Atticus, who is in a sense the great star of Philostratos' work, and repeatedly defended by him'; Papalas 1979, 96. See also Kemezis 2014, 209, for the idea that Philostratos' Herodes is 'the embodiment of everything a sophist should be'. Cf. Kemezis 2011, 8–11.

[20] For a depiction of Polemon as having similar social issues, but from the perspective of psychological dysfunction, see Lauwers 2015.

[21] See *VS* 1.0.481 for Philostratos' conception of the 'Second Sophistic' and the importance of *epideixis* in character. See also Whitmarsh 2001, 42.

Corinth and its as-yet-undug canal. This scene serves as a fine introduction to Philostratos' rhetorical portrait of Herodes Attikos and forms the subject of the first section of the chapter. The second section examines how Philostratos crafts Herodes as tyrannical, especially in the political sphere of the empire, and Marcus Aurelius' imperial rule as a form of circumscribed democracy. The third section explores Herodes' kingly role within the limited sophistic scene at Athens. In section four, the trial at Sirmium is dissected and the implications of Herodes' tyrannical and Marcus' philosophical casting analysed. The final section explores Herodes' assimilation to Theseus and how Philostratos uses this affinity to comment on Herodes' political aspirations within Athens in the context of imperial Greek culture more broadly, as well as how Philostratos reinterprets Herodes' own self-fashioning to shape his image for posterity.

6.1 THE ISTHMUS OF CORINTH: HERO, KING, TYRANT, GOD?

> Herodes was driving to Corinth with Ktesidemos sitting by his side; on arriving at the Isthmus, Herodes said: 'Poseidon, I want to do it, but no one will let me!' Amazed ($\theta\alpha\nu\mu\acute{a}\sigma\alpha\varsigma$) at what he had said, Ktesidemos asked him the reason for his remark. So Herodes replied: 'For a long time I have been striving ($\dot{a}\gamma\omega\nu\acute{\iota}\zeta\omega\mu\alpha\iota$) to leave behind ($\dot{\nu}\pi\omega\lambda\epsilon\acute{\iota}\pi\epsilon\sigma\theta\alpha\iota$) to men that come after me some sign ($\sigma\eta\mu\epsilon\hat{\iota}o\nu$) of an intention ($\delta\iota\alpha\nu o\acute{\iota}\alpha\varsigma$) that reveals me as a man ($\delta\eta\lambda o\acute{\nu}\sigma\eta\varsigma$ $\check{a}\nu\delta\rho\alpha$), and I consider that I have not yet achieved this reputation ($\delta\acute{o}\xi\eta\varsigma$)'. Then Ktesidemos narrated praises ($\dot{\epsilon}\pi\alpha\acute{\iota}\nu o\nu\varsigma$ $\delta\iota\acute{\eta}\iota\epsilon\iota$) of his words and his deeds ($\lambda\acute{o}\gamma\omega\nu$ $\alpha\dot{\nu}\tau o\hat{\nu}$ $\kappa\alpha\grave{\iota}$ $\tau\hat{\omega}\nu$ $\check{\epsilon}\rho\gamma\omega\nu$) which no other man could surpass ($\dot{\nu}\pi\epsilon\rho\beta o\lambda\acute{\eta}\nu$). But Herodes replied: 'All this that you speak of is perishable ($\varphi\theta\alpha\rho\tau\acute{a}$) and liable to conquest by time ($\chi\rho\acute{o}\nu\omega\iota$ $\dot{a}\lambda\omega\tau\acute{a}$), and others will dig into and plunder ($\tau o\iota\chi\omega\rho\nu\chi o\hat{\nu}\sigma\iota\nu$) my speeches, criticizing now this, now that. But the cutting of the Isthmus is an immortal achievement ($\check{\epsilon}\rho\gamma o\nu$ $\dot{a}\theta\acute{a}\nu\alpha\tau o\nu$) and unbelievable by nature ($\dot{a}\pi\iota\sigma\tau o\acute{\nu}\mu\epsilon\nu o\nu$ $\tau\hat{\eta}$ $\varphi\acute{\nu}\sigma\epsilon\iota$), for it seems to me that to cleave through the Isthmus requires Poseidon rather than a mere man' ($\Pi o\sigma\epsilon\iota\delta\hat{\omega}\nu o\varsigma$ $\delta\epsilon\hat{\iota}\sigma\theta\alpha\iota$ $\mathring{\eta}$ $\dot{a}\nu\delta\rho\acute{o}\varsigma$). (*VS* 2.1.552)

This passage reveals three important aspects of Philostratos' Herodes: his ambition to make a mark on the world that is unique and appropriate to his self-conception; his fear of mortality and the loss of control over his reputation which it ensures; his desire for a heroic form of immortal fame. The language Philostratos assigns to Herodes identifies the metaphorical framework within which he is to be located: he is striving ($\dot{a}\gamma\omega\nu\acute{\iota}\zeta\omega\mu\alpha\iota$) to leave a sign ($\sigma\eta\mu\epsilon\hat{\iota}o\nu$) of a purpose/intention ($\delta\iota\acute{a}\nu o\iota\alpha$) that reveals him as a man ($\dot{a}\nu\acute{\eta}\rho$); yet, in this case, $\dot{a}\nu\acute{\eta}\rho$ is best taken as meaning the (great) man that he is. In Philostratos' *In Honour of Apollonios of Tyana*, for example, $\acute{o}$ $\dot{a}\nu\acute{\eta}\rho$ is used to refer to the protagonist honorifically, meaning something akin to 'the great man' (e.g. *VA* 1.2, 1.5, 1.6). Here, juxtaposed as it is to Poseidon, the accusative ἄνδρα also recalls Homer's Odysseus.[22] As the hero who tells his own story to ensure his κλέος ('fame'), Odysseus is a fitting mythic analogue to the sophistic Herodes.

The verb ἀγωνίζομαι signals a contest and, in the context of the passage, indicates that Herodes is striving with himself, future generations, and the past, in that he wants to leave something indelible, remarkable, and unique. From Homer onwards, the word σημεῖον has invoked a funeral monument or tomb marker, as we saw in chapter 4 with respect to its cognate σῆμα.[23] Herodes' σημεῖον must also be a concrete, physical item and not open to misinterpretation, unlike his words, which have brought him contemporary fame, but which can be manipulated by future audiences, with the implied potential consequence of manipulating his memory. This is the opposite attitude to that of Favorinus and Apuleius in the previous chapter, who championed text as a medium capable of preserving their speeches accurately and rivalling a physical monument.[24] It also conflicts with Philostratos' own presentation of his sophistic hall of fame, which Shane Butler evocatively describes as akin to a 'jukebox', since the abundant quotations of past rhetors recorded by Philostratos are treated as though they preserve individual voices whose speeches can be experienced again when read.[25] Philostratos' Herodes, then, is not on the same page as his sophistic peers.

At the same time, ἀγωνίζομαι suggests rivalry with the past, since carving the Isthmus places Herodes in competition with all those men who have tried and failed at this deed before him.[26] The phrase, 'an immortal task and unbelievable in nature', stresses the 'man-made' character of the hypothetical canal, but also the vast scale of the project. Thus it is fitting that Herodes' words and deeds are praised, two attributes that, when paired, recall both Homer and Thucydides, and which are fitting to the 'hero' (ἥρως) that Herodes' name (Ἡρώδης) conjures and on which Philostratos puns throughout his anecdotal biography.[27] This notion of altering nature is consistent with the earlier, pre-Troy, questing generation of mythic heroes, who performed a civilizing function on the natural world, and the Isthmus is strongly associated with the Athenian hero-king, Theseus, who erected a pillar there demarcating the boundary between the Peloponnese and Ionia (Strabo 3.5.5, 9.1.6–7; Plut. *Thes.* 25.4).

---

[22] See van Dijk 2009 for intertextual connections between the *VA* and the *Od*.

[23] Section 4.1; Steiner 2001, 254–9. For σημεῖον being equivalent to σῆμα, see *LSJ* s.v. σημεῖον.

[24] See Sections 5.3 and 5.5.   [25] Butler 2015, 34.

[26] The following figures also dreamt of cutting the Isthmus: Periander (Diog. Laert. 1.99), Demetrios Poliorketes (Strabo 1.3.11), Julius Caesar (Suet. *Iul.* 44.3; Plut. *Caes.* 58.4), Nero (Philostr. *VS* 2.1.551, *Ner.* 2, *VA* 4.24), Caligula (Suet. *Calig.* 21). See Tobin 1997, 314, and Whitmarsh 1999, 142 n. 3.

[27] Coté 2010 argues that Herodes approximates a modern version of the Homeric hero.

A link to Theseus is not created solely by mythic tradition. Herodes embedded himself physically in Isthmia by donating chryselephantine statues of Poseidon, Amphitrite, and Melikertes/Palaimon to the temple of Poseidon (*VS* 2.1.551; Paus. 2.1.8) only about twenty years after a new colossal marble complex, which constituted the cult statues, had been set up. Herodes' group probably functioned as supplementary cult statues or, at least, were designed to give the impression of being cult statues.[28] They indicate a desire to represent himself monumentally as a 'new Theseus', an aspect of his self-characterization that is crucial to understanding Philostratos' portrait.[29] The son of Poseidon, Theseus was believed to have transformed the Isthmian games from funeral contests for Melikertes into an event in honour of his father (Plut. *Thes.* 25.4). Herodes too may have hoped his offerings at the temple would be interpreted as a filial act. A bath complex at Isthmia with a large mosaic floor featuring Poseidon and Amphitrite has also been identified as a donation of Herodes in Polydeukion's honour that would have reinforced his association with this divine family.[30] Already in chapter 3 I noted the intertextual relationship between Herodes' Marathonian arch, Theseus' Isthmian pillar, and Hadrian's Arch in Athens.[31] One other Herodean monumental work recalls Theseus: the bull on the nymphaion dedicated by Regilla at Olympia may well have been intended to remind the viewer of the Marathonian bull captured and sacrificed by Theseus (Paus. 1.27.10; Plut. *Thes.* 14.1), as well as Theseus' triumph over the Minotaur.[32]

Like heroes, however, tyrants too are renowned in literary sources as trying to control and shape the natural world. By implication, especially if Philostratos is the author of the *Nero* dialogue in the corpus of Lucian,[33] any attempt to cut through the Isthmus would also place Herodes in direct rivalry with that emperor, who himself tried to create an Isthmian canal. Indeed, David Pettegrew has convincingly posited that Herodes' outburst to Ktesidemos should be understood as being prompted by the remaining visible signs of Nero's efforts: the abandoned canal trenches and piled debris.[34] Needless to say, Nero was a tyrannical figure. In the *Nero*, *Lives of the Sophists*, and *Apollonios of Tyana*, cutting through the Isthmus is cast as a great deed of heroic proportions by the men who wish to do

---

[28] See Sturgeon 1987, 4, 76–113 (on the cult statue group); 4, 8, 84–5, 91–4 (on the relationship between the colossal marble group and Herodes' group). Sturgeon does not accept that Herodes' statues were intended as cult statues, but Pausanias' description and their material indicates they serve this purpose (Paus. 2.1.7–8; cf. *VS* 2.1.551). Broneer (1971, 88–90) interprets them as cult statues and Lapatin (2001, 127–8) as monumental.

[29] See Tobin 1997, 312–14, for all of Herodes' monumental efforts at the Isthmus. See also, Schowalter 2014, 171.

[30] Reinhard 2005, 36–69, 250.

[31] See Section 3.1; Tobin 1997, 243–4, 314–22, and Gleason 2010, 135–8.

[32] On this bull, see further Section 5.2.

[33] On the text as Philostratean, see Whitmarsh 1999, 143–4.   [34] Pettegrew 2016, 187.

it (*VS* 2.1.551, *Ner.* 2, *VA* 4.24);[35] all three works, however, mock this notion. When Nero personally abandons the task, for example, Philostratos notes that he went to Corinth 'believing he had surpassed all the deeds of Herakles (τὰ Ἡρακλέους δοκῶν ὑπερβεβῆσθαι πάντα)' (*Ner.* 3). Nero's self-belief, like that of Herodes, is raised to a heroic register and Herakles is the one hero who, in some traditions, achieved immortality.

It is also in this implication that Philostratos undermines Herodes' rhetoric, since in the *Nero* the emperor's attempt to cut the Isthmus boils down to a lot of show, little personal effort, and less effect: he turns a clod of earth with a golden fork and then leaves the task to slaves, eventually calling off the effort entirely (*Ner.* 3). This image of the ineffectual Nero wielding a two-pronged fork (δί-κελλα) is designed to contrast negatively with Poseidon and his trident and ties into Herodes' lament that the cutting of the Isthmus is a task fit only for that god (Ποσειδῶνος δεῖσθαι ἢ ἀνδρός, *VS* 2.1.552), with the effect of mocking Nero and belittling Herodes' aspirations. This impression is enhanced by the allusion to the water-channeller simile of *Iliad* 21.257–64 via μάκελλα ('mattock', 21.259) that compares the failure of a farmer to control the flow of an artificial irrigation channel to Skamander overwhelming Achilles, 'since gods are greater than mortals' (θεοὶ δέ τε φέρτεροι ἀνδρῶν, 21.264).

Nero's efforts are even teased at the site of the aborted excavation by a rock-cut relief (Figure 6.1). This weathered carving most probably depicts Nero (since it is similar to how that emperor appears on Corinthian coins of AD 67/68) or Herakles (since the figure also resembles the pose of the Farnese-type Herakles) and, quite possibly, Nero as Herakles within a framing *naiskos* that suggests both deification (if interpreted as a temple) and death (if interpreted as the typical *naiskos* frame of funerary art).[36] Thus Nero's ambitions and their failure are here imprinted on the landscape that he altered but failed to control by an image that mocks his pretentions in Greece to assimilate to the demi-god Herakles, who was himself a master of waterways.[37] Indeed it is perhaps this relief that Philostratos is responding to, in negatively comparing the tasks of the emperor and hero in the *Nero*, as much as Nero's own efforts to shape his image in the likeness of the son of Zeus and Alkmene.

---

[35] On Nero's ambition, see also Cass. Dio 58.16–9, Suet. *Ner.* 19, and Joseph. *BJ* 3.540.

[36] Pettegrew (2016, 188–9) summarizes interpretations of this relief. On the Corinthian coinage, see Amandry 1988, pls 40–1 (Issue XXIII for the year AD 67/68). On the relief as depicting Herakles, see Wiseman 1978, 50–1, fig. 46; Salowey 1994, 94, pl. 29a; Werner 1997, 115. On the Farnese type Herakles and its possible connection to Corinth, see Stafford 2012, 129 (it appeared on a Corinthian coin *c*.300 BC and, so, may have been made for display in Corinth); Salowey (1994, 94) discusses the relief as the Farnese type Herakles. On the relief showing Nero as Herakles, see Salowey 1994, 94; Champlin 2003, 137–8; Stafford 2012, 153–4.

[37] On Herakles and waterworks, see Salowey 1994; Luce 2006; Pettegrew 2016, 188–9.

FIGURE 6.1 Relief of Herakles or Nero as Herakles carved into the wall of an ancient canal trench of the Corinthian canal, almost a kilometre from the Corinthian Gulf, Isthmia.

The connection between Herodes and Nero is strengthened by Philostratos' *Apollonios of Tyana* 4.24, in which the same motive given to Herodes at *Lives of the Sophists* 2.1.551—that of wishing to reduce the length of the sea voyage—is attributed also to Nero. Herodes' statement, 'no one will allow me', however, implies permission is withheld by the current emperor. Philostratos confirms this, stating that Herodes was too scared to broach the subject 'lest he be accused of grasping at an intention (διανοίας), which not even Nero brought to fruition' (*VS* 2.1.551). Herodes' great ambition (that purpose or διάνοια that reveals him to posterity) is kept in check by those who have power over him, and in this particular case he is compared negatively and ironically to Nero.

The stress Herodes places on the commemorative potential of an Isthmian canal recalls the actions of another tyrant in Herodotos' assessment of Xerxes' canal through Mt Athos: 'he wanted to show his power (δύναμιν ἀποδείκνυσθαι) and to leave something by which to be remembered (μνημόσυνα λιπέσθαι)' (7.24).[38] Xerxes' actions are invoked as tyrannical by Herodotos, Dio Chrysostom (*Or.* 3.31–41), and the *Nero*'s Musonius Rufus (*Ner.* 2), who labels the cutting of Athos and the chaining of the Hellespont examples of tyrannical obsession.[39] So here Philostratos stresses the authoritarian nature of Herodes' quest for self-

[38] See also Diod. 2.7–15 on Semiramis.   [39] Cf. Whitmarsh 1999, 149.

commemoration. At the same time, he has connected or contrasted Herodes to the legendary Athenian hero-king Theseus, the god Poseidon (albeit demeaningly), and Roman emperors (whose power surpasses his own). As we will see, Herodes' apparent emulation of Theseus and Philostratos' handling of the idea play an important role in Herodes' biography, as Theseus' shade comes to symbolize a competing paradigm of governance to the imperial family.

Finally, if the comparison with Nero holds, there must also be an implied contrast to Musonius Rufus: the philosopher who was exiled to the Aegean island of Gyara by Nero and who is the philosophical foil of that emperor in the *Nero* dialogue.[40] Aligned with a tyrannical emperor, who stands for Roman power, and opposed to a philosopher, who although an Etruscan represents Greek culture (at least in the *Nero*),[41] is an odd position for the greatest of imperial sophists to find himself in. This is not an isolated incident in Philostratos' *Lives* and points to other philosophical paradigms who come into conflict with Herodes, the most sustained of which is Marcus Aurelius. Throughout the biography, the relationship between Herodes, Roman emperors, tyranny, and philosophy is essential to understanding his characterization, and it is to this dynamic that I now turn.

6.2 SOPHISTIC TYRANNY, IMPERIAL DEMOCRACY

This section establishes the common rhetorical casting of Greek elites as tyrannical in their home cities and how Herodes' interaction with Athens as presented by Philostratos fits into this schema. In addition, how the Roman empire was regularly shaped as a form of circumscribed democracy if ruled by a good emperor will also be explored, again with particular reference to Philostratos and Marcus Aurelius. These two competing paradigms provide a framework for better understanding Philostratos' rhetorical crafting of Herodes via sophistic *exempla*.

Roman citizenship provided opportunities for personal advancement and broadened the avenues to commemoration for the provincial Greek elite. Their relationship with both their *poleis* and Rome nevertheless remained complex. Although a circumscribed autonomy remained within provincial cities, the broader context of Roman imperial rule limited political and personal expression.[42] Local offices and Roman administrative positions were one way to gain political influence; yet the primary means of creating a lasting presence in public consciousness was to grant benefactions to cities and to construct funerary

---

[40] See Whitmarsh 1999.
[41] On Musonius' cultural positioning in the *Nero* dialogue, see Whitmarsh 1999, 150–9.
[42] On Greek culture and Roman power, see especially Whitmarsh 1998; 2001, 2–4.

monuments. Indeed, this had been the normal practice amongst elite Greeks since well before the principate.[43]

The boundaries of personal expression thus remained elastic and, in his building activities and political interactions, we see Herodes Attikos distinctively rivalling and imitating imperial behaviours. His efforts at construction especially approach those of Hadrian.[44] Philostratos, however, does not compare Herodes to Hadrian and, as I will argue, does not envision him as particularly emperor-like at all. Generous public building in the provinces could in fact place one on shaky political ground locally. Although tyrannies should not have been able to exist within the Roman empire, there are numerous examples of the language of tyranny applied to prominent citizens. Indeed, it was a common perception that any individual who came to dominate a given *polis* fiscally and politically laid himself open to the accusation of tyrannical behaviour, especially from his political rivals.[45] Herodes' own grandfather had been condemned as a tyrant under Domitian, a circumstance mentioned in the first paragraphs of his Philostratean 'Life' (*VS* 2.1.548).[46]

Nigel Kennell has made a compelling case in support of a genuine perception of Herodes as tyrannical in Athens.[47] He has shown that an inscription (EM 13366; Figure 6.2)—found in the Athenian agora and recording a letter from Marcus Aurelius to the Athenians[48]—deals predominantly with Herodes and his relationship to the people of Athens.[49] As Kennell explains, 'Marcus Aurelius' main and indeed probably only motive in sending this letter was to settle suits involving Herodes, either directly or indirectly, and thus end the *stasis* that had racked Athens for so long'.[50] Plutarch, in his *Precepts of Statecraft*, warns that political *stasis*, which he characterizes as marked primarily by 'ambition and contentiousness of the first citizens' ($\pi\lambda\epsilon o\nu\epsilon\xi\iota\alpha$ $\kappa\alpha\iota$ $\varphi\iota\lambda o\nu\epsilon\iota\kappa\iota\alpha$ $\tau\tilde{\omega}\nu$ $\pi\rho\acute{\omega}\tau\omega\nu$, 815a), can lead to devastating forms of intervention by Roman authority and should thus be avoided

[43] See Smith 1998, especially 70–7, and Gleason 2010 for the incorporation of diverse cultural elements into Roman Greek monuments. See Thomas 2007 on Greek monuments in public space, and König 2014 for the tension in elite Greek and Roman interactions in Philostratos' *VS*. Cormack 2004 details the social function and meaning of tombs in the eastern empire. Mitchell 1987 and Zuiderhoek 2009 examine the nuances of elite euergetism. On the Greek tradition of euergetism, see Gygax 2016.

[44] See Tobin 1997, 292–3, for a summary of how Herodes emulated Hadrian. See also Gleason 2010 and Arafat 1996, 191. Kemezis (2014, 213–14) perceptively argues that a figure like Herodes could exist only in a provincial centre because Rome was the emperor's city and a private citizen could never mark its cityscape in the same way. Cf. Eck 1984, 139–45; Bodel 1997, 30.

[45] See Kennell 1997, 351–5, for examples. See also Tobin 1997, 285–94, and Dio Chrys. *Or.* 47.

[46] On Hipparchos, see Tobin 1997, 14–17, 286–7.

[47] Kennell 1997. Tobin 1997, esp. 285–94, also makes this argument.

[48] *SEG* 29.127. See Oliver 1970b, 1–40; Jones 1971; Follet 1979; Ameling 1983b, 182–205, no. 189; Tobin 1997, 41–7; Civiletti 2002, 591 n. 98 and 99.

[49] Kennell 1997, esp. 347–9.   [50] Kennell 1997, 349.

FIGURE 6.2 Inscribed letter from Marcus Aurelius to the Athenians regarding Herodes Attikos and the social advancement of freedmen (plaque 2). Epigraphic Museum, Athens (EM 13366; SEG 29.127). Height: 2.3 m; Width: 0.8 m.

at all costs.[51] The *stasis* to which Kennell refers here is the conflict between Herodes and the *dêmos*, which is mentioned by Philostratos and which resulted in the Athenian assembly claiming they lived under a tyranny before the

---

[51] See Hogan 2017 for a discussion of Pausanias' attitude towards *stasis* with bibliography.

proconsuls of the day, the Quintilii brothers (*VS* 2.1.559). Kennell convincingly argues that this letter derives from the aftermath of the resulting trial before Marcus Aurelius at Sirmium in AD 174. Moreover, the focus in the emperor's letter on the social advancement of freedmen and their descendants is indicative of the Athenian perception that Herodes had tyrannical aspirations over their city: by flooding its institutions with former slaves loyal to himself, Herodes increased his political power.[52]

Dio Chrysostom's 47th *Oration*, in which he defends himself against the impression of tyranny for embellishing his native city of Prusa, provides further insight into the connection between building and tyranny as well as a parallel to Herodes' experiences in Athens (cf. *Or.* 45.12–14).[53] The most salient passage claims that certain attributes, which are regularly invoked as marking out a tyrant, may also be considered the qualities of a king if viewed in a different light:

Is it because I built an expensive house and don't let it fall down? Or because I wear purple and not a cheap cloak? Or is it that I grow my hair long and sport a beard? But perhaps this is not the sign of a tyrant ($\tau \upsilon \rho \alpha \nu \nu \iota \kappa \acute{o} \nu$), but of a king ($\beta \alpha \sigma \iota \lambda \iota \kappa \acute{o} \nu$)? Indeed someone said that to be slandered ($\tau \grave{o} \ \kappa \alpha \kappa \hat{\omega} s \ \acute{\alpha} \kappa o \acute{\upsilon} \epsilon \iota \nu$) through doing good deeds ($\kappa \alpha \lambda \hat{\omega} s \ \pi o \iota o \hat{\upsilon} \nu \tau \alpha$) is also the mark of a king.   (*Or.* 47.25)

Dio here demonstrates how blurred the popular distinction between tyranny and kingship is, and hints at the rhetorical and subjective nature of both words. Athenaios and Lucian also associate tyranny with wealthy or prominent citizens and point to the subjectivity and even arbitrariness of such a charge (Lucian, *Saturnalia* 26; *Slander* 13; Ath. 5.54). In response to his public building Herodes is criticized in a similar way. One example of this is the backlash against his decision to reject the terms of his father's will and, instead of granting a yearly allowance to all Athenian citizens, build the Panathenaic stadium (*VS* 2.1.549). Another is that of the rumours insisting he built the Odeion of Regilla solely to assuage his guilt over her alleged murder (*VS* 2.1.555–7). I will cover these incidents in more detail below. Note, however, that despite the backlash to his monumentalizing and commemorative activities Herodes persisted in them. The best explanation for this is that he was more concerned about his legacy than his contemporary reputation.

Despite Herodes' prolific public and private building, throughout his 'Life' Philostratos describes or mentions only his public benefactions: the water-supply at Alexandria Troas (*VS* 2.1.548–9), the Panathenaic stadium (2.1.550), the

---

[52] See Kennell 1997. Kennell also convincingly argues that Lucian's *Assembly of the Gods* is a satire on the situation in Athens and targets Herodes and his freedmen (355–6). Note that Herodes' relationship with his father's freedmen was far more negative (*VS* 2.1.549).

[53] Tobin 1997, 285–94. See also Kennell 1997, 353–4.

Odeion of Regilla (2.1.551), the theatre at Corinth, statues at the Isthmus, the stadium at Delphi, an aqueduct at Olympia, bathing pools at Thermopylai (2.1.551). He completely ignores Herodes' private monumental accomplishments, except for the statues he sets up of his τρόφιμοι ('foster-sons', 2.1.559). This neglect of Herodes' private monumentalization is significant, given that in imperial times tyrants were often identified more by their excessive private than by their public constructions, such as the emperor Nero and his golden house (Tac. *Ann.* 15.41–2; Suet. *Ner.* 31; cf. Suet. *Cal.* 22). Dio's *Oration* 47.23–5 also shows that private displays of wealth were particularly open to criticism by political opponents. Lucian's *Ikaromenippos* 18, moreover, mocks the insignificance of a rich man's possessions from the title character's bird's-eye view as he flies above the earth and these possessions just happen to correspond to those of Herodes' family.[54]

Philostratos' silence can be understood to stem from a desire to focus the reader's attention on the ambiguity surrounding Herodes' hold over Athens—is it emperor-like, kingly, or tyrannical? The inconclusiveness of Herodes' euergetistic aims in the text is highlighted by the contrast between his apparent aspiration to present himself in a similar light to Hadrian in life and Philostratos' insistence rather on aligning him with the more negative imperial exemplar of Nero.[55] The ability of an audience to misconstrue actively or passively euergetistic intent has been well demonstrated by Jaś Elsner. He has revealed how warped the literary depiction of Nero's building became once his tyrannical nature had been established by later writers, and how fraught imperial (and by analogy elite provincial) building could be as a means of shaping a personal image for posterity.[56] Both Herodes and Nero do everything right and, indeed, others such as Augustus and Hadrian are praised for the same efforts, but tradition crafts Nero and Herodes in a tyrannical mould. Herodes' ambitions thus exposed him to a judgement by future generations that could be either fame/greatness or infamy/depravity: in the rhetorical world of Philostratos' Second Sophistic, Herodes manages ever to embody both potentialities.

Within the *Lives of the Sophists*, the words τύραννος (including its cognate verb) and βασιλεύς are used in very specific ways, unlike in the case of Lucian, for instance, who uses both terms interchangeably.[57] Of the eighty-three times Philostratos employs βασιλεύς, it is applied eight times to the Persian king, once

---

[54] See Mestre and Gómez 2009, 98–9.

[55] See Tobin 1997, 292–3, on Herodes and Hadrian.   [56] Elsner 1994a.

[57] See Mestre and Gómez 2009, 101–4, for how Dio Chrysostom and Lucian use τύραννος. Dio's use is more in line with Philostratos', where τύραννος is pejorative, but Lucian uses τύραννος and βασιλεύς as synonyms with the exception that there can be a legitimacy allowed to kingship that is not present in Lucian's attitude to tyranny. See also Whitmarsh 1999, 144, and Dio Chrys. *Or.* 1.66–84, on the contemporary negativity of τύραννος, and 2001, 206–8, also on Dio Chrysostom.

to the king of Bosporos, twice to Herodes with respect to his eloquence, and all other times to a Roman emperor. On the other hand, τύραννος is used once in Philostratos' description of the nature of the Second Sophistic (1.0.481), and once in an epideictic theme (2.4.569), eight times to denote Dionysios of Syracuse (1.15.499–500), once to describe Kritias and once the Thessalians (in relation to Kritias, 1.16.501–2), once to label the council of the 400 in 411 BC at Athens (1.15.498), twice to denote Domitian (in relation to Dio Chrysostom, 1.7.488), twice for Heliogabalos (in Aelian's opinion, 2.31.625), once for the charge against Herodes' grandfather, Hipparchos (2.1.547), and finally once for the similar charge against Herodes (2.1.559).

Thus, in the *Lives*, τύραννος is far more flexible than βασιλεύς. Where βασιλεύς overwhelmingly denotes the office of emperor and is used as a straightforward, honorific, political designation as in most imperial Greek literature,[58] τύραννος is loaded with moral judgement and applied to 'bad' emperors, classical tyrants, or contemporary prominent provincial elites who also happen to be part of Herodes' family. Within the *Lives*' rhetorical landscape, then, βασιλεύς describes legitimacy and τύραννος the overstepping of bounds or transgression of accepted power roles.[59] The emperor as legitimate βασιλεύς also meant that the phenomenon of the tyrant was always localized. In reality more so than rhetoric, moreover, the individual concerned needed to walk a fine line so as not to tread on the toes of Rome in his ambitions, as Herodes' grandfather had done, since it was ultimately the emperor who determined the validity of and punishment for any such charge.[60] There were therefore very real potential consequences for Herodes' commemorative ambition.

The section of Herodes' life which describes the charge of tyranny made before the Quintilii further elucidates the power relationship the *Lives of the Sophists* constructs between legitimate and illegitimate kingship. Philostratos explains: 'when these two men were both governing Greece, after the Athenians invited them to a meeting of the assembly, they launched speeches (φωνὰς ἀφῆκαν) that they were being tyrannized (τυραννευομένων), meaning by Herodes; and finally begged that what they had said might be passed on to the emperor's ears (τὰ βασίλεια ὦτα)' (2.1.559). There are two elements of interest here. The first is the juxtaposition of βασίλειος, referring to the emperor, with tyranny, referring to Herodes. Given the rhetorical landscape of the text, this language use marks

---

[58] See Mason 1974, 120–1, for a discussion of the official and literary use of βασιλεύς for the Roman emperor. It is in literary use by the first century AD and begins to appear in inscriptions around the time of Hadrian, but it is not used with formal imperial titles in inscriptions until the time of Gordian III.

[59] More broadly, τύραννος and τυραννεύω can be used in imperial Greek literature neutrally for an absolute (usually non-dynastic) ruler.

[60] Kennell 1997, especially 356.

Herodes' aspirations as illegitimate.[61] Moreover, Herodes' response, that the Quintilii were plotting against him to incite the Athenians (2.1.559), is very much that of a man concerned for his power over the city. In stark contrast to Herodes' own position, when Philostratos describes the charge of tyranny against Herodes' grandfather, he stresses that the Athenians did not bring it (ἃς Ἀθηναῖοι μὲν οὐκ ἐπῆργον, 2.1.548).

The second element of interest is the apparent contempt with which Philostratos reports the charge. The phrase φωνὰς ἀφῆκαν invokes the Athenians throwing their words at Herodes like petty missiles. Thus Philostratos' tone suggests he is less convinced by the Athenians' complaints than the Quintilii were. This scene, however, also underscores the power imbalance between the *dêmos* and the sophist: as I will show below, in the *Lives of the Sophists* no one, at least in Athens, has the verbal weaponry to match Herodes. Philostratos also introduces this episode merely in order to explain the bad blood that existed between Herodes and the Quintilii, which is surely less important than the charge of tyranny itself.[62] Philostratos therefore presents the accusation as politically motivated and his portrait of the Athenians is not overly sympathetic.

In the section following the intervention of the Quintilii, Philostratos relates the 'escape' (ὑπεξῆλθον) of Herodes' accusers to seek refuge and understanding from Marcus Aurelius, who is labelled δημοτικώτερος (*VS* 2.1.560). This word is regularly translated as 'quite/somewhat/unusually democratic', although the core meaning of δημοτικός is 'populist'. In context, the straight comparative 'more democratic' is implied and the figure of contrast can only be the τύραννος Herodes. This definition of Marcus Aurelius as more democratic than Athens' leading citizen is striking, especially since Athens was ever the champion of democracy and prided itself on having overthrown or resisted a number of tyrannies in the past.[63] In relation to classical tyrannies, on which Philostratos is undoubtedly playing, the use of δημοτικώτερος for Marcus and in contrast to Herodes renders the latter less Athenian and more monarchical than the Roman

---

[61] See Parker 1998 for the development of the word τύραννος in literature. He notes that the negative associations are most clear in Athenian sources and suggests that this is a development in response to the fact that Athens became democratic so early in its history. See Rosivach 1988 for the concept of the tyrant in classical Greece; and Ferrill 1978 for τύραννος in Herodotos and in wider classical literature in opposition to βασιλεύς. Tobin (1997, 286) notes that, in the archaizing context of Roman Athens, the concept of tyranny would recall classical tyrants, many of whom were known for their artistic patronage and building programmes as much as their abuse of power. Cf. Mestre and Gómez 2009, 101–4.

[62] See Kuhn 2012 for the relations between Herodes and the Quintilii and their parallel careers.

[63] Parker (1998, 169) notes the sharp distinction between kingship and tyranny in Attic speech already in Classical times. See also Atack 2014 and, especially, 2020, 68–91. The word 'δημοτικώτερος' is unusual but appears in Aristotle and Isokrates in reference to the reforms of Kleisthenes in particular, and always in contrast to tyrants and tyrannical behaviours at Athens. See Arist. [*Ath. Pol.*] 22.1, 27.1, 41.2 and Isoc. *On the Peace* 8.13, 8.108 and *Areopagitikos* 7.17, 7.23. See also Lys. *For Polystratos* 13.

emperor.[64] This is the rhetorical force of the word, but in practice Philostratos is suggesting Herodes' accusers believed Marcus would be more impartial and open to the notional suffering of the people of Athens, to the ideological position of Rome governing for the good of all citizens regardless of wealth or rank, and to the argument that Rome's authority ought not to be usurped by a local citizen who had gained too much power.

This notion of the Roman empire as a democracy is key to Philostratos' presentation of Herodes and is not an isolated instance but recurs several times in imperial Greek literature. Notable instances include Dio Cassius 52.14.3–5, through the contrasting advice of Agrippa and Maecenas to Augustus on how to shape his government, Aelius Aristeides' encomium *To Rome* 60, and most significantly in Philostratos again, but this time in his *Apollonios of Tyana*, in which the hero advises Vespasian against abdication and restoration of democracy, saying:[65]

I do not think the human herd should perish for lack of a just (δικαίου) and reasonable (σώφρονος) herdsman. For just as one man of exceptional virtue (εἷς ἀρετῇ προὔχων) changes democracy so as to make it appear the rule of one man better than the rest, so the rule of one man who is always looking out for the common good is democracy.[66]

(*VA* 5.35.4)

This is a variation on the debate in Herodotos (3.80–3) on the best type of government—monarchy, oligarchy, or democracy—with the conclusion that monarchy is best if ruled by the best man who has the interests of all at heart.[67] Such a monarchy is nevertheless hard to sustain, a point stressed by Otanes to his fellow Persians in that text. Both Philostratos' Apollonios and Dio's Maecenas assert in different ways that classical Athenian-style democracy would be anachronistic and dysfunctional in the changed circumstances of the late republic and early empire. Dio's Maecenas in particular holds that monarchic democracy should consist of a definite hierarchy that places individuals in their most effective

---

[64] Parker 1998, 169, on the Athenian aversion to tyranny. Cf. Mestre and Gomez 2009, 103.

[65] See Starr 1952, particularly 13–16, for examples from imperial Greek literature. Markov 2013 summarises and evaluates various scholarly interpretations of Agrippa's and Maecenas' speeches in Dio Cass. 52. Espinosa Ruiz 1987 argues that Dio's Agrippa and Maecenas champion the same political ideal: a combination of δημοκρατία and μοναρχία, where δημοκρατία is equivalent to *libertas*. Kemezis (2014, 126–35, esp. 130–5) argues convincingly that Maecenas' speech in favour of monarchy is about an ideal system rather than an ideal ruler and that Dio is not interested in the monarch's character; rather Maecenas' system is designed to function even with a 'bad' emperor. On Aristeides' relationship to Rome, see Pernot 2008, especially 188–90.

[66] Translation after Jones 2005b.

[67] The belief that just rule always involves governing for the benefit of the *dêmos* is also Plato's view in the *Republic*. See Lane 2018 on book 8.

positions according to their particular talents and socio-economic station.[68] The definition of the rule of one man who acts for the common good being like democracy nevertheless well describes Philostratos' attitude to Marcus Aurelius in the *Lives* and contrasts sharply with his portrait of Herodes. The latter's political interventions and euergetism appear predominantly selfish, since their primary aims are to increase his civic influence and preserve his and his family's memory. It is no accident that, in the *Apollonios*, Philostratos puts the above words into the mouth of the eponymous philosophical sage, and it is precisely Marcus' association with philosophy and Herodes' lack of this characteristic that colours their respective representations and interactions in the *Lives of the Sophists*.

Philostratos presents Herodes as trying to dominate Athens in both the cultural and political spheres. Oddly, then, within the actual 'Life of Herodes', Philostratos focuses very little on his oratory, devoting only one brief section at the very end to a description of his style.[69] Yet this section paints Herodes as both tyrannical and strongly traditional. Philostratos says Herodes' style was inseparable from that of Kritias and that he acquainted the Greeks better with that orator, who had previously been overlooked (*VS* 2.1.564).[70] That Herodes chose to imitate an orator whom Philostratos designates as obscure (though this is clearly Philostratean hyperbole) is typical of his textual representation. Instead of emulating the more famous Demosthenes, as Polemon did, modelling himself on Kritias demonstrates his uniqueness, discernment, and breadth of classical knowledge. At the same time, he strengthens the canonical status of Kritias by increasing that orator's airplay if only through μίμησις. Moreover, Kritias himself was a tyrannical figure, being the leading member and most brutal of the Thirty Tyrants, and it is for this reason that Philostratos suggests the Greeks neglected him (1.16.502). Indeed, in his 'Life of Kritias', Philostratos calls the sophist in his opinion 'the worst man amongst all who are notorious for wrong-doing' (1.16.501). Nevertheless, although he labels Kritias a tyrant, Philostratos condemns him specifically for aiding Sparta and for bloodthirstiness, rather than for overthrowing the democracy, which he considers to have been in disarray anyway (*VS* 1.16.501). Philostratos' position, then, is not against autocratic rule as such but rather opposed to the perceived betrayal of Athens and persecution of the *dêmos*.

The use of the word προστήκομαι ('to cling to', 'to give oneself up to') to connect Herodes to Kritias is evocative and implies that Philostratos intends for it

---

[68] See Markov 2013, esp. 226–9. Dio Chrysostom makes a similar argument at *Or.* 3.42–50. See the discussion of Madsen 2014, 21–8. See also Thucydides on Perikles (e.g. 2.65).

[69] Cf. Kemezis 2014, 208; Coté 2010, paragraph 8.

[70] One speech survives, which has been attributed tentatively to Herodes, but which has also been identified as the work of Kritias himself. See Wade-Gery 1945; Anderson 1986, 113; Civiletti 2002, 528 n.140.

to refer to more than simply his oratorical style.[71] In the sentence directly following the oratorical comparison, Philostratos notes that all of Greece called Herodes one of the Ten, referring to the canon of orators, in which Kritias was not represented. Nevertheless, the mention of this group so close to Kritias' name would readily highlight his membership of that other numbered group—the Thirty—and subtly damn Herodes by association. The importance of this tyrannical perception of Herodes is that it demonstrates clear contemporary backlash against his personal promotion, but the backlash did not temper his commemorative efforts. Rather, he persisted in single-mindedly trying to craft his image for posterity despite the negative reaction of his *polis*. This is yet further evidence of Herodes' long view of Greek cultural history and his aspirations for future cultural eminence. Moreover, politically and in his personal emulation of Kritias, Philostratos' Herodes appears decidedly tyrannical in a negative sense, but in his governance of the sophistic sphere, to which I now turn, his role is presented quite differently. In this way, Philostratos creates two competing realities—a sophistic world centred in Athens and the political realm of the Roman empire.

6.3 THE KING OF WORDS

Philostratos' *Lives* establishes Athens as the centre of sophistic activity and characterizes Herodes as ruling the Athenian sophistic scene.[72] He manages with great success within the city itself. When he is removed from it and placed before the emperor, however, his sophistic performances fail. This is an aspect of his Philostratean presentation which is indicative of the two realities created by Philostratos that this section explores. Herodes is labelled 'the king of words' ($\tau o\nu$ $\beta\alpha\sigma\iota\lambda\acute{\epsilon}\alpha$ $\tau\hat{\omega}\nu$ $\lambda\acute{o}\gamma\omega\nu$) by Hadrian of Tyre (2.10.586) and as 'the master ($\delta\epsilon\sigma\pi\acute{o}\tau\eta\nu$) [...] and the tongue of the Greeks ($E\lambda\lambda\acute{\eta}\nu\omega\nu$ $\gamma\lambda\hat{\omega}\tau\tau\alpha\nu$) and king of words ($\lambda\acute{o}\gamma\omega\nu$ $\beta\alpha\sigma\iota\lambda\acute{\epsilon}\alpha$)' (2.17.598) by Rufus of Perinthos, both of whom were students of the great man in Athens. These metaphorical uses of $\beta\alpha\sigma\iota\lambda\epsilon\acute{\upsilon}\varsigma$ are the only times that it does not refer to a legitimate king or the emperor of Rome. Accordingly, when invoking Herodes' sophistic activities, it transfers that sense of legitimacy to his cultural rule. As described by Philostratos, Herodes' negotiation of various situations within the Athenian sophistic scene validates this characterization, while his behaviour before emperors beyond Attica serves to undermine it. Here, I will give two brief examples of the interactions between sophists in Herodes' Athens,

---

[71] Breitenbach 2003 is an important discussion of Kritias, Herodes, style, and tyranny.

[72] Cf. Kemezis 2011, 8–10.

which highlight his sophistic rule: one involving Philagros of Kilikia, who negotiates it poorly, and the other Alexander the Clay Plato, who negotiates it well.[73]

As detailed in chapter 2, Philagros commits several mistakes on his visit to Herodes' Athens; notably, these occur in relation to his attempts to further or fight for his reputation.[74] Primarily, Philagros fails to abide by Herodes' sophistic rules: he inserts personal material into an *epideixis* (*VS* 2.8.579), thus breaking the sophistic spell; he tries to reperform a published speech instead of improvising (2.8.579); he lets the sophistic mask drop with the ἔκφυλον ῥῆμα ('outlandish word'), on the back of which he asserts his canonicity (2.8.578–9). Most damningly, he challenges Herodes' authority over sophistic protocol and invests greater value in writing than speech, thus failing to prioritize his contemporary Athenian audience (*VS* 2.8.579). All of these aberrations make him thoroughly ἔκφυλος himself if the term is taken to highlight his exclusion from the tribes (φυλαί) and thus the civic society of Athens.[75]

Yet it is a concern for self-promotion and commemoration which also mark Herodes as transgressive and difficult in Philostratos' biography. Indeed, the anecdote of Philagros' visit to Athens is a microcosm of Herodes' existence beyond Athens in the empire at large. Philagros' primary blunders are misjudging his audience and his inability to control his emotions before Herodes, Athens' King of Words, a form of failure before mastery that Herodes ironically repeats before the emperors Hadrian and Marcus. To drive the point home, Philagros even misfires a second time in Athens when, overcome by emotion during his performance, he literally loses the ability to speak: 'his voice was stifled by his wrath' (ἐσβέσθη τὸ φθέγμα ὑπὸ τῆς χολῆς, 2.8.580).[76] In Herodes' Athens, Philagros thus achieves infamy alone. Philagros is, however, far from a perpetual failure. As Philostratos tells us, he was later appointed to the Chair of Rhetoric in Rome, the highest and most prestigious of such chairs, thus indicating the level of respect he attained at the centre of empire. Philostratos here again creates two spheres of sophistic activity with vastly different value systems.

Alexander the Clay Plato, in comparison, negotiates Athens and Herodes entirely successfully (2.5.571–3) but encounters difficulties in Rome (2.5.571).[77] In Athens, having been forced to begin his declamation before Herodes' arrival, Alexander stops as soon as the great man appears in order to seek advice on the continuation of his performance. Should he reperform the current oration or address a different theme? Herodes defers to the audience, who choose to hear the current theme

---

[73] Cf. Kemezis 2011, 10–11.

[74] On this episode, see Section 2.3; Eshleman 2012, 7–10; Kemezis 2011, 3–4 and 11; Papalas 1979.

[75] Whitmarsh 2005, 34. Cf. Eshleman 2012, 8–10, on Philagros as an outsider.

[76] On Philagros' and other sophists' anger in the *VS*, see Bowie 2006, 144–5.

[77] On Alexander in Athens, see also Kemezis 2011, 10.

again. Alexander, understanding the performance constructs of Herodes' Athens, improvises a completely different speech on the same topic by varying his vocabulary and rhythms (2.5.572–3). This anecdote demonstrates how great Herodes' sway over the art of sophistry in Athens is and how 'democratic' he can be in this sphere. It also reveals that Alexander recognizes his subservience to Herodes in the city and that he must enact deference to succeed. Alexander's behaviour in Rome, however, is strikingly combative and leads to ridicule at the hands of the emperor Antoninus Pius. In contrast to his submissiveness before Herodes, halfway through his speech he demands unceremoniously that the emperor pay more attention to him. The emperor responds by dismissively and wittily focusing on Alexander's carefully constructed appearance rather than his rhetorical ability (2.5.571), demonstrating that in his mind this sophist is all show and no substance. In Rome, Alexander needs more than oratorical versatility to make an impact, with the result that he overestimates his own importance and underestimates the emperor's verbal mastery. The different experiences and behaviours of Philagros and Alexander in Herodes' Athens and the emperors' Rome shed light on Herodes' own oratorical exploits. What is clear is that Athens and Rome are not the same fora and what stands in one will not in the other.

Throughout the *Lives of the Sophists*, Herodes is said to declaim brilliantly twice in Athens (*VS* 1.25.539, 2.5.574). Specifically in Philostratos' 'Life of Herodes', however, two more of the sophist's speeches are mentioned, both of which are made before emperors far from his sophistic stronghold: one before Hadrian in his youth (2.1.565) and the other before Marcus Aurelius in defence against the charge of tyranny (2.1.561). In both cases, the greatest of orators fails and the circumstances of each aborted speech bracket the brief section in which Philostratos praises Herodes' skill. This sandwiching of flattery between failures has the effect of calling into question the sincerity of Philostratos' praise and highlights the imperial circumstances of Herodes' sophistic misadventures, to which I now turn.

6.4 ROMAN PHILOSOPHER, GREEK TYRANT

Philostratos' presentation of Herodes' failure before Marcus juxtaposes the emperor and the tyrant, the philosopher and the sophist, and illustrates the power of Philostratos' narrative to shape the reception of both individuals. It reveals Marcus Aurelius as fitting the paradigm of Apollonios' 'good shepherd' and diminishes Herodes to make him resemble Philagros in his excess of emotion and unwise challenge to greater authority. The episode also helps to highlight that the empire functions under very different rules to Herodes' sophistic Athens and that there are very real potential consequences for his attempt to dominate his *polis.* Herodes' persistence in investing in his material and fiscal dominance of Athens, despite these consequences, moreover, reveals his greater concern for his future legacy than his contemporary reputation. At the trial, the sophist is upset over the chance death of two favoured female servants and takes this out on Marcus, attacking him without any semblance of rhetorical disguise (2.1.560–1). Herodes' displays of excess emotion, most often in association with death, are a recurring theme in Philostratos' *Lives* and regularly expose him to the ridicule of philosophers.[78] On this occasion, despite Herodes' slander (διαβολή) of the emperor (2.1.561), Marcus punishes the sophist's freedmen rather than Herodes himself by placing checks on their social mobility (*VS* 2.1.561, EM 13366). This has the effect of reducing Herodes' power base without chastising him directly.

Moreover, despite curtailing Herodes' ability to assert his tyrannical tendencies in this way, Marcus is savvy enough to legitimate his prestige in Athens by replying to Herodes' epistolary accusations of neglect with a request that Herodes, as priest at Eleusis, initiate him into the mysteries (2.1.562–3). Philostratos describes this letter as Marcus' ἀπολογία ('defence speech') and calls it both φιλάνθρωπος and ἐρρωμένη ('kindly' and 'powerful'/'formidable', 2.1.563). Φιλανθρωπία is an imperial virtue and championed by Dio Chrysostom in his *Orations* 1–4, on kingship, which were presented as mild advice to Trajan upon his inauguration.[79] Moreover, the participle ἐρρωμένη seems out of place, given Philostratos' stress on the gentleness of Marcus' discourse and disposition. Philostratos is perhaps, then, intending a pun on the Greek word for 'Rome', Ῥώμη, which also means 'strength' or 'might', and as such draws attention to the fact that Marcus' philanthropic and philosophical response comes from a position of Roman power. Herodes' correspondence, on the other hand, is described as containing 'not a defence, but an accusation' (οὐκ ἀπολογίαν [...] ἀλλ' ἔγκλημα, *VS* 2.1.562), wording which places him in the wrong in this particular interaction. Notably, Herodes' letter comes from Athens, his sophistic capital, where he is accustomed to being the first citizen, and its contents stress his inability to play an appropriate imperial (i.e., political) role beyond that city.

Philostratos is regularly seen as excusing or defending Herodes' behaviour in this episode by foregrounding the effect of his grief and emphasizing there was no lasting ill will. It is, however, Marcus' restraint and philosophical nature that save their relationship, so that they remain on good terms despite Herodes' poor behaviour. Additionally, once the reader reaches the life of Philagros, s/he would be struck by how Herodes' belligerent conduct before the imperial

---

[78] See Lucian, *Demon.* 24 and 33 with *Catapl.* with Mestre and Gómez 2009, who connect Herodes' reputation for excessive grief with his supposed tyranny. See also Gell. 19.12.

[79] See Madsen 2014; Moles 1990; Whitmarsh 1998; 2001, 200–16; 2005, 60–3. Moles in particular explores whether the orations were intended as advice or praise and argues persuasively for the former.

authority of Marcus mirrors Philagros' deportment in the face of Herodes' sophistic rule in Athens. Both Herodes and Philagros are undone by their emotions and unwise challenge to superior power. Marcus' response does not mirror Herodes' admonishment of Philagros, however, but rather gently defines Herodes' sphere of influence for him by acknowledging his relative importance within the confines of Athens. Still, the presumptuousness of Herodes' behaviour is emphasized by Marcus' wry command to the complainants in the case, which Philostratos marks as an exemplary philosophical moment: 'make your defence (ἀπολογεῖσθε), Athenians, though Herodes does not allow it (μὴ ξυγχωρεῖ)' (2.1.561). This one comment highlights the expanse between Herodes' imagined position over the Athenians and his actual position beneath the emperor Marcus. Philostratos takes a similar stance with respect to Favorinus' imperial difficulties: in response to the sophist's boast that he quarrelled with an emperor and lived, Philostratos rather praises the restraint of Hadrian, because he controlled his anger against a man over whom he had the power of life and death (1.8.489).

Despite Philostratos inserting praise of Herodes' oratorical skills, then, and mentioning the compliments of others, when Herodes does speak in the *Lives*, he is less the 'king of words' and more a slave to his own emotions, much as Philagros appeared to him in Athens. It is damning that Marcus is moved to tears by the rhetoric of Herodes' opponents rather than Herodes himself. Marcus, in contrast, is praised by Philostratos as behaving ever in a manner worthy of a philosopher (ταῦτα μὲν δὴ ὧδε ἐφιλοσοφεῖτο τῷ Μάρκῳ, 2.1.561): he fails to lose his temper, defuses the situation in a way that is acceptable to both Herodes and the *dêmos*, and restores the correct imperial hierarchy. Nevertheless, the episode also reveals that the Roman administration was aware of the potential for conflict presented by overly ambitious provincial elites and were careful to avoid it.

This situation between Marcus and Herodes inverts the paradigm of the philosopher and the king, described above in connection with Apollonios' advice to Vespasian.[80] Normally, the philosopher wisely counsels or challenges the ruler, whose philosophic virtue or tyrannical nature is revealed in whether or not he follows the sage's advice.[81] Apollonios himself comes across both kinds of rulers in Vespasian, Titus, and Nerva, on the one hand, and Domitian and Nero, on the other. Both Plutarch, in his treatise *The Philosopher Should Above All Discuss with*

---

[80] On the relationship between philosophers and rulers with numerous examples, see Flinterman 1995, 162–92. On the ambivalence towards philosophy in the imperial period, see Trapp 2007. For an overview of the prevalence and variety of philosophy, philosophers, and elite philosophical engagement in the imperial period, see Trapp 2014. See also the essays in Bosman 2019, esp. Jażdżewska 2019 on sophists and emperors.

[81] Flinterman 1995, 162; Whitmarsh 1999, 145. See also Kemezis 2014, 219, who highlights that Philostratos' Apollonios was acting during a moment of crisis in the empire, unlike the stability of the Antonine years that form the backdrop to the *VS*.

Persons in Leading Positions, and Dio Chrysostom, in his *Oration* 1, exploit this paradigm and present the way to become a good and wise ruler as a process of listening to and learning from the right adviser.[82] Importantly, it should be a Greek philosopher who advises a Roman emperor (or other foreign king), and this role was perceived as evidence for the value of Greek culture in the empire.[83] In Philostratos' *In Honour of Apollonios*, for instance, the sage's Greekness is as important as his wisdom in qualifying him as a mentor. He is in fact introduced to the Parthian king, Vardanes, as 'a wise man ($\sigma o\phi\acute{o}s$), a Greek ($\H{E}\lambda\lambda\eta\nu$), and a good counsellor ($\xi\acute{v}\mu\beta o\nu\lambda os\ \grave{a}\gamma a\theta\acute{o}s$)' (*VA* 1.28).

At the same time as being the best adviser to the good and willing ruler, the philosopher is also the truest opponent of the tyrant and a philosopher's behaviour before tyranny reveals his special nature. So Philostratos' Apollonios asserts: 'I know tyrannies ($\tau\grave{a}s\ \tau\upsilon\rho a\nu\nu\acute{\iota}\delta as$), as they are the truest test of men who philosophize ($\grave{a}\rho\acute{\iota}\sigma\tau\eta\ \beta\acute{a}\sigma a\nu os\ \grave{a}\nu\delta\rho\hat{\omega}\nu\ \phi\iota\lambda o\sigma o\phi o\acute{v}\nu\tau\omega\nu$)' (*VA* 7.1).[84] In all these cases, there is an underlying struggle between (Greek) wisdom and (Roman) power, and Jason König has demonstrated that throughout the *Lives of the Sophists* every relationship between Greek and Roman elites, except perhaps that established by Philostratos between himself and the Gordian of his preface, emits at least some level of dissonance.[85]

With this in mind, Marcus' meeting with Herodes at the latter's trial becomes laced with a complex set of meanings. Ostensibly, the roles are clear: Herodes is an elite provincial Greek *pepaideumenos* straining at the limits of his power and Marcus is a Roman emperor trying to maintain the smooth functioning of his empire. Herodes is never labelled philosopher by Philostratos, unlike several others including Favorinus and Dio Chrysostom, who he says were philosophers but called sophists because of their eloquence (1.0.484). Indeed, his behaviour is corrected or admonished by philosophers on several occasions, including by Peregrinus Proteus (2.1.563–4), Sextus the philosopher (2.1.558) and a certain Lucius (2.1.556–7), the latter two of whom ridicule Herodes' outrageous grief. In this trial too Marcus is cast in the role of a philosopher trying to correct an errant 'ruler' in Herodes to free the Athenians from his perceived tyranny. In this respect, Philostratos' praise for one of the speeches against Herodes that was given by a

---

[82] See Flinterman 1995, 173–5.

[83] Flinterman 1995, 173. See also Crawford 1978, 197; Rawson 1989, 235; Whitmarsh 1998; König 2014. Cf. Swain 1996, 396–400. Flinterman 2004 argues that, despite superficial similarities between sophists and philosophers, a sophist would not act as an imperial adviser. See Jażdżewska 2019 for an overview of interactions between sophists and rulers in Philostratos' *VS*, characterized as entertainment, persuasion, and 'dangerous encounters' (168).

[84] See Philostr. *VA* 7.1–3 for further examples of philosophers confronting tyrants.

[85] König 2014, especially 252–8, on sophists and emperors. See Whitmarsh 1998 for the relationship of Greek *paideia* and Roman power in the figure of Dio Chrysostom.

certain Demostratos (2.1.563) is also pertinent. This individual, although historical, nevertheless possesses a rhetorically fitting name indeed for the champion of the Athenians, a coincidence that is exploited by Philostratos and that accentuates the strife between the *dêmos* and the sophist.[86]

Marcus is the most philosophical of the emperors in Philostratos' text. Even he, however, cannot quite manage to gain equal cultural footing with Greek *pepaideumenoi* more broadly nor can he escape the superiority of his social and political station. This is shown by König through analysis of the mockery suffered by Marcus at the hands of the Greek Lucius, who teases the emperor over his desire to learn Greek wisdom (2.1.557) by highlighting how unbecoming it is for a Roman emperor to wait in the role of client before a Greek's door, even should he prove a philosopher.[87] This must be the implication of ἐρρωμένη above: this seeming philosopher king who saves Herodes, a Greek *pepaideumenos*, from himself and instructs him on how best to govern is in reality the Roman emperor.[88] Strikingly, Marcus' encounter with Lucius occurs in the 'Life of Herodes' and is framed by philosophical criticism of Herodes' grief—the same grief that leads to the confrontation between the supremely philosophical Marcus and the errant Herodes in Sirmium. Thus, although there is something not quite right in the Roman emperor Marcus' pursuit of Greek philosophy, his credentials are more than sufficient when confronted by the volatile and tyrannical *pepaideumenos* Herodes.

This circumstance turns the accepted wisdom of the relationship between Greek learning and Roman power on its head. It is particularly conspicuous given that in the 'Life of Theodotos', which follows that of Herodes, Philostratos mentions that Marcus assigned Herodes the task of choosing the inaugural Chairs of Philosophy at Athens, while he himself chose the Chair of Rhetoric (2.2.566–7). This detail underscores the topsy-turvy nature of Herodes and Marcus' relationship.[89] Additionally, Marcus' choice, Theodotos, spoke against Herodes at his trial. Thus the emperor's intervention changes the dynamic, at least symbolically, of the sophistic and political landscape of Herodes' Athens. Harry Sidebottom, moreover, has shown that sophists and philosophers, particularly in the *Lives*, are delineated not by education or knowledge, but by outward signs such as physical aesthetic (clothes, expression, grooming) and the way they communicate (gestures, tone, style of speaking).[90] In Aulus Gellius' *Attic Nights*,

---

[86] On the identification of this individual, see Civiletti 2002, 520 n. 102.

[87] König 2014, 254–5.

[88] See Boulet 2014 on the idea of Plato's 'philosopher king' in imperial Greek literature generally, but especially Plutarch.

[89] On this episode, see Civiletti 2002, 535 nn. 8–9.

[90] Sidebottom 2009, especially 72–87. See also Lauwers 2013. Bowersock 2002 sees the categories as more of a continuum and the circumstances of the second century as bringing the two categories closer together. Cf. Stanton 1973; Jones 1974; Moles 1978; Brancacci 1986.

Herodes is reported as specifically damning the practice of claiming the title of 'philosopher' based on outward signs (Gell. 9.2.1–11).[91] Yet it is in similar symbolic, representational terms that Herodes comes to appear tyrannical and Marcus philosophical in the *Lives of the Sophists*. Philostratos thus exploits the stereotypes of 'sophist', 'philosopher', 'tyrant', and 'king' for their rhetorical potency. His manipulation of these categories serves to upset expectations about his protagonists and highlight the in-fact-quite-rigid power relationships between the emperor and his provincial subjects, no matter how wealthy, ambitious, or cultured. Herodes' role as ruler of the sophistic scene in Athens is thus shown to be limited absolutely to this bizarre, localized cultural anomaly.

Herodes' recklessness before Marcus' authority is the only aspect of his behaviour which one might interpret as reminiscent of a philosopher's, in that his outspoken pique resembles philosophical fearlessness before power.[92] Indeed, Flinterman has shown that advising an emperor on anything other than literature or rhetoric is beyond the accepted place of a sophist.[93] Yet, although Herodes is willing to face death by speaking his mind (*VS* 2.1.561), Philostratos emphasizes that it is his (very unphilosophical) emotions that drive this temerity. Thus his careless audacity and excess emotion should rather be seen as peculiar to yet another stock rhetorical figure: the hero. Indeed, in the vein of a Homeric hero, Herodes' uncontrollable grief and habit of stepping outside the social norm because of it are two of his most persistent qualities.[94] Nevertheless, once more Philostratos' depiction is ambiguous as to whether this exceptional grief should be interpreted as tyrannical or heroic. In its quality, it approaches a mythic, heroic intensity, but it also tends to bring Herodes into conflict with philosophers and can be generated by questionable circumstances.[95]

One such episode in the *Lives* revolves around Herodes' odeion built into the slopes of the Akropolis in Athens (Figure 6.3). The odeion is mentioned twice by Philostratos.[96] In the first instance, it is praised along with the Panathenaic stadium as being the greatest of monuments in the empire (2.1.551). In the second, the circumstance surrounding its construction is discussed: the death of Herodes' wife, Regilla (2.1.555–7), whose family accused him of murder.

---

[91] See this episode in Gellius with Eshleman (2012), 1–2, who demonstrates how such labels needed to be constantly defended and reasserted.

[92] See Flinterman 2004, 361–4.   [93] Flinterman 2004, 376. Cf. Rawson 1989, 253.

[94] On the quality of Herodes' grief, see Gleason 2010, 156–62. On Herodes as a rhetorical Homeric hero, see Coté 2010. In his high-strung nature and fearlessness, Herodes also comes to resemble Alexander, a hero king whose personal excesses tradition held the philosopher Aristotle tried to tame. This is represented in the traditions surrounding Alexander by the letters of Aristotle to the Makedonian king as well as his position as teacher in his youth. See Plut. *Alex.* 7.1–8.4.

[95] See Bowie 2006 for the idea of excessive emotion shaping Philostratos' sophists in a Homeric way.

[96] On the structure of the odeion, see Tobin 1997, 185–94; Galli 2002, 32–7; Korres 2015.

FIGURE 6.3 View from the Akropolis into the Odeion of Herodes Attikos and Regilla, Athens.

Pausanias also focuses on these two aspects in his mention of the odeion in connection to the one in Patras:

the odeion is in every way the most remarkable (ἀξιολογώτατα) in Greece, except of course for the one in Athens: for this is unrivalled (ὑπερῆρκε) in size (μεγέθει) and all its construction (τὴν πᾶσαν κατασκευήν), an Athenian man made it (ἀνὴρ [...] Ἀθηναῖος ἐποίησεν), Herodes, in memory (μνήμην) of his dead wife. (7.20.6)

Regilla's apparent murder connects Herodes once more to Nero. The accusation against him claimed that he had commanded one of his freedmen to beat her when she was eight months pregnant, leading to death during premature childbirth brought on by a blow to her stomach.[97] This scenario is almost identical to that described by Suetonius in which Nero beat to death his pregnant wife, whom he claimed to love greatly (*Ner.* 35.3), or the story in Herodotos about the Corinthian tyrant Periander committing a similar crime (3.50).[98] In Greek and Roman tradition, the murder of pregnant wives is typically tyrannical, and the murder charge may have been based less on fact and more on the desire both of the *dēmos* and of Regilla's family to represent Herodes as tyrannical and of

---

[97] See Fronto, *To Marcus* 3.3, for the accusation that Herodes beat and murdered some of his freedmen.
[98] See Ameling 1986 on the pattern of pregnant-wife-killing tyrants (Nero, Kambyses, Periander, and Herodes) and their urges to create canals. Cf. Pomeroy 2007, 121–3. See Pomeroy 2007, 119–36, for a speculative discussion of the murder and trial.

Herodes himself to appear emperor-like or kingly.[99] Herodes dedicates the theatre to Regilla as part of his show of extravagant grief, a circumstance which Philostratos attributes to helping him in his defence on the murder charge (2.1.556). Thus the odeion stands as a memorial to Herodes' wife and, consequently, to Herodes himself, to the controversy surrounding Regilla's death, and to his tyrannical leanings, which associate him with an extravagant, tyrannical emperor like Nero rather than the benefactor Hadrian or the philosophical Marcus, whose role as a philosopher king I established above. Herodes' commitment to this type of commemorative construction nevertheless demonstrates once more that his concern is predominantly with his legacy rather than his contemporary reputation.

Philostratos uses the odeion specifically to focus on Herodes' grief. Throughout his Philostratean 'Life' Herodes is cast as emotionally volatile and the odeion's construction introduces a litany of episodes of excessive grieving for Regilla, his daughters, and the three τρόφιμοι (2.1.556–9). Maud Gleason has shown that, in the context of Greek and Roman cultural practices in imperial times, Herodes' mourning is not so unusual for Greeks but was exceptional for Romans. She has further perceptively argued that his bicultural nature and the cross-gendered character of grief allowed him the leeway to express himself to the degree that he did.[100] An important proviso to this picture is that Herodes' grief is deliberately crafted in epic proportions, resembling that of Achilles after the death of Patroklos or Herakles after he murders his own family.[101] In this respect, the odeion is less a memorial to Regilla and more a monument to Herodes' own heroic suffering.

His grieving over Regilla, which causes him to redecorate his house entirely in black, introduces an extended anecdote that once more pits Herodes against a philosopher. On this occasion, the wise man Lucius curbs his emotional excesses through the employment of ridicule (*VS* 2.1.556–7). This is the same individual who mocks Marcus' desire to learn Greek wisdom and who was a student of Musonius Rufus, the philosophical foil in Philostratos' *Nero* dialogue. Having warned Herodes that his behaviour jeopardizes his great reputation (περὶ τῇ δόξῃ κινδυνεύων, 2.1.557) to no effect, Lucius' resorts to mockery which is reported to Herodes by his slaves. It is significant that here in Athens, the sophistic capital, as opposed to before Marcus in Sirmium, the 'king of words' does check his antisocial lack of restraint when his performance is lampooned. Only a direct and demonstrable threat to his reputation, however, can break his self-indulgence.

Herodes' grief is also a focus for other writers, including Lucian, Aulus Gellius, and Fronto. Lucian reports two mocking quips by the philosopher Demonax aimed at Herodes' mourning over Regilla and Polydeukion, and his theatrical

---

[99] See Vout 2007, 87, for Herodes imitating Hadrian and Nero, and for Nero as tyrannical. See Connolly 2008 for the suggestion that the murder of Regilla was a rhetorical construct and that Herodes may have deliberately drawn attention to the similarity with Nero.

[100] Gleason 2010, 158–60.   [101] Cf. Gleason 2010, 157; Bowie 2006; Coté 2010.

insistence on persisting as though the latter were still alive, so that he would have dinner served for the boy or his chariot made ready (*Demon.* 24 and 33). As Lucian tells it, Demonax exploits Herodes' grief for a punchline:

Demonax went to him and said, 'I am bringing you a message from Polydeuces.' Herodes was pleased and thought that Demonax, like everyone else, was falling in with his humour; so he said: 'Well, what does Polydeuces want, Demonax?' 'He finds fault with you,' said he, 'for not going to join him at once!' (24)[102]

In this case, the philosopher's ridicule is not connected directly to tyranny, but rather to an intemperate nature. Nevertheless, noting that others (οἵ ἄλλοι) are indulging Herodes certainly implies pandering to power. As shown by Francesca Mestre and Pilar Gómez, moreover, the title character of Lucian's *Downward Journey or the Tyrant*, Megapenthes, is also a comic portrait of Herodes who is mocked for both his sorrow and tyrannical life.[103] This is revealed even in Lucian's careful choice of pseudonym, which has the double meaning of 'one who causes great suffering' and 'one who suffers great grief'.

Aulus Gellius, on the other hand, reports a speech by Herodes in response to a Stoic philosopher's accusation that he failed to endure his grief over the death of a beloved boy with sufficient wisdom (*minus sapienter*) and manliness (*parum viriliter*) (Gell. 19.12.1–10). This Stoic admonition is reinforced in a letter Fronto writes to Herodes at the behest of Marcus Aurelius, urging him to bear the death of an infant son rationally and focus rather on the future ('To Herodes from Fronto'/*Greek Letters* 3). Herodes' defence against such Stoic attacks crafts his emotional volatility as the result of having a great soul. He casts Stoic ἀπάθεια ('lack of feeling') as itself excessive and equivalent to a living death: 'with all the soul's more vigorous emotions cut out (*amputatis*), they (i.e. adherents of ἀπάθεια) grow old in the numbness of a spiritless (*torpore ignavae*) and practically inanimate (*quasi enervatae*) life' (Gell. 19.12.10). Herodes' grief and his response to it, therefore, is interpreted in wider contemporary literature in the same conflicting terms as Philostratos' characterization: his excesses are indicative of both tyranny and heroism. These capacities are often juxtaposed, in fact, to accentuate one depiction over the other. In Lucian's *Downward Journey*, for instance, it is a lack of μεγαλοψυχία ('greatness of soul') that characterizes Megapenthes, the Herodes-like tyrant, whose trappings and appearance had made him seem a ὑπεράνθρωπος ('superman') in life, but in death he is reduced to an everyman (16).

Herodes' excessive grief for Polydeukion and his other foster-sons also calculatedly imitates that exhibited by Hadrian for Antinoos,[104] including his

---

[102] Translated by Harmon 1913. See Anderson 1989, 168, for the unlikely suggestion that Philostratos' Lucius is in fact our Lucian.

[103] Mestre and Gómez 2009.   [104] See Gleason 2010, 158.

heroization of Polydeukion and erection of herms of the τρόφιμοι all over Attica.[105] Nevertheless, the connection is not drawn by Philostratos, who avoids any Hadrianic comparison, preferring instead to imply affinities with Nero and distinctions from Marcus Aurelius. Marcus' function in the 'Life of Herodes' is especially pointed: in the Sirmium episode, Marcus assumes less the guise of an emperor or judge and more that of a philosophical mentor, and Herodes resembles both a ruler, who must be taught how best to rule, and a hero, whose personal expression is not governed by the same rules as society more generally. Moreover, Philostratos creates a clear differentiation between the social, political, and cultural formalities of Herodes' sophistic Athens and the Roman empire at large.

Herodes' rhetorical failure before Hadrian, although a tale of youthful inexperience, nevertheless reinforces this picture and is used by Philostratos to introduce one of the primary concerns of his sophists: the potential that mortality has to affect one's reputation. The aborted speech in Pannonia (2.1.565) is mentioned by Philostratos immediately after his praise of Herodes' rhetorical skills (2.1.563–5) and comes just prior to his description of the sophist's death and burial (2.1.565–6). Philostratos states that 'words failed [Herodes]' (λόγου τινός [...] ἐκπεσεῖν, 2.1.565), comparing this to Demosthenes failing before Philip, though Demosthenes still expected acclaim whereas Herodes wished to die. Philostratos explains Herodes' suicidal impulse by noting that his desire for fame as a rhetor was so overpowering that 'he assessed the penalty of failure as death' (ὡς θανάτου τιμᾶσθαι τὸ σφαλῆναι, 2.1.565). It is striking that Philostratos turns immediately from this statement of wished-for death to Herodes' eventual actual death: 'he assessed the penalty of failure as death. He died [...]'. It is impossible for the reader not to connect the two trains of thought and conclude that, for an orator, silence may as well be death. This same sentiment dominated the episode of Polemon's live burial, discussed in chapter 4.[106]

Moreover, Philostratos has just connected death with failure. This notion is similarly expressed in Lucian's *Downward Journey* 29, where the tyrant Megapenthes' punishment for his earthly wickedness is to be denied a draught from Lethe, the river of forgetfulness, so that his shade may be conscious forever of the worldly power and circumstances he has lost. As a punishment for Herodes, who was clearly obsessed with commemorating himself and his loved ones, self-remembrance of his efforts amongst a crowd of forgetful shades is particularly apt, given it is a place in other people's memories that he truly desired. What death's failure represents for Herodes in Philostratos' *Lives of the Sophists* is, equally fittingly, an end to any control he may possess over his own reputation and commemoration. Thus it is appropriate that Philostratos' account of Herodes' death has him once more playing a series of rhetorical roles.

[105] See Sections 4.2.3 and 5.4.   [106] See Section 4.1.

6.5 HERODES AND THESEUS

Herodes' burial alludes to the sophist as both kingly and heroic in the vein of Theseus. It also reveals some surprising elements, given Philostratos' presentation of the poor relations between the Athenian *dêmos* and the great sophist. Philostratos' account has Herodes truly accepted in Athens only after his death, but the Athenians' actions take control of his commemoration against his express wishes. The conflict between Herodes and the *dêmos*, moreover, centres on his monumental benefactions, especially the place of his purported burial, the Panathenaic stadium. The conflict is thus largely about the issues raised by Herodes' prioritizing of his legacy over the need of his contemporary Athenians for appropriate benefactions. Philostratos uses this tension to explore Herodes' political potential in the Roman empire and the limitations of power placed on provincial elites. In doing so, he reinterprets Herodes' legacy in a way that discourses on the role of Greek culture in the empire more broadly.

Philostratos describes the burial as follows:

He died at the age of about seventy-six of a wasting sickness. And although he passed away at Marathon and had commanded his freedmen to bury him there (ἐκεῖ θάπτειν), the Athenians, having snatched him away by the hands of the ephebes (ταῖς τῶν ἐφήβων χερσὶν ἁρπάσαντες), bore him into the city (ἐς ἄστυ), and every age came out to meet (προαπαντῶντες) the bier with tears and wailing, as would sons (παῖδες) who were bereft of a worthy father (χρηστοῦ πατρός).   (*VS* 2.1.565–6)

Joseph Rife has covered this episode extensively from a rigorously historical perspective.[107] In what follows, I will approach it from a more textual, literary one. In its spontaneity, processional nature, the involvement of the entire *dêmos*, and the use of the verb προαπαντάω ('to come out to meet', often in an official capacity), this scene recalls an inscription found reused as a threshold in the village of Bey near Marathon (*IG* II² 3606). The rectangular block records in elegiac distich Herodes' return from the Sirmium trial as a triumphant entrance greeted by all the people of Athens and accompanied by various gods (Figure 6.4).[108] The allusive poem, which holds back the honorand's name until well down the stone (l. 32) and is aimed at an educated audience, is incomplete because the *stêlê* is broken diagonally at the base, so that the lower lines are preserved to a progressively lesser degree. Despite the loss of lines, a clear picture is gained of the city accepting Herodes back with both pomp and open arms:

[107] Rife 2008.

[108] Ameling 1983b, 205–11, no. 190; Tobin 1997, 272–5; Skenteri 2005, 86–110; Bowie 2019, 146–7. Rife (2008, 100–1) also makes the connection between the Bey inscription and Herodes' funeral, noting that the funeral bears characteristics of an ἀπάντησις ceremony. See Rife 2009 for other Philostratean deaths and elite funerary practices.

FIGURE 6.4 Poetic inscription from the village of Bey near Marathon, describing Herodes Attikos' triumphal return from his trial for tyranny before Marcus Aurelius in Sirmium. Archaeological Museum of Marathon (Inv. 22; *IG* II² 3606). Height: 0.88 m; Width: 0.61 m; Depth: 0.08 m.

ὄλβιος, ὦ Μαραθών, νῦν ἔπλεο, καὶ μελεδαντός
ἀνδράσιν ἠὲ πάρος, φαίδιμον Ἀλκαΐδην
νοστήσαντ' ἐσορῶν ἀβίων ἀπὸ Σαυροματάων
γαίης ἐκ νεάτης, ἔνθα φιλοπτολέμῳ
Αὐσονίων βασιλῆι συνέσπετο τῆλ' ἐλάοντι.   5
τὸν μὲν ὁ κισσοφόρος παῖς Διὸς ἱρέα ὃν

αὐτὸς ἄγεν πάτρην ἐς ἀοίδιμον Εἰραφιώτης,
   ἐξόπιθεν δὲ θεῷ δωσιβίῳ πρόεσαν.
τοῖσι δ' Ἀθηναίη πολιήοχος ἀντεβόλησε
   ἐρχομένοις Ῥειτώ, Χαλκιδικὼ ποταμώ,   10
Θρειῶζ', ἔνθ' ἁλίῳ συμβάλλετον οἶδμα ῥόος τε,
   λαὸν ἄγουσα ἔτας πάντας ὁμηγερέας,
ἱρῆας μὲν πρῶτα θεῶν κομόωντας ἐθείραις
   κόσμῳ τῷ σφετέρῳ, πάντας ἀριπρεπέας,
ἱρείας δὲ μεταῦθι σαόφρονα Κύπριν ἐχούσας,   15
   τῆς δ' ἔπι κυδαλίμους παῖδας ἀοιδοπόλους
Ζηνὶ θεηκολέοντας Ὀλυμπίῳ, ἵμασι κύδρους,
   τοῖσι δ' ἔπ' ἠϊθέους ἵστορας ἠνορέης,
παῖδας Ἀθηναίων χαλκῷ γανάοντας ἐφήβους,
   τοὺς αὐτός, λήθην πατρὸς ἀκειόμενος   20
Αἰγείδεω, λώβης δ<ν>οφοείμονος ἔσχεθε κούρο[υς]
   ἀργυφέαις χλαίναις οἴκοθεν ἀμφιέσας,
δωρηθεὶς γ' ἐνετῇσι κατωμαδὸν ἠλέκτροιο.
   τῶν δ' ὄπιθεν βουλὴ κεκριμένη Κεκρόπων
ἔξαιτος προτέρω κίον ἀθρόοι, ἡ μὲν ἀρείω[ν],   25
   ἡ δ' ἑτέρη μείων ἕσπετο τῇ κατόπιν.
πάντες δ' ἐστολάδαντο νεόπλυτα φάρ[εα λευκά]·
   τῶν δ' ἀγχοῦ προβάδην ἔστιχ[εν ἄλλος ὄχλος]
ἐνδήμων ξείνων τε καὶ αι — —
   οὐδέ τις οἰκοφύλαξ λείπ[ετ' ἐνὶ μεγάροις]   30
οὐ παῖς, οὐ κούρη λευ[κώλενος, ἀλλ' ἀγέροντο]
   δέγμενοι Ἡρώδην — —
ὡς δ' ὅτε παῖδα γε — —
   ἀμφιπέσῃ μή[τηρ — —]
τηλόθεν ἐ[ξ ἀπίης γαίης — —]   35
   χαιροσύ[νῃ — —]
πλήν — —
   ὦ[ρ]σ[ε? — —]

Blessed are you now, Marathon, and a concern
   to men more than before, as the radiant descendant of Herakles
you beheld returning from the Sarmatian nomads
   from the outermost edge of the earth, to there he had followed
the war-loving, far-travelling king of the Ausonians.   5
   Him, Eiraphiotes, the ivy-bearing child of Zeus, himself conducted
his own priest to his fatherland, famous in song.
   Behind came along the two life-giving goddesses.
Athena, protectress of the city, met them

as they were approaching the Rheitoi—two rivers of Chalkis—,   10
at Thria, where the salty swell and stream dash together.
   She led the people, all the citizens assembled together:
first the priests of the gods with long flowing hair,
   in their own regalia, all glittering,
and, after, the priestesses, in company with temperate Aphrodite;   15
   next to them the renowned boys, devoted to song,
a choir for Olympian Zeus, clothed in distinction;
   behind them the unwed youth, becoming experts in manhood,
sons of the Athenians, the ephebes, gleaming in their bronze,
   whom he himself, making amends for his forgetfulness of his father,   20
the son of Aegeus sundered from the dark garments of shame,
   by clothing them in silver-white cloaks from his own stores,
he bestowed the gift fastened with an amber clasp at the shoulder;
   behind them the select council of the Kekropians,
standing out in precedence, marched thronged together, the higher
rank first,   25
   the other, lesser followed behind.
All were arrayed in the newly washed, [white] cloaks.
   Close by them advanced onwards all the masses
of foreign residents, and even — —
   No guardsman was left [in the halls],   30
no boy, no white[-armed] maiden [but all were gathered]
   to welcome Herodes — —
as when a child — —
   a mother embraces — —
from afar [from a distant land — —]   35
   rejoicing — —
except — —
   [he urged on? — —]

It cannot be determined who the poet was, but Herodes was surely involved in the composition.[109] Equally, it is impossible to say whether its content reflects a genuine occurrence, how much it exaggerates if the episode is genuine, or even if Philostratos knew this poetic inscription, since it was most probably on Herodes' private Marathon estate, given its find spot at Bey. If he did, however, Philostratos perverts Herodes' poem of heroic triumph in this funerary scene to stress his mortality. Furthermore, in keeping with the notion of a tyrannical Herodes, the procession described in the Bey inscription calls to mind the similar triumphal

[109] See Skenteri 2005, 108–10.

THE KING OF ATHENS 281

processions and ἀπαντήσεις ceremonies for Hellenistic kings (themselves figures of benefaction and tyranny), Roman governors, or even the *adventus* ritual for the arrival of an emperor.[110] Polybios' *Histories*, for instance, describes the arrival of Attalos I of Pergamon at Athens in similar terms: 'he was met (ἀπήντων), not only by all the magistrates and the knights, but by all the citizens with their children and wives' (16.25). Thus in this poem Herodes conceives of and actively promotes himself as kingly after the fashion of Hellenistic rulers and implies he serves as a representative of the Roman emperor (at least in Athens), an attitude he also assumed iconographically on the Olympia nymphaion.[111] Such posturing only adds to the subversive effect of Philostratos' funeral scene.[112] Significantly, Philostratos mentions no such welcome for Herodes after the Sirmium trial; rather upon his return Philostratos' Herodes retired to a less visible life in Kephisia and Marathon.

The removal of Herodes' body from Marathon and its transference to Athens call to mind another monarch from Athens' legendary past, namely Theseus. This hero-king has two homecomings: the first mythic following his triumph over the Minotaur, when the hero's forgetfulness inadvertently led to the death of his father Aegeus (Plut. *Thes.* 22.1–6), an episode alluded to in Herodes' poem (ll. 20–3); the second literal, when on the advice of the Delphic oracle Kimon found and brought back from the island of Skyros what he claimed to be Theseus' bones (Plut. *Thes.* 36, *Cim.* 8.5–6; Thuc. 1.98.2).[113] Plutarch records the event in the following way:

There a coffin was found of a man of extraordinary size, a bronze spear lying by its side, and a sword. When these relics were brought home on his trireme by Kimon, the Athenians were delighted, and received them with splendid processions (πομπαῖς [...] λαμπραῖς) and sacrifices (θυσίαις), as though Theseus himself were returning to the city. And now he lies buried (κεῖται) in the middle of the city (τῇ πόλει), near the present gymnasium.[114]

(*Thes.* 36.2)

---

[110] See Polyb. 30.25–6; Ath. 5.196a–203e; cf. Plut. *Dem.* 9–13; Ath. 6.253d-f. Skenteri (2005), 95–103, discusses the text and procession of Herodes' poem. See also Kuhn 2012, 449; Robert 1987, 470–4; Rife 2008, 101–2 and 101 n. 60.

[111] See Section 5.2.

[112] Veyne (1990, 125) claims such processions were common for benefactors and not just the privilege of kings or governors; however, he cites no primary evidence in support. Cf. Tobin 1997, 275 n. 95. See Pont 2008 for the ritual welcomes given to governors, and Robert 1987, 470–4, and Rife 2008, 101 n. 60, for some more literary examples of such communal welcomes.

[113] Thucydides does not mention Theseus' bones, but he does mention Kimon's expedition to Skyros. See Podlecki 1971, 141–3, on Kimon's motivations for retrieving the bones. See also Walker 1995, 55–64, on Kimon and Theseus in general.

[114] Translation after Perrin 1914.

One parallel between this description of Theseus' interment in Athens and Herodes' interment in Philostratos that is not clear from the passages is that Theseus had gone to Skyros in exile (Paus. 1.17.5–6) and, although it is denied by Philostratos, Herodes was rumoured to have been exiled for a time to Orikos in Epeiros after the Sirmium trial (*VS* 2.1.562). A form of exile is alluded to by Marcus Aurelius in his letter to the Athenians through his explanation that his pronouncements are designed to enable Herodes to take his rightful place among them again in the future (EM 13366 ll. 87–94). That Kimon retrieves Theseus' bones is important, since a family connection exists between Kimon, Miltiades, and Herodes, as well as a shared association with Marathon. Significantly, Kimon and Miltiades, of whom Philostratos says Herodes was proud, were both tyrannical figures (*VS* 2.1.546–7). Indeed, Miltiades had been an actual τύραννος in the Thracian Chersonese, and Herodes named one of his daughters Elpinike after Miltiades' own child. Kimon himself died far from Athens in Cyprus and his remains were also repatriated at a later date (Plut. *Cim.* 19.1–4).[115] Theseus' link to Marathon was equally strong through his capture of the Marathonian bull (Paus. 1.27.10) and the legend that his apparition appeared to the Athenians before the Battle of Marathon where he charged against the enemy in front of them (Plut. *Thes.* 35.8; Paus. 1.15.3). Pausanias even directly connects the victory at Marathon to Kimon's retrieval of Theseus' bones with the implication of gratitude for the hero's aid (1.17.6).

Herodes' attachment to Marathon was so strong that he wished to be buried there.[116] Yet, like Theseus before him, he was instead interred at Athens, above one of his benefactions to the city (Figure 6.5). Unlike Theseus, however, Herodes was buried extramurally:

They buried him in the Panathenaic [stadium], and inscribed over him (ἐπιγράψαντες) this brief and great epigram:

'Herodes, son of Attikos, of Marathon, to whom all this belongs,
lies here in this grave, but his good fame is everywhere.'

Ἀττικοῦ Ἡρώδης Μαραθώνιος, οὗ τάδε πάντα,
κεῖται τῷδε τάφῳ, πάντοθεν εὐδόκιμος

That is all (τοσαῦτα) I have to say concerning Herodes the Athenian (Ἡρώδου τοῦ Ἀθηναίου); part of it has been told by others, but part was unknown. (*VS* 2.1.566)

Above is the translation of Herodes' epitaph that is championed by Joseph Rife; however, there are two ways to read this inscription.[117] If the comma after πάντα is

---

[115] See also Shapiro 1992, especially 48–9.

[116] On Herodes and Marathon, see Bowie 2013, 251–3. See, too, Athanassaki 2016 for Herodes' attempts to connect his family to the Marathon messenger.

[117] See Rife 2008, 112–13.

FIGURE 6.5 The Panathenaic Stadium, Athens. It was rebuilt for the first modern Olympics in 1896. The sarcophagus and inscribed altar are situated midway along the right-hand arm of the stadium on the eastern slope of the hill above.

removed, which is how most modern editions print the text, then the epitaph reads: 'Herodes, son of Attikos, of Marathon, of whom all that remains lies here in this tomb, but his good fame is everywhere'.[118] In this rendering, οὗ τάδε πάντα connects nicely to the idea of Theseus' (and Kimon's) bones returned to Athens. Rife, however, sets forth a strong case for keeping the comma, including that the main clause lacks a verb if κεῖται τῷδε τάφῳ becomes part of the relative clause. He also notes that, although κεῖται τῷδε τάφῳ is unique in Greek poetry, its common substitute ἐνθάδε κεῖται is always in the main clause.[119] If the comma is retained and οὗ τάδε πάντα is taken to mean 'to whom all this belongs', the epitaph becomes more interesting rhetorically. In this case, the sentiment behind it mocks the very notion that one's memory can be preserved the way one desires, since it can be read to imply that the epitaph was intended for the environs of Herodes' Marathonian estate and Philostratos wants us to think that it too was transferred to Athens along with the body.

The way Philostratos reports it, moreover, derides Herodes' ambitions to dominate Athens while still living. The inscription identifies Herodes as belonging to Marathon (Μαραθώνιος), which is immediately countered by Philostratos' description of him as Athenian (Ἡρώδου τοῦ Ἀθηναίου). Although the deme of Marathon is inextricable from Athens proper and Herodes' identification in the

[118] This is how it appears in Kayser's Teubner. See Rife 2008, 112. [119] Rife 2008, 112.

epitaph is the usual epigraphic formula for an Athenian (name, patronymic, deme), in Philostratos' *Lives of the Sophists* a tension and opposition are created between the two locales through the Athenian *dêmos*' hostility to Herodes and Herodes' powerful and pointed connection to the deme. When Philostratos denies Herodes' post-Sirmium exile, he places him instead on his private estates at Kephisia and Marathon (*VS* 2.1.562), and it is to Marathon that Herodes' Bey inscription refers as the place of his triumphant return (*IG* II^2 3606, ll. 1–3). If one follows the Thesean paradigm precisely, Marathon then becomes Herodes' location of exile.

In part the division is temporal. Herodes' affinity to Marathon is also symbolic of a bond to Athens' glorious past, which his contemporary Athenians fail to emulate except in Herodes' sophistic scene. Marathon is also from where Herodes must be recalled with all the Athenian youth ($\tau\grave{\eta}\nu$ $\nu\epsilon\acute{o}\tau\eta\tau\alpha$ [...] $\pi\^{\alpha}\sigma\alpha\nu$), referred to as his 'Greeks' ($\H{E}\lambda\lambda\eta\nu\epsilon\varsigma$, *VS* 2.5.571), by Alexander the Clay Plato before he is willing to speak in Athens. Thus Philostratos' constructed opposition between Marathon and Athens parallels his alternate realities of a sophistic Athens, over which Herodes rules supreme, and an imperial Athens, in which Herodes abuses his social and political position. In the material record too it is on his private estates, such as at Marathon, Kephisia, Loukou, and surrounding sacred and historically significant locales that Herodes embeds himself most personally and expressively. Further, within the Bey inscription, there is an allusion to the epigram inscribed on the *stêlê* of the Erechtheid fallen at the Battle of Marathon, removed from the *soros* by Herodes and transferred to his estate at Loukou-Eva Kynouria.[120] The phrase 'outermost edge of the earth' ($\gamma\alpha\acute{\iota}\eta\varsigma$ $\grave{\epsilon}\kappa$ $\nu\epsilon\acute{\alpha}\tau\eta\varsigma$, *IG* II^2 3606, l. 4), used on the Bey *stêlê* to describe Sirmium and the place from which Herodes returns triumphant from the trial before the 'war-loving king of the Ausonians' ($\varphi\iota\lambda o\pi\tau o\lambda\acute{\epsilon}\mu\varphi$ | $A\mathring{\upsilon}\sigma o\nu\acute{\iota}\omega\nu$ $\beta\alpha\sigma\iota\lambda\^{\eta}\iota$, l. 4–5; i.e. Marcus Aurelius), recalls 'the ends of the earth' ($\H{\epsilon}\sigma\chi\alpha\tau\alpha$ $\gamma\alpha\acute{\iota}\epsilon\varsigma$), used on the *stêlê* to indicate the extent of the *Marathonomachoi*'s fame.

Philostratos' re-identification of Herodes in the epitaph is thus jarring for two reasons: first, due to Herodes' express wish to be buried at Marathon, a task he had entrusted to his freedmen; secondly, on account of the prior scene of his corpse being welcomed into the city in comparison to Herodes' own poem of triumphant return after Sirmium. The latter was inscribed at Marathon and may or may not have been invented, but was surely exaggerated given the tensions in the city before the trial.[121] The juxtaposition of the *dêmos* and Herodes' freedmen

---

[120] See Section 4.4.

[121] Note that Kuhn (2012, 449) accepts the procession and Herodes' description of it as accurate and as evidence the Athenians took note of Marcus Aurelius' exhortation at the end of his post-Sirmium inscribed letter: 'When their care has been worked out in all matters, is it not possible for the Athenians to love my – and their very own – Herodes ($\tau\grave{o}\nu$ $\grave{\epsilon}\mu\grave{o}\nu$ $\kappa\alpha\grave{\iota}$ $\tau\grave{o}\nu$ $\H{\iota}\delta[\iota]o\nu$ $\alpha\mathring{\upsilon}\tau\^{\omega}\nu$ $H\rho\acute{\omega}\iota\delta\eta\nu$ $\sigma\tau\acute{\epsilon}\rho\gamma\epsilon\iota\nu$), since no other major conflict

only heightens the effect. The phrase οὗ τάδε πάντα ('to whom all this belongs') in Philostratos' epitaph claims that the dead Herodes owns the stadium but also beyond that and in the context of Philostratos' *Lives* his Athenian surrounds, a notion that ridicules his political ambitions while still living and that again highlights his lack of acceptance within the city itself. The second reading, 'of whom all that remains', only enhances the impression, since the epitaph has an inherent ambiguity and both meanings would have suggested themselves to the educated reader concurrently, stressing that, far from owning his surrounds, Herodes is rather a pile of entombed bones within them. This effect neatly undercuts Herodes in a similar way to Lucian's Megapenthes of *Downward Journey* 16, who seemed a ὑπεράνθρωπος in life, but was just one of the masses in death, or Alexander in Arrian's *Anabasis* 7.1.6,[122] who is reminded by the wise Indians that, despite his attempts to conquer the world, he will ultimately possess only enough of the earth to cover his corpse.

The phrase also strengthens the case for Philostratos presenting this epitaph as intended for a Marathonian burial, since much of the area around Marathon indeed did belong to Herodes.[123] Moreover, as noted by Rife, οὗ τάδε πάντα is an allusion to a much-quoted fragment of Antimachos concerning Nemesis: 'there is a great goddess Nemesis, who has obtained all these things (τάδε πάντα) | from the blessed ones' (Strabo 13.1.13), where τάδε πάντα signifies a region.[124] Not only do the sanctuary at Rhamnous and deme of Marathon belong to the same Attic-littoral complex, but they were also intimately connected in contemporary Athenian thought by the story, related by Pausanias (1.33.2–3), that the cult statue of Nemesis at Rhamnous was carved from Parian marble brought by the Persians to Greece in preparation for a victory monument, but that Nemesis fell on them at Marathon for their *hubris*.[125] Thus the cult statue replaced the Persians' hypothetical victory monument and served as both sacred object and memorial to the Athenian victory at Marathon.

Herodes' material footprint reveals that he too gave special attention to the cult of Nemesis at Rhamnous. A portrait bust of Herodes was found there along with busts of Marcus Aurelius and Lucius Verus, which were dedicated by Herodes and which match another set of three portraits from his Egyptianizing complex at

---

(με[γάλου] | ἀντικρούοντος) still hinders their good will (εὐνοίαι)?' (EM 13366, ll. 92–4). Translation adapted from Kennell 1997, 361, and Oliver 1970b, 32. This is an overly optimistic reading of the situation, given the trial.

[122] Quoted in Section 4.2.1.   [123] See Section 3.1.

[124] Rife 2008, 113. See Matthews 1996, 313–21, especially 319. Matthews thinks τάδε πάντα in the Antimachos epigram means 'everything here on earth', but also cites Wyss 1936, who more convincingly thought it referred to a specific region.

[125] Cf. Section 3.1.

Brexiza (Figures 3.5–7).[126] Herodes' father, Attikos, had previously dedicated statues of Hadrian and Antinoos there.[127] A now-lost fragment of a curse inscription (*IG* II² 13208) was also discovered in the sanctuary, which is surprising given that this warning has otherwise been found only on monuments situated on his private land.[128] Tobin plausibly suggests that Herodes felt such a connection to Rhamnousian Nemesis that he considered the sanctuary part of his domain—he did, after all, feel comfortable enough to resituate the memorials to the *Marathonomachoi* from the *soros* at Marathon.[129] He is known to have established her cult at his Roman villa on the Via Appia as well. Moreover, as noted on the inscribed base of a statue of Polydeukion dedicated in the sanctuary by Herodes to Nemesis, Herodes and Polydeukion would regularly sacrifice there (Figure 6.6):[130]

```
ψηφ[ίσα]μένης τῆς ἐξ Ἀ-
[ρείου Πάγ]ου βουλῆς καὶ
[τῆ]ς βουλῆ[ς τῶ]ν πεντακ-
        καὶ τοῦ δ[ήμο]υ
[ο]σίων Ἡρώδης Βιβούλλι-                    5
[ο]ν Πολυδευκίωνα ἱππέ[α]
[Ῥ]ωμαίων ὁ θρέψας καὶ φι-
[λ]ήσας ὡς υἱὸν, τῇ Νεμέ-
[σει], ᾗ μετ' αὐτοῦ ἔθυεν, [εὐμ]-
[ε]νῆ καὶ ἀίμνηστον τὸν [τρό]-              10
        φιμον.
```

By decree of the Bou-
le of the Areopagos and
of the Boule of the Five-Hun-
        and of the people
dred, Herodes [sets up/dedicates] Vibull-   5
us Polydeukion, an Equestrian
of Rome, whom he raised and loved as a son, to Neme-
sis, to whom he used to sacrifice with him, the kindly and ever-remembered foster-   10
        son.

---

[126] See Section 3.1; Petrakos 1995, 114; Ameling 1983b, 163, 169–70; Tobin 1997, 265, 278–80. Petrakos 1999a, 291. See Mazurek 2018 on the Brexiza triad.

[127] Karanastasi 2019.

[128] The association of the curses with Herodes' estates was already noticed by Graindor 1930, 115.

[129] Tobin 1997, 138, 279.

[130] *SEG* 49.209. The text follows that of Petrakos 1999b, 126–7, no. 159. Petrakos argues that due to the size of the base, which offers a platform 1.87×1.01 m, the statue most likely showed Polydeukion hunting with a dog and his prey. The base certainly supported a group rather than an individual statue. See also Petrakos 1999a, 291–3.

FIGURE 6.6 Statue base of Polydeukion dedicated by Herodes at the Sanctuary of Nemesis at Rhamnous. Archaeological site of Rhamnous (Inv. Λ505). The inscription describes Polydeukion as an equestrian, and repeated sacrifices by Polydeukion and Herodes to Nemesis (*SEG* 49.209). Full height: 1.54 m; Full width: 1.075 m; Full depth: 1.865 m. Height between mouldings: 0.70 m; Width (at the level of inscription): 0.55 m; Depth (at the level of inscription): 1.36 m.

The dedication has been permitted by the Areopagos, Council of the Five-Hundred, and the people of Athens, but note that the phrase, καὶ τοῦ δήμου ('and of the people [of Athens]'), is inserted awkwardly and in much smaller lettering between the third and fourth line of the inscription, as though as an afterthought. Syntactically, it should come after πεντακοσίων, but on the stone it splits the word. This appears to be an initial oversight by the inscriber, which serendipitously reflects the tension between Herodes and the *dêmos*.

Finally, Rhamnous, Marathon, and Herodes are brought together in one further artefact: a sarcophagus made for his daughter Elpinike. It was found in Kephisia in 1866, and decorated (unusually for a sarcophagus, particularly an Athenian sarcophagus) with scenes from the myth of the birth of Helen and the Dioskouroi, who appear on the front, each figure disconnected and isolated from the other two (Figure 6.7).[131] On the short, left side, Leda is depicted with the swan and, on the right side, Eros is stringing his bow. This focus on Spartan mythology reflects Herodes' unusually strong ties to that city. His father was a citizen, a status most likely granted to him when the family moved there in exile

---

[131] On this sarcophagus, see Perry 2001; 2005, 65–76; Galli 2002, 158–60.

FIGURE 6.7 Front panel of the Leda Sarcophagus. Roman tomb, Kephisia. Found with three other sarcophagi, it was designed for Herodes' daughter Elpinike and her husband. The panel shows Helen between the Dioskouroi. All three are depicted as though statues in the round and disconnected from each other.

following Herodes' grandfather Hipparchos' conviction for tyranny at Athens, and Herodes was probably also enrolled as an ephebe there.[132] The detached posing of the siblings on the frontal surface has been interpreted as the influence of sculpture in the round and these figures may well be reproductions of famous statues.[133] Ellen Perry, moreover, has perceptively demonstrated that this posing matches the style of figures represented on the bases of classical-era cult statues, such as the Mantinea base and the base of Rhamnousian Nemesis. This latter also depicts Helen being led by Leda (in the role of step-mother) to her mother, Nemesis, in accord with the local version of the myth.[134] Thus the sarcophagus manages to highlight the close association of Herodes' family with Marathon, Rhamnous, and Sparta, and helps elucidate why the allusion in Philostratos' epitaph to Antimachos' poem via the phrase οὗ τάδε πάντα serves both to bind Herodes and the epitaph more closely to Marathon and its surrounds and to alienate him further from Athens.

With this reading of the epitaph, the words πάντοθεν εὐδόκιμος ('his good fame is everywhere') must be ironic. Philostratos' 'Life of Herodes' has consistently demonstrated that Herodes' reputation was mixed, being part-fame and part-infamy, especially in Athens, and in the end it is the Athenians who dominate Herodes rather than the other way around. In fact, the whole scenario sees

---

[132] The connections of Herodes' family with Sparta are detailed in Spawforth 1980; 1984. Also see Perry 2001, 468–75.
[133] See Perry 2005, 69–70; Tobin 1997, 223; Benndorf 1868, 38; Robert 1890, 10.
[134] Perry 2001, 475–83; 2005, 70–5; Stafford 2013, 211–14.

Philostratos granting the *dêmos* ultimate revenge for Herodes' apparent tyranny. His freedmen, who were detested by the *dêmos*, prove ineffectual, and his final wishes for his burial and commemoration are usurped. Catherine Connors has shown how biographical deaths in Latin literature, particularly those of literary artists, tend to encapsulate their artistic lives: 'the moment of death is artfully contrived to be the final utterance of a writing life'.[135] Herodes' Philostratean death, with its undertones of exile, kingship/tyranny, and heroism, adheres to this pattern by nodding to his sophistic powers in life but also undermining his life-long attempts to shape his legacy monumentally in Athens, Greece, and beyond. It reveals Herodes' life to have been something of a sophistic performance: ephemeral, artificial, and open to future manipulation.

Additionally, the counterargument that Herodes' strongly stated desire for a Marathonian burial and the post-mortem actions of the Athenians have a semblance of *recusatio imperii* about them does not hold water. Certainly, the burial in Athens should be considered an honour that would please its recipient despite any protests and it does fit the Thesean paradigm, since he too was belatedly honoured by the *dêmos* in such a manner. Had Philostratos presented Herodes as beloved at Athens, *recusatio imperii* would indeed be a valid interpretation. As it is, however, any affinity to the ritual in this episode must again be ironic. Philostratos' Athenians do not appreciate Herodes' dominance of their city and the stadium site is in fact conspicuously extramural to both Hadrian's and Theseus' cities.[136] Thus Herodes lies close to Athens, but remains excluded, and, given his careful construction as Marathonian, that deme is a far more fitting place for his desired burial. Moreover Herodes' death leaves him incapable of appreciating his belated acceptance and popular celebration: if the Athenians really did repent of their resentment, it came too late and it was also short lived.

There are further circumstances that make Philostratos' description of Herodes' burial charged. Beyond the typical biographical ending that briefly relates Herodes' death and interment,[137] in his earlier description of the Panathenaic stadium (*VS* 2.1.550), Philostratos fails to describe or even mention Herodes' tomb (Figure 6.8). He simply notes that on the other side of the stadium was a temple of Tyche without explicitly stating what stood opposite this shrine, although the flow of the narrative suggests the temple is being counterposed to the mooring place of the Panathenaic ship.[138] Philostratos perhaps supresses a description of the tomb out of a desire to shape Herodes' image in the way he wants rather than giving voice to Herodes' own funerary iconography. This feat is enhanced by his

---

[135] Connors 1994, 230. See also Barthes 1972, 100–2.   [136] See Theocharaki 2011.

[137] See Rife 2009 for a discussion of the other concluding deaths and burials in the *VS*.

[138] See Tobin 1993; 1997, 177–85. Rife 2008, 109–11, convincingly refutes her argument.

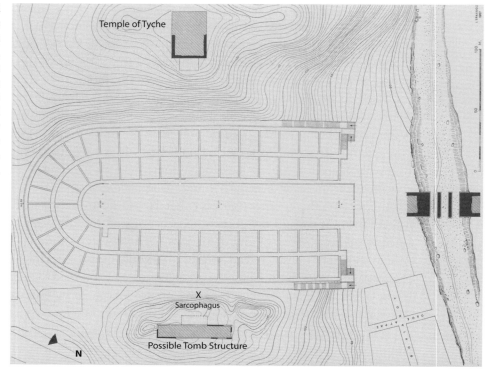

FIGURE 6.8 Ground plan of the Panathenaic Stadium and surrounds, showing the temple of Tyche on the western slope of the Ardittos hill and the long, narrow structure that may be a tomb on the eastern slope.

withholding of the epitaph to the very end, so that if it is not his own composition, it is at least forced to serve the thrust of his narrative.

Alternatively, if the sarcophagus discovered in 1904 above the eastern side of the stadium did originally belong to Herodes (Figure 6.9), the tomb may already have been disturbed by the time Philostratos was writing the *Lives of the Sophists* in the late 230s or early 240s.[139] Herodes died in the late 170s and the burial discovered within the possibly reused sarcophagus dates from after AD 250.[140] The best reasons for associating this sarcophagus with Herodes are Philostratos' description and an inscribed altar, which is dedicated to 'the hero of Marathon' by

---

[139] See Galli 2002, 18–19, for an illustration of the stadium's layout. For the initial excavation of the sarcophagus, see Skias 1905.

[140] See Rife 2008, 107. Cf. Tobin 1993, 83–4, who believes that the sarcophagus was unlikely to have originally belonged to Herodes and then been reused, because most examples of its type date to the third century AD. Rife argues, on stylistic grounds, that the sarcophagus dates to the last quarter of the second century. He is following Goette 1991, who dates this type of Attic sarcophagus from *c.* AD 180–230/40, meaning that, if it belonged to Herodes, it would have been one of the earliest of its kind. Rife 2008, 106–7, also makes the compelling point that the haste of the unplanned burial explains the sarcophagus' half-finished state. The dating of the burial is based on a coin of Decius (AD 249–51) that was found in the mouth of the skeleton. See also Galli 2002, 20–1.

FIGURE 6.9 Sarcophagus above the eastern side of the Panathenaic stadium with associated altar (see Figure 6.10). Panathenaic Stadium, Athens. The sarcophagus is unfinished, and the lid ill-fitting.

parties unknown and which was built into a wall of the chamber surrounding the reused sarcophagus (*IG* II² 6791, Figure 6.10):[141]

⟦Ἐ — —⟧
ἥρωϊ
τῶι
Μαραθωνίωι
⟦— —⟧

The presence of this altar does not indicate Herodes was definitively buried there, since hero cults did not need to be connected with a tomb; often a locale strongly associated with the 'hero' would suffice.[142] What it does reveal is that at least some faction at Athens conceived of Herodes as heroic at some point, so that, like the sophist's apparent material emulation of Theseus, the notion and the pun on Ἡρώδης/ἥρως are not invented by Philostratos, but rather something he chooses to emphasize and manipulate. Identifying Herodes as the hero of Marathon is again a nod to Theseus, given the latter's reported role in the Battle of Marathon. The inscription also reflects its imperial Greek context with the inconsistent archaizing of *E* for *H* but retaining the *Ω* instead of *O*. Importantly, both the

[141] See Rife 2008, 105–6; Ameling 1983b, 212–13, no. 193; Tobin 1997, 181–3.
[142] See Cormack 2004, 35–7, for tombs associated with existing public structures, such as stadiums or gymnasiums, in Asia Minor.

FIGURE 6.10 Altar dedicated to 'the hero of Marathon' with both the name of the dedicant and the dedicator erased (*IG* II² 6791). Panathenaic Stadium, Athens. Height: 0.95 m, Width: 0.49 m; Depth: 0.41 m.

dedicator and the dedicatee have been obliterated in what must be a form of *damnatio memoriae*,[143] which in itself is fitting to Herodes' tyrannical aspirations and the Athenians' apparent animosity. This antipathy is clear in Philostratos' *Lives* while Herodes is alive but evaporates upon his death. The vandalized altar belies Philostratos' version of events, or, at least, it shows either that the animosity returned at some point following the elaborate funeral, or that those who resented Herodes outweighed those who worshipped him. This idea is supported by the altar being a private dedication, since the erasure of ὁ δῆμος in the position of dedicator would be unparalleled.[144] It is striking now, as it must have been shortly after Herodes' death (given the tomb was reused in the 250s), that Herodes' presence via his monumental accomplishments is all over Athens, but his tomb—that metonymic symbol of post-mortem identity—has been obliterated. Rather, it is the monuments that are most associated with Herodes' supposed tyranny that remain most conspicuous: the Panathenaic stadium and the Odeion of Regilla. This once more indicates Herodes' greater interest in his Athenian legacy as a euergetist than in his contemporary reputation, as well as the ability of posterity and its recorders like Philostratos to shape his reception.

[143] Rife 2008, 118–20.   [144] See Rife 2008, 105–6.

Another potential reason for Philostratos' initial silence is that he thought a description of the location and form of the tomb unnecessary because it was so conspicuous and well known. Yet, even were this the case, it is odd to neglect these details in a work that ostensibly celebrates the fame of its subjects and discusses the possible tombs of the work's secondary focus, Polemon, at some length and in some detail (*VS* 1.25.543–4). Whatever his reasons, rhetorically, the passage describing the burial sees Herodes alienated from his beloved Marathon and installed (almost) in Athens. This, if reminiscent of Theseus' similar return, inverts the notion of exile, since Herodes, who is labelled Μαραθώνιος in his epitaph, is claimed as Ἀθηναῖος by Philostratos, who in this case has the last word. If indeed Herodes were buried at the stadium, all that now remains of him and his burial is the epitaph reported by Philostratos, which given its focus on Marathon may well have been invented by the author as a way of stressing Herodes' eternal displacement. Rife argues that the epitaph must be genuine, since οὗ τάδε πάντα is replicated in a late second- or third-century epitaph (*IG* II² 13161), which he believes must have been copied from Herodes' tomb.[145] This is certainly possible, but not absolutely certain: Philostratos could have lifted his literary version as easily from this later epitaph or it could be independently referencing Antimachos. If Philostratos' epitaph is genuine, it may not have been intended for an Athenian location; at the very least, Philostratos' narrative encourages reading it as implying Herodes' dislocation.

Another important consideration relating to the idea of an honorific Herodean tomb above the Panathenaic stadium is that, in Philostratos' text, this monument is the source of initial tensions between Herodes and the *dêmos* of Athens (*VS* 2.1.548–9). Consequently, it is an odd place for the *dêmos* to choose for his eternal commemoration, unless they wanted to remember Herodes resentfully. According to Philostratos, the construction of the stadium emerged from a dispute over the will of Herodes' father. Attikos had bequeathed the sum of a *mina* annually to all Athenian citizens. Herodes baulked at this arrangement and offered them five *minai* as a one-off payment instead. When they came to collect the money, however, Herodes demanded payment for all the debts incurred to his family by the citizens and their families, so that very few received any money at all and many found themselves in debt anew (2.1.549). Philostratos claims that this created a groundswell of resentment amongst the Athenians. As he describes it: 'they never stopped hating him, not even when he thought he was bestowing the greatest benefits (τὰ μέγιστα εὐεργετεῖν) on them' (2.1.549).

Philostratos' wording here (τὰ μέγιστα εὐεργετεῖν) could be an allusion to Plato's *Apology* 36b–c, in which Sokrates explains that he refrained from

---

[145] Rife 2008, 112.

the activities that most men value—money-making (χρηματισμοῦ), property (οἰκονομίας), military offices (στρατηγιῶν), public speaking (δημηγοριῶν), political offices (ἀρχῶν), amongst others—to instead bestow on each Athenian citizen what he believed to be the greatest benefit (εὐεργετεῖν τὴν μεγίστην εὐεργεσίαν): the exhortation to seek virtue and wisdom for themselves.[146] This possible allusion is strengthened by Herodes' material posturing as a wise adviser to Marcus and Lucius in the Rhamnous and Brexiza busts,[147] by his mediating/guiding role implied by the Olympia nymphaion,[148] by the bust of Sokrates found somewhere in Marathon that may have been connected to Herodes' self-fashioning,[149] and by Philostratos' casting of him as a problematic Athenian teacher, who was embraced by the *polis* too late, as well as his consistent contrasting of Herodes to philosophers. So here Herodes' euergetism is juxtaposed to Sokrates' moral and ethical interventions that, according to Plato's Sokrates, were possible only in Athens but that also determined his enforced suicide at the hands of Athenian law.[150] Sokrates was, at least in Plato, exemplary: 'ethical and even-tempered, courageous on the battlefield and in civic affairs, obedient to the laws of the *polis*'—quite unlike Philostratos' Herodes.[151] Yet Sokrates too was rejected by Athens, only apparently to be accepted again in hindsight.

As a potential tyrant, king, or hero, how might Philostratos' Socratic casting of Herodes work? As Tim Whitmarsh has shown, in narratives of Sokrates' trial, 'punishment becomes implicitly an index of the punisher's intolerance, not of the sufferer's culpability'.[152] In this light, the Athenians who accuse Herodes of tyranny and reject him, though he sees himself as a great benefactor, are failing to embrace a potential saviour. That the Athenians appeal to the authority of Rome to subdue Herodes' influence casts him as a misunderstood 'martyr' for Hellenism and implies that, as in Sokrates' day, the Athenian *dêmos* are unable to discern what is actually good for them. On the other hand, the comparison to

---

[146] See also Xen. *Mem.* 4.8.9–10.   [147] See Section 3.1.   [148] See Section 5.2.

[149] See Galli 2002, 165, and Section 3.1. Dodwell 1819, 161, reports the discovery of a Sokrates bust at Brexiza as described in Fauvel's notebooks, but Petrakos 1995, 68–9, 114–18, using the notebooks, does not mention this bust, and Tobin 1997, 253, is adamant it was found elsewhere in Marathon. Galli speculates that the slight twist to Herodes' portrait head might allude to the Type B portrait of Sokrates. See Richter 1965a, s.v. Sokrates Type B, figs 503, 513, 524–6, 560–2, 563a, 569. He thus connects the Marathon bust with Herodes. On the portraits of Sokrates more generally, see Lapatin 2006.

[150] On Sokrates' belief that Athens was the only place where he could practice his form of philosophy, see Colson 1989, 40–8, especially 47.

[151] The quotation comes from Beck 2014, 463. Beck persuasively argues that Plato's presentation of Sokrates as exemplary led his character to become symbolic of the debate over the relationship of philosophy to politics.

[152] Whitmarsh 2001, 284. On the importance of Sokrates as a paradigm for imperial writers, see Moles 1978, 98. Dio Chrysostom, for instance, compares himself (as a persecuted and falsely charged individual) to Sokrates in *Or.* 43.8–12.

Sokrates also works ironically to damn Herodes' grasp for local power. First, as revealed in Plato's description of Sokrates' sentiments above, the Athenian sage rejects the very things in which Herodes excels: money-making, politics, public speaking, property ownership. Philosophy and euergetism, it turns out, are quite different pursuits. Thus, in this case, the Socratic paradigm can be read to signal that Herodes, with his extravagant building, is misplacing his energies in an inferior Roman/tyrannical brand of rule, when he should be investing in and setting an example through Greek thought and culture. In this, we are reminded of Philostratos' negative allusions to Nero.

Second, both Herodes and Sokrates do not fit into their respective sociocultural milieux. Judging by the Socratic and Thesean comparison, this is not entirely Herodes' fault, but rather a failure on the part of the *dêmos* to embrace him. There is a sense of missed opportunity: that if Herodes had been allowed to continue his plans to dominate Athens, a different future might have arisen for the city. But Herodes' anachronism and inappropriate approach ensure this is impossible: the Roman empire cannot permit an Athenian king, especially one who is modelled on a Roman emperor. Once more, Philostratos' juxtaposition of Herodes and Marcus (as the figure of Roman authority) enforces the ironic spin. Marcus, though inferior to the Greek philosopher Lucius, is philosophically superior to Herodes, whose intemperate, aphilosophical nature is a complex mix of out-moded kingship-turned-tyranny and heroism that fails to deliver on its potential in contemporary society. In this, we are reminded through the figure of Sokrates of the Platonic doctrine of 'great natures' and how great men are capable of both great good and great evil depending on their nurture, especially their relationship to philosophy.[153]

So, although in Philostratos' text Herodes conceives of the stadium as a great benefaction, it is not received in the same light, and, indeed, the Athenians 'in fact declared the Panathenaic ($Παναθηναϊκόν$) stadium well named ($εὖ ἐπωνομάσθαι$), for [Herodes] had built it with money of which all Athenians ($Ἀθηναῖοι πάντες$) were being robbed' (*VS* 2.1.549). Herodes did not, however, deprive the Athenians of their inheritance because he wished to hoard his money, but rather because he wanted to use it in a way that would bring him a lasting presence in the city. In other words, Herodes' benefactions were not aimed at appeasing or pleasing his contemporary Athenians, but at impressing future viewers of his monuments. Moreover, his refusal to honour Attikos' will had the effect of maintaining his fiscal control over the city, since the annual grant would certainly have strengthened the average citizen's position while simultaneously weakening that of Herodes.[154]

---

[153] See Sokrates' explication of 'great natures' in Pl. *Resp.* 491b-5b with Duff 1999.
[154] Cf. Tobin 1997, 27–9, 163–5.

Philostratos describes the decision to build the stadium as follows:[155]

> he held the office of eponymous archon at Athens and curatorship of the Panhellenic festival; and when crowned by the charge of the Panathenaic festival he announced: 'I will welcome you, Athenians, and those Hellenes that will attend, and the athletes who are to compete, in a stadium of white marble.' And, having said this, he completed within four years the stadium on the other side of the Ilisos, and thus constructed a monument ($\check{\epsilon}\rho\gamma o\nu$) beyond all marvels ($\acute{v}\pi\grave{\epsilon}\rho$ $\pi\acute{a}\nu\tau a$ $\tau\grave{a}$ $\theta a\acute{v}\mu a\tau a$), for no theatre can rival it.   (*VS* 2.1.549–50)

With this move, Herodes claims the Panathenaia as his own. Hadrian had only recently promoted it to sacred iselastic ($\epsilon\acute{i}\sigma\epsilon\lambda a\sigma\tau\iota\kappa\acute{o}s$) status, which granted victorious athletes the right of triumphal entrance to their own *poleis*, thus increasing its importance.[156] In this way, another connection is made between Herodes and Theseus, who as Plutarch relates founded this festival shortly after the *synoikism* of Athens (Plut. *Thes.* 24.3). In her study of elites and religious change in Roman Athens, Elena Muñiz Grijalvo demonstrated that one way in which provincial elites increased their social prestige and controlled the political landscape by public spending was the increasing oligarchization of religious power. This process suited both Roman officials and local elites, and is another instance of Rome supporting the leading citizens of the Greek east in distinguishing themselves in their local political sphere.[157] She highlights Herodes Attikos as a specific and conspicuous example of a provincial elite who continued to show economic initiative in religious affairs when this role had mostly been adopted by the imperial family or other foreign benefactors.[158] The Panathenaic festival was particularly symbolic in these terms, since although it was closely connected to imperial cult, the festival's traditional focus was paradoxically on Athenian military might and democracy.[159] In building the stadium, moreover, Herodes forever attaches his name to this festival and connects himself to Theseus as founder of the festival and instigator of the *synoikism* of Athens.[160]

In Philostratos' account, the decision to build the stadium is immediately followed by another Herodean intervention in the Athenian landscape, only this time in the city's sacred landscape: Herodes has the Athenian ephebes' cloaks changed from black to white (*VS* 2.1.550). If independent evidence, in an inscription (*IG* II^2 2090) from Eleusis that dates the innovation to 165/6, did not exist, one would assume from Philostratos' account that the change was instigated for the Panathenaia of 143/4.[161] This is indicative of Philostratos'

---

[155] On the stadium in general, its reception, and its relationship to other stadiums, see Galli 2002, 12–28.

[156] Spawforth and Walker 1985, 90–1; Boatwright 2000, 100; see also Muñiz Grijalvo 2005, 264.

[157] Muñiz Grijalvo 2005.   [158] Muñiz Grijalvo 2005, 270.

[159] See Shear 2001, 634–50; Muñiz Grijalvo 2005, 264.

[160] For other mythic and literary associations with the founding of the games, see Galli 2002, 30–1.

[161] For other such changes to mourning dress, see Plut. *Arat.* 53; Paus. 2.3.6; Philostr. *Heroikos* 53.

artfulness and tendency to wilfully mislead. Herodes' substitution recalls Theseus' failure to do the same with his ship's sails and 'undoes' the mourning for either Aegeus (according to Herodes' Bey inscription, *IG* II² 3606, ll. 19–23) or the more usual Kopreus (according to Philostr. *VS* 2.1.550 and Hom. *Il.* 15.639) that the black cloaks signified.[162] The white cloaks reflect the marble (λίθου λευκοῦ, *VS* 2.1.550) used to clothe the stadium and may be the reason why Philostratos chose to place the anecdote at this confusing point in his narrative. Additionally, the black mourning cloaks had been worn by the ephebes on all festal or processional occasions, and, consequently, another reason for Philostratos to connect the cloaks with the stadium and the Athenians' resentment appears: in the *Lives*, Herodes' corpse is carried off from Marathon by the ephebes, whose white garb signals celebration rather than mourning.

Given the emphasis in Philostratos' account on the negativity that the *dêmos* felt towards Herodes and the Panathenaic stadium, as well as their ironic change of heart upon his death, the multi-layered epitaph that mocks Herodes' ambitions in life, and all the other ambiguities attached to the stadium addressed above, it becomes the perfect and most meaningful burial spot for Philostratos' literary design. This raises the possibility that Herodes was not buried at the Panathenaic stadium at all and that this tradition was invented by our author.[163] Philostratos is a sophisticated, playful writer, who does have a tendency to fictionalize in order to enhance his narrative purpose; consequently, his production of anecdotal history in the *Lives of the Sophists* should not be accepted as completely reliable.[164] This option, therefore, is not beyond the realms of possibility, however improbable, and the Panathenaic stadium is a nice complement to the gymnasium of Ptolemy where Theseus' bones were supposedly interred (Plut. *Thes.* 36.2).

Rife makes a strong circumstantial case for locating Herodes' tomb at the stadium. He bases his arguments predominantly on Philostratos, the altar and sarcophagus, and the rectangular structure (*c.*11 × 60 m) above the eastern side of the stadium (Figure 6.9), of which only minimal foundations remain but which

---

[162] See Skenteri 2005, 99–100, on the two interpretations. See Plut. *Thes.* 17.4, 22 on Aegeus' suicide. Graindor 1912, 88: Philostratos' version comes from Herodes being a member of the *genos* of the Kerykes, of whom Kopreus was the eponymous ancestor, and so he was capable of purifying the ephebes of his ancestor's murder. Herodes, however, clearly connects the black cloaks to Aegeus. Also see Galli 2002, 29–30.

[163] Note that most of Herodes' family was buried at Kephisia, and an inscription of mourning for a child built into one of these tombs hints that Herodes intended to be buried there too (*SEG* 26.290); however, no evidence of the fulfilment of this promise exists. See Ameling 1983b, 143, no. 140; Tobin 1997, 225–6.

[164] Bowie 1994, 181. Swain 1991 argues that the *VS* is as reliable as an account based on oral sources can be. Swain's position, however, denies Philostratos' literary agency. Cf. Jones 1974. See Schmitz 2009's convincing characterization of the narrator of Philostratos' *VS* as designed to project authority and a sense of non-fiction; see especially 68, for the text as deliberately unstable, sophistic, and bewildering. Kemezis 2011 also perceptively reads the *VS* as a literary text with a carefully planned overall structure and purpose.

may have been an altar-shaped tomb, whose form is known from Asia Minor.[165] The altar and sarcophagus are not definitive, and there is not enough left of the rectangular structure to determine its function with any certainty. Tobin, for instance, based on Philostratos' account, argues (less convincingly) that it was the place of mooring for the Panathenaic ship during the festival and that Herodes was rather buried beneath the race track.[166] It would be bold indeed of Philostratos to fabricate the tomb's whereabouts. Although he does toy with the many possible locations of Polemon's burial, the *Lives'* secondary focus, before vaguely locating it somewhere in Laodikeia on his own authority and against predominant tradition (*VS* 1.25.543–4), he has been proved more accurate with the tomb of Dionysios of Miletos (*VS* 1.22.526), which was discovered close to where Philostratos placed it in central Ephesos.[167]

Rather, then, it is the way Philostratos crafts his tale that builds a picture of Herodes trying to leave his mark on an unappreciative city, a tale in which the Panathenaic stadium becomes the locus of resentment. Both the Odeion of Regilla and the stadium are singled out by Philostratos as Herodes' greatest constructions: 'these two monuments [...] are such as exist nowhere else in the Roman empire' (2.1.551). Yet both monuments were built under problematic circumstances that colour Herodes as tyrannical and/or heroic. The odeion results from the murder of Regilla, but also from Herodes' excessive, heroic grief; the stadium memorializes the swindling of the *dêmos* and a desire to mark public space, but also recalls Theseus' foundation of Athens as a *polis*. In the *Lives of the Sophists*, Philostratos uses θαῦμα and θαυμάζω to describe the performances of his sophists and their effect on the audience.[168] In these cases, the word almost always refers to speech. In the 'Life of Herodes', however, there is only one occasion where the sophist's speech causes wonder and that is when he cries out to Poseidon lamenting his inability, despite his desire, to cut through the Isthmus of Corinth. On the two other occasions the word is used in reference to Herodes, it describes the Panathenaic stadium and the two daughters of Alkimedon, whose deaths so upset Herodes at his Sirmium trial. So, although Herodes is the greatest of sophists, his greatness is defined in Philostratos by his desire to monumentalize (and concurrently memorialize) and his helplessness in the face of death.

As well as Philostratos associating Herodes' monumentalizing impulse with Nero rather than Hadrian, another undercurrent of meaning in the Nero

---

[165] See Rife 2008, 104. Tobin 1997, 177–8, following Gasparri 1974–75, 376–83, figs 78–88, argues for dimensions of 9.5×42 m. However, Travlos 1971, 498–501, and Ziller 1870 agree with Rife's measurements.

[166] Tobin 1993; 1997, 177–85; Rife 2008, 109–11, and Galli 2002, 20–1, refute her argument.

[167] See Section 3.1; Rife 2009, 114–19.

[168] See, for example, *VS* 1.18.510, 1.19.511, 1.20.513, 1.21.515, 1.21.517, 1.21.518–21. Cf. Whitmarsh 1999, 151.

paradigm is that of an unrealized potential in Herodes to bring freedom to the Athenians as a new Theseus. Nero himself had granted 'freedom' to the province of Achaia in AD 67. In reality this was simply tax immunity and lasted only until Vespasian used civil unrest as an excuse to retract the grant. Yet the parallel in striving for Greek rule over Athens and failure in that goal is pertinent.

The association of Herodes with Theseus does not stem solely from Philostratus—Herodes instigated his own material programme to do so. It is Herodes, not Philostratos, who connects the black cloaks to Aegeus rather than Kopreus, who 'refounds' the Panathenaia by building the stadium, who mimics the concept of Theseus' Isthmian pillar with his Marathonian arch,[169] and who revives the temple of Poseidon at Isthmia by supplementing the cult statues in what appears a filial act. Nevertheless, Philostratos picks up this posturing and crafts it to serve his own narrative of failed heroism and kingship become tyranny.

This notion of Herodes as a failed Theseus is important given the limited political potential of elite Greeks in the empire. Theseus was considered responsible for the *synoikism* of the Athenians (Paus. 1.22.3; Thuc. 2.15.2),[170] and, although he began as a purely monarchic figure, he came to possess a democratic reputation, so that his two identities—heroic king and father of democracy—existed contiguously.[171] Euripides' *Suppliants* is the first clear expression of this paradox, when Theseus the King says the following of the *dêmos*: 'for I put them in charge | when I set this city free, all now with an equal vote' (352–3). According to Plutarch, Theseus gathered all the people of Attica into the city. The common folk were more than happy to join him, but he enticed the nobles by promising to lay down his absolute rule and institute a form of democracy, in which he would have only the power to command in war and be the guardian of laws (*Thes.* 24.1–2). At this point he instituted the Panathenaic festival. Nevertheless, Plutarch later reports that his monarchic quasi-democracy failed, since:

Menestheus [...] united and stirred up the powerful men in Athens. These had long felt oppressed by Theseus and thought that he had robbed each of the country nobles of his royal office, and then shut them all up in a single city, where he treated them as subjects (ὑπηκόοις) and slaves (δούλοις). The common people he also threw into confusion and misled. They thought they had a vision of liberty, he said, but in reality they had been robbed of their native homes and religions in order that, in the place of many good kings of

---

[169] For the argument that Hadrian tried to present himself as a new Theseus, see Karivieri 2002.

[170] The festival of the Synoikia was also dedicated to him. On Theseus in this context, see Atack 2020, 76–84.

[171] Gouschin 1999. See Walker 1995 for the transformation of Theseus from self-centred violent hero to democratic leader and Mills 1997 for Theseus as consistently imagined as representing Athenian core values. See Calame 1990 for the relationship of the Theseus myth to Attic cult.

their own blood, they might look obediently to one master (ἕνα δεσπότην) who was an immigrant (ἔπηλυν) and an alien (ξένον) (*Thes.* 32.1).[172]

The events described above closely match those surrounding the charge of tyranny brought against Herodes by the Athenians. It is after the people turn against Theseus that he exiles himself and, similarly, it is after the trial at Sirmium that 'some' (as Philostratos says) record the exile of Herodes (Plut. *Thes.* 35.3; Philostr. *VS* 2.1.562). In Pausanias' version (1.17.5–6), in contrast, it is Menestheus who establishes the democracy by expelling Theseus and courting the favour of the *dêmos*. Patrick Hogan has demonstrated that Pausanias presents monarchy as the best form of government and that for him it is rather Menestheus' democracy that threatens Athens' greatness. He argues that Pausanias is drawing a parallel with his own second-century context and cautioning against providing Rome with an excuse to intervene locally through elite disunity, as the Dioskouroi did in the struggle between Menestheus and those loyal to Theseus, and as Vespasian did to retract Nero's grant of freedom. Pausanias therefore presents Theseus as wronged by the *dêmos* and then later redeemed through the agency of Kimon.[173] There is no hint in Pausanias that his attitude to Theseus extends to Herodes Attikos, but anyone reading the text who was aware of Herodes' self-fashioning as a new Theseus could well have drawn the connection.

Philostratos' narrative of Herodes follows a similar pattern but is far less certain about the rightful outcome. In Athenian traditions, Theseus manages to be both a heroic king and the embodiment of Athenian democracy.[174] The strong strain of allusion throughout Philostratos' 'Life of Herodes' to the figure of Theseus and the concurrent ambivalence towards the protagonist stems from Herodes' posturing as a Thesean figure and signals Philostratos' mixed feelings about the implications of any attempt to restore a Thesean-style monarchy. Philostratos' own crafting of Herodes thus complements Pausanias' presentation of Theseus, and considering the two accounts side by side opens the latter up to a reading that is strongly (if unintentionally) subversive of the Roman empire. Philostratos' presentation of the conflict between Herodes and the *dêmos* is thus less about provincial tyranny and more about larger issues of empire. On the one hand, a Thesean Herodes could be the champion Athens needs to cast off the shackles of Rome; on the other, such a figure would entail the substitution of one kind of monarchy for another (albeit a potentially 'democratic' one) and, if unsuccessful,

---

[172] Translation adapted from Perrin 1914. Cf. Paus. 1.3.3.

[173] See Hogan 2017. Hogan draws compelling parallels between Pausanias' characterizations of Theseus and Themistokles in a similar way to how I have compared Theseus and Herodes. Compare also Habicht's discussion of Pausanias' view of monarchy, tyranny, and democracy, which largely corresponds to Hogan's, in Habicht 1985, 109–11.

[174] See Walker 1995, 113–69, especially 144–6, for a discussion of the two parallel traditions.

would bring heavy-handed Roman intervention on the *polis*. In the world of Philostratean rhetoric, the contradictory, ambiguous figure of Theseus offers an effective mythical analogue for the enigmatic Herodes. Herodes (Ἡρώδης) can be presented as the hero (ἥρως) of Athens, who challenges the absolute control of the city by Rome. Yet, at the same time, he must always fail, given Athens' love of democracy and freedom, and the incongruity (even in classical times) of the civic veneration of its legendary king.[175] Not to mention the prevalence of the concept of 'imperial democracy' in contemporary Greek literature and the reality that, politically, Athens was but one small cog in the greater imperial machine.

In this light, Philostratos' 'Life of Herodes' becomes a commentary on the limitations to individual greatness placed on the provincial Greek elite in the Roman empire, and it is probable Philostratos sees himself and his own cultural and political constraints in the figure of Herodes.[176] In the *Lives*, Herodes is heroic, but because of his very heroism—his larger than life, domineering, and often antisocial behaviour—he fails to negotiate imperial society successfully and, at the same time, he also exists in tension with the Athenian *dêmos*, because the empire can brook no King of Athens and a true democracy has no place for supermen.[177] The kind of imperial democracy described by Philostratos, Aelius Aristeides, or Dio Cassius is indicative of an acceptance that the advent and persistence of the empire and the emperor signify an absolute end to real political freedom.[178] This notion must also lie behind the passage from Plutarch quoted above (*Thes.* 32.1), in which 'democratic' monarchy promises liberty, but ultimately fails to deliver. Harry Sidebottom has argued that 'philosopher' and 'sophist', especially in Philostratos' *Lives*, function as 'supra-*polis* symbolic roles [...] with enough symbolic capital to operate on a level with Roman power'.[179] Philostratos' 'Life of Herodes', however, suggests the opposite. Herodes' sophistic realm is cast as escapist and constructed, juxtaposed as it is to the political reality of the empire, within which there is no longer any room for the Thesean figure Herodes approximates (unless it be the emperor himself).

For Philostratos, then, Herodes fails to be a new Theseus, but the text's attitude towards this failure is ambivalent. He presents two, superimposed versions of Athens—the sophistic cultural centre ruled graciously by Herodes and the minor political entity governed by Rome, in which Herodes oversteps his bounds. This dual presentation signals that the incongruity of Philostratos' heroic, sophistic Herodes in the wider empire is a critique of the 'Second Sophistic' itself, in its harking back to the glory days of a city that is now part of another's empire and the notion that cultural expression can compete with Roman might. Alternatively,

---

[175] See Walker 1995, 3; Atack 2014. [176] On Philostratos' life, see Bowie 2009, 19–25.
[177] On the notion of the incongruity of supermen in a democratic *polis*, see Walker 1995, 147.
[178] Starr 1952, 16. [179] Sidebottom 2009, 98.

Philostratos' ambivalence can be read to imply that Herodes does not go far enough but rather fails to unite culture and power successfully. So, although his sophistic realm functions independently of Rome and, as Jason König has established, is founded absolutely in Hellenic culture and traditions,[180] Herodes betrays Athens and Greece in limiting his political challenges to Roman authority through rather a single-minded focus on his continuing monumental and cultural presence, just as Athens fails him by not accepting his attempts to rule. It is in Athens' inability to accept Herodes in life that Philostratos' allusive comparison of him to Sokrates becomes significant. Yet Sokrates Herodes is not. Additionally, it is striking that in a passage describing Theseus' interment, which pre-empts Philostratos' account of Herodes' spontaneous funeral, Plutarch notes that his tomb became a sanctuary for runaway slaves and those who fear men in power (*Thes.* 36.2). Protector of the downtrodden is certainly not a quality that emerges from the Herodes of the *Lives of the Sophists* and is rather more associated with Marcus Aurelius. This failure of the man and the city to be worthy of each other explains the discrepancy between the epitaph recorded by Philostratos that labels Herodes 'Marathonian' and Philostratos' last words on the matter, τοσαῦτα περὶ Ἡρώδου τοῦ Ἀθηναίου (2.1.566), that, as well as conveying the sense of having exhausted the subject, also surely imply a dismissive undertone of 'so much for Herodes the Athenian' (2.1.566).

6.6 CONCLUSION

Philostratos' *Lives of the Sophists* constructs two, superimposed versions of Athens: the isolated, anachronistic, and unreal sophistic city and the Roman Greek *polis* that functions in the empire at large and in relation to Rome. Philostratos' Herodes appears as a very different character in each version of the city. In sophistic Athens, where he is the 'king of words', he rules supreme and with a generous, democratic nature; in Roman Athens, however, he is an ambiguous, domineering mix of hero and tyrant, who never fulfils his kingly potential. The two ultimately incompatible paradigms offer competing visions of a utopic possibility and a difficult reality.

Philostratos' written portrait of Herodes, then, is a complex mix of praise and blame that draws on Herodes' own commemorative posturing as a 'new Theseus' and his euergetistic imitation of Hadrian, which Philostratos turns around to suggest a closer affinity with Nero. Indeed, the complete absence of Hadrian, except as a figure of authority and power before whom Athens' 'king of words' loses the ability to speak, demonstrates Philostratos' power over the shaping of

[180] König 2014, 258–70.

Herodes' memory and how effectively he can record euergetism as tyranny and failed heroic kingship. Philostratos crafts his character rhetorically, using his own sophistic tools against him, by aligning him alternatively with the figures of the hero, tyrant, and king, and contrasting him to the philosopher. Indeed, the only philosopher that Philostratos associates with Herodes through literary allusion is Sokrates, who was also rejected by Athens, but the allusion serves to underscore the differences between what Herodes and Sokrates respectively conceived of as 'the greatest benefits' to bestow on the Athenians: public monuments designed to commemorate the donor and extend his political influence versus moral and ethical improvement. It is striking that Marcus Aurelius, a Roman emperor, proves a far more philosophical figure than Herodes himself and that Philostratos implies that Herodes' failure to be a suitable 'king of Athens' partly lies in his need to be schooled in Greek philosophy. At the same time, Herodes fails to learn from his own lessons to Philagros in his sophistic microcosm and exceeds the limits of his power and position in the reality of the Roman empire. The text's ambivalence to Herodes and the superimposition of cultural utopia and Roman reality implies an inherent, unresolvable tension in being a Greek *pepaideumenos* and a politically active Roman citizen. Even Herodes, whose wealth, status, education, connections, and ambition are second to none, fails to unite culture and power successfully, and, consequently, to craft a positive lasting self-image for posterity.

The very unreality of Herodes' sophistic Athens underscores the political anachronism of Philostratos' 'Second Sophistic' and a figure like that of Philagros introduces uncertainty even about its cultural validity. The textual and innovative Philagros, who dispenses with contemporary fame by breaking with the past and convention, two elements on which the Second Sophistic itself depends, challenges the primacy of improvised *epideixis* and, contiguously, Herodes' conception of cultural supremacy. In Herodes' sophistic Athens, he fails dismally, but it is a different story in Rome, where the textual Philagros thrives and the performer Alexander the Clay Plato bombs. Moreover, as I argued in chapter 2, there is a textual affinity between Philagros and Philostratos, who himself is creating a new canon—that of the Second Sophistic—through the act of writing the sophists.[181] Philostratos' depiction of Herodes, then, presents a vision of Greek rhetorical culture that is uncertain of its place in a Roman world and Philostratos' attempts to capture it textually—to preserve the cultural artefact—may be symptomatic of its increasing cultural specificity and functional isolation. Philostratos exhibits great respect for and even awe at Herodes—he too is a $\theta\alpha\hat{v}\mu\alpha$ at which to marvel—as well as affection for his 'Second Sophistic', but (in the 'Life of Herodes', at least) the sense of anachronism, displacement, and unsustainability is overwhelming.

---

[181] See Section 2.3.

Alexei Zadorojnyi has argued compellingly that in Greek and Roman biography literacy is a sign of despotism and tyranny,[182] and this tendency can be seen in Philostratos' two Herodeis and two Athenses as well. Herodes' Athens is one of sophistic oratory, but when he does write, it is to exert his authority over individuals such as Philagros; in the reality of the Roman empire, he writes to accuse Marcus Aurelius of neglect. Thus, in both realms, writing is seen as a weapon in the arsenal of the struggle for power and, in particular, power over how one is perceived, either locally or more broadly. Equally, Herodes' monumentalizing impulse performs a similar function to writing, in that it records a specific personal intention and authority in a lasting medium, writing it into the landscape, and was likewise used by the Athenians as evidence of tyranny. What is striking in the case of Herodes is that despite this public pushback and the very real possibility of execution for tyranny, Herodes persists in crafting monuments designed to preserve his legacy. Philostratos himself asserts his authority over the memory of Herodes through text and here lies another reason for Philostratos raising the spectre of Sokrates. In the inherently agonistic environment of sophistic activity, not only does Philostratos score a virtual victory over his illustrious forerunner by controlling his image, but he also sets up a similar complex relationship as that which exists between the textual Plato and the oral Sokrates. In both cases, the writer (i.e. Philostratos/Plato) and his character (i.e. the literary Herodes/Sokrates) come to stand for the subject himself (i.e. the historical Herodes/Sokrates), who essentially disappears by being written out of the literary record (or, more precisely, written over).

Significantly, in the *Lives of the Sophists*, Herodes fails to live up to any of the roles Philostratos creates for him. Philostratos' project is aided by the failure of any of Herodes' literary works to survive from antiquity and his adherence to *epideixis*, so that even if the speech in the style of Kritias that has been associated with Herodes were by his hand, it would give no clearer picture of the man. Commemorative ambition, therefore, whether literary or material, is also in essence tyrannical—an effort to dominate space, time, and cultural memory—and the loss of ability to shape one's own reception, as exemplified by Philostratos' Herodes Attikos, is the trade-off for acquiring a foothold in cultural consciousness.

---

[182] Zadorojnyi 2006.

SEVEN

The Politics of Posterity

Posterity is as likely to be wrong as anybody else.
– Heywood Broun, *Sitting on the World*.[1]

The past that fascinates Roman-era Greeks has traditionally been conceived of as limiting and dwarfing their cultural output. More recently, this perception has morphed into a learned assessment that their cultural efforts are valuable both as art and in terms of cultural history *despite* their commitment to a backwards-looking gaze. One aim of this book has been to demonstrate that it is rather *because of* this embroilment in the past that imperial Greeks manage to position their cultural efforts as worthy of canonicity in their own right. By investing in the past, imperial Greeks create a context for their cultural innovations that is founded on an artificially constructed sense of continuity between past, present, and posterity. Not only does this allow meaningful contemporary self-fashioning, but it also ensures (rhetorically) a receptive audience in the future.

Whether through a Janus-like, bi-directional gaze that forges a movable temporal perspective, competitive imitation that displaces and supersedes a cultural or historical icon, or originality, imperial Greek cultural expression rescales Greek and Roman cultural and political history, so that someone glancing back from a hypothetical future moment might view imperial Greeks as an equal notch on (or potentially even the climax of) a long, culturally inclusive timeline. One result of this temporally expansive outlook is to subordinate reception in the Roman present to that in the future.

Herodes Attikos' material posturing as the 'hero of Marathon' or a Theseus-style 'king of Athens', for instance, was resisted by his fellow citizens. This is evinced by his need to apply curse inscriptions to his monuments, by the defacement of the 'hero of Marathon' altar in Athens, by the Delphians' dismissive reference to Polydeukion as 'Herodes' hero', and by the Athenians' outrage over the construction of the Panathenaic stadium instead of honouring Attikos' will. Despite this push back from his fellow Greeks and political repercussions in the form of his trial on the capital charge of tyranny before Marcus Aurelius, Herodes

[1] Broun 1924, 62.

Fashioning the Future in Roman Greece: Memory, Monuments, Texts. Estelle Strazdins, Oxford University Press.
© Estelle Strazdins 2023. DOI: 10.1093/oso/9780192866103.003.0007

persisted in shaping such provocative commemorative identities. Similarly, Aelius Aristeides rejected a typical sophistic career that strove for provincial followed by imperial recognition through statue honours, local liturgies and offices, a following of students, and perhaps an imperial chair of rhetoric. Instead he embraced a written account of seclusion, physical suffering, and divine recognition, protection, and instruction leading to his transformation into an object of wonder and oratorical supremacy. Both Herodes and Aristeides, then, were not averse to mortgaging the present to gamble on the future.

This attitude to cultural production provides an alternative explanation for the tension created between Roman power and Greek culture in this period. Rather than seeing it as deriving from a rhetorical, nostalgic response to loss of political freedom, one can instead trace this tension in the empowerment that comes from allowing imperial Greeks a stake in the future. Arrian's *Anabasis*, for example, uses Alexander's experience of space and time in his conquest of Asia to highlight the inevitable waxing and waning of political power within a greater cycle of history. Not only does this elucidate Alexander's desperate efforts to shape his legacy, but it also implies that Rome's own position of dominance over her Mediterranean empire is ultimately unstable. Thus Tony Spawforth might see imperial Greek fascination with the past as dancing to a Roman tune, but the threat contained in the kind of ambivalent heroic identities Herodes creates must have registered with Roman rulers too and lies behind such acts as Marcus Aurelius' transference of blame for Herodes' tyranny over Athens from the man himself to his freed slaves: don't poke the hornets' nest. Moreover, the ambivalence of such identities in the Roman present is central to their ability to speak powerfully to future audiences, as shown by Philostratos' retrospective engagement with Herodes' political potential but ultimate failure.

These commemorative strategies derive their power from their location within memorial land- and cityscapes, punctuated by monuments, and in relation to the classical literary canon. Time, topography, text, and artefact are woven together to form a personalized commemorative narrative that fashions the Roman east as an arena of self-aggrandizement. These memorial spaces are physical, but also virtual in their multitemporality, so that horses whinny and men battle each night on the plain of Marathon, as Pausanias tells us, at the same time as Herodes establishes portraits of the emperors Marcus and Lucius Verus there, loots the memorial to the Athenian dead, and claims ownership of Marathon (possibly all of Attica or even Greece) as 'Herodes' space' on his Gate of Eternal Concord. The monuments of the Greek past are the keys to communication between pre-existing temporal layers and provide the guarantee that one's own material efforts will also function as commemorative time machines. The reshaping of memorial space displaces and diminishes classical authority in favour of one's own. It asserts a new plural, temporally elastic, and materially bound form of cultural expression, which exists in the textual as much as physical realm, so that Arrian's writings turn Asia into a funerary inscription for Alexander and his *Anabasis* into his tomb, or bring Mt Theches to Trapezous and reconstruct the Ten Thousand's cairn as a monument to Hadrian and Arrian's literary works.

The intertextuality and intermediality of imperial Greek cultural output are thus pivotal to our understanding of the cultural and historical positioning of the 'Second Sophistic'. Indeed, it is impossible to gain an accurate and complete impression of this period without considering text and monument together. Likewise, restricting temporal investigation both limits the ability of Roman-period Greek culture to signal its own aspirations—commemorative, artistic, personal, political—and impedes scholarship from perceiving the full range of its possible meanings. For one thing, the idea of posterity nuances how we understand the political messages contained in imperial Greek texts and monuments, the more contentious of which become clearer when viewed as aimed beyond rather than simply in spite of a present audience. For another, it provides a richer comprehension of imperial Greek reuse of the past: classical Greek culture is not a monolith in whose shadow to cower, but a context in which to be understood and a paradigm from which to depart. Finally, it also explains the frequent ambivalence as to the prospect of success in imperial Greek commemorative efforts. The very processes of manipulation, appropriation, and reapplication of past culture that the Second Sophistic embraces highlight the impossibility of controlling the reception of one's own art no matter how carefully shaped or curated in its moment of production. Thus, despite the numerous strategies deployed to fashion and control one's image that this book has examined, imperial Greek awareness of the potential to misread culture creatively is the quality that opens it, like the chameleon god Antinoos, to a plurality of readings. This paradox in imperial Greek cultural output infuses it with pathos, but also the complexity, stratification, variety, richness, and even desperation that have made it such a powerful voice capable of speaking to and affecting diverse audiences across time and space.

BIBLIOGRAPHY

ADAMS, A. 1989. 'The Arch of Hadrian in Athens', in eds. S. WALKER and A. CAMERON, *The Greek Renaissance in the Roman Empire*, *BICS* Supplement 55, pp. 10–17. London.

ADAMS, C. 2007. 'Travel and the Perception of Space in the Eastern Desert', in ed. M. RATHMANN, *Wahrnehmung und Erfassung geographischer Räume in der Antike*, pp. 211–20. Mainz am Rhein.

ADLER, F. 1892. 'Exedra den Herodes Attikos', in eds. F. ADLER, R. BORRMANN, W. DÖRPFELD, F. GRAEBER, and P. GRAEF, *Olympia. Ergebnisse der von dem Deutschen Reich veranstalteten Ausgrabung II: Die Baudenmäler*, pp. 134–9. Berlin.

AERTS, W. J. 1994. 'Alexander the Great and Ancient Travel Stories', in ed. Z. VOB MARTELS, *Travel Fact and Travel Fiction: Studies on Fiction, Literary Tradition, Scholarly Discovery and Observation in Travel Writing*, pp. 30–8. Leiden.

AICHER, P. 1989. 'Ennius' Dream of Homer', *AJPhil* 110.2: 227–32.

AITKEN, E. B. and J. K. B. MACLEAN eds. 2001. *Flavius Philostratus: Heroikos*. Atlanta.

AITKEN, E. B. and J. K. B. MACLEAN eds. 2005. *Philostratus' Heroikos: Religion and Cultural Identity in the Third Century CE*. Leiden and Boston.

ALCHERMES, J. 1994. 'Spolia in Roman Cities of the Late Empire: Legislative Rationales and Architectural Reuse', *Dumbarton Oaks Papers* 48: 167–78.

ALCOCK, S. E. 1996. 'Landscapes of Memory and the Authority of Pausanias', in ed. J. BINGEN, *Pausanias Historien*, pp. 241–76. Geneva.

ALCOCK, S. E. 2002. *Archaeologies of the Greek Past: Landscape, Monuments, and Memories*. Cambridge.

ALCOCK, S. E. 2005. 'Material Witness: An Archaeological Context for the *Heroikos*', in eds. J. K. B. MACLEAN and E. B. AITKEN, *Philostratus's Heroikos: Religion and Cultural Identity in the Third Century C.E.*, pp. 159–68. Leiden.

ALCOCK, S. E. 2015. 'Kaleidoscopes and the Spinning of Memory in the Eastern Roman Empire', in eds. K. GALINSKY and K. LAPATIN, *Cultural Memories in the Roman Empire*, pp. 24–32. Los Angeles, CA.

ALCOCK, S., J. CHERRY, and J. ELSNER eds. 2001. *Pausanias: Travel and Memory in Roman Greece*. Oxford.

ALLEN, J. 2017. 'Herodes Atticus, Memnon of Ethiopia and the Athenian *Ephebeia*', in eds. W. VANACKER and A. ZUIDERHOEK, *Imperial Identities in the Roman World*, pp. 162–75. Los Angeles, CA.

ALZINGER, W. 1970. 'Ephesos B. Archäologischer Teil', in eds. A. PAULY and G. WISSOWA, *Real-Encyclopädie der Classischen Altertumswissenschaft* (1893–1978). Supplementband XII, pp. 1588–704. Stuttgart.

AMANDRY, M. 1988. *Le Monnayage des Duovirs Corinthiens*, *BCH* Supplément XV. Paris.

AMANDRY, M. and A. BURNETT eds. in collaboration with J. Mairat 2015. *Roman Provincial Coinage* III. *From Nerva to Hadrian (AD 96–138)*. London and Paris.

AMATO, E. ed. 2005. *Favorinos D'Arles: Oeuvres I*. Paris.

AMELING, W. 1983a. *Herodes Atticus I: Biographie*. Zürich.

AMELING, W. 1983b. *Herodes Atticus II: Inschriftenkatalog.* Zürich.

AMELING, W. 1984. 'L. Flavius Arrianus Neos Xenophon', *Epigraphica Anatolica* 4: 119–22.

AMELING, W. 1986. 'Tyrannen und schwangere Frauen', *Historia* 35.4: 507–8.

AMELING, W. 2011. 'Die Gefallenen der Phyle Erechtheis im Jahr 490 v. Chr', *ZPE* 176: 10–23.

ANDERSON, G. 1986. *Philostratus: Biography and Belles Lettres in the Third Century* A.D. London.

ANDERSON, G. 1989. 'The *Pepaideumenos* in Action: Sophists and Their Outlook in the Early Empire', *ANRW* 2.33.1: 79–208.

ANDERSON, G. 1993. *The Second Sophistic: A Cultural Phenomenon in the Roman Empire.* London.

ANDO, C. 2000. *Imperial Ideology and Provincial Loyalty in the Roman Empire.* Berkeley, CA.

ANGUISSOLA, A. 2014. 'Remembering with Greek Masterpieces: Observations on Memory and Roman Copies', in ed. K. GALINSKY, *Memoria Romana: Memory in Rome and Rome in Memory*, pp. 117–34. Ann Arbor, MI.

ARAFAT, K. W. 1996. *Pausanias' Greece: Ancient Artists and Roman Rulers.* Cambridge.

ARISTODEMOU, G. A. 2018. 'Fountain Figures from the Greek Provinces: Monumentality in Fountain Structures of Roman Greece as Revealed through their Sculptural Display Programs and their Patrons', in eds. G. A. ARISTODEMOU and T. P. TASSIOS, *Great Waterworks in Roman Greece: Aqueducts and Monumental Fountain Structures. Function in Context*, pp. 193–217. Oxford.

ARRINGTON, N. T. 2015. *Ashes, Images, and Memories: The Presence of the War Dead in Fifth-Century Athens.* Oxford.

ASSMAN, J. 1995. 'Collective Memory and Cultural Identity', *New German Critique* 65: 125–33.

ATACK, C. 2014. 'The Discourse of Kingship in Classical Athenian Thought', *Histos* 8: 329–62.

ATACK, C. 2020. *The Discourse of Kingship in Classical Greece.* London.

ATHANASSAKI, L. 2016. 'Who was Eucles? Plutarch and his Sources on the Legendary Marathon-Runner (*De gloria Atheniensium* 347CD)', in eds. J. OPSOMER, G. ROSKAM, and F. B. TITCHENER, *A Versatile Gentleman: Consistency in Plutarch's Writing. Studies Offered to Luc Van Der Stockt on the Occasion of his Retirement*, pp. 213–28. Leuven.

AUJAC, G. ed. 1992. *Denys D'Halicarnasse: Opuscules Rhétoriques 5.* Paris.

BAGNALL, R. S. 2011. *Everyday Writing in the Graeco-Roman East*, Sather Lectures 69. Berkeley, CA.

BAIRD, J. A. and C. TAYLOR. 2011. 'Ancient Graffiti in Context: Introduction', in eds. J. A. BAIRD and C. TAYLOR, *Ancient Graffiti in Context*, pp. 1–19. New York and Abingdon.

BARIGAZZI, A. ed. 1966. *Favorino di Arelate: Opere: Introduzione, Testo Critico e Commento.* Florence.

BARTHES, R. 1972. *Critical Essays*, translated by R. HOWARD. Evanston.

BARTHES, R. 1975. *The Pleasure of the Text*, translated by R. MILLER. New York, NY.

BARTSCH, S., and J. ELSNER. 2007. 'Ekphrasis. Introduction: Eight Ways of Looking at Ekphrasis', *Classical Philology* 102.1: i–vi.

BAUMGART, H. 1874. *Aelius Aristides als Repräsentant der sophistischen Rhetorik des zweiten Jahrhunderts der Kaiserzeit.* Leipzig.

BAZ, F. 2007. 'Ein neues Ehrenmonument für Flavius Arrianus', *ZPE* 163: 123–7.

BEARD, M. 1991. 'Writing and Religion: *Ancient Literacy* and the Function of the Written Word in Roman Religion: Question: What was the Role of Writing in Graeco-Roman Paganism?', in ed. J. H. HUMPHREY, *Literacy in the Roman World: JRA* Supplement 3, pp. 35–58. Ann Arbor, MI.

BEARD, M. 1998. 'Vita Inscripta', in ed. W. W. EHLERS, *La Biographie Antique: huit exposéssuivis de discussions*, pp. 83–118. Geneva.

BECK, M. 2014. 'The Socratic Paradigm', in ed. M. BECK, *A Companion to Plutarch*, pp. 463–78. Malden, MA, Oxford, and Chichester.

BEHR, C. 1968. *Aelius Aristides and the Sacred Tales.* Amsterdam.

BEHR, C. 1981. *P. Aelius Aristides: The Complete Works Volume II. Orations XVII–LIII.* Leiden.

BELTRÁN FORTES, J. 1992. 'Arriano de Nicomedia y la Bética, de nuevo', *Habis* 23: 171–96.

BENEDIKTSON, D. T. 2000. *Literature and the Visual Arts in Ancient Greece and Rome.* Norman, OK.

BENNDORF, O. 1868. 'Römisches Grab in Kephisia', *Archäologische Zeitung* 26: 35–40.

BENNDORF, O. 1899. 'Porträtskopf des Platon', *Jahreshefte des Österreichischen archäologischen Instituts in Wien* 2: 250–4.

BERGMANN, B. 1994. 'The Roman House as Memory Theatre: The House of the Tragic Poet in Pompeii', *Art Bulletin* 76.2: 225–56.

BETTENWORTH, A. 2007. 'The Mutual Influence of Inscribed and Literary Epigram', in eds. P. BING and J. S. BRUSS, *Brill's Companion to Hellenistic Epigram: Down to Philip*, pp. 69–93. Leiden.

BETTINI, M. 1991. *Anthropology and Roman Culture: Kinship, Time, Images of the Soul*, translated by J. VAN SICKLE. Baltimore and London.

BETTINI, M. 1999. *The Portrait of the Lover.* Translated by L. GIBBS. Berkeley, CA and London.

BING, P. 1998. 'Between Literature and the Monuments', in eds. M. A. HARDER, R. F. REGTUIT, and G. C. WAKKER, *Genre in Hellenistic Poetry*, pp. 21–43. Groningen.

BING, P. 2002. 'The Un-Read Muse? Inscribed Epigram and its Readers in Antiquity', in eds. M. A. HARDER, R. F. REGTUIT, and G. C. WAKKER, *Hellenistic Epigrams*, pp. 39–66. Leuven.

BING, P. 2008. *The Well-Read Muse: Present and Past in Callimachus and the Hellenistic Poets.* Ann Arbor, MI.

BINGEN, J. 1987. 'Aelius Aristides, OGIS 709 et les "Grecs d'Égypte"', in eds. J. SERVAIS, T. HACKENS, and B. SERVAIS-SOYEZ, *Stemmata: mélanges de philologie, d'histoire et d'archéologie grecques offerts à Jules Labarbe*, pp. 173–85. Louvain.

BINGEN, J. ed. 1996. *Pausanias Historien.* Geneva.

BINGEN, J. 2005. *Pages d'Épigraphie grecque II: Égypte (1983–2002).* Brussels.

BIRLEY, A. 1997. *Hadrian: The Restless Emperor.* London and New York.

BLANCK, H. 1969. *Wiederverwendung alter Statuen als Ehrendenkmäler bei Griechen und Römern*. Rome.

BLANSHARD, A. J. L. 2007. 'Alexander's Mythic Journey into India', in eds. H. PRAHBA RAY and D. T. POTTS, *Memory as History: The Legacy of Alexander in Asia*, pp. 28–39. New Delhi.

BLOOM, H. 1973. *The Anxiety of Influence: A Theory of Poetry*. Oxford.

BLOOM, H. 1994. *The Western Canon: The Books and School of Ages*. New York, NY.

BOATWRIGHT, M. T. 1993. 'The City Gate of Plancia Magna in Perge', in ed. E. D'AMBRA, *Roman Art in Context: An Anthology*, pp. 189–207. Englewood Cliffs, NJ.

BOATWRIGHT, M. T. 2000. *Hadrian and the Cities of the Roman Empire*. Princeton, NJ.

BODEL, J. 1997. 'Monumental Villas and Villa Monuments', *JRA* 10: 5–35.

BODEL, J. 2001. 'Epigraphy and the Ancient Historian', in ed. J. BODEL, *Epigraphic Evidence: Ancient History from Inscriptions*, pp. 1–56. London and New York.

BOEDER, M. 1996. *Visa est vox: Sprache und Bild in der Spätantiken Literatur*. Frankfurt.

BOL, R. 1984. *Das Statuenprogramm des Herodes-Atticus-Nymphäums. Olympische Forschungen* XV. Berlin.

BOL, R. 1998. 'Die Porträts des Herodes Atticus und seiner Tochter Athenais', *Antike Kunst* 41: 118–29.

BOMPAIRE, J. 1958. *Lucien écrivain: Imitation et création*. Paris.

BORG, B. E. 2004. 'Glamorous Intellectuals: Portraits of *Pepaideumenoi* in the Second and Third Centuries AD', in ed. B. E. BORG, *Paideia: The World of the Second Sophistic*, pp. 157–78. Berlin and Boston.

BÖRKER, C. and R. MERKELBACH with help from H. ENGELMANN and D. KNIBBE eds. 1979. *Die Inschriften von Ephesos*, Part II: Nr. 100–599 (Repertorium). Bonn.

BOSMAN, P. R. ed. 2019. *Intellectual and Empire in Greco-Roman Antiquity*. London and New York.

BOSWORTH, A. B. 1972. 'Arrian's Literary Development', *Classical Quarterly* 22.1: 163–85.

BOSWORTH, A. B. 1976. 'Arrian in Baetica', *Greek, Roman, and Byzantine Studies* 17.1: 55–64.

BOSWORTH, A. B. 1980. *A Historical Commentary on Arrian's History of Alexander Vol. 1*. Oxford.

BOSWORTH, A. B. 1988. *From Arrian to Alexander: Studies in Historical Interpretation*. Oxford.

BOSWORTH, A. B. 1993. 'Arrian and Rome: The Minor Works', *ANRW* II.34.1: 226–75.

BOSWORTH, A. B. 1995. *A Historical Commentary on Arrian's History of Alexander Vol. 2*. Oxford.

BOSWORTH, A. B. 2007. 'Arrian, Alexander, and the Pursuit of Glory', in ed. J. MARINCOLA, *A Companion to Greek and Roman Historiography*, pp. 447–53. Malden, MA and Oxford.

BOULET, B. 2014. 'The Philosopher-King', in ed. M. BECK, *A Companion to Plutarch*, pp. 449–62. Chichester.

BOWERSOCK, G. W. 1967. 'A New Inscription of Arrian', *Greek, Roman, and Byzantine Studies* 8.4: 279–80.

BIBLIOGRAPHY 313

BOWERSOCK, G. W. 1969. *Greek Sophists in the Roman Empire*. Oxford.

BOWERSOCK, G. W. 2002. 'Philosophy in the Second Sophistic', in eds. G. CLARK and T. RAJAK, *Philosophy and Power in the Graeco-Roman World*, pp. 157–70. Oxford.

BOWIE, E. L. 1974. 'Greeks and their Past in the Second Sophistic', in ed. M. I. FINLEY, *Studies in Ancient Society*, pp. 166–209. London.

BOWIE, E. L. 1982. 'The Importance of Sophists', *Yale Classical Studies* 27: 29–59.

BOWIE, E. L. 1994. 'Philostratus: Writer of Fiction', in eds. J. R. MORGAN and R. STONEMAN, *Greek Fiction: The Greek Novel in Context*, pp. 181–99. London.

BOWIE, E. L. 1996. 'Past and Present in Pausanias', in ed. J. BINGEN, *Pausanias Historien*, pp. 207–40. Geneva.

BOWIE, E. L. 2001. 'Inspiration and Aspiration: Date, Genre, and Readership', in eds. S. E. ALCOCK, J. F. CHERRY, and J. ELSNER, *Pausanias: Travel and Memory in Roman Greece*, pp. 21–32. Oxford.

BOWIE, E. L. 2004. 'The Geography of the Second Sophistic: Cultural Variations', in ed. B. E. BORG, *Paideia: The World of the Second Sophistic*, pp. 65–83. Berlin and Boston.

BOWIE, E. L. 2006. 'Portrait of the Sophist as a Young Man', in eds. B. McGING and J. MOSSMAN, *The Limits of Ancient Biography*, pp. 141–53. Swansea.

BOWIE, E. L. 2008. 'Literary Milieux', in ed. T. WHITMARSH, *The Cambridge Companion to the Greek and Roman Novel*, pp. 17–38. Cambridge.

BOWIE, E. L. 2009. 'Philostratus: The Life of a Sophist', in eds. E. BOWIE and J. ELSNER, *Philostratus*, pp. 19–32. Cambridge.

BOWIE, E. L. 2012. 'The Philotimia of Aristides', in eds. G. ROSKAM, M. DE POURCQ, and L. VAN DER STOCKT, *The Lash of Ambition: Plutarch, Imperial Greek Literature and the Dynamics of Philotimia*, pp. 229–51. Louvain.

BOWIE, E. L. 2013. 'Marathon in the Greek Culture of the Second Century AD', in eds. C. CAREY and M. EDWARDS, *Marathon—2500 Years. Proceedings of the Marathon Conference*, pp. 241–53. London.

BOWIE, E. L. 2015. 'Teachers and Students in Roman Athens', in eds. R. ASH, J. MOSSMAN, and F. B. TITCHENER, *Fame and Infamy: Essays for Christopher Pelling on Characterization in Greek and Roman Biography and Historiography*, pp. 239–54. Oxford.

BOWIE, E. L. 2016. 'Xenophon's Influence in Imperial Greece', in ed. M. A. FLOWER, *The Cambridge Companion to Xenophon*, pp. 403–15. Cambridge.

BOWIE, E. L. 2019. 'Marcus Aurelius, Greek Poets, and Greek Sophists: Friends or Foes', in ed. P. R. BOSMAN, *Intellectual and Empire in Greco-Roman Antiquity*, pp. 143–59. London and New York.

BOWMAN, A. K. and G. WOOLF eds. 1994. *Literacy and Power in the Ancient World*. Cambridge.

BOYD, M. J. 1957. 'Longinus, the "Philological Discourses", and the Essay "On the Sublime"', *Classical Quarterly* 7.1: 39–46.

BRANCACCI, A. 1986. 'Seconde Sophistique, Historiographie et Philosophie (Philostrate, Eunape, Synésios)', in ed. B. CASSIN *Le plaisir de parler: Études de sophistique comparée*, pp. 87–110. Paris.

BRANHAM, R. B. 1985. 'Introducing a Sophist: Lucian's Prologues', *TAPA* 115: 237–43.

BRANHAM, R. B. 1989. *Unruly Eloquence: Lucian and the Comedy of Traditions*. Cambridge, MA.

BRAUND, D. 1986. 'The Caucasian Frontier: Myth, Exploration and the Dynamics of Imperialism', in eds. P. FREEMAN and D. KENNEDY, *The Defence of the Roman and Byzantine East: Proceedings of a Colloquium Held at the University of Sheffield in April 1986 Part 1*, pp. 31–49. Oxford.

BRAUND, D. 1994. *Georgia in Antiquity: A History of Colchis and Transcaucasian Iberia 550 BC—AD 562*. Oxford.

BREITENBACH, A. 2003. 'Kritias und Herodes Attikos: Zwei Tyrannen in Philostrats Sophistenviten', *Wiener Studien* 116: 109–13.

BRIANT, P. 2002. *From Cyrus to Alexander*. Winona Lake.

BRILLIANT, R. 1963. *Gesture and Rank in Roman Art: The Use of Gestures to Denote Status in Roman Sculpture and Coinage*. New Haven, CT.

BRINK, C. O. 1972. 'Ennius and the Hellenistic Worship of Homer', *AJPhil* 93.4: 547–67.

BRIXHE, C. 1984. *Essai sur le grec anatolien au début de notre ère*. Lorraine.

BRONEER, O. 1971. *Isthmia: Excavations by the University of Chicago under the Auspices of the American School of Classical Studies at Athens* I: *Temple of Poseidon*. Princeton, NJ.

BROSIUS, M. 2003. 'Alexander and the Persians', in ed. J. ROISMAN, *Brill's Companion to Alexander the Great*, pp. 169–93. Leiden.

BROUN, H. 1924. *Sitting on the World*. New York, NY.

BROWN, P. 1978. *The Making of Late Antiquity*. Cambridge, MA.

BRUNT, P. A. ed. and trans. 1976. *Arrian Vol. 1: Anabasis of Alexander Vol. 1 (Books 1–4)*, LCL 236. Cambridge, MA.

BRUNT, P. A. ed. and trans. 1983. *Arrian Vol. 2: Anabasis of Alexander Vol. 2 (Books 5–7. Indica)*, LCL 269. Cambridge, MA.

BRUNT, P. A. 1994. 'The Bubble of the Second Sophistic', *Bulletin of the Institute of Classical Studies* 39: 25–52.

BURRELL, B. 2009. 'Reading, Hearing, and Looking at Ephesos', in eds. W. A. JOHNSON and H. N. PARKER, *Ancient Literacies: The Culture of Reading in Ancient Rome*, pp. 69–95. Oxford.

BUSSELS, S. 2012. *The Animated Image: Roman Theory on Naturalism, Vividness and Divine Power*. Leiden and Berlin.

BUTLER, S. 2015. *The Ancient Phonograph*. New York, NY.

BUTZ, P. A. 2015. 'The Stoichedon Arrangement of the New Marathon Stele from the Villa of Herodes Atticus at Kynouria', in eds. J. BODEL and N. DIMITROVA, *Ancient Documents and their Contexts: First North American Congress of Greek and Latin Epigraphy 2011*, pp. 82–97. Leiden and Boston.

CALAME, C. 1990. *Thésée et l'imaginaire Athénien: Légende et culte en Grèce antique*. Lausanne.

CALANDRA, E. 1996. *Oltre la Grecia: alle origini del filellenismo di Adriano*. Naples.

CALANDRA, E. and B. ADEMBRI eds. 2014. *Adriano e la Grecia: Villa Adriana tra classicità ed ellenismo. Studi e ricerche*. Milan.

CAMPANILE, M. D. 1999. 'La construzione del sofista: note sul βίος di Polemone', *Studie ellenistici* 12: 269–315.

CARLSEN, J. 2014. 'Greek History in a Roman Context: Arrian's *Anabasis of Alexander*', in eds. J. M. MADSEN and R. REES, *Roman Rule in Greek and Latin Writing: Double Vision*, pp. 210–23. Leiden and Boston.

CARROLL, M. 2011. '*Memoria* and *Damnatio Memoriae*: Preserving and Erasing Identities in Roman Funerary Commemoration', in eds. M. CARROLL and J. REMPEL, *Living through the Dead: Burial and Commemoration in the Classical World*, pp. 65–90. Oxford.

CASEVITZ, M. ed. 1992. *Pausanias: Description de la Grèce I*, traduit par J. Pouilloux, commenté par F. Chamoux. Paris.

CASEVITZ, M. ed. 1998. *Pausanias: Description de la Grèce VIII*, traduit et commenté par M. Jost. Paris.

CHAMPLIN, E. 2003. *Nero.* Cambridge, MA.

CHANDLER, R. 1776. *Travels in Greece: Or an Account of a Tour Made at the Expense of the Society of Dilettanti.* Oxford.

CHANIOTIS, A. 2012. 'Listening to Stones: Orality and Emotions in Ancient Inscriptions', in eds. J. DAVIES and J. WILKES, *Epigraphy and the Historical Sciences*, Proceedings of the British Academy 177, pp. 299–328. Oxford.

CHANIOTIS, A. 2018. 'Who Wants to Study Inscriptions? Greek Inscriptions in the Poetic Work of C. P. Cavafy', *Journal of Epigraphic Studies* 1: 11–26.

CHARITONIDIS, S. 1968. *Αι επιγραφαί της Λέσβου. Συμπλήρωμα.* Athens.

CHOAY, F. 2001. *The Invention of the Historic Monument*, translated by L. M. O'CONNELL. Cambridge.

CHUGG, A. 2002. 'The Sarcophagus of Alexander the Great', *Greece and Rome* 49.1: 8–26.

CIVILETTI, M. ed. 2002. *Filostrato: Vite dei Sofisti.* Milan.

CLARK, D. L. 1951. 'Imitation: Theory and Practice in Roman Rhetoric', *Quarterly Journal of Speech* 37.1: 11–22.

CLASSEN, C. J. 1995. 'Rhetoric and Literary Criticism: Their Nature and Their Functions in Antiquity', *Mnemosyne* 48.5: 513–35.

CLIFFORD, J. 1988. *The Predicament of Culture: Twentieth-Century Ethnography, Literature, and Art.* Cambridge, MA.

COHOON, J. W. ed. and trans. 1932. *Dio Chrysostom Vol. 1: Discourses 1–11*, LCL 257. Cambridge, MA.

COHOON, J. W. 1940. *Dio Chrysostom Vol. 3: Discourses 31–36*, LCL 358. Cambridge, MA.

COLE, M. 1993. 'Remembering the Future', in eds. G. A. MILLER and G. HARMAN, *Conceptions of the Human Mind: Essays in Honor of George A. Miller*, pp. 247–65. Hillsdale, NJ.

COLE, M. 2016. 'Remembering the Future', in eds. N. VAN DEUSEN and L. M. KOFF, *Time: Sense, Space, Structure*, pp. 375–87. Leiden and Boston.

COLSON, D. D. 1989. '*Crito* 51a-c: To What Does Socrates Owe Obedience?', *Phronesis* 34.1: 27–55.

CONNOLLY, J. 2001. 'Reclaiming the Theatrical in the Second Sophistic', *Helios* 28.1: 75–96.

CONNOLLY, J. 2008. 'Wife-Beating in Ancient Rome', *The Times Literary Supplement*, 9 November 2008.

CONNORS, C. 1994. 'Famous Last Words: Authorship and Death in the *Satyricon* and Neronian Rome', in eds. J. ELSNER and J. MASTERS, *Reflections of Nero: Culture, History, and Representation*, pp. 225–35. London.

BIBLIOGRAPHY

CONSTANTINE, D. 2011. *In the Footsteps of the Gods: Travellers to Greece and the Quest for the Hellenic Ideal*. London.

COOK, A. B. 1925. *Zeus: A Study in Ancient Religion, Volume 2.2*. Cambridge.

COOK, A. B. 1940. *Zeus: A Study in Ancient Religion, Volume 3.2*. Cambridge.

COOLEY, A. E. 2000. 'Inscribing History at Rome', in ed. A. E. COOLEY, *The Afterlife of Inscriptions: Reusing, Rediscovering, Reinventing and Revitalizing Ancient Inscription*, pp. 7–20. London.

COOLEY, A. E. ed. 2009. *Res Gestae Divi Augusti: Text, Translation, and Commentary*. Cambridge.

COOLEY, A. E. 2018. 'New Approaches to the Epigraphy of the Roman World', *Journal of Epigraphic Studies* 1: 27–46.

CORDOVANA, O. D. and M. GALLI eds. 2007. *Arte e memoria culturale nell'età della Seconda Sofistica*. Catania.

CORMACK, S. 2004. *The Space of Death in Roman Asia Minor*. Vienna.

COTÉ, D. 2010. 'Sophistique et pouvoir chez Philostrate', *Cahiers des études anciennes* [En ligne] 47: 475–502, URL: http://etudesanciennes.revues.org/157.

CRAWFORD, M. H. 1978. 'Greek Intellectuals and the Roman Aristocracy in the First Century BC', in eds. P. D. A. GARNSEY and C. R. WHITTAKER, *Imperialism in the Ancient World*, pp. 193–207. Cambridge.

CUEVA, E. P. and S. N. BYRNE eds. 2014. *A Companion to the Ancient Novel*. Chichester.

D'ANGOUR, A. 2011. *The Greeks and the New: Novelty in Ancient Greek Imagination and Experience*. Cambridge.

DANZIGER, K. 2008. *Marking the Mind: A History of Memory*. Cambridge.

DATSOULIS-STAVRIDIS, A. 1977. 'Συμβολή στην εικονογραφία του Πολυδεύκη', *Athens Annals of Archaeology* 10: 126–48.

DATSOULIS-STAVRIDIS, A. 1978. 'Συμβολὴ στην εἰκονογραφία τοῦ Ἡρώδη τοῦ Ἀττικου', *Athens Annals of Archaeology* 11: 214–32.

DATSOULIS-STAVRIDIS, A. 1985. *Ρωμαϊκά Πορτραίτα στο Εθνικό Αρχαιολογικό Μουσείο της Αθήνας*. Athens.

DAVIES, J. K. 2005. 'The Origins of the Inscribed Greek Stela', in eds. P. BIENKOWSKI, C. MEE, and E. A. SLATER, *Writing and Ancient Near Eastern Society: Papers in Honour of A. R. Millard*, pp. 283–300. New York, NY.

DAUX, G. 1962. 'Chronique des fouilles et découvertes archéologiques en Grèce en 1961', *BCH* 86.2: 629–975.

DAUX, G. 1963. 'Chronique des fouilles et découvertes archéologiques en Grèce en 1962', *BCH* 87.2: 689–879.

DAUX, G. and A. SALAĆ eds. 1932. *Fouilles de Delphes, III. Épigraphie*. Fasc. 3: *Inscriptions depuis le trésor des Athéniens jusqu'aux bases de Gélon*, Vol. 1. Paris.

DAY, J. W. 1989. 'Rituals in Stone: Early Greek Grave Epigrams and Monuments', *JHS* 109: 16–28.

DAY, J. W. 2000. 'Epigram and Reader: Generic Force as (Re-)Activation of Ritual', in eds. M. DEPEW and D. OBBINK, *Matrices of Genre: Authors, Canons, and Society*, pp. 37–57. Cambridge, MA.

DAY, J. W. 2007. 'Poems on Stone: The Inscribed Antecedents of Hellenistic Epigram', in eds. P. BING and J. S. BRUSS, *Brill's Companion to Hellenistic Epigram: Down to Philip*, pp. 29–47. Leiden.

DAY, J. W. 2010. *Archaic Greek Epigram and Dedication: Representation and Reperformance*. Cambridge.

DE ARNIM, J. ed. 1893. *Dionis Prusaensis quem vocat Chrysostomum Quae Extant Omnia I*. Berlin.

DE ARNIM, J. ed. 1896. *Dionis Prusaensis quem vocat Chrysostomum Quae Extant Omnia II*. Berlin.

DE LANNOY, L. ed. 1977. *Flavius Philostratus: Heroicus*. Leipzig.

DERDERIAN, K. 2001. *Leaving Words to Remember: Greek Mourning and the Advent of Literacy*. Leiden.

DE ROMILLY, J. ed. 1953. *Thucydide: La Guerre du Péloponnèse I*. Paris.

DERRIDA, J. 1981. *Dissemination*, translated by B. JOHNSON. King's Lynn.

DESTRÉE, P. and P. MURRAY. 2015. 'Introduction', in eds. P. DESTRÉE and P. MURRAY, *A Companion to Ancient Aesthetics*, pp. 1–12. Hoboken, NJ.

DE TEMMERMAN, K. ed. 2020. *The Oxford Handbook of Ancient Biography*. Oxford.

DEVINE, A. M. 1993. 'Arrian's "Tactica"', *ANRW* II.34.1: 312–37.

DEVOTO, J. G. ed. 1993. *Flavius Arrianus: Τέχνη Τακτικά and Ἔκταξις κατὰ Ἀλανῶν*. Chicago, IL.

DICKENSON, C. P. 2017. *On the Agora: The Evolution of Public Space in Hellenistic and Roman Greece (c.323 BC to 267 AD)*. Leiden and Boston.

DICKENSON, C. P. and O. M. VAN NIJF. 2013. 'Introduction', in eds. C. P. DICKENSON and O. M. VAN NIJF, *Public Space in the Post-Classical City: Proceedings of a One Day Colloquium Held at Fransum 23rd July 2007*, pp. xi–xxi. Leuven.

DILLON, S. 1996. 'The Portraits of a Civic Benefactor of 2nd-C. Ephesos', *JRA* 9: 261–74.

DI NAPOLI, V. 2016. 'Looking at the Classical Past: Tradition, Identity, and Copies of Nobilia Opera in Roman Greece', in eds. S. E. ALCOCK, M. EGRI, and J. F. D. FRAKES, *Beyond Boundaries: Connecting Visual Cultures in the Provinces of Ancient Rome*, pp. 307–25. Los Angeles, CA.

DITTENBERGER, W. and K. PURGOLD eds. 1896. *Die Inschriften von Olympia*. Berlin.

DOBROV, G. W. 2002. 'The Sophist on his Craft: Art, Text, and Self-Construction in Lucian', *Helios* 29: 173–94.

DODWELL, E. 1819. *A Classical and Topographical Tour through Greece: During the Years 1801, 1805, and 1806*, Vol. 2. London.

DOWNIE, J. 2008. 'Proper Pleasures: Bathing and Oratory in Aelius Aristides' *Hieros Logos* I and *Oration* 33', in eds. W. V. HARRIS and B. HOLMES, *Aelius Aristides between Greece, Rome, and the Gods*, pp. 115–30. Leiden.

DOWNIE, J. 2013. *At the Limits of Art: A Literary Study of Aelius Aristides' Hieroi Logoi*. Oxford.

DUBEL, S. 1994. 'Dialogue and Autoportrait: Les Masques de Lucien', in ed. A. BILLAULT, *Lucien de Samosate: Actes du colloque international de Lyon organisé au Centre d'Études Romaines et Gallo-Romaines (les 30 septembre–1ᵉʳ octobre 1993)*, pp. 19–26. Lyon.

DUFF, T. 1999. 'Plutarch, Plato and "Great Natures"', in eds. A. PÉREZ JIMÉNEZ, J. GARCÍA LÓPEZ, and R. M. AGUILAR, *Plutarco, Platón y Aristóteles (Actas del V Congreso Internacional de la I.P.S. Madrid-Cuenca, 4–7 de Mayo de 1999)*, pp. 313–32. Madrid.

EASTMOND, A. 2015. 'Introduction: Viewing Inscriptions', in ed. A. EASTMOND, *Viewing Inscriptions in the Late Antique and Medieval World*, pp. 1–9. Cambridge.

ECK, W. 1984. 'Senatorial Self-Representation: Developments in the Augustan Period', in eds. F. MILLAR and E. SEGAL, *Caesar Augustus: Seven Aspects*, pp. 129–67. Oxford.

EICHLER, F. 1969. 'Ephesos: Grabungsbericht 1968', *Anzeiger: Österreichische Akademie der Wissenschaften, Wien, Philologisch-historische Klasse* 106: 131–46.

EIDSON, D. 2013. 'The Celsus Library at Ephesus: Spatial Rhetoric, Literacy, and Hegemony in the Eastern Roman Empire', *Advances in the History of Rhetoric* 16.2: 189–217.

ELIOT, T. S. 1932a. 'Tradition and the Individual Talent', in *Selected Essays*, pp. 13–22. New York, NY.

ELIOT, T. S. 1932b. 'The Function of Criticism', in *Selected Essays*, pp. 23–34. New York, NY.

ELIOT, T. S. 1932c. 'A Commentary', *Criterion* 12: 73–9.

ELIOT, T. S. 1945. *What is a Classic?* London.

ELSNER, J. 1992. 'Pausanias: A Greek Pilgrim in the Roman World', *Past and Present* 135: 3–29.

ELSNER, J. 1994a. 'Constructing Decadence: The Representation of Nero as Imperial Builder', in eds. J. ELSNER and J. MASTERS, *Reflections of Nero: Culture, History, and Representation*, pp.112–27. London.

ELSNER, J. 1994b. 'From the Pyramids to Pausanias and Piglet: Monuments, Travel, and Writing', in eds. S. GOLDHILL and R. OSBORNE, *Art and Text in Ancient Greek Culture*, pp. 224–54. Cambridge.

ELSNER, J. 1995. *Art and the Roman Viewer*. Cambridge.

ELSNER, J. 1996. 'Inventing Imperium: Texts and the Propaganda of Monuments in Augustan Rome', in ed. J. ELSNER, *Art and Text in Roman Culture*, pp. 32–53. Cambridge.

ELSNER, J. 1997. 'Hagiographic Geography: Travel and Allegory in the Life of Apollonius of Tyana', *JHS* 117: 22–37.

ELSNER, J. 1998. *Imperial Rome and the Christian Triumph*. Oxford.

ELSNER, J. 2001a. 'Describing Self in the Language of the Other: Pseudo (?) Lucian at the Temple of Hierapolis', in ed. S. GOLDHILL, *Being Greek under Rome: Cultural Identity, the Second Sophistic and the Development of Empire*, pp. 123–53. Cambridge.

ELSNER, J. 2001b. 'Structuring "Greece": Pausanias's *Periegesis* as a Literary Construct', in eds. S. E. ALCOCK, J. F. CHERRY, and J. ELSNER, *Pausanias: Travel and Memory in Roman Greece*, pp. 3–20. Oxford.

ELSNER, J. 2003. 'Iconoclasm and the Preservation of Memory', in eds. R. S. NELSON and M. OLIN, *Monuments and Memory, Made and Unmade*, pp. 209–31. Chicago, IL.

ELSNER, J. 2006. 'Classicism in Roman Art', in ed. J. I. PORTER, *Classical Pasts: The Classical Traditions of Greece and Rome*, pp. 270–97. Princeton, NJ.

ELSNER, J. 2007a. *Roman Eyes: Visuality and Subjectivity in Art and Text*. Princeton, NJ.

ELSNER, J. 2007b. 'Prologue', in *Roman Eyes: Visuality and Subjectivity in Art and Text*, xi–xvii. Princeton, NJ.

ELSNER, J. 2007c. 'Between Mimesis and Divine Power: Visuality in the Greco-Roman World', in *Roman Eyes: Visuality and Subjectivity in Art and Text*, pp. 1–26. Princeton, NJ.

ELSNER, J. 2007d. 'Image and Ritual: Pausanias and the Sacred Culture of Greek Art', in *Roman Eyes: Visuality and Subjectivity in Art and Text*, pp. 29–48. Princeton, NJ.

ELSNER, J. 2007e. 'Discourses of Style: Connoisseurship in Pausanias and Lucian', in *Roman Eyes: Visuality and Subjectivity in Art and Text*, pp. 49–66. Princeton, NJ.

ELSNER, J. 2009. 'A Protean Corpus', in eds. E. BOWIE and J. ELSNER, *Philostratus*, pp. 3–18. Cambridge.

ELSNER, J. 2014. 'Introduction', in eds. J. ELSNER and M. MEYER, *Art and Rhetoric in Roman Culture*, pp. 1–34. Cambridge.

ELSNER, J. and M. MEYER eds. 2014. *Art and Rhetoric in Roman Culture*. Cambridge.

ENGELMANN, H. 1993. 'Celsus Bibliothek und Auditorium', *Jahreshefte des Österreichischen Archäologischen Institutes in Wien* 62: 105–11.

ENGELMANN, H. 1995. 'Philostrat und Ephesos', *ZPE* 108: 77–87.

ENGELMANN, H., D. KNIBBE, and R. MERKELBACH eds. 1980. *Die Inschriften von Ephesos*, Part III: Nr. 600–1000 (Repertorium). Bonn.

ERLL, A. 2010. 'Cultural Memory Studies: An Introduction', in eds. A. ERLL, A. NÜNNING, and S. YOUNG, *A Companion to Cultural Memory Studies*, pp. 1–15. Berlin and New York.

ERLL, A. 2011. *Memory in Culture*, translated by S. B. YOUNG. Houndmills.

ERSKINE, A. 2001. *Troy between Greece and Rome: Local Tradition and Imperial Power*. Oxford.

ERSKINE, A. 2002. 'Life after Death: Alexandria and the Body of Alexander', *Greece and Rome* 49.2: 163–79.

ESHLEMAN, K. 2008. 'Defining the Circle of the Sophists: Philostratus and the Construction of the Second Sophistic', *Classical Philology* 103.4: 395–413.

ESHLEMAN, K. 2012. *The Social World of Intellectuals in the Roman Empire: Sophists, Philosophers, Christians*. Cambridge.

ESPINOSA RUIZ, U. 1987. 'El problema de la historicidad en el debate Agripa-Mecenas de Dion Cassio', *Gerion* 5: 289–316.

EVANGELIDIS, V. 2014. 'Agoras and Fora: Developments in the Central Public Space of the Cities of Greece during the Roman Period', *Annual of the British School at Athens* 109: 335–56.

EWEGEN, S. M. 2014. *Plato's* Cratylus: *The Comedy of Language*. Bloomington.

FARAONE, C. A. 1992. *Talismans and Trojan Horses: Guardian Statues in Ancient Greek Myth and Ritual*. Oxford.

FEENEY, D. 1995. 'Criticism Ancient and Modern', in eds. D. INNES, H. HINE, and C. PELLING, *Ethics and Rhetoric: Classical Essays for Donald Russell on his Seventy-Fifth Birthday*, pp. 301–12. Oxford.

FEENEY, D. 2007. *Caesar's Calendar*. Berkeley and Los Angeles, CA.

FEIN, S. 1994. *Die Bezeihungen der Kaiser Trajan und Hadrian zu den Litterati*. Stuttgart.

320 BIBLIOGRAPHY

FERGUSON, J. 1975. *Utopias of the Classical World*. London.

FERRILL, A. 1978. 'Herodotus on Tyranny', *Historia* 27.3: 385–98.

FIELDS, D. 2008. 'Aristides and Plutarch on Self-Praise', in eds. W. V. HARRIS and B. HOLMES, *Aelius Aristides between Greece, Rome, and the Gods*, pp. 149–72. Leiden.

FIELDS, D. 2013. 'The Reflections of Satire: Lucian and Peregrinus', *TAPA* 143.1: 213–45.

FITTSCHEN, K. 2021. *Privatporträts mit Repliken: zur Sozialgeschichte römischer Bildnisse der mittleren Kaiserzeit*. Wiesbaden.

FLACELIÈRE, R. ed. 1974. *Plutarque: Oeuvres Morales VI*. Paris.

FLINTERMAN, J.-J. 1995. *Power,* Paideia *and Pythagoreanism: Greek Identity, Conceptions of the Relationship between Philosophers and Monarchs and Political Ideas in Philostratus'* Life of Apollonius. Amsterdam.

FLINTERMAN, J.-J. 2004. 'Sophists and Emperors: A Reconnaissance of Sophistic Attitudes', in ed. B. E. BORG, *Paideia: The World of the Second Sophistic*, pp. 359–76. Berlin and Boston.

FLOWER, H. I. 2006. *The Art of Forgetting: Disgrace and Oblivion in Roman Political Culture*. Chapel Hill, NC.

FOCCARDI, D. 1987. 'Religious Silence and Reticence in Pausanias', in ed. M. CIANI, *The Regions of Silence. Studies in the Difficulty of Communicating*, pp. 67–113. Amsterdam.

FOLLET, S. 1977. 'La datation de l'archonte Dionysius (*IG* II² 3968): ses conséquences archéologiques, littéraires et épigraphiques', *Revue des études grecques* 90: 47–54.

FOLLET, S. 1979. 'Lettre de Marc-Aurèle aux Athéniens (EM 13366): Nouvelles lectures et interprétations', *Revue de Philologie* 53: 29–43.

FORD, A. 1992. *Homer: The Poetry of the Past*. Ithaca, NY.

FOULON, E. ed. 1995. *Polybe: Histoires Livres XIII–XVI*, traduit par R. Weil. Paris.

FOWLER, D. P. 1991. 'Narrate and Describe: The Problem of Ekphrasis', *JRS* 81.1: 25–35.

FOWLER, D. P. 2000. *Roman Constructions: Readings in Postmodern Latin*. Oxford.

FRANCIS, J. A. 2003. 'Living Icons: Tracing a Motif in Verbal and Visual Representation from the Second to Fourth Centuries C.E.', *AJPhil* 124.4: 575–600.

FRASER, P. M. 1972. *Ptolemaic Alexandria: Volume 2*. Oxford.

FRAZIER, F. and C. FROIDEFOND eds. 1990. *Plutarque: Oeuvres Morales V.1*. Paris.

FREEDBERG, D. 1989. *The Power of Images: Studies in the History of Theory and Response*. Chicago, IL.

GAIFMAN, M. 2006. 'Statue, Cult and Reproduction', in eds. J. TRIMBLE and J. ELSNER, *Art and Replication: Greece, Rome, and Beyond. Art History* (Special Issue) 29.2: 258–79.

GALINSKY, K. ed. 2014. *Memoria Romana: Memory in Rome and Rome in Memory*. Ann Arbor, MI.

GALINSKY, K. 2015. 'Introduction', in eds. K. GALINSKY and K. LAPATIN, *Cultural Memories in the Roman Empire*, pp. 1–22. Los Angeles, CA.

GALINSKY, K. ed. 2016. *Memory in Ancient Rome and Early Christianity*. Oxford.

GALLI, M. 2002. *Die Lebenswelt eines Sophisten: Untersuchungen zu den Bauten und Stiftungen des Herodes Atticus*. Mainz am Rhein.

GALLI, M. 2007. '*Et Graeci quidem eum consecraverunt*: la creazione del mito di Antinoo', in eds. O. D. CORDOVANA and M. GALLI, *Arte e memoria culturale nell'età della Seconda Sofistica*, pp. 189–210. Catania.

GARCIA JR, L. F. 2013. *Homeric Durability: Telling Time in the Iliad*, Centre for Hellenic Studies Series 58. Washington, DC. http://nrs.harvard.edu/urn-3:hul.ebook:CHS_GarciaL.Homeric_Durability_Telling_Time_in_the_Iliad.2013.

GARDNER, A. 1961. 'The Egyptian Memnon', *Journal of Egyptian Archaeology* 47: 91–9.

GASPARRI, C. 1974–75. 'Lo Stadio Panatenaico', *Annuario della Scuola archeologica di Atene e delle Missioni italiane in Oriente* 52–53: 313–92.

GAZDA, E. K. 1977. *Roman Portraiture: Ancient and Modern Revivals*. Ann Arbor, MI.

GAZDA, E. K. 1980. 'A Portrait of Polydeukion', *Bulletin of the Museum of Art and Archaeology* 3: 1–13.

GAZDA, E. K. 2002. 'Beyond Copying: Artistic Originality and Tradition', in ed. E. K. GAZDA, *The Ancient Art of Emulation: Studies in Artistic Originality and Tradition from the Present to Classical Antiquity*, pp. 1–24. Ann Arbor, MI.

GEAGAN, D. J. 1964. 'A New Herodes Epigram from Marathon', *Mitteilungen des Deutschen Archäologischen Instituts Athenische Abteilung* 79: 149–56.

GEIGER, J. 1985. *Cornelius Nepos and Ancient Political Biography*. Stuttgart.

GEIGER, J. 2014. 'The Project of the *Parallel Lives*: Plutarch's Conception of Biography', in ed. M. BECK, *A Companion to Plutarch*, pp. 292–303. Malden, MA, Oxford, Chichester.

GEORGIADOU, A. and D. H. J. LARMOUR eds. 1998. *Lucian's Science Fiction Novel, True Histories: Interpretation and Commentary*. Leiden.

GERGEL, R. A. 2004. 'Agora S 166 and Related Works: The Iconography, Typology, and Interpretation of the Eastern Hadrianic Breastplate Type', *Hesperia Supplements* 33: 371–409.

GLEASON, M. W. 1995. *Making Men: Sophists and Self-Presentation in Ancient Rome*. Princeton, NJ.

GLEASON, M. 2010. 'Making Space for Bicultural Identity: Herodes Atticus Commemorates Regilla', in ed. T. WHITMARSH, *Local Knowledge and Microidentities in the Imperial Greek World*, pp. 125–62. Cambridge.

GOETTE, H. R. 1991. 'Attische Klienen-Riefel-Sarkophage', *Mitteilungen des Deutschen Archäologischen Instituts Athenische Abteilung* 106: 309–38.

GOETTE, H. R. 2001. 'Heroenreliefs von Herodes Atticus für seine Trophimoi', in ed. D. PENDIMELIS, *ΑΓΑΛΜΑ: μελέτες για την αρχαία πλαστική προς τιμήν του Γιώργου Δεσπίνη*, pp. 419–27. Thessaloniki.

GOETTE, H. R. 2019. 'The Portraits of Herodes Atticus', in ed. O. PALAGIA, *The Handbook of Greek Sculpture*, pp. 225–58. Berlin.

GOLDHILL, S. 2000. 'Viewing and the Viewer: Empire and the Culture of Spectacle', in ed. T. SIEBERS, *The Body Aesthetic: From Fine Art to Body Modification*, pp. 44–51. Ann Arbor, MI.

GOLDHILL, S. 2001. 'The Erotic Eye: Visual Stimulation and Cultural Conflict', in ed. S. GOLDHILL, *Being Greek under Rome: Cultural Identity, the Second Sophistic, and the Development of Empire*, pp. 154–94. Cambridge.

GOLDHILL, S. 2002. *Who Needs Greek? Contests in the Cultural History of Hellenism*. Cambridge.

GOLDSCHMIDT, N. and B. GRAZIOSI eds. 2018. *Tombs of the Ancient Poets: Between Literary Reception and Material Culture*. Oxford.

322 BIBLIOGRAPHY

GORAK, J. 1991. *The Making of the Modern Canon: Genesis and Crisis of a Literary Idea*. London.

GOUŠCHIN, V. 1999. 'Athenian Synoikism of the Fifth Century B.C., or Two Stories of Theseus', *Greece and Rome* 46.2: 168–87.

GRAHAM, A. S. 2013. 'The Word is Not Enough: A New Approach to Assessing Monumental Inscriptions. A Case Study from Roman Ephesus', *AJArch* 117: 383–412.

GRAINDOR, P. 1912. 'Un Épisode de la vie d'Hérode Atticus', *Musée belge* 16: 69–90.

GRAINDOR, P. 1914. 'Inscriptions attiques d'époque impériale', *BCH* 38: 351–443.

GRAINDOR, P. 1915a. 'Les cosmètes du Musée d'Athènes', *BCH* 39: 241–401.

GRAINDOR, P. 1915b. 'Tête du Nègre du Musée de Berlin', *BCH* 39: 402–12.

GRAINDOR, P. 1930. *Un milliardaire antique: Hérode Atticus et sa famille*. Cairo.

GREEN, R. P. H. ed. 1999. *Decimi Magni Ausonii Opera*. Oxford.

GREENSMITH, E. 2020. *The Resurrection of Homer in Imperial Greek Epic: Quintus of Smyrnaeus'* Posthomerica *and the Poetics of Impersonation*. Cambridge.

GREENWOOD, E. 2006. *Thucydides and the Shaping of History*. London.

GROSS, K. 1992. *The Dream of the Moving Statue*. Ithaca and London.

GROSSARDT, P. 2008. 'How to Become a Poet? Homer and Apollonius Visit the Mound of Achilles', in eds. K. DEMOEN and D. PRAET, *Theios Sophistes: Essays on Flavius Philostratus'* Vita Apollonii, pp. 75–94. Boston, MA.

GRUBE, G. M. A. 1957. 'Notes on the Περὶ Ὕψους', *AJPhil* 78.4: 355–74.

GRUBE, G. M. A. 1965. *The Greek and Roman Critics*. London.

GSELL, S. 1922. *Inscriptiones latines de l'Algérie*. Paris.

GUARDUCCI, M. 1978. *Epigrafia Greca* Vol. IV. Rome.

GUAST, W. 2016. 'Greek Declamation in Context'. Unpublished DPhil Thesis. University of Oxford.

GUERLAC, S. 1985. 'Longinus and the Subject of the Sublime', *New Literary History* 16.2: 275–89.

GYGAX, M. D. 2016. *Benefaction and Rewards in the Ancient Greek City: The Origins of Euergetism*. Cambridge.

HABICHT, C. 1969. *Die Inschriften des Asklepieions*. Berlin.

HABICHT, C. 1985. *Pausanias' Guide to Ancient Greece*, Sather Classical Lectures 50. Berkeley and Los Angeles, CA.

HÄGG, T. 2012. *The Art of Biography in Antiquity*. Cambridge.

HÄGG, T. and P. ROUSSEAU 2000. 'Introduction', in eds. T. HÄGG and P. ROUSSEAU, *Greek Biography and Panegyric in Late Antiquity*, pp. 1–28. Berkeley and Los Angeles, CA.

HALBWACHS, M. 1980. *The Collective Memory*, translated by F. J. DITTER and V. Y. DITTER. New York, NY.

HALBWACHS, M. 1992. *On Collective Memory*, edited, translated, and with an introduction by L. A. COSER. Chicago, IL.

HALFMANN, H. 1979. *Die Senatoren aus dem östlichen Teil des Imperium Romanum: bis zum Ende des 2. Jahrhunderts n. Chr.* Göttingen.

HALL, E. 2017. 'Sublime to the Ridiculous', *The Times Literary Supplement*, 6 January 2017.

HALLETT, C. H. 2005. 'Emulation versus Replication: Redefining Roman Copying', *JRA* 18: 419–35.

HANINK, J. 2014. *Lycurgan Athens and the Making of Classical Tragedy*. Cambridge.

HANSEN, W. 2003. 'Strategies of Authentication in Ancient Popular Literature', in eds. S. PANAYOTAKIS, M. ZIMMERMAN, and W. H. KEULEN, *The Ancient Novel and Beyond*, pp. 301–14. Leiden.

HARMON, A. M. ed. and trans. 1913. *Lucian Vol. 1*, LCL 14. Cambridge, MA.

HARRIS, W. V. 1989. *Ancient Literacy*. Cambridge, MA.

HARRISON, E. B. 1990. 'Repair, Reuse, and Reworking of Ancient Sculpture', in eds. M. TRUE and J. PODAMY, *Marble: Art Historical and Scientific Perspectives on Ancient Sculpture*, pp. 163–85. Malibu.

HARRISON, S. J. 2000. *Apuleius: A Latin Sophist*. Oxford.

HARRISON, S. J. 2001. 'General Introduction: Life and Writings of Apuleius', in ed. S. HARRISON, *Apuleius: Rhetorical Works*, translated and annotated by S. HARRISON, J. HILTON, and V. HUNINK, pp. 1–10. Oxford.

HEATH, M. 1999. 'Longinus, *On Sublimity*', *Proceedings of the Cambridge Philological Society* 45: 43–74.

HEKLER, A. 1940. 'Philosophen- und Gelehrtenbildnisse der mittleren Kaiserzeit: Beiträge zur Antiken Bildungsgeschichte', *Die Antike* 16: 115–41.

HELBIG, W. 1886. 'Über die Bildnisse des Platon', *Jahrbuch des Deutschen Archäologischen Instituts* 1: 71–8.

HELM, R. ed. 1959. *Apuleius II.2: Florida*. Leipzig.

HENDERSON, J. 2002. *Pliny's Statue: The Letters, Self-Portraiture, and Classical Art*. Exeter.

HERBERT, F. 1965. *Dune*. London.

HERTZ, N. 1983. 'A Reading of Longinus', *Critical Inquiry* 9.3: 579–96.

HERZFELD, E. 1901. 'Pasargadae', *Klio* 8: 36–43.

HIGBIE, C. 2017. *Collectors, Scholars, and Forgers in the Ancient World: Object Lessons*. Oxford.

HILTON, J. 2001. 'Apuleius *Florida*: Introduction and Translation', in ed. S. J. HARRISON *Apuleius: Rhetorical Works*, translated and annotated by S. HARRISON, J. HILTON, and V. HUNINK, pp. 123–76. Oxford.

HINCK, H. ed. 1873. *Polemonis Declamationes: Quae Supersunt Duae*. Leipzig.

HIRST, A. ed. 2007. *C. P. Cavafy: The Collected Poems*. Oxford.

HOGAN, P. P. 2017. '*Pausanias Politicus*: Reflections on Theseus, Themistocles, and Athenian Democracy in Book 1 of the *Periegesis*', *Classical World* 110.2: 187–210.

HOLFORD-STREVENS, L. 1997. 'Favorinus: The Man of Paradoxes', in eds. J. BARNES and M. GRIFFIN, *Philosophia Togata II: Plato and Aristotle at Rome*, pp. 189–217. Oxford.

HÖLSCHER, T. 2004. *The Language of Images in Roman Art*. Cambridge.

HOLZBERG, N. 1996. 'Novel-like Works of Extended Prose Fiction II', in ed. G. SCHMELING, *The Novel in the Ancient World*, pp. 621–53. Leiden.

HOOPER-GREENHILL, E. 2000. *Museums and the Interpretation of Visual Culture*. London and New York.

HOPKINS, K. 1974. 'Elite Mobility in the Roman Empire', in ed. M. I. FINLEY, *Studies in Ancient Society*, pp. 103–20. London.

HØJTE, J. M. 2002. 'Cultural Interchange? The Case of Honorary Statues in Greece', in ed. E. N. OSTENFELD, with the assistance of K. BLOMQUIST and L. NEVETT, *Greek Romans and Roman Greeks: Studies in Cultural Interaction*, pp. 53–63. Copenhagen.

HUDE, C. ed. 1927a. *Herodoti Historiae I*. Oxford.

HUDE, C. ed. 1927b. *Herodoti Historiae II*. Oxford.

HUDE, C. ed. 1972. *Xenophon: Expeditio Cyri*, editionem correctiorem curavit J. Peters. Leipzig.

HUMBLE, N. and K. SIDWELL 2006. 'Dreams of Glory: Lucian as Autobiographer', in eds. B. McGING and J. MOSSMAN, *The Limits of Ancient Biography*, pp. 213–25. Swansea.

HUMPHREY, J. H. ed. 1991. *Literacy in the Ancient World*, JRA Supplementary Series 3. Ann Arbor, MI.

HUNINK, V. ed. 2001. *Apuleius of Madauros: Florida*. Amsterdam.

HUTTON, W. 2005. *Describing Greece: Landscape and Literature in the Periegesis of Pausanias*. Cambridge.

HUTTON, W. 2010. 'Pausanias and the Mysteries of Hellas', *TAPA* 140: 423–59.

HUTTON, W. 2017. 'Pausanias', in eds. W. A. JOHNSON and D. S. RICHTER, *The Oxford Handbook of the Second Sophistic*, pp. 357–70. Oxford.

INNES, D. C. 1995a. 'Longinus: Structure and Unity', in eds. J. G. J. ABBENES, S. R. SLINGS, and I. SLUITER, *Greek Literary Theory after Aristotle: A Collection of Papers in Honour of D. M. Schenkeveld*, pp. 111–24. Amsterdam.

INNES, D. C. 1995b. 'Longinus, Sublimity, and the Low Emotions', in eds. D. INNES, H. HINE, and C. PELLING, *Ethics and Rhetoric: Classical Essays for Donald Russell on his Seventy-Fifth Birthday*, pp. 323–33. Oxford.

INNES, D. C. 2002. 'Longinus and Caecilius: Models of the Sublime', *Mnemosyne* 55: 259–84.

JACKSON, C. R. 2017. 'Dio Chrysostom', in eds. W. A. JOHNSON and D. S. RICHTER, *The Oxford Handbook of the Second Sophistic*, pp. 217–32. Oxford.

JACQUEMIN, A. 1991. 'Delphes au IIe siècle après J.-C.: un lieu de la mémoire grecque', in ed. S. SAÏD, *ΈΛΛΗΝΙΣΜΟΣ: Quelques Jalons pour une Histoire de L'Identité Grecque. Actes du colloque de Strasbourg 25–27 Octobre 1989*, pp. 217–31. Leiden.

JACOBY, F. 1923. 'Onesikritos von Astypalaia (134)', in ed. F. JACOBY, *Die Fragmente der Griechischen Historiker Part I–III*. Berlin.

JAMES, L. 1996. '"Pray Not to Fall into Temptation and Be on Your Guard": Pagan Statues in Christian Constantinople', *Gesta* 35.1: 12–20.

JANKO, R. 2014. 'The New Epitaph for the Fallen at Marathon', *ZPE* 190: 11–12.

JANSEN, K. 2006. 'Herodes Atticus und seine Trophimoi', unpublished doctoral dissertation. Münster.

JAŻDŻEWSKA, K. 2019. 'Entertainers, Persuaders, Adversaries: Interactions of Sophists and Rulers in Philostratus' *Lives of the Sophists*', in ed. P. R. BOSMAN, *Intellectual and Empire in Greco-Roman Antiquity*, pp. 160–77. London and New York.

JOHNSON, F. 1931. *Corinth IX. Sculpture 1896–1923*. Cambridge, MA.

JOHNSON, W. A. and H. N. PARKER eds. 2009. *Ancient Literacies: The Culture of Reading in Greece and Rome*. Oxford.

JOHNSON, W. A. and D. S. RICHTER eds. 2017. *The Oxford Handbook of the Second Sophistic*. Oxford.

JOHNSTON, S. I. 1991. "Crossroads." *ZP* 88: 217–24.

JOLOWICZ, D. 2021. *Latin Poetry in the Ancient Greek Novels*. Oxford.

JONES, C. P. 1971. 'A New Letter of Marcus Aurelius to the Athenians', *ZPE* 8: 161–83.

JONES, C. P. 1974. 'The Reliability of Philostratus', in ed. G. W. BOWERSOCK, *Approaches to the Second Sophistic*, pp. 11–16. University Park, PA.

JONES, C. P. 1978. 'Three Foreigners in Attica', *Phoenix* 32.3: 222–34.

JONES, C. P. 1996. 'The Panhellenion', *Chiron* 26: 29–56.

JONES, C. P. ed. and trans. 2005a. *Philostratus: Apollonius of Tyana Vol. I (Books 1–4)*, LCL 16. Cambridge, MA.

JONES, C. P. ed. and trans. 2005b. *Philostratus: Apollonius of Tyana Vol. II (Books 5–6)*, LCL 17. Cambridge, MA.

JONES, C. P. 2010. *New Heroes in Antiquity: From Achilles to Antinoos*. Cambridge, MA.

JONES, C. P. 2014. 'Apuleius, Corinth, and Two Epigrams from Nemea', *ZPE* 192: 115–20.

JUNG, M. 2006. *Marathon und Plataiai: Zwei Perserschlachten als 'lieux de mémoire' im antiken Griechenland*. Göttingen.

JUNG, M. 2013. 'Marathon and the Construction of the Persian Wars in Antiquity and Modern Times. Part I: Antiquity', in eds. C. CAREY and M. EDWARDS, *Marathon—2,500 Years: Proceedings of the Marathon Conference 2010*, pp. 255–66. London.

KAHANE, A. 2011. 'Image, Word, and the Antiquity of Ruins', *European Revue of History: Revue europeenne d'histoire* 18.5–6: 829–50.

KALINOWSKI, A. 2021. *Memory, Family, and Community in Roman Ephesos*. Cambridge.

KALTSAS, N. 2002. *Sculpture in the National Archaeological Museum Athens*, trans. by D. HARDY. Los Angeles, CA.

KAPETANOPOULOS, E. A. 1989. 'Polydeukion and the Archon Dionysios', *Horos* 7: 35–40.

KARANASTASI, P. 2019. 'Ἕνα νέο πορτρέτο του Ἀντινόου ἀπό το ιερό της Νεμέσεως στον Ραμνοῦντα', in eds. H. R. GOETTE and I. LEVENTI, *ΑΡΙΣΤΕΙΑ. ΜΕΛΕΤΕΣ ΠΡΟΣ ΤΙΜΗΝ ΤΗΣ ΟΛΓΑΣ ΠΑΛΑΓΓΙΑ/Excellence. Studies in Honour Of Olga Palagia*, pp. 289–300. Rahden/Westf.

KARIVIERI, A. 2002. 'Just One of the Boys: Hadrian in the Company of Zeus, Dionysus, and Theseus', in ed. E. N. OSTENFELD, *Greek Romans and Roman Greeks: Studies in Cultural Interaction*, pp. 40–54. Aarhus.

KARUSU, S. 1969. 'Die Antiken vom Kloster Luku in der Thyreatis', *Mitteilungen des Deutschen Archäologischen Instituts, Römische Abteilung* 76: 253–65.

KASSEL, R. 1983. 'Dialoge mit Statuen', *ZPE* 51: 1–12.

KASSEL, R. and C. AUSTIN eds. 1989. *Poetae Comici Graeci Volume VII: Menecrates—Xenophon*. Berlin.

KASTORXIS, E. 1882. 'Ἡρώδου Ἀττικοῦ Ἐπιγραφὴ ἐν Μαραθῶνα', *Ἀθήναιον* 10: 538–41.

KAYSER, C. L. ed. 1870. *Flavii Philostrati Opera I*. Leipzig.

KAYSER, C. L. ed. 1871. *Flavii Philostrati Opera II*. Leipzig.

KEESLING, C. M. 2012. 'The Marathon Casualty List from Eva-Loukou and the Plinthedon Style in Attic Inscriptions', *ZPE* 180: 139–48.

KEESLING, C. M. 2017. *Early Greek Portraiture: Monuments and Histories*. Cambridge.

KEIL, B. ed. 1898. *Aelii Aristidis Smyrnaei Quae Supersunt Omnia II*. Berlin.

KEIL, J. 1932. 'XVI. Vorläufiger Bericht über die Ausgrabungen in Ephesos', *Jahreshefte der Österreichischen archäologischen Instituts in Wien, Beiblatt* 27: 5–72.

326 BIBLIOGRAPHY

Kellum, B. 2015. 'Imperial Messages', in eds. E. A. Friedland, M. G. Sobocinski, and E. K. Gazda, *The Oxford Handbook of Roman Sculpture*, pp. 423–35. Oxford.

Kemezis, A. M. 2011. 'Narrative of Cultural Geography in Philostratus's *Lives of the Sophists*', in eds. T. Schmidt and P. Fleury, *Perceptions of the Second Sophistic and Its Times—Regards sur la Seconde Sophistique et son époque*, pp. 3–22. Toronto.

Kemezis, A. M. 2014. *Greek Narratives of the Roman Empire under the Severans: Cassius Dio, Philostratus and Herodian*. Cambridge.

Kennedy, G. 1974. 'The Sophists as Declaimers', in ed. G. W. Bowersock, *Approaches to the Second Sophistic*, pp. 17–22. University Park, PA.

Kennell, N. M. 1997. 'Herodes Atticus and the Rhetoric of Tyranny', *Classical Philology* 92.4: 346–62.

Kent, J. H. 1966. *Corinth: Results of Excavations Conducted by the American School of Classical Studies at Athens* VIII.3: *The Inscriptions 1926–1950*. Princeton, NJ.

Kent, R. G. 1950. *Old Persian: Grammar, Texts, Lexicon*. New Haven, CT.

Kerkhecker, A. 1999. *Callimachus' Book of* Iambi, pp. 11–16. Oxford.

Kermode, F. 1975. *The Classic: Literary Images of Permanence and Change*. New York, NY.

Kermode, F. 2004a. 'Change', in ed. R. Alter, *Pleasure and Change: The Aesthetics of Canon*, pp. 32–50. Oxford.

Kermode, F. 2004b. 'Pleasure', in ed. R. Alter, *Pleasure and Change: The Aesthetics of Canon*, pp. 15–31. Oxford.

Kienast, H. J. 2014. *Der Turm der Winde in Athen*. Weisbaden.

Kilburn, K. ed. 1959. *Lucian VI* (LCL 430). Cambridge, MA.

Kim, L. 2010. *Homer between History and Fiction in Imperial Greek Literature*. Cambridge.

King, D. 2017. *Experiencing Pain in Imperial Greek Culture*. Oxford.

Kinney, D. 1997. '*Spolia*: *Damnatio* and *Renovatio Memoriae*', *Memoirs of the American Academy in Rome* 42: 117–48.

Kleiner, D. E. E. 1983. *The Monument of Philopappos in Athens*. Rome.

Klose, D. O. A. 1987. *Die Münzprägung von Smyrna in der römischen Kaiserzeit*. Berlin.

Knoepfler, D. and M. Piérart eds. 2001. *Éditer, traduire, commenter Pausanias en l'an 2000. Receuil de travaux publiés par la Faculté de Lettres et Sciences Humaines Université de Neuchâtel 49*. Geneva.

König, J. 2001. 'Favorinus' *Corinthian Oration* in its Corinthian Context', *Proceedings of the Cambridge Philological Society* 47: 141–71.

König, J. 2005a. 'The Cynic and Christian Lives of Lucian's Peregrinus', in eds. J. Mossman and B. McGing, *The Limits of Ancient Biography*, pp. 227–54. Swansea.

König, J. 2005b. *Athletics and Literature in the Roman Empire*. Cambridge.

König, J. 2014. 'Images of Elite Community in Philostratus: Re-Reading the Preface to the *Lives of the Sophists*', in eds. J. M. Madsen and R. Rees, *Roman Rule in Greek and Latin Writing: Double Vision*, Impact of Empire Vol. 18, pp. 246–70. Leiden and Boston.

Korenjak, M. 2000. *Publikum und Redner: ihre Interaktion in der sophistischen Rhetorik der Kaiserzeit*. Munich.

KORENJAK, M. 2005. ' "Unbelievable Confusion": Weshalb sind die "Hieroi Logoi" des Aelius Aristides so wirr?', *Hermes* 133: 215–34.

KORENJAK, M. 2012. 'Conversing with Posterity: Hermogenes, Aristides, and Sophistic *φιλοτιμία*', in eds. G. ROSKAM, M. DE POURCQ, and L. VAN DER STOCKT, *The Lash of Ambition: Plutarch, Imperial Greek Literature and the Dynamics of* Philotimia, pp. 253–66. Louvain.

KORRES, M. 2015. *The Odeion Roof of Herodes Atticus and other Giant Spans*. Athens.

KOSMIN, P. J. 2018. *Time and its Adversaries in the Seleucid Empire*. Cambridge, MA.

KOUSSER, R. 2015. 'Monument and Memory in Ancient Greece and Rome: A Comparative Perspective', in eds. K. GALINSKY and K. LAPATIN, *Cultural Memories in the Roman Empire*, pp. 33–48. Los Angeles, CA.

KRITZAS, CH. B. 1992. '*Δύο ἐπιγράμματα ἀπό το Πετρί Νεμέας*', in ed. A. INTZESSILOGLOU, *Διεθνές Συνέδριο γιά την Ἀρχαία Θεσσαλία: στη μνήμη του Δημήτρη Π. Θεοχάρη: Πρακτικά*, pp. 398–413. Athens.

KRUMAICH, R. 2004. ' "Klassiker" im Gymnasion. Bildnisse attischer Kosmeten der mittleren und späten Kaiserzeit zwischen Rom und griechischer Vergangenheit', in ed. B. E. BORG, *Paideia: The World of the Second Sophistic*, pp. 131–56. Berlin.

KUHN, A. B. 2012. 'Herodes Atticus and the Quintilii of Alexandria Troas: Elite Competition and Status Relations in the Graeco-Roman East', *Chiron* 42: 421–58.

KURKE, L. 2013. *The Traffic in Praise: Pindar and the Poetics of Social Economy*. Berkeley, CA.

LANE, M. 2018. 'How to Turn History into Scenario: Plato's *Republic* Book 8 on the Role of Political Office in Constitutional Change', in eds. D. ALLEN, P. CHRISTESEN and P. MILLETT, *How to Do Things with History: New Approaches to Ancient Greece*, pp. 81–108. Oxford.

LANGDON, M. K. 1985. 'Hymettianai', *Hesperia* 54: 257–70.

LAPATIN, K. 2001. *Chryselephantine Statuary in the Ancient Mediterranean World*. Oxford.

LAPATIN, K. 2006. 'Picturing Socrates', in eds. S. AHBEL-RAPPE and R. KAMTEKAR, *A Companion to Socrates*, pp. 110–55. Chichester.

LATTIMORE, R. 1942. *Themes in Greek and Latin Epitaphs*. Urbana.

LATTIMORE, S. 1996. *Isthmia: Excavations by the University of California at Los Angeles and the Ohio State University under the Auspices of the American School of Classical Studies at Athens* VI: *Sculpture II: Marble Sculpture, 1967–1980*. Princeton, NJ.

LAUWERS, J. 2012. 'Reading Books, Talking Culture: The Performance of *Paideia* in Imperial Greek Literature', in ed. E. MINCHIN, *Orality, Literacy and Performance in the Ancient World*, pp. 227–44. Leiden and Boston.

LAUWERS, J. 2013. 'Systems of Sophistry and Philosophy: The Case of the Second Sophistic', *Harvard Studies in Classical Philology* 107: 331–63.

LAUWERS, J. 2015. 'Narcissism and Sophistry: Reading Philostratus' Life of Polemo of Laodicea', *Materiali e discussioni per l'analisi dei testi classici* 74: 143–80.

LAVALLE NORMAN, D. 2019. *The Aesthetics of Hope in Late Greek Imperial Literature*. Cambridge.

LAZZARINI, M. L. 1986. 'L'arcaismo nelle epigrafi greche di età imperiale', *AIΩN: Annali del dipartimento di studi del mondo classico e del mediterraneo antico, sezione linguistica* 8: 147–53, figs 1–4.

LEAKE, W. M. 1830. *Travels in the Morea II*. London.

LEATHERBURY, S. V. 2017. 'Writing, Reading and Seeing between the Lines: Framing Late-Antique Inscriptions as Texts and Images', in eds. V. PLATT and M. SQUIRE, *The Frame in Classical Art: A Cultural History*, pp. 544–81. Cambridge.

LEE, B. T. 2005. *Apuleius' Florida: A Commentary*. Berlin.

LE GOFF, J. 1992. *History and Memory*, translated by S. RENDALL and E. CLAMAN. New York, NY.

LENDON, J. E. 1997. *Empire of Honour: The Art of Government in the Roman World*. Oxford.

LENORMANT, F. 1866. 'Inscriptionum Graecarum Ineditarum Centuria Secunda et Tertia', *Rheinisches Museum für Philologie* 21: 362–404.

LEON, D. W. 2021. *Arrian the Historian: Writing the Greek Past in the Roman Empire*. Austin, TX.

LEVI, C. 1961. *Il futuro ha un cuore antico: viaggio nell'Unione Sovietica*. Turin.

LEVINE, D. B. 2005. 'EPATON BAMA ('Her Lovely Footstep'): The Erotics of Feet in Ancient Greece', in ed. D. CAIRNS, *Body Language in the Greek and Roman Worlds*, pp. 55–72. Swansea.

LIANERI, A. ed. 2016. *Knowing Future Time in and through Greek Historiography*. Berlin and Boston.

LIDDLE, A. ed. 2003. *Arrian: Periplus Ponti Euxini*. Bristol.

LIGHTFOOT, J. L. ed. 2003. *Lucian, On the Syrian Goddess*. Oxford.

LIOTSAKIS, V. 2019. *Alexander the Great in Arrian's Anabasis*. Berlin.

LISSARRAGUE, F. 1992. '*Graphein*: écrire et dessiner' in eds. C. BRON and E. KASSAPOGLOU, *L'Image en jeu: de l'antiquité à Paul Klee*, pp. 189–203. Paris.

LOLLING, H. G. 1873. 'Inscrizioni d'esecrazione in Cefissia', *Bullettino dell'Instituto di corrispondenza archeologica per l'anno 1873*: 218–22.

LONGFELLOW, B. 2011. *Roman Imperialism and Civic Patronage: Form, Meaning, and Ideology in Monumental Fountain Complexes*. Cambridge.

LOW, P. 2012. 'The Monuments to the War Dead in Classical Athens: Form, Contexts, Meanings', in eds. P. LOW, G. OLIVER, and P. J. RHODES, *Cultures of Commemoration: War Memorials, Ancient and Modern*, pp. 13–39. Oxford.

LUCAS, G. 2005. *The Archaeology of Time*. London.

LUCE, J.-M. 2013. 'Hérode Atticus et le Land Art: Une archéologie de l'acte esthétique', *Pallas* 93: 207–14.

LUCE, J. V. 2006. 'Heracles and Hydraulics', *Hermathena* 181: 25–39.

MA, J. 2006. 'The Two Cultures: Connoisseurship and Civic Honours', in eds. J. TRIMBLE and J. ELSNER, *Art and Replication: Greece, Rome, and Beyond. Art History* (Special Issue) 29.2: 325–38.

MA, J. 2007. 'Hellenistic Honorific Statues and their Inscriptions', in eds. Z. NEWBY and R. LEADER-NEWBY, *Art and Inscriptions in the Ancient World*, pp. 203–20. Cambridge.

MA, J. 2013. *Statues and Cities: Honorific Portraits and Civic Identities in the Hellenistic World*. Oxford.

MACLEOD, M. D. ed. 1972. *Luciani Opera I*. Oxford.

MACLEOD, M. D. ed. 1974. *Luciani Opera II*. Oxford.

MACLEOD, M. D. ed. 1980. *Luciani Opera III*. Oxford.

MACLEOD, M. D. ed. 1987. *Luciani Opera IV*. Oxford.

MACLEOD, M. D. ed. 1991. *Lucian: A Selection*. Warminster.

MACMULLEN, R. 1982. 'The Epigraphic Habit in the Roman Empire', *AJPhil* 103.3: 233–46.

MADSEN, J. M. 2006. 'Intellectual Resistance to Roman Hegemony and its Representivity', in ed. T. BEKKER-NIELSEN, *Rome and the Black Sea Region*, pp. 63–83. Aarhus.

MADSEN, J. M. 2009. *Eager to be Roman: Greek Responses to Roman Rule in Pontus and Bithynia*. London.

MADSEN, J. M. 2014. 'Patriotism and Ambitions: Intellectual Response to Roman Rule in the High Empire', in eds. J. M. MADSEN and R. REES, *Roman Rule in Greek and Latin Writing: Double Vision*, pp. 16–38. Leiden and Boston.

MADSEN, J. M. and R. REES 2014. 'Introduction: A Roman Greek', in eds. J. M. MADSEN and R. REES, *Roman Rule in Greek and Latin Writing: Double Vision*, pp. 1–15. Leiden and Boston.

MAIRS, R. 2011. 'Egyptian "Inscriptions" and Greek "Graffiti" at El Kanais in the Egyptian Eastern Desert', in eds. J. A. BAIRD and C. TAYLOR, *Ancient Graffiti in Context*, pp. 153–64. New York and Abingdon.

MALLWITZ, A. 1964. '*ΟΜΟΝΟΙΑΣ ΑΘΑΝΑΤΟΥ ΠΥΛΗ*', *Mitteilungen des Deutschen Archäologischen Instituts Athenische Abteilung* 79: 157–64.

MARINCOLA, J. M. 1989. 'Some Suggestions on the Proem and 'Second Preface' of Arrian's *Anabasis*', *JHS* 109: 186–9.

MARKOV, K. V. 2013. 'The Concepts of "Democracy" and "Tyranny" in the Speech of Agrippa in Cassius Dio 52.1-13: Conventional Rhetoric or Political Theory?', in eds. A. MEHL, A. V. MAKHLAYUK and O. GABELKO, *Ruthica Classica Aetatis Novae: A Collection of Works by Russian Scholars in Ancient Greek and Roman History*, pp. 215–31. Stuttgart.

MARTIN, F. 1996. 'The Importance of Honorific Statues: A Case-Study', *Bulletin of the Institute of Classical Studies* 41: 53–70.

MARTINDALE, C. 1993. *Redeeming the Text: Latin Poetry and the Hermeneutics of Reception*. Cambridge.

MARTINDALE, C. 2006. 'Introduction: Thinking through Reception', in eds. C. MARTINDALE and R. F. THOMAS, *Classics and the Uses of Reception*, pp. 1–13. Malden, MA and Oxford.

MARTINDALE, C. 2013. 'Reception – A New Humanism? Receptivity, Pedagogy, the Transhistorical', *Classical Receptions Journal* 5.2: 169–83.

MASON, H. 1974. *Greek Terms for Roman Institutions: A Lexicon and Analysis*. Toronto.

MATTHEWS, V. J. ed. 1996. *Antimachus of Colophon: Text and Commentary, Mnemosyne* Supplement 155. Leiden.

MATTHAIOU, A. P. 2003. 'Ἀθηναίοισι τεταγμένοισι ἐν τεμένει Ἡρακλέους', in eds. P. DEROW and R. PARKER, *Herodotus and His World*, pp. 197–8. Oxford and New York.

MAYOR, A. 2018. *Gods and Robots: Myths, Machines, and Ancient Dreams of Technology.* Princeton.

MAZUREK, L. A. 2018. 'The Middle Platonic Isis: Text and Image in the Sanctuary of the Egyptian Gods at Herodes Atticus' Marathon Villa', *AJArch* 122.4: 611–44.

McCREDIE, J. 1966. *Fortified Military Camps in Attica, Hesperia* Supplement 11. Princeton, NJ.

McGING, B. and J. MOSSMAN 2006. 'Introduction', in eds. B. McGING and J. MOSSMAN, *The Limits of Ancient Biography*, pp. ix–xx. Swansea.

McIVER, C. A. 2016. 'Truth, Narration, and Interpretation in Lucian's *Verae Historiae*, *AJPhil* 137.2: 219–50.

MEADOWS, A. and J. WILLIAMS 2001. '*Moneta* and the Monuments: Coinage and Politics in Republican Rome', *JRS* 91: 27–49.

MERKELBACH, R. 1971. 'Gefesselte Götter', *Antaios* 12: 549–65.

MERITT, B. D. ed. 1931. *Corinth: Results of Excavations Conducted by the American School of Classical Studies at Athens* VIII.1: *Greek Inscriptions 1896–1927.* Cambridge, MA.

MESTRE, F. and GÓMEZ, P. 2009. 'Power and the Abuse of Power in the Works of Lucian', in ed. A. BARTLEY, *A Lucian for our Times*, pp. 93–108. Newcastle upon Tyne.

MEYER, E. A. 1990. 'Explaining the Epigraphic Habit in the Roman Empire: The Evidence of Inscriptions', *JRS* 80: 74–96.

MEYER, H. 1985. 'Vibullius Polydeukion: Ein archaeologisch-epigraphischer Problemfall', *Mitteilungen des Deutschen Archäologischen Instituts, Athenische Abteilung* 100: 393–404.

MEYER, H. 1991. *Antinoos: Die archäologischen Denkmäler unter Einbeziehung des numismatischen und epigraphischen Materials sowie der literarischen Nachrichten.* München.

MILES, G. 2018. *Philostratus: Interpreters and Interpretation.* London and New York.

MILES, R. 2000. 'Communicating Culture, Identity, Power', in ed. J. HUSKINSON, *Experiencing Rome: Culture, Identity and Power in the Roman Empire*, pp. 29–62. London.

MILLS, S. 1997. *Theseus, Tragedy, and the Athenian Empire.* Oxford.

MINAKARAN-HIESGEN, E. 1970. 'Untersuchungen zu den Porträts des Xenophon und Isokrates', *Jahrbuch des Deutschen Archäologischen Instituts* 85: 112–57.

MINCHIN, E. 2012. 'Commemoration and Pilgrimage in the Ancient World: Troy and the Stratigraphy of Cultural Memory', *Greece and Rome* 59.1: 76–89.

MITCHELL, S. 1987. 'Imperial Building in the Eastern Roman Provinces', *Harvard Studies in Classical Philology* 91: 333–65.

MITFORD, T. B. 1974. 'Some Inscriptions from the Cappadocian Limes', *JRS* 64: 160–75.

MITFORD, T. B. 1991. 'Inscriptiones Ponticae: Sebastopolis', *ZPE* 87: 181–243.

MITFORD, T. B. 2000. '*Thalatta, Thalatta*: Xenophon's View of the Black Sea', *Anatolian Studies* 50: 127–31.

MITFORD, T. B. 2018a. *East of Asia Minor: Rome's Hidden Frontier*, Vol. 1. Oxford.

MITFORD, T. B. 2018b. *East of Asia Minor: Rome's Hidden Frontier*, Vol. 2. Oxford.

MOLES, J. L. 1978. 'The Career and Conversion of Dio Chrysostom', *JHS* 98: 79–100.

MOLES, J. L. 1985. 'The Interpretation of the 'Second Preface' in Arrian's *Anabasis*', *JHS* 105: 162–8.

MOLES, J. L. 1990. 'The Kingship Orations of Dio Chrysostom', *Papers of the Leeds International Latin Seminar* 6: 297–375.

MOLES, J. L. 1999. '*Ἀνάθημα καὶ κτῆμα*: The Inscriptional Inheritance of Ancient Historiography', *Histos* 3: 27–69.

MOMIGLIANO, A. 1958. 'The Place of Herodotus in the History of Historiography', *History* 43.147: 1–13.

MOMIGLIANO, A. 1993. *The Development of Greek Biography*. Cambridge, MA and London.

MONRO, D. B. and ALLEN, T. W. eds. 1920a. *Homeri Opera I: Iliadis Libros I–XII*. Oxford.

MONRO, D. B. and ALLEN, T. W. eds. 1920b. *Homeri Opera II: Iliadis Libros XIII–XXIV*. Oxford.

MOORHEAD, S. and D. STUTTARD 2012. *The Romans who Shaped Britain*. London.

MOREWOOD, J. 2012. *Hadrian*. London.

MOSSMAN, J. 1991. 'Plutarch's Use of Statues', in eds. M. A. FLOWER and M. TOHER, *Georgica: Greek Studies in Honour of George Cawkwell*, pp. 98–119. London.

MOSSMAN, J. 2006. 'Travel Writing, History, and Biography', in eds. B. McGING and J. MOSSMAN, *The Limits of Ancient Biography*, pp. 281–303. Swansea.

MUÑIZ GRIJALVO, E. 2005. 'Elites and Religious Change in Roman Athens', *Numen* 52.2: 255–82.

NASRALLAH, L. S. 2010. *Christian Responses to Roman Art and Architecture: The Second-Century Church amid the Spaces of Empire*. Cambridge.

NELSON, R. S. and M. OLIN 2003. 'Introduction', in eds. R. S. NELSON and M. OLIN, *Monuments and Memory: Made and Unmade*, pp. 1–10. Chicago, IL and London.

NESSELRATH, H. G. 1990. 'Lucian's Introductions', in ed. D. A. RUSSELL, *Antonine Literature*, pp. 111–40. Oxford.

NEUGEBAUER, K. A. 1934. 'Herodes Atticus, ein antiker Kunstmäzen', *Die Antike* 10: 92–121.

NEWBY, Z. 2002a. 'Reading Programs in Greco-Roman Art: Reflections on the Spada Reliefs', in ed. D. FREDRICK, *The Roman Gaze: Vision, Power, and the Body*, pp. 110–48. Baltimore.

NEWBY, Z. 2002b. 'Testing the Boundaries of Ekphrasis: Lucian's *On the Hall*', in ed. J. ELSNER, *The Verbal and the Visual: Cultures of Ekphrasis in Antiquity. Ramus* 31.1–2: 126–35.

NEWBY, Z. 2005. *Greek Athletics in the Roman World*. Oxford.

NG, D. Y. 2016. 'Monuments, Memory, and Status Recognition in Roman Asia Minor', in ed. K. GALINSKY, *Memory in Ancient Roman and Early Christianity*, pp. 235–60. Oxford.

NÍ MHEALLAIGH, K. 2008. 'Pseudo-Documentarism and the Limits of Ancient Fiction', *AJPhil* 129.3: 403–31.

NÍ MHEALLAIGH, K. 2009. 'Monumental Fallacy: The Teleology of Origins in Lucian's *Verae Historiae*', in ed. A. BARTELY, *A Lucian for Our Times*, pp. 11–28. Newcastle.

NÍ MHEALLAIGH, K. 2014. *Reading Fiction with Lucian: Fakes, Freaks, and Hyperreality*. Cambridge.

NORA, P. 1996. 'From *Lieux de Mémoire* to Realms of Memory', in ed. L. D. KRITZMAN, under the direction of P. Nora and translated by A. GOLDHAMMER, *Realms of Memory*. Vol. 1: *Conflicts and Divisions*, pp. xv–xxiv. New York, NY.

OLIVER, J. H. 1970a. 'Arrian and the Gellii of Corinth', *Greek, Roman, and Byzantine Studies* 11.4: 335–8.

OLIVER, J. H. 1970b. *Marcus Aurelius: Aspects of Civic and Cultural Policy in the East. Hesperia Supplements* 13. Princeton, NJ.

OLIVER, J. H. 1972. 'Herm at Athens with Portraits of Xenophon and Arrian', *AJArch* 76.3: 327–8.

OLIVER, J. H. 1982. 'Arrian in Two Roles', *Hesperia Supplements* 19: 122–9.

OLIVIER, L. 2011. *The Dark Abyss of Time: Archaeology and Memory*, translated by A. GREENSPAN. Plymouth.

OLSON, S. D. 2016. 'Reading the New Erechtheid Casualty List from Marathon', in eds. G. COLESANTI and L. LULLI, *Submerged Literature in Ancient Greek Culture: Case Studies*, pp. 41–66. Berlin and Boston.

ONDAATJE, M. 1993. *The English Patient*. London.

OPPER, T. 2008. *Hadrian: Empire and Conflict*. Cambridge, MA.

ORWELL, G. 1949. *1984*. New York, NY.

PAPADIMITRIOU, I. 1963. 'The Sanctuary of Artemis at Brauron', *Scientific American* 208.6: 111–20.

PAPAIOANNOU, M. 2018. 'Villas in Roman Greece', in eds. A. MARZANO and G. P. R. MÉTRAUX, *The Roman Villa in the Mediterranean Basin: Late Republic to Late Antiquity*, pp. 328–76. Cambridge.

PAPALAS, A. J. 1979. 'Herodes Atticus and the Wrath of Philagrus', *Rivista di Cultura Classica e Medioevale* 21: 93–104.

PARKER, V. 1998. 'Τύραννος: The Semantics of a Political Concept from Archilochus to Aristotle', *Hermes* 126.2: 145–72.

PEARCE, S. M. 1995. *On Collecting: An Investigation into Collecting in the European Tradition*. London.

PEARCY, L. T. 1988. 'Theme, Dream, and Narrative: Reading the Sacred Tales of Aelius Aristides', *TAPA* 118: 377–91.

PEPPAS-DELMOUZOU, D. 1970. 'Βάσις ἀνδριάντος τοῦ Ἀρριανοῦ', *Athens Annals of Archaeology* 3: 377–80.

PERKINS, J. 2009. *Roman Imperial Identities in the Early Christian Era*. Abingdon and New York.

PERNOT, L. 2002. 'Les *Discours Sacrés* d'Aelius Aristide entre medicine, religion et rhétorique', *Atti Accademia Pontaniana* 51: 369–83.

PERNOT, L. 2008. 'Aelius Aristides and Rome', in eds. W. V. HARRIS and B. HOLMES, *Aelius Aristides between Greece, Rome, and the Gods*, pp. 175–202. Leiden and Boston.

PERNOT, L. 2015. *Epideictic Rhetoric: Questioning the Stakes of Ancient Praise*. Austin, TX.

PERRIN, B. ed. and trans. 1914. *Plutarch Lives Vol 1*, LCL 46. Cambridge, MA.

PERRY, E. E. 2001. 'Iconography and the Dynamics of Patronage: A Sarcophagus from the Family of Herodes Atticus', *Hesperia* 70: 461–92.

PERRY, E. E. 2002. 'Rhetoric, Literary Criticism, and the Roman Aesthetics of Artistic Imitation', in ed. E. K. GAZDA, *The Ancient Art of Emulation: Studies in Artistic Originality and Tradition from the Present to Classical Antiquity*, pp. 153–71. Ann Arbor, MI.

PERRY, E. E. 2005. *The Aesthetics of Emulation in the Visual Arts of Ancient Rome*. Cambridge.

PETRAKOS, B. CHR. (Πετράκος, Β. Χ.) 1995. Ὁ Μαραθών. Athens.

PETRAKOS, B. 1999a. Ο Δήμος του Ραμνούντος: σύνοψη των ανασκαφών και των ερευνών, *1813–1998. I. Τοπογραφία*. Athens.

PETRAKOS, B. 1999b. Ο Δήμος του Ραμνούντος: σύνοψη των ανασκαφών και των ερευνών, *1813–1998. II. Οι επιγραφές*. Athens.

PETRAKOS, B. 2002. 'Το κτήμα του Ηρώδου στον Μαραθώνα', Πρακτικά της Ακαδημίας Αθηνών 77: 83–90.

PETROVIC, A. 2013. 'The Battle of Marathon in Pre-Herodotean Sources: on Marathon Verse-Inscriptions (IG I^3 503/504; SEG LVI 430)', in eds. C. CAREY and M. EDWARDS, *Marathon—2,500 Years: Proceedings of the Marathon Conference 2010*, pp. 47–53. London.

PETSALIS-DIOMIDIS, A. 2006. 'Sacred Writing, Sacred Reading: The Function of Aelius Aristides' Self-Presentation as Author in the *Sacred Tales*', in eds. B. MCGING and J. MOSSMAN, *The Limits of Ancient Biography*, pp. 193–211. Swansea.

PETSALIS-DIOMIDIS, A. 2007. 'Landscape, Transformation, and Divine Epiphany', in eds. S. SWAIN, S. HARRISON, and J. ELSNER, *Severan Culture*, pp. 250–89. Cambridge.

PETSALIS-DIOMIDIS, A. 2008. 'The Body in the Landscape: Aristides' *Corpus* in Light of *The Sacred Tales*', in eds. W. V. HARRIS and B. HOLMES, *Aelius Aristides between Greece, Rome, and the Gods*, pp. 131–50. Leiden and Boston.

PETSALIS-DIOMIDIS, A. 2010. *Truly beyond Wonders: Aelius Aristides and the Cult of Asklepios*. Oxford.

PETTEGREW, D. K. 2016. *The Isthmus of Corinth: Crossroads of the Mediterranean World*. Ann Arbor, MI.

PHILADELPHEUS, A. 1919. Ἑρμαϊκὴ στήλη Ἡρώδου τοῦ Ἀττικοῦ, Ἀρχαιολόγικον Δέλτιον 5: 38–40.

PHILADELPHEUS, A. 1920. 'Un Hermès d'Hérode Atticus', *BCH* 44: 170–80.

PITT, R. K. 2014–15. 'Recent Discoveries and Resources in Athenian Epigraphy', *Archaeological Reports* 61: 51.

PLATT, V. 2007. '"Honour Takes Wing": Unstable and Anxious Orators in the Greek Tradition', in eds. Z. NEWBY and R. LEADER-NEWBY, *Art and Inscriptions in the Ancient World*, edited by, pp. 247–71. Cambridge.

PLATT, V. 2011. *Facing the Gods: Epiphany and Representation in Graeco-Roman Art, Literature and Religion*. Cambridge.

PODLECKI, A. J. 1971. 'Cimon, Skyros, and Theseus' Bones', *JHS* 91: 141–3.

POMEROY, S. B. 2007. *The Murder of Regilla: A Case of Domestic Violence in Antiquity*. Cambridge, MA.

PONT, A.-V. 2008. 'Rituels civiques (*apantêsis* et acclamations) et gouverneurs en Asie Mineure à l'époque romaine', in eds. O. HEKSTER, S. SCHMIDT-HOFNER and C. WITSCHEL, *Ritual Dynamics and Religious Change in the Roman Empire: Proceedings of the Eighth Workshop of the International Network 'Impact of Empire'* (Heidelberg, 5–7 July 2007), pp. 185–211. Leiden.

PORTER, J. I. 2001. 'Ideals and Ruins: Pausanias, Longinus, and the Second Sophistic', in eds. S. E. ALCOCK, J. F. CHERRY, and J. ELSNER, *Pausanias: Travel and Memory in Roman Greece*, pp. 63–92. Leiden.

PORTER, J. I. 2005. 'What is "Classical" about Classical Antiquity? Eight Propositions', *Arion* 13.1: 27–62.

PORTER, J. I. 2006. 'Feeling Classical: Classicism and Ancient Literary Criticism', in ed. J. I. PORTER, *Classical Pasts: The Classical Traditions of Greece and Rome*, pp. 301–52. Princeton, NJ.

PORTER, J. I. 2010. *The Origins of Aesthetic Thought in Ancient Greece: Matter, Sensation, and Experience*. Cambridge.

PORTER, J. I. 2011. 'Sublime Monuments and Sublime Ruins in Ancient Aesthetics, *European Revue of History: Revue europeenne d'histoire* 18.5–6: 685–96.

PORTER, J. I. 2012. 'Is the Sublime an Aesthetic Value?', in eds. I. SLUITER and R. M. ROSEN, *Aesthetic Value in Classical Antiquity*, pp. 47–70. Leiden and Boston.

PORTER, J. I. 2016. *The Sublime in Antiquity*. Cambridge.

POULSEN, F. 1945. 'Talking, Weeping and Bleeding Sculptures: A Chapter in the History of Religious Fraud', *Acta Archaeologica* 16: 178–95.

PRETZLER, M. 2007. *Pausanias: Travel Writing in Ancient Greece*. London.

PRETZLER, M. 2010. 'From One Connoisseur to Another: Pausanias as Winckelmann's Guide to Analysing Greek Art', *Classical Receptions Journal* 2.2: 197–218.

PRICE, S. R. F. 1984. *Rituals and Power: The Roman Imperial Cult in Asia Minor*. Cambridge.

PROIETTI, G. 2012. 'La memoria delle Guerre Persiane in età imperiale: il classicismo di Erode Attico e la "Stele dei Maratonomachi"', *Annario della Scuola Archaeologica di Atene* 90: 97–117.

PROIETTI, G. 2013. 'The Marathon Epitaph from Eua-Loukou: Some Notes about Its Text and Historical Context', *ZPE* 185: 24–30.

PROIETTI, G. 2020. 'La stele dei Maratonomachi (o 'stele di Loukou')', *Axon* 4.1: 31–50.

PUECH, B. 2002. *Orateurs et sophistes grecs dans les inscriptions d'époque impériale*. Paris.

PURVES, A. C. 2010. *Space and Time in Ancient Greek Narrative*. Cambridge.

QUATEMBER, U. and SCHEILBELREITER-GAIL, V. 2017. 'T. Flavius Damianus und der Grabbau seiner Familie', *Jahreshefte des österreichischen archäologischen Institutes in Wien* 86: 221–354.

QUET, M.-H. 1992. 'L'inscription de Vérone en l'honneur d'Aelius Aristides et le rayonnement de la seconde sophistique chez les "Grecs d'Égypte"', *Revue des études anciennes* 94: 379–401.

RADT, S. ed. 2004. *Strabons Geographika Band 3*. Göttingen.

RADT, S. ed. 2005. *Strabons Geographika Band 4*. Göttingen.

RAWSON, E. 1989. 'Roman Ruler and the Philosophic Adviser', in eds. M. GRIFFIN and J. BARNES, *Philosophia Togata: Essays on Philosophy and Roman Society*, pp. 233–57. Oxford.

READER, W. 1996. *The Severed Hand and the Upright Corpse: The Declamations of Marcus Antonius Polemo*, in collaboration with A. J. CHVALA-SMITH. Atlanta.

REARDON, B. P. ed. 2004. *Chariton Aphrodisiensis: De Callirhoe Narrationes Amatoriae*. Munich and Leipzig.

REINHARD, J. H. 2005. 'The Roman Bath at Isthmia: Decoration, Cult and Herodes Atticus', Unpublished PhD Dissertation. University of Minnesota.

REITZ, B. 2012. '*Tantae Molis Erat*: On Valuing Roman Imperial Architecture', in eds. I. SLUITER and R. M. ROSEN, *Aesthetic Value in Classical Antiquity*, pp. 317–44. Leiden and Boston.

RICCARDI, L. A. 2007. 'The Bust-Crown, The Panhellenion, and Eleusis: A New Portrait from the Athenian Agora', *Hesperia* 76.2: 365–90.

RICHARDSON, R. B. 1900. 'Pirene', *AJArch* 4: 204–39.

RICHTER, G. M. A. 1959. *Greek Portraits II: To What Extent Were They Faithful Likenesses?* Brussels.

RICHTER, G. M. A. 1965a. *The Portraits of the Greeks Vol. 1*. London.

RICHTER, G. M. A. 1965b. *The Portraits of the Greeks Vol. 2*. London.

RICHTER, G. M. A. 1965c. *The Portraits of the Greeks Vol. 3*. London.

RIEGL, A. 1982. 'The Modern Cult of Monuments: Its Character and Its Origins' translated by K.W. FORSTER and D. GHIRARDO, *Oppositions* 25: 21–51.

RIFE, J. L. 2008. 'The Burial of Herodes Atticus: Elite Identity, Urban Society, and Public Memory in Roman Greece', *JHS* 128: 92–127.

RIFE, J. L. 2009. 'The Deaths of the Sophists: Philostratean Biography and Elite Funerary Practices', in eds. E. BOWIE and J. ELSNER, *Philostratus*, pp. 100–28. Cambridge.

RIZAKIS, A. 2007. 'Urban Elites in the Roman East: Enhancing Regional Positions and Social Superiority', in ed. J. RÜPKE, *A Companion to Roman Religion*, pp. 317–30. Malden and Oxford.

ROBERT, C. 1890. *Die antiken Sarkophagreliefs*, vol. 2. Berlin.

ROBERT, L. 1937. *Études Anatoliennes: Reserches sur les inscriptions greques de l'Asie Mineure*. Paris.

ROBERT, L. 1978. 'Malédictions Funéraires Grecques', *Comptes rendus des séances de l'Académie des Inscriptions et Belles-Lettres* 122.2: 241–89.

ROBERT, L. 1979. 'Deux inscriptions de l'époque impériale en Attique', *AJPhil* 100: 153–65.

ROBERT, L. 1980. 'Deux poètes grecs à l'époque impériale', in eds. Σωματείο φίλων του Νικολάου Κοντολέοντος, ΣΤΗΛΗ: Τόμος εις μνήμην Νικολαου Κοντολέοντος. Athens.

ROBERT, L. 1987. *Documents d'Asie Mineure*. Athens and Paris.

ROBINSON, B. A. 2011. *Histories of Peirene: A Corinthian Fountain in Three Millennia*. Princeton, NJ.

ROGERS, D. K. 2021. 'Sensing Water in Roman Greece: The Villa of Herodes Atticus at Eva-Loukou and the Sanctuary of Demeter and Kore at Eleusis', *AJArch* 125.1: 91–122.

ROHDE, E. 1960 [1914]. *Der griechische Roman und seine Vorläufer*, 4th edition, with a foreword by KARL KERÉNYI. Leipzig.

ROLLER, D. W. 2018. *A Historical and Topographical Guide to the Geography of Strabo*. Cambridge.

ROMIOPOULOU, K. 1997. Ελληνορωμαϊκά Γλυπτά του Εθνικού Αρχαιολογικού Μουσείου. Athens.

ROMM, J. 1990. 'Wax, Stone, and Promethean Clay: Lucian as Plastic Artist', *Classical Antiquity* 9: 74–98.

ROMM, J. 1992. *The Edges of the Earth in Ancient Thought: Geography, Exploration, and Fiction*. Princeton, NJ.

ROOD, T. 2004. *The Sea! The Sea! The Shout of the Ten Thousand in the Modern Imagination*. London.

ROOD, T. 2011. 'Black Sea Variations: Arrian's *Periplus*', *Cambridge Classical Journal* 57: 137–63.

ROOS, A. G. ed. 1967. *Flavius Arrianus I: Alexandri Anabasis*. Leipzig.

ROSE, C. B. 2015. 'The Homeric Memory Culture of Roman Ilion', in eds. K. GALINSKY and K. LAPATIN, *Cultural Memories in the Roman Empire*, pp. 134–52. Los Angeles, CA.

ROSIVACH, V. J. 1988. 'The Tyrant in Athenian Democracy', *Quaderni Urbinati di Cultura Classica* 30.3: 43–57.

ROSSI, A. 2001. 'Remapping the Past: Caesar's Tale of Troy (Lucan, *BC* 9.964-999)', *Phoenix* 55.3: 313–26.

ROSTOVTZEFF, M. I. 1909. 'Novye latinskiye nadpisi s Yuga Rossii', *Izvestiya Arkheologischeskoy Kommissii* 33: 1–22.

RUSSELL, D. A. ed. 1964. *'Longinus': On the Sublime*, edited with Introduction and Commentary. Oxford.

RUSSELL, D. A. 1981. 'Longinus Revisited', *Mnemosyne* 34.1/2: 72–86.

RUSSELL, D. A. 1983. *Greek Declamation*. Cambridge.

RUSSELL, D. A. and WINTERBOTTOM, M. eds. 1989. *Classical Literary Criticism*. Oxford.

RUTHERFORD, I. 1992. 'Inverting the Canon: Hermogenes on Literature', *Harvard Studies in Classical Philology* 94: 355–78.

RUTLEDGE, S. 2012. *Ancient Rome as a Museum: Power, Identity, and the Culture of Collecting*. Oxford.

SAÏD, S. 1993. 'Le "Je" de Lucien', in eds. M-F. BASLEZ, P. HOFFMANN and L. PERNOT, *L'Invention de l'Autobiographie d'Hésiode à Saint Augustin: Actes du deuxième colloque de l'Équipe de Recherche sur l'Hellénisme Post-Classique (Paris, École normale supérieure, 14–16 juin 1990)*, pp. 253–70. Paris.

SALOWEY, C. A. 1994. 'Herakles and the Waterworks: Mycenaean Dams, Classical Fountains, Roman Aqueducts', in ed. K. A. SHEEDY, *Archaeology in the Peloponnese: New Excavations and Research*, pp. 77–94. Oxford.

SANDY, G. N. 1997. *The Greek World of Apuleius: Apuleius and the Second Sophistic*. Leiden.

SAUNDERS, N. J. 2006. *Alexander's Tomb: The Two Thousand Year Obsession to Find the Lost Conqueror*. New York.

SCHENKEVELD, D. M. 1992. 'Prose usages of "to read"', *Classical Quarterly* 42: 129–41.

SCHMITZ, T. 1997. *Bildung und Macht: Zur Sozialen und Politischen Funktion der zweiten Sophistik in der griechischen Welt der Kaiserzeit*. Munich.

SCHMITZ, T. 1999. 'Performing History in the Second Sophistic', in ed. M. ZIMMERMANN, *Geschichtsschreibung und politischer Wandel im 3. Jh. N. Chr.*, pp. 71–92. Stuttgart.

SCHMITZ, T. 2009. 'Narrator and Audience in Philostratus' *Lives of the Sophists*', in eds. E. BOWIE and J. ELSNER, *Philostratus*, pp. 49–68. Cambridge.

SCHMITZ, T. 2017. 'Professionals of Paideia?: The Sophists as Performers', in eds. D. S. RICHTER and W. A. JOHNSON, *The Oxford Handbook to the Second Sophistic*, pp. 169–80. Oxford.

SCHOWALTER, D. N. 2014. 'Regilla Standing By: Reconstructed Statuary and Re-Inscribed Bases in Fourth-Century Corinth', in eds. S. J. FRIESEN, S. A. JAMES, and D. N. SCHOWALTER, *Corinth in Contrast: Studies in Inequality*, pp. 166–83. Leiden and Boston.

SEGAL, C. P. 1959. '῞Υψος and the Problem of Cultural Decline in the *De Sublimitate*', *Harvard Studies in Classical Philology* 64: 121–46.

SEGAL, C. P. 1987. 'Writer as Hero: The Heroic Ethos in Longinus, *On the Sublime*', in eds. J. SERVAIS, T. HACKENS, and B. SERVAIS-SOYEZ, *Stemmata: Mélanges de Philologie, d'Histoire et d'Archéologie Grecques Offerts à Jules Labarbe*, pp. 209–17. Louvain-la-Neuve.

SHAPIRO, H. A. 1992. 'Theseus in Kimonian Athens: The Iconography of Empire', *Mediterranean Historical Review* 7.1: 29–49.

SHAW, B. D. 2019. 'Did the Romans have a Future?', *JRS* 109: 1–26.

SHAYA, J. 2015. 'Ancient Analogs of Museums', in eds. E. A. FRIEDLAND, M. G. SOBOCINSKI, and E. K. GAZDA, *Oxford Handbook of Roman Sculpture*, pp. 622–37. Oxford.

SHEAR, J. L. 2001. *Polis and Panathenaia: The History and Development of Athena's Festival*. Ann Arbor.

SHEAR, J. L. 2007. 'Reusing Statues, Rewriting Inscriptions and Bestowing Honours in Roman Athens', in eds. Z. NEWBY and R. LEADER-NEWBY, *Art and Inscriptions in the Ancient World*, pp. 221–46. Cambridge.

SIDEBOTTOM, H. 2009. 'Philostratus and the Symbolic Roles of the Sophist and the Philosopher', in eds. E. BOWIE and J. ELSNER, *Philostratus*, pp. 69–99. Cambridge.

SILBERMAN, A. 1993. 'Arrien, "Périple du Pont Euxin": Essai d'interprétation et d'évaluation des données historiques et géographiques', *ANRW* II.34.1: 276–311.

SILBERMAN, A. 1995. *Arrien, Périple du Pont-Euxin*. Paris.

SISKOU, L. 2011. 'The Male Egyptianizing Statues from the Sanctuary of the Egyptian Gods at Marathon', in eds. L. BRICAULT and R. VEYMIERS, *Bibliotheca Isiaca II*, pp. 79–96. Bordeaux.

SKENTERI, F. 2005. *Herodes Atticus Reflected in Occasional Poetry of Antonine Athens*. Lund.

SKIAS, A. N. 1905. Αἱ ἀνασκαφαὶ τοῦ Παναθηναϊκοῦ Σταδίου, *Νέος Ἑλληνομνήμων* 2: 257–65.

SLATER, N. 2009. 'Reading Inscriptions in the Ancient Novel', in eds. M. PASCHALIS, S. PANAYOTAKIS, and G. SCHMELING, *Readers and Writers in the Ancient Novel*, pp. 64–78. Groningen.

SMALL, J. P. 1997. *Wax Tablets of the Mind: Cognitive Studies of Memory and Literacy in Classical Antiquity*. London.

SMALL, J. P. 2008. 'Visual Copies and Memory', in ed. A. MACKAY, *Orality, Literacy, Memory in the Ancient Greek and Roman World*, pp. 227–51. Leiden.

SMITH, R. R. R. 1990. 'Late Roman Philosopher Portraits from Aphrodisias', *JRS* 80: 127–55, 177.

SMITH, R. R. R. 1998. 'Cultural Choice and Political Identity in Honorific Portrait Statues in the Greek East in the Second Century A.D.', *JRS* 88: 56–93.

SMITH, R. R. R. 1999. 'Review of *Die Maske des Sokrates. Das Bild des Intellektuellen in der antiken Kunst* by Paul Zanker', *Gnomon* 71.5: 448–57.

SMITH, R. R. R. 2007. 'Pindar, Athletes, and the Early Greek Statue Habit', in eds. S. HORNBLOWER and C. MORGAN, *Pindar's Poetry, Patrons, and Festivals: From Archaic Greece to the Roman Empire*, pp. 83–140. Oxford.

SMITH, R. R. R. 2016. 'Statue Practice in the Late Roman Empire: Numbers, Costumes, Styles', in eds. R. R. R. SMITH and B. WARD-PERKINS, *The Last Statues of Antiquity*. Oxford.

SOURVINOU-INWOOD, C. 1995. *'Reading' Greek Death: To the End of the Classical Period*. Oxford.

SOTERIADES, G. 1933. 'Ἀνασκαφή Μαραθῶνος', Πρακτικά της εν Αθήναις Αρχαιολογικής Εταιρείας 88: 31–46.

SPAWFORTH, A. J. S. 1980. 'Sparta and the Family of Herodes Atticus: A Reconsideration of the Evidence', *Annual of the British School at Athens* 75: 203–20.

SPAWFORTH, A. J. S. 1984. 'Review of W. Ameling, *Herodes Attikos. I. Biographie. II. Inschriftenkatalog*', *JRS* 74: 214–17.

SPAWFORTH, A. J. S. 1994. 'Symbol of Unity? The Persian-Wars Tradition in the Roman Empire', in ed. S. HORNBLOWER, *Greek Historiography*, pp. 233–48. Oxford.

SPAWFORTH, A. J. S. 1999. 'The Panhellenion Again', *Chiron* 9: 339–52.

SPAWFORTH, A. J. S. 2012. *Greece and the Augustan Cultural Revolution*. Cambridge.

SPAWFORTH, A. J. and S. WALKER 1985. 'The World of the Panhellenion. I. Athens and Eleusis', *JRS* 75: 78–104.

SPIVEY, N. 1997. 'Bionic Statues', in ed. A. POWELL, *The Greek World*. London: 442–59.

SPYROPOULOS, G. 2001. *Drei Meisterwerke der griechischen Plastik aus der Villa des Herodes Atticus zu Eva/Loukou*. Frankfurt.

SPYROPOULOS, G. (Σπυρόπουλος, Γ.) 2006a. Η Έπαυλη του Ηρώδη Αττικού στην Εύα/Λουκού Κυνουρίας. Athens.

SPYROPOULOS, G. 2006b. Νεκρόδειπνα, Ηρωικά Ανάγλυφα και ο Ναός-Ηρώο του Αντίνοου στην Έπαυλη του Ηρώδη Αττικού. Athens.

SPYROPOULOS, G. 2009. Οι Στήλες των Πεσόντων στην Μάχη του Μαραθώνα από την Έπαυλη του Ηρώδη Αττικού στην Εύα Κυνουρίας. Athens.

SPYROPOULOS, G. In press. 'Appropriation and Synthesis in the Villa of Herodes Atticus at Eva (Loukou), Greece', in eds. T. POTTS, J. SPIER, and S. E. COLE, *Egypt, Greece, Rome: Cross-Cultural Encounters in Antiquity*. Los Angeles.

SPYROPOULOS, G. and T. SPYROPOULOS 1996. The Villa of Herodes Atticus at Eva (Loukou) in Arcadia. Unpublished manuscript.

SQUIRE, M. 2009. *Image and Text in Graeco-Roman Antiquity*. Cambridge.

SQUIRE, M. 2015. 'Theories of Reception', in ed. C. MARCONI, *The Oxford Handbook of Greek and Roman Art and Architecture*, pp. 637–61. Oxford.

STADTER, P. 1967. 'Flavius Arrianus: The New Xenophon', *Greek, Roman, and Byzantine Studies* 8.2: 155–161.

STADTER, P. 1980. *Arrian of Nicomedia*. Chapel Hill, NC.

STAFFORD, E. 2012. *Herakles*. London.

STAFFORD, E. 2013. '"The People to the goddess Livia". Attic Nemesis and the Roman Imperial Cult', *Kernos* 26: 205–38.

STEINHAUER, G. (Σταϊνχάουερ, Γ.) 2004–09. 'Στήλη Πεσόντων τῆς Ἐρεχθηίδος', ΗΟΡΟΣ 17–21: 679–92.

STEINHAUER, G. 2009. *Marathon and the Archaeological Museum*. Athens.

STEINHAUER, G. 2010. 'Οἱ στήλες τῶν Μαραθωνομάχων ἀπό τὴν ἔπαυλη τοῦ Ἡρώδη Ἀττικού στὴ Λουκού Κυνουρίας', in eds. K. BURASELIS and K. MEIDANI, *Μαραθών: Η μάχη και ο Αρχαίος Δῆμος*, pp. 99–108. Athens.

STANTON, G. R. 1973. 'Sophists and Philosophers: Problems of Classification', *AJPhil* 94: 350–64.

STARR, C. G. 1952. 'The Perfect Democracy of the Roman Empire', *American Historical Review* 58.1: 1–16.

STEINER, D. T. 2001. *Images in Mind: Statues in Archaic and Classical Greek Literature and Thought*. Princeton, NJ.

STEWART, A. 1979. *Attika: Studies in Athenian Sculpture of the Hellenistic Age*. London.

STEWART, A. 1990. *Greek Sculpture: An Exploration*. New Haven, CT.

STEWART, P. 2003. *Statues in Roman Society: Representation and Response*. Oxford.

STIRLING, L. M. 2008. 'Pagan Statuettes in Late Antique Corinth: Sculpture from the Panayia Domus', *Hesperia* 77.1: 89–161.

STONEMAN, R. 1995. 'Riddles in Bronze and Stone: Monuments and their Interpretation in the *Alexander Romance*', in *Groningen Colloquia on the Novel Volume VI*, pp. 159–70. Groningen.

STOOP, J. 2017. 'Between City and Empire: Awarding Statues to Romans in Greek Cities', *Past and Present* 235: 3–36.

STRAZDINS, E. 2008. 'The Sophistic Dilemma: Contemporary Fame Versus a Literary Legacy in Lucianus's Dream', in ed. MUSTAFA ÇEVIK, *Uluslararasi Samsatli Lucianus Sempozyumu/International Symposium on Lucianus of Samosata*, pp. 99–110. Adıyaman.

STRAZDINS, E. 2019. 'The King of Athens: Philostratus' Portrait of Herodes Atticus', *Classical Philology* 114.2: 238–64.

STRAZDINS, E. 2022a. 'Herodes Atticus and the Sanctuaries of Achaea: Reinterpreting the Roman Present via the Greek Past', in A. KOUREMENOS (ed.), *The Province of Achaea in the Second Century CE: The Past Present*, pp. 166–90. London.

STRAZDINS, E. 2022b. '*Anabasis* as Monument: Arrian, Xenophontic Space, and Cultural Authority', in eds. T. ROOD and M. TAMIOLAKI, *Xenophon's Anabasis and its Reception*, pp. 311–28. Berlin.

STRAZDINS, E. In press. 'Herodes Atticus, Hadrian, and the Antonines: Mediating Power and Self-Promotion in Achaea through Public and Private Display', in eds. C. DAVENPORT and S. MALIK, *Representing Rome's Emperors: Historical and Cultural Perspectives through Time*. Oxford.

STRAZDINS, E. Forthcoming. 'Herodes Atticus, Material Memories, and the Expression and Reception of Grief', in eds. G. KAZANTZIDIS and D. SPATHARAS, *Memory and Emotions in Classical Antiquity*. Berlin.

STRONACH, D. 1971. 'A Circular Symbol on the Tomb of Cyrus', *Iran* 9: 155–9.

STRONACH, D. 1978. *Pasargadae: A Report on the Excavations Conducted by the British Institute of Persian Studies from 1961 to 1963*. Oxford.

STRONACH, D. 1985. 'Pasargadae', in ed. I. GERSHEVITCH, *The Cambridge Ancient History of Iran II*, pp. 838–41. Cambridge.

STRUBBE, J. H. M. ed. 1991. 'Cursed Be He That Moves My Bones', in eds. C. A. FARAONE and D. OBBINK, *Magika Hiera: Ancient Greek Magic and Religion*, pp. 33–59. Oxford.

STRUBBE, J. H. M. 1997. *ΑΡΑΙ ΕΠΙΤΥΜΒΙΟΙ: Imprecations against Desecrators of the Grave in the Greek Epitaphs of Asia Minor. A Catalogue*. Bonn.

STUART, J. and N. REVETT 1762–1830. *The Antiquities of Athens. Measured and Delineated by James Stuart, FRS and FSA, and Nicholas Revett, Painters and Architects*, 5 vols. London.

STURGEON, M. C. 1987. *Isthmia: Excavations by the University of Chicago under the Auspices of the American School of Classical Studies at Athens* IV: *Sculpture I: 1952–1967*. Princeton, NJ.

SVENBRO, J. 1993. *Phrasikleia: An Anthropology of Reading in Ancient Greece*. Ithaca, NY.

SWAIN, S. C. R. 1991. 'The Reliability of Philostratus's *Lives of the Sophists*', *Classical Antiquity* 10.1: 148–63.

SWAIN, S. C. R. 1996. *Hellenism and Empire: Language, Classicism, and Power in the Greek World AD 50–250*. Oxford.

SWAIN, S. C. R. 1997. 'Biography and Biographic in the Literature of the Roman Empire', in eds. M. J. EDWARDS and S. SWAIN, *Portraits: Biographical Representation in the Greek and Latin Literature of the Roman Empire*, pp. 1–38. Oxford.

SYME, R. 1982. 'The Career of Arrian', *Harvard Studies in Classical Philology* 86: 181–211.

SYME, R. 1988. *Roman Papers IV*, ed. A. R. BIRLEY. Oxford.

SZEWCZYK, M. 2015. 'Nouveaux éléments pour l'étude d'un portrait de notable éphésien du musée du Louvre', *Revue des études anciennes* 117.1: 129–51.

TAGLIABUE, A. 2016. 'Aelius Aristides' Sacred Tales: A Study of the Creation of the "Narrative about Asclepius"', *Classical Antiquity* 35.1: 126–46.

TAMIOLAKI, M. 2016. 'Writing for Posterity in Ancient Historiography: Lucian's Perspective', in ed. A. LANIERI, *Knowing Future Time in and through Greek Historiography*, pp. 293–308. Berlin and Boston.

TANRIVER, C. 2013. *Mysia'dan Yeni Epigrafik Buluntular*. Izmir.

TATUM, J. 1978. *Apuleius and the Golden Ass*. Ithaca, NY.

TAYLOR, C. 2011. 'Graffiti and the Epigraphic Habit: Creating Communities and Writing Alternate Histories in Classical Attica', in eds. J. A. BAIRD and C. TAYLOR, *Ancient Graffiti in Context*, pp. 90–109. Berlin and Boston.

TENTORI MONTALTO, M. 2013. 'Nuove considerazioni sulla stele della tribù Erechtheis dalla villa di Erode Attico a Eva-Loukou', *ZPE* 185: 31–52.

TENTORI MONTALTO, M. 2014. 'La stele dei caduti della tribù Erechtheis dalla villa di Erode Attico a Loukou – Eva Kynourias (SEG LVI 430): la datazione e l'epigramma', *ZPE* 192: 34–44.

TESORIERO, C. A. 2005. 'Trampling over Troy: Caesar, Virgil, Lucan', in ed. C. WALDE, *Lucan im 21. Jahrhundert*, pp. 202–15. Munich and Leipzig.

THEOCHARAKI, A. M. 2011. 'The Ancient Circuit Wall of Athens: Its Changing Course and the Phases of Construction', *Hesperia* 80.1: 71–156.

THOMAS, E. 2007. *Monumentality and the Roman Empire*. Oxford.

THOMAS, E. 2013. 'Translating Roman Architecture into Greek Regional Identities', in eds. P. SCHUBERT, P. DUCREY, and P. DERRON, *Le Grecs Héritiers des Romains*, pp. 147–202. Geneva.

THOMAS, E. 2014. 'On the Sublime in Architecture', in eds. J. ELSNER and M. MEYER, *Art and Rhetoric in Roman Culture*, pp. 37–88. Cambridge.

THOMAS, E. 2015. 'The Beauties of Architecture', in eds. P. DESTRÉE and P. MURRAY, *A Companion to Ancient Aesthetics*, pp. 274–90. Hoboken.

THOMAS, E. 2017. 'Performance Space', in eds. D. S. RICHTER and W. A. JOHNSON, *The Oxford Handbook to the Second Sophistic*, pp. 181–202. Oxford.

THOMAS, R. 1992. *Literacy and Orality in Ancient Greece*. Cambridge.

THOMAS, R. 2003. 'Prose Performance Texts: *Epideixis* and Written Publication in the Late Fifth and Early Fourth Centuries', in ed. H. YUNIS, *Written Texts and the Rise of Literate Culture in Ancient Greece*, pp. 162–88. Cambridge.

THOMPSON, H. A. 1987. 'The Impact of Roman Architects and Architecture on Athens: 170 B.C. – A.D. 170', in eds. S. MACREADY and F. H. THOMPSON, *Roman Architecture in the Greek World*, pp. 1–17. London.

TILG, S. 2010. *Chariton of Aphrodisias and the Invention of the Greek Love Novel*. Oxford.

TOBIN, J. 1993. 'Some New Thoughts on Herodes Atticus' Tomb, his Stadium of 143/4, and Philostratus *VS* 2.550', *AJArch* 97.1: 81–9.

TOBIN, J. 1997. *Herodes Attikos and the City of Athens: Patronage and Conflict under the Antonines*. Amsterdam.

TOMPKINS, J. P. 1980. 'The Reader in History: The Changing Shape of Literary Response', in ed. J. P. TOMPKINS, *Reader-Response Criticism: From Formalism to Post-Structuralism*, pp. 201–32. Baltimore.

TOO, Y. L. 1996. 'Statues, Mirrors, Gods: Controlling Images in Apuleius', in ed. J. ELSNER, *Art and Text in Roman Culture*, pp. 133–52. Cambridge.

TOO, Y. L. 1998. *The Idea of Ancient Literary Criticism*. Oxford.

TRAPP, M. 1990. 'Plato's *Phaedrus* in Second-Century Greek Literature', in ed. D. A. RUSSELL, *Antonine Literature*, pp. 141–73. Oxford.

TRAPP, M. 2007. 'What is this *Philosophia* Anyway?', in eds. J. R. MORGAN and M. JONES, *Philosophical Presences in the Ancient Novel*, pp. 1–22. Groningen.

TRAPP, M. 2014. 'The Role of Philosophy and Philosophers in the Imperial Period', in ed. M. BECK, *A Companion to Plutarch*, pp. 43–57. Malden, MA, Oxford, Chichester.

TRAVLOS, J. 1971. *Pictorial Dictionary of Ancient Athens*. New York, NY.

TRAVLOS, J. 1988. *Bildlexicon zur Topographie des antiken Attika*. Tübingen.

VAN DIJK, G.-J. 2009. 'The *Odyssey* of Apollonius: An Intertextual Paradigm', in eds. E. BOWIE and J. ELSNER, *Philostratus*, pp. 176–204. Cambridge.

VAN DYKE, R. M. 2008. 'Memory, Place, and the Memorialization of Landscape', in eds. B. DAVID and J. THOMAS, *Handbook of Landscape Archaeology*, pp. 277–84. Walnut Creek, CA.

VANDERPOOL, E. 1961. 'News Letter from Greece', *AJArch* 65: 299–303.

VANDERPOOL, E. 1970. 'Some Attic Inscriptions', *Hesperia* 39.1: 40–6.

VAN GRONINGEN, B. A. 1965. 'General Literary Tendencies in the Second Century A.D.', *Mnemosyne* 18: 41–56.

VAN NIJF, O. 2000. 'Inscriptions and Civic Memory in the Roman East', in ed. A. E. COOLEY, *The Afterlife of Inscriptions: Reusing, Rediscovering, Reinventing and Revitalizing Ancient Inscriptions*, pp. 23–36. London.

VARNER, E. R. 2004. *Mutilation and Transformation: Damnatio Memoriae and Roman Imperial Portraiture*. Leiden.

VARNER, E. R. 2006. 'Reading Replications: Roman Rhetoric and Greek Quotations', in eds. J. TRIMBLE and J. ELSNER, *Art and Replication: Greece, Rome, and Beyond. Art History* (Special Issue) 29.2: 280–303.

VARNER, E. R. 2015. 'Reuse and Recarving: Technical Evidence', in eds. E. A. FRIEDLAND, M. G. SOBOCINSKI, and E. K. GAZDA, *Oxford Handbook of Roman Sculpture*, pp. 123–38. Oxford.

VERMEULE, C. C. III 1954. 'Review of Harrison, *The Athenian Agora. Results of Excavations conducted by the American School of Classical Studies at Athens: Vol. 1, Portrait Sculpture*', *AJArch* 58: 253–5.

VERMEULE, C. C. III 1977. *Greek Sculpture and Roman Taste*. Ann Arbor, MI.

VERNANT, J.-P. 1991. 'A "Beautiful Death" and the Disfigured Corpse in Homeric Epic', in ed. F. I. ZEITLIN, *Mortals and Immortals: Collected Essays*, pp. 50–74. Princeton, NJ.

VETTERS, H. 1978. 'Ephesos: Vorläufiger Grabungsbericht 1976', *Anzeiger: Österreichische Akademie der Wissenschaften, Wien, Philologisch-historische Klasse* 114: 194–212.

VEYNE, P. 1990. *Bread and Circuses: Historical Sociology and Political Pluralism*, abridged with an introduction by O. MURRAY, translated by B. PEARCE. London.

VIDAL-NAQUET, P. 1984. 'Flavius Arrien entre deux mondes', in Arrien, *Histoire d'Alexandre: l'Anabase d'Alexandre le Grand et l'Inde*, translated by PIERRE SAVINEL, pp. 309–94. Paris.

VON FREEDEN, J. 1983. *Oikia Kyrrestou: Studien zum sogenannten Turm der Winde in Athen (Archaeologica)*. Rome.

VON MÖLLENDORF, P. 2014. 'Mimet(h)ic *Paideia* in Lucian's *True History*', in eds. E. P. CUEVA and S. N. BYRNE, *A Companion to the Ancient Novel*, pp. 522–34. Malden, MA and Oxford.

VON MOOCK, D. W. 1998. *Die figürlichen Grabstelen Attikas in der Kaiserzeit. Studien zur Verbreitung, Chronologie, Typologie und Ikonographie*. Mainz.

VON SCHEFOLD, K. 1943. *Die Bildnisse der antiken Dichter, Redner und Denker*. Basel.

VOUT, C. 2003. 'A Revision of Hadrian's Portraiture', in eds. L. DE BLOIS, P. ERDKAMP, O. HEKSTER, G. DE KLEIJN, and S. MOLS, *The Representation and Perception of Roman Imperial Power*, pp. 442–57. Amsterdam.

VOUT, C. 2005. 'Antinous, Archaeology, and History', *JRS* 95: 80–96.

VOUT, C. 2006. 'Biography as Fantasy, History as Image', in *Antinous: The Face of the Antique*, pp. 23–39. Leeds.

VOUT, C. 2007. *Power and Eroticism in Imperial Rome*. Cambridge.

VOUTIRAS, E. 2008. 'Representing the "Intellectual" or the Active Politician? The Portrait of Herodes Atticus', in eds. A. D. RIZAKIS and F. CAMIA, *Pathways to Power: Civic Elites in the Eastern Part of the Roman Empire*, pp. 209–20. Athens.

WADE-GERY, H. T. 1945. 'Kritias and Herodes', *Classical Quarterly* 39: 19–33.

WAELKENS, M. 1987. 'The Adoption of Roman Building Techniques in the Architecture of Asia Minor', in eds. S. MACREADY and F. H. THOMPSON, *Roman Architecture in the Greek World*, pp. 94–105. London.

WAGNER, P. 1996. 'Ekphrasis, Iconotexts, and Intermediality – the State(s) of the Art(s)', in ed. P. WAGNER, *Icon—Texts—Iconotexts: Essays on Ekphrasis and Intermediality*, pp. 1–40. Berlin.

WALKER, H. J. 1995. *Theseus and Athens*. Oxford.

WALKER, S. 1989. 'Exhibits at Ballot: A Marble Head of Herodes Atticus from Winchester City Museum', *The Antiquities Journal* 69: 324–6.

WALLACE-HADRILL, A. 2008. *Rome's Cultural Revolution*. Cambridge.

WALSH, G. B. 1988. 'Sublime Method: Longinus on Language and Imitation', *Classical Antiquity* 7.2: 252–69.

WEBB, P. A. 2017. *The Tower of the Winds in Athens. Greeks, Romans, Christians, and Muslims: Two Millennia of Continual Use*. Philadelphia.

WEBB, R. 2006. 'Fiction, *Mimesis* and the Performance of the Greek Past in the Second Sophistic', in eds. D. KONSTAN and S. SAÏD, *Greeks on Greekness: Viewing the Greek Past under the Roman Empire*, pp. 27–46. Cambridge.

WEBB, R. 2009. *Ekphrasis, Imagination and Persuasion in Ancient Rhetorical Theory and Practice*. Farnham.

WEBER, H. 1956. 'Eine spätgriechische Jünglingstatue', in ed. E. KUNZE, *Bericht über die Ausgrabungen in Olympia*, pp. 128–48. Berlin.

WELCH, K. 1998. 'Greek Stadia and Roman Spectacles: Asia, Athens, and the Tomb of Herodes Atticus', *JRA* 11: 117–45.

WELSH, M. K. 1904–05. 'Honorary Statues in Ancient Greece', *The Annual of the British School at Athens* 11: 32–49.

WERNER, W. 1997. 'The Largest Ship Trackway in Ancient Times: The Diolkos of the Isthmus of Corinth, Greece, and Early Attempts to Build a Canal', *International Journal of Nautical Archaeology and Underwater Exploration* 26: 98–119.

WHITEHEAD, A. 2009. *Memory*. London.

WHITBY, M. 2016. 'Onesikritos (134)', in ed. I. WORTHINGTON, *Brill's New Jacoby*. Leiden.

WHITMARSH, T. 1998. 'Reading Power in Roman Greece: The *Paideia* of Dio Chrysostom', in eds. Y. L. TOO and N. LIVINGSTONE, *Power and Pedagogy: Rhetorics of Classical Learning*, pp. 192–213. Cambridge.

WHITMARSH, T. 1999. 'Greek and Roman in Dialogue: The Pseudo-Lucianic Nero', *JHS* 119: 142–60.

WHITMARSH, T. 2001. *Greek Literature and the Roman Empire: The Politics of Imitation*. Oxford.

WHITMARSH, T. 2002. 'Alexander's Hellenism and Plutarch's Textualism', *Classical Quarterly* 52.1: 174–92.

WHITMARSH, T. 2004. 'Aelius Aristides', in ed. I. J. F DE JONG, *Narrators, Narratees, and Narratives in Ancient Greek Literature Vol. 1*, pp. 441–7. Leiden.

WHITMARSH, T. 2005. *The Second Sophistic*. Oxford.

WHITMARSH, T. 2006a. 'True Histories: Lucian, Bakhtin, and the Pragmatics of Reception', in eds. C. MARTINDALE and R. F. THOMAS, *Classics and the Uses of Reception*, pp. 104–15. Malden, MA and Oxford.

WHITMARSH, T. 2006b. 'Quickening the Classics: The Politics of Prose in Roman Greece', in ed. J. I. PORTER, *Classical Pasts: The Classical Traditions of Greece and Rome*, pp. 353–74. Princeton, NJ.

WHITMARSH, T. ed. 2008. *The Cambridge Companion to the Greek and Roman Novel*. Cambridge.

WHITMARSH, T. 2011. 'Hellenism, Nationalism, Hybridity: The Invention of the Novel', in eds. G. BHAMBRA, D. ORRELLS, and T. ROYNON, *African Athena: New Agendas*, pp. 210–24. Oxford.

WHITMARSH, T. 2012. 'Philostratus', in ed. I. J. F. DE JONG, *Space in Ancient Greek Literature*, pp. 463–79. Oxford.

WHITMARSH, T. 2013a. *Beyond the Second Sophistic: Adventures in Postclassicism*. Berkeley, CA.

WHITMARSH, T. 2013b. 'Resistance is Futile? Greek Literary Tactics in the Face of Rome', in eds. P. SCHUBERT, P. DUCREY, and P. DERRON, *Le Grecs Héritiers des Romains*, pp. 57–78. Geneva.

WHITMARSH, T. 2015. 'The Mnemology of Empire and Resistance: Memory, Oblivion, and Periegesis in Imperial Greek Culture', in eds. K. GALINSKY and K. LAPATIN, *Cultural Memories in the Roman Empire*, pp. 49–64. Los Angeles, CA.

WHITMARSH, T. 2018. *Dirty Love: The Genealogy of the Ancient Greek Novel*. Oxford.

WILHELM, A. 1933. 'Zwei Hermes des Herodes Atticus', *Jahreshefte des Österreichischen archäologischen Instituts in Wien* 28: 168–82.

WINIARCZYK, M. 2002. *Euhemeros von Messene: Leben, Werk und Nachwirkung*. Munich.

WIRTH, G. 1963. 'Ἀρριανὸς ὁ φιλόσοφος', *Klio* 41: 221–3.

WISEMAN, J. 1978. *The Land of the Ancient Corinthians*. Göteborg.

WITSCHEL, C. 2014. 'Epigraphische Monumente und städtische Öffentlichkeit im Westen des Imperium Romanum', in eds. W. ECK and P. FUNKE, *Öffentlichkeit— Monument—Text. XIV Congressus Internationalis Epigraphiae Graecae et Latinae, Berlin 2012—Akten*, pp. 105–33. Berlin and Boston.

WOOLF, G. 1996. 'Monumental Writing and the Expansion of Roman Society in the Early Empire', *JRS* 86: 22–39.

WREDE, H. 1972. *Die spätantike Hermengalerie von Welschbillig: Untersuchung zur Kunsttradition im 4. Jahrhundert n. Chr. und zur allgemeinen Bedeutung des antiken Hermenmals*. Berlin.

WREDE, H. 1986. *Die Antike Herme*. Mainz.

WRIGHT, W. C. ed. and trans. 1968. *Philostratus: Lives of the Sophists. Eunapius: Lives of Philosophers*, LCL 134. Cambridge, MA.

WYLER, S. 2006. 'Roman Replications of Greek Art at the Villa della Farnesina', in eds. J. TRIMBLE and J. ELSNER, *Art and Replication: Greece, Rome, and Beyond. Art History* (Special Issue) 29.2: 213–32.

WYSS, B. ed. 1936. *Antimachi Colophonii Reliquiae*. Berlin.

YATES, F. A. 1966. *The Art of Memory*. London.

YOURCENAR, M. 1963. *Memoirs of Hadrian and Reflections on the Composition of Memoirs of Hadrian*, translated by G. FRICK in collaboration with M. Yourcenar. New York, NY.

ZADOROJNYI, A. V. 2006. 'Lords of the Flies: Literacy and Tyranny in Imperial Biography', in eds. B. McGING and J. MOSSMAN, *The Limits of Ancient Biography*, pp. 351–94. Swansea.

ZADOROJNYI, A. V. 2013. 'Shuffling Surfaces: Epigraphy, Power, and Integrity in the Graeco-Roman Narratives', in eds. P. LIDDEL and P. LOW, *Inscriptions and their Uses in Greek and Latin Literature*, pp. 365–82. Oxford.

ZADOROJNYI, A. V. 2018. 'The Aesthetics and Politics of Inscriptions in Imperial Greek Literature', in eds. A. PETROVIC, I. PETROVIC, and E. THOMAS, *The Materiality of Text—Placement, Perception, and Presence of Inscribed Texts in Classical Antiquity*, pp. 48–68. Leiden.

ZANKER, P. 1995. *The Mask of Socrates: The Image of the Intellectual in Antiquity*, translated by A. SHAPIRO. Berkeley.

ZIEGLER, K. ed. 1970. *Plutarchi Vitae Parallelae I.1*. Leipzig.

ZIEGLER, K. ed. 1994. *Plutarchi Vitae Parallelae II.2*, editionem correctiorem cum addendis curavit H. Gärtner. Stuttgart and Leipzig.

ZILLER, E. 1870. 'Ausgrabungen am panathenaïschen Stadion', *Zeitschrift für Bauwesen* 20: 485–92.

ZUIDERHOEK, A. 2009. *The Politics of Munificence in the Roman Empire: Citizens, Elites and Benefactors in Asia Minor*. Cambridge.

ZUIDERHOEK, A. 2013. 'Cities, Buildings and Benefactions in the Roman East', in eds. C. P. DICKENSON and O. M. VAN NIJF, *Public Space in the Post-Classical City: Proceedings of a One Day Colloquium Held at Fransum 23rd July 2007*, pp. 173–92. Leuven.

GENERAL INDEX

Note: Figures are indicated by an italic *"f"*, and notes are indicated by "n." following the page number.

For the benefit of digital users, indexed terms that span two pages (e.g., 52–53) may, on occasion, appear on only one of those pages

Achilles (foster-son of Herodes Attikos) 147, 149*f*, 151n.109, 152–3, 155, 227*f*, 228–30,
Achilles (hero) 72, 131, 131n.43, 132n.48, 133n.51, 156n.121, 161–3, 162n.137, 174, 177, 182, 182n.207, 185, 191, 228, 254, 274
  lyre of 162
  tomb of 159–66, 173–4, 228
Aegeus, father of Theseus 112, 280, 281, 296–7, 299
Agrippa, Marcus Vipsanius 111, 263
Aigisthos 116–17
Aischines 2–3, 5, 7, 83–6, 84*f*, 88–9, 204, 249–50
Ajax 174, 182n.207
  tomb of 174
Akropolis, Athenian, *see* Athens
Alexander the Clay Plato / of Seleukeia 98–9, 265–7, 284, 303
Alexander the Great 14, 50, 51n.79, 55–8, 70, 85–6, 89n.39, 111, 121, 123–4, 133n.51, 134–44, 146, 157–74, 182–3, 191, 193, 215–17, 237–8, 272n.94, 284–5, 306–7
  and tomb of Achilles 161–6
  and tomb of Kyros the Great 166–74
  tomb of 133n.51, 134–6, 160, 164–6, 170
Alexander of Kotiaion 67, 72
Alexander (Paris), *see* Paris-Alexandros
Alexandria 81nn.13 and 18, 89n.39, 133n.51, 146n.102, 164–5, 170, 242, 242n.188
Alexandria Troas 81nn.13 and 18, 89, 177, 259–60
Alkibiades 38, 205–6
Andronikos of Kyrrhos 14, 15*f*
Andokides 44
Antinoos 81n.13, 86n.33, 89n.37, 177, 182, 185, 188–90, 189*f*, 221–6, 222*f*, 222*f*, 223*f*, 224*f*, 225*f*, 228–33, 243–4, 275–6, 285–6, 307

as Apollo 221–3
as Dionysos 182, 185, 221–3
and Ganymede 221–6
and imperial cult 188, 190, 232n.154
as Osiris 177, 221–3, 222*f*, 232–3
and Polydeukion 223–6, 224*f*, 225*f*, 228–33, 243–4, 275–6
Antipater 41–2
Antoninus Pius 93n.45, 94–5, 111–12, 131–2, 207–10, 209*f*, 266–7
Apollo 138–9, 198–9, 221, 237n.268
Apollonios of Tyana 80n.8, 129n.35, 130n.36, 138–44, 156n.121, 157–9, 161n.136, 251–2, 263–4, 267–70, *see also* Philostratos
Apuleius 4n.23, 24–5, 194, 199–200, 238–44, 252
  Apologia 4n.23
  Florida 16 4n.23, 199–200, 238–41
  and statues 199–200, 238–41, 244
Aratos 14
Arch of Hadrian, *see* Athens
Argive Hera 111, 113
Argo, the 106, 108–10
Aristeides, Aelius 4n.23, 8–9, 24–5, 29–30, 60, 67–75, 85–6, 100–1, 105–8, 110–11, 113–14, 117–20, 123–4, 133–6, 194, 200–1, 203–4, 203*f*, 217–19, 240–3, 263, 301, 305–6
  Against Those Who Criticize Him Because He Does Not Declaim (Or. 33) 133–4
  altar from Mytilene 73–4, 74*f*
  and Alexander 134–6, 141, 166
  and artefactual memory 105–8, 110–11, 113–14, 117–20
  and Asklepios 67–75, 134–6, 218–19
  and Demosthenes 68, 70–2
  and dreams 68–9, 71–5, 85–6, 133–6, 200–1, 218–19, 221, 241–3
  Isthmian Oration 105–8, 114
  Oration 28 68

348 GENERAL INDEX

Aristeides, Aelius (*cont.*)
  Panathenaic Oration 61–2
  and performance 68–75, 135–6, 242–3
  Sacred Tales 60, 67–75, 100–1, 108, 123–4,
    133–6, 166, 200–1, 218–19, 241–3
  statue of 70–1, 203–4, 203*f*, 242
  and statues 200–1, 218–19, 221, 241–2
  as spectacle (θέαμα) 70–1, 74–5, 140,
    305–6
  To Rome 263
  and training (ἄσκησις) 67–8, 70
  and writing 72–5, 133–6, 241–3, 305–6
Aristoboulos (officer of Alexander the
    Great) 166–8, 172
Aristotle 86–8, 262n.63, 272n.94
Arrian, Lucius Flavius 1–2, 22–5, 29–30,
    47n.68, 48–59, 63–4, 78, 80, 100–1,
    108–14, 117–21, 134–40, 159–74,
    188–9, 191, 194, 198, 203–4, 237–8,
    241, 285, 306–7
  Anabasis of Alexander 50, 56n.94, 121,
    123–4, 134–5, 138–40, 159–74, 188,
    285, 306–7
  and artefactual memory 23, 108–11,
    113–14, 117–20
  Battle Order Against the Alani 50, 51n.79
  Bithyniaka 56n.94
  and commemorative landscapes 1–2,
    50–9, 63–4, 100–1, 110, 161–6
  Discourses 56n.94
  Events After Alexander 56n.94, 164–5
  and Hadrian 1, 22–3, 50–1, 53–9, 54*f*,
    108–9, 164–5, 306–7
  herm from Athens 51–3, 52*f*, 58–9
  Indika 50, 56n.94
  and inscriptions 48–9, 49*f*, 56–7, 110,
    162–8, 172
  and literary authority 50–9, 100–1, 110,
    165–6, 237–8
  On Hunting 50–3
  Parthika 56n.94
  and Phasine 108–9, 112–13, 168n.159
  Periplous 1–2, 22–3, 50–9, 78, 85–6,
    108–10, 125, 134
  and statues 55–9, 108–10, 136–7, 198,
    203–4, 237–8
  Tactical Handbook 50
  and Trapezous 1, 50–9, 100–1, 110, 134,
    136–7, 160–1, 306–7
  and Xenophon 1, 22–3, 47n.68, 50–9,
    52*f*, 63–4, 100–1, 110, 203–4

Asklepios 8–9, 45–6, 67–75, 74*f*, 134–6,
    177, 200–1, 218–19
Asklepieion
  at Athens 177
  at Mytilene 73–4, 74*f*
  at Pergamon 44–6, 45*f*, 67–8, 70,
    205n.62
Astros 175, 190
Athena 68, 72, 138–9, 161–2,
    161n.134, 184n.220, 200–1,
    278–9
  Parthenos 108–9, 200–1
  Promachos 108–9
Athenais (daughter of Herodes
    Attikos) 207–10, 217n.94
Athens 2–3, 7, 14, 18n.88, 19–22, 24–5,
    48, 51–3, 60–3, 66–8, 81–3, 88–95,
    98–101, 107n.92, 108–9, 111–13,
    126–7, 177–8, 180, 182, 185, 190,
    202, 210–11, 219, 226, 230–3, 236,
    241, 249–51, 256–306
  Agora 14, 15n.73, 83–5, 83*f*, 111,
    215n.91, 257–9
  Akropolis 23, 108–9, 112–13, 200–1,
    205n.60, 272–3
  Arch of Hadrian 90–5, 94*f*, 99, 253
  Archon 19, 23, 226, 296
  Dêmosion Sêma 177–8
  Metroon 108
  Mouseion Hill 19–23, 20*f*
  Odeion of Agrippa 111
  Odeion of Regilla 126–7, 259–60, 272–4,
    273*f*, 291–2, 298
  Olympieion 92–3, 202, 202*f*, 223–6
  Panathenaia 296–7, 299
  Panathenaic ship 289–90, 297–8
  Panathenaic stadium 100–1, 259–60,
    272–3, 277, 282, 283*f*, 289–93,
    290*f*, 291*f*, 292*f*, 295–8,
    305–6
  Philopappos Monument 15n.73,
    19–23, 20*f*, 21*f*, 22*f*, 100–1,
    211–12
  Roman Agora 14, 15*f*
  Temple of Olympian Zeus, *see*
    Olympieion
  Tower of the Winds 14, 15*f*
Atlantis 146–7
Attica 77–8, 80, 86–8, 93n.45, 98, 105,
    180–1, 182n.209, 190–1, 226–8,
    265–6, 275–6, 299, 306–7

GENERAL INDEX **349**

Attikos (father of Herodes Attikos) 98n.62,
175, 211–12, 282–3, 285–6, 293, 295,
305–6
Attikos Bradua 147–51, 207–10
audience 2–4, 11–12, 23n.99, 29–40,
42n.44, 43, 47, 58–67, 69–75,
69n.145, 77, 85–9, 98–9, 104, 108–9,
111–20, 127–9, 133, 135–8, 140–1,
143, 146–7, 153, 159n.130, 168–70,
174, 190, 194, 219, 226–8, 235–9,
244, 249, 252, 260, 266–7, 277,
298, 305–7
Augustus 55–6, 89n.37, 136–8, 170, 260,
263
    Res Gestae 136–8
authenticity 4–5, 38, 109–10, 112, 180–1,
191–2, 203–4
author(s) 4–6, 10–13, 18, 23–5, 29–33,
35–7, 38n.36, 39–44, 42n.49,
47–8, 50–3, 59–60, 62, 65–9, 75–6,
80–1, 96n.53, 97–9, 108, 112,
114–16, 118, 124–7, 129, 131–3,
137–8, 141, 144–7, 158–61,
163–6, 168, 172–3, 188–9, 191, 193,
200, 203–7, 217–18, 223–6,
237–8, 241–4, 247–8, 253–4,
260, 274–5, 293, 294n.152,
297, 304
Avlona 90–1, 98–9, 98n.62

Bakkhylides 72–3
Behr, Charles 69–70
benefaction, *see* euergetism
Black Sea 1, 47–8, 50, 53, 108–10
book(s) 34, 38–40, 72, 109–10, 127, 166,
240–3
Bowie, Ewen 6, 72
Brexiza, *see* Sanctuary of the Egyptian Gods
Brown, Peter 13–14
Bull(s)
    Marathonian 210–11, 253, 282
    Minotaur 210–11, 253
    Nymphaion at Olympia 210–11, 210*f*, 253
Burrell, Barbara 101
Butz, Patricia 184–5

Caecilius of Kaleakte 30–1
canon, the 3–4, 7–8, 11–13, 29–48, 55,
62–3, 65–7, 75–6, 111–13, 131–2,
143n.90, 144–6, 163, 165–6, 264–5,
303, 306–7

canonicity 3–4, 7–8, 12–13, 25–6, 29–48,
74–5, 119–20, 145–6, 165–6,
266, 305
Caracalla 161–2, 170
Chaironeia 35
Chairs of Philosophy 271–2
Chairs of Rhetoric 66–8, 266, 271–2,
305–6
Chandler, Richard 99–100
Chaniotis, Angelos 4–5
Charon 41–2
citizenship, Roman 1–2, 13–16,
19–22, 24–5, 45–6, 101–2, 104,
106–7, 147–51, 177, 205–6,
211–12, 217, 256–7, 262–3, 296,
302–3
classic 29–30, 62–3, 65, 204, 242
classical 2–4, 6–8, 14, 17, 22–3, 25–6,
29–48, 50–3, 58–9, 62–4, 69–70,
75–6, 79–86, 92–3, 97–8, 100–1,
108–10, 115–16, 131–2, 160–1, 172,
175, 182, 191, 204, 221–3, 226–8,
243–4, 261–4, 262n.61, 288–9,
300–1, 306–7
classicism 13, 25, 30–48, 76
classicizing 2, 6–7, 10, 13
Cole, Michael 12
collective memory, *see* memory
Connolly, Joy 6
consul 19, 22*f*, 23, 48–9, 49*f*, 83–5, 101,
136–7, 212–13
copy 65, 79–85, 86n.33, 93n.45,
136–7, 180–2, 188, 191–2, 204,
230–1, 293
Corinth 24–5, 81–3, 89, 105–8,
113–14, 117–18, 158, 159*f*, 177,
183n.213, 200–1, 205–6, 217–18,
220, 233–7, 244, 250–1, 253–4,
259–60, 273–4
    and Favorinus 200–1, 205–6, 217–18,
    220–1, 236–8, 244
    and Herakles 253–4, 255*f*
    Isthmus of 92–3, 250–6, 255*f*, 259–60,
    298
        Theseus' pillar 92–5, 252, 299
    and Nero 253–6, 255*f*
    Peirene Fountain 233–7, 234*f*, 234*f*,
    235*f*
    and Regilla 233–7, 234*f*, 234*f*,
    235*f*
cultural memory, *see* memory

350 GENERAL INDEX

Damianos, T. Flavius 80, 100–1, 185n.226
damnatio memoriae 206, 291–2
Delphi 24–5, 41–3, 81–3, 89, 128–9, 138–9,
    177, 180–1, 213n.87, 217n.94, 223*f*,
    231–2, 232*f*, 235–6, 243–4, 259–60,
    281, 305–6
Delphic oracle 41–3, 128–9, 180–1, 281
dêmos 14–16, 83–5, 177, 190, 194–7, 199,
    258, 262, 263n.67, 264, 269–71, 273–4,
    277, 283–5, 287–9, 291–5, 297–301
Demosthenes 31, 35–6, 44–8, 45*f*, 53, 68,
    70–2, 83–6, 83*f*, 88–9, 143n.92,
    204–6, 264, 276
    On the Crown 35–6
Dio Cassius 49n.72, 55–6, 161–2, 170,
    254n.35, 263–4, 301
Dio Chrysostom 4n.23, 24, 37–40, 47, 59–62,
    77, 109–10, 194, 200n.35, 205–6,
    239n.182, 242, 255–6, 257n.45,
    259–61, 264n.68, 268–71, 294n.152
    Orations 1–4 (on Kingship) 14n.71, 268–70
    Oration 21, 29–30, 37–40, 47, 109–10
    Rhodian Oration (*Or.* 31) 205–6, 218n.96
    Oration 47 257n.45, 259–60
Diodoros Siculus 137n.64, 144–5,
    161n.134, 164–5, 170, 255n.38
Dionysios
    of Halikarnassos 40–1
    Longinos 30n.4
    of Miletos 78–80, 103–5, 103*f*, 104*f*,
        119–20, 297–8
        Sarcophagus of, *see* Ephesos
    of Syracuse 260–1
    Titus Claudius Flavianus, *see* of Miletos
Dionysos 138, 142–4, 146, 161n.134, 177,
    182, 184n.220, 185, 221–3
    and Antinoos 177, 182, 185, 221–3
    and Herakles 138, 142–4, 146
Downie, Janet 68, 70, 242–3
dream(s) 17, 41–2, 44–6, 45*f*, 65n.126,
    68–9, 71–5, 85–6, 133–6, 200–1,
    218–21, 238, 241–3

ekphrasis 8–9, 63–5, 80, 109, 111, 114–15,
    117, 119
Eleusis 81–3, 93n.45, 268, 296–7
Eliot, T.S. 32–3
Elpinike, daughter of Herodes Attikos 183–4,
    207–10, 217n.94, 282, 287–8, 288*f*

Elsner, Jaś 109, 111, 260
emotions 3, 61–2, 97–8, 100, 147, 156,
    158–9, 266–9, 272, 274–5
    grief 62, 95, 97–8, 191, 268–76, 298
emperors 19n.90, 48, 53, 55–8, 72, 81–3,
    85–6, 93n.45, 98–9, 106, 107n.95,
    123–4, 131–2, 139–40, 170, 175, 177,
    182–3, 188–9, 204, 211–14, 217,
    221–3, 232n.154, 250, 255–76,
    280–1, 295, 301–3
empire, *see* imperialism, imperial power
    (Roman)
emulation (ζῆλος) 8, 13, 31, 38, 41, 46–8,
    53, 63, 132, 138n.67, 160, 175n.185,
    184, 193, 221, 231, 255–6, 264–5,
    284, 291–2
energeia ('vividness') 115
Ennius 41–2
Ephesos 15n.73, 71, 77–83, 100–5,
    106n.90, 185–9, 207, 297–8
    Library of Kelsos 15n.73, 78–9, 101–4,
        102*f*, 123, 189, 204n.50, 207
    tomb of Titus Claudius Flavianus Dionysios
        78–80, 103–5, 103*f*, 104*f*, 297–8
    tomb of T. Flavius Damianos 80, 101
    Vedii Antonini family 83n.20, 101, 185–8,
        186*f*, 187*f*, 221–3
epideixis 2–4, 34–5, 48n.69, 59–60,
    61n.109, 64–70, 72, 117–18, 130–3,
    191, 206–7, 219, 238, 244, 249–50,
    250n.21, 260–1, 266, 303–4
Eshleman, Kendra 6, 249–50
eternal, *see* temporality
eternity, *see* temporality
euergetism 5, 8–9, 13–17, 19–26, 81–5,
    100–1, 106–8, 111–12, 123–4, 174,
    177, 182, 188, 193–5, 201, 205–6,
    207n.72, 211, 214–17, 232–3, 235–6,
    240–4, 248–9, 256–7, 259–60, 263–4,
    273–4, 277, 280–2, 291–6, 302–3
Euhemeros 144–6
Euripides 117, 131n.43, 299

fake 38, 65
false 66, 129–30, 145–7, 160, 238,
    294n.152
fame 1–2, 4, 14, 17–18, 23–5, 29–30, 33–4,
    36, 40, 42–3, 45–8, 53, 58–61, 63–8,
    72–3, 81–3, 105, 125–7, 129–32, 134–6,

140–1, 159–62, 164–6, 169–70, 172–4, 181, 192–6, 214–15, 217–18, 237–41, 244, 251–2, 260, 276, 282–4, 288–9, 293, 303, *see also* κλέος
Faustina the Elder 94–5, 207–10, 209*f*
Faustina the Younger 81, 183–4, 207–10, 209*f*
Favorinus 5n.30, 24–5, 60, 194–5, 200–1, 205–6, 217–18, 220–1, 236–8, 241, 244, 252, 268–71
  Corinthian Oration 200–1, 205–6, 217–18, 236–8
future, *see* temporality
futurity, *see* temporality

Galinsky, Karl 13
Geagan, Daniel 96
Gellius, Aulus 247–9, 268n.78, 271–2, 274–5
Gleason, Maud 6, 90–3, 96, 98, 274
Gorgon 116–17, 188
Gorgoneion 188, 189*f*
Graham, Abigail 101

Hadrian 1, 22–3, 50–9, 86–8, 89n.37, 90–5, 94*f*, 99, 101, 108–12, 123–4, 136–8, 161–2, 164–5, 174–5, 184, 188–9, 189*f*, 202, 204–5, 207–11, 212*f*, 213–14, 215n.91, 221–6, 231–3, 253, 257, 260, 261n.58, 266–7, 273–6, 286, 298–300, 299n.169, 306–7
  and Antinoos 188–9, 189*f*, 221–6, 231–3, 275–6
  Arch of, *see* Athens
Hektor 135n.55, 161n.136,
  statue of 200–1, 237
Herakles 121, 131, 138–9, 142–7, 161n.134, 177, 185, 191, 253–4, 255*f*, 274, 278–9
  and Dionysos 138, 142–4, 146
  pillars of 138, 142–7
herms, *see* Herodes Attikos
Hermes 54, 58–9, 153, 155–6, 163n.143, 184n.220, 221–3
Herodes Attikos 15n.73, 19–22, 24–5, 44, 46–7, 62–3, 66–7, 78–103, 105–7, 111–12, 119–20, 123–4, 126–7, 129–30, 138, 147–59, 169n.163, 173–92, 194, 201, 204, 207–17, 221–37, 243–4, 247–307
  and Athens 256–304

Bey inscription 277–81, 278*f*, 284–5
  and Demosthenes 44, 46–7, 83–6, 88–9, 276
  Ephesos 188
  foster-sons, *see* Achilles, Memnon, Polydeukion
  Gate of Eternal Concord, *see* Marathon
  and grief 95–8, 100, 182, 184–5, 191, 268–76
  and 'Greeks', the 98–9, 284
  and Hadrian 86–8, 89n.37, 90–5, 99, 111–12, 175, 184, 188–9, 189*f*, 207–11, 213–14, 215n.91, 221–6, 231–3, 253, 257, 260, 266–7, 273–6, 286, 298–300, 299n.169
  and Herakles 177, 185, 191, 253–4, 274, 278
  and herms 147–59
  as 'Hero of Marathon' 190–1, 194, 232, 290–2, 291*f*, 292*f*, 305–6
  Klepsydrion 98–9
  and Kritias 44, 264
  Loukou estate 147, 174–92, 226, 228–30, 232n.155, 284
  and Marathon 24–5, 81, 86–100, 147, 155–6, 174–92, 210–11, 223–6, 232, 277–94, 296–7, 299, 301–2, 305–7
  and Marcus Aurelius 81, 86–9, 257–9, 258*f*, 261–4, 267–72, 274–6, 283–5, 306
  and Nero 253–6, 259–60, 269–70, 273–6, 294–5, 298–300, 302–3
  and nymphaion at Olympia 207–17
  Odeion of Regilla, *see* Athens
  and Philagros 62–3, 66–7, 266
  and philosophers 214–15, 267–77
  portrait(s) 81–9, 82*f*, 87*f*
  Sirmium trial 207–10, 213–14, 248, 250–1, 257–9, 267–71, 274–85, 298, 300
  and Sokrates 86–8, 293–5, 301–4
  stêlê of the fallen of the Erechtheis tribe, *see* Marathon
  and Theseus 92–5, 210–11, 250–3, 255–6, 277–303, 305–6
  tomb of 277–85, 288–98
  and tyranny 248, 250–1, 255–65, 267–77, 280–2, 287–9, 291–2, 294–5, 298–304
  and Xerxes 255–6

Herodotos 13n.64, 29n.3, 50, 86–8, 115n.126, 117n.135, 163, 169–70, 180–1, 242, 255–6, 262n.61, 263–4, 273–4

Homer 10–11, 16–19, 31, 41–3, 47–8, 50, 65n.130, 72, 96, 99, 124–6, 129n.35, 131, 142n.83, 144–6, 160–3, 174, 182–3, 190–1, 193, 228, 232–3, 238–9, 242n.188, 251–2, 272

   Homer's reincarnation 41–3

   Iliad 19n.89, 125–6, 125n.6, 131, 135n.55, 144, 162–3, 237n.168, 254, 296–7

   Odyssey 125–6, 125n.6, 142, 144–6, 238, 252n.22

honorific 14, 23–5, 46–8, 70–3, 78, 85–6, 92–3, 98, 102–3, 105, 111, 119–20, 123–4, 128, 177, 182, 188, 194–244, 261, 293

   arch 90–5, 98

   statue(s) 14, 23–5, 46–7, 70–1, 78, 85–6, 102–3, 111, 119–20, 128, 177, 188, 194–244

   inscription(s) 23–4, 48, 123–4, 177, 196–9, 201, 233–7, 242

Horace 126, 131–2, 193

   Odes 3.30 126

hubris 37, 88, 137–8, 206, 242, 285

Hyphasis River 55–6, 137–9, 143, 157–8, 160–1

identity 6–7, 10, 19, 22–3, 32–3, 53n.85, 65, 100, 118, 173–4, 195, 201, 203–7, 228, 232–3, 239–40, 299

   bicultural 90–1, 212–13, 248, 274

   commemorative 19, 22–3, 47–8, 77, 79, 97–101, 127, 151n.110, 160, 162, 168, 177, 184, 188–9, 191–3, 201, 231–3, 243–4, 247–9, 291–2, 305–6

   cultural 1n.2, 48, 61–3, 76, 94–5, 98–9, 106, 119–20, 134–5, 169–70, 182, 191–3, 205–6, 248–9, 306

   personal 19, 23, 41–4, 46–50, 62–3, 65, 77, 90–1, 94–5, 97–9, 102–3, 112–13, 119–20, 127, 146–7, 159–60, 162, 168–70, 184, 190–1, 194–6, 215–17, 247–9, 306

imitation (see *mimesis*)

immortality 1–2, 19n.89, 25, 41, 47–8, 65–7, 69, 125n.6, 126, 130–6, 139, 144–7, 156, 158–61, 164–5, 168, 218–19, 238–9, 242, 251–4

imperial building 19–22, 98, 106, 136–7, 177, 196n.11, 214–15, 226–8, 232–3, 257, 260

imperial cult 89n.37, 188, 190, 232–3, 296

imperial democracy 251, 256, 262–4, 300–1

imperial family 81, 177, 190, 195, 196n.11, 207–17, 223–6, 228–30, 256, 296

imperial harmony 6–7, 88, 175, 189, 270–1

imperial funding 15–16

imperialism 16–17, 106–8, 136–8, 166–74, 193, 195, 215–17, 221–3, 232–3, 243–4, 257

imperial portraits 85–9, 106, 177, 188, 195–6, 196n.11, 207–17, 221–3, 228–30

imperial power (Roman) 7, 16–17, 25, 56–7, 86–8, 94–5, 106, 109–10, 138, 173, 193, 211, 215–17, 221–3, 243–4, 250–1, 257, 259–60, 264–5, 268–9, 277, 295, 300–4, 306

imperium 56–7, 86–8, 188, 211–12

India(ns) 55–6, 70, 138–41, 143, 147–51, 157–8, 160, 170, 284–5

innovation(s) 11–12, 17, 32n.13, 34–5, 41, 62–4, 66–7, 69, 75, 77, 182, 214–15, 223–6, 296–7, 305

innovative 42n.44, 62, 66, 80, 123, 303

intermediality 8–9, 23, 77–80, 307

intertextuality 23, 56n.94, 58, 60, 93n.43, 94–5, 98, 146, 165n.151, 252n.22, 253, 307

Ionia 7, 61, 92–3, 252

Isle of the Blessed 65–6, 69, 144–7

Isthmia 89, 105, 177, 253–5, 299, *see also* Corinth, Isthmus of

Isthmian Canal 251–6, 255*f*

Jason (hero) 109–10

Julius Caesar 107–8, 161–2, 252n.26

Kallimachos 64n.123, 219–21

Kappadokia 1n.2, 49, 55–8, 108, 110, 198

Kemezis, Adam 7, 249–50

Kephisia 81–3, 96n.53, 98–9, 147–53, 183–5, 190–1, 226, 228–31, 280–1, 283–4, 287–8, 297n.163
Kermode, Frank 32–3
kleos (κλέος) 17–18, 123–6, 130–1, 160–1, 172, 182–3, 251–2, *see also* fame
Klepsydrion 98–9
König, Jason 270, 301–2
Kolchis 109–10
Kommagene 19–23
Korenjak, Martin 4
Kroisos (king of Lydia) 86–8
Kybele 108–9
Kynegeiros 64n.123, 219
Kyros the Great 38, 50–1, 51n.79, 159–60, 166–74
    tomb of 166–74, 171*f*

Laodameia 96–8
Laodikeia 44, 129–30, 202, 297–8
Leake, Martin 182
library 13, 218
    of Kelsos 15n.73, 78–9, 101–4, 102*f*, 123, 189, 204n.50, 207
literary authority 7–8, 18, 30–7, 39–59, 61–3, 65n.130, 66–7, 105–15, 117–18, 138–47, 159–74, 192–3, 217–21, 236, 241, 248–9, 297–8, 304
literary monument(s) 48–59, 105–15, 124–36, 138–47, 159–74, 217–21, 236–43
Longinos (Pseudo-), *On the Sublime* 29–44, 47, 49, 59–62, 65, 70, 107n.95, 111–12, 115n.126, 146n.102, 242–4
Loukou 147, 174–92, 226, 228–30, 232n.155, 284
Lucian 4n.23, 8n.40, 12n.59, 24–5, 29–30, 37n.35, 41–2, 48, 50, 53, 60, 109, 115, 119–20, 138, 142–7, 158–9, 173–4, 191, 214–15, 247–9, 253–4, 259–61
    Alexander the False Prophet 48, 117n.134
    and novelty 63–6
    Assembly of the Gods 259n.52
    Charon or the Inspectors 41–2
    Death of Peregrinus 65, 214–15
    Demonax 158, 268n.78, 274–5

Dionysos 64n.124
Dream or the Cock 220
Downward Journey 268n.78, 275–6, 284–5
Essays in Portraiture 117n.134, 236n.165
How to Write History 146n.102
Ikaromenippos 259–60
Lover of Lies 191–2
on artistic originality and canonicity, see *True Stories*
on text and image, see *On the Hall*
On the Hall 78, 116–19
On the Syrian Goddess 109
Prometheus in Words 37n.35, 64n.124
Saturnalia 259
Slander 259
Teacher of Rhetoric 143n.92
True Stories 65–6, 69, 123–4, 138, 142–7
Zeuxis or Antiochos 63–5, 115
Lucius (philosopher in *VS*) 270–1, 274, 275n.102, 295
Lucius Verus 81, 86–8, 88*f*, 175, 207–10, 285–6, 293–4, 306–7
Lykourgos 100–1
Lysias 69, 83–6, 85*f*, 204

Marathon 24–5, 81–3, 86n.34, 91*f*, 98–9, 147–59, 175, 177, 180–5, 190–2, 211, 219–21, 223–6, 243–4, 277, 281–5, 287–9, 291–4, 296–7, 301–2, 306–7
    Battle of (490BC) 64n.123, 88, 156, 174–5, 177–8, 180–2, 190–2, 219, 282, 284–5, 291–2, 306–7
    Bey 277–81
    Estate of Herodes Attikos 79, 81, 90–101, 147–59, 175, 183–5, 190–1, 280–3, 306–7
        Brexiza, *see* Sanctuary of the Egyptian Gods
        Gate of Eternal Concord 90–101, 90*f*, 91*f*, 92*f*, 93*f*, 96*f*, 253, 299
    soros 81, 98, 177–8, 180–1, 285–6
    stêlê of the fallen of the Erechtheis tribe 174–92, 178*f*, 284–6
Marathonomachoi 35, 180, 182, 184–5, 189, 191–2, 284–6
Marcus Aurelius 81, 86–9, 87*f*, 175, 207–10, 213–14, 213*f*, 214*f*, 243, 248, 250–1, 256–77, 282, 284–6, 284n.121, 293–5, 301–7

354 GENERAL INDEX

Martindale, Charles 114
material memory, *see* memory
Megapenthes 275–6, 284–5
Memnon (foster-son of Herodes Attikos)
    81, 147–51, 152*f*, 216n.92
memory 1, 9–10, 18, 34, 57, 100–1, 109,
    113, 115–20, 124–7, 138–92,
    218, 249, 252, 263–4, 273, 282–3,
    302–3
  collective 10n.51, 100, 160–2
  cultural 9–10, 18, 23, 59, 88–9, 100, 106–7,
    119, 123–4, 158–9, 174, 183–4, 304
  future 18–19
  historical 57–9, 88–9, 99–100, 158–9,
    192–3
  material 35, 79–120, 124–7, 138–47,
    159–93, 206, see also *damnatio*
    memoriae
  spatial 9–10, 19, 48–59, 77–8, 100,
    106–7, 115–16, 119, 124–7, 138–74,
    182–5, 226–8
mimesis (μίμησις) 3, 31, 34, 34n.27, 39–60,
    48n.69, 65–6, 70, 75, 79–80, 92–3,
    143n.89, 146, 161n.136, 171, 191–2,
    194, 225n.124, 243–4, 248, 257, 264,
    274n.99, 275–6, 299, 302–3, 305
  passive 40–8, 65, 70
  competitive 40–60, 70, 75, 305
mnêma (μνῆμα) 16–17, 23, 168, 172n.171,
    241–2
monumentum 16–17, 126
Mt Theches 54–5, 57, 134, 306–7
Mouseion hill 19–23
Mousaios 19–23
munificence, *see* euergetism
Musonius Rufus 255–6

naiskos 97–8, 254
Nemea 182–3, 183*f*
Nemesis 88–9, 285–8
  Cult statue of 88, 285, 287–8
  Sanctuary at Rhamnous 81, 88–9, 147,
    183–4, 285–6, 287*f*
Nero 24n.104, 37–9, 205–6, 253–6, 255*f*,
    259–60, 269–70, 273–6, 294–5,
    298–300, 302–3
  Nero dialogue by Philostratos,
    see Philostratos
Newby, Zara 8–9

novelty (καινός, καινότης) 29–30, 33–7, 59–67,
    75, 143, 214–15, *see also* originality
numinosity 18–19, 112

Odysseus 53n.85, 72, 131, 139n.71, 142,
    145–7, 251–2
Oinoe 90–1, 98–9
Oliver, James 51–3
Olympia 37, 65, 81–3, 89, 108–9, 111, 134–5,
    140, 177, 197, 207, 211–13, 215–17,
    223–6, 243–4, 253–4, 259–60, 278
  Antinoos of Olympia 223–6, 224*f*
  nymphaion of Herodes Attikos 207–17,
    253–4, 280–1, 293–4
  Philippeion 207
Olympieion, *see* Athens
Onesikritos (officer of Alexander the
    Great) 171–2
oreichalkinos 146
Orestes 116–17
originality 3, 29–30, 32, 59, 62, 64–75,
    79–80, 101n.73, 130–1, 136–8, 142,
    143n.90, 146, 168, 173–4, 180–1,
    191–2, 305, *see also* novelty
οὗ τάδε πάντα 282–5, 287–8

Panchaia 144–5
Panhellenion 211
Paris-Alexandros 162
Pasargadae 166–74
  tomb of Kyros the Great 166–74, 171*f*
past, *see* temporality
patrician 90–1, 212–13
patron 79–80, 135
patronage 13–14, 211, 262n.61
Pausanias 8–9, 18, 22–5, 58n.100, 78, 88,
    108, 109nn.100 and 103, 110–14,
    117–20, 156, 180–1, 241, 247–9,
    253n.28, 258n.51, 272–3, 282, 285,
    300–1, 306–7
pepaideumenoi 5, 9–10, 14, 23, 80, 85–6,
    100–1, 105, 128–9, 141–2, 204–5,
    270–1, 302–3
Peregrinus Proteus 65, 214–15, 270–1
performance 2, 2n.5, 4–6, 29–30, 34, 38–9,
    59–63, 65n.129, 66, 68n.140, 69–72,
    77, 106–7, 126–7, 130–1, 133, 135–6,
    191, 206–7, 238–9, 242–4, 265–7,
    274, 288–9, 298

GENERAL INDEX 355

Pergamon 8–9, 44–6, 53, 67–8, 70, 134, 205n.62, 280–1
Perikles 104, 264n.68
Persia 166, 170
Persian Empire 168, 172n.171
Persian King 260–1
  Darius I (the Great) 171–2, 172n.173, 175
  Xerxes 137–8, 169–70, 175, 180–1, 255–6
Persian(s) 37–8, 88, 166–72, 175, 180–1, 185, 189, 210–11, 263–4, 285
Persian Wars 17, 88, 175, 177–8, 180–1, 185, 189, 210–11, 219–20, 285
Petsalis-Diomidis, Alexia 8–9
phantasia (φαντασία) 80, 115–16
Phasine, *see* Arrian
Pheidias 108–9, 112–13, 200–1
Philagros of Kilikia 59–64, 66–7, 74–5, 265–9, 302–4
Philiskos of Thessaly 62
Philip II of Makedon 88–9, 111, 207, 217, 276
Philopappos, Gaius Julius Antiochos Epiphanes 15n.73, 19–23, 20*f*, 21*f*, 22*f*, 211–12
Philopappos monument, *see* Athens
philosophical 2–3, 41, 86–8, 96, 100, 139–40, 162, 202, 204–5, 235–6, 240, 250–1, 256, 268–76, 295, 302–3
philosopher(s) 25, 48–9, 49*f*, 65, 71–2, 85–8, 104, 138, 196–7, 199, 202*f*, 203–5, 203*f*, 214–15, 219, 235–6, 240–1, 250, 256, 267–77, 293–5, 301–3
philosopher king 271, 273–4
philosophy 40n.39, 139–40, 225n.122, 256, 263–4, 269–70, 294–5, 302–3
Philostratos 2, 25, 31, 60, 72, 81–3, 100–1, 123–4, 136, 173–4, 193–4, 197, 201
  and the 'Second Sophistic' 2–8, 11–12, 23–6, 29–30, 34, 44, 66–7, 159n.130, 193, 201, 204, 232–3, 247–304, 306–7
  Heroikos 156, 174, 200–1, 237
  In Honour of Apollonios of Tyana 80n.8, 108, 138–43, 147–51, 158–9, 251–5, 263–4, 269–70
  Lives of the Sophists 2, 4, 34, 44, 46–7, 72, 247–8

Life of Aelius Aristeides 242–3
Life of Alexander the Clay Plato 266–7
Life of Dionysios of Miletos 104–5
Life of Favorinus 60
Life of Herodes Attikos 147–51, 157–8, 248–9, 251–304, 306
Life of Philagros 60–3, 66–7, 266
Life of Polemon 129–34, 202, 249–50
Nero 252n.26, 253–6, 274
philotimia 13–14
Pindar 14, 18n.87, 72–3, 126, 133, 161n.134, 163–4, 188–9, 193, 218
  Pythian 6 126, 133, 193, 218
Plato 4n.22, 29, 31, 41–3, 41n.42, 42n.46, 50, 69, 114, 117n.135, 143n.92, 146, 204–5, 225n.122, 238, 240–3, 263n.67, 271n.88, 293–5, 304
  Apology 293–5
  Meno 238
  Cratylus 133n.51, 160
  Critias 146
  Gorgias 133n.51
  Phaidros 4n.22, 114
  Republic 117n.135, 263n.67
Platt, Verity 8–9, 112
plurality 9–10, 32–3, 184n.220, 189, 307
Plutarch 115n.126, 139–40, 205n.61, 271n.88, 296n.161
  Life of Alexander 14, 93n.43, 139–40, 237–8, 237n.168, 272n.94
    on Alexander at Troy 161–2
    on Kyros' tomb 167–70, 172–3
  Life of Cimon 281–2
  Life of Theseus 93n.43, 210–11, 252–3, 296–7, 301–2,
    on Theseus' burial 281–2, 297
    on Theseus and democracy 299–301
    on Theseus and the Panathenaia 296
  On the Oracles at Delphi 128–9
  On the Fortune of Alexander 138n.68
  Precepts of Statecraft on *stasis* 257–9
  The Philosopher Should Above All Discuss with Persons in Leading Positions 270
Polemon, Marcus Antonius 5n.30, 24–5, 44–7, 53, 64n.123, 67, 70, 73, 133–6, 194, 202–6, 202*f*, 217, 219, 221, 232n.155, 240, 249–50, 250n.20, 264, 276, 293, 297–8

356 GENERAL INDEX

Polemon, Marcus Antonius (*cont.*)
  and Demosthenes 44–7, 45*f*, 53
  tomb of 129–33, 136, 276, 293, 297–8
Polydeuces, *see* Polydeukion
Polydeukion, Vibullus (foster–son of Herodes
    Attikos) 81, 86n.33, 147–59, 183–4,
    221–37, 253, 274–6, 285–7, 305–6
  and Antinoos 223–6, 224*f*, 225*f*, 228–33,
    243–4, 275–6
  and *sôphrosynê* 231, 232*f*
Porter, James I. 4–5, 30–1, 42–3, 47
Poseidon 14, 105, 146, 251–6, 298–9
postclassicism 7–8, 17, 25, 29–48, 247–8
posterity, *see* temporality
present, *see* temporality
Protesilaos 65n.130, 96–8, 143n.92, 156,
    161n.134, 201
Pseudo-Longinos, *see* Longinos
Ptolemy, son of Lagos 164–6
Ptolemy II and Arsinoë II, monument at
    Olympia of 207, 215–17
Ptolemy III, gymnasium of 297
Ptolemy X 170
puerility (μειρακιώδες) 61–2

reception 62–7, 72–3, 77–8, 81–3, 86–9,
    114, 117–20, 126n.13, 140, 144–7,
    171–2, 189, 206–7, 242, 247–9,
    267–8, 281, 293, 295, 296n.155,
    304–5, 307
rededication 89n.37, 200n.35, 201, 205–6,
    235n.160
Regilla 90–100, 126–7, 147, 153n.113,
    183n.213, 207–17, 233–7, 253,
    259–60, 272–5, 291–2, 298
  Gate of Eternal Concord 90–100
  Mandra tis Grias 90–2, 91*f*, 99–100
  murder of 259, 272–4, 298
  nymphaion at Olympia 207–17, 253
  Odeion of 126–7, 259–60, 272–4, 291–2,
    298
  Peirene fountain 233–6
  priestess of Demeter Chamyne 210–11
  and *sôphrosynê* 233–6
Regillus, son of Herodes Attikos 207–10,
    217n.94
replication 39, 73, 101–2, 111, 134–5,
    191–2, 194–5, 200n.37, 213–14,
    221–37, 241, 243–4

reputation 1, 10–11, 14, 23, 42, 45–6,
    59–62, 66–7, 71–2, 105, 117n.135,
    132, 135, 160–2, 165–6, 174, 192–3,
    198, 200, 207, 218, 241–3, 251–2,
    259, 266–8, 273–4, 276, 288–9,
    291–2, 299
Rhamnous 81, 86–9, 101–2, 147, 147n.108,
    175, 183–4, 204–5, 215–17, 285–8,
    293–4
Rhea 108–9, 112–13, 168n.159
rhetor / orator 2–3, 5, 24–5, 29–30, 30n.5,
    34–5, 40–1, 43n.54, 44–7, 60–2,
    64–8, 70, 72, 83–6, 88–9, 100–1, 104,
    115–16, 131–3, 197, 199, 203–4, 219,
    242–3, 264–7, 276
rhetoric / oratory 2–5, 8–9, 11–12, 25,
    29–30, 34, 34n.24, 38–9, 39n.37,
    44–6, 60–1, 63, 65–75, 77–8, 80,
    107–8, 114–19, 130–2, 133n.51,
    134–6, 141, 182, 206–7, 212n.84,
    221, 235–8, 242–4, 248, 250–1, 254,
    256, 259–72, 274n.99, 276, 282–3,
    293, 303–6
Robinson, Betsey 233
Rome 6–8, 10–11, 13, 18–22, 37–9, 55, 60,
    66–8, 76, 81–3, 88–9, 98–9, 98n.60,
    106–7, 126, 134–7, 141, 158–9, 170,
    174–5, 177, 189, 193, 195–6,
    203n.49, 204–5, 211–13, 249–50,
    256–7, 257n.44, 261–3, 265–8, 286,
    294–6, 300–3, 306
Rood, Tim 53, 110

Sanctuary of the Egyptian Gods 81, 86–9,
    87*f*, 87*f*, 88*f*, 91*f*, 99n.65, 101–2,
    175, 183–4, 215–17, 223–6, 225*f*,
    285–6, 293–4
sapheneia ('clarity') 115
sarcophagus
  of Dionysios of Miletos 79, 103–5, 103*f*,
    104*f*, 297–8
  of Elpinike 183–4, 287–8
  of Kyros 166–8, 173
  'Leda Sarcophagus', *see* sarcophagus of
    Elpinike
  at the Panathenaic Stadium 283*f*, 290–1,
    290*f*, 291*f*, 297–8
Sardis 83n.20, 101
Schmitz, Thomas 6

Sebastopolis (Kappadokian) 56–7, 110
Sebastopolis-Dioskourias 56–7, 110
'Second Sophistic' 1–12, 16–17, 23–6, 34, 40n.39, 50–1, 66–7, 79, 105, 110n.109, 118, 244, 247–50, 248n.11, 260–1, 301–3, 307
σῆμα 16–17, 105, 125–7, 130, 132–3, 160, 164–5, 177–8, 238, 252, *see also* tombs
σημεῖον 16–17, 167–8, 251–2, *see also* tombs
Shaw, Brent 11–12
Sidebottom, Harry 271–2, 301
Smith, R.R.R. 19, 83–5, 101, 204
Smyrna 44–6, 67, 71–2, 129–32, 203*f*, 218, 232n.155, 242–3, 242n.188
Sokrates 68, 86–8, 114, 238, 293–5, 301–4
Solon 86–8
sophistic dilemma 4, 132
sophistic 2–4, 6, 13–14, 39–40, 44, 60–2, 66–8, 72, 75, 130–3, 136, 159n.130, 201, 242–4, 248–52, 256–69, 271–2, 274–6, 284, 288–9, 301–6
sophistry 39–40, 72–3, 238, 266–7
sophist(s) 4–8, 11–12, 24–5, 31, 34–5, 44, 60–1, 61n.109, 66–7, 69–70, 72–3, 80–3, 101n.75, 104, 123–4, 129–32, 193, 195, 197, 199, 201–2, 232–3, 238, 240, 247–51, 253–6, 262, 264–72, 266n.76, 269nn.80 and 83, 270n.85, 276–7, 291–2, 298, 301, 303
Sophokles 29, 69, 116–17
sôphrosynê 231, 232*f*, 233–6, 234*f*
soros, the 81, 88–9, 177–8, 180–1, 183–4, 284–6
Sparta 18n.88, 89, 128–9, 175, 236, 264, 287–8
spatial memory, *see* memory
Spawforth, Tony 6–7, 13, 306
Squire, Michael 8–9, 77–8
stasis 257–9
Statue(s)
  honorific, *see* honorific
  animated 237–43
  sweating 237–8
Stesichoros 41–2
Strabo 93n.43, 137n.64, 138n.67, 142, 164–5, 167–8, 170–2, 240, 242, 252, 285

style
  architectural 48, 214–15
  rhetorical (χρῶμα) 30–1, 39, 42n.44, 44, 61–2, 127, 264–5, 271–2, 304
  visual 85–6, 109, 185n.222, 199, 288–9
sublime, the (ὕψος) 30–7, 39–40, 42, 43, 62, 62n.112, 107–8

Tacitus 11–12, 38–9
temple 146, 161–2, 220, 254
  of Asklepios at Smyrna 218
  of Athena at Troy 161–2, 161n.134
  of Dionysos–Antinoos at Loukou 182, 185
  of Hermes at Trapezous 54, 58–9
  of Homer 242n.188
  of Hygeia at Pergamon 69–70
  of Olympian Zeus, *see* Athens
  of Poseidon at Isthmia 253, 299
  of Plato 241–3
  of Tyche, Panathenaic stadium 289–90
  of Zeus Asklepios at Pergamon 134–5
temporality 1–3, 5, 10–11, 13, 17–18, 23, 25, 29–40, 43, 57–8, 75–7, 94–5, 100, 106, 119–20, 123–4, 126–7, 131–2, 141, 160–1, 191, 193, 201, 205–6, 230–3, 242–4, 284, 305–7
  anachronism 3–4, 8, 22–3, 31–2, 46–7, 51n.79, 108–9, 263–4, 302
  archaizing 2–3, 111–12, 181n.203, 235–6, 262n.61, 291–2
  atemporality 69, 96, 126–7
  contemporary 2, 4, 8–9, 11–13, 22–3, 25–6, 29–31, 34–40, 43, 46–8, 58, 60–8, 74–8, 80, 83–5, 88–9, 100, 111–12, 114–15, 119, 123–4, 129–30, 132, 136–7, 141, 153, 160, 185, 191, 199, 206, 214–17, 226, 232–3, 238–9, 247–8, 252, 259, 261, 264–8, 273–5, 284–5, 291–2, 295, 300–1, 303, 305
  eternal 1, 17–18, 33, 37n.34, 69, 72–4, 90*f*, 91*f*, 92, 94–8, 96*f*, 100, 105, 130–1, 134–6, 146, 158, 160–1, 173, 175, 293, 306–7
  eternity 10–11, 11n.57, 31, 33n.19, 36, 37n.34, 43, 47, 97–8, 116–17, 137–8, 145n.100, 206–7

358 GENERAL INDEX

temporality (*cont.*)
  future 6–7, 10–14, 16–19, 23–6, 29–48,
    55, 58–61, 63–4, 66–7, 72–3, 75–6,
    99–100, 105–6, 108, 110–14,
    119–20, 123–4, 126–7, 132, 136–7,
    146–7, 152–3, 159, 161–3, 166,
    172–3, 190–3, 200, 226–8, 235–6,
    242, 244, 247–9, 252, 260, 264–5,
    268, 275, 282, 288–9, 295, 305–6
  futurity 11–12, 17–19, 24–6, 29–32, 34,
    36–7, 39, 66, 119–20
  moveable temporal perspective 4, 36–7,
    39, 43, 75–6, 111–12, 119–20,
    131–2, 141, 146n.102, 191, 193,
    242–4, 305–7
  multitemporal 18, 77, 94–5, 112, 141,
    193, 205–6, 232–3, 284, 306–7
  past 1–4, 6–14, 16–18, 22–3, 25–6,
    29–40, 42–4, 47–8, 58–9, 61–2, 65,
    69, 72, 75–6, 78, 92–3, 95–6, 106,
    108–14, 119–20, 123–7, 131, 141,
    144–7, 160–1, 166–8, 170, 172–5,
    180, 184–5, 188–9, 191, 193, 206,
    226–8, 243–4, 248, 252, 262–3, 281,
    284, 303, 305–7
  posterity 1–2, 4–6, 15–16, 18–19, 22–3,
    30, 32–6, 39, 56–7, 59, 61n.109,
    65n.129, 67–8, 71–2, 75–6, 79, 81–3,
    99–101, 108, 111–13, 118–19,
    123–4, 133–4, 139–40, 142, 144–5,
    146n.102, 161–2, 170, 172, 188–9,
    191, 214–15, 242–3, 248–51, 255,
    260–1, 264–5, 291–2, 302–3, 305–7
  present 4, 6, 9–17, 23, 25–6, 29–40,
    42–3, 47, 55, 57–60, 62–4, 66–7,
    69, 72, 75, 77, 88, 95–6, 99, 101–2,
    108, 110–14, 119–20, 126–7, 129–30,
    133, 137–8, 141, 144, 146n.102, 156,
    159n.130, 167–8, 180–1, 188–9, 191,
    193, 195–6, 206, 226–8, 240, 243–4,
    255, 266–7, 281, 305–7
textuality 4–5, 19n.89, 58, 115–16, 125,
  125n.6, 136
textual materiality 4–5, 18–19, 24–5, 59, 76–7,
  80, 103, 103n.79, 105–19, 124–36,
  138–47, 159–74, 217–21, 236–43
  see also *ekphrasis*, literary monument(s)
thauma (θαῦμα) 18, 33, 41–3, 69n.145, 71,
  111–12, 135, 251, 296, 298, 303

Thermopylai 89, 175, 177, 260
Theseus 92–5, 112–13, 210–11, 250–3,
  255–6, 277–303, 305–6
  pillar at Isthmia 92–5, 253
Thomas, Edmund 17, 101, 106
Thucydides 18n.88, 29, 31, 34n.26, 68,
  104–5, 115n.126, 125n.7, 163,
  177–8, 252, 264n.68, 281, 299
time, *see* temporality
tomb(s) 16–23, 65n.130, 78, 80–1, 88–9,
  96n.53, 98, 101–5, 119–20, 123–37,
  139, 144, 153, 159–74, 177–8, 180–4,
  220, 226, 238, 252, 257n.43, 282–5,
  289–93, 297–8, 301–2, 306–7
  of Achilles, *see* Achilles
  of Ajax, *see* Ajax
  of Alexander, *see* Alexander
  of the Athenians from the Battle of
    Marathon, see *soros*
  of Herodes Attikos, *see* Herodes Attikos
  of Kelsos, *see* Ephesos
  of Kyros, *see* Kyros
  Philopappos Monument, *see* Athens
  of Polemon, *see* Polemon
  of T. Flavius Damianos, *see* Ephesos
Tower of the Winds, *see* Athens
Trajan 19–23, 19n.93, 55–8, 60, 101,
  111n.116, 268
Trapezous, *see* Arrian
travel 2, 18, 41–2, 78, 97n.57, 98–100,
  105, 106n.85, 108, 113n.120, 127,
  137–40, 143–4, 146n.101, 161–2,
  163n.142, 166, 238, 241, 278
trophimoi (τρόφιμοι) 147–59, 223–30
Troy 89, 172–3, 200–1, 237, 252
  tomb of Achilles 161–6
  tomb of Ajax 174
tyranny 88–9, 207–10, 213–14, 248,
  256–65, 267, 270–1, 275, 280–1,
  287–9, 293–5, 299–306
tyrant 25, 163–4, 247, 250–1, 253–65,
  267–76, 280–2, 293–5, 298, 302–4

Xenophon 1, 19, 47–8, 50–9, 52*f*, 63–4,
  101, 110, 160–1, 162n.137, 163–5,
  203–4
  Anabasis 1, 50–1, 53, 55–7, 160–1,
    165n.151
Xerxes 137–8, 169–70, 175, 180–1, 255–6

GENERAL INDEX 359

Vedii Antonini, family of the 83n.20, 101,
    185–8, 186*f*, 186*f*, 187*f*, 187*f*, 221–3
Vidal–Naquet, Pierre 48, 188–9
Villa of Herodes Attikos (Loukou),
    see Herodes Attikos

Wagner, Peter 77–8
Wallace–Hadrill, Andrew 6–7
Webb, Ruth 115
Whitmarsh, Tim 6–8, 10–11, 47, 294–5
writing(s) 1, 4–6, 11–13, 18, 24–5, 29–31,
    34–8, 41–2, 47–8, 53, 55, 57, 59–61,
    63, 66–7, 71–5, 97–8, 100–1, 103,

106, 109–11, 113–16, 115n.126,
    123–8, 133–6, 141–2, 144–5, 158–9,
    163, 165–7, 171–2, 196n.11, 206–7,
    217–18, 237–44, 248–9, 266, 275,
    288–91, 302–7

Zeus 108–9, 129n.35, 133–5, 140,
    144–5, 201, 207–13, 223–6, 232–3,
    254, 278
  Olympian 108–9, 134, 138–9, 223–6, 278
  Zeus Asklepios 134
Zeuxis 63–5
Zuiderhoek, Arjan 15–16

INDEX LOCORUM

Note: Figures are indicated by an italic "*f*", and notes are indicated by "*n.*" following the page number

For the benefit of digital users, indexed terms that span two pages (e.g., 52–53) may, on occasion, appear on only one of those pages.

AELIAN
  VH
    13.22 42n.47, 242n.188
ALEXANDER ROMANCE
    1.30 167n.158, 172n.174
    1.32 167n.158, 172n.174
    1.33–4 172n.174
    1.42 161–2, 172n.174
    2.27 169n.163
    3.5–17 172n.174
    3.6 139
    3.24 172n.174
    3.28 172n.174
    3.34 164–5
APOLLODOROS
  Bibl.
    1.140–2 237n.168
APOLLONIOS OF RHODES
  Argon.
    4.1639–93 237n.168
APULEIUS
  Florida
    16.3 199–200
    16.6–10 238–9
    16.10 239
    16.16–17 238–9
    16.19 239
    16.20–2 239
    16.22 239–40
    16.32–3 239–40
    16.39–44 240
    16.47–8 240–1, 244
ARISTEIDES, AELIUS
  HL
    1.17 218–19
    2.21 71
    2.40 71–2

    2.41–3 200–1
    2.51–5 71
    2.70 67–8
    2.74–8 71
    2.82 71
    3.4 71–2
    3.44 67–8
    3.47 200–1
    4.14 67–8
    4.15 68
    4.17 69–70
    4.18 67–8
    4.18–19 70
    4.19 71–2
    4.22 60, 70–1
    4.45 72–3
    4.47 73
    4.48 100–1, 134
    4.49 134–5, 166
    4.50 200–1, 219
    4.57 69
    4.59 69
    4.60 69
    4.61 69
    4.62 69n.145
    5.36 71n.154
    5.52 133–4
    5.56 72, 242–3
    5.57–67 241–2
    5.61 242
    5.62 241
    5.63 241–2
    5.66 242–3
  Or.
    1 (*Panathenaic Or.*) 61–2
    26.60 (*To Rome*) 263
    28 60–1
    33 133–4

INDEX LOCORUM 361

46.22–7 106
46.28 105–8
46.29 106
ARISTOTLE
[*Ath. Pol.*]
22.1 262n.63
27.1 262n.63
41.2 262n.63
De an.
427b 18–20 116n.132
Mem.
450a 30–2 116n.130
ARRIAN
An.
1.0.1–1.0.3 163
1.9.10 14n.71, 161n.134
1.11.2 237–8
1.11.5 161n.134
1.11.6–7 55–6, 137n.64
1.11.7 161n.134
1.11.7–8 161–2
1.12.1 161–3
1.12.1–5 161n.134
1.12.2 163–5, 237–8
1.12.2–4 237–8
1.12.4 163–5
1.12.4–5 161–2, 165–6
1.12.5 134–5, 163–6
1.16.5 161n.134
2.3.7 161n.134
2.5.9 161n.134
2.7.8–9 161n.134
2.24.6 121
3.3.1–2 161n.134
4.10.1–2 165
4.10.1–11.9 165n.153
4.28.1–5 138
5.1.1–2 138
5.1.5 161n.134
5.26.4 160–1
5.29.1 55–6
5.29.1–2 137n.64
6.3.4–5 138
6.9.3 161n.134
6.9.5 161n.134
6.24.2–3 170
6.29.4 166, 170
6.29.4–6 166–7

6.29.8 168
6.29.9 167–8
6.29.10 167–8
6.29.11 172–3
6.30.1 170
7.1.6 139–40, 160, 284–5
7.2.2–4 139–40
7.24–8 141n.79
7.9.6 161n.134
7.30.2 163–4
Battle Order Against the Alani
10 51n.79
22 51n.79
Cyn.
1.4 50
16.7 51–3
21.2 51–3
25.4 51–3
Events after Alexander
9.25 164–5
Peripl.
1.1 50–3, 55–7, 164–5
1.2 57
1.3 55, 58, 110
1.3–4 201
1.4 1, 55, 58
2 54
2.3 55–6
6.2 50
9.2 108–10, 168n.159
10.1 50
11.1 55–6
12.5 51–3, 55–6
13.6 51–3, 55–6
14.4 55–6
16.3 55–6
25.1 51–3, 55–6
ATHANASIOS
Apologia contra Arianos
III 5.230 221n.115
ATHENAIOS
5.215b–c [5.54] 259
5.196a–203e 281n.110
6.253d–f 281n.110
AUSONIUS
Epigrams
37.9–10 123

INDEX LOCORUM

CASSIUS DIO
51.16.5 170
52.14.3–5 263
58.16–9 254n.35
68.29.1 55–6
68.39.1 55–6
76.13.2 170
78.7–8, 22–3 170
78.16.7 161–2

CICERO
Ad Quintem
1.1 38–9
Arch.
9 242n.188
24 161–2
De or.
2.354–60 116n.132

CURTIUS RUFUS, Q.
8.10.2 138n.68
8.11.2 138n.68
8.14.11 138n.68
9.2.29 138n.68
9.3.19 137n.64
10.1.30–8 167
10.1.32 173n.176
10.10.13 170
10.10.20 164–5

DEMOSTHENES
On the Crown
18.208 35

DIO CHRYSOSTOM
Or.
2.33 14n.71
3.31–41 255–6
3.42–50 264n.68
21.1 37–8
21.2 37, 39, 242
21.3–6 37–8
21.6–8 37
21.11 38–40
21.12 38–9, 109–10
21.15 37–8
31.9 205–6
31.30 206
31.89 218n.96
43.8–12 294n.152
45.12–14 259

47.23–5 259–60
47.25 259

DIODOROS SICULUS
2.7–15 130n.38
6.1.4–10 144–5
17.17.3 161n.134
17.95.1–2 137n.64
18.3.5 164–5
18.26–8 164–5
18.26.3 170

DIOGENES LAIRTIOS
1.99 252n.26

DIONYSIOS OF HALIKARNASSOS
On Dinarchos
7–8 40–1

EURIPIDES
Hec.
109–15 131n.43
Supp.
352–3 299

FAVORINUS
Corinthian Oration
37.8 200–1
37.9 238
37.10 237
37.16 200
37.22 200
37.25–8 236
37.28 218, 220
37.31 200
37.40 205–6
37.46 138
37.47 217–18

FRONTO
Ep. ad Marcum Caesarum
3.3 273n.97
4.12.6 195n.7
Ep. Graec.
3 275

GELLIUS, AULUS
9.2.1–11 271–2
19.12.1–10 275

HESIOD
Op.
659 163n.143
763–4 218

INDEX LOCORUM 363

HERODIAN
    4.8.1–5 161–2
    4.8.9 170
HERODOTOS
    1.1.0 29n.3
    1.5.3 163
    1.5.4 13n.64, 170
    1.29–33 86–8
    2.4 242
    3.50 273–4
    3.80–3 263–4
    7.24 255–6
    7.45.1–46.2 169
    8.40–96 169
HOMER
    Il.
      2.701 96
      6.168 125n.9
      7.87–91 125n.8
      9.189 131
      9.438–43 131
      15.639 296–7
      16.40–2 132n.48
      18.417–18, 375–7 237n.168
      21.257–64 254
      23.326–33 125–6
    Od.
      1.82–3 145n.99
      4.584 125n.8
      9.67–83 142
      11.204–22 238
      11.222 238
      24.80 125n.8
HOM. HYMN TO HERMES
    464–5 163n.143
HORACE
    Carm.
      3.30.1–9 11n.57, 126
      3.30.8–9 126
INSCRIPTIONS
    Charitonidis 1968, no. 33 73–4, 74*f*
    Corinth 8.1, no. 85 158, 159*f*
    Corinth 8.1, no. 86 233–6, 234*f*
    Corinth 8.3, no.124 49n.72
    Corinth 8.3, no. 128 183n.213,
      233n.159, 236n.164
    Corinth 8.3, no. 337 233n.159

Corinth 8.3, no. 343 233n.159
FD III.3.1, no. 74 231–2, 232*f*
Gsell 1922, 1.2115 239–40
Habicht 1969, no. 33 44–6, 45*f*, 205n.62
I.Ephesos 2.426 103–4
I.Ephesos 3.640 188n.229
IG II^2 1006 184n.219
IG II^2 2090 296–7
IG II^2 3606 277–81, 278*f*, 283–4, 296–7
IG II^2 3968 226
IG II^2 3969 147–51, 287*f*
IG II^2 3970 156, 157*f*
IG II^2 3973 226n.131
IG II^2 3974 226
IG II^2 3975 226
IG II^2 3977 152–3, 155–6
IG II^2 4776 226n.131
IG II^2 5185 92–3
IG II^2 5189 38–9, 92, 93*f*, 158, 299
IG II^2 5189a 90–2, 92*f*
IG II^2 6791 290–2, 292*f*
IG II^2 13161 293
IG II^2 13188 152n.111
IG II^2 13191/3 150*f*, 152–3
IG II^2 13192 152n.111
IG II^2 13194 153–5, 154*f*
IG II^2 13195 149*f*, 153
IG II^2 13200 147n.105, 151*f*
IG II^2 13201 148*f*, 157–8
IG II^2 13202 150*f*
IG II^2 13208 285–6
IG XII, 5 891, ll.1–2 14
I.Olympia, no. 476 197
I.Olympia no. 610 210–11, 210*f*
I.Smyrna 901 242
L'Année Epigraphique 1905, 44,
    no. 175 56n.96, 110
Mitford 1974, no. 1 54, 54*f*
Mitford 1991, no. 8 57n.97, 110
SEG 23.121 95–9, 96*f*
SEG 26.290 96n.53, 297n.163
SEG 29.127 257–9, 258*f*, 267–8, 282,
    284n.121
SEG 30.159 48
SEG 41.273 182–3, 183*f*
SEG 49.209 89n.37, 285–7, 287*f*
SEG 55.1279 242
SEG 58.1665 198–9, 198*f*

364 INDEX LOCORUM

INSCRIPTIONS (*cont.*)
Steinhauer 2004–2009 [*SEG* 56.430]
178–82, 178*f*, 184–5,
189–92, 284

ISOKRATES
Or.
4.186 126n.12
7.17 262n.63
7.23 262n.63
8.13 262n.63
8.108 262n.63
15.7 126n.12

JOSEPHOS
BJ
3.540 254n.35

JUSTIN
Epit.
11.5.12 161n.134
12.13.3–10 141n.79
12.8.16 137n.64

JUVENAL
Sat.
3 38–9

KALLISTRATOS
Descriptiones
1.3 237n.169
2.3 237n.169
3.2 237n.169
6.3 237n.169
7.3 237n.169
9.1 237n.169
11.2 237n.169

LONGINOS (PS.-)
Subl.
1.3–4 33, 47
3.4 62
3.5 61–2
4.7 47
5.1 35, 60–1
7.2 35
7.3 34
9.3 47
12.3–4 107n.95
13.2–4 41
13.3 42–3
13.4 42–3
14.1–3 31, 36

14.3 36–7, 47
16.2 35
26.2 115n.126
36.2 47
44.1 47
44.4 47
44.8 47
44.9 47

LUCAN
9.964–99 161–2
9.974–9 161n.136
10.14–52 170

LUCIAN
Alex.
2 48
3 117n.134
Catapl.
16 275, 284–5
29 276
Charon or the Inspectors
7 41–2
Demon.
24 158, 268n.78, 274–5
33 158, 268n.78, 274–5
Dionysos
5 64n.124
Dream or the Cock
24 220
How to Write History
61–3 146n.102
Ikaromennipos
18 259–60
Iupp. trag.
8 220
Lover of Lies
18 191–2
On the Hall
3 118n.141
13 116–17
18 116–17
19 116–17
20 116–17
21 116–17
32 117
Peregr.
19–20 214–15
Prometheus in Words
3 37n.35, 63n.117

Saturnalia
26 259
Slander
13 259
Syr. D
15 109
Teacher of Rhetoric
9 143n.92
True Stories
1.4 142–4
1.5 142
1.7 142–4
2.5–29 65
2.28 144–7
Zeuxis
2 63
3 65
3–7 63
4 63–4
5 63–4
8–11 63

LYSIAS
Or.
20.13 262n.63

OVID
Met. 13.441–50 131n.43

PAUSANIAS
1.3.3 300n.172
1.3.5 108–9
1.5.5 111–12
1.7.1 164–5
1.8.2 111
1.8.6–13.9 111
1.17.5–6 282, 300
1.18.6 226n.127
1.19.6 111–12
1.22.3 299
1.25.8 23
1.27.8 112–13
1.27.10 210–11, 253
1.32.3 177–8, 180–1
1.32.4 156
1.33.2–3 88, 285
1.35.4–5 174n.177
2.1.8 253
2.3.6 296n.161
2.17.4 111
2.38.6 190

2.38.7 175
3.11.1 110–11, 113
7.20.6 111–12, 272–3
8.43.3–6 111–12
8.53.5 237n.168
9.36.5 18

PHILOSTRATOS
Her.
8.1 161–2, 174
9.6–7 201
13.3 143n.92, 156
19.1–7 200–1
19.4 237
19.5 201
53 296n.161
Nero
2 252n.26, 253–6
3 253–4
VA
1.2 251–2
1.5 251–2
1.6 140, 251–2
1.28 269–70
2.22.5 80n.8
2.43 55–6, 138–42
3.11 147–51
4.11–16 131n.43, 156n.121
4.24 252n.26, 253–5
5.35.4 263–4
7.1 270
7.1–3 270n.84
8.15 140
8.30–1 130n.36, 139–40
8.31.3 129n.35
VS
1.0.481 2–3, 5, 250, 260–1, 270–1
1.7.488 60, 260–1
1.8.489 268–9
1.8.490–1 5n.30
1.8.491–2 60
1.15.498 260–1
1.15.499–500 260–1
1.16.501–2 260–1, 264
1.18.510–11 5, 298n.168
1.19.511 298n.168
1.20.513 298n.168
1.21.515 298n.168
1.21.516 131n.45

366 INDEX LOCORUM

PHILOSTRATOS (*cont.*)
  1.21.517 298n.168
  1.21.518–21 298n.168
  1.21.519 131n.45
  1.22.526 105, 297–8
  1.25.533 202
  1.25.536 5n.30
  1.25.539 44, 205n.62, 267
  1.25.540 131–2
  1.25.541 5n.30, 131
  1.25.542–3 46n.64, 130n.39
  1.25.543–4 129–30, 132–3, 293,
    297–8
  2.1.546–7 182–4, 282
  2.1.547 260–1
  2.1.548 257, 261–2
  2.1.548–9 259–60, 293
  2.1.549 259, 259n.52, 293–5
  2.1.549–50 296–7
  2.1.550 259–60, 289–90,
    296–7
  2.1.551 252n.26, 253–5, 259–60,
    272–3, 298
  2.1.552 251–6
  2.1.555–7 259, 272–3
  2.1.556 273–4
  2.1.556–7 270–1, 274
  2.1.556–9 274
  2.1.557 271, 274
  2.1.558 147–51, 270–1
  2.1.558–9 157–8, 226–8
  2.1.559 248–9, 257–62
  2.1.560 262–4
  2.1.560–1 267–8
  2.1.561 267–9, 272
  2.1.562 268, 282, 284, 300
  2.1.562–3 268
  2.1.563 268, 270–1
  2.1.563–4 270–1
  2.1.563–5 276
  2.1.564 44, 264
  2.1.565 267, 276
  2.1.565–6 276–85
  2.1.566 282–5, 287–9, 293,
    301–2
  2.2.566–7 271–2
  2.4.569 260–1
  2.5.571 98–9, 266–7, 284
  2.5.571–3 266–7

  2.5.572–3 266–7
  2.5.574 267
  2.8.578 66
  2.8.578–9 62–3, 266
  2.8.579 61–3, 66, 266
  2.8.580 66, 266
  2.9.582 242–3
  2.9.582–3 72
  2.9.585 72
  2.10.585–6 98–9
  2.10.586 265–6
  2.17.598 265–6
  2.23.606 100–1
  2.30.623 62
  2.31.625 260–1

PINDAR
  Pyth.
    6.5, 7–14 126
PLATO
  Ap.
    36b–c 293–5
  Cra.
    400b–c 133n.51, 160
  Crit.
    119c 146–7
  Euthphr.
    11c–d 238
  Grg.
    493a 133n.51
  Ion
    533c–e 41n.42
  Meno
    97d 238
  Phdr.
    275b–276a 114
  Resp.
    491b–5b 295n.153
  Tht.
    191c–e 116n.130
PLINY
  HN
    7.109 14n.71
PLUTARCH
  Alex.
    7.1–8.4 272n.94
    11.12 14n.71
    14.8–9 237–8
    15.4 161–2
    15.4–5 162

24.4 237n.168
69.1–3 167
69.2–3 169–70
62.7–8 137n.64
73–7 141n.79

Arat.
53 296n.161

Artax.
8.1 115n.126

Caes.
58.4 252n.26

Cim.
8.5–6 281
19.1–4 282

De fort. Rom.
326b 138n.68

Dem.
9–13 281n.110

De Pyth. or.
395a–b 128–9

Prae. ger. reip.
815a 257–9

Thes.
14.1 210–11, 253
17.4 297n.162
22.1–6 281
24.1–2 299
24.3 296
25.4 93n.43, 252–3
32.1 299–301
35.3 300
36 281
36.2 281–2, 297, 301–2

POLEMON
Kallimachos
3 219n.104
10–12 219n.104
51 219n.104
51–2 219–21
54 219n.104
58 219n.104
60 219n.104
61 219
Kynegeiros
7 219n.104
8 64n.123
10 219
22–3 219n.104
30 219n.104

33 219n.104
39 219

POLYBIOS
16.25 280–1
30.25–6 281n.110

QUINTILLIAN
Inst.
3.7.18 238–9
10.1.72 238–9
11.2 116n.132

RHETORICA AD HERENNIUM
3.16.28–24.30 116n.132

SEVERIAN OF GABALA
On the Creation of the World
5.5 195n.7

STRABO
1.3.11 252n.26
3.5.5 93n.43, 137n.64, 138n.67,
  142, 252
9.1.6–7 252
13.1.13 285
14.1.37 242n.188
15.1.6–9 138n.68
15.3.7 167–8, 172
15.3.8 171–2
17.1.8 164–5, 170

SUETONIUS
Aug.
18 170
Calig.
21 252n.26
31 259–60
Iul.
44.3 252n.26
Ner.
19 254n.35
28 37
31 259–60
35.3 273–4

TACITUS
Ann.
15.41–2 259–60

THUCYDIDES
1.1.1 163
1.22.4 29
1.98.2 281
2.15.2 299

368 INDEX LOCORUM

THUCYDIDES (*cont.*)
  2.34.5–6 177–8
  2.43.3 104–5

XENOPHON
  An.
    4.7.24 53

4.7.25 57
4.8.22 51, 57
Cyr.
  5.3.34–45 51–3
Mem.
  4.8.9–10 294n.146